# Collected Poems of
# THOMAS PARNELL

# Collected Poems of
# THOMAS
# PARNELL

*Edited by*
Claude Rawson *and* F. P. Lock

**DELAWARE**

*Newark: University of Delaware Press*
*London and Toronto: Associated University Presses*

PR
3616
A17
1989

Associated University Presses
440 Forsgate Drive
Cranbury, NJ 08512

Associated University Presses
25 Sicilian Avenue
London WC1A 2QH, England

Associated University Presses
P.O. Box 488, Port Credit
Mississauga, Ontario
Canada L5G 4M2

The paper used in this publication meets the
requirements of the American National Standard for
Permanence of Paper for Printed Materials Z39.48-1984.

**Library of Congress Cataloging-in-Publication Data**

Parnell, Thomas, 1679–1718.
  Collected poems of Thomas Parnell.

  Includes indexes.
  1. Rawson, Claude Julien.   II. Lock, F. P.
III. Title.
PR3616.A17   1989      821′.5        85-41023
ISBN 0–87413–154–5 (alk. paper)

Printed in the United States of America

*To Christopher Patrick Parnell,*
*eighth baron Congleton, and*
*in memory of William Jared Parnell,*
*seventh baron Congleton (1925–67)*

# Contents

## List of Illustrations

# Acknowledgments

Our principal debt is to Christopher, eighth baron Congleton, and to his late brother, the seventh baron, who generously put at our disposal their family papers and to whom this edition is gratefully dedicated.

Other friends and colleagues have greatly assisted us at various stages of preparation. Five, who are now dead, were especially helpful in the early stages: John Butt, Herbert Davis, J. C. Maxwell, George Sherburn, and Sir Harold Williams. We wish also warmly to thank C. F. Burgess, W. J. Cameron, Vin Carretta, Reinhard Düchting, J. D. Fleeman, David Foxon, S. F. Gallagher, Philip Gaskell, David Hayton, Ian Higgins, Maynard Mack, Frederick Nash, D. G. Neill, David Nokes, Yseulte Parnell, Pat Rogers, Margaret M. Smith, Tom Woodman (whose Twayne volume on Thomas Parnell appeared as this edition was going to press), H.-J. Zimmermann.

We wish also to thank the librarians and staff of the following libraries: the Bodleian Library, the British Library, the Brotherton Library, the Cambridge University Library, the William Andrews Clark Memorial Library, the Columbus Academy (and especially Pat Clements and the headmaster, W. Boulton Dixon), the Library of Congress, the Houghton Library, the Huntington Library, the Library of the University of Illinois at Urbana-Champaign, the National Library of Ireland, the Newberry Library, the Library of the University of Newcastle upon Tyne, the University of Nottingham Library, the University of Queensland Library, the Library of Trinity College Cambridge, the Library of Trinity College Dublin (and especially William O'Sullivan), the Victoria and Albert Museum, the University of Warwick Library, the Yale University Library.

Grants in aid of research were at various time provided by the American Philosophical Society, the Australian Academy of the Humanities and the Myer Foundation, the University of Illinois at Urbana-Champaign, the Universities of Newcastle upon Tyne and Warwick, and the University of Queensland.

# Introduction

Thomas Parnell presents the unusual editorial problem of a poet most of whose work was published posthumously. Born in 1679, Parnell wrote his earliest datable poem on the death of Queen Mary II (who died on 28 December 1694). Yet when Swift reported to Stella in December 1712 that Parnell "outdoes all our Poets here a Barrs Length" (*J.S.* 2 : 586) not one of his poems had been printed. When Parnell died in 1718,only nine of his poems had been published.[1] This edition prints nearly one hundred and fifty. For almost all these poems there is thus a degree of uncertainty about how far the extant texts represent Parnell's intentions about the way he would have liked them to have appeared in print. Many of the poems printed here were probably not written for publication at all.

These unusual circumstances have determined both the arrangement and the editorial policies adopted in this edition. It is unlikely that Parnell himself ever contemplated a complete edition of his poems, and we certainly do not know how he would have arranged one. Too few of his poems can be dated for a chronological arrangement to be possible, nor would any grouping by subject or genre be free from serious objection. We have therefore chosen to present the poems in a way that reflects how the Parnell corpus has grown. Thus we place first those poems that were published in Parnell's lifetime, followed by the poems first printed in the posthumous collection, *Poems on Several Occasions* (1722), edited by Pope. These are the poems by which Parnell was chiefly known until the 1750s. In 1758 a substantial body of *Posthumous Works* was published. Although it is a carelessly edited and printed collection, the order of the poems within it seems to be authorial. We have therefore placed its contents next after the poems first published by Pope and have generally retained its order. For the actual texts of the poems, however, we have used alternative copy-texts whenever they are available. The contents of the 1758 collection are followed by the handful of stray poems that were printed in other sources between 1721 and 1755, but which do not appear in the 1758 edition. Finally, there are the poems now published for the first time. The present edition more than doubles the number of poems known to be Parnell's, being the first to make use of an extensive collection of manuscripts preserved in the family of the poet's younger brother John and generously made available to us by their owner, the present Lord Congleton. Also first collected in this edition are the poems from a notebook discovered by the late Paul S. Schoedinger and included as an appendix in his 1940 Yale dissertation. Our arrangement has the advantages that it keeps together those poems that Parnell and Pope thought the best, and allows the reader to follow the growth of the published corpus of Parnell's poems.

This edition is the first to attempt the establishment of a reliable text of Parnell's poems, based on a study of all the available manuscripts and editions of any authority. Our editorial policies have been determined by our aim of making available an authoritative text of the poems, primarily addressed to a scholarly readership.[2] Thus we have tried to present texts with the minimum of editorial interference, reproducing the authorities for the texts (emended, of course, where necessary, and as duly noted) as faithfully as possible. In the case of the poems now first printed from the manuscripts, this means the form in which Parnell left the poems. His manuscripts are very lightly, often defectively, punctuated; but for us to have supplied punctuation would effectively have determined how the poems were to be read. This policy leads to occasional difficulties, but in our view these are greatly outweighed by the gains. Before enlarging on our treatment of the text, however, we need to outline the peculiar publishing history of Parnell's poems, for it is this history that has created the unusual editorial problem.

# 1
## Poems Published by Parnell

Parnell seems to have been remarkably free of any ambition to make a public reputation as a poet. Although he had been writing poetry since at least 1695, it seems entirely possible that, had he not met and been encouraged by Swift and Pope, he might never have published any. Only nine of his poems were published in his lifetime. Of the two long poems, Swift was certainly responsible for appearance of the *Essay on the Different Styles of Poetry* in March 1713. The *Journal to Stella* records Swift's struggle with Parnell's diffidence or laziness about the poem (e.g., *J.S.* 2:604, 17 January 1713), and it was Swift who persuaded him to insert the compliments to Bolingbroke and to dedicate the poem to the minister. Pope was responsible for the publication of *Homer's Battle of the Frogs and Mice* (which appeared in May 1717). The poem had been completed as early as 1715, but Parnell was curiously reluctant or indifferent about sending it to Pope for publication. Of course neither Swift nor Pope was acting entirely without ulterior motives in thus encouraging Parnell as a poet. Swift was anxious to have recorded and celebrated the achievements of the Tory government, and (as with his project for an English academy) to associate it with learning and the patronage of the arts (hence his stage-managing in January 1713 of Lord Oxford's seeking out Parnell; *J.S.* 2:611–12). For Pope, the publication of *Homer's Battle* and its attendant prose pieces served a double purpose. It was a graceful tribute to have his own translation of the *Iliad* recognized as a modern classic, directly in the compliments paid him in the preface to the "Life of Zoilus" and indirectly through the publication of a translation of the pseudo-Homeric mock-epic into his own idiom. In the "Life" and "Remarks of Zoilus," Pope's chief critical enemy, John Dennis, was amusingly identified with Zoilus, the ancient critic notorious for his malicious but unsuccessful attacks on the reputation of Homer. If Dennis was the modern Zoilus, Pope was the modern Homer.

The publication of the seven short pieces can also be connected with Parnell's literary friends. *The Horse and the Olive* was separately published as a folio half-sheet by Swift's friend and publisher, John Morphew, in April 1713, and it seems likely that Swift arranged publication. Four short poems appeared in *Poetical Miscellanies* (1714, though actually published late in 1713): "A Hymn on Contentment," "Song" ("My days have been"), "To a Young Lady, on her Translation of the Story of Phoebus and Daphne from Ovid," and "Anacreontick" ("Gay Bacchus"). This collection was edited by Richard Steele, to whose *Spectator* and *Guardian* Parnell had earlier contributed prose essays. We do not know whether Parnell knew Steele independently, or whether they had been brought together by Swift or Pope. "To Mr. Pope" was printed among the commendatory poems prefixed to the collected edition of Pope's own *Works* (1717). The "Translation of Part of the First Canto of *The Rape of the Lock* into Leonine Verse" was published in *Poems on Several Occasions* (1717), a miscellany edited by Pope himself and now better known as *Pope's Own Miscellany*, the title under which it was edited by Norman Ault (1935). Sometime before his death Parnell was planning a collection of his poems, but characteristically he seems to have intended to entrust the actual business of publication to Pope. Returning to Ireland in 1718, however, Parnell died unexpectedly at Chester, and the collection edited by Pope became a memorial rather than a midcareer retrospective.

## 2
### Pope's Edition: *Poems on Several Occasions* (1722)

Writing to Parnell on 6 July 1717, Pope praised *Homer's Battle of the Frogs and Mice* (which had recently appeared) and referred to the "other pieces you entrusted to my care" as being "preserved with the same veneration as relics," before alluding rather obscurely to having "meant to have told you the reason that your poems are not published." Later in the same letter Pope speaks of "the present violent bent to politics" (meaning the "whig split" of 1717), but this remark could refer either backwards to Parnell's poems or forward to the comments about Pope's own poems (*Pope Corr.* 1:415–16). There are two possible explanations of these "other pieces" entrusted to Pope's care. One is that they had been intended for *Poems on Several Occasions* (1717; *Pope's Own Miscellany*). As we have seen, the only poem by Parnell actually included was his "Translation of Part of the First Canto of *The Rape of the Lock*," but Pope may at one stage have intended to print more of his work. The second possibility is that Parnell had already given Pope the material for a collected edition of his own poems, and that the reference in the letter means that Pope had decided that immediate publication was inadvisable. The political situation may only have been a pretext; Pope may well have been too busy with his own collected *Works* and with his translation of the *Iliad* to have felt able to take on the additional task of supervising the appearance of Parnell's poems. Thus there is at least the possibility that the genesis of the 1722 *Poems on Several Occasions* goes back as far as 1717. At some time after Parnell's death (in 1718), Pope replied to a letter in which Charles Jervas had chided him for overlooking the death of Rowe (who died in December 1718), that his oversight had been because "*Parnelle* was too much in my mind, to whose Memory I am erecting the best Monument I can. What he gave me to publish was but a small part of what he left behind him, but it was the best, and I will not make it worse by enlarging it" (*Pope Corr.* 2:24). Sherburn dates this letter in 1720; the extant text is a fabrication. Its statements must therefore be accepted with some caution, but they are not inherently improbable. Pope's phrase "what he gave me to publish" implies that Parnell had decided on a selected rather than a collected edition, and that Parnell himself had made a selection. Pope disclaims the idea of enlarging this selection, but it is possible that he omitted some poems that Parnell himself would have included.

The "Monument" to which Pope referred in his letter to Jervas, his edition of Parnell's *Poems on Several Occasions*, prefaced by a poem of his own dedicating the volume to the earl of Oxford, was published in December 1721, though with 1722 on the title page. It is a modest octavo of some 230 uncrowded pages, and includes (besides Pope's own) only twenty poems. Its physical appearance contrasts strongly with the large quarto monument to himself, the *Works* of 1717, that Pope had previously erected, and with the two bulky, pompous volumes of the duke of Buckingham's *Works* that Pope edited and that appeared in 1723. The modesty of the format of Parnell's *Poems* was appropriate to the nature of the enterprise as Pope saw it, a small collection of the best that Parnell had given him to publish. Yet doubts remain about whether the contents of Pope's edition were exactly such as Parnell would himself have chosen. It seems hard to imagine that Parnell would not have wanted to reprint his *Essay on the Different Styles of Poetry*. When Swift saw the Dublin edition of the collection, he was surprised at the omission of the *Essay* and attributed it to the malign influence of Parnell's younger brother (*Swift Corr.* 2:424).

It is also odd that a volume called *Poems on Several Occasions* should include five prose "Visions" (of which four had previously appeared in the *Spectator* and the *Guardian*), amounting to almost a fifth of the whole volume (39 pages).[3] Parnell's own poems, indeed, occupy only 165 of the 217 pages of text; the rest are taken up with Pope's dedicatory poem, the prose, the Latin text of the *Pervigilium Veneris,* and the passage from *The Rape of the Lock* that Parnell turned into Latin. Pope's claim, in the letter to Jervas, that he had more poems than he intended to print, was certainly correct. He later thought Parnell's version of Donne's "Third Satire" good enough to print among his own versifications of Donne in 1738. What other poems he had copies of is unknown. Joseph Spence recorded that Pope burned his remaining Parnell manuscripts.[4] Presumably, then, none of the subsequently published poems, nor any of the extant manuscripts, are to be traced back to the collection Parnell left with Pope. In his decision to print the prose pieces to the exclusion of more poems, Pope may have been influenced by a desire to record Parnell's connection with the *Spectator* and the *Guardian,* to both of which he had himself contributed.

Apart from the *Essay on the Different Styles of Poetry,* Pope excluded two of the shorter poems that Parnell had published: *The Horse and the Olive* and "To a Young Lady," from Steele's *Poetical Miscellanies.* He also printed *Homer's Battle of the Frogs and Mice* without the substantial prose pieces with which it had orginally been published. Various conjectures may be advanced for these exclusions. The *Essay* had been dedicated to Bolingbroke, in 1721 still an attainted rebel living in exile in France. But it seems unlikely that political prudence determined its exclusion. The references to Bolingbroke could have been excised as easily as they had been inserted (at Swift's suggestion) by Parnell; and Pope's own dedicatory poem to the disgraced earl of Oxford shows that he was not afraid of making a political gesture unfriendly to the government. A more plausible explanation is that in building his friend's monument he wished to exclude, not only a slight piece like *The Horse and the Olive,* but also poems that could only invite unfavorable comparison with his own. The *Essay on the Different Styles of Poetry* had from the first been overshadowed by Pope's own *Essay on Criticism.* It was probably to allow *Homer's Battle* to be appreciated independently as a translation of an amusing classical poem, detached from its original context in the Grub Street pamphlet warfare that surrounded Pope's own translation of the *Iliad,* that determined Pope to omit the "Zoilus" prose. The version of the "The Book-Worm" published in Pope's edition has fewer topical allusions than the longer version that survives in manuscript, and whether it was Parnell or Pope who was responsible for the changes, they are consistent with the general aim of classical permanence that was clearly the effect that Pope (and presumably also Parnell) wanted in *Poems on Several Occasions.*

Parnell thus appears in Pope's edition as a minor classic, as a poet of versatility and accomplishment rather than originality. Translations, poems related to classical models, and the minor genres (songs, eclogues, anacreontics) predominate. Pope's edition was skillfully arranged to display Parnell's variety and to present the poems in a sensible reading order. The lighter side of Parnell's talent is first displayed with "Hesiod" and the songs; the two long classical translations stand at the center of the book; and the more serious, meditative, and philosophical poems are reserved for the end. The following poems appeared in Pope's edition; they are here listed in the order in which Pope printed them. For the poems marked with an asterisk Pope's edition is the only textual authority; and briefly noted are the alternative texts of the other poems ("1755" refers to the *Works in Verse and Prose* of that date):

| | |
|---|---|
| "Hesiod: or, The Rise of Woman" | "Variations" in 1755 |
| "Song ("When thy beauty")" | Congleton MS |
| "Song ("Thyrsis")" | Congleton MS; "Variations" in 1755 |
| "Song ("My days have been")" | *Poetical Miscellanies* |
| "Anacreontic" ("When spring") | Congleton MS |
| "Anacreontic" ("Gay Bacchus") | Congleton MS; *Poetical Miscellanies* |
| "A Fairy Tale" | * |
| "The Vigil of Venus" | * |
| *Homer's Battle* | 1717 edition |
| "To Mr. Pope" | Pope's *Works* |

| | |
|---|---|
| "A Translation of Part of *The Rape of the Lock*" | *Pope's Own Miscellany* |
| "Health: An Eclogue" | Congleton MS |
| "The Flies: An Eclogue" | * |
| "An Elegy to an Old Beauty" | * |
| "The Book-Worm" | Congleton MS |
| "An Allegory on Man" | Congleton MS |
| "An Imitation of Some French Verses" | * |
| "A Night-Piece on Death" | "Variations" in 1755 |
| "A Hymn on Contentment" | *Poetical Miscellanies* |
| "The Hermit" | "Variations" in 1755 |

Apart from his responsibility for the selection and arrangement of the poems, Pope would certainly have regarded any improvements he could make to the texts of the poems as a legitimate and indeed necessary part of a friend's editorial duty. The poems that had been previously published appear in Pope's edition practically unchanged; this is not surprising, since at least three of them had passed through Pope's hands already on their way to their original publication. It is impossible to determine the extent of any improvements that Pope made to the poems that he was publishing for the first time in Parnell's *Poems on Several Occasions,* for we do not have the manuscripts from which he worked, or any manuscripts that we can confidently suppose textually close to Pope's manuscripts. Where we have manuscript evidence, it seems probable that these manuscripts are Parnell's penultimate drafts, from which he made the copies that he gave to Pope, rather than that Parnell retained duplicates of his final versions. This problem will be more fully discussed below, in relation to the 1755 *Works in Verse and Prose,* but attempted here is a note on the general character of the supposed Pope revisions. We have some form of pre-Pope text for nine of the fourteen poems first printed in Pope's edition. For three of these poems ("Hesiod," "A Night-Piece on Death," and "The Hermit") the only evidence is the "Variations" printed in the 1755 *Works in Verse and Prose.* The differences between these "Variations" and Pope's texts are of two kinds: some short passages (rarely longer than four lines) are found in the 1755 "Variations" but not in Pope's text, while Pope's text incorporates some small verbal improvements. For the "Song" ("Thyrsis"), we have, besides the "Variations," a manuscript of an early draft of the first stanza. Taking the three stages of the text together, we find the first stanza compressed and improved between the manuscript and the 1755 "Variations" and the whole song further compressed and improved between the 1755 "Variations" and Pope's text.

It would be wrong to build too much on the evidence of one poem, but it does show Parnell himself undertaking the same kind of pruning and polishing that is characteristic of the differences between the 1755 "Variations" and Pope's text. In the case of "The Book-Worm" we have some manuscript evidence for the whole poem as well as the 1755 "Variations" (which agree in the main with the manuscript). The poem is reduced from 136 lines in the manuscript to 100 lines in Pope's text, and the omissions (together with other changes) significantly alter the character of the poem. "The Book-Worm" is the only poem that is really changed in substance, as well as being shortened and improved, in Pope's edition. These changes are discussed below; here it is sufficient to say that they cannot be attributed conclusively either to Pope or to Parnell. For four other poems manuscripts are extant. Three of these manuscripts are evidently fair copies, only lightly corrected. The textual differences between these and Pope's text are much the same as have already been noted between the 1755 "Variations" and Pope's text: small-scale excisions and verbal improvements. These poems ("Song" ["When thy beauty"], "Health," and "An Allegory on Man") were evidently brought to almost their final state by Parnell; again, either he or Pope may have been responsible for their final form as they appear in Pope's edition.

Much more interesting is the surviving manuscript of the fourth poem, the "Anacreontic" ("When spring came on").[5] This seems also to have been begun as a fair copy, and about half the poem is only lightly corrected. But two passages of about ten lines each are very heavily worked over, and a third passage moderately heavily revised, clear evidence that what began as a fair copy could become a working manuscript. Although we cannot tell how often Parnell reworked his poems in this way, the "Anacreontic" manuscript is very important evidence of what might sometimes happen. It allows us to suppose that, even where we have a fair copy of a poem in Parnell's hand, discrepancies between that copy and Pope's text need not be attributed to Pope, for Parnell might have revised the poem in a subsequent manuscript before giving it to Pope.

Faced with the textual problems presented by Pope's edition, an editor has two main choices: to accept Pope's texts, or (whenever possible) to use an alternative, pre-Pope text. In this edition we have taken the second course only for the poems that were printed in Parnell's lifetime. With these poems the differences are slight, and we can be confident that these texts represent the poems in a form of which Parnell approved the publication. With the poems that first appeared in Pope's edition, however, we have preferred to accept Pope's texts; for in the case of these poems, we cannot be confident that the alternative texts we have (derived from the Congleton manuscripts and the 1755 "Variations") represent the poems in forms that Parnell would have approved for publication. To have based texts of these poems on extant manuscripts, and to have incorporated the 1755 "Variations" into the texts of the poems, would have been to risk rejecting authorial improvements and revisions and perpetuating texts that Parnell himself had rejected. On balance it has seemed better to us not to take this risk, even at the cost of admitting into the text some alterations that may be Pope's rather than Parnell's own.

Pope's idea of the duties of an editor and literary executor who was also a personal friend was one that sanctioned much greater liberties than would be thought proper today. If Parnell had lived to see his *Poems on Several Occasions,* he would probably have thought himself fortunate in the friendship of a great poet and tactful editor. The measure of how well Pope served his friend is that when, in 1758, a large collection of *Posthumous Works* was published, it was denounced as spurious on the grounds that the poems were too bad to have been written by the poet whose monument Pope had erected.[6] When Pope's dealings with his friends are assessed, this episode should be remembered to his credit.

### 3
### Uncollected Poems, 1721–1738

Although Pope was, in an informal sense, Parnell's literary executor and had been entrusted with the important manuscripts that would serve as the basis for *Poems on Several Occasions,* he did not gain possession of the entire collection of Parnell's literary manuscripts. Pope may have corresponded with Parnell's younger brother, but if so no evidence survives. It seems likely that the greater the proportion of the manuscripts in Pope's possession, the more limited would have been the growth of the Parnell canon. We do not know how careful Parnell was with his literary manuscripts; his unexpected death at Chester may have left them in greater disorder than would otherwise have been the case. Apart from those entrusted to Pope, the existence of the following important manuscripts is either known or can be inferred:

(1) the collection that passed to his brother and remained in the family, the residue of which forms part of the present Congleton papers;

(2) the manuscripts that were printed in 1758 as *Posthumous Works,* apparently presented to Benjamin Everard by Parnell himself; and British Library Add. MS 31114, which stands in a close but uncertain relationship to the Everard manuscripts;

(3) the manuscript used by the editor of the 1755 *Works in Verse and Prose.*

Each of these manuscripts will require separate and detailed treatment; between them they account for the greatest part of the posthumously published poems. We can also infer the existence of a number of less important manuscripts, possibly given or loaned by Parnell to friends in London and Dublin, some of which found their way into print. Ten new Parnell poems were published between 1721 and 1727; an eleventh was released by Pope himself in 1738. These poems are in no sense a group, having nothing in common beyond the accident of their circumstances of first publication. What little is known of these poems can be usefully summarized here.

The composition of the first to appear, "On the Death of Mr. Viner," must have been soon after Viner's death in November 1716. Although Parnell did not publish the poem, it is likely that manuscript copies circulated in Dublin, where Viner had been a prominent musician for many years. The poem was twice printed in 1721, apparently from independent manuscripts. A "John Parnel" is listed among the subscribers to *A Miscellaneous Collection of Poems*, edited by "T. M." (2 vols., Dublin, 1721). If we could be sure that he was the poet's younger brother, the appearance of the poem in the collection could be presumed to have been authorized by him. He might even have supplied the manuscript. No such presumption can be made in favor of the poem's appearance in *The Pleasures of Coition*, a Curll publication that was advertised in January 1721. We have been unable to date the appearance of the Dublin *Miscellaneous Collection*, and therefore to determine the priority between these two printings.

An edition of the *Carmina* published by Jacob Tonson (1720) seems to have suggested to Edmund Curll the idea of a translation of the poems of Jean Bonnefons (Johannes Bonefonius, 1554–1614). Bonnefons was not a prolific poet (his poems fill only seventy-five pages in the Tonson edition). It is an interesting example of Curll's publishing techniques that he chose to bulk out the Bonnefons poems with quite unrelated material to make three pamphlets, extending to over two hundred pages. The three pamphlets (often found bound together in libraries, and later reissued by Curll as a single volume) are as follows:

(1) *The Pleasures of Coition.* This contains a translation of Bonnefons's "Pervigilium Veneris" (pp. 7–22), together with other poems by various hands (pp. 23–56), including Parnell's "On the Death of Mr. Viner" (pp. 53–56). It is apparently the volume advertised in the *Post Boy* of 31 January as "Ten New Poems" (a more exact title); in the advertisement Parnell's poem is called "The Power of Musick."

(2) *Pancharis, Queen of Love.* This pamphlet prints selections from Bonnefons's "Basia" (pp. 1–30), together with other poems by various

hands (pp. 31–52), including six attributed to Parnell (pp. 36–46). This volume was advertised in the *Daily Post* on 27 March.

(3) *Cupid's Bee-Hive: or, The Sting of Love*. This publishes further translations from the "Basia" (pp. 1–10, 35–75, 89–90), mixed with other poems by various hands (pp. 10–34, 76–88, 91–94), but nothing by Parnell. It was advertised in the *Daily Post* on 21 April.[7]

The six poems attributed to Parnell in *Pancharis, Queen of Love,* are: "Chloris Appearing in a Looking Glass"; "On the Castle of Dublin"; "Love in Disguise"; "On a Lady with a Foul Breath"; "On the Number Three"; and the "Epigram" ("The greatest gifts"). Nothing is known of the source of these poems, for which (unlike "On the Death of Mr. Viner") Curll's edition is the only authority. There seems no reason to doubt the attribution, however; they are not unlike other Parnell poems, and we have accepted them as genuine.

"Piety: or, The Vision" and "Bacchus: or, The Vines of Lesbos" were printed in the *Dublin Weekly Journal* for 4 June 1726. At this time (1725–27) the regular literary feature of the *Journal* (usually an essay) took the form of a letter from "Hibernicus" (James Arbuckle). The two Parnell poems were printed under a covering letter from "Musophilus," another pseudonym for Arbuckle himself. Arbuckle (a Scot) arrived in Dublin from Glasgow in 1724, so cannot have known Parnell. In Dublin he was connected with the Molesworth circle and published a poem critical of Swift; he may have known John Parnell. Several copies of these two poems were evidently in existence, for they were both later printed (in each case apparently from independent manuscripts) in the 1755 *Works in Verse and Prose* and in the 1758 *Posthumous Works*.

"A Riddle" was published in the second volume of *Miscellanea* (2 vols., 1727), another Curll miscellany, among a group of poems attributed (not always correctly) to Swift and his friends. The accuracy of the Parnell attribution in this instance, however, is confirmed by the poem's reappearance in the 1758 *Posthumous Works*. The source of Curll's manuscript is again unknown, but several of the poems in the "Swift" group are evidently of Irish origin, and an Irish source is likely. The notes explaining the riddle are not found in the 1758 edition, and for them Curll's text is the sole authority.

Pope was responsible for the appearance in two of the 1738 printings of his own *Works*, volume 2, part 2, of "The Third Satire of Dr. John Donne." Pope's motive is clear; he wanted Parnell's poem to fill the gap between his own versifications of Donne's second and fourth satires. Yet he had presumably rejected the poem for *Poems on Several Occasions,* and he seems to have reverted to his earlier opinion of it, since he dropped it from later editions of his own *Works*.

**4**

*Works in Verse and Prose*
**(Glasgow, 1755)**

Despite the occasional printing of new Parnell poems, Pope's selection remained standard for over thirty years. Many editions of *Poems on Several Occasions* (for which see the Bibliography) added the "Zoilus" prose that Pope had omitted. Some Dublin editions added the *Essay on the Different Styles of Poetry* (it is tempting to see Swift's influence at work here, since we know he was annoyed at the poem's omission from Pope's edition; but there is no direct evidence of it). But the first edition to expand significantly on Pope's was the *Works in Verse and Prose*, published in Glasgow by the Foulis brothers in 1755. It remained respectful enough of Pope as editor to preserve the integrity of his selection, printing its additions at the end. These comprised the "Life" and "Remarks of Zoilus" (which had already been added to several earlier editions), and (much more important) some material previously unpublished: "Variations" from Pope's text said to be taken from Parnell's manuscript, and five new poems (strictly speaking three, since two had been printed in the *Dublin Weekly Journal* in 1726). These "Variations" were advertised as "taken from a MS. communicated by a Gentleman of Taste in Ireland; and are published as a Specimen of Mr. POPE's Alterations of the Verses of his Friend, such as he has himself given of his own Verses, in the latest Editions of his Works." The new poems are described as "published from the manuscript from which the foregoing variations were taken." We have no clue as to the identity of the "Gentleman of Taste," nor is the manuscript itself now extant. However, the genuineness of the manuscript can be accepted without question: two of the "new" poems survive in holograph manuscripts among the Congleton papers, which also contain manuscripts of "The Book-Worm," which authenticate the "Variations" in the text of that poem as printed in 1755. It should be noted, however, that although the editor of the *Works* seems to have respected the words of his manuscript (printing an incomplete line in "The Ecstasy," line 66), the edition modernizes spelling and the use of capitals and italic (this applies, of course, to the portions reprinted from Pope's edition as well as to the new material). Unless the manuscript was very unlike the surviving Parnell manuscripts, which are very lightly punctuated, the editor was also largely responsible for the punctuation of the new material in the 1755 edition. Nor does the editor seem to have retained the arrangement of his manuscript. The "Variations" are printed in the order in which the poems appear in Pope's edition ("Hesiod," "Song" ["Thyrsis"], "The Book-Worm," "A Night-Piece on Death," and "The Hermit"), which is most unlikely to have been that of the manuscript. The order of the new poems ("Bacchus," "Elysium," "To Dr. Swift," "Piety," and "Ecstasy") may reflect their sequence in the manuscript, where however they were surely found interspersed with the poems that Pope had printed. As we shall see after reviewing all the evidence, the manuscript used was probably a working notebook.

The editor of the 1755 *Works* assumed that the differences between his manuscript and Pope's text of the poems could be ascribed to Pope. Whether, or how far, this assumption was correct is one of the most difficult of the problems faced by an editor of Parnell's poems. Fortunately, much more evidence is now available to help solve the problem. There can be little doubt that Pope made some improvements to the texts of his friend's poems. While he was arranging for the printing and publication of *Homer's Battle of the Frogs and Mice,* Pope wrote to Parnell that "I scarce see any thing to be altered in this whole piece; in the poems you sent I will take the liberty you allow me. . . . Let me know how far my commission is to extend, and be confident of my punctual perform-ance of whatever you enjoin" (*Pope Corr.* 1 : 396). While we do not know exactly what was "the liberty you allow me" in relation to the (unspec-ified) "poems you sent," it is a natural inference that Pope was to correct them as he had previously been commissioned to correct the *Battle.* Since Pope later destroyed all his Parnell manuscripts, we have no way of knowing how extensive were his improvements to the poems he pub-lished for the first time. But an examination of the texts of the individual poems allows us to reach certain conclusions about the nature of the manuscript used by the editor of the 1755 edition.

For three of these poems ("Hesiod," "A Night-Piece on Death," and "The Hermit"), the 1755 "Variations" are the only evidence that allows us to see behind the texts that Pope printed. The differences are of two kinds; the "Variations" preserve a number of short passages omitted in Pope's edition and a number of lines that the editor thought had been improved by Pope. On literary grounds, Pope's texts are certainly to be preferred; and while Pope may have been responsible for the excisions and improvements, there is no reason at all to suppose that Parnell himself was incapable of making them. In the case of a fourth poem ("Song" ["Thyrsis"]), we do have evidence of Parnell himself making alterations of this kind. A draft of the first stanza of this poem exists among the Congleton papers; it consists of ten lines. An eight-line version of the stanza appears in the 1755 "Variations"; in Pope's text it is further reduced to six lines. If Parnell could make the first alteration, he could certainly have made the second.

More problematical is the case of the fifth poem, "The Book-Worm." Here we have two Congleton manuscripts: an imperfect holograph (lacking the first part of the poem) and a later transcript that seems, however, to preserve substantially the same text as the holograph. With one important exception, the 1755 "Variations" agree with the manuscripts. Pope's text omits ten brief passages (thirty lines in all) that are found both in the manuscripts and in the 1755 "Variations." There is, however, a twelve-line passage in the manuscripts that is not found among the 1755 "Variations" and that is replaced in Pope's text by six lines not found elsewhere. This passage raises a nontextual problem as well, for it contains an elaborate compliment to the duke of Marlborough that seems out of place and that complicates the question of the poem's date. "The Book-Worm" is the only poem whose character is really changed in Pope's text, for besides the Marlborough passage several of the shorter omissions in Pope's text remove topical references. As we have already suggested, one of the principles on which Pope seemed to work in editing *Poems on Several Occasions* was the avoidance of the topical; in the case of this poem, then, it may be thought that the balance of probabilities favors assigning responsibility for the revisions to Pope himself.

Two of the "new" poems in the *Works in Verse and Prose* ("Bacchus" and "Piety") had already been printed in the *Dublin Weekly Journal* in 1726, and would again appear in Parnell's *Posthumous Works* (Dublin, 1758; this edition is discussed in more detail below). It is difficult to determine the relationships between the three texts of these poems; what evidence there is suggests that each of the three printings was based on an independent manuscript, and that the verbal variants in the 1755 text are superior. It seems likely that, in the case of these two poems, the 1755 text was based on a manuscript that contained later readings than the manuscripts behind the other printings.

For the three poems that were printed for the first time in the *Works in Verse and Prose,* however, we can show that its texts are inferior. "To Dr. Swift" was later printed in Swift's *Works* (1765) from a different and clearly later manuscript. It is a reasonable conjecture that the 1765 text was printed from the copy of the poem that Parnell actually sent to Swift, and that, being found among Swift's papers, would naturally find its way into print among Swift's own literary remains; whereas the 1755 text was printed from an earlier draft of the poem that Parnell retained in his own possession. Manuscripts of the two remaining poems, "Elysium" and "Ecstasy", survive among the Congleton papers, the latter in two versions. The 1755 text of "Elysium" can be shown to be intermediate between the two manuscript texts: it prints an incomplete line (line 66) that is clearly a transitional stage between the two manuscripts; and it preserves readings found only in the earlier manuscript (line 90) or canceled in the later one (line 9). Similarly the 1755 text of "Elysium" can be shown to be earlier than the extant manuscript of the poem.

All the evidence points to the conclusion that the manuscript used by the editor of the *Works in Verse and Prose* was a working notebook containing poems in different stages of composition. Some of its poems had been copied from earlier texts in other notebooks or loose papers; some would in turn be copied elsewhere. Each time the poem was copied it would naturally be revised, if only in small ways. Since we know that in the case of three of the poems ("To Dr. Swift," "The Ecstasy," and "Elysium") Parnell himself made later, more authoritative copies of the poems, it is probable that he did so in the case of some of the other seven poems and possible that he did so for them all. The alterations that the 1755 editor ascribed to Pope may well have been present in the manuscripts that Parnell supplied to Pope; some of them may indeed be Pope's own, but we have no way of knowing which these were. Our editorial policy, as noted above in discussing Pope's *Poems on Several Occasions,* has been to accept Pope's texts of the poems first published in his edition. To have incorporated the 1755 "Variations" into the texts of the poems would have risked excluding some of Parnell's own revisions, a serious risk since the manuscript on which they were based certainly contained poems that Parnell had recopied and revised elsewhere. (If, as we have suggested, the text of "To Dr. Swift," a poem written for Swift's birthday in 1713, is a penultimate draft, that would indicate that the notebook was in use during 1713.)

## 5
### *Posthumous Works* (Dublin, 1758)

This edition, which was reissued in London in the same year with a new title page, is an important but problematical volume. It contains twenty-eight poems, of which only five had been previously printed; and for eighteen poems it furnishes our only text. The anonymous editor left it to his readers to decide "how far these Productions come up to, if not excel any of his former" poems. At the same time he anticipated that "they might be doubted really his," and to allay such doubts he printed what purported to be both a note of provenance and a certificate of authenticity:

> The following POEMS were given by the Author to the late *Benjamin Everard,* Esq; and since his Death, found by his Son among several other valuable Manuscripts, who gave them to the Editor; The

Receipt annexed in Dean SWIFT's own hand Writing, and found at the same time, shews an Acknowledgment that they are actually Genuine.
   Dec. 5, 1723.
   Then Received from *Benjamin Everard* Esq; the above Writings of the late Doctor PARNELL, in four stitched Volumes of Manuscript; which I Promise to restore to him on Demand,
                    JONATHAN SWIFT.

The genuineness of the poems was, nevertheless, denied by the reviewer of the volume in the *Gentleman's Magazine,* principally on the ground of their poor quality.[8] This review was given wider circulation by being reprinted in the *Scots Magazine* and (in part) in the *London Chronicle.* A different opinion was expressed by the *Monthly Review,* which accepted the poems as probably genuine, though certainly inferior.[9]

   The authenticity of the poems in the 1758 edition was established by C. J. Rawson.[10] Most important, six of the poems are extant in holograph manuscripts; four in British Library Additional MS 31114, and two among the Congleton papers. Indirect evidence is found in the appearance of four of the poems (including the two for which we have Congleton manuscripts) in the 1755 *Works in Verse and Prose,* whose new material can in turn be authenticated by the Congleton manuscripts. Further testimony to the "four stitched Volumes" having really existed is provided by textual evidence that, where the 1758 collection prints a previously published poem, its text is independent of the earlier printings.

   The existence of Benjamin Everard can also be corroborated, and his connections with Parnell demonstrated. In 1711–13, a Benjamin Everard was a churchwarden of Finglas, of which Parnell became vicar in 1716. Everard and Parnell are found acting together in the establishment of a parish library and in the improvement of the church fabric. Copies of *An Essay on the Different Stiles of Poetry,* 1713, and *Homer's Battle of the Frogs and Mice,* 1717, inscribed in Parnell's hand "For Benj: Everard Esq," are in the Nickell Collection at the University of Illinois at Urbana-Champaign. A Benjamin Everard (who cannot, unfortunately, be positively identified with the churchwarden) is known to have married and to have become the father of twin sons in 1736. This Benjamin Everard died in 1756; his will connects him with Finglas (he left money to the poor of the parish, and gave directions for his burial there) and establishes that he owned "Books Manuscrips papers" sufficiently important to be mentioned in such a document. In 1758 his sons (or a surviving son) would recently have come of age, and the conclusion seems inescapable that one of them provided the manuscripts on which the *Posthumous Works* was based. The editor says that the manuscripts were given by the poet himself to the elder Everard, and while this may be only a family tradition it does tend to strengthen the identification between Parnell's churchwarden and the Everard who died in 1756.

While there is no reason to doubt the genuineness of Swift's receipt, it does raise problems. The original reviewer in the *Gentleman's Magazine* made the point that such a receipt would have been surrendered when the volumes were returned by Swift to Everard. Yet the point of the receipt may have been, not that Everard did not trust Swift, but rather that he wanted it as an authentication of the poems being really Parnell's. The receipt (and the list to which it was presumably originally subjoined) may have been kept available for inspection by the curious and doubtful, though it has since disappeared.

If, as seems most likely, the Everard to whom Parnell gave the volumes of manuscript poetry was the churchwarden, this would be consistent with the predominance of religious poetry in the collection. It is even plausible to identify the volume now in the British Library with one of the four volumes given to Everard, for its four poems occupy 76½ pages, or about one-quarter of the 286 pages that the entire Everard corpus occupies in the 1758 edition. Close examination, however, shows that this cannot have been the case. The British Library volume is not marked in any way that would suggest that it had been used as printer's copy. More important, where the manuscript has been corrected or revised (in Parnell's hand), the 1758 edition has sometimes the earlier reading, sometimes the later one. If Add. MS 31114 were directly behind the 1758 text, it could be expected that the printer would have chosen in most instances at least the more legible reading. But this is not the case. A small but clinching point is the evidence from two lines ("Moses," lines 502 and 650) where Parnell's revised reading is written directly on top of the original, all but obliterating it. No compositor, with the British Library manuscript as his copy, would have set these original readings, yet they are in the 1758 text. This must mean that the *Posthumous Works* was set neither from this manuscript, nor from a transcript of it in its present state (though it could have been set from a transcript of the manuscript in an earlier state). Nevertheless, the differences between the two texts are few and minor enough for it to be clear that the 1758 text derives from a manuscript textually close to the British Library one. Most probably the lost manuscript was a transcript made before Parnell had added to the surviving manuscript his latest revisions. This conclusion raises the further question of why Parnell should have wanted to copy out a nearly identical manuscript of the lengthy biblical paraphrases.[11] It cannot have been for publication, for it seems clear that these poems were written with no thought or expectation of being printed. To attempt to answer this question leads to a consideration of the nature and order of the poems in the 1758 edition.

There seems no reason to doubt that the 1758 edition prints the poems as they were found in the "four stitched Volumes." In the following list summary details of other substantive texts of the individual poems are added; for the poems marked * the 1758 edition is our only text:

| | |
|---|---|
| "The Gift of Poetry" | |
| "Moses" | British Library Add. MS |
| "Deborah" | 31114 |
| "Hannah" | |
| "David" | * |
| "Solomon" | * |
| "Jonah" | * |
| "Hezekiah" | * |
| "Habakkuk" | * |
| "The Vision of Piety" | *Dublin Weekly Journal*, 1726; *Works in Verse and Prose*, 1755 |
| "A Hymn for Morning" | * |
| "A Hymn for Noon" | * |
| "A Hymn for Evening" | * |
| "The Soul in Sorrow" | * |
| "The Happy Man" | * |
| "The Way to Happiness" | * |
| "The Convert's Love" | * |
| "A Desire to Praise" | * |
| "On Happiness in this Life" | * |
| "Ecstasy" | Congleton MSS (two versions); *Works in Verse and Prose*, 1755 |
| "On Divine Love" | * |
| "On Queen Anne's Peace" | * |
| "Elysium" | Congleton MS; *Works in Verse and Prose*, 1755 |
| "The Judgment of Paris" | * |
| "Bacchus" | *Dublin Weekly Journal*, 1726; *Works in Verse and Prose*, 1755 |
| "A Riddle" | *Miscellanea*, 1727 |
| "On Mrs. Arabella Fermor" | * |
| "On the Bishop of Sarum" | Swift's *Works*, 1765 |

As we have seen, the first four poems (those in the British Library manuscript) occupy 76½ pages in the 1758 edition. The remaining biblical poems (from "David" to "Habakkuk") fill 135 pages, and so would fit into two volumes of about the same size as Add. MS 31114. The remaining poems are all short; they occupy only 74 pages in 1758 and would fit into a single volume of the same size. Here, then, is a plausible reconstruction of the contents of the "four stitched Volumes" that Swift saw.

We may further observe that, with the single exception of the British Library manuscript, all the poems for which we have alternative texts would have appeared in the fourth volume. In conjunction with other evidence, some important inferences can be drawn from this. The biblical paraphrases form a self-contained group and are likely to be early poems; the shorter poems are more miscellaneous, and some ("On Queen Anne's Peace" and "On the Bishop of Sarum") can be no earlier than 1713. We do not know when Parnell became acquainted with the Benjamin Everard to whom it seems likely that he gave a collection of his poems. It could have been as early as 1705, when there was a possibility of Parnell's being appointed vicar of Finglas, or as late as 1716, when he was actually appointed. The most likely time for such a gift would surely have been at or about the time of appointment. Yet it seems most unlikely that, as late as 1716, Parnell would have had the inclination to write out a presentation copy of the long biblical paraphrases, which he must then have regarded as no more than juvenilia. There is a strong possibility, however, that in 1716 Parnell may have had two copies of these poems. In "Hannah" an autobiographical passage describes the poet as "a gift devoted in the womb . . . Like Samuel vowd before my breath I drew" (lines 234–35). There is other evidence that Parnell's mother wanted him to become a priest. It seems quite possible that the biblical poems were written, at least in part, to please his mother, and probable that he may have copied them out for her. The poet's mother died in 1708, at which time her copies of his poems would naturally have come back into his own possession. They would thus have been available for presentation to an important parishioner with whom Parnell hoped to establish a close working relationship (as we have seen Parnell did with the churchwarden Everard). To the three volumes of biblical poems Parnell could have added a fourth containing a selection of his more recent poems, especially copied out (not necessarily by the poet himself) for presentation. The inclusion of the two topical poems of 1713 ("On Queen Anne's Peace" and the satirical poem "On the Bishop of Sarum") suggests that in politics Everard was a Tory.

Of the poems that would have been contained in the fourth of the Everard volumes, the group from "A Hymn for Morning" to "On Happiness in this Life" stands out as a long sequence of poems that exist in no alternative texts. Among the Congleton manuscripts is a list or inventory of Parnell's writings that refers to a number of works not now known and that implies the existence of manuscripts apparently no longer extant. This list (which is not in Parnell's hand) includes two groups of poems that were evidently thought of as sequences or units. The list gives the number of lines in each of the poems, and also the total number of lines in each of the two groups. One of the groups is called "The Gift of Poetry" and includes the eight biblical poems. The other, and much less obvious, sequence is called "The Affections of Divine Poetry" and comprises, in the same order, the seven poems printed in 1758 from "A Hymn for Morning" to "The Convert's Love," with two further poems listed as "On yᵉ Divine Love" and "On Contentment." We can plausibly reconstruct how Parnell adapted this group of poems to fill part of the fourth Everard volume. He prefixed "Piety: or, The Vision" as an introduction to the whole group (much as "The Gift of Poetry" serves as an introduction to the biblical poems). "On yᵉ Divine Love" is probably the same poem as "On Divine Love, by Meditating on the Wounds of Christ," which occurs in the 1758 collection at a slightly later point than might have been expected from its position in the Congleton list. If (as the similar number of lines in the two poems suggests) "On Contentment" is the same poem as the "Hymn to Contentment" that had been printed in Steele's *Poetical Miscellanies* (1714), Parnell might well have preferred to substitute for it the still-unpublished "Ecstasy." The fact that "Ecstasy" survives in two slightly different versions among the Congleton manuscripts and that it was also among the poems in the working notebook used by the editor of the 1755 *Works in Verse and Prose* may be further evidence that it was a later poem than those listed in the "Affections of Divine Poetry" group. This account is admittedly conjectural, assuming the existence of some manuscripts that are no longer extant. The four Everard volumes have disappeared, as was normal for printer's copy in the eighteenth century. Of the three volumes containing Parnell's own copies of the biblical poems, one has survived and the others may yet be found. On the whole, we may be reasonably confident that the 1758 *Posthumous Works* was indeed printed, as its editor claimed, from a four-volume collection of his unpublished poetry given by Parnell to Everard.

If the authenticity of the poems is beyond doubt, the question of the reliability of the actual texts (an important consideration since for eighteen poems it is our only text) is more problematical. On this point all the evidence points to the *Posthumous Works* being a careless and unreliable text. The most important evidence is provided by a comparison between Add. MS 31114 and the poems as printed in 1758. A few figures and examples will briefly indicate the nature of the differences between the manuscript and the printed text. The four poems extend to a total of 1,496 lines (excluding from the count lines that are canceled in the manuscript). The manuscript is corrected or revised in some 150 passages, usually by a new reading written above the earlier one, but sometimes (possibly indicating that Parnell had not finally made up his mind) by a new reading entered above without deletion of the old. In some eighty-six passages, 1758 follows the corrected manuscript reading, in some thirty-four it reproduces the original reading; but there is no consistent relationship between this pattern and whether the original reading is actually canceled or not.[12] For example, in "Deborah," where "assures" is written above the original uncanceled "secures" (line 58), 1758 prints "secures"; yet only two lines later, where "furling" is written above the similarly uncanceled "Waving" (line 60), 1758 prints "furling." The evidence of the revised passages is that 1758 was based on a transcript of the British Library manuscript, probably made by Parnell himself, on which he continued to work but without always making the same changes to both his copies. This is consistent with the hypothesis advanced above, that the Everard manuscript of the biblical poems may originally have been copied for Parnell's mother.

Apart from the passages revised in the manuscript, the 1758 edition departs from the reading of the surviving manuscript in some 123 instances that involve a difference in a word rather than spelling or punctuation. Most of these are probable errors on 1758's part, some being due to likely misreadings of Parnell's hand, such as "burning" for "turning" ("Moses," line 764) and "perishing" for "persisting" ("Hannah," line 195). Such examples are evidence that the transcript was authorial. More frequent are errors due to carelessness (although some of these, too, might be ascribed to misreading if we could see the actual manuscript from which the 1758 compositor worked). The commonest classes of such errors (of which numerous examples will be found in the textual notes) are the addition or omission of final *s* (less commonly *d*), and confusion and substitution between such similar words as *the, thy, their,* and *her* (although some of these examples might well be authorial substitutions). Authors transcribing their own work are liable to make the same kinds of error as other transcribers, and will introduce some "indifferent" variants and unconscious substitutions. The hypothesis that 1758 was printed from an authorial transcript is supported by the evidence of some variants that are at least possibly authorial. The most convincing evidence is a small group of readings that may be characterized as "intermediate revisions," where 1758 seems to preserve a reading later than the original manuscript reading but earlier than the manuscript revision. Such readings are difficult to account for except on the hypothesis of an authorial transcript behind 1758. The best example is from "Deborah," where the beginning of line 27 originally read (in the manuscript) "A mossy bank upon its root." In 1758 the line begins "Near the firm root a mossy bank"; in the manuscript the line is revised to read "Near the broad root a mossy bank." In the same poem, line 43 originally ended "beneath thy sword." Parnell started to revise this to read "thine edg——," but before finishing "edge" he deleted "ed" and made the word into "glittering," without, however, making the necessary change of "thine" back to "thy." In 1758, the line ends "thine edged sword." In both these lines, 1758 may be correctly reproducing the readings of the transcript in which Parnell made his first attempts to revise these passages. Other examples are less certain, since they could also be errors on 1758's part (see the textual notes on "The Gift of Poetry," line 11; "Moses," lines 608, 701, 726; and "Deborah," line 304).

Some features of the 1758 text suggest that it was not edited in the modern sense, but that its compositors were responsible for (for example) its very poor punctuation. A very odd feature is the printing of whole words in capitals (usually, but not always, proper names). This never occurs in the British Library manuscript, nor does it occur in signatures B-D (pp. 1–24) of 1758; from signature E onwards, however, it occurs erratically. The words so printed are not always underlined, or spelled with even an initial capital, in the manuscript (the most absurd example is "PENNONS," "Deborah," line 116). Here we have what is surely a compositorial quirk, and we have felt justified in removing it from our texts of the poems printed from 1758. We know from the body of the surviving manuscripts that Parnell punctuated very lightly; the compositors of 1758 scattered marks of punctuation throughout the text, but it was clearly done stick-in-hand on an almost line-by-line basis. Patently, little attempt was made by an editor or proofreader to punctuate for sense.

All the evidence so far adduced can be readily explained on the hypothesis that 1758 was carelessly printed from an authorial transcript of Additional MS 31114 (and its lost companions) when in an only partially revised state. Supporting evidence can be produced from the shorter poems. Wherever we have an alternative text, 1758's text is clearly inferior and exhibits the same classes of error (especially the confusion between singular and plural caused by the addition or omission of final s) as we have seen in comparing 1758 with the British Library manuscript. It follows that, as a textual authority, 1758 must always be treated with suspicion, especially when a variant belongs to one of its typical kinds of error. Even so, of course, each variant must be treated on its merits, since changes between singular and plural are possibly authorial. The texts where 1758 is our only witness need particular scrutiny; many corruptions are likely to have crept in, but the uncertainties involved in speculative emendation have induced us (except in rare cases) to prefer 1758's reading to a plausible correction.

Although we have respected its words, the "1758 only" poems are in general so badly punctuated that we have (as explained below) in their case taken greater liberties with their punctuation.

After 1758, no new poems were printed as Parnell's. In 1786, however, the Foulis Press of Glasgow (which had printed the 1755 *Works in Verse and Prose*) published a splendid folio edition (see Bibliography, B29) of nearly all of Parnell's known poems (omitting only the seven uncollected poems that had appeared in 1721). The edition was dedicated to Sir John Parnell, a descendant of the poet's younger brother, but no use seems to have been made of any family manuscripts. Great care, however, was evidently expended on the printing of the edition. In 1790, an even fuller edition (omitting only "To a Young Lady") was published as Volume 27 of *The Works of the English Poets* (Bibliography, B30).

## 6
## New Poems in This Edition

This edition provides the first substantial expansion of the corpus of Parnell's poetry since 1758. This new material is derived from manuscripts preserved among the papers of the descendants of Parnell's younger brother, and kindly made available to us by the present Lord Congleton.[13] By 1758 sixty poems had been printed as Parnell's. This edition adds sixty-seven new English poems and seven fragments, besides ten poems in Latin. Only a summary account of this new material is given here; fuller details of the manuscripts themselves are provided in the commentary.

Most important is the "Satires" Notebook. This is largely in Parnell's hand and is the source of twenty-five new English poems and of three in Latin. In addition, it supplies texts of eight of the poems printed in the eighteenth century. It contains thirty-seven items in all, and no pages seem to have been removed. An indication of the date on which Parnell began to use it is supplied by the first poem ("In Librum hunc"), which is dated 1702; some poems earlier than 1702 seem to have been copied into it, however, and Parnell must still have been using it early in 1713, the most likely date of composition for *The Horse and the Olive*.

Much smaller is the "Lyrics" Notebook, almost entirely in Parnell's hand and containing fifteen items, of which eleven are new English poems. Many pages of this notebook have been removed, leaving two fragmentary endings of poems. In addition, it contains early drafts of the first stanza of the "Song" ("Thyrsis") and of the whole of the "Song" ("When thy beauty").

Four other notebooks contain material of literary interest. One contains a late (probably nineteenth-century) transcript of "The Book-Worm." (An incomplete holograph of the poem is also preserved among the loose manuscripts [see below], but the transcript, which claims to have been copied "from y^e original," is of textual value). The "Homer" Notebook contains autograph texts of the unpublished dedication and of the published preface to the "Life of Zoilus." The "Zoilus" Notebook is largely nonautograph, but contains not only the dedication and preface, but also the "Life of Zoilus." The last few pages of the "Life" are in Parnell's hand. The "Essay" Notebook contains an autograph text of the *Essay on the Different Styles of Poetry*. Apart from the unused dedication, these notebooks contain no new material, but they provide interesting glimpses of Parnell at work on both his prose and his verse. The manuscript of the *Essay* is particularly important for the confirmation it provides of Swift's role in the revision and publication of the poem. Three of these notebooks were formerly enclosed in a blue envelope, which included also two loose manuscripts. One of these is the very important sheet of "Epigrams," the most interesting of the new poems, which have already been published by the present editors.[14] The other loose manuscript (not in Parnell's hand) is a text of an anonymous poem of 1697.[15]

Apart from the notebooks, a collection of twenty-eight manuscripts, formerly kept in a blue envelope similar to the one that enclosed the material mentioned above, contains many items of literary interest, including an inventory (not autograph) or list of Parnell's works. Between them, these loose manuscripts provide holograph texts of five poems not found elsewhere, of two poetic fragments, and of a prose essay containing three passages in verse. In addition there are texts (not all autograph) of some of the published poems and of some of the poems found in the "Satires" Notebook. The most interesting are the autograph text of part of "The Book-Worm" and the heavily corrected working manuscript of "Anacreontic" ("When spring comes on").[16] There is also a sheet containing eight Latin poems in Parnell's hand, probably student exercises. Finally, there are five poems (none in Parnell's hand) which we regard as, for various reasons, not Parnell's; these are described in the Appendix, where our reasons for rejecting them are set out.

A single unpublished poem, "For Philip Ridgate, Esq.," was among a collection of Parnell-related manuscripts from the Congleton papers that came to light earlier than the major find described above.[17]

A small but interesting notebook containing fourteen poems, thirteen of which must be the earliest of Parnell's poems to survive (the fourteenth is probably by Parnell's father), was purchased in England in 1925 by Paul S. Schoedinger. Its earlier provenance is unknown, but it must once have formed part of the main body of Parnell manuscripts. These poems were included as an appendix to Schoedinger's Ph.D. dissertation "The Life and Works of Thomas Parnell" (Yale University, 1940). The notebook itself is now on deposit among the archives of the Columbus Academy, Gahanna, Ohio.

The arrangement of these new poems presents a problem of order. We have decided to respect the integrity of the notebooks as units, and to print the new poems in the following order: the "Schoedinger" Notebook (which clearly contains the earliest poems, several dated in the 1690s); the "Satires" Notebook (which was begun in 1702); the "Lyrics" Notebook (the remaining contents of which seem later than the first poems in the "Satires" Notebook); and finally the poems from the loose manuscripts, in what we believe to be a logical order for reading.

## 7
## Editorial Principles and Practices of This Edition

The long and complicated textual history of Parnell's poems thus briefly summarized presents his modern editors with some awkward choices and difficult problems. Those few poems that were published either by Parnell himself or by Pope were carefully printed, and their texts offer few difficulties either for editor or reader. The posthumous poems, however, create a variety of different textual problems, including the problem of how best to present them to a modern reader. In the case of the 1758 *Posthumous Works* (our sole text for eighteen poems), we can check about one-quarter of its text against an autograph manuscript, and we know that its system (if it can be so called) of capitalization and punctuation is neither Parnell's own nor in itself either intelligent or consistent. In the case of the many poems now first published from (mainly) autograph manuscripts, the texts are generally very lightly punctuated. Parnell himself uses a number of forms (ampersands, superscript letters, abbreviations) that would certainly have been regularized if the poems had been printed in his own time, nor is he consistent in following such conventions as beginning a new line of poetry with a capital letter. Faced with this variety of textual sources, an editor has three main choices: scrupulous fidelity to the forms of the texts from which the poems are taken; regularization, inevitably involving partial or total modernization; or some compromise between the more extreme courses, such as leaving the poems published by Parnell and Pope in their original published forms, while taking greater liberties with (for example) the punctuation of the posthumous and manuscript texts.

Each of these courses has its attractions and drawbacks, and each might be suitable for a particular kind of edition. We have chosen the first course as the most suitable for the scholarly audience for whom this edition is primarily intended.[18] Regularization and modernization would be the right policy for a selection of Parnell's poems edited for a general readership, but scholars will want to read a text as close as possible to what Parnell wrote and with the minimum of editorial interference. Nor, in practice, is it possible to make a satisfactory compromise between fidelity to the original and regularization without losing more than is gained. The very inconsistencies between poems, some of which appear in careful eighteenth-century style while others are taken from rough, unfinished manuscripts, is itself an advantage. Readers will be reminded by the appearance of the poem whether it is one published by Parnell or Pope, or whether it is now first printed (and perhaps never given its final form by Parnell).

In the case of poems printed from earlier printed texts, our general aim (apart from the silent suppression of the long $s$) has been to reproduce the spelling and punctuation of the original exactly. All departures from the copy-text are recorded in the notes. Where (exceptionally) we have changed the punctuation of the copy-text without the authority of a better text (as in the case of the "1758 only" poems), this is recorded, so that it is always possible to reconstruct the original form as well as wording of the copy-text. In the case of poems printed from manuscript sources, we have tried to print what seems to have been Parnell's final intention, recording earlier readings in the notes wherever they are decipherable. In general, where it is uncertain whether a letter is intended as a capital or not (as happens frequently with $s$), we have treated it as lower case unless it begins a proper name or a line of verse. Ampersands, contractions, and superscript letters are preserved, but Parnell's occasional use of the tailed $q$ has been treated as "que." Parnell's manuscripts are very lightly punctuated, and to punctuate them is often to impose on the reader the editor's reading of a phrase or a line. Where we have felt it would help the reader to have guidance with difficult or ambiguous syntax, we have provided this in the commentary, not in the text itself. Thus where the punctuation (or lack of it) is Parnell's own, we have been careful not to interfere with it; but where (as in the case of the "1758 only" poems) it seems to be largely compositorial, we have felt free (though conservatively) to emend.

Apart from recording departures from the copy-text, the textual notes record all significant variants from all the texts of any authority. The exact scope of the textual notes varies according to the particular textual situation, and is explained in the headnote to each poem or group of poems. Some general points may be noted here. Except in rare cases, the text of a poem printed from a manuscript copy-text will contain the latest readings of the manuscripts, and the earlier ones will be recorded in the textual notes. Where a reading is canceled in the manuscript, it is placed within angle brackets ⟨ ⟩; where an earlier reading is left uncanceled (usually with the later one written above), it is placed in scrolled brackets, { }. Textual authorities in agreement are separated by a comma; alternative readings are separated by a semicolon. Since we almost never record differences in spelling, the agreement implied is with the word or mark of punctuation involved, not necessarily the way a word is spelled. With some forms that might give rise to confusion (such as & in a manuscript and *and* in a printed text), we have given both forms. While we have not attempted to record every stroke of Parnell's pen, we have tried to present all the evidence that has a bearing on the text, sometimes recording (for example) the fact of an illegible deletion as evidence of Parnell's having revised the text at that point. Parnell frequently retained part of a rejected reading to form part of the revised one. Because of this, it is not possible to indicate economically exactly which words or letters he actually deleted. In the textual notes, therefore, the canceled reading as a whole is placed in angle brackets, even though some of the words or letters may have been left to stand as part of the new reading. This system facilitates the easy comparison of different readings. More complicated cases defy such presentation, and have been explained in words.

In the explanatory notes we have tried to provide such literary and historical information as is needed for a reading and understanding of the poems. Since the poems are of uneven interest, however, we have not treated each on the same scale. Some of the poems, such as the songs and lyrics, hardly require notes at all. In the case of the long biblical paraphrases, we have been content to point out the main passages from the Bible from which Parnell was working. We have tried to indicate Parnell's sources and to explicate his allusions, but inevitably some of both will have escaped us.

## Notes

1. For the abbreviated citations used in the Introduction, see the list in the headnote to the Commentary.

2. The arguments in favor of minimal regularization of manuscript texts when they are transferred to print are developed at length in G. Thomas Tanselle, "The Editing of Historical Documents," *Studies in Bibliography* 31 (1978): 1–56. Although Tanselle is there primarily concerned with historical documents, his arguments apply equally to texts such as Parnell's unpublished poems.

3. The four visions that had been previously published were *Spectator*, Nos. 460 (18 August 1712) and 501 (4 October 1712); ed. Donald F. Bond (Oxford: Clarendon Press,

1965, 4:121–24, 276–79; and *Guardian*, Nos. 56 (15 May 1713) and 66 (27 May 1713); ed. John C. Stephens (Lexington: University of Kentucky Press, 1982), 217–20, 250–53. The fifth vision (an allegory of a library) may also have been written for one of the periodical papers, but its first appearance in print was in *Poems on Several Occasions*.

4. *Anecdotes*, ed. James M. Osborn (Oxford: Clarendon Press, 1966), No. 139.

5. This manuscript is reproduced on pp. 134–37 of this edition.

6. See note 8 below.

7. These oddly-composed volumes are not untypical of Curll; see the handlist of his publications in Ralph Straus, *The Unspeakable Curll* (1927), especially (for 1721) pp. 265–69.

8. *The Gentleman's Magazine* 28 (June 1758): 282–84. Reviewing Johnson's edition, the *Gentleman's Magazine* admitted (49 [December 1779]: 599) that it had "somewhat too severely censured" the 1758 volume. Nichols, the proprietor of the *Gentleman's Magazine*, had a financial interest in Johnson's edition, but he had also an antiquarian interest in poetry, and was the first (for example) to collect the Parnell poems that had appeared in *Pancharis, Queen of Love* in 1721.

9. *The Monthly Review* 19 (October 1758): 380–85. A particularly interesting comment in this review is the suggestion that the biblical poems might be late rather than (as one might more naturally suppose) early: "His advancing years, and his probable retirement from court . . . might naturally concur to dispose his muse to the choice of scriptural and religious subjects" (p. 380). Although general probability counts heavily against the idea, there is one piece of evidence that might support this view, the virtual absence of triplets in the biblical poems (there is only one, in "David"). The author of the review was James Kirkpatrick, a regular contributor of reviews of medical works (he was an M.D.) and occasionally of poetry (B. C. Nangle, *The Monthly Review, First Series, 1749–1789: Indexes of Contributors and Articles* [Oxford: Clarendon Press, 1934], 24, 171).

10. "Swift's Certificate to Parnell's *Posthumous Works*," *Modern Language Review* 57 (1962): 179–82. The following paragraphs draw on the evidence about the Everards that is assembled in this article.

11. It is, of course, possible that only the first volume ever existed in duplicate.

12. These figures are only approximate; the complexities involved, and the number of doubtful and intermediate readings, make it impossible to give exact numbers. But the proportions are about right.

13. These manuscripts were briefly described in C. J. Rawson, "New Parnell Manuscripts," *The Scriblerian* 1.2 (Spring 1969): 1–2.

14. C. J. Rawson and F. P. Lock, "Scriblerian Epigrams by Thomas Parnell," *Review of English Studies* 33 (1982): 138–47.

15. The poem is *Advice to a Painter*, for which see the Appendix.

16. See note 5 above.

17. These were described and discussed in C. J. Rawson, "Some Unpublished Letters of Pope and Gay: And Some Manuscript Sources of Goldsmith's Life of Thomas Parnell," *Review of English Studies* 10 (1959): 371–87.

18. That is, our "aim is historical—the reproduction of a particular text or the reconstruction of what the author intended"; see G. Thomas Tanselle, "Recent Editorial Discussion and the Central Questions of Editing," *Studies in Bibliography* 34 (1981): 23–65. The quotation is from p. 60.

# Collected Poems of
# THOMAS PARNELL

*For Benj: Everard Esq*
*The Author*
*Tho Parnell*

# An E S S A Y

## O N   T H E

## Different Stiles

### O F

# P O E T R Y.

Parnell's First Published Poem, with half-title showing Parnell's inscription to Benjamin Everard. *(Courtesy of the University of Illinois at Urbana-Champaign.)*

# AN
# ESSAY
## ON THE
## 𝕯𝖎𝖋𝖋𝖊𝖗𝖊𝖓𝖙 𝕾𝖙𝖎𝖑𝖊𝖘
## OF
# POETRY.

---

—*Vatibus addere calcar,*
*Ut ſtudio majore petant Helicona virentem.*

---

---

*LONDON:*

Printed for Benj. Tooke, at the *Middle-Temple-*
*Gate* in *Fleet-ſtreet.* M DCC XIII.

# Texts

## An Essay on the Different Stiles of Poetry

*—Vatibus addere calcar,*
*Ut studio majore petant Helicona virentem.*

---

## Preface.

Allegory *is in it self so retired a way of Writing, that it was thought proper to say something beforehand concerning this Piece which is intirely fram'd upon it.*

*The* Design *therefore is to show the several* Stiles *which have been made use of by those who have endeavour'd to write in Verse. The* Scheme 5
*by which it is carry'd on, supposes an old* Grecian Poet *couching his Observations or Instructions within an* Allegory; *which* Allegory *is wrought out upon the single word* Flight, *as in the* figurative *way it signifies a Thought above the common Level: Here* Wit *is made to be* Pegasus, *and the* Poet *his* Rider, *who flies by several* Countries *where* 10
*he must not touch, by which are meant so many vicious* Stiles, *and arrives at last at the* Sublime.

*This way of Writing is not only very engaging to the Fancy whenever it is well perform'd, but it has been thought also one of the first that the* Poets *made use of. Hence arose many of those Stories concerning the* Heathen 15
Gods, *which at first were invented to insinuate Truth and Morality more pleasingly, and which afterwards made* Poetry *it self more solemn, when they happen'd to be receiv'd into the* Heathen Divinity. *And indeed there*

47

*seems to be no likelier way by which a* Poetical Genius *may yet appear as
an* Original, *than that he should proceed with a full compass of Thought    20
and Knowledge, either to design his Plan, or to beautify the Parts of it, in
an* Allegorical *manner. We are much beholden to* Antiquity *for those
excellent Compositions by which Writers at present form their Minds; but it
is not so much requir'd of us to adhere meerly to their Fables, as to observe
their Manner. For if we preclude or own Invention, Poetry will    25
consist only in Expression, or Simile, or the Application of old Stories; and
the utmost Character to which a Genius can arrive, will depend on
Imitation, or a borrowing from others, which we must agree together not to
call Stealing, because we take only from the Ancients. There have been
Poets amongst our selves, such as* Spencer *and* Milton, *who have suc-    30
cessfully ventur'd further. These Instances may let us see that Invention is
not bounded by what has been done before, they may open our Imagina-
tions, and be one Method of preserving us from Writing without Schemes.*

*As for what relates any further particularly to this Poem, the Reader
will observe, that its Aim is* Instruction. *Perhaps a representation of    35
several Mistakes and Difficulties which happen to many who write Poetry,
may deter some from attempting what they have not been made for: And
perhaps the description of several Beauties belonging to it, may afford
Hints towards forming a Genius for delighting and improving Mankind.
If either of these happen the Poem is useful; and upon that Account its    40
Faults may be more easily excused.*

# An Essay on the Different Stiles of Poetry.

## To HENRY, Lord Viscount BOLINGBROKE.

---

I Hate the *Vulgar* with untuneful Mind,
Hearts uninspir'd, and Senses unrefin'd.
Hence ye *Prophane,* I raise the sounding String,
And BOLINGBROKE descends to hear me sing.

    When *Greece* cou'd Truth in *Mystick* Fable shroud,        5
And with Delight instruct the list'ning Crowd,
An ancient *Poet* (*Time* has lost his Name)
Deliver'd Strains on Verse to future *Fame.*
Still as he sung he touch'd the trembling Lyre,
And felt the Notes a rising Warmth inspire.        10
Ye sweet'ning *Graces* in the Musick Throng,
Assist my *Genius,* and retrieve the Song
From dark *Oblivion.* See, my *Genius* goes
To call it forth. 'Twas thus the *Poem* rose.

    W*IT* is the *Muses* Horse, and bears on high        15
The daring *Rider* to the *Muses* Sky:
Who, while his strength to mount aloft he tries,
By *Regions* varying in their Nature, flies.

    At first he riseth o'er a *Land* of Toil,
A barren, hard, and undeserving Soil,        20
Where only Weeds from heavy Labour grow,
Which yet the Nation prune, and keep for show.
Where *Couplets* jingling on their Accent run,
Whose point of *Epigram* is sunk to *Pun.*

49

Where *Wings by *Fancy* never feather'd fly,                    25
Where Lines by measure form'd in *Hatchets* lie;
Where *Altars* stand, erected *Porches* gape,
And Sense is cramp'd while Words are par'd to shape;
Where mean *Acrosticks* labour'd in a Frame,
On scatter'd Letters raise a painful Scheme;                    30
And by Confinement in their Work controul
The great Enlargings of the boundless Soul.
Where if a Warriour's elevated Fire
Wou'd all the brightest Strokes of Verse require,
Then streight in *Anagram* a wretched Crew                      35
Will pay their undeserving Praises too;
While on the rack his poor disjointed *Name*
Must tell its Master's Character to *Fame*.
And (if my Fire and Fears aright presage)
The lab'ring Writers of a future Age                            40
Shall clear new ground, and Grotts and Caves repair,
To civilize the babbling *Ecchoes* there.
Then while a Lover treads a lonely Walk,
His Voice shall with its own Reflection talk,
The closing Sounds of all the vain Device,                     45
Select by trouble frivolously nice,
Resound through Verse, and with a false Pretence
Support the Dialogue, and pass for Sense.
Can things like these to lasting Praise pretend?
Can any *Muse* the worthless Toil befriend?                     50
Ye sacred *Virgins*, in my Thoughts ador'd,
Ah, be for ever in my Lines deplor'd!
If Tricks on Words acquire an endless Name,
And Trifles merit in the Court of *Fame*.

"At this the *Poet* stood concern'd a while,                    55
"And view'd his Objects with a scornful Smile:
"Then other *Images* of diff'rent kind,
"With diff'rent Workings enter'd on his Mind;
"At whose Approach he felt the former gone,
"And shiver'd in Conceit, and thus went on.                     60

By a cold *Region* next the *Rider* goes,
Where all lies cover'd in eternal Snows;

---

*These and the like Conceits of putting Poems into several Shapes by the different Lengths
of Lines, are frequent in old Poets of most Languages.

Where no bright *Genius* drives the Chariot high,
To glitter on the Ground, and gild the Sky.
Bleak level *Realm,* where *Frigid Stiles* abound,          65
Where never yet a daring Thought was found,
But counted Feet is *Poetry* defin'd;
And starv'd *Conceits* that chill the Reader's Mind
A little Sense in many Words imply,
And drag with loit'ring numbers slowly by.          70
Here dry sententious *Speeches* half asleep,
Prolong'd in Lines, o'er many Pages creep;
Nor ever shew the Passions well exprest,
Nor raise like Passions in another's Breast.
Here flat *Narrations* fair Exploits debase,          75
In Measures void of ev'ry shining Grace;
Which never arm their *Hero* for the Field,
Nor with *Prophetick Story* paint the Shield,
Nor fix the Crest, or make the Feathers wave,
Or with their Characters reward the Brave;          80
Undeck'd they stand, and unadorn'd with Praise,
And fail to profit while they fail to please.
Here forc'd *Description* is so strangely wrought,
It never stamps its Image on the Thought;
The liveless Trees may stand for ever bare,          85
And Rivers stop, for ought the Readers care;
They see no Branches trembling in the Woods,
Nor hear the Murmurs of encreasing Floods,
Which near the Roots with ruffled Waters flow,
And shake the shadows of the Boughs below.          90
Ah sacred *Verse,* replete with heav'nly Flame,
Such cold Endeavours wou'd invade thy Name!
The *Writer* fondly wou'd in these survive,
Which wanting Spirit never *seem'd* alive:
But if *Applause* or *Fame* attend his Pen,          95
Let breathless Statues pass for breathing Men.

   "Here seem'd the *Singer* touch'd at what he sung,
"And Grief a while delay'd his Hand and Tongue:
"But soon he check'd his Fingers, chose a Strain,
"And flourish'd shrill, and thus arose again.          100

   Pass the next *Region* which appears to show,
'Tis very open, unimprov'd, and low;
No noble Flights of elevated Thought,

No nervous strength of Sense maturely wrought,
Possess this Realm; but common *Turns* are there,                    105
Which idely sportive move with childish Air.
On callow Wings, and like a Plague of Flies,
The little *Fancies* in a *Poem* rise,
The jaded *Reader* ev'ry where to strike,
And move his Passions ev'ry where alike.                            110
There all the graceful *Nymphs* are forc'd to play
Where any Water bubbles in the way:
There shaggy *Satyrs* are oblig'd to rove
In all the Fields, and over all the Grove:
There ev'ry Star is summon'd from its Sphear,                       115
To dress one Face, and make *Clorinda* fair:
There *Cupids* fling their Darts in ev'ry Song,
While Nature stands neglected all along:
Till the teiz'd *Hearer,* vex'd at last to find
One constant Object still assault the Mind,                         120
Admires no more at what's no longer new,
And hastes to shun the persecuting View.
There bright *Surprizes* of *Poetick* Rage,
(Whose Strength and Beauty more confirm'd in Age
For having lasted, last the longer still)                          125
By weak Attempts are imitated ill,
Or carry'd on beyond their proper Light,
Or with Refinement flourish'd out of sight.
There *Metaphors* on *Metaphors* abound,
And Sense by differing Images confound:                            130
Strange injudicious Management of Thought,
Not born to Rage, nor into Method brought.
Ah, sacred *Muse!* from such a Realm retreat,
Nor idly waste the Infl'ence of thy Heat
On shallow Soils, where quick Productions rise,                    135
And wither as the Warmth that rais'd them dies.

"Here o'er his Breast a sort of Pity roll'd,
"Which something lab'ring in the Mind controul'd,
"And made him touch the loud-resounding Strings,
"While thus with Musick's stronger Tones he sings.                 140

Mount higher still, still keep thy faithful Seat,
Mind the firm Reins, and curb thy *Courser's* Heat;
Nor let him touch the *Realms* that next appear,
Whose hanging Turrets seem a Fall to fear,

And strangely stand along the Tracts of Air                    145
Where Thunder rolls, and bearded Comets glare.
The *Thoughts* that most extravagantly soar,
The *Words* that sound as if they meant to *roar;*
For *Rant* and *Noise* are offer'd here to Choice,
And stand elected by the *Publick Voice.*                      150
All *Schemes* are slighted which attempt to shine
At once with strange and probable Design;
'Tis here a mean Conceit, a vulgar View,
That bears the least Respect to seeming true;
While ev'ry trifling turn of things is seen                    155
To move by Gods descending in Machine.
Here swelling *Lines* with stalking Strut proceed,
*And in the Clouds terrifick Rumblings breed:*
*Here single* Heroes *deal grim Deaths around,*
*And Armies perish in tremendous Sound:*                       160
*Here fearful* Monsters *are preserv'd to die,*
*In such a Tumult as affrights the Sky;*
*For which the Golden* Sun *shall hide with dread,*
*And* Neptune *lift his sedgy-matted Head,*
*Admire the Roar, and dive with dire Dismay,*                  165
*And seek his deepest Chambers in the Sea.*
To raise their Subject thus the Lines devise,
And false *Extravagance* wou'd fain surprize;
Yet still, ye Gods, ye live untouch'd by Fear,
And undisturb'd at bellowing Monsters here:                    170
But with Compassion guard the Brain of Men,
If thus they bellow through the *Poet's* Pen:
So will the *Readers* Eyes discern aright
The rashest *Sally* from the noblest *Flight,*
And find that only *Boast* and *Sound* agree                   175
To seem the *Life* and *Voice of Majesty,*
When WRITERS rampant on *Apollo* call,
And bid him enter and possess them all,
And make his Flames afford a wild Pretence
To keep them unrestrain'd by common Sense.                     180
Ah, sacred *Verse!* lest *Reason* quit thy Seat,
Give none to such, or give a gentler Heat.

   " 'Twas here the *Singer* felt his Temper wrought
"By fairer Prospects, which arose to Thought;

"And in himself a while collected sat,                           185
"And much admir'd at this, and much at that;
"Till all the beauteous *Forms* in order ran,
"And then he took their Track, and thus began.

Above the Beauties, far above the Show
In which weak *Nature* dresses here below,                       190
Stands the great *Palace* of the *Bright* and *Fine*,
Where fair Ideas in full Glory shine,
Eternal Models of exalted Parts,
The Pride of Minds, and Conquerors of Hearts.

Upon the first Arrival here, are seen                            195
Rang'd Walks of *Bay*, the *Muses ever-Green*,
Each sweetly springing from some sacred Bough,
Whose circling Shade adorn'd a *Poet*'s Brow,
While through the Leaves, in unmolested Skies,
The gentle breathing of *Applauses* flies,                      200
And flatt'ring Sounds are heard within the Breeze,
And pleasing Murmur runs among the Trees,
And falls of Water join the flatt'ring Sounds,
And Murmur soft'ning from the Shore rebounds.
The warbled Melody, the lovely Sights,                          205
The Calms of Solitude inspire Delights,
The dazzled Eyes, the ravish'd Ears, are caught,
The panting Heart unites to purer Thought,
And grateful Shiverings wander o'er the Skin,
And wondrous *Ecstasies* arise within,                          210
Whence *Admiration* overflows the Mind,
And leaves the Pleasure felt, but undefin'd.
Stay, daring *Rider*, now no longer rove;
Now pass to find the *Palace* through the *Grove;*
Whate'er you see, whate'er you feel, display                    215
The *Realm* you sought for, daring *Rider* stay.

Here various *Fancy* spreads a vary'd Scene,
And *Judgment* likes the sight, and looks serene,
And can be pleas'd its self, and helps to please,
And joins the Work, and regulates the Lays.                     220
Thus on a Plan, design'd by double Care,
The *Building* rises in the glittering Air,
With just Agreement fram'd in ev'ry part,
And smoothly polish'd with the nicest Art.

Here Lawrel-boughs, which ancient *Heroes* wore,                225
Now not so fading as they prov'd before,
Wreath round the Pillars which the *Poets* rear,
And slope their Points to make a *Foliage* there.
Here Chaplets pull'd in gently-breathing Wind,
And wrought by *Lovers* innocently kind,                        230
Hung o'er the Porch, their fragrant Odours give,
And fresh in lasting Song for ever live.
The Shades, for whom with such indulgent care
*Fame* wreaths the Boughs or hangs the Chaplets there,
To deathless Honours thus preserv'd above,                      235
For Ages conquer, or for Ages love.

Here bold *Description* paints the Walls within,
Her Pencil touches, and the *World* is seen:
The Fields look beauteous in their flow'ry Pride,
The Mountains rear aloft, the Vales subside,                    240
The Cities rise, the Rivers seem to play,
And hanging Rocks repell the foaming Sea;
The foaming Seas their angry Billows show,
Curl'd White above, and darkly roll'd below,
Or cease their Rage, and as they calmly lie,                    245
Return the pleasing Pictures of the Sky;
The Skies extended in an open View,
Appear a lofty distant Arch of *Blue,*
In which *Description* stains the painted Bow,
Or thickens Clouds, and feathers out the Snow,                  250
Or mingles Blushes in the Morning ray,
Or gilds the Noon, or turns an Evening gray.

Here on the *Pedestalls* of *War* and *Peace,*
In diff'rent Rows, and with a diff'rent Grace,
Fine *Statues* proudly ride, or nobly stand,                    255
To which *Narration* with a pointing Hand
Directs the Sight, and makes Examples please
By boldly vent'ring to dilate in Praise,
While chosen Beauties lengthen out the Song,
Yet make her Hearers never think it long.                       260
Or if with closer Art, with sprightly Mien,
Scarce like her self, and more like *Action* seen,
She bids their Facts in Images arise,
And seem to pass before the *Readers* Eyes,
The Words like Charms inchanted Motion give,                    265

And all the *Statues* of the *Palace* live.
Then Hosts embattel'd stretch their Lines afar,
Their Leaders Speeches animate the War,
The Trumpets sound, the feather'd Arrows fly,
The Sword is drawn, the Lance is toss'd on high,                    270
The Brave press on, the fainter Forces yield,
And *Death* in differing Shapes deforms the Field.
Or shou'd the Shepherds be dispos'd to play,
*Amintor*'s jolly Pipe beguiles the Day,
And jocund *Ecchoes* dally with the Sound,                          275
And *Nymphs* in measures trip along the ground,
And e're the Dews have wet the Grass below,
Turn homewards singing all the way they go.

Here, as on Circumstance *Narrations* dwell,
And tell what moves, and hardly seem to tell,                       280
The Toil of *Heroes* on the dusty Plains,
Or on the Green the Merriment of *Swains*,
*Reflection* speaks, then all the *Forms* that rose
In Life's inchanted Scene themselves compose;
Whilst the grave Voice, controlling all the Spells                  285
With solemn Utt'rance, thus the *Moral* tells:
*So* PUBLICK WORTH *its Enemies destroys,*
*Or* PRIVATE INNOCENCE *it self enjoys.*

Here all the *Passions*, for their greater sway,
In all the Pow'r of Words themselves array;                        290
And hence the soft *Pathetick* gently charms,
And hence the Bolder fills the Breast with Arms.
Sweet *Love* in Numbers finds a World of *Darts*,
And with *Desirings* wounds the tender Hearts.
Fair *Hope* displays its Pinnions to the Wind,                      295
And flutters in the Lines, and lifts the Mind.
Brisk *Joy* with Transport fills the rising Strain,
Breaks in the Notes, and bounds in ev'ry Vein.
Stern *Courage*, glittering in the sparks of *Ire*,
Inflames those Lays that set the Breast on fire.                    300
*Aversion* learns to fly with swifter Will,
In Numbers taught to represent an Ill.
By frightful Accents *Fear* produces Fears.
By sad Expression *Sorrow* melts to Tears.
And dire *Amazement* and *Despair* are brought                      305

By words of *Horror* through the Wilds of Thought.
'Tis thus tumultuous *Passions* learn to roll;
Thus arm'd with *Poetry* they win the Soul.

Pass further through the *Dome,* another View
Wou'd now the Pleasures of thy Mind renew,                310
Where oft *Description* for the Colours goes,
Which raise and animate its native Shows;
Where oft *Narration* seeks a florid Grace
To keep from sinking e're 'tis time to cease;
Where easy turns *Reflection* looks to find,              315
When *Morals* aim at Dress to please the Mind;
Where lively *Figures* are for Use array'd,
And these an *Action,* those a *Passion,* aid.

There modest *Metaphors* in order sit,
With unaffected undisguising Wit,                         320
That leave their own, and seek anothers place,
Not forc'd, but changing with an easy pace,
To deck a Notion faintly seen before,
And *Truth* preserves her shape, and shines the more.

By these the beauteous *Similes* reside,                  325
In look more open, in Design ally'd,
Who, fond of Likeness, from anothers Face
Bring ev'ry Feature's corresponding Grace,
With near approaches in Expression flow,
And take the turn their Pattern loves to show;           330
As in a Glass the Shadows meet the Fair,
And dress and practice with resembling Air.
Thus *Truth,* by Pleasure doth her Aim pursue,
Looks bright, and fixes on the doubled View.

There *Repetitions* one another meet,                     335
Expresly strong, or languishingly sweet,
And raise the sort of Sentiment they please,
And urge the sort of Sentiment they raise.

There close in order are the *Questions* plac'd,
Which march with Art conceal'd in shows of haste,        340
And work the *Reader* till his Mind be brought
To make its Answers in the *Writers* Thought.

For thus the moving *Passions* seem to throng,
And with their Quickness force the Soul along;
And thus the Soul grows fond they shou'd prevail,          345
When ev'ry *Question* seems a fair Appeal;
And if by just degrees of Strength they soar,
In Steps as equal each affects the more.

There strange *Commotion* naturally shown,
Speaks on regardless that we speak alone,          350
Nor minds if they to whom she talks be near,
Nor cares if that to which she talks can hear.
The warmth of *Anger* dares an absent *Foe;*
The words of *Pity* speaks to Tears of *Woe;*
The *Love* that hopes, on Errands sends the Breeze;          355
And *Love despairing* moans to naked Trees.

There stand the new *Creations* of the *Muse,*
*Poetick Persons,* whom the *Writers* use
Whene'er a Cause magnificently great,
Wou'd fix Attention with peculiar weight.          360
'Tis hence that humbled *Provinces* are seen
Transform'd to *Matrons* with neglected Mien,
Who call their *Warriors* in a mournful Sound,
And shew their Crowns of *Turrets* on the ground,
While over *Urns* reclining *Rivers* moan          365
They shou'd enrich a Nation not their own.
'Tis hence the *Virtues* are no more confin'd
To be but Rules of Reason in the Mind;
Their heav'nly *Forms* start forth, appear to breath,
And in bright Shapes converse with Men beneath,          370
And, as a *God,* in Combat *Valour* leads,
In Council *Prudence* as a *Goddess* aids.

There *Exclamations* all the Voice employ
In sudden Flushes of *Concern* or *Joy:*
Then seem the Sluices which the *Passions* bound,          375
To burst asunder with a speechless Sound;
And then with Tumult and Surprize they roul,
And shew the Case important in the Soul.

There rising *Sentences* attempt to speak,
Which *Wonder, Sorrow, Shame,* or *Anger,* break;          380
But so the *Part* directs to find the rest,

That what remains behind is more than ghest.
Thus fill'd with Ease, yet left unfinish'd too,
The Sense looks large within the Readers View:
He freely gathers all the *Passion* means,                                    385
And artful *Silence* more than Words explains.

   Methinks a thousand *Graces* more I see,
And I cou'd dwell— But when wou'd Thought be free?
Engaging *Method* ranges all the Band,
And smooth *Transition* joins them hand in hand:                               390
Around the Musick of my Lays they throng,
Ah too deserving Objects of my Song!
Live wondrous *Palace*, live secure of Time,
To Senses *Harmony,* to Souls *sublime,*
And just *Proportion* all, and great *Design,*                                395
And lively *Colours,* and an *Air divine.*

   'Tis here, that guided by the *Muses* Fire,
And fill'd with sacred Thought, her *Friends* retire,
Unbent to Care, and unconcern'd with Noise,
To taste Repose and elevated Joys,                                            400
Which in a deep untroubled Leisure meet,
Serenely ravishing politely sweet.
From hence the *Charms* that most engage they choose,
And as they please the glittering Objects use;
While to their *Genius* more than *Art* they trust,                           405
Yet *Art* acknowledges their Labours just.
From hence they look, from this exalted Show,
To choose their Subject in the World below,
And where an *Hero* well deserves a Name,
They consecrate his Acts in Song to *Fame;*                                    410
Or if a *Science* unadorn'd they find,
They smooth its Look to please and teach the Mind;
And where a *Friendship*'s generously strong,
They celebrate the Knot of Souls in Song;
Or if the *Verses* must inflame *Desire,*                                      415
The Thoughts are melted, and the Words on fire:
But when the *Temples* deck'd with Glory stand,
And Hymns of *Gratitude* the *Gods* demand,
Their Bosoms kindle with *Celestial Love,*
And then alone they cast their Eyes above.                                     420
Hail sacred *Verse!* ye sacred *Muses* hail!
Cou'd I your Pleasures with your Fire reveal,

The World might then be taught to know you right,
And court your Rage, and envy my Delight.
But whilst I follow where your pointed Beams      425
My Course directing shoot in golden Streams,
The bright Appearance dazzles *Fancy*'s Eyes,
And weary'd out the fix'd *Attention* lies,
Enough my *Verses* have you work'd my Breast,
I'll seek the sacred *Grove*, and sink to Rest.      430

   "No longer now the ravish'd *Poet* sung,
"His Voice in easy Cadence left the Tongue;
"Nor o'er the Musick did his Fingers fly,
"The Sounds ran tingling, and they seem'd to die.

O BOLINGBROKE! O Fav'rite of the Skies,      435
   O born to Gifts by which the Noblest rise,
Improv'd in Arts by which the Brightest please,
Intent to Business, and polite for Ease;
Sublime in Eloquence, where loud *Applause*
Hath stil'd thee *Patron* of a Nation's Cause.      440
'Twas there the *World* perceiv'd and own'd thee great,
Thence ANNA call'd thee to the Reins of State;
Go, said the Greatest *Queen*, with OXFORD go,
And still the Tumults of the World below,
Exert thy Powers, and prosper; he that knows      445
To move with OXFORD never shou'd repose.
She spoke: the *Patriot* overspread thy Mind,
And all thy Days to publick Good resign'd.
Else might thy Soul so wonderfully wrought
For ev'ry depth and turn of curious Thought,      450
To this the *Poet*'s sweet *Recess* retreat,
And thence report the Pleasures of the Seat,
Describe the Raptures which a *Writer* knows,
When in his Breast a Vein of Fancy glows,
Describe his Business while he works the Mine,      455
Describe his Temper when he sees it shine,
Or say when *Readers* easy Verse insnares,
How much the *Writers* Mind can act on theirs:
Whence *Images* in charming Numbers set,
A sort of Likeness in the Soul beget,      460
And what fair *Visions* oft we fancy nigh
By fond Delusions of the swimming Eye,

Or further pierce through *Natures* Maze to find
How *Passions* drawn give *Passions* to the Mind.

Oh what a sweet Confusion! what Surprize!      465
How quick the shifting Views of Pleasure rise!
While lightly skimming, with a transient Wing,
I touch the Beauties which I wish to sing.
Is *Verse* a sov'raign Regent of the *Soul*,
And fitted all its Motions to controul?      470
Or are they Sisters, tun'd at once above,
And shake like *Unisons* if either move?
For when the Numbers sing an eager Fight,
I've heard a Soldier's Voice express Delight;
I've seen his Eyes with crowding Spirits shine,      475
And round his Hilt his Hand unthinking twine.
When from the Shore the fickle *Trojan* flies,
And in sweet Measures poor *Eliza* dies,
I've seen the Book forsake the Virgins Hand,
And in their Eyes the Tears but hardly stand.      480
I've known them blush at soft *Corinna's* Name,
And in red Characters confess a Flame:
Or wish Success had more adorn'd his Arms,
Who gave the World for *Cleopatra's* Charms.

Ye Sons of *Glory*, be my first Appeal,      485
If here the Pow'r of Lines these Lines reveal.
When some great Youth has with impetuous Thought
Read o'er Atchievements which another wrought,
And seen his *Courage* and his *Honour* go
Through crowding Nations in *Triumphant* Show,      490
His Soul enchanted by the Words he reads
Shines all impregnated with sparkling Seeds,
And *Courage* here, and *Honour* there, appears
In brave Design that soars beyond his Years,
And *this* a Spear, and *that* a Chariot lends,      495
And War and Triumph he by turns attends:
Thus gallant Pleasures are his waking Dream,
Till some fair Cause have call'd him forth to Fame.
Then form'd to Life on what the *Poet* made,
And breathing Slaughter, and in Arms array'd,      500
He marches forward on the daring Foe,
And *Emulation* acts in ev'ry Blow.

Great *Hector's* Shade in Fancy stalks along,
From Rank to Rank amongst the Martial Throng,
While from his Acts he learns a Noble Rage,                    505
And shines like *Hector* in the present Age.
Thus Verse will raise him to the Victor's Bays,
And Verse, that rais'd him, shall resound his Praise.

    Ye tender *Beauties*, be my Witness too,
If Song can charm, and if my Song be true.                    510
With sweet Experience oft a *Fair* may find
Her Passions mov'd by Passions well design'd;
And then she longs to meet a gentle Swain,
And longs to Love, and to be lov'd again.                    515
And if by chance an Am'rous Youth appears,
With Pants and Blushes she the Courtship hears;
And finds a Tale that must with theirs agree,
And he's *Septimius,* and his *Acme* she:
Thus lost in Thought her melted Heart she gives,
And the rais'd *Lover* by the *Poet* lives.                    520

*FINIS.*

# HOMER's BATTLE

## OF THE

## Frogs and Mice.

### WITH THE

## REMARKS of ZOILUS,

To which is Prefix'd,

The *LIFE* of the faid ZOILUS.

---

*Vide quam iniqui funt divinorum munerum Æfti-*
*matores, etiam quidam Profeffi Sapientiam.*
Seneca.

---

## LONDON,

Printed for BERNARD LINTOT, between
the *Temple*-Gates. M DCC XVII.

First Edition of *Homer's Battle of the Frogs and Mice,* 1717.

# Homer's Battle of the Frogs and Mice with the Remarks of Zoilus. To Which Is Prefixed The Life of the Said Zoilus

*Vide quam iniqui sunt divinorum munerum Æstimatores, etiam quidam Professi
Sapientiam.*     Seneca.

## Preface

H AVING *some Time ago heard, that the Translation of* Homer's Iliad
*wou'd be attempted, I resolv'd to confer with the Gentleman who
undertook it. I found him of a tall Presence, and thoughtful Countenance,
with his Hands folded, his Eyes fix'd, and his Beard untrimm'd. This I
took to be a good Omen, because he thus resembled the* Constantino-     5
politan *Statue of* HOMER *which* Cedrenus *describes, and surely nothing
cou'd have been liker, had he but arriv'd at the Character of Age and
Blindness. As my Business was to be my Introduction, I told him how much
I was acquainted with the secret History of* HOMER; *that no one better
knows his own Horse, than I do the Camel of* Bactria, *in which his*     10
*Soul resided at the Time of the* Trojan *Wars; that my Acquaintance
continued with him, as he appear'd in the Person of the* Grecian *Poet; that
I knew him in his next Transmigration into a Peacock; was pleas'd with his
Return to Manhood, under the Name of* Ennius *at* Rome; *and more
pleas'd to hear he wou'd soon revive under another Name, with all his full*     15
*Lustre, in* England. *This particular Knowledge, added I, which sprung
from the Love I bear him, has made me fond of a Conversation with you,
in Order to the Success of your Translation.*

*The civil Manner in which he receiv'd my Proposal encouraging me to
proceed, I told him, there were* Arts *of Success, as well as* Merits *to obtain*     20
*it; and that he, who now dealt in* Greek, *should not only satisfy himself*

65

*with being a good* Grecian, *but also contrive to hasten into the Repute of
it. He might therefore write in the Title-Page,* Translated *from the
Original* GREEK, *and select a* Motto *for his Purpose out of the same
Language. He might obtain a Copy of Verses written in it to prefix to*          25
*the Work; and not call the Titles of each Book, The First, and Second, but
Iliad* Alpha, *and* Beta. *He might retain some* Names *which the World is
least acquainted with, as his old Translator* Chapman *uses* Ephaistus
*instead of* Vulcan, Baratrum *for* Hell; *and if the* Notes *were fill'd
with* Greek *Verses, it wou'd more increase the Wonder of many Readers.*          30
*Thus I went on; when he told me, smiling, I had shewn him indeed a Set of
Arts very different from Merit, for which Reason, he thought, he ought not
to depend upon them. A Success, says he, founded on the Ignorance of
others, may bring a temporary Advantage, but neither a conscious Satis-
faction, nor future Fame to the Author. Men of Sense despise the Affecta-*          35
*tion which they easily see through, and even they who were dazzled with it
at first, are no sooner inform'd of its being an Affectation, but they
imagine it also a Veil to cover Imperfection.*

   *The next Point I ventur'd to speak on, was the Sort of Poetry he intended
to use; how some may fancy, a Poet of the greatest Fire wou'd be*          40
*imitated better in the Freedom of Blank Verse, and the Description of
War sounds more pompous out of Rhime. But, will the Translation,
said he, be thus remov'd enough from Prose, without greater Inconve-
niences? What Transpositions is* Milton *forc'd to, as an Equivalent for
Want of Rhime, in the Poetry of a Language which depends upon a*          45
*natural Order of Words? And even this wou'd not have done his
Business, had he not given the fullest Scope to his Genius, by
choosing a Subject upon which there could be no Hyperboles. We
see (however he be deservedly successful) that the* Ridicule *of his
Manner succeeds better than the* Imitation *of it; because Transpositions,*          50
*which are unnatural to a Language, are to be fairly derided, if
they ruin it by being frequently introduced; and because Hyper-
boles, which outrage every lesser Subject where they are seriously
us'd, are often beautiful in Ridicule. Let the* French, *whose Lan-
guage is not copious, translate in Prose; but ours, which exceeds it in*          55
*Copiousness of Words, may have a more frequent Likeness of Sounds, to
make the Unison or Rhime easier; a Grace of Musick, that attones for the
Harshness our Consonants and Monosyllables occasion.*

   *After this, I demanded what Air he would appear with? whether
antiquated, like* Chapman's *Version, or modern, like* La Motte's *Con-*          60
*traction. To which he answer'd, by desiring me to observe what a Painter*

*does who would always have his Pieces in Fashion. He neither chooses to
draw a Beauty in a* Ruff, *or a* French-Head; *but with its Neck un-
cover'd, and in its natural Ornament of Hair curl'd up, or spread
becomingly: So may a Writer choose a natural Manner of expressing
himself which will always be in Fashion, without affecting to borrow an
odd Solemnity and unintelligible Pomp from the past Times, or humouring
the present by falling into its Affectations, and those Phrases which are
born to die with it.*                                                              65

   *I ask'd him, lastly, whether he would be strictly litteral, or expatiate with*          70
*further Licenses? I wou'd not be litteral, replies he, or ty'd up to Line for
Line in such a Manner, wherein it is impossible to express in one Lan-
guage what has been deliver'd in another. Neither wou'd I so expatiate, as
to alter my Author's Sentiments, or add others of my own. These Errors are
to be avoided on either Hand, by adhering not only to the Word, but the*          75
*Spirit and Genius of an Author; by considering what he means, with what
beautiful Manner he has express'd his Meaning in his own Tongue, and
how he would have express'd himself, had it been in ours. Thus we ought to
seek for* HOMER *in a Version of* HOMER: *Other Attempts are but Transfor-
mations of him; such as* Ovid *tells us, where the Name is retain'd, and the*      80
*Thing alter'd: This will be really what you mention'd in the Compliment
you began with, a Transmigration of the Poet from one Country into
another.*

   *Here ended the serious Part of our Conference. All I remember further
was, that having ask'd him, what he design'd with all those Editions and*          85
*Comments I observ'd in his Room? he made Answer, That if any one, who
had a Mind to find Fault with his Performance, wou'd but stay 'till it was
entirely finish'd, he shou'd have a very cheap Bargain of them.*

   *Since this Discourse, I have often resolv'd to try what it was to translate
in the Spirit of a Writer, and at last, chose the* Battle of the Frogs and           90
Mice, *which is ascrib'd to* HOMER; *and bears a nearer Resemblance to his*
Iliad, *than the* Culex *does to the Æneid of* Virgil. Statius *and others
think it a Work of Youth, written as a Prelude to his greater Poems.*
Chapman *thinks it the Work of his Age, after he found Men ungrateful;
to shew he cou'd give Strength, Lineage and Fame as he pleas'd, and*                95
*praise a Mouse as well as a Man. Thus, says he, the Poet professedly flung
up the World, and apply'd himself at last to Hymns. Now, tho' this Reason
of his may be nothing more than a Scheme form'd out of the Order in which*
HOMER's *Works are printed, yet does the Conjecture that this Poem was
written after the* Iliad, *appear probable, because of its frequent Allusions*     100

to that *Poem, and particularly that there is not a* Frog *or a* Mouse *kill'd, which has not its parallel Instance there, in the Death of some Warrior or other.*

   *The Poem itself is of the Epick Kind; the Time of its Action the Duration of two Days; the Subject (however in its Nature frivolous, or ridiculous)*    105
*rais'd, by having the most shining Words and Deeds of Gods and Heroes accommodated to it: And while other Poems often compare the illustrious Exploits of great Men to those of Brutes, this always heightens the Subject by Comparisons drawn from Things above it. We have a great Character given it with Respect to the Fable in* Gaddius de Script. non Eccles. *It*    110
*appears, says he, nearer Perfection than the* Iliad, *or* Odysses, *and excels both in Judgment, Wit, and exquisite Texture, since it is a Poem perfect in its own Kind. Nor does* Crusius *speak less to its Honour, with Respect to the Moral, when he cries out in an Apostrophe to the Reader; "Whoever "you are, mind not the Names of these little Animals, but look into the*    115
*"Things they mean; call them Men, call them Kings, or Counsellors, or "humane Polity itself, you have here Doctrines of every Sort." And indeed, when I hear the* Frog *talk concerning the Mouse's Family, I learn, Equality shou'd be observ'd in making Friendships; when I hear the* Mouse *answer the* Frog, *I remember, that a Similitude of Manners shou'd*    120
*be regarded in them; when I see their Councils assembling, I think of the Bustles of humane Prudence; and when I see the Battle grow warm and glorious, our Struggles for Honour and Empire appear before me.*

   *This Piece had many Imitations of it in Antiquity, as the Fight of the Cats, the Cranes, the Starlings, the Spiders, &c. That of the Cats is in the*    125
Bodleian *Library, but I was not so lucky as to find it. I have taken the Liberty to divide my Translation into Books (tho' it be otherwise in the Original) according as the Fable allow'd proper Resting-Places, by varying its Scene, or Nature of Action: This I did, after the Example of* Aristarchus *and* Zenodotus *in the* Iliad. *I then thought of carrying the*    130
*Grammarians Example further, and placing Arguments at the Head of each, which I fram'd as follows, in Imitation of the short Ancient* Greek Inscriptions *to the* Iliad.

BOOK I.

*In* Alpha, *the Ground*    135
*Of the Quarrel is found.*

BOOK II.

*In* Beta, *we*
*The Council see.*

## BOOK III.                                    140
*Dire* Gamma *relates*
*The Work of the Fates.*

*But as I am averse from all Information which lessens our Surprize, I only mention these for a Handle to quarrel with the Custom of long Arguments before a Poem. It may be necessary in Books of Controversy or* 145 *abstruse Learning, to write an Epitome before each Part; but it is not kind to forestal us in a Work of Fancy, and make our Attention remiss by a previous Account of the End of it.*

*The next Thing which employ'd my Thoughts was the Heroes Names. It might perhaps take off somewhat from the Majesty of the Poem, had I cast* 150 *away such noble Sounds as,* Physignathus, Lycopinax, *and* Crambophagus, *to substitute* Bluffcheek, Lickdish, *and* Cabbage-Eater, *in their Places. It is for this Reason I have retain'd them untranslated: However, I place them in* English *before the Poem, and sometimes give a short Character extracted out of their Names; as in* Polyphonus, Pter- 155 nophagus, *& c. that the Reader may not want some sight of their Humour in the Original.*

*But what gave me a greater Difficulty was, to know how I shou'd follow the Poet, when he inserted Pieces of Lines from his Iliad, and struck out a Sprightliness by their new Application. To supply this in my Translation, I* 160 *have added one or two of* HOMER's *Particularities; and us'd two or three Allusions to some of our* English *Poets who most resemble him, to keep up some Image of this Spirit of the Original with an equivalent Beauty. To use more might make my Performance seem a Cento rather than a Translation, to those who know not the Necessity I lay under.* 165

*I am not ignorant, after all my Care, how the World receives the best Compositions of this Nature. A Man need only go to a Painter's, and apply what he hears said of a Picture to a Translation, to find how he shall be us'd upon his own, or his Author's Account. There one Spectator tells you, a Piece is extreamly fine, but he sets no Value on what is not like the Face it* 170 *was drawn for, while a second informs you, such another is extreamly like, but he cares not for a Piece of Deformity, tho' its Likeness be never so exact.*

*Yet notwithstanding all which happens to the best, when I translate, I have a Desire to be reckon'd amongst them; and I shall obtain this, if the World will be so good-natur'd as to believe Writers that give their own* 175 *Characters: Upon which Presumption, I answer to all Objections beforehand, as follows:*

*When I am litteral, I regard my Author's Words; when I am not, I
translate in his Spirit. If I am low, I choose the narrative Style; if high, the
Subject requir'd it. When I am enervate, I give an Instance of ancient*          180
*Simplicity; when affected, I show a Point of modern Delicacy. As for
Beauties, there never can be one found in me which was not really
intended; and for any Faults, they proceeded from too unbounded Fancy,
or too nice Judgment, but by no means from any Defect in either of those
Faculties.*          185

# THE LIFE OF ZOILUS.

*Pendentem volo Zoilum videre.*
Martial.

---

THEY who have discours'd concerning the Nature and Extent of Criticism, take Notice, That Editions of Authors, the Interpretations of them, and the Judgment which is pass'd upon each, are the three Branches into which the Art divides itself. But the last of these, that directs in the Choice of Books, and takes Care to prepare us for reading them, is by the learned *Bacon* call'd the *Chair* of the *Criticks.* In this Chair (to carry on the Figure) have sate *Aristotle, Demetrius Phalereus, Dionysius Halicarnassensis, Cicero, Horace, Quintillian,* and *Longinus;* all great Names of Antiquity, the *Censors* of those Ages which went before, and the *Directors* of those that come after them, with Respect to the natural and perspicuous Manners of Thought and Expression, by which a correct and judicious *Genius* may be able to write for the Pleasure and Profit of Mankind.

But whatever has been advanc'd by Men really great in themselves, has been also attempted by others of Capacities either unequal to the Undertaking, or which have been corrupted by their Passions, and drawn away into partial Violences: So that we have sometimes seen the Province of *Criticism* usurp'd, by such who judge with an *obscure Diligence,* and a certain *Dryness of Understanding,* incapable of comprehending a figurative Stile, or being mov'd by the Beauties of Imagination; and at other Times by such, whose natural *Moroseness in general,* or *particular Designs* of Envy, has render'd them indefatigable against the Reputation of others.

In this last Manner is ZOILUS represented to us by Antiquity, and with a Character so abandon'd, that his Name has been since made Use of to brand all succeeding Criticks of his Complexion. He has a Load of Infamy thrown upon him, great, in Proportion

to the Fame of HOMER, against whom he oppos'd himself: If the          30
one was esteem'd as the very Residence of Wit, the other is
describ'd as a Profligate, who wou'd destroy the Temple of *Apollo*
and the *Muses,* in Order to have his Memory preserv'd by the
envious Action. I imagine it may be no ungrateful Undertaking to
write some Account of this celebrated Person, from whom so          35
many derive their Character; and I think the Life of a *Critick* is
not unseasonably put before the Works of his *Poet,* especially
when his Censures accompany him. If what he advances be just,
he stands here as a Censor; if otherwise, he appears as an Addi-
tion to the Poet's Fame, and is placed before him with the Justice          40
of Antiquity in its Sacrifices, when, because such a Beast had
offended such a Deity, he was brought annually to his Altar to be
slain upon it.

ZOILUS was born at *Amphipolis* a City of *Thrace,* during the Time
in which the *Macedonian* Empire flourish'd. Who his Parents were          45
is not certainly known, but if the Appellation of *Thracian Slave,*
which the World apply'd to him, be not meerly an Expression of
Contempt, it proves him of mean Extraction. He was a Disciple of
one *Polycrates* a Sophist, who had distinguish'd himself by writing
against the great Names of the Ages before him; and who,          50
when he is mention'd as his Master, is said to be particularly
famous for a bitter Accusation or Invective against the Memory of
*Socrates.* In this Manner is ZOILUS set out to Posterity, like a Plant
naturally baneful, and having its Poison render'd more acute and
subtile by a Preparation.          55

In his Person he was tall and meagre, his Complexion was pale,
and all the Motions of his Face were sharp. He is represented by
*Ælian,* with a Beard nourish'd to a prodigious Length, and his
Head kept close shav'd, to give him a Magisterial Appearance: His
Coat hung over his Knees in a slovenly Fashion; his Manners were          60
form'd upon an Aversion to the Customs of the World. He was
fond of speaking ill, diligent to sow Dissention, and from the
constant Bent of his Thought, had obtain'd that Sort of Readiness
for Slander or Reproach, which is esteem'd Wit by the light
Opinion of some, who take the Remarks of ill Nature for an          65
Understanding of Mankind, and the abrupt Lashes of Rudeness
for the Spirit of Expression. This, at last, grew to such a Heighth
in him, that he became careless of concealing it; he threw off all
Reserves and Managements in Respect of others, and the Passion
so far took the Turn of a Frenzy, that being one Day ask'd, why he          70
spoke ill of every one? "It is (says he) because I am not able to do
"them Ill, tho I have so great a Mind to it." Such extravagant

Declarations of his general Enmity made Men deal with him as
with the Creature he affected to be; they no more spoke of him as
belonging to the Species he hated; and from henceforth his          75
learned Speeches or fine Remarks cou'd obtain no other Title for
him, but that of *The Rhetorical Dog.*

While he was in *Macedon* he employ'd his Time in writing, and
reciting what he had written in the Schools of Sophists. His
Oratory (says *Dionisius Halicarnassensis*) was always of the demon-   80
strative Kind, which concerns itself about Praise or Dispraise. His
Subjects were the most approv'd Authors, whom he chose to
abuse upon the Account of their Reputation; and to whom, with-
out going round the Matter in *faint Praises* or *artificial Insinuations*,
he us'd to deny their own *Characteristicks.* With this Gallantry of   85
Opposition did he censure *Zenophon* for Affectation, *Plato* for
vulgar Notions, and *Isocrates* for Incorrectness. *Demosthenes*, in his
Opinion, wanted Fire, *Aristotle* Subtilty, and *Aristophanes* Humour.
But, as to have Reputation was with him a sufficient Cause of
Enmity, so to have that Reputation universal, was what wrought      90
his Frenzy to its wildest Degree; for which Reason it was HOMER
with whom he was most implacably angry. And certainly, if Envy
choose its Object for the Power to give Torment, it shou'd here (if
ever) have the Glory of fully answering its Intentions; for the Poet
was so worship'd by the whole Age, that his Critick had not the     95
common Alleviation of the Opinion of one other Man, to concur
in his Condemnation.

ZOILUS however went on with indefatigable Industry in a volu-
minous Work which he entitled, *The Ψόγος, or Censure of* HOMER:
'Till having at last finish'd it, he prepares to send it into the World   100
with a pompous Title at the Head, invented for himself by Way of
Excellency, and thus inserted after the Manner of the Ancients.

ZOILUS, *the Scourge of* HOMER, *writ this against that Lover of Fables.*

Thus did he value himself upon a Work, which the World has
not thought worth transmitting to us, and but just left a Specimen   105
in five or six Quotations, which happen to be preserv'd by the
Commentators of that Poet against whom he writ it. If any One be
fond to form a Judgment upon him from these Instances, they
are as follows:

*Il.*1. He says, HOMER is very ridiculous (a Word he was noted to   110
apply to him) when he makes such a God as *Apollo* employ himself
in killing Dogs and Mules.

*Il.*5. HOMER is very ridiculous in describing *Diomedes*'s Helmet
and Armour, as sparkling, and in a Blaze of Fire about him, for
then why was he not burn'd by it?                                   115

*Il.*5. When *Idæus* quitted his fine Chariot, which was entangl'd
in the Fight, and for which he might have been slain, the Poet was
a Fool for making him leave his Chariot, he had better have run
away in it.

*Il.*24. When *Achilles* makes *Priam* lie out of his Tent, lest the          120
*Greeks* shou'd hear of his being there, the Poet had no Breeding,
to turn a King out in that Manner.

*Od.*9. The Poet says, *Ulysses* lost an equal Number out of each
Ship. The Critick says, that's impossible.

*Od.*10. He derides the Men who were turn'd into Swine, and          125
calls them HOMER'S poor little blubbering Pigs. The first five of
these Remarks are found in *Didymus,* the last in *Longinus.*

Such as these are the cold Jests and trifling Quarrels, which
have been registred from a Composition that (according to the
Representation handed down to us) was born in Envy, liv'd a short          130
Life in Contempt, and lies for ever bury'd with Infamy.

But, as his Design was judg'd by himself wonderfully well ac-
complish'd, *Macedon* began to be esteem'd a Stage too narrow for
his Glory; and *Ægypt,* which had then taken Learning into its
Patronage, the proper Place where it ought to diffuse its Beams,          135
to the Surprize of all whom he wou'd perswade to reckon them-
selves hitherto in the Dark, and under the Prejudices of a false
Admiration. However as he had prepar'd himself for the Journey,
he was suddenly diverted for a while by the Rumour of the
*Olympick* Games, which were at that Time to be celebrated.          140
Thither he steer'd his Course full of the Memory of *Herodotus,*
and others who had successfully recited in that large Assembly;
and pleas'd to imagine he shou'd alter all *Greece* in their Notions of
Wit before he left it.

Upon his Arrival, he found the Field in its Preparation for          145
Diversion. The Chariots stood for the Race, carv'd and gilded, the
Horses were led in costly Trappings, some practis'd to wrestle,
some to dart the Spear, (or whatever they design'd to engage at) in
a Kind of Flourish beforehand: Others were looking on to amuse
themselves; and all gaily dress'd according to the Custom of those          150
Places. Through these did ZOILUS move forward, bald-headed,
bearded to the Middle, in a long sad-colour'd Vestment, and
inflexibly stretching forth his Hands fill'd with Volumns roll'd up
to a vast Thickness: a Figure most venerably slovenly! able to
demand Attention upon Account of its Oddness. And indeed, he          155
had no sooner fix'd himself upon an Eminence, but a Crowd
flock'd about him to know what he intended. Then the Critick
casting his Eyes on the Ring, open'd his Volume slowly, as consid-

ering with what Part he might most properly entertain his Au-
dience. It happen'd, that the Games at *Patroclus*'s Obsequies came 160
first into his Thought; whether it was that he judg'd it suitable to
the Place, or knew that he had fall'n as well upon the Games
themselves, as upon HOMER for celebrating them, and cou'd not
resist his natural Disposition to give Mankind Offence. Every One
now intently fasten'd upon him, while he undertook to prove, that 165
those Games signify'd nothing to the Taking of *Troy*, and there-
fore only furnish'd an impertinent Episode: that the Fall of the
Lesser *Ajax* in Cow-dung, the Squabble of the Chariot-Race, and
other Accidents which attend such Sports, are mean or trifling:
and a World of other Remarks, for which he still affirm'd HOMER 170
to be a Fool, and which they that heard him took for study'd
Invectives against those Exercises they were then employ'd in.
Men who frequent Sports, as they are of a chearful Disposition, so
are they Lovers of Poetry: This, together with the Opinion they
were affronted, wrought them up to Impatience and further 175
Licenses: There was particularly a young *Athenian* Gentleman
who was to run three Chariots in those Games, who being an
Admirer of HOMER, cou'd no longer contain himself, but cry'd out,
"What in the Name of *Castor* have we here, ZOILUS from *Thrace*?"
and as he said it, struck him with a Chariot-Whip. Immediately 180
then a Hundred Whips were seen curling round his Head; so that
his Face, naturally deform'd, and heighten'd by Pain to its utmost
*Caricatura*, appear'd in the Midst of them, as we may fancy the
Visage of Envy, if at any Time her Snakes rise in Rebellion to lash
their Mistress. Nor was this all the Punishment they decreed him, 185
when once they imagin'd he was ZOILUS: The *Scyronian* Rocks were
near 'em, and thither they hurried him with a general Cry, to that
speedy Justice which is practis'd at Places of Diversion.

It is here, that, according to *Suidas*, the Critick expir'd. But we
following the more numerous Testimonies of other Authors, con- 190
clude he escap'd either by the Lowness of those Rocks whence he
was thrust, or by Bushes which might break his Fall; and soon
after following the Courses of his first Intention, he set Sail for
*Ægypt*.

*Ægypt* was at this Time govern'd by *Ptolomy Philadelphus*, a 195
Prince passionately fond of Learning, and learned Men; par-
ticularly an Admirer of HOMER to Adoration. He had built the
finest Library in the World, and made the choicest, as well as most
numerous Collection of Books. No Encouragements were
wanting from him to allure Men of the brightest Genius to his 200
Court, and no Time thought too much which he spent in their

Company. From hence it is that we hear of *Eratosthenes* and *Aristophanes*, those universal Scholars, and candid Judges of other Mens Performances: *Callimachus*, a Poet of the most easy, courteous Delicacy, famous for a Poem on the Cutting of *Berenice's*   205
Hair; and whom *Ovid* so much admired as to say, "It was Reason "enough for him to love a Woman, if she wou'd but tell him he "exceeded *Callimachus;*" *Theocritus*, the most famous in the Pastoral Way of Writing; And among the young Men, *Aristarchus* and *Apollonius Rhodius*, the one of whom prov'd a most judicious   210
Critick, the other a Poet of no mean Character.

These and many more fill'd the Court of that munificent Prince, whose liberal Dispensations of Wealth and Favour became Encouragements to every One to exert their Parts to the utmost; like Streams which flow through different Sorts of Soils, and   215
improve each in that for which it was adapted by Nature.

Such was the Court when ZOILUS arriv'd; but before he enter'd *Alexandria,* he spent a Night in the Temple of *Isis,* to enquire of the Success of his Undertaking; not that he doubted the Worth of his Works, but his late Misfortune had instructed him, that others   220
might be ignorant of it. Having therefore perform'd the accustom'd Sacrifice, and compos'd himself to rest upon the Hide, he had a Vision which foretold of his future Fame.

He found himself sitting under the Shade of a dark Yew, which was cover'd with Hellebore and Hemlock, and near the   225
Mouth of a Cave, where sate a Monster, pale, wasted, surrounded with Snakes, fost'ring a Cockatrice in her Bosom; and cursing the Sun, for making the Work of the Deities appear in its Beauty. The sight of this bred Fear in him; when she suddenly turning her sunk Eyes, put on a hideous Kind of a loving Grin, in which he   230
discover'd a Resemblance to some of his own Features. Then turning up her Snakes, and interlacing them in the Form of a Turbant to give him less Disgust, she thus address'd herself: "Go "on, my Son, in whom I am renew'd, and prosper in thy brave "Undertakings on Mankind: Assert their Wit to be Dulness; prove   235
"their Sense to be Folly; know Truth only when it is on thy own "Side; and acknowledge Learning at no other Time to be use- "ful. Spare not an Author of any Rank or Size; let not thy "Tongue or Pen know Pity; make the living feel thy Accusations; "make the Ghosts of the dead groan in their Tombs for their   240
"violated Fame. But why do I spend Time in needless Advice, "which may be better us'd in Encouragement? Let thy Eyes "delight themselves with the future Recompence which I have "reserv'd for thy Merit." Thus spoke the Monster, and shriek'd

the Name of zoilus: The Shades who were to bear the same 245
Name after him became obedient, and the Mouth of the Cave was
fill'd with strange supercilious Countenances, which all crowded
to make their Appearance. These began to march before him
with an Imitation of his Mien and Manners: Some crown'd with
wild Sorrel, others having Leaves of dead Bays mingl'd amongst 250
it; while the Monster still describ'd them as they pass'd, and
touch'd each with a livid Track of malignant Light that shot from
her Eye, to point where she meant the Description. "They (says
"she) in the Chaplets of wild Sorrel, are my Writers of Prose, who
"erect Scandal into Criticism: They who wear the wither'd Bay 255
"with it, are such who write Poems, which are professedly to
"answer all Rules, and be left for Patterns to Men of Genius.
"These that follow shall attack others, because they are excell'd by
"them. The next Rank shall make an Author's being read a
"sufficient Ground of Opposition. Here march my Grammarians 260
"skill'd to torture Words; there my Sons of Sophistry, ever ready
"to wrest a Meaning. Observe how faint the foremost of the
"Procession appear; and how they are now lost in yonder Mists
"which roll about the Cave of Oblivion! This shews, it is not for
"themselves that they are to be known; the World will consider 265
"them only as managing a Part of thy Endowments, and so know
"them by thy Name while they live, that their own shall be lost for
"ever. But see how my Cave still swarms! how every Age produces
"Men, upon whom the Preservation of thy Memory devolves. My
"Darling, the Fates have decreed it! Thou art zoilus, and zoilus 270
"shall be eternal: Come, my Serpents, applaud him with your
"Hisses, that is all which now can be done; in modern Times my
"Sons shall invent louder Instruments, and artificial Imitations,
"Noises which drown the Voice of Merit, shall furnish a Consort to
"delight them." Here she arose to clasp him in her Arms, a 275
strange Noise was heard, the Critick started at it, and his Vision
forsook him.

   It was with some Confusion, that he lay musing a while upon
what he had seen; but reflecting, that the Goddess had giv'n him
no Answer concerning his Success in *Ægypt*, he strengthen'd his 280
Heart in his ancient Self-Love and Enmity to others, and took all
for an idle Dream born of the Fumes of Indigestion, or produc'd
by the dizzy Motion of his Voyage. In this Opinion, he told it at his
Departure to the Priest, who admiring the extraordinary Relation,
registred it in Hieroglyphicks at *Canopus*. 285

   The Day when he came to *Alexandria* was one on which the King
had appointed Games to *Apollo* and the *Muses,* and Honours and

Rewards for such Writers as shou'd appear in them. This he took
for a happy Omen at his Entrance, and, not to lose an Opportu-
nity of shewing himself, repair'd immediately to the publick    290
Theatre, where, as if every Thing was to favour him, the very first
Accident gave his Spleen a Diversion, which we find at large in the
Proem of the seventh Book of *Vitruvius*. It happen'd that when the
Poets had recited, six of the Judges decreed the Prizes with a full
Approbation of all the Audience. From this *Aristophanes* alone    295
dissented, and demanded the first Prize for a Person whose
bashful and interrupted Manner of speaking made him appear
the most disgustful: For he (says the Judge) is alone a Poet, and all
the rest Reciters; and they who are Judges shou'd not approve
Thefts, but Writings. To maintain his Assertion, those Volumns    300
were produc'd from whence they had been stoll'n: Upon which
the King order'd them to be formally try'd for Theft, and dis-
miss'd with Infamy; but plac'd *Aristophanes* over his Library, as
One, who had given a Proof of his Knowledge in Books. This
Passage ZOILUS often afterwards repeated with Pleasure, for the    305
Number of Disgraces which happen'd in it to the Pretenders in
Poetry; tho' his Envy made him still careful not to name
*Aristophanes*, but a Judge in general.

However, Criticism had only a short Triumph over Poetry,
when he made the next Turn his own, by stepping forward into    310
the Place of reciting. Here he immediately rais'd the Curiosity,
and drew the Attention of both King and People: But, as it
happen'd, neither the one nor the other lasted; for the first
Sentence where he had registred his own *Name*, satisfied their
Curiosity; and the next, where he offer'd to prove to a Court so    315
devoted to *Homer*, that he was ridiculous in every thing, went near
to finish his Audience. He was nevertheless heard quietly for
some Time, till the King seeing no End of his Abusing the Prince
of Philological Learning, (as *Vitruvius* words it) departed in Dis-
dain. The Judges follow'd, deriding his Attempt as an    320
Extravagance which cou'd not demand their Gravity; and the
People taking a License from the Precedent, hooted him away
with Obloquy and Indignation. Thus *Zoilus* fail'd at his first Ap-
pearance, and was forc'd to retire, stung with a most impatient
Sense of publick Contempt.    325

Yet notwithstanding all this, he did not omit his Attendance at
Court on the Day following, with a Petition that he might be put
upon the Establishment of Learning, and allow'd a Pension. This
the King read, but return'd no Answer: So great was the Scorn he
conceiv'd against him. But ZOILUS still undauntedly renew'd his    330

Petitions, 'till *Ptolomy,* being weary of his Persecution, gave him a
flat Denial. HOMER, (says the Prince) who has been dead these
Thousand Years, has maintain'd Thousands of People; and
ZOILUS, who boasts he has more Wit than he, ought not only to
maintain himself, but many others also.          335

His Petitions being thrown carelessly about, were fall'n into the
Hands of Men of Wit, whom, according to his Custom, he had
provok'd, and whom it is unsafe to provoke if you wou'd live
unexpos'd. I can compare them to nothing more properly, than to
the Bee, a Creature wing'd and lively, fond to rove through the          340
choicest Flowers of Nature, and blest at home among the Sweets
of its own Composition: Not ill-natur'd, yet quick to revenge an
Injury; not wearing its Sting out of the Sheath, yet able to wound
more sorely than its Appearance wou'd threaten. Now these being
made personal Enemies by his malicious Expressions, the Court          345
rung with Petitions of ZOILUS transvers'd; new Petitions drawn up
for him; Catalogues of his Merits, suppos'd to be collected by
himself; his Complaints of Man's Injustice set to a Harp out of
Tune, and a Hundred other Sports of Fancy, with which their
Epigrams play'd upon him. These were the Ways of Writing          350
which ZOILUS hated, because they were not only read, but retain'd
easily, by Reason of their Spirit, Humour, and Brevity; and be-
cause they not only make the Man a Jest upon whom they are
written, but a further Jest, if he attempt to answer them gravely.
However, he did what he cou'd in Revenge; he endeavour'd to set          355
those whom he envy'd at Variance among themselves, and in-
vented Lies to promote his Design. He told *Eratosthenes,* that
*Callimachus* said, his Extent of Learning consisted but in a super-
ficial Knowledge of the Sciences; and whisper'd *Callimachus,* that
*Eratosthenes* only allow'd him to have an artful habitual Knack of          360
Versifying. He would have made *Aristophanes* believe, that *The-*
*ocritus* rally'd his Knowledge in Editions as a curious Kind of
Triffling; and *Theocritus,* that *Aristophanes* derided the rustical
Simplicity of his Shepherds. Tho' of all his Stories, that which he
most valu'd himself for, was his constant Report, that every one          365
whom he hated was a Friend to *Antiochus* King of *Syria,* the Enemy
of *Ptolomy.*

But Malice is unsuccessful when the Character of its Agent is
known: They grew more Friends to one another, by imagining,
that even what had been said, as well as what had not, was all of          370
ZOILUS's Invention; and as he grew more and more the common
Jest, their Derision of him became a Kind of Life and Cement to
their Conversation.

Contempt, Poverty, and other Misfortunes had now so assaulted
him, that even they who abhorr'd his Temper, contributed some-          375
thing to his Support, in common Humanity. Yet still his Envy, like
a vitiated Stomach, converted every Kindness to the Nourishment
of his Disease; and 'twas the whole Business of his Life to revile
HOMER, and those by whom he himself subsisted. In this Humour
he had Days, which were so given up to *impatient Ill-nature,* that he          380
cou'd neither write any Thing, nor converse with any One. These
he sometimes employ'd in throwing Stones at Children; which was
once so unhappily return'd upon him, that he was taken up for
dead: And this occasion'd the Report in some Authors, of his
being ston'd to Death in *Ægypt.* Or, sometimes he convey'd him-          385
self into the Library, where he blotted the Name of HOMER wher-
ever he could meet it, and tore the best Editions of several
Volumns; for which the Librarians debarr'd him the Privilege of
that Place. These and other Mischiefs made him universally
shunn'd; nay, to such an Extravagance was his Character of Envy          390
carry'd, that the more superstitious *Ægyptians* imagin'd they were
fascinated by him, if the Day were darker, or themselves a little
heavier than ordinary; some wore Sprigs of Rue, by Way of
Prevention; and others, Rings made of the Hoof of a wild Ass for
Amulets, lest they shou'd suffer, by his fixing an Eye upon them.          395
 It was now near the Time, when that splendid Temple which
*Ptolomy* built in Honour of HOMER, was to be open'd with a solemn
Magnificence: For this the Men of Genius were employ'd in
finding a proper Pageant. At last, they agreed by one Consent, to
have ZOILUS, the utter Enemy of HOMER, hang'd in Effigie; and the          400
Day being come, it was on this Manner they form'd the Proces-
sion. Twelve beautiful Boys, lightly habited in white, with purple
Wings representing the *Hours,* went on the foremost: After these
came a Chariot exceeding high and stately, where sate one repre-
senting *Apollo,* with another at his Feet, who in this Pomp sustain'd          405
the Person of HOMER: *Apollo's* Lawrel had little gilded Points, like
the Appearance of Rays between its Leaves; HOMER's was bound
with a blue Fillet, like that which is worn by the Priests of the
Deity: *Apollo* was distinguish'd by the golden Harp he bore; HO-
MER, by a Volumn, richly beautify'd with Horns of inlaid Ivory,          410
and Tassels of Silver depending from them. Behind these came
three Chariots, in which rode nine Damsels, each of them with
that Instrument which is proper to each of the Muses; among
whom, *Calliope,* to give her the Honour of the Day, sate in the
Middle of the second Chariot, known by her richer Vestments.          415
After these march'd a solemn Train aptly habited, like those

Sciences which acknowledge their Rise or Improvement from this Poet. Then the Men of Learning who attended the Court, with Wreaths, and Rods or Scepters of Lawrel, as taking upon themselves the Representation of *Rhapsodists,* to do Honour, for the 420 Time, to HOMER. In the Rear of all was slowly drawn along an odd Carriage, rather than a Chariot, which had its Sides artfully turn'd, and carv'd so as to bear a Resemblance to the Heads of snarling Mastiffs. In this was born, as led in Triumph, a tall Image of Deformity, whose Head was bald, and wound about with Net- 425 tles for a Chaplet. The Tongue lay lolling out, to shew a Contempt of Mankind, and was fork'd at the End, to confess its Love to Detraction. The Hands were manacled behind, and the Fingers arm'd with long Nails, to cut deep through the Margins of Authors. Its Vesture was of the Paper of *Nilus,* bearing inscrib'd upon 430 its Breast in Capital Letters, ZOILUS *the* HOMERO-MASTIX; and all the rest of it was scrawl'd with various Monsters of that River, as Emblems of those Productions with which that Critick us'd to fill his Papers. When they had reach'd the Temple, where the King and his Court were already plac'd to behold them from its Galler- 435 ies, the Image of ZOILUS was hung upon a Gibbet, there erected for it, with such loud Acclamations as witness'd the Peoples Satisfaction. This being finish'd, the *Hours* knock'd at the Gates, which flew open, and discover'd the Statue of HOMER magnificently seated, with the Pictures of those Cities which contended for his 440 Birth, rang'd in Order around him. Then they who represented the Deities in the Procession, laying aside their Ensigns of Divinity, usher'd in the Men of Learning with a Sound of Voices, and their various Instruments, to assist at a Sacrifice in Honour of *Apollo* and his Favourite HOMER. 445

It may be easily believ'd, that ZOILUS concluded his Affairs were at the utmost Point of Desperation in *Ægypt;* wherefore, fill'd with Pride, Scorn, Anger, Vexation, Envy, (and whatever cou'd torment him, except the Knowledge of his Unworthiness) he flung himself aboard the first Ship which left that Country. As it happen'd, the 450 Vessel he sail'd in was bound for *Asia Minor,* and this landing him at a Port the nearest to *Smyrna,* he was a little pleas'd amidst his Misery to think of decrying HOMER in another Place where he was ador'd, and which chiefly pretended to his Birth. So incorrigible was his Disposition, that no Experience taught him any Thing 455 which might contribute to his Ease and Safety.

And as his Experience wrought nothing on him, so neither did the Accidents, which the Opinion of those Times took for ominous Warnings: For, he is reported to have seen the Night he

came to *Smyrna,* a venerable Person, such as HOMER is describ'd by    460
Antiquity, threatning him in a Dream; and in the Morning he
found a Part of his Works gnaw'd by *Mice,* which, says *Ælian,* are
of all Beasts the most prophetick; insomuch that they know when
to leave a House, even before its Fall is suspected. Envy, which has
no Relaxation, still hurry'd him forward, for it is certainly true    465
that a Man has not firmer Resolution from Reason, to stand by a
good Principle, than Obstinacy from perverted Nature, to adhere
to a bad one.

    In the Morning as he walk'd the Street, he observ'd in some
Places Inscriptions concerning HOMER, which inform'd him where    470
he liv'd, where he had taught School, and several other Par-
ticularities which the *Smyrneans* glory to have recorded of him; all
which awaken'd and irritated the Passions of ZOILUS. But his
Temper was quite overthrown, by the venerable Appearance
which he saw, upon entring the *Homereum;* which is a Building    475
compos'd of a Library, Porch, and Temple erected to HOMER. Here
a Phrenzy seiz'd him which knew no Bounds; he rav'd violently
against the Poet, and all his Admirers; he trampled on his Works,
he spurn'd about his Commentators, he tore down his Busts from
the Niches, threw the Medals that were cast of him out of the    480
Windows, and passing from one Place to another, beat the aged
Priests, and broke down the Altar. The Cries which were occa-
sioned by this Means brought in many upon him; who observ'd
with Horror how the most sacred Honours of their City were
prophan'd by the frantick Impiety of a Stranger; and immediately    485
dragg'd him to Punishment before their Magistrates, who were
then sitting. He was no sooner there, but known for ZOILUS by
some in Court, a Name a long Time most hateful to *Smyrna;*
which, as it valu'd itself upon the Birth of HOMER, so bore more
impatiently than other Places, the Abuses offer'd him. This made    490
them eager to propitiate his Shade, and claim to themselves a
second Merit by the Death of ZOILUS; wherefore they sentenc'd
him to suffer by Fire, as the due Reward of his Desecrations; and
order'd, that their City shou'd be purify'd by a Lustration, for
having entertain'd so impious a Guest. In Pursuance to this Sen-    495
tence, he was led away, with his Compositions born before him by
the publick Executioner: Then was he fasten'd to the Stake,
prophesying all the while how many shou'd arise to revenge his
Quarrel: particularly, that when *Greek* shou'd be no more a Lan-
guage, there shall be a *Nation* which will both *translate* HOMER into    500
*Prose,* and *contract* him in *Verse.* At last, his Compositions were
lighted to set the Pile on Fire, and he expir'd sighing for the Loss

of them, more than for the Pain he suffer'd: And perhaps too, because he might foresee in his prophetick Rapture, that there shou'd arise a Poet in another Nation, able to do HOMER Justice,          505 and make him known amongst his People to future Ages.

Thus dy'd this noted Critick, of whom we may observe from the Course of the History, that as several Cities contended for the Honour of the Birth of HOMER, so several have contended for the Honour of the Death of ZOILUS. With him likewise perish'd his          510 great Work on the *Iliad,* and the *Odysses;* concerning which we observe also, that as the known Worth of HOMER's Poetry makes him survive himself with Glory; so the bare Memory of ZOILUS's Criticism makes him survive himself with Infamy. These are deservedly the Consequences of that *ill Nature* which made him fond          515 of Detraction, that *Envy,* which made him choose so excellent a Character for its Object, and those *partial Methods* of *Injustice* with which he treated the Object he had chosen.

Yet how many commence Criticks after him, upon the same unhappy Principles? How many labour to destroy the Monu-          520 ments of the dead, and summon up the Great from their Graves to answer for Trifles before them? How many, by Misrepresentations, both hinder the World from favouring Men of Genius, and discourage them in themselves; like Boughs of a baneful and barren Nature, that shoot a-cross a Fruit-Tree; at once to screen          525 the Sun from it, and hinder it by their Droppings from producing any Thing of Value? But if these who thus follow ZOILUS, meet not the same Severities of Fate, because they come short of his Indefatigableness, or their Object is not so universally the Concern of Mankind; they shall nevertheless meet a Proportion of it in the          530 inward Trouble they give themselves, and the outward Contempt others fling upon them: A Punishment which every one has hitherto felt, who has really deserv'd to be call'd a ZOILUS; and which will always be the natural Reward of such Mens Actions, as long as ZOILUS is the proper Name of *Envy.*          535

## Names *of the* MICE.

PSYCARPAX, *One who plunders Granaries.*
Troxartas, *A Bread-eater.*
Lychomile, *A Licker of Meal.*
Pternotractas, *A Bacon-eater.*
Lychopinax, *A Licker of Dishes.*
Embasichytros, *A Creeper into Pots.*
Lychenor, *A Name from Licking.*
Troglodytes, *One who runs into Holes.*
Artophagus, *Who feeds on Bread.*
Tyroglyphus, *A Cheese-Scooper.*
Pternoglyphus, *A Bacon-Scooper.*
Pternophagus, *A Bacon-Eater.*
Cnissodioctes, *One who follows the Steam of Kitchens.*
Sitophagus, *An Eater of Wheat.*
Meridarpax, *One who plunders his Share.*

## Names *of the* FROGS.

PHYSIGNATHUS, *One who swells his Cheeks.*
Peleus, *A Name from Mud.*
Hydromeduse, *A Ruler in the Waters.*
Hypsiboas, *A loud Bawler.*
Pelion, *From Mud.*
Seutlæus, *Call'd from the Beets.*
Polyphonus, *A great Babbler.*
Lymnocharis, *One who loves the Lake.*
Crambophagus, *Cabbage-eater.*
Lymnisius, *Call'd from the Lake.*
Calaminthius, *From the Herb.*
Hydrocharis, *Who loves the Water.*
Borborocates, *Who lies in the Mud.*
Prassophagus, *An Eater of Garlick.*
Pelusius, *From Mud.*
Pelobates, *Who walks in the Dirt.*
Prassæus, *Call'd from Garlick.*
Craugasides, *from Croaking.*

# Homer's Battle of the Frogs and Mice.

## Book I.

To fill my rising Song with sacred Fire,
Ye tuneful *Nine,* ye sweet Celestial Quire!
From *Helicon*'s imbow'ring Height repair,
Attend my Labours, and reward my Pray'r.
The dreadful Toils of raging *Mars* I write,                          5
The Springs of Contest, and the Fields of Fight;
How threatning *Mice* advanc'd with warlike Grace,
And wag'd dire Combats with the *croaking* Race.
Not louder Tumults shook *Olympus'* Tow'rs,
When Earth-born Giants dar'd Immortal Pow'rs.                          10
These equal Acts an equal Glory claim,
And thus the *Muse* records the Tale of Fame.
   Once on a Time, fatigu'd and out of Breath,
And just escap'd the stretching Claws of Death,
A Gentle *Mouse,* whom Cats pursu'd in vain,                          15
Flies swift-of-foot across the neighb'ring Plain,
Hangs o'er a Brink, his eager Thirst to cool,
And dips his Whiskers in the standing Pool;
When near a courteous *Frog* advanc'd his Head,
And from the Waters, hoarse-resounding said,                          20
   What art thou, Stranger? What the Line you boast?
What Chance hath cast thee panting on our Coast?
With strictest Truth let all thy Words agree,
Nor let me find a faithless Mouse in thee.
If worthy Friendship, proffer'd Friendship take,                      25
And entring view the pleasurable Lake:
Range o'er my Palace, in my Bounty share,
And glad return from hospitable Fare.
This Silver Realm extends beneath my Sway,
And me, their Monarch, all its Frogs obey.                            30
Great *Physignathus* I, from *Peleus'* Race,
Begot in fair *Hydromeduse'* Embrace,

Where by the nuptial Bank that paints his Side,
The swift *Eridanus* delights to glide.
Thee too, thy Form, thy Strength, and Port proclaim,                    35
A scepter'd King; a Son of Martial Fame;
Then trace thy Line, and aid my guessing Eyes.
Thus ceas'd the *Frog*, and thus the *Mouse* replies.
    Known to the Gods, the Men, the Birds that fly
Thro' wild Expanses of the midway Sky,                                  40
My Name resounds; and if unknown to thee,
The Soul of Great *Psycarpax* lives in me.
Of brave *Troxartas'* Line, whose sleeky Down
In Love compress'd *Lychomile* the brown.
My Mother she, and Princess of the Plains                               45
Where-e're her Father *Pternotroctas* reigns:
Born where a Cabin lifts its airy Shed,
With Figs, with Nuts, with vary'd Dainties fed.
But since our Natures nought in common know,
From what Foundation can a Friendship grow?                            50
These curling Waters o'er thy Palace roll;
But Man's high Food supports my Princely Soul.
In vain the circled Loaves attempt to lie
Conceal'd in Flaskets from my curious Eye,
In vain the Tripe that boasts the whitest Hue,                         55
In vain the gilded Bacon shuns my View,
In vain the Cheeses, Offspring of the Pale,
Or honey'd Cakes, which Gods themselves regale.
And as in Arts I shine, in Arms I fight,
Mix'd with the bravest, and unknown to Flight.                         60
Tho' large to mine the humane Form appear,
Not *Man* himself can smite my Soul with Fear.
Sly to the Bed with silent Steps I go,
Attempt his Finger, or attack his Toe,
And fix indented Wounds with dext'rous Skill,                          65
Sleeping he feels, and only seems to feel.
Yet have we Foes which direful Dangers cause,
Grim *Owls* with Talons arm'd, and *Cats* with Claws,
And that false *Trap*, the Den of silent Fate,
Where *Death* his Ambush plants around the Bait;                       70
All-dreaded these, and dreadful o'er the rest
The potent Warriours of the tabby Vest,
If to the dark we fly, the Dark they trace,
And rend our Heroes of the *nibling* Race.
But me, nor Stalks, nor watrish Herbs delight,                         75

Nor can the crimson Radish charm my Sight,
The Lake-resounding *Frogs* selected Fare,
Which not a *Mouse* of any Tast can bear.
　　As thus the downy Prince his Mind exprest,
His Answer thus the croaking King addrest.　　　　　80
　　Thy Words luxuriant on thy Dainties rove,
And, stranger, we can boast of bounteous *Jove:*
We sport in Water, or we dance on Land,
And born amphibious, Food from both command.
But trust thy self where Wonders ask thy View,　　　85
And safely tempt those Seas, I'll bear thee through:
Ascend my Shoulders, firmly keep thy Seat,
And reach my marshy Court, and feast in State.
　　He said, and leant his Back; with nimble Bound
Leaps the light Mouse, and clasps his Arms around,　90
Then wond'ring floats, and sees with glad Survey
The winding Banks dissemble Ports at Sea.
But when aloft the curling Water rides,
And wets with azure Wave his downy Sides,
His Thoughts grow conscious of approaching Woe,　　95
His idle Tears with vain Repentance flow,
His Locks he rends, his trembling Feet he rears,
Thick beats his Heart with unaccustom'd Fears;
He sighs, and chill'd with Danger, longs for Shore:
His Tail extended forms a fruitless Oar,　　　　　100
Half-drench'd in liquid Death his Pray'rs he spake,
And thus bemoan'd him from the dreadful Lake.
　　So pass'd *Europa* thro' the rapid Sea,
Trembling and fainting all the vent'rous Way;
With oary Feet the *Bull* triumphant rode,　　　105
And safe in *Crete* depos'd his lovely Load.
Ah safe at last! may thus the *Frog* support
My trembling Limbs to reach his ample Court.
　　As thus he sorrows, Death ambiguous grows,
Lo! from the deep a Water-*Hydra* rose;　　　　110
He rolls his sanguin'd Eyes, his Bosom heaves,
And darts with active Rage along the Waves.
Confus'd, the Monarch sees his hissing Foe,
And dives to shun the sable Fates below.
Forgetful *Frog!* The Friend thy Shoulders bore,　　115
Unskill'd in Swimming, floats remote from Shore.
He grasps with fruitless Hands to find Relief,
Supinely falls, and grinds his Teeth with Grief,

Plunging he sinks, and struggling mounts again,          120
And sinks, and strives, but strives with Fate in vain.
The weighty Moisture clogs his hairy Vest,
And thus the *Prince* his dying Rage exprest.
   Nor thou, that flings me flound'ring from thy Back,
As from hard Rocks rebounds the shatt'ring Wrack,
Nor thou shalt 'scape thy Due, perfidious King!          125
Pursu'd by Vengeance on the swiftest Wing:
At Land thy Strength could never equal mine,
At Sea to conquer, and by Craft, was thine.
But Heav'n has Gods, and Gods have searching Eyes:
Ye *Mice,* ye *Mice,* my great Avengers rise!          130
   This said, he sighing gasp'd, and gasping dy'd.
His Death the young *Lychopinax* espy'd,
As on the flow'ry Brink he pass'd the Day,
Bask'd in the Beams, and loyter'd Life away:
Loud shrieks the *Mouse,* his Shrieks the Shores repeat;     135
The nibbling Nation learn their Heroe's Fate:
Grief, dismal Grief ensues; deep Murmurs sound,
And shriller Fury fills the deafen'd Ground;
From Lodge to Lodge the *sacred Heralds* run,
To fix their Council with the rising Sun;          140
Where great *Troxartas* crown'd in Glory reigns,
And winds his length'ning Court beneath the Plains;
*Psycarpax* Father, Father now no more!
For poor *Psycarpax* lies remote from Shore;
Supine he lies! the silent Waters stand,          145
And no kind Billow wafts the *Dead* to Land!

# Book II.

WHEN rosy-finger'd Morn had ting'd the Clouds,
Around their *Monarch-Mouse* the Nation crouds,
Slow rose the Monarch, heav'd his anxious Breast,
And thus, the Council fill'd with Rage, addrest.
   For lost *Psycarpax* much my Soul endures,          5
'Tis mine the private Grief, the publick, yours.
Three warlike Sons adorn'd my nuptial Bed,
Three Sons, alas, before their Father dead!
Our Eldest perish'd by the rav'ning *Cat,*

As near my Court the *Prince* unheedful sate.                                     10
Our next, an Engine fraught with Danger drew,
The Portal gap'd, the Bait was hung in View,
Dire *Arts* assist the *Trap*, the *Fates* decoy,
And Men unpitying kill'd my *gallant Boy!*
The last, his *Country's* Hope, his *Parent's* Pride,       15
Plung'd in the Lake by *Physignathus*, dy'd.
Rouse all the War, my Friends! avenge the Deed,
And bleed that *Monarch,* and his *Nation* bleed.
    His Words in ev'ry Breast inspir'd Alarms,
And careful *Mars* supply'd their Host with Arms.           20
In verdant Hulls despoil'd of all their Beans,
The buskin'd Warriours stalk'd along the Plains,
Quills aptly bound, their bracing Corselet made,
Fac'd with the Plunder of a Cat they flay'd,
The Lamp's round Boss affords their ample Shield,          25
Large Shells of Nuts their cov'ring Helmet yield;
And o'er the Region, with reflected Rays,
Tall Groves of Needles for their Lances blaze.
Dreadful in Arms the marching *Mice* appear:
The wond'ring *Frogs* perceive the Tumult near,            30
Forsake the Waters, thick'ning form a Ring,
And ask, and hearken, whence the Noises spring;
When near the Croud, disclos'd to publick View,
The valiant Chief *Embasichytros* drew:
The sacred Herald's Scepter grac'd his Hand,               35
And thus his Words exprest his King's Command.
    Ye *Frogs!* the *Mice* with Vengeance fir'd, advance,
And deckt in Armour shake the shining Lance;
Their hapless Prince by *Physignathus* slain,
Extends incumbent on the watry Plain.                      40
Then arm your Host, the doubtful Battle try;
Lead forth those *Frogs* that have the Soul to die.
    The Chief retires, the Crowd the Challenge hear,
And proudly-swelling, yet perplex'd appear,
Much they resent, yet much their *Monarch* blame,          45
Who rising, spoke to clear his tainted Fame.
    O Friends, I never forc'd the *Mouse* to Death,
Nor saw the Gaspings of his latest Breath.
He, vain of Youth, our Art of Swimming try'd,
And vent'rous, in the Lake the Wanton dy'd.                50
To Vengeance now by false Appearance led,

They point their Anger at my guiltless Head.
But wage the rising War by deep Device,
And turn its Fury on the crafty *Mice.*
Your *King* directs the Way; my Thoughts elate     55
With Hopes of Conquest, form Designs of Fate.
Where high the Banks their verdant Surface heave,
And the steep Sides confine the sleeping Wave,
There, near the Margin, and in Armour bright,
Sustain the first impetuous Shocks of Fight:     60
Then where the dancing Feather joins the Crest,
Let each brave *Frog* his obvious *Mouse* arrest;
Each strongly grasping, headlong plunge a Foe,
'Till countless Circles whirl the Lake below;
Down sink the *Mice* in yielding Waters drown'd;     65
Loud flash the Waters; ecchoing Shores resound:
The *Frogs* triumphant tread the conquer'd Plain,
And raise their glorious Trophies of the slain.
    He spake no more, his prudent Scheme imparts
Redoubling Ardour to the boldest Hearts.     70
Green was the Suit his arming Heroes chose,
Around their Legs the Greaves of Mallows close,
Green were the Beetes about their Shoulders laid,
And green the Colewort, which the Target made.
Form'd of the vary'd Shells the Waters yield,     75
Their glossy Helmets glist'ned o'er the Field;
And tap'ring Sea-Reeds for the polish'd Spear,
With upright Order pierc'd the ambient Air.
Thus dress'd for War, they take th' appointed Height,
Poize the long Arms, and urge the promis'd Fight.     80
    But now, where *Jove's* irradiate Spires arise,
With Stars surrounded in Æthereal Skies,
(A Solemn Council call'd) the brazen Gates
Unbar; the Gods assume their golden Seats:
The Sire superiour leans, and points to show     85
What wond'rous Combats Mortals wage below:
How strong, how large, the num'rous Heroes stride;
What Length of Lance they shake with warlike Pride:
What eager Fire, their rapid March reveals;
So the fierce *Centaurs* ravag'd o'er the Dales;     90
And so confirm'd, the daring *Titans* rose,
Heap'd Hills on Hills, and bid the Gods be Foes.
    This seen, the Pow'r his sacred Visage rears,

He casts a pitying Smile on worldly Cares,
And asks what heav'nly Guardians take the List,                95
Or who the *Mice,* or who the *Frogs* assist?
   Then thus to *Pallas.* If my Daughter's Mind
Have join'd the *Mice,* why stays she still behind?
Drawn forth by sav'ry Steams they wind their Way,
And sure Attendance round thine Altar pay,                100
Where while the Victims gratify their Tast,
They sport to please the Goddess of the Feast.
   Thus spake the Ruler of the spacious Skies,
When thus, resolv'd, the Blue-Ey'd Maid replies.
In vain, my Father! all their Dangers plead,                105
To such, thy *Pallas* never grants her Aid.
My flow'ry Wreaths they petulantly spoil,
And rob my chrystal Lamps of feeding Oil.
(Ills following Ills) but what afflicts me more,
My Veil, that idle Race profanely tore.                110
The Web was curious, wrought with Art divine;
Relentless Wretches! all the Work was mine.
Along the Loom the purple Warp I spread,
Cast the light Shoot, and crost the silver Thread;
In this their Teeth a thousand Breaches tear,                115
The thousand Breaches skilful Hands repair,
For which vile earthly Dunns thy Daughter grieve,
And Gods, that use no Coin, have none to give.
And Learning's Goddess never less can owe,
Neglected Learning gets no Wealth below.                120
Nor let the *Frogs* to gain my Succour sue,
Those clam'rous Fools have lost my Favour too.
For late, when all the Conflict ceast at Night,
When my stretch'd Sinews work'd with eager Fight,
When spent with glorious Toil, I left the Field,                125
And sunk for Slumber on my swelling Shield,
Lo from the Deep, repelling sweet Repose,
With noisy Croakings half the Nation rose:
Devoid of Rest, with aking Brows I lay,
'Till Cocks proclaim'd the crimson Dawn of Day.                130
Let all, like me, from either Host forbear,
Nor tempt the flying Furies of the Spear.
Let heav'nly Blood (or what for Blood may flow)
Adorn the Conquest of a meaner Foe,
Who, wildly rushing, meet the wond'rous Odds,                135

Tho' Gods oppose, and brave the wounded Gods.
O'er gilded Clouds reclin'd, the Danger view,
And be the Wars of Mortals Scenes for you.
　So mov'd the *blue-ey'd Queen*, her Words persuade,
Great *Jove* assented, and the rest obey'd.                    140

# BOOK III.

N ow Front to Front the marching Armies shine,
　　Halt e'er they meet, and form the length'ning Line,
The Chiefs conspicuous seen, and heard afar,
Give the loud Sign to loose the rushing War;
Their dreadful Trumpets deep-mouth'd Hornets sound,             5
The sounded Charge remurmurs o'er the Ground,
Ev'n *Jove* proclaims a Field of Horror nigh,
And rolls low Thunder thro' the troubled Sky.
　First to the Fight the large *Hypsiboas* flew,
And brave *Lychenor* with a Javelin slew.                      10
The luckless Warriour fill'd with gen'rous Flame,
Stood foremost glitt'ring in the Post of Fame;
When in his Liver struck, the Jav'lin hung;
The *Mouse* fell thund'ring, and the Target rung;
Prone to the Ground he sinks his closing Eye,                  15
And soil'd in Dust his lovely Tresses lie.
A Spear at *Pelion Troglodytes* cast,
The missive Spear within the Bosom past;
Death's sable Shades the fainting *Frog* surround,
And Life's red Tide runs ebbing from the Wound.               20
*Embasichytros* felt *Seutlæus*' Dart
Transfix, and quiver in his panting Heart;
But great *Artophagus* aveng'd the slain,
And big *Seutlæus* tumbling loads the Plain,
And *Polyphonus* dies, a *Frog* renown'd,                     25
For boastful Speech and Turbulence of Sound;
Deep thro' the Belly pierc'd, supine he lay,
And breath'd his Soul against the Face of Day.
The strong *Lymnocharis*, who view'd with Ire,
A Victor triumph, and a Friend expire;                        30
And fiercely flung where *Troglodytes* fought,
With heaving Arms a rocky Fragment caught,
A Warriour vers'd in Arts, of sure Retreat,

Yet Arts in vain elude impending Fate;
Full on his sinewy Neck the Fragment fell, 35
And o'er his Eye-lids Clouds eternal dwell.
*Lychenor* (second of the glorious Name)
Striding advanc'd, and took no wand'ring Aim;
Thro' all the *Frog* the shining Jav'lin flies,
And near the vanquish'd *Mouse* the Victor dies; 40
The dreadful Stroke *Crambophagus* affrights,
Long bred to Banquets, less inur'd to Fights,
Heedless he runs, and stumbles o'er the Steep,
And wildly flound'ring flashes up the Deep;
*Lychenor* following with a downward Blow 45
Reach'd in the Lake his unrecover'd Foe;
Gasping he rolls, a purple Stream of Blood
Distains the Surface of the Silver Flood;
Thro' the wide Wound the rushing Entrails throng,
And slow the breathless Carkass floats along. 50
*Lymnisius* good *Tyroglyphus* assails,
Prince of the *Mice* that haunt the flow'ry Vales,
Lost to the milky Fares and rural Seat,
He came to perish on the Bank of Fate.
The dread *Pternoglyphus* demands the Fight, 55
Which tender *Calaminthius* shuns by Flight,
Drops the green Target, springing quits the Foe,
Glides thro' the Lake, and safely dives below.
The dire *Pternophagus* divides his Way
Thro' breaking Ranks, and leads the dreadful Day. 60
No nibbling Prince excell'd in Fierceness more,
His Parents fed him on the savage Boar;
But where his Lance the Field with Blood imbru'd,
Swift as he mov'd *Hydrocharis* pursu'd,
'Till fall'n in Death he lies, a shatt'ring Stone 65
Sounds on the Neck, and crushes all the Bone,
His Blood pollutes the Verdure of the Plain,
And from his Nostrils bursts the gushing Brain.
*Lycopinax* with *Borbocætes* fights
A blameless *Frog,* whom humbler Life delights; 70
The fatal Jav'lin unrelenting flies,
And Darkness seals the gentle Croaker's Eyes.
Incens'd *Prassophagus* with spritely Bound,
Bears *Cnissiodortes* off the rising Ground,
Then drags him o'er the Lake depriv'd of Breath, 75
And downward plunging, sinks his Soul to Death.

But now the great *Psycarpax* shines afar,
(Scarce he so great whose Loss provok'd the War)
Swift to revenge his fatal Jav'lin fled,
And thro' the Liver struck *Pelusius* dead;                            80
His freckled Corps before the Victor fell,
His Soul indignant sought the Shades of Hell.
This saw *Pelobates,* and from the Flood
Lifts with both Hands a monst'rous Mass of Mud,
The Cloud obscene o'er all the Warrior flies,                          85
Dishonours his brown Face, and blots his Eyes.
Enrag'd, and wildly sputtring, from the Shore
A Stone immense of Size the Warrior bore,
A Load for lab'ring Earth, whose Bulk to raise,
Asks ten degen'rate *Mice* of modern Days.                            90
Full to the Leg arrives the crushing Wound,
The *Frog* supportless, wriths upon the Ground.
Thus flush'd, the Victor wars with matchless Force,
'Till loud *Craugasides* arrests his Course,
Hoarse-croaking Threats precede, with fatal Speed                     95
Deep thro' the Belly runs the pointed Reed,
Then strongly tug'd, return'd imbru'd with Gore,
And on the Pile his reeking Entrails bore.
The lame *Sitophagus* oppress'd with Pain,
Creeps from the desp'rate Dangers of the Plain;                      100
And where the Ditches rising Weeds supply,
To spread their lowly Shades beneath the Sky,
There lurks the silent *Mouse* reliev'd of Heat,
And safe imbower'd, avoids the Chance of Fate.
But here *Troxartes, Physignathus* there,                            105
Whirl the dire Furies of the pointed Spear:
Then where the Foot around its Ankle plies,
*Troxartes* wounds, and *Physignathus* flies,
Halts to the Pool, a safe Retreat to find,
And trails a dangling Length of Leg behind.                          110
The *Mouse* still urges, still the *Frog* retires,
And half in Anguish of the Flight expires;
Then pious Ardor young *Prassæus* brings,
Betwixt the Fortunes of contending Kings:
Lank, harmless *Frog!* with Forces hardly grown,                     115
He darts the Reed in Combats not his own,
Which faintly tinkling on *Troxartes'* Shield,
Hangs at the Point, and drops upon the Field.
    Now nobly tow'ring o'er the rest appears

A gallant Prince that far transcends his Years,                    120
Pride of his Sire, and Glory of his House,
And more a *Mars* in Combat than a *Mouse:*
His Action bold, robust his ample Frame,
And *Meridarpax* his resounding Name.
The Warrior singled from the fighting Crowd,                    125
Boasts the dire Honours of his Arms aloud;
Then strutting near the Lake, with Looks elate,
Threats all its Nations with approaching Fate.
And such his Strength, the Silver Lakes around,
Might roll their Waters o'er unpeopled Ground.                    130
But pow'rful *Jove* who shews no less his Grace
To *Frogs* that perish, than to human Race,
Felt soft Compassion rising in his Soul,
And shook his sacred Head, that shook the Pole.
Then thus to all the gazing Pow'rs began,                    135
The Sire of *Gods*, and *Frogs*, and *Mouse,* and *Man.*
   What Seas of Blood I view, what Worlds of slain,
An Iliad rising from a Day's Campaign!
How fierce his Jav'lin o'er the trembling Lakes
The black-fur'd Hero *Meridarpax* shakes!                    140
Unless some fav'ring Deity descend,
Soon will the *Frogs* loquacious Empire end.
Let dreadful *Pallas* wing'd with Pity fly,
And make her *Ægis* blaze before his Eye:
While *Mars* refulgent on his ratling Car,                    145
Arrests his raging Rival of the War.
   He ceas'd, reclining with attentive Head,
When thus the glorious God of Combats said.
Nor *Pallas, Jove!* tho' *Pallas* take the Field,
With all the Terrors of her hissing Shield,                    150
Nor *Mars* himself, tho' *Mars* in Armour bright
Ascend his Car, and wheel amidst the Fight;
Nor these can drive the desp'rate *Mouse* afar,
And change the Fortunes of the bleeding War.
Let all go forth, all Heav'n in Arms arise,                    155
Or launch thy own red Thunder from the Skies.
Such ardent Bolts as flew that wond'rous Day,
When Heaps of *Titans* mix'd with Mountains lay,
When all the Giant-Race enormous fell,
And huge *Enceladus* was hurl'd to Hell.                    160
   'Twas thus th' Armipotent advis'd the Gods,
When from his Throne the Cloud-Compeller nods,

Deep length'ning Thunders run from Pole to Pole,
*Olympus* trembles as the Thunders roll.
Then swift he whirls the brandish'd Bolt around,                    165
And headlong darts it at the distant Ground,
The Bolt discharg'd inwrap'd with Light'ning flies,
And rends its flaming Passage thro' the Skies,
Then Earth's Inhabitants the Niblers shake,
And *Frogs*, the Dwellers in the Waters, quake.                     170
Yet still the *Mice* advance their dread Design,
And the last Danger threats the croaking Line,
'Till *Jove* that inly mourn'd the Loss they bore,
With strange Assistants fill'd the frighted Shore.
    Pour'd from the neighb'ring Strand, deform'd to View,           175
They march, a sudden unexpected Crew,
Strong Sutes of Armor round their Bodies close,
Which, like thick Anvils, blunt the force of Blows;
In wheeling Marches turn'd oblique they go,
With harpy Claws their Limbs divide below,                          180
Fell Sheers the Passage to their Mouth command,
From out the Flesh the Bones by Nature stand,
Broad spread their Backs, their shining Shoulders rise,
Unnumber'd Joints distort their lengthen'd Thighs,
With nervous Cords their Hands are firmly brac'd,                   185
Their round black Eye-balls in their Bosom plac'd,
On eight long Feet the wond'rous Warriors tread,
And either End alike supplies a Head.
These, mortal Wits to call the *Crabs*, agree;
The Gods have other Names for Things than we.                       190
    Now where the Jointures from their Loins depend,
The Heroes Tails with sev'ring Grasps they rend.
Here, short of Feet, depriv'd the Pow'r to fly,
There, without Hands upon the Field they lie.
Wrench'd from their Holds, and scatter'd all around,                195
The bended Lances heap the cumber'd Ground.
Helpless Amazement, Fear pursuing Fear,
And mad Confusion thro' their Host appear,
O'er the wild Wast with headlong Flight they go,
Or creep conceal'd in vaulted Holes below.                          200
    But down *Olympus* to the Western Seas,
Far-shooting *Phœbus* drove with fainter Rays,
And a whole War (so *Jove* ordain'd) begun,
Was fought, and ceas'd, in one revolving Sun.

# Zoilus's Remarks.

*Ingenium magni Livor detractat Amici,*
*Quisquis & ex illo Zoile nomen Habes.*

I MUST do my Reader the Justice, before I enter upon these
NOTES of ZOILUS, to inform him, that I have not in any Author
met this Work ascrib'd to him by its Title, which has made me not
mention it in the LIFE. But thus much in general appears, that he
wrote several Things besides his Censure on the *Iliad*, which, as it          5
gives Ground for this Opinion, encourages me to offer an Ac-
count of the Treatise.

Being acquainted with a grave Gentleman who searches after
Editions, purchases Manuscripts, and collects Copies, I apply'd to
him for some Editions of this Poem, which he readily oblig'd me          10
with. But, added he, taking down a Paper, I doubt I shall dis-
courage you from your Translation, when I show this Work,
which is written upon the Original, by ZOILUS, the famous Adver-
sary of HOMER. ZOILUS! said I with Surprize, I thought his Works
had long since perish'd. They have so, answer'd he, all, except this          15
little Piece, which has a PREFACE annex'd to it accounting for its
Preservation. It seems, when he parted from *Macedon,* he left this
behind him where he lodg'd, and where no one enter'd for a long
Time, in Detestation of the Odiousness of his Character, 'till
*Mævius* arriving there in his Travels, and being desirous to lie in          20
the same Room, luckily found it, and brought it away with him.
This the Author of the PREFACE imagins the Reason of *Horace's*
wishing *Mævius* in the 10th *Epode,* such a Shipwrack as HOMER
describes; as it were with an Eye to his having done something
disadvantageous to that Poet. From *Mævius,* the Piece came into          25
the Hand of *Carvilius Pictor,* (who, when he wrote against *Virgil,*
call'd his Book, with a respectful Imitation of ZOILUS, the
*Æneidomastix*) and from him into the Hands of others who are

97

unknown, because the World apply'd to them no other Name than
that of ZOILUS, in Order to sink their own in Oblivion. Thus it ever          30
found some learned Philologist or Critick, to keep it secret from
the Rage of HOMER's Admirers; yet not so secret, but that it has still
been communicated among the *Literati*. I am of Opinion, that our
Great *Scaliger* borrow'd it, to work him up when he writ so sharply
against *Cardan;* and perhaps *Le Clerc* too, when he prov'd *Q.*          35
*Curtius* ignorant of every particular Branch of Learning.

This formal Account made me give Attention to what the Book
contain'd; and I must acknowledge, that whether it be his, or the
Work of some Grammarian, it appears to be writ in his Spirit. The
open Profession of Enmity to great Genius's, and the Fear of          40
nothing so much as that he may not be able to find Faults enough,
are such Resemblances of his strongest Features, that any one
might take it for his own Production. To give the World a Notion
of this, I have made a Collection of some REMARKS, which most
struck me, during that short Time in which I was allow'd to          45
peruse the Manuscript.

## THE REMARKS OF ZOILUS UPON HOMER'S 'BATTLE OF THE FROGS AND MICE'

VERSE 1. To fill my rising Song.] *As* Protagoras *the Sophist found
fault with the Beginning of the* Iliad, *for its speaking to
the* Muse *rather with an abrupt Command, than a solemn Invocation; so
I, says* ZOILUS, *do on the other Hand find Fault with him for using any
Invocation at all before this Poem, or any such Trifles as he is Author of. If*          5
*he must use one,* Protagoras *is in the right; if not, I am: This I hold for
true Criticism, notwithstanding the Opinion of* Aristotle *against us. Nor
let any one lay a Stress on* Aristotle *in this Point; he alas! knows nothing
of Poetry but what he has read in* HOMER; *his Rules are all extracted from
him, or founded in him. In short,* HOMER's *Works are the Examples of*          10
Aristotle's *Precepts; and* Aristotle's *Precepts the Methods* HOMER
*wrought by.* From hence it is to be concluded as the Opinion of this
Critick, that whoever wou'd intirely destroy the Reputation of
HOMER, must renounce the Authority of *Aristotle* before-hand.
The Rules of Building may be of Service to us, if we design to          15
judge of an Edifice, and discover what may be amiss in it for the
Advantage of future Artificers; but they are of no Use to those
who only intend to overthrow it utterly.

After the Word [*Song,*] in the first Line the Original adds, [*What*

*I have written in my Tablets.*] These Words, which are dropp'd in the
Translation as of no Consequence, the Great ZOILUS has thought
fit to expunge; asserting for a Reason, without backing it with
farther Proof, *That Tablets were not of so early Invention.* Now, it must
be granted, this Manner of *proving by Affirmation* is of an ex-
traordinary Nature, but however it has its End with a Set of
Readers for whom it is adapted. One Part of the World knows not
with what Assurance another Part can express itself. They imag-
ine a reasonable Creature will not have the Face to say any Thing
which has not some Shadow of Reason to support it; and run
implicitly into the Snare which is laid for good Nature, by these
daring Authors of definitive Sentences upon bare Assertion.

VERSE 15. *Whom Cats pursu'd.*] The *Greek* Word here expresly
signifies a *Cat:* ZOILUS, whom *Perizonius* follows, affirms, *It was
Weezils which the Mouse fled from;* and then objects against its Proba-
bility. But it is common with one Sort of Criticks, to shew an
Author means differently from what he really did, and then to
prove, that the Meaning which *they* find out for him is good for
nothing.

VERSE 25. *If worthy Friendship.*] In this Proposal begins the Moral
of the whole Piece, which is, that hasty, ill-founded, or unnatural
Friendships and Leagues, will naturally end in War and Discord.
But ZOILUS, who is here mightily concern'd to take off from
HOMER all the Honour of having design'd a Moral, asserts on the
other Hand, *That the Poet's whole Intent was to make a Fable; that a
Fable he has made, and one very idle and triffling; that many Things are
ascrib'd to* HOMER, *which poor* HOMER *never dream'd of; and he who
finds them out rather shews his own Parts than discovers his Author's
Beauties.* In this Opinion has he been follow'd by several of those
Criticks, who only dip into Authors when they have Occasion to
write against them. And yet even these shall speak differently
concerning the Design of Writers, if the Question be of their own
Performances; for to their own Works they write *Prefaces,* to
display the Grandness of the Moral, Regularity of the Scheme,
Number and Brightness of the Figures, and a Thousand other
Excellencies, which if they did not tell, no one wou'd ever imag-
ine. For others, they write *Remarks,* which tend to contract their
Excellencies within the narrow Compass of their partial Ap-
prehension. It were well if they cou'd allow such to be as wise as
themselves, whom the World allows to be much wiser: But their
being naturally Friends to themselves, and professedly Adver-
saries to some greater Genius, easily accounts for these different
Manners of Speaking. I will not leave this Note, without giving

20

25

30

35

40

45

50

55

60

you an Instance of its Practice in the great *Julius Scaliger:* He has
been free enough with HOMER in the *Remarks* he makes upon him;
but when he speaks of himself, I desire my Reader wou'd take          65
Notice of his Modesty; I give his own Words, *Lib. 3. Poet. Cap.*
112. *In Deum Patrem Hymnum cum scriberemus tanquam rerum om-*
*nium conditorem, ab orbis ipsius creatione ad nos nostraq; usq; dux-*
*imus.—In quo abduximus animum nostrum a corporis carcere ad liberos*
*campos contemplationis quæ me in illum transformaret. Tum autem sanc-*    70
*tissimi Spiritus ineffabilis vigor ille tanto ardore celebratus est, ut cum*
*lenissimis numeris esset inchoatus Hymnus, repentino divini Ignis impetu*
*conflagravit.*

    VERSE 53. *The circled Loaves.*] ZOILUS *here finds Fault with the*
*Mention of Loaves, Tripes, Bacon and Cheese, as Words below the Dignity*    75
*of the* Epick, *as much,* (says he) *as it wou'd be to have opprobious Names*
*given in it.* By which Expression we easily see, he hints at the First
Book of the *Iliad.* Now, we must consider in Answer, that it is a
Mouse which is spoken of, that Eating is the most appearing
Characteristick of that Creature, that these Foods are such as          80
please it most; and to have describ'd particular Pleasures for it in
any other Way, would have been as incongruous, as to have de-
scrib'd a haughty loud Anger without those Names which it
throws out in its Fierceness, and which raise it to its Pitch of
Phrenzy. In the one Instance you still see a Mouse before you,          85
however the Poet raises it to a Man; in the other you shall see a
Man before you; however the Poet raises him to a Demi-God. But
some call that *low,* which others call *natural.* Every Thing has two
Handles, and the Critick who sets himself to censure all he meets,
is under an Obligation still to lay hold on the worst of them.          90

    VERSE 75. *But me, nor Stalks.*] In this Place ZOILUS *laughs at the*
*Ridiculousness of the Poet, who* (according to his Representation)
*makes a Prince refuse an Invitation in Heroicks, because he did not like*
*the Meat he was invited to.* And, that the Ridicule may appear in as
strong a Light to others as to himself, he puts as much of the          95
Speech as concerns it into Burlesque Airs and Expressions. This is
indeed a common Trick with *Remarkers,* which they either practice
by Precedent from their Master ZOILUS, or are beholding for it to
the same Turn of Temper. We acknowledge it a fine Piece of Satyr,
when there is Folly in a Passage, to lay it open in the Way by which    100
it naturally requires to be expos'd: Do this handsomely, and the
Author is deservedly a Jest. If, on the contrary, you dress a
Passage which was not originally foolish, in the highest Humour
of Ridicule, you only frame something which the Author himself
might laugh at, without being more nearly concern'd than an-           105
other Reader.

VERSE 103. *So pass'd* Europa.] This Simile makes ZOILUS, who sets up for a profess'd Enemy of Fables, to exclaim violently. *We had,* says he, *a Frog and a Mouse hitherto, and now we get a Bull and a Princess to illustrate their Actions: When will there be an End of this* 110 *Fabling-Folly and Poetry, which I value my self for being unacquainted with? O great* Polycrates, *how happily hast thou observ'd in thy Accusation against* Socrates, *That whatever he was before, he deserv'd his Poison when he began to make Verses!* Now, if the Question be concerning HOMER's good or bad Poetry, this is an unqualifying 115 Speech, which affords his Friends just Grounds of Exception against the Critick. Wherefore, be it known to all present and future Censors, who have, or shall presume to glory in an Ignorance of Poetry, and at the same Time take upon them to judge of Poets, that they are in all their Degrees for ever excluded the Post 120 they would usurp. In the first Place, they who know neither the Use, nor Practice of the Art; in the second, they who know it but by Halves, who have Hearts insensible of the Beauties of Poetry, and are however able to find Fault by Rules; and, thirdly, they who, when they are capable of perceiving Beauties and pointing 125 out Defects, are still so ignorant in the Nature of their Business, as to imagine the Province of Criticism extends itself only on the Side of Dispraise and Reprehension. How cou'd any one at this Rate be seen with his proper Ballance of Perfection and Error? or what were the best Performances in this Indulgence of ill Nature, 130 but as Apartments hung with the Deformities of Humanity, done by some great Hand, which are the more to be abhorr'd, because the Praise and Honour they receive, results from the Degree of Uneasiness, to which they put every Temper of common Goodness? 135

VERSE 130. *Ye Mice, ye Mice.*] The Ancients believ'd that Heroes were turn'd into Demi-Gods at their Death; and in general, that departing Souls have something of a Sight into Futurity. It is either this Notion, or a Care which the Gods may take to abate the Pride of insulting Adversaries, which a Poet goes upon, when he 140 makes his Leaders die foretelling the End of those by whom they are slain. ZOILUS however is against this Passage. He says, *That every Character ought to be strictly kept; that a General ought not to invade the Character of a Prophet, nor a Prophet of a General.* He is positive, *That nothing shou'd be done by any one, without having been* 145 *hinted at in some previous Account of him.* And this he asserts, without any Allowance made either for a Change of States, or the Design of the Gods. To confirm this Observation, he strengthens it with a Quotation out of his larger Work on the *Iliads,* where he has these Words upon the Death of *Hector: How foolish is it in* HOMER *to make* 150

Hector (*who thro' the whole Course of the* Iliad *had made Use of* Helenus, *to learn the Will of the Gods*) *become a Prophet just at his Death? Let every one be what he ought, without falling into those Parts which others are to sustain in a Poem.* This he has said, not distinguishing rightly between our natural Dispositions and accidental Offices.           155
And this he has said again, not minding, that tho' it be taken from another Book, it is still from the same Author. However, Vanity loves to gratify itself by the Repetition of what it esteems to be written with Spirit, and even when we repeat it our selves, pro-
vided another hears us. Hence has he been follow'd by a Mag-           160
isterial Set of Men who quote themselves, and swell their new Performances with what they admire in their former Treatises. This is a most extraordinary Knack of Arguing, whereby a Man can never want a Proof, if he be allow'd to become an Authority for his own Opinion.           165

VERSE 146. *And no kind Billow.*] *How impertinent is this Case of Pity, says* ZOILUS, *to bemoan, that the Prince was not toss'd towards Land: It is enough he lost his Life, and there is an End of his Suffering where there is an End of his Feeling. To carry the Matter farther is just the same foolish Management as* HOMER *has shewn in his* Iliads, *which he spins out into*           170
*forty Triffles beyond the Death of* Hector. But the Critick must allow me to put the Readers in Mind, that Death was not the last Distress the Ancients believ'd was to be met upon Earth. The last was the remaining unbury'd, which had this Misery annex'd, that while the Body was without its Funeral-Rites in this World, the Soul was           175
suppos'd to be without Rest in the next, which was the Case of the Mouse before us. And accordingly the *Ajax* of *Sophocles* continues after the Death of its Heroe more than an Act, upon the Contest concerning his Burial. All this ZOILUS knew very well: But ZOILUS is not the only one, who disputes for Victory rather than Truth.           180
These foolish Criticks write even Things they themselves can answer, to shew how much they can write against an Author. They act unfairly, that they may be sure to be sharp enough; and triffle with the Reader, in order to be voluminous. It is needless to wish them the Return they deserve: Their Disregard to Candour is no           185
sooner discover'd, but they are for ever banish'd from the Eyes of Men of Sense, and condemn'd to wander from Stall to Stall, for a temporary Refuge from that Oblivion which they can't escape.

BOOK II. VERSE 9. *Our Eldest perish'd.*] ZOILUS has here taken *the Recapitulation of those Misfortunes which happen'd to the Royal Family,*           190
*as an Impertinence that expatiates from the Subject;* tho' indeed there seems nothing more proper to raise that Sort of Compassion,

which was to inflame his Audience to War. But what appears
extreamly pleasant is, that at the same Time he condemns
the Passage, he shou'd make Use of it as an Opportunity, to fall          195
into *an ample Digression on the various Kinds of Mouse-Traps,* and
display that minute Learning which every Critick of his Sort is
fond to shew himself Master of. This they imagine is tracing of
Knowledge thro' its hidden Veins, and bringing Discoveries to
Day-light, which Time had cover'd over. Indefatigable and useless          200
Mortals! who value themselves for Knowledge of no Con-
sequence, and think of gaining Applause by what the Reader is
careful to pass over unread. What did the Disquisition signify
formerly, whether *Ulysses*'s Son, or his Dog, was the elder? or how
can the Account of a Vesture, or a Player's Masque, deserve that          205
any shou'd write the Bulk of a Treatise, or others read it when it is
written? A Vanity thus poorly supported, which neither affords
Pleasure nor Profit, is the unsubstantial Amusement of a Dream
to our selves, and a provoking Occasion of our Derision to others.

   Book II. verse 23. *Quills aptly bound—Fac'd with the Plunder of a*          210
*Cat they flay'd.*] This Passage is something difficult in the Original,
which gave zoilus the Opportunity of inventing an Expression,
which his Followers conceitedly use when any Thing appears dark
to them. *This,* say they, *let* Phœbus *explain;* as if what exceeds their
Capacity must of Necessity demand Oracular Interpretations, and          215
an Interposal of the God of Wit and Learning. The Basis of such
Arrogance is the Opinion they have of that Knowledge they as-
cribe to themselves. They take Criticism to be beyond every other
Part of Learning, because it gives Judgment upon Books written
in every other Part. They think in Consequence, that every Critick          220
must be a greater Genius than any Author whom he censures;
and therefore if they esteem themselves Criticks, they set en-
thron'd Infancy at the Head of Literature. Criticism indeed de-
serves a noble Elogy, when it is enlarg'd by such a comprehensive
Learning as *Aristotle* and *Cicero* were Masters of; when it adorns its          225
Precepts with the consummate Exactness of *Quintilian,* or is ex-
alted into the sublime Sentiments of *Longinus.* But let not such
Men tell us they participate in the Glory of these great Men, and
place themselves next to *Phœbus,* who, like zoilus, entangle an
Author in the Wrangles of Grammarians, or try him with a          230
positive Air and barren Imagination, by the Set of Rules they have
collected out of others.

   Book II. verse 37. *Ye Frogs, the Mice.*] At this Speech of the
Herald's, which recites the Cause of the War, zoilus is angry with
the Author, *for not finding out a Cause entirely just; for,* says he, *it*          235

*appears not from his own Fable, that* Physignathus *invited the Prince
with any malicious Intention to make him away.* To this we answer, 1st.
That it is not necessary in relating Facts to make every War have a
just Beginning. 2dly, This doubtful Cause agrees better with the
Moral, by shewing that ill-founded Leagues have Accidents to                    240
destroy them, even without the Intention of Parties. 3dly, There
was all Appearance imaginable against the Frogs; and if we may
be allow'd to retort on our Adversary the Practice of his Posterity,
there is more Humanity in an Hostility proclaim'd upon the
Appearance of Injustice done us, than in their Custom of attack-               245
ing the Works of others as soon as they come out, purely because
they are esteem'd to be good. Their Performances, which cou'd
derive no Merit from their own Names, are then sold upon the
Merit of their Antagonist: And if they are sensible of Fame, or
even of Envy, they have the Mortification to remember, how much            250
by this Means they become indebted to those they injure.

BOOK II. VERSE 57. *Where high the Banks.*] This Project is not put
in Practice during the following Battle, by Reason of the Fury of
the Combatants: Yet the Mention of it is not impertinent in this
Place, forasmuch as the probable Face of Success which it carries          255
with it tended to animate the Frogs. ZOILUS however cannot be so
satisfied; *It were better,* says he, *to cut it intirely out; nor wou'd* HOMER
*be the worse if half of him were serv'd in the same Manner; so,* continues
he, *they will find it, whoever in any Country shall hereafter undertake so
odd a Task, as that of Translating him.* Thus Envy finds Words to put       260
in the Mouth of Ignorance; and the Time will come, when Igno-
rance shall repeat what Envy has pronounced so rashly.

BOOK II. VERSE 77. *And tap'ring Sea-Reed.*] If we here take the
Reed for that of our own Growth, it is no Spear to match the long
Sort of Needles with which the Mice had arm'd themselves; but               265
the Cane, which is rather intended, has its Splinters stiff and
sharp, to answer all the Uses of a Spear in Battle. Nor is it here to
be lightly past over, since ZOILUS moves a Question upon it, that
the Poet cou'd not choose a more proper Weapon for the Frogs,
than that which they choose for themselves in a defensive War               270
they maintain with the Serpents of *Nile. They have this Strategem,*
says *Ælian, to protect themselves; they swim with Pieces of Cane across
their Mouths, of too great a Length for the Breadth of the Serpents
Throats; by which Means they are preserv'd from being swallow'd by
them.* This is a Quotation so much to the Point, that I ought to have        275
usher'd in my Author with more Pomp to dazzle the Reader.
ZOILUS and his Followers, who seldom praise any Man, are how-

ever careful to do it for their own Sakes, if at any Time they get an
Author of their Opinion: Tho' indeed it must be allow'd, they still
have a Drawback in their Manner of Praise, and rather choose to          280
drop the Name of their Man, or darkly hint him in a Periphrasis,
than to have it appear that they have directly assisted the per-
petuating of any one's Memory. Thus, if a *Dutch* Critick were to
introduce for Example *Martial,* he wou'd, instead of naming him,
say, *Ingeniosus ille Epigrammaticus Bilbilicus.* Or, if one of our own    285
were to quote from among ourselves, he wou'd tell us how it has
been remark'd *in the Works of a learned Writer, to whom the World is
oblig'd for many excellent Productions,* &c. All which Proceeding is
like boasting of our great Friends, when it is to do our selves an
Honour, or the Shift of dressing up one who might otherwise be         290
disregarded, to make him pass upon the World for a responsible
Voucher to our own Assertions.

BOOK II. VERSE 81. *But now where* Jove's.] At this fine Episode, in
which the Gods are introduced, ZOILUS has no Patience left him to
remark; but runs some Lines with a long String of such Ex-            295
pressions as *Triffler, Fabler, Lyar, foolish, impious,* all which he lav-
ishly heaps upon the Poet. From this Knack of calling Names,
joyn'd with the several Arts of finding Fault, it is to be suspected,
that our ZOILUS's might make very able Libellers, and dangerous
Men to the Government, if they did not rather turn themselves to       300
be ridiculous Censors: For which Reason I cannot but reckon the
State oblig'd to Men of Wit; and under a Kind of Debt in Grati-
tude, when they take off so much Spleen, Turbulency, and Ill-
nature, as might otherwise spend it self to the Detriment of the
Publick.                                                              305

BOOK II. VERSE 98. *If my Daughter's Mind.*] This Speech, which
*Jupiter* speaks to *Pallas* with a pleasant Kind of Air, ZOILUS takes
gravely to Pieces; and affirms, *It is below* Jupiter's *Wisdom, and only
agreeable with* HOMER's *Folly, that he shou'd borrow a Reason for her
assisting the Mice from their Attendance in the Temple, when they waited*   310
*to prey upon those Things which were sacred to her.* But the Air of
the Speech rendering a grave Answer unnecessary; I shall only
offer ZOILUS an Observation in Return for his. There are
upon the Stone that is carv'd for the Apotheosis of HOMER,
Figures of Mice by his Footstool, which, according to *Cuperus,* its      315
Interpreters, some have taken to signify this Poem; and others
those Criticks, who tear or vilify the Works of great Men. Now, if
such can be compar'd to Mice, let the Words of ZOILUS be brought
home to himself and his Followers for their Mortification: *That no*

*one ought to think of meriting in the State of Learning only by debasing the*     320
*best Performances, and as it were preying upon those Things which shou'd*
*be sacred in it.*

BOOK II. VERSE 105. *In vain my Father.*] The Speech of *Pallas* is
dislik'd by ZOILUS, *because it makes the Goddess carry a Resentment*
*against such inconsiderable Creatures;* tho' he ought to esteem them     325
otherwise when they represent the Persons and Actions of Men,
and teach us how the Gods disregard those in their Adversities
who provoke them in Prosperity. But, if we consider *Pallas* as the
Patroness of Learning, we may by an allegorical Application of
the Mice and Frogs, find in this Speech two Sorts of Enemies to     330
Learning; they who are maliciously mischievous, as the Mice; and
they who are turbulent through Ostentation, as the Frogs. The
first are Enemies to Excellency upon Principle; the second acci-
dentally by the Error of Self-Love, which does not quarrel with
the Excellence itself, but only with those People who get more     335
Praise than themselves by it. Thus, tho' they have not the same
Perversness with the others, they are however drawn into the
same Practices, while they ruin Reputations, lest they shou'd not
seem to be learn'd; as some Women turn Prostitutes, lest they
shou'd not be thought handsome enough to have Admirers.     340

BOOK III. VERSE 5. *The dreadful Trumpets.*] Upon the reading of
this, ZOILUS becomes full of Discoveries. He recollects, *that* HOMER
*makes his* Greeks *come to Battle with Silence, and his* Trojans *with*
*Shouts,* from whence he discovers, *that he knew nothing of Trumpets.*
Again, he sees, *that the* Hornet *is made a Trumpeter to the Battle,* and     345
hence he discovers, *that the Line must not be* HOMER'*s.* Now had he
drawn his Consequences fairly, he cou'd only have found by the
one, that Trumpets were not in use at the taking of *Troy;* and by
the other, that the Battle of *Frogs* and *Mice* was laid by the Poet for
a later Scene of Action than that of the *Iliad.* But the Boast of     350
Discoveries accompanies the Affectation of Knowledge; and the
Affectation of Knowledge is taken up with a Design to gain a
Command over the Opinions of others. It is too heavy a Task for
some Criticks to sway our Judgments by rational Inferences; a
pompous Pretence must occasion Admiration, the Eyes of Man-     355
kind must be obscur'd by a Glare of Pedantry, that they may
consent to be led blindfold, and permit that an Opinion shou'd be
dictated to them without demanding that they may be reason'd
into it.

BOOK III. VERSE 24. *Big* Seutlæus *Tumbling.*] ZOILUS has hap-     360
pen'd to brush the Dust of some old Manuscript, in which the
Line that kills *Seutlæus* is wanting. And for this cause he fixes a

general Conclusion, *that there is no Dependance upon any thing which is handed down for* HOMER's, *so as to allow it Praise; since the different Copies vary amongst themselves.* But is it fair in ZOILUS, or any of his          365
Followers, to oppose one Copy to a Thousand? and are they impartial who wou'd pass this upon us for an honest Ballance of Evidence? When there is such an Inequality on each Side, is it not more than probable that the Number carry the Author's Sense in them, and the single one its Transcribers Errors? It is Folly or          370
Madness of Passion to be thus given over to Partiality and Preju- dices. Men may flourish as much as they please concerning the Value of a new found Edition, in order to byass the World to particular Parts of it; but in a Matter easily decided by common Sense, it will still continue of its own Opinion.          375

BOOK III. VERSE 69. *With* Borbocætes *fights.*] Through the Grammatical Part of ZOILUS's Work he frequently rails at HOMER for his Dialects. *These,* says he in one place, *the Poet made use of because he could not write pure* Greek; and in another, *they strangely contributed to his Fame, by making several Cities who observ'd some-*          380
*thing of their own in his mix'd Language, contend for his being one of their Natives.* Now since I have here practis'd a License in Imitation of his, by short'ning the Word *Borbocætes* a whole Syllable, it seems a good Opportunity to speak for him where I defend myself. Remember then, that any great Genius          385
who introduces Poetry into a Language, has a Power to polish it, and of all the Manners of speaking then in use, to settle that for Poetical which he judges most adapted to the Art. Take Notice too, that HOMER has not only done this for Necessity but for Ornament, since he uses various Dialects to humour his Sense          390
with Sounds which are expressive of it. Thus much in Behalf of my Author to answer ZOILUS: As for myself, who deal with his Followers, I must argue from Necessity, that the Word was stub- born and wou'd not ply to the Quantities of an English Verse, and therefore I alter'd it by the *Dialect* we call *Poetical,* which makes my          395
Line so much smoother, that I am ready to cry with their Brother *Lipsius,* when he turn'd an O into an I, *Vel ego me amo, vel me amavit* Phœbus *quando hoc correxi.* To this let me add a Recrimination upon some of them: As first, such as choose Words written after the Manner of those who preceded the purest Age of a Language,          400
without the Necessity I have pleaded, as *regundi* for *regendi, perduit* for *perdidit,* which Restoration of obsolete Words deserves to be call'd a *Critical License* or *Dialect.* 2dly, Those who pretending to Verse without an Ear, use the *Poetical Dialect* of *Abbreviation,* so that the Lines shall run the rougher for it. And, *3dly,* Those who          405

presume by their *Critical Licenses* to alter the Spellings of Words; an Affectation which destroys the Etymology of a Language, and being carry'd on by private Hands for Fancy or Fashion, wou'd be a Thing we shou'd never have an End.

BOOK III. VERSE 149. *Nor* Pallas, Jove.] *I cannot, says* ZOILUS,    410
*reflect upon this Speech of* Mars, *where a* Mouse *is oppos'd to the God of War, the Goddess of Valour, the Thunder of* Jupiter, *and all the Gods at once, but I rejoyce to think that* Pythagoras *saw* HOMER's *Soul in Hell hanging on a Tree and surrounded with Serpents for what he said of the Gods.* Thus he who hates Fables answers one with another, and    415
can rejoyce in them when they flatter his Envy. He appears at the Head of his Squadron of Criticks, in the full Spirit of one utterly devoted to a Party; with whom Truth is a Lye, or as bad as a Lye, when it makes against him; and false Quotations, pass for Truth, or as good as Truth, when they are necessary to a Cause.    420

BOOK III. VERSE 203. *And a whole War.*] *Here, says* ZOILUS, *is an End of a very foolish Poem, of which by this Time I have effectually convinc'd the World, and silenc'd all such for the future, who, like* HOMER, *write Fables to which others find Morals, Characters whose Justness is question'd, unnecessary Digressions, and impious Episodes.*    425
But what Assurance can such as ZOILUS have, that the World will ever be convinc'd against an establish'd Reputation, by such People whose Faults in writing are so very notorious? who judge against Rules, affirm without Reasons, and censure without Manners? who quote themselves for a Support of their Opinions,    430
found their Pride upon a Learning in Trifles, and their Superiority upon the Claims they magisterially make? who write of Beauties in a harsh Style, judge of Excellency with a Lowness of Spirit, and pursue their Desire to decry it with every Artifice of Envy? There is no Disgrace in being censur'd, where there is no    435
Credit to be favour'd. But, on the contrary, Envy gives a Testimony of some Perfection in another; and one who is attack'd by many, is like a Heroe whom his Enemies acknowledge for such, when they point all the Spears of a Battle against him. In short, an Author who writes for every Age, may even erect himself a    440
Monument of those Stones which Envy throws at him: While the Critick who writes against him can have no Fame because he has no Success; or if he fancies he may succeed, he shou'd remember, that by the Nature of his Undertaking he wou'd but undermine his own Foundation; for he is to sink of Course when the Book    445
which he writes against, and for which alone he is read, is lost in Disrepute or Oblivion.

*FINIS.*

# The Horse and the Olive: Or, War and Peace

WITH *Moral* Tale let Ancient *Wisdom* move,
   Which thus I sing to make the *Moderns* wise:
Strong *Neptune* once with sage *Minerva* strove,
   And rising *Athens* was the *Victor*'s Prize.

By *Neptune, Plutus* (Guardian Pow'r of Gain),           5
   By Great *Minerva,* Bright *Apollo* stood:
But *Jove* superior bad the Side obtain
   Which best contriv'd to do the *Nation* Good.

Then *Neptune* striking, from the parted Ground
   The Warlike *Horse* came pawing on the Plain,        10
And as it toss'd its Mane, and pranc'd around,
   By this, he cries, I'll make the *People* Reign.

The *Goddess* smiling gently bow'd the Spear,
   And, rather thus they shall be bless'd, she said;
Then upwards shooting in the Vernal Air           15
   With loaded Boughs the fruitful *Olive* spread.

*Jove* saw what Gifts the *Rival Pow'rs* design'd,
   And took th' impartial Scales, resolv'd to show,
If greater Bliss in *Warlike Pomp* we find,
   Or in the *Calm* which *Peaceful Times* bestow.       20

On *Neptune*'s part he plac'd *Victorious Days,*
   Gay *Trophies* won, and *Fame* extending wide:
But *Plenty, Safety, Science, Arts,* and *Ease,*
   *Minerva*'s Scale with greater Weight supply'd.

Fierce *War* devours whom gentle *Peace* wou'd save,      25
   Sweet *Peace* restores what angry *War* destroys,

*War* made for *Peace* with that rewards the Brave,
   While *Peace* its Pleasures from it self enjoys.

Hence vanquish'd *Neptune* to the Sea withdrew,
   Hence wise *Minerva* rul'd *Athenian* Lands,          30
Her *Athens* hence in Arts and Honour grew,
   And still her *Olives* deck *pacifick* Hands.

From *Fables* thus disclos'd, a Monarch's Mind
   May form just Rules to chuse the Truly-Great:
And *Subjects* weary'd with Distresses find          35
   Whose kind Endeavours most befriend the State.

Ev'n *Britain* here may learn to place her Love,
   If *Cities* won her *Kingdoms* Wealth have cost,
If *ANNA*'s Thoughts the PATRIOT-SOULS approve
   Whose Cares restore that Wealth the Wars had lost.       40

But if we ask the *Moral* to disclose
   Whom best EUROPA's *Patroness* it calls,
Great *ANNA*'s Title no Exception knows,
   And unapply'd in this the *Fable* falls.

With Her no *Neptune* or *Minerva* vyes;       45
   Whene'er she pleas'd her *Troops* to Conquest flew,
Whene'er she pleases *Peaceful Times* arise:
   She gave the *Horse*, and gives the *Olive* too.

# Poems from Steele's *Poetical Miscellanies*

## A Hymn on Contentment.

Lovely lasting *Peace* of *Mind,*
  Sweet delight of Human Kind,
Heav'nly born, and bred on high,
To crown the Fav'rites of the Sky
With more of Happiness below,                   5
Than Victors in a Triumph know:
Whither, O whither art thou fled,
To lay thy meek contented Head?
What happy Region dost thou please
To make the Seat of Calms and Ease?         10

  *Ambition* searches all its Sphere
Of Pomp and State to find thee there.
Encreasing *Avarice* wou'd find
Thy Presence in its Gold enshrin'd.
The bold Advent'rer ploughs his way       15
Through Rocks amidst the foaming Sea
To gain thy Love, and then perceives
Thou wer't not in the Rocks and Waves.
The silent Heart whom Grief assails,
Treads soft and lonesome o'er the Vales,    20
Sees Daizies open, Rivers run,
And seeks (as I have vainly done)
Amusing Thought; but learns to know
That *Solitude*'s a Nurse of Woe.
No real Happiness is found                25
In trailing Purple o'er the Ground:
Or in a Soul exalted high

To range the *Circuit* of the Sky,
Converse with *Stars* above, and know
All *Nature* in its Forms below;               30
The Rest it seeks in seeking dies,
And Doubts at last for Knowledge rise.

    Lovely lasting *Peace* appear;
This World it self, if thou art here,
Is once again with *Eden* bless'd,            35
And Man contains it in his Breast.

    'Twas thus, as under Shade I stood,
I sung my Wishes to the Wood,
And, lost in Thought, no more perceiv'd
The Branches whisper as they wav'd;       40
It seem'd as if the quiet Place
Confess'd the Presence of the *Grace*,
When thus she spoke—Go rule thy Will,
Bid thy wild Passions all be still,
Know God—and bring thy Heart to know     45
The Joys which from Religion flow;
Then ev'ry *Grace* shall prove its Guest,
And I'll be there to crown the rest.

    Oh! by yonder Mossie Seat,
In my Hours of sweet Retreat,            50
Might I thus my Soul employ
With sense of Gratitude and Joy,
Rais'd, as Ancient *Prophets* were,
In heav'nly Vision, Praise, and Pray'r,
Pleasing all Men, hurting none,           55
Pleas'd and bless'd with God alone.

    Then, while the Gardens take my Sight,
With all the Colours of Delight,
While Silver Waters glide along,
To please my Ear, and court my Song;      60
I'll lift my Voice, and tune my String,
And Thee, great SOURCE of NATURE, sing.

    The Sun that walks his airy Way,
To light the World, and give the Day;
The Moon that shines with borrow'd Light,    65

The Stars that gild the gloomy Night,
The Seas that roll unnumber'd Waves,
The Wood that spreads its shady Leaves,
The Field whose Ears conceal the Grain,
The yellow Treasure of the Plain;                    70
All of these, and all I see,
Wou'd be sung, and sung by me,
They speak their *Maker* as they can,
But want and ask the Tongue of Man.

   Go search among your idle Dreams          75
Your busie or your vain Extreams,
And find a *Life* of equal Bliss,
Or own the *next* begun in *this*.


## SONG.


M Y Days have been so wondrous Free,
   The little Birds that flie
With careless Ease from Tree to Tree,
   Were but as bless'd as I.

Ask gliding Waters, if a Tear                        5
   Of mine encreas'd their Stream?
Or ask the flying Gales, if ere
   I lent a Sigh to them?

But now my former Days retire,
   And I'm by Beauty caught,
The tender Chains of sweet Desire                    10
   Are fix'd upon my Thought.

An eager Hope within my Breast
   Does ev'ry Doubt controul,
And charming *Nancy* stands confest                  15
   The Fav'rite of my Soul.

Ye Nightingales ye twisting Pines,
   Ye Swains that haunt the Grove,
Ye gentle Ecchoes, breezy Winds,
   Ye close Retreats of Love;                     20

With all of Nature, all of Art,
   Assist the dear Design;
O teach a young unpractis'd Heart
   To make Her ever Mine.

The very Thought of Change I hate,           25
   As much as of Despair;
And hardly covet to be great,
   Unless it be for Her.

'Tis true, the Passion in my Mind
   Is mix'd with soft Distress;           30
Yet while the Fair I love is kind,
   I cannot wish it Less.

# To a YOUNG LADY, ON Her Translation of the Story of *Phoebus* and *Daphne,* from *Ovid.*

IN *Phœbus Wit* (as *Ovid* said)
   Enchanting *Beauty* woo'd;
In *Daphne Beauty* coily fled,
   While vainly *Wit* pursu'd.

But when you trace what *Ovid* writ,         5
   A diff'rent Turn we view;
*Beauty* no longer flies from *Wit,*
   Since both are joyn'd in You.

Your Lines the wondrous Change impart,
   From whence our Lawrels spring;        10
In Numbers fram'd to please the Heart,
   And merit what they Sing.

Methinks thy *Poet*'s gentle Shade
   Its Wreath presents to Thee;
What *Daphne* owes you as a Maid,        15
   She pays you as a Tree.

## ANACREONTICK.

### I.

G AY *Bacchus* liking *Estcourt's* Wine,
　A noble Meal bespoke;
And for the Guests that were to Dine,
　Brought *Comus, Love,* and *Joke.*

### II.

The God near *Cupid* drew his Chair,                    5
　And *Joke* near *Comus* plac'd;
Thus *Wine* makes *Love* forget its Care,
　And *Mirth* exalts a Feast.

### III.

The more to please the sprightly God,
　Each sweet engaging *Grace*                          10
Put on some Cloaths to come abroad,
　And took a Waiters Place.

### IV.

Then *Cupid* nam'd at every Glass
　A Lady of the Sky;
While *Bacchus* swore he'd Drink the Lass,              15
　And had it Bumper high.

### V.

Fat *Comus* tost his Brimmers o're,
   And always got the most;
For *Joke* took care to fill him more,
   When-e'er he mist the Toast.          20

### VI.

They call'd, and drank at every Touch,
   Then fill'd, and drank again;
And if the Gods can take too much,
   'Tis said, they did so then.

### VII.

Free Jests run all the Table round,         25
   And with the Wine conspire,
(While they by sly Reflection wound,)
   To set their Heads on Fire.

### VIII.

Gay *Bacchus* little *Cupid* stung,
   By reck'ning his Deceits;         30
And *Cupid* mock'd his stammering Tongue,
   With all his staggering Gaits.

### IX.

*Joke* droll'd on *Comus'* greedy Ways,
   And Tales without a Jest;
While *Comus* call'd his witty Plays,         35
   But Waggeries at Best.

## X.

Such Talk soon set 'em all at Odds;
    And, had I *Homer*'s Pen,
I'd sing ye, how they drunk, like Gods,
    And how they fought, like Men.           40

## XI.

To part the Fray, the *Graces* fly,
    Who make 'em soon agree;
And had the *Furies* selves been nigh,
    They still were Three to Three.

## XII.

*Bacchus* appeas'd, rais'd *Cupid* up,          45
    And gave him back his Bow;
But kept some Darts to stir the Cup,
    Where Sack and Sugar flow.

## XIII.

*Joke* taking *Comus'* rosie Crown,
    In Triumph wore the Prize,          50
And thrice, in Mirth, he pusht him down,
    As thrice he strove to rise.

## XIV.

Then *Cupid* sought the Myrtle Grove,
    Where *Venus* did recline,
And *Beauty* close embracing *Love,*          55
    They join'd to Rail at *Wine.*

XV.


And *Comus* loudly cursing *Wit*,
    Roll'd off to some Retreat,
Where boon Companions gravely sit,
    In fat unweildy State.                                    60


XVI.


*Bacchus* and *Joke,* who stay behind,
    For one fresh Glass prepare;
They Kiss, and are exceeding kind,
    And Vow to be sincere.


XVII.


But part in Time, whoever hear                              65
    This our Instructive Song;
For tho' such Friendships may be dear,
    They can't continue long.

# From Pope's *Works*

## To Mr. *Pope.*

To praise, and still with just respect to praise
A Bard triumphant in immortal bays,
The Learn'd to show, the Sensible commend,
Yet still preserve the province of the Friend,
What life, what vigour must the lines require?            5
What Music tune them, what affection fire?
    O might thy Genius in my bosom shine!
Thou should'st not fail of numbers worthy thine;
The brightest Ancients might at once agree,
To sing within my lays, and sing of thee.                10
    *Horace* himself wou'd own thou dost excell
In candid arts to play the Critic well.
*Ovid* himself might wish to sing the Dame,
Whom *Windsor*-Forest sees a gliding stream:
On silver feet, with annual Osier crown'd,               15
She runs for ever thro' Poetic ground.
    How flame the glories of *Belinda*'s Hair,
Made by thy Muse the envy of the Fair?
Less shone the tresses *Ægypt*'s Princess wore,
Which sweet *Callimachus* so sung before.                20
Here courtly trifles set the world at odds;
Belles war with Beaus, and Whims descend for Gods.
The new Machines, in names of ridicule,
Mock the grave frenzy of the Chimick fool.
But know, ye fair, a point conceal'd with art,           25
The Sylphs and Gnomes are but a woman's heart.
The Graces stand in sight; a Satyr-train,
Peeps o'er their head, and laughs behind the scene.

In Fame's fair Temple o'er the boldest wits,
Inshrin'd on high, the sacred *Virgil* sits,                              30
And sits in measures, such as *Virgil's* Muse,
To place thee near him, might be fond to chuse.
How might he tune th' alternate reed with thee,
Perhaps a *Strephon* thou, a *Daphnis* he;
While some old *Damon*, o'er the vulgar wise,                            35
Thinks he deserves, and thou deserv'st the Prize.
Rapt with the thought, my fancy seeks the plains,
And turns me shepherd while I hear the strains.
Indulgent nurse of ev'ry tender gale,
Parent of flowrets, old *Arcadia* hail!                                  40
Here in the cool my limbs at ease I spread,
Here let thy Poplars whisper o'er my head!
Still slide thy waters soft among the trees,
Thy Aspins quiver in a breathing breeze!
Smile, all ye valleys, in eternal spring,                                45
Be hush'd, ye winds! while *Pope* and *Virgil* sing.
    In *English* lays, and all sublimely great,
Thy *Homer* warms with all his ancient heat;
He shines in Council, thunders in the fight,
And flames with ev'ry sense of great delight.                            50
Long has that Poet reign'd, and long unknown,
Like Monarchs sparkling on a distant throne;
In all the majesty of *Greek* retir'd,
Himself unknown, his mighty name admir'd;
His language failing, wrapt him round with night;                        55
Thine, rais'd by thee, recalls the work to light.
So wealthy Mines, that ages long before
Fed the large realms around with golden Oar,
When choak'd by sinking banks, no more appear,
And shepherds only say, *The mines were here:*                           60
Should some rich youth (if nature warm his heart,
And all his projects stand inform'd with art)
Here clear the caves, there ope the leading vein;
The mines detected flame with gold again.
    How vast, how copious are thy new designs!                           65
How ev'ry Music varies in thy lines!
Still, as I read, I feel my bosom beat,
And rise in raptures by another's heat.
Thus in the wood, when summer dress'd the days,
When *Windsor* lent us tuneful hours of ease,                           70
Our ears the lark, the thrush, the turtle blest,

And *Philomela* sweetest o'er the rest:
The shades resound with song—O softly tread,
While a whole season warbles round my head.
 This to my friend—and when a friend inspires, 75
My silent harp its master's hand requires,
Shakes off the dust, and makes these rocks resound;
For fortune plac'd me in unfertile ground.
Far from the joys that with my soul agree,
From wit, from learning—very far from thee. 80
Here moss-grown trees expand the smallest leaf;
Here half an Acre's corn is half a sheaf;
Here hills with naked heads the tempest meet,
Rocks at their sides, and torrents at their feet;
Or lazy lakes, unconscious of a flood, 85
Whose dull, brown *Naiads* ever sleep in mud.
Yet here Content can dwell, and learned ease,
A Friend delight me, and an Author please;
Ev'n here I sing, when *Pope* supplies the theme,
Shew my own love, tho' not increase his fame. 90

# From Pope's *Poems on Several Occasions*

---

## *Part of the first Canto of the* Rape of the Lock.

Aɴᴅ now, unveil'd, the *Toilet* stands display'd,
Each Silver vase in mystic order laid.
First, rob'd in white, the Nymph intent adores
With head uncover'd, the *Cosmetic* pow'rs.
A heav'nly Image in the Glass appears,        5
To that she bends, to that her eyes she rears;
Th' inferior Priestess, at her altar's side,
Trembling, begins the sacred rites of Pride.
Unnumber'd treasures ope at once, and here
The various off'rings of the world appear;      10
From each she nicely culls with curious toil,
And decks the goddess with the glitt'ring spoil.
This casket *India*'s glowing Gems unlocks,
And all *Arabia* breaths from yonder box.
The tortoise here and elephant unite,        15
Transform'd to combs, the speckled, and the white.
Here files of pins extend their shining rows,
Puffs, powders, patches, bibles, billet-doux.
Now awful beauty puts on all its arms,
The fair each moment rises in her charms,      20
Repairs her smiles, awakens ev'ry grace,
And calls forth all the wonders of her face;
Sees by degrees a purer blush arise,
And keener Lightnings quicken in her eyes.
The busy *Sylphs* surround their darling care;   25
These set the head, and those divide the hair,
Some fold the sleeve, while others plait the Gown,
And *Betty*'s prais'd for Labours not her own.

# A TRANSLATION *of part of the first Canto of the* Rape of the Lock, *into Leonine Verse, after the manner of the ancient Monks.*

E *T nunc dilectum speculum, pro more retectum,*
    *Emicat in mensâ, quæ splendet pyxide densâ:*
*Tum primum lymphâ, se purgat candida Nympha;*
*Jamque sine mendâ, cœlestis imago videnda,*
*Nuda caput, bellos retinet, regit, implet, ocellos.*                    5
*Hâc stupet explorans, seu cultus numen adorans.*
*Inferior claram Pythonissa apparet ad aram,*
*Fertque tibi cautè, dicatque superbia! lautè,*
*Dona venusta; oris, quæ cunctis, plena laboris,*
*Excerpta explorat, dominamque deamque decorat.*                        10
*Pyxide devotâ, se pandit hic* India *tota,*
*Et tota ex istâ transpirat* Arabia *cistâ;*
*Testudo hic flectit, dum se mea Lesbia pectit;*
*Atque elephas lentè, te pectit Lesbia dente;*
*Hunc maculis nôris, nivei jacet ille coloris.*                         15
*Hic jacet & mundè, mundus muliebris abundè;*
*Spinula resplendens æris longo ordine pendens,*
*Pulvis suavis odore, & epistola suavis amore.*
*Induit arma ergo, Veneris pulcherrima virgo;*
*Pulchrior in præsens tempus de tempore crescens;*                      20
*Jam reparat risus, jam surgit gratia visûs,*
*Jam promit cultu, mirac'la latentia vultu.*
*Pigmina jam miscet, quo plus sua Purpura gliscet,*
*Et geminans bellis splendet magè fulgor ocellis.*
*Stant* Lemures *muti, Nymphæ intentique saluti,*                       25
*Hic figit Zonam, capiti locat ille Coronam,*
*Hæc manicis formam, plicis dat & altera normam;*
*Et tibi vel* Betty, *tibi vel nitidissima* Letty!
*Gloria factorum temerè conceditur horum.*

# POEMS

## ON

## Several Occasions.

Written by

## Dr. *THOMAS PARNELL,*

Late Arch-Deacon of *Clogher:*

## A N D

*Published by Mr.* POPE.

*Dignum laude Virum Musa vetat mori.* HOR.

*LONDON:*
Printed for B. LINTOT, at the *Cross-Keys,* between
the *Temple Gates* in *Fleet-street,* 1722.

First Collected Edition, edited by Pope.

# Poems from *Poems on Several Occasions,* 1722

## *HESIOD:* OR, THE Rise of WOMAN.

W HAT antient Times (those Times we fancy wise)
  Have left on long Record of *Woman's* Rise,
What Morals teach it, and what Fables hide,
What Author wrote it, how that Author dy'd,
All these I sing. In *Greece* they fram'd the Tale          5
(In *Greece,* 'twas thought, a *Woman* might be frail)
Ye modern Beauties! where the Poet drew
His softest Pencil, think he dreamt of you;
And warn'd by him, ye wanton Pens, beware
How Heav'n's concern'd to vindicate the Fair.          10
The Case was *Hesiod's*; he the Fable writ;
Some think with Meaning, some with idle Wit:
Perhaps 'tis either, as the Ladies please;
I wave the Contest, and commence the Lays.

  In days of yore, (no matter where or when,          15
'Twas e're the low Creation swarm'd with Men)
That one *Prometheus,* sprung of heav'nly Birth,
(Our Author's Song can witness) liv'd on Earth.
He carv'd the Turf to mold a manly Frame,
And stole from *Jove* his animating Flame.          20
The sly Contrivance o'er *Olympus* ran,
When thus the Monarch of the Stars began.

  Oh vers'd in Arts! whose daring Thoughts aspire
To kindle Clay with never-dying Fire!
Enjoy thy Glory past, That Gift was thine;          25
The next thy Creature meets, be fairly mine:

125

And such a Gift, a Vengeance so design'd,
As suits the Counsel of a God to find;
A pleasing Bosom-cheat, a specious Ill,
Which felt they curse, yet covet still to feel.                    30

    He said, and *Vulcan* strait the Sire commands,
To temper Mortar with etherial Hands;
In such a Shape to mold a rising Fair,
As Virgin-goddesses are proud to wear;
To make her Eyes with Diamond-water shine,                         35
And form her Organs for a Voice divine.
'Twas thus the Sire ordain'd; the Pow'r obey'd;
And work'd, and wonder'd at the Work he made;
The fairest, softest, sweetest Frame beneath,
Now made to seem, now more than seem, to breathe.                  40

    As *Vulcan* ends, the chearful *Queen* of *Charms*
Clasp'd the new-panting Creature in her Arms;
From that Embrace a fine Complexion spread,
Where mingled Whiteness glow'd with softer red.
Then in a Kiss she breath'd her various Arts,                      45
Of trifling prettily with wounded Hearts;
A Mind for Love, but still a changing Mind;
The Lisp affected, and the Glance design'd;
The sweet confusing Blush, the secret Wink,
The gentle-swimming Walk, the courteous Sink,                      50
The Stare for Strangeness fit, for Scorn the Frown,
For decent yielding Looks declining down,
The practis'd Languish, where well-feign'd Desire
Wou'd own its melting in a mutual Fire;
Gay Smiles to comfort; *April* Show'rs to move;                    55
And all the Nature, all the Art, of Love.

    Gold-scepter'd *Juno* next exalts the Fair;
Her Touch endows her with imperious Air,
Self-valuing Fancy, highly-crested Pride,
Strong sov'reign Will, and *some* Desire to chide:                 60
For which, an Eloquence, that aims to vex,
With native Tropes of Anger, arms the Sex.

    *Minerva* (skillful Goddess) train'd the Maid
To twirl the Spindle by the twisting Thread,
To fix the Loom, instruct the Reeds to part,                       65

Cross the long Weft, and close the Web with Art,
An useful Gift; but what profuse Expence,
What world of Fashions, took its Rise from hence!

Young *Hermes* next, a close-contriving God,
Her Brows encircled with his Serpent Rod:                    70
Then Plots and fair Excuses, fill'd her Brain,
The Views of breaking am'rous Vows for Gain,
The Price of Favours; the designing Arts
That aim at Riches in Contempt of Hearts;
And for a Comfort in the Marriage Life,                      75
The little, pilf'ring Temper of a *Wife*.

Full on the Fair his Beams *Apollo* flung,
And fond Persuasion tip'd her easy Tongue;
He gave her Words, where oyly Flatt'ry lays
The pleasing Colours of the Art of Praise;                   80
And Wit, to Scandal exquisitely prone,
Which frets another's Spleen to cure its own.

Those sacred *Virgins* whom the Bards revere,
Tun'd all her Voice, and shed a Sweetness there,
To make her Sense with double Charms abound,                 85
Or make her lively Nonsense please by Sound.

To dress the Maid, the decent *Graces* brought
A Robe in all the Dies of Beauty wrought,
And plac'd their Boxes o'er a rich Brocade
Where pictur'd *Loves* on ev'ry cover plaid;                 90
Then spread those Implements that *Vulcan*'s Art
Had fram'd to merit *Cytherea*'s Heart;
The Wire to curl, the close-indented Comb
To call the Locks that lightly wander, home;
And chief, the Mirrour, where the ravish'd Maid             95
Beholds and loves her own reflected Shade.

Fair *Flora* lent her Stores, the purpled *Hours*
Confin'd her Tresses with a Wreath of Flow'rs;
Within the Wreath arose a radiant Crown;
A Veil pellucid hung depending down;                         100
Back roll'd her azure Veil with Serpent fold,
The purfled Border deck'd the Floor with Gold.
Her Robe (which closely by the Girdle brac't

Reveal'd the Beauties of a slender Waste)
Flow'd to the Feet; to copy *Venus* Air,                         105
When *Venus*'s Statues have a Robe to wear.

    The newsprung Creature finish'd thus for Harms,
Adjusts her Habit, practises her Charms,
With Blushes glows, or shines with lively Smiles,
Confirms her Will, or recollects her Wiles:                      110
Then conscious of her Worth, with easy Pace
Glides by the Glass, and turning views her Face.

    A finer Flax than what they wrought before,
Thro' Time's deep Cave the *Sister Fates* explore,
Then fix the Loom, their Fingers nimbly weave,                   115
And thus their Toil prophetick Songs deceive.

    Flow from the Rock my Flax! and swiftly flow,
Pursue thy Thread; the Spindle runs below.
A Creature fond and changing, fair and vain,
The Creature *Woman*, rises now to reign.                        120
New Beauty blooms, a Beauty form'd to fly;
New Love begins, a Love produc'd to dye;
New Parts distress the troubled Scenes of Life,
The fondling Mistress, and the ruling Wife.

    Men, born to Labour, all with Pains provide;                 125
*Women* have Time, to sacrifice to Pride:
They want the Care of Man, their Want they know,
And dress to please with heart-alluring Show,
The Show prevailing, for the Sway contend,
And make a Servant where they meet a Friend.                     130

    Thus in a thousand wax-erected Forts
A loytering Race the painful Bee supports,
From Sun to Sun, from Bank to Bank he flies,
With Honey loads his Bag, with Wax his Thighs,
Fly where he will, at home the Race remain,                      135
Prune the silk Dress, and murm'ring eat the Gain.

    Yet here and there we grant a gentle Bride,
Whose Temper betters by the Father's side;
Unlike the rest that double humane Care,

Fond to relieve, or resolute to share:                                    140
Happy the Man whom thus his Stars advance!
The Curse is gen'ral, but the Blessing Chance.

   Thus sung the *Sisters,* while the Gods admire
Their beauteous Creature, made for Man in Ire;
The young *Pandora* she, whom all contend                                  145
To make too perfect not to gain her End:
Then bid the Winds that fly to breath the Spring,
Return to bear her on a gentle Wing;
With wafting Airs the Winds obsequious blow,
And land the shining Vengeance safe below.                                 150
A golden Coffer in her Hand she bore,
(The Present treach'rous, but the Bearer more)
'Twas fraught with Pangs; for *Jove* ordain'd above,
That Gold shou'd aid, and Pangs attend on Love.

   Her gay Descent the Man perceiv'd afar,                   155
Wond'ring he run to catch the falling Star;
But so surpriz'd, as none but he can tell,
Who lov'd so quickly, and who lov'd so well.
O'er all his Veins the wand'ring Passion burns,
He calls her Nymph, and ev'ry Nymph by turns.                             160
Her Form to lovely *Venus* he prefers,
Or swears that *Venus* must be such as hers.
She, proud to rule, yet strangely fram'd to teize,
Neglects his Offers while her Airs she plays,
Shoots scornful Glances from the bended Frown,                            165
In brisk Disorder trips it up and down,
Then hums a careless Tune to lay the Storm,
And sits, and blushes, smiles, and yields, in *Form.*

   "Now take what *Jove* design'd (she softly cry'd)
"This box thy Portion, and my self thy Bride:"                            170
Fir'd with the Prospect of the double Charms,
He snatch'd the Box, and Bride, with eager Arms.

   Unhappy Man! to whom so bright she shone,
The fatal Gift, her tempting self, unknown!
The Winds were silent, all the Waves asleep,                              175
And Heav'n was trac'd upon the flatt'ring Deep;
But whilst he looks unmindful of a Storm,

And thinks the Water wears a stable Form,
What dreadful Din around his Ears shall rise!
What Frowns confuse his Picture of the Skies!    180

At first the Creature Man was fram'd alone,
Lord of himself, and all the World his own.
For him the Nymphs in green forsook the Woods,
For him the Nymphs in blue forsook the Floods,
In vain the Satyrs rage, the Tritons rave,    185
They bore him Heroes in the secret Cave.
No Care destroy'd, no sick Disorder prey'd,
No bending Age his sprightly Form decay'd,
No Wars were known, no Females heard to rage,
And Poets tell us, 'twas a golden Age.    190

When *Woman* came, those Ills the Box confin'd
Burst furious out, and poison'd all the Wind,
From Point to Point, from Pole to Pole they flew,
Spread as they went, and in the Progress grew:
The Nymphs regretting left the mortal Race,    195
And alt'ring Nature wore a sickly Face:
New Terms of Folly rose, new States of Care;
New Plagues, to suffer, and to please, the Fair!
The Days of whining, and of wild Intrigues,
Commenc'd, or finish'd, with the Breach of Leagues;    200
The mean Designs of well-dissembled Love;
The sordid Matches never joyn'd above;
Abroad, the Labour, and at home the Noise,
(Man's double Suff'rings for domestick Joys)
The Curse of Jealousy; Expence, and Strife;    205
Divorce, the publick Brand of shameful Life;
The Rival's Sword; the Qualm that takes the Fair;
Disdain for Passion, Passion in Despair—
These, and a thousand, yet unnam'd, we find;
Ah fear the thousand, yet unnam'd behind!    210

THUS on *Parnassus* tuneful *Hesiod* sung,
The Mountain echo'd, and the Valley rung,
The sacred Groves a fix'd Attention show,
The chrystal *Helicon* forbore to flow,
The Sky grew bright, and (if his Verse be true)    215
The *Muses* came to give the Laurel too.
But what avail'd the verdant Prize of Wit,

If *Love* swore Vengeance for the Tales he writ?
Ye Fair offended, hear your Friend relate
What heavy Judgment prov'd the Writer's Fate,                       220
Tho' *when* it happen'd, no Relation clears,
'Tis thought in five, or five and twenty Years.

   Where, dark and silent, with a twisted Shade
The neighb'ring Woods a native Arbour made,
There oft a tender Pair for am'rous Play                            225
Retiring, toy'd the ravish'd Hours away;
A *Locrian* Youth, the gentle *Troilus* he,
A fair *Milesian,* kind *Evanthe* she:
But swelling Nature in a fatal Hour
Betray'd the Secrets of the conscious Bow'r;                        230
The dire Disgrace her Brothers count their own,
And track her Steps, to make its Author known.

   It chanc'd one Evening, ('twas the Lover's Day)
Conceal'd in Brakes the jealous Kindred lay;
When *Hesiod* wand'ring, mus'd along the Plain,                     235
And fix'd his Seat where Love had fix'd the Scene:
A strong Suspicion strait possest their Mind,
(For Poets ever were a gentle kind.)
But when *Evanthe* near the Passage stood,
Flung back a doubtful Look, and shot the Wood,                     240
"Now take, (at once they cry) thy due Reward,"
And urg'd with erring Rage, assault the Bard.
His Corps the Sea receiv'd. The Dolphins bore
('Twas all the Gods would do) the Corps to Shore.

   Methinks I view the Dead with pitying Eyes,                     245
And see the Dreams of antient Wisdom rise;
I see the *Muses* round the Body cry,
But hear a *Cupid* loudly laughing by;
He wheels his Arrow with insulting Hand,
And thus inscribes the Moral on the Sand.                          250
"Here *Hesiod* lies: Ye future Bards, beware
"How far your Moral Tales incense the Fair:
"Unlov'd, unloving, 'twas his Fate to bleed;
"Without his Quiver *Cupid* caus'd the Deed:
"He judg'd this Turn of Malice justly due,                          255
"And *Hesiod* dy'd for Joys he never knew.

# SONG.

W<small>HEN</small> thy Beauty appears
   In its Graces and Airs,
All bright as an Angel new dropt from the Sky;
   At distance I gaze, and am aw'd by my Fears,
   So strangely you dazzle my Eye!             5

   But when without Art,
   Your kind Thoughts you impart,
When your Love runs in Blushes thro' ev'ry Vein;
   When it darts from your Eyes, when it pants in your Heart,
   Then I know you're a Woman again.        10

   There's a Passion and Pride
   In our Sex, (she reply'd,)
And thus (might I gratify both) I wou'd do:
   Still an Angel appear to each Lover beside,
   But still be a Woman to you.        15

# A SONG.

T<small>HYRSIS</small>, a young and am'rous Swain,
   Saw two, the Beauties of the Plain;
     Who both his Heart subdue:
Gay *Cælia's* Eyes were dazzling fair,
*Sabina's* easy Shape and Air        5
     With softer Magick drew.

He haunts the Stream, he haunts the Grove,
Lives in a fond Romance of Love,
     And seems for each to dye;
'Till each a little spiteful grown,        10
*Sabina Cælia's* Shape ran down,
     And she *Sabina's* Eye.

Their Envy made the Shepherd find
Those Eyes, which Love cou'd only blind;
     So set the Lover free:        15
No more he haunts the Grove or Stream,

Or with a True-love Knot and Name
   Engraves a wounded Tree.

Ah *Cælia!* (sly *Sabina* cry'd)
Tho' neither love, we're both deny'd;         20
Now, to support the Sex's Pride,
   Let either fix the Dart.
Poor Girl! (says *Cælia*) say no more;
For shou'd the Swain but one adore,
That Spite which broke his Chains before,     25
   Wou'd break the other's Heart.


## ANACREONTICK.


WHEN Spring came on with fresh Delight,
   To cheer the Soul, and charm the Sight,
While easy Breezes, softer Rain,
And warmer Suns salute the Plain;
'Twas then, in yonder Piny Grove,
That *Nature* went to meet with *Love.*      5

   Green was her Robe, and green her Wreath,
Where-e'er she trod, 'twas green beneath;
Where-e'er she turn'd, the Pulses beat
With new recruits of *Genial* Heat;      10
And in her Train the Birds appear,
To match for all the coming Year.

   Rais'd on a Bank, where Daizys grew,
And Vi'lets intermix'd a Blew,
She finds the *Boy* she went to find;     15
A thousand *Pleasures* wait behind,
Aside, a thousand Arrows lye,
But all unfeather'd wait to fly.

   When they met, the *Dame* and *Boy,*
Dancing *Graces,* idle *Joy,*      20
Wanton *Smiles,* and airy *Play,*
Conspir'd to make the Scene be gay;
*Love* pair'd the Birds through all the Grove,
And *Nature* bid them sing to *Love,*

The Heavily Corrected Manuscript of "When Spring came on." (*Courtesy of Lord Congleton.*)

Of every dart can boast a kind
That suits a proper turn of mind
From the towering Eagles plume
The gen'rous hearts ~~~~~
Shot by the Peacocks ~~~~ eye
The vain ~~~~~~~~~~~~~~~
~~~~ carefully ~~~~~~~~~~
~~~~~~~~~ on speckled ~~~~~~
~~~~~~~~~~~~~~~~~~~~~~
~~~~~~~~ with ~~~~ love
~~~~~~~~~~ silver from ye doves;

2  When from the Dove the passions spring
The ~~~-serene affords a wing;
1  The eyes of parrots deck ye dart
When warbling ~~~ the panting hearts;
Together by ye sparrow strung
~~~ down ye wanton & the young;
If fledg'd by geese the weapons fly
When others love they know not why
All this of late I changed by ~~~~~
That I view'd in yonder ~~~~~
I see, says Love which calls me near
How much I ~~~~ by Nature here,
How each ~~~~~~ a proper part
I've given ~~ the feather & the dart
~~~~~~~~~~~~~~~~~~~~~~~~
~~~~~~~~~~~~~~~~~~~~~~~~
~~~~~~~~~~~~~~~~~~~~~~~~
~~~~~~~~~~~~~~~~~~~~~~~~
~~~~~~~~~~~~~~~~~~~~~~~~
~~~~~~~~~~~~~~~~~~~~~~~~
But if I soul alike the found
From both to both I dart ye wound

They why should Mortall pride        
& match with & foule(?) averse to their sphere?
fondly court(?) & idely sigh;
If Nature Cross them so do I.
                    for my weapon unfeather'd flys
& falter(?) shuffles in the sky.
But if         common charms I find
Where nature joyns y mind to Mind,
Then         my heart & for the dark
And                both from         hearts.
& strike through         through

         ever for foles averse to sigh
If nature cross you so do I

the Street —

Sitting, hopping, flutt'ring, sing,                                    25
And pay their Tribute from the Wing,
To fledge the Shafts that idly lye,
And yet unfeather'd wait to fly.

'Tis thus, when Spring renews the Blood,
They meet in ev'ry trembling Wood,                                     30
And thrice they make the Plumes agree,
And ev'ry Dart they mount with three,
And ev'ry Dart can boast a Kind,
Which suits each proper turn of Mind.

From the tow'ring *Eagle's* Plume                                      35
The *Gen'rous Hearts* accept their Doom;
Shot by the *Peacock's* painted Eye
The *vain* and *airy Lovers* dye:
For *careful* Dames and *frugal* Men,
The Shafts are speckled by the *Hen.*                                  40
The *Pyes* and *Parrots* deck the Darts,
When *Prattling* wins the panting Hearts:
When from the *Voice* the Passions spring,
The warbling *Finch* affords a Wing:
Together, by the *Sparrow* stung,                                      45
Down fall the *wanton* and the *young:*
And fledg'd by *Geese* the Weapons fly,
When others love *they know not why.*

All this (as late I chanc'd to rove)
I learn'd in yonder waving Grove.                                      50
And see, says *Love,* (who call'd me near)
How much I deal with *Nature* here,
How both support a proper Part,
She gives the Feather, I the Dart:
Then cease for Souls averse to sigh,                                   55
If *Nature* cross ye, so do I;
My Weapon there unfeather'd flies,
And shakes and shuffles through the Skies.
But if the *mutual Charms* I find
By which she links you, Mind to Mind,                                  60
They wing my Shafts, I poize the Darts,
And strike from both, through both your Hearts.

# A Fairy Tale in the *Ancient* English *Style*.

I N *Britain's* Isle and *Arthur's* days,
  When Midnight *Faeries* daunc'd the Maze,
    Liv'd *Edwin* of the Green;
*Edwin,* I wis, a gentle Youth,
Endow'd with Courage, Sense and Truth,          5
    Tho' badly Shap'd he been.

His Mountain Back mote well be said
To measure heigth against his Head,
    And lift it self above:
Yet spite of all that Nature did          10
To make his uncouth Form forbid,
    This Creature dar'd to love.

He felt the Charms of *Edith's* Eyes,
Nor wanted Hope to gain the Prize,
    Cou'd Ladies took within;          15
But one Sir *Topaz* dress'd with Art,
And, if a Shape cou'd win a Heart,
    He had a Shape to win.

*Edwin* (if right I read my Song)
With slighted Passion pac'd along          20
    All in the Moony Light:
'Twas near an old enchaunted Court,
Where sportive *Faeries* made Resort
    To revel out the Night.

His Heart was drear, his Hope was cross'd,          25
'Twas late, 'twas farr, the Path was lost
    That reach'd the Neighbour-Town;
With weary Steps he quits the Shades,
Resolv'd the darkling Dome he treads,
    And drops his Limbs adown.          30

But scant he lays him on the Floor,
When hollow Winds remove the Door,
    A trembling rocks the Ground:
And (well I ween to count aright)

At once an hundred Tapers light                    35
  On all the Walls around.

Now sounding Tongues assail his Ear,
Now sounding Feet approachen near,
  And now the Sounds encrease:
And from the Corner where he lay                   40
He sees a Train profusely gay
  Come pranckling o'er the Place.

But (trust me *Gentles!*) never yet
Was dight a Masquing half so neat,
  Or half so rich before;                          45
The Country lent the sweet Perfumes,
The Sea the Pearl, the Sky the Plumes,
  The Town its silken Store.

Now whilst he gaz'd, a *Gallant* drest
In flaunting Robes above the rest,                 50
  With awfull Accent cry'd;
What *Mortall* of a wretched Mind,
Whose Sighs infect the balmy Wind,
  Has here presum'd to hide?

At this the *Swain* whose vent'rous Soul           55
No Fears of *Magick* Art controul,
  Advanc'd in open sight;
'Nor have I Cause of Dreed, he said,
'Who view by no Presumption led
  'Your Revels of the Night.

                                                   60

"Twas Grief, for Scorn of faithful Love,
'Which made my Steps unweeting rove
  'Amid the nightly Dew.
'Tis well, the *Gallant* crys again,
We *Faeries* never injure Men                      65
  Who dare to tell us true.

Exalt thy Love-dejected Heart,
Be mine the Task, or e'er we part,
  To make thee Grief resign;
Now take the Pleasure of thy Chaunce;              70

Whilst I with *Mab* my part'ner daunce,
    Be little *Mable* thine.

He spoke, and all a sudden there
Light Musick floats in wanton Air;
    The *Monarch* leads the *Queen:*                    75
The rest their *Faerie* Partners found,
And *Mable* trimly tript the Ground
    With *Edwin* of the Green.

The Daucing past, the Board was laid,
And siker such a Feast was made                        80
    As Heart and Lip desire;
Withouten Hands the Dishes fly,
The Glasses with a Wish come nigh,
    And with a Wish retire.

But now to please the *Faerie King,*                   85
Full ev'ry deal they laugh and sing,
    And antick Feats devise;
Some wind and tumble like an Ape,
And other-some transmute their Shape
    In *Edwin's* wond'ring Eyes.                        90

'Till one at last that *Robin* hight,
(Renown'd for pinching Maids by Night)
    Has hent him up aloof;
And full against the Beam he flung,
Where by the Back the *Youth* he hung                  95
    To spraul unneath the Roof.

From thence, "Reverse my Charm, he crys,
"And let it fairely now suffice
    "The Gambol has been shown.
But *Oberon* answers with a Smile,                     100
Content thee *Edwin* for a while,
    The Vantage is thine own.

Here ended all the Phantome-play;
They smelt the fresh Approach of Day,
    And heard a Cock to crow;                          105
The whirling Wind that bore the Crowd

Has clap'd the Door, and whistled loud,
　To warn them all to go.

Then screaming all at once they fly,
And all at once the Tapers dy;　　　　　　　　　　110
　Poor *Edwin* falls to Floor;
Forlorn his State, and dark the Place,
Was never Wight in sike a Case
　Through all the Land before.

But soon as Dan *Apollo* rose,　　　　　　　　　　115
Full Jolly Creature home he goes,
　He feels his Back the less;
His honest Tongue and steady Mind
Han rid him of the Lump behind
　Which made him want Success.　　　　　　　　　120

With lusty livelyhed he talks,
He seems a dauncing as he walks,
　His Story soon took wind;
And beautious *Edith* sees the Youth,
Endow'd with Courage, Sense and Truth,　　　　　125
　Without a Bunch behind.

The Story told, Sir *Topaz* mov'd,
(The Youth of *Edith* erst approv'd)
　To see the Revel Scene:
At close of Eve he leaves his home,　　　　　　　130
And wends to find the ruin'd Dome
　All on the gloomy Plain.

As there he bides, it so befell,
The Wind came rustling down a Dell,
　A shaking seiz'd the Wall:　　　　　　　　　　135
Up spring the Tapers as before,
The *Faeries* bragly foot the Floor,
　And Musick fills the Hall.

But *certes* sorely sunk with woe
Sir *Topaz* sees the *Elphin* show,　　　　　　　140
　His Spirits in him dy:
When *Oberon* crys, 'a *Man* is near,

'A mortall Passion, cleeped Fear,
  'Hangs flagging in the Sky.

With that Sir *Topaz* (Hapless Youth!)                       145
In Accents fault'ring ay for Ruth
  Intreats them Pity graunt;
For als he been a mister Wight
Betray'd by wand'ring in the Night
  To tread the circled Haunt;
                                                             150
'Ah Losell Vile, at once they roar!
'And little skill'd of *Faerie* lore,
  'Thy Cause to come we know:
'Now has thy Kestrell Courage fell;
'And *Faeries*, since a Ly you tell,                         155
  'Are free to work thee Woe.

Then *Will*, who bears the wispy Fire
To trail the Swains among the Mire,
  The Caitive upward flung;
There like a Tortoise in a Shop                              160
He dangled from the Chamber-top,
  Where whilome *Edwin* hung.

The Revel now proceeds apace,
Deffly they frisk it o'er the Place,
  They sit, they drink, and eat;                             165
The time with frolick Mirth beguile,
And poor Sir *Topaz* hangs the while
  'Till all the Rout retreat.

By this the Starrs began to wink,
They skriek, they fly, the Tapers sink,                      170
  And down ydrops the *Knight*.
For never Spell by *Faerie* laid
With strong Enchantment bound a Glade
  Beyond the length of Night.

Chill, dark, alone, adreed, he lay,                          175
'Till up the Welkin rose the Day,
  Then deem'd the Dole was o'er:
But wot ye well his harder Lot?

His seely Back the *Bunch* has got
   Which *Edwin* lost afore.                             180

This Tale a *Sybil-Nurse* ared;
She softly strok'd my youngling Head,
   And when the Tale was done,
'Thus some are born, my Son (she cries)
'With base Impediments to rise,                  185
   'And some are born with none.

'But Virtue can it self advance
'To what the Fav'rite Fools of Chance
   'By Fortune seem'd design'd;
'Virtue can gain the Odds of Fate,              190
'And from it self shake off the Weight
   'Upon th' unworthy *Mind*.

*Cras amet, qui numquam amavit ; quique ama-*
*vit, cras amet.*

Tunc liquore de superno, spameo ponti e globo,

Cærulas inter catervas, inter & bipedes equos,

Fecit undantem Dionen de maritis imbribus.

*Cras amet, qui numquam amavit ; quique ama-*
*vit, cras amet.*

Ipsa gemmas purpurantem pingit annum floribus,

Ipsa surgentis papillas de Favonî spiritu

Urguet in totos pentes ; ipsa roris lucidi,

Noctis aura quem relinquit, spargit umentis aquas,

Et micant lacrymæ trementes decidito pondere.

Gutta præceps orbe parvo sustinet casus suos.

In pudorem florulentæ prodiderunt purpuræ.

Umor ille, quem serenis astra rorant noctibus,

Mane virgineas papillas solvit umenti peplo.

Ipsa

The Uncancelled Page of "Pervigilium Veneris" in the Cambridge copy of *1722*.
*(Courtesy of the Cambridge University Library.)*

## PERVIGILIUM VENERIS.

C*RAS amet, qui numquam amavit; Quique amavit, cras amet.*
Ver novum, ver jam canorum: vere natus orbis est,
Vere concordant amores, vere nubent alites,
Et nemus comam resolvit de maritis imbribus.
Cras amorum copulatrix inter umbras arborum                    5
Implicat casas virentes de flagello myrteo.
Cras Dione jura dicit, fulta sublimi throno.
  *Cras amet, qui numquam amavit; quique amavit,*
    *cras amet.*

  Tunc cruore de superno, spumeo ponti e globo,
Cærulas inter catervas, inter & bipedes equos,              10
Fecit undantem Dionen de maritis imbribus.
  *Cras amet, qui numquam amavit; quique amavit,*
    *cras amet.*

  Ipsa gemmas purpurantem pingit annum floribus,
Ipsa turgentes papillas de Favonî spiritu,
Urguet in toros stupentes; ipsa roris lucidi,              15
Noctis aura quem relinquit, spargit umentis aquas,
Et micant lacrymæ trementes decidivo pondere.
Gutta præceps orbe parvo sustinet casus suos.
In pudorem florulentæ prodiderunt purpuræ.

# THE VIGIL of *VENUS*.

*Written in the Time of* JULIUS CÆSAR, *and by some ascrib'd to* CATULLUS.

L*ET those love now, who never lov'd before,*
  *Let those who always lov'd, now love the more.*

The *Spring,* the new, the warb'ling Spring appears,
The youthful Season of reviving Years;
In Spring the *Loves* enkindle mutual Heats,           5
The feather'd Nation chuse their tuneful Mates,
The Trees grow fruitful with descending Rain
And drest in diff'ring Greens adorn the Plain.
She comes; to morrow *Beauty's Empress* roves
Thro' Walks that winding run within the Groves;     10
She twines the shooting Myrtle into Bow'rs,
And ties their meeting Tops with Wreaths of Flow'rs,
Then rais'd sublimely on her easy Throne
From Nature's pow'rful Dictates draws her own.
  *Let those love now, who never lov'd before,*       15
*Let those who always lov'd, now love the more.*


  'Twas on that Day which saw the teeming Flood
Swell round, impregnate with celestial Blood;
Wand'ring in Circles stood the finny Crew,
The midst was left a void Expanse of Blue,         20
There Parent *Ocean* work'd with heaving Throes,
And dropping wet the fair *Dione* rose.
  *Let those love now, who never lov'd before,*
*Let those who always lov'd, now love the more.*


  She paints the purple Year with vary'd show,     25
Tips the green Gem, and makes the Blossom glow.
She makes the turgid Buds receive the Breeze,
Expand to Leaves, and shade the naked Trees.
When gath'ring damps the misty Nights diffuse,
She sprinkles all the Morn with balmy Dews;      30
Bright trembling Pearls depend at ev'ry spray,

Umor ille, quem serenis astra rorant noctibus,        20
Mane virgines papillas solvit umenti peplo.
Ipsa jussit mane ut udæ virgines nubant rosæ
Fusæ prius de cruore deque amoris osculis,
Deque gemmis, deque flammis, deque Solis purpuris.
Cras ruborem qui latebat veste tectus ignea,        25
Unica marito nodo non pudebit solvere.
    *Cras amet, qui numquam amavit; quique amavit,*
      *cras amet.*

    Ipsa Nimfas Diva luco jussit ire myrteo,
Et Puer comes puellis. Nec tamen credi potest
Esse Amorem feriatum, si sagittas vexerit.        30
Ite Nimfæ: posuit arma, feriatus est Amor.
Jussus est inermis ire, nudus ire jussus est:
Neu quid arcu, neu sagitta, neu quid igne læderet.
Sed tamen cavete Nimfæ, quod Cupido pulcer est:
Totus est inermis idem, quando nudus est Amor.        35
    *Cras amet, qui numquam amavit; quique amavit,*
      *cras amet.*

    Compari Venus pudore mittit ad te virgines.
Una res est quam rogamus, cede virgo Delia,
Ut nemus sit incruentum de ferinis stragibus.
Ipsa vellet ut venires, si deceret virginem:        40
Jam tribus choros videres feriatos noctibus:
Congreges inter catervas ire per saltus tuos,
Floreas inter coronas, myrteas inter casas.

And kept from falling, seem to fall away.
A glossy Freshness hence the *Rose* receives,
And blushes sweet through all her silken Leaves;
(The Drops descending through the silent Night,     35
While Stars serenely roll their golden Light,)
Close 'till the Morn, her humid Veil she holds;
Then deckt with Virgin Pomp the Flow'r unfolds.
Soon will the Morning blush: Ye Maids! prepare,
In rosy Garlands bind your flowing Hair     40
'Tis *Venus*' Plant: The Blood fair *Venus* shed,
O'er the gay Beauty pour'd immortal Red;
From *Love*'s soft Kiss a sweet *Ambrosial* Smell
Was taught for ever on the Leaves to dwell;
From Gemms, from Flames, from orient Rays of Light     45
The richest Lustre makes her Purple bright;
And she to morrow weds; the sporting Gale
Unties her Zone, she bursts the verdant Veil;
Thro' all her Sweets the rifling *Lover* flies,
And as he breaths, her glowing Fires arise.     50
    *Let those love now, who never lov'd before,*
*Let those who always lov'd, now love the more.*


    Now fair *Dione* to the Myrtle Grove
Sends the gay *Nymphs*, and sends her tender *Love*.
And shall they venture? is it safe to go?     55
While *Nymphs* have Hearts, and *Cupid* wears a Bow?
Yes safely venture, 'tis his Mother's Will;
He walks unarm'd and undesigning ill,
His Torch extinct, his Quiver useless hung,
His Arrows idle, and his Bow unstrung.     60
And yet, ye *Nymphs*, beware, his Eyes have Charms,
And *Love* that's naked, still is *Love* in Arms.
    *Let those love now, who never lov'd before,*
*Let those who always lov'd, now love the more.*


    From *Venus* Bow'r to *Delia*'s Lodge repairs     65
A Virgin Train compleat with modest Airs:
'Chast *Delia*! grant our Suit! or shun the Wood,
'Nor stain this sacred Lawn with savage Blood.
'*Venis, O Delia!* if she cou'd persuade,
'Wou'd ask thy Presence, might she ask a Maid.     70

Nec Ceres, nec Bacchus absunt, nec Poetarum Deus;
Decinent & tota nox est pervigila cantibus.                                45
Regnet in silvis Dione: tu recede Delia.
  *Cras amet, qui numquam amavit; quique amavit,*
    *cras amet.*


  Jussit Hiblæis tribunal stare Diva floribus.
Præsens ipsa jura dicit, adsederunt Gratiæ.
Hibla totos funde flores quidquid annus adtulit.                          50
Hibla florum rumpe vestem, quantus Ennæ campus est.
Ruris hic erunt puellæ, vel puellæ montium,
Quæque silvas, quæque lucos, quæque fontes incolunt.
Jussit omnis adsidere pueri Mater alitas,
Jussit & nudo puellas nil Amori credere.                                  55
  *Cras amet, qui numquam amavit; quique amavit,*
    *cras amet.*


  Et recentibus virentes ducat umbras floribus.
Cras erit qui primus æther copulavit nuptias,
Ut pater roris crearet vernis annum nubibus,
In sinum maritus imber fluxit almæ conjugis,                              60
Ut fœtus immixtus omnis aleret magno corpore.
Ipsa venas atque mentem permeante spiritu
Intus occultis gubernat procreatrix viribus,
Perque cœlum, perque terras, perque pontum subditum,

Here chearful Quires for three auspicious Nights
With Songs prolong the pleasurable Rites:
Here Crouds in Measures lightly-decent rove;
Or seek by Pairs the Covert of the Grove,
Where meeting Greens for Arbours arch above,                    75
And mingling Flowrets strow the Scenes of Love.
Here dancing *Ceres* shakes her golden Sheaves:
Here *Bacchus* revels, deckt with viny Leaves:
Here Wit's enchanting God in Lawrel crown'd
Wakes all the ravish'd Hours with silver Sound.                    80
Ye Fields, ye Forests, own *Dione*'s Reign,
And *Delia*, Huntress *Delia*, shun the Plain.
   *Let those love now, who never lov'd before,*
*Let those who always lov'd, now love the more.*


   Gay with the Bloom of all her opening Year,                    85
The *Queen* at *Hybla* bids her Throne appear;
And there presides; and there the fav'rite Band
(Her smiling *Graces*) share the great Command.
Now beauteous *Hybla!* dress thy flow'ry Beds
With all the Pride the lavish Season sheds,                    90
Now all thy Colours, all thy Fragrance yield,
And rival *Enna*'s Aromatick Field.
To fill the Presence of the gentle Court
From ev'ry Quarter rural *Nymphs* resort,
From Woods, from Mountains, from their humble Vales,                    95
From Waters curling with the wanton Gales.
Pleas'd with the joyful Train, the *laughing Queen*
In Circles seats them round the Bank of green;
And 'lovely Girls, (she whispers) guard your Hearts;
'My Boy, tho' stript of Arms, abounds in Arts.                    100
   *Let those love now, who never lov'd before,*
*Let those who always lov'd, now love the more.*


   Let tender Grass in shaded Allys spread,
Let early Flow'rs erect their painted Head.
To morrow's Glory be to morrow seen,                    105
That Day, old *Ether* wedded *Earth* in green.
The *Vernal Father* bid the Spring appear,
In Clouds he coupled to produce the Year,
The Sap descending o'er her Bosom ran,

Pervium sui tenorem seminali tramite                                65
Imbuit, jussitque mundum nosse nascendi vias.
　　*Cras amet, qui numquam amavit; quique amavit,*
　　*cras amet.*


　Ipsa Trojanos nepotes in Latino transtulit;
Ipsa Laurentem puellam conjugem nato dedit;
Moxque Marti de sacello dat pudicam virginem.                       70
Romuleas ipsa fecit cum Sabinis nuptias,
Unde Rames & Quirites, proque prole posterûm
Romoli matrem crearet & nepotem Cæsarem.
　　*Cras amet, qui numquam amavit; quique amavit,*
　　*cras amet.*


　Rura fœcundat voluptas: rura Venerem sentiunt.                    75
Ipse Amor puer Dionæ rure natus dicitur.
Hunc ager cum parturiret, ipsa suscepit sinu,
Ipsa florum delicatis educavit osculis.
　　*Cras amet, qui numquam amavit; quique amavit,*
　　*cras amet.*


　Ecce, jam super genestas explicant tauri latus.                  80
Quisque tutus quo tenetur conjugali fœdere.
Subter umbras cum maritis ecce balantum gregem.
Et canoras non tacere Diva jussit alites.
Jam loquaces ore rauco stagna cygni perstrepunt,
Adsonat Terei puella subter umbram populi,                          85
Ut putas motus Amoris ore dici musico,
Et neges queri sororem de marito barbaro.

And all the various sorts of Soul began. 110
By Wheels unknown to Sight, by secret Veins
Distilling Life, the fruitful Goddess reigns,
Through all the lovely Realms of native Day,
Through all the circled Land, and circling Sea;
With fertil Seed she fill'd the pervious Earth, 115
And ever fix'd the mystick Ways of Birth.
   *Let those love now, who never lov'd before,*
*Let those who always lov'd, now love the more.*


   'Twas she the *Parent*, to the *Latian* Shore
Through various Dangers *Troy*'s Remainder bore. 120
She won *Lavinia* for her warlike Son,
And winning her, the *Latian* Empire won.
She gave to *Mars* the Maid, whose honour'd Womb
Swell'd with the *Founder* of immortal *Rome*.
Decoy'd by Shows the *Sabin* Dames she led, 125
And taught our vig'rous Youth the Means to wed.
Hence sprung the *Romans*, hence the Race divine
Thro' which great *Cæsar* draws his *Julian* Line.
   *Let those love now, who never lov'd before,*
*Let those who always lov'd, now love the more.* 130


   In rural Seats the Soul of *Pleasure* reigns;
The Life of *Beauty* fills the rural Scenes;
Ev'n *Love* (if *Fame* the Truth of *Love* declare)
Drew first the breathings of a rural Air.
Some pleasing Meadow pregnant *Beauty* prest, 135
She laid her Infant on its flow'ry Breast,
From Nature's Sweets he sipp'd the fragrant Dew,
He smil'd, he kiss'd them, and by kissing grew.
   *Let those love now, who never lov'd before,*
*Let those who always lov'd, now love the more.* 140


   Now Bulls o'er Stalks of Broom extend their Sides,
Secure of Favours from their lowing Brides.
Now stately Rams their fleecy Consorts lead,
Who bleating follow thro' the wand'ring Shade.
And now the *Goddess* bids the Birds appear, 145
Raise all their Musick, and salute the Year:

Illa cantat: nos tacemus: quando ver venit meum?
Quando faciam ut chelidon, ut tacere desinam?
Perdidi Musam tacendo, nec me Phœbus respicit.                    90
Sic Amyclas, cum tacerent, perdidit silentium.
    *Cras amet, qui numquam amavit; quique amavit,*
      *cras amet.*

Then deep the Swan begins, and deep the Song
Runs o'er the Water where he sails along;
While *Philomela* tunes a treble Strain,
And from the Poplar charms the list'ning Plain.          150
We fancy Love exprest at ev'ry Note,
It melts, it warbles, in her liquid Throat.
Of barb'rous *Tereus* she complains no more,
But sings for Pleasure as for Grief before.
And still her Graces rise, her Airs extend,          155
And all is Silence 'till the *Syren* end.


   How long in coming is my lovely Spring?
And when shall I, and when the Swallow sing?
Sweet *Philomela* cease,—Or here I sit,
And silent lose my rapt'rous Hour of Wit:          160
'Tis gone, the Fit retires, the Flames decay,
My tuneful *Phœbus* flies averse away.
His own *Amycle* thus, as Stories run,
But once was silent, and that once undone.
   *Let those love now, who never lov'd before,*          165
*Let those who always lov'd, now love the more.*

# HEALTH, *an* ECLOGUE.

N ow early Shepherds o'er the Meadow pass,
  And print long Foot-steps in the glittering Grass;
The Cows neglectful of their Pasture stand,
By turns obsequious to the Milker's Hand.

When *Damon* softly trod the shaven Lawn,                5
*Damon* a Youth from City Cares withdrawn;
Long was the pleasing Walk he wander'd thro',
A cover'd Arbour clos'd the distant view;
There rests the *Youth,* and while the feather'd Throng
Raise their wild Musick, thus contrives a Song.          10

Here wafted o'er by mild *Etesian* Air,
Thou Country *Goddess,* beauteous *Health!* repair;
Here let my Breast thro' quiv'ring Trees inhale
Thy rosy Blessings with the Morning Gale.
What are the Fields, or Flow'rs, or all I see?           15
Ah! tastless all, if not enjoy'd with thee.

Joy to my Soul! I feel the *Goddess* nigh,
The Face of Nature cheers as well as I;
O'er the flat Green refreshing Breezes run,
The smiling Dazies blow beneath the Sun,                 20
The Brooks run purling down with silver Waves,
The planted Lanes rejoice with dancing Leaves,
The chirping Birds from all the Compass rove
To tempt the tuneful Echoes of the Grove:
High sunny Summits, deeply shaded Dales,                 25
Thick Mossy Banks, and flow'ry winding Vales,
With various Prospect gratify the Sight,
And scatter fix'd Attention in Delight.

Come, Country *Goddess,* come, nor thou suffice,
But bring thy Mountain-Sister, *Exercise.*               30
Call'd by thy lively Voice, she turns her Pace,
Her winding Horn proclaims the finish'd Chace;
She mounts the Rocks, she skims the level Plain,
Dogs, Hawks, and Horses, crowd her early Train;
Her hardy Face repels the tanning Wind,                  35
And Lines and Meshes loosely float behind.

All these as Means of Toil the Feeble see,
But these are helps to Pleasure join'd with thee.

Let *Sloth* lye softning 'till high Noon in Down,
Or lolling fan her in the sult'ry Town,                    40
Unnerv'd with Rest; and turn her own Disease,
Or foster others in luxurious Ease:
I mount the Courser, call the deep mouth'd Hounds,
The Fox unkennell'd flies to covert Grounds;
I lead where Stags thro' tangled Thickets tread,          45
And shake the Saplings with their branching Head;
I make the Faulcons wing their airy Way,
And soar to seize, or stooping strike their Prey;
To snare the Fish I fix the luring Bait;
To wound the Fowl I load the Gun with Fate.               50
'Tis thus thro' change of Exercise I range,
And Strength and Pleasure rise from ev'ry Change.
   Here beautious *Health* for all the Year remain,
   When the next comes, I'll charm thee thus again.

Oh come, thou *Goddess* of my rural Song,                 55
And bring thy Daughter, calm *Content*, along,
Dame of the ruddy Cheek and laughing Eye,
From whose bright Presence Clouds of Sorrow fly:
For her I mow my Walks, I platt my Bow'rs,
Clip my low Hedges, and support my Flow'rs;              60
To welcome her, this Summer Seat I drest,
And here I court her when she comes to Rest;
When she from Exercise to learned Ease
Shall change again, and teach the Change to please.

Now Friends conversing my soft Hours refine,             65
And *Tully's Tusculum* revives in mine:
Now to grave Books I bid the Mind retreat,
And such as make me rather Good than Great.
Or o'er the Works of easy *Fancy* rove,
Where Flutes and Innocence amuse the Grove:             70
The native *Bard* that on *Sicilian* Plains
First sung the lowly Manners of the Swains;
Or *Maro's* Muse, that in the fairest Light
Paints rural Prospects and the Charms of Sight;
These soft *Amusements* bring *Content* along,          75
And *Fancy,* void of Sorrow, turns to *Song.*

Here beauteous *Health* for all the Year remain,
When the next comes, I'll charm thee thus again.

## *The* FLIES. *An* ECLOGUE.

WHEN in the River Cows for Coolness stand,
And Sheep for Breezes seek the lofty Land,
A Youth whom *Æsop* taught that ev'ry Tree
Each Bird and Insect spoke as well as he:
Walk'd calmly musing in a shaded Way                          5
Where flow'ring Hawthorn broke the sunny Ray,
And thus instructs his Moral Pen to draw
A Scene that obvious in the Field he saw.

Near a low Ditch, where shallow Waters meet,
Which never learnt to glide with liquid Feet,                10
Whose *Naiads* never prattle as they play,
But screen'd with Hedges slumber out the Day,
There stands a slender Fern's aspiring Shade,
Whose answ'ring Branches regularly layd
Put forth their answ'ring Boughs, and proudly rise           15
Three Stories upward, in the nether Skies.

For Shelter here, to shun the Noon-day Heat,
An airy Nation of the *Flies* retreat;
Some in soft Air their silken Pinions ply,
And some from Bough to Bough delighted fly,                  20
Some rise, and circling light to perch again;
A pleasing Murmur hums along the Plain.
So, when a Stage invites to pageant Shows,
(If great and small are like) appear the *Beaus,*
In Boxes some with spruce Pretension sit,                    25
Some change from Seat to Seat within the Pit,
Some roam the Scenes, or turning cease to roam;
Preluding Musick fills the lofty Dome.

When thus a Fly (if what a Fly can say
Deserves attention) rais'd the rural Lay.                    30

Where late *Amintor* made a Nymph a Bride,
Joyful I flew by young *Favonia's* side,

Who, mindless of the Feasting, went to sip
The balmy Pleasure of the Shepherd's Lip.
I saw the Wanton, where I stoop'd to sup,   35
And half resolv'd to drown me in the Cup;
'Till brush'd by careless Hands, she soar'd above:
Cease, Beauty, cease to vex a tender Love.

 Thus ends the Youth, the buzzing Meadow rung,
And thus the Rival of his Musick sung.   40

 When Suns by thousands shone in Orbs of Dew,
I wafted soft with *Zephyretta* flew;
Saw the clean Pail, and sought the milky Chear,
While little *Daphne* seiz'd my roving Dear.
Wretch that I was! I might have warn'd the Dame,   45
Yet sat indulging as the Danger came,
But the kind Huntress left her free to soar:
Ah! guard, ye *Lovers*, guard a Mistress more.

 Thus from the Fern, whose high-projecting Arms,
The fleeting Nation bent with dusky Swarms,   50
The *Swains* their Love in easy Musick breathe,
When Tongues and Tumult stun the Field beneath.
Black *Ants* in Teams come darkning all the Road,
Some call to march, and some to lift the Load;
They strain, they labour with incessant Pains   55
Press'd by the cumbrous weight of single Grains.
The Flies struck silent gaze with Wonder down:
The busy *Burghers* reach their earthy Town;
Where lay the Burthens of a wint'ry Store,
And thence unwearied part in search of more.   60
Yet one grave *Sage* a Moment's space attends,
And the small City's loftiest Point ascends,
Wipes the salt Dew that trickles down his Face,
And thus harangues them with the gravest Grace.

 Ye foolish *Nurslings* of the Summer Air,   65
These gentle Tunes and whining Songs forbear;
Your *Trees* and whisp'ring *Breeze*, your *Grove* and *Love*,
Your Cupids Quiver, and his Mother's Dove:
Let Bards to Business bend their vig'rous Wing,
And sing but seldom, if they love to sing:   70
Else, when the Flourets of the Season fail,

And this your Ferny Shade forsakes the Vale,
Tho' one would save ye, not one Grain of Wheat
Shou'd pay such Songsters idling at my Gate.

He ceas'd: The Flies, incorrigibly vain,                          75
Heard the *May'r's Speech*, and fell to sing again.


## AN ELEGY, *To an Old* BEAUTY.


I N vain, poor Nymph, to please our youthful sight
   You sleep in Cream and Frontlets all the Night,
Your Face with Patches soil, with Paint repair,
Dress with gay Gowns, and shade with foreign Hair.
If Truth in spight of Manners must be told,                       5
Why really *Fifty Five* is something old.

   Once you were young; or one, whose Life's so long
She might have born my Mother, tells me wrong.
And once (since Envy's dead before you dye,)
The Women own, you play'd a sparkling Eye,                       10
Taught the light Foot a modish little Trip,
And pouted with the prettiest purple Lip—

   To some new Charmer are the Roses fled,
Which blew, to damask all thy Cheek with red;
*Youth* calls the *Graces* there to fix their Reign,            15
And *Airs* by thousands fill their easy Train.
So parting Summer bids her flow'ry Prime
Attend the Sun to dress some foreign Clime,
While with'ring Seasons in Succession, here,
Strip the gay Gardens, and deform the Year.                     20

   But thou (since Nature bids) the World resign,
'Tis now thy Daughter's Daughter's time to shine.
With more Address, (or such as pleases more)
She runs her Female Exercises o'er,
Unfurls or closes, raps or turns the Fan,                       25
And smiles, or blushes at the Creature Man.
With quicker Life, as guilded Coaches pass,
In sideling Courtesy she drops the Glass.

With better Strength, on Visit-days she bears
To mount her fifty Flights of ample Stairs.          30
Her Mein, her Shape, her Temper, Eyes and Tongue
Are sure to conquer.—for the Rogue is young;
And all that's madly wild, or oddly gay,
We call it only pretty *Fanny*'s way.

   Let Time that makes you homely, make you sage,          35
The Sphere of Wisdom is the Sphere of Age.
'Tis true, when Beauty dawns with early Fire,
And hears the flatt'ring Tongues of soft Desire,
If not from Virtue, from its gravest Ways
The Soul with pleasing Avocation strays.          40
But Beauty gone, 'tis easier to be wise;
As Harpers better, by the loss of Eyes.

   Henceforth retire, reduce your roving Airs,
Haunt less the Plays, and more the publick Pray'rs,
Reject the *Mechlin* Head, and gold Brocade,          45
Go pray, in sober *Norwich* Crape array'd.
Thy pendent Diamonds let thy *Fanny* take,
(Their trembling Lustre shows how much you shake;)
Or bid her wear thy Necklace row'd with Pearl,
You'll find your *Fanny* an obedient Girl.          50
So for the rest, with less Incumbrance hung,
You walk thro' Life, unmingled with the young;
And view the *Shade* and *Substance* as you pass
With joint Endeavour trifling at the Glass,
Or *Folly* drest, and rambling all her Days,          55
To meet her Counterpart, and grow by *Praise:*
Yet still sedate your self, and gravely plain,
You neither fret, nor envy at the Vain.

   'Twas thus (if Man with Woman we compare)
The wise *Athenian* crost a glittering Fair,          60
Unmov'd by Tongues and Sights, he walk'd the place,
Thro' Tape, Toys, Tinsel, Gimp, Perfume, and Lace;
Then bends from *Mars*'s Hill his awful Eyes,
And *What a World I never want?* he cries;
But cries unheard: For *Folly* will be free.          65
So parts the buzzing gaudy Crowd, and He:
As careless he for them, as they for him;
He wrapt in *Wisdom*, and they whirl'd by *Whim*.

# *The* BOOK-WORM.

COME hither, Boy, we'll hunt to Day  
    The *Book-Worm,* ravening Beast of Prey,  
Produc'd by Parent *Earth,* at odds  
(As Fame reports it) with the *Gods.*  
Him frantick Hunger wildly drives                 5  
Against a thousand Authors Lives:  
Thro' all the Fields of Wit he flies;  
Dreadful his Head with clust'ring Eyes,  
With Horns without, and Tusks within,  
And Scales to serve him for a Skin.              10  
Observe him nearly, lest he climb  
To wound the Bards of antient Time,  
Or down the Vale of Fancy go  
To tear some modern Wretch below:  
On ev'ry Corner fix thine Eye,                15  
Or ten to one he slips thee by.

   See where his Teeth a Passage eat:  
We'll rouse him from the deep Retreat.  
But who the Shelter's forc'd to give?  
'Tis Sacred *Virgil* as I live!                20  
From Leaf to Leaf, from Song to Song,  
He draws the tadpole Form along,  
He mounts the gilded Edge before,  
He's up, he scuds the Cover o'er,  
He turns, he doubles, there he past,          25  
And here we have him, caught at last.

   Insatiate *Brute,* whose Teeth abuse  
The sweetest Servants of the *Muse.*  
(Nay never offer to deny,  
I took thee in the Fact to fly.)              30  
His *Roses* nipt in ev'ry Page,  
My poor *Anacreon* mourns thy Rage.  
By thee my *Ovid* wounded lies;  
By thee my *Lesbia's Sparrow* dies:  
Thy rabid Teeth have half destroy'd        35  
The Work of Love in *Biddy Floyd,*  
They rent *Belinda's* Locks away,  
And spoil'd the *Blouzelind* of *Gay.*

For all, for ev'ry single Deed,
Relentless *Justice* bids thee bleed.    40
Then fall a *Victim* to the *Nine*,
My self the *Priest*, my Desk the *Shrine*.

   Bring *Homer, Virgil, Tasso* near,
To pile a sacred Altar here;
Hold, Boy, thy Hand out-run thy Wit,    45
You reach'd the Plays that *D——s* writ;
You reach'd me *Ph——s* rustick Strain;
Pray take your mortal Bards again.

   Come bind the Victim,— there he lies,
And here between his num'rous Eyes    50
This venerable Dust I lay,
From *Manuscripts* just swept away.

   The Goblet in my Hand I take,
(For the Libation's yet to make)
A Health to Poets! all their Days    55
May they have Bread, as well as Praise;
Sense may they seek, and less engage
In Papers fill'd with Party-Rage.
But if their Riches spoil their Vein
Ye *Muses,* make them poor again.    60

   Now bring the Weapon, yonder Blade,
With which my tuneful Pens are made.
I strike the Scales that arm thee round,
And twice and thrice I print the Wound;
The sacred Altar floats with red,    65
And now he dies, and now he's dead.

   How like the Son of *Jove* I stand,
This *Hydra* stretch'd beneath my Hand!
Lay bare the Monster's Entrails here,
To see what Dangers threat the Year:    70
Ye Gods! what Sonnets on a Wench?
What lean Translations out of *French?*
'Tis plain, this Lobe is so unsound,
*S——* prints, before the Months go round.

   But hold, before I close the Scene,    75

The sacred Altar shou'd be clean.
Oh had I *Sh——ll's* Second Bays,
Or *T——!* thy pert and humble Lays!
(Ye Pair, forgive me, when I vow
I never miss'd your Works till now)                    80
I'd tear the Leaves to wipe the Shrine,
(That only way you please the *Nine*)
But since I chance to want these two,
I'll make the Songs of *D——y* do.

   Rent from the Corps, on yonder Pin,                 85
I hang the Scales that brac't it in;
I hang my studious Morning Gown,
And write my own *Inscription* down.

   'This *Trophy* from the *Python* won,
'This *Robe,* in which the Deed was done,             90
'These, *Parnell* glorying in the Feat,
'Hung on these Shelves, the *Muses* Seat.
'Here *Ignorance* and *Hunger* found
'Large Realms of Wit to ravage round;
'Here *Ignorance* and *Hunger* fell;                  95
'Two Foes in one I sent to Hell.
'Ye *Poets,* who my Labours see,
'Come share the Triumph all with me!
'Ye *Criticks!* born to vex the *Muse,*
'Go mourn the *grand Ally* you lose.                  100

# An ALLEGORY on MAN.

A Thoughtful Being, long and spare,
   Our Race of Mortals call him *Care:*
(Were *Homer* living, well he knew
What Name the Gods have call'd him too)
With fine Mechanick Genius wrought,                    5
And lov'd to work, tho' no one bought.

   This Being, by a Model bred
In *Jove's* eternal sable Head,
Contriv'd a Shape impow'rd to breathe,
And be the *Worldling* here beneath.                  10

The *Man* rose staring, like a Stake;
Wond'ring to see himself awake!
Then look'd so wise, before he knew
The Bus'ness he was made to do;
That pleas'd to see with what a Grace     15
He gravely shew'd his forward Face,
*Jove* talk'd of breeding him on high,
An *Under-something* of the Sky.

But e'er he gave the mighty *Nod,*
Which ever binds a *Poet's God:*     20
(For which his Curls Ambrosial shake,
And Mother *Earth's* oblig'd to quake:)
He saw old Mother *Earth* arise,
She stood confess'd before his Eyes;
But not with what we read she wore,     25
A Castle for a Crown before,
Nor with long Streets and longer Roads
Dangling behind her, like Commodes:
As yet with Wreaths alone she drest,
And trail'd a Landskip-painted Vest.     30
Then thrice she rais'd, (as *Ovid* said)
And thrice she bow'd, her weighty Head.

Her Honours made, Great *Jove,* she cry'd,
This *Thing* was fashion'd from my Side;
His Hands, his Heart, his Head are mine;     35
Then what hast thou to call him thine?

Nay rather ask, the *Monarch* said,
What boots his Hand, his Heart, his Head,
Were what I gave remov'd away?
Thy Part's an idle Shape of Clay.     40

Halves, more than Halves! cry'd honest *Care,*
Your Pleas wou'd make your Titles fair,
You claim the Body, you the Soul,
But I who join'd them, claim the whole.

Thus with the Gods Debate began,     45
On such a trivial Cause, as *Man.*
And can Celestial Tempers rage?
(Quoth *Virgil* in a later Age.)

As thus they wrangled, *Time* came by;
(There's none that paint him such as I,                    50
For what the Fabling *Antients* sung
Makes *Saturn* old, when *Time* was young.)
As yet his Winters had not shed
Their silver Honours on his Head;
He just had got his Pinions free                           55
From his old Sire *Eternity.*
A Serpent girdled round he wore,
The Tail within the Mouth before;
By which our *Almanacks* are clear
That learned *Ægypt* meant the Year.                       60
A Staff he carry'd, where on high
A Glass was fix'd to measure by,
As Amber Boxes made a Show
For Heads of Canes an Age ago.
His Vest, for Day, and Night, was py'd;                    65
A bending Sickle arm'd his Side;
And Spring's new Months his Train adorn;
The other Seasons were unborn.

Known by the Gods, as near he draws,
They make him *Umpire* of the Cause.                       70
O'er a low Trunk his Arm he laid,
(Where since his *Hours* a *Dial* made;)
Then leaning heard the nice Debate,
And thus pronounc'd the Words of *Fate.*

Since *Body* from the Parent *Earth,*                      75
And *Soul* from *Jove* receiv'd a Birth,
Return they where they first began;
But since their *Union* makes the *Man,*
'Till *Jove* and *Earth* shall part these two,
To *Care* who join'd them, *Man* is due.                   80

He said, and sprung with swift Career
To trace a Circle for the Year;
Where ever since the *Seasons* wheel,
And tread on one another's Heel.

'Tis well, said *Jove,* and for consent                    85
Thund'ring he shook the Firmament.
Our Umpire *Time* shall have his Way,

With *Care* I let the Creature stay:
Let Bus'ness vex him, Av'rice blind,
Let Doubt and Knowledge rack his Mind,                    90
Let Error act, Opinion speak,
And Want afflict, and Sickness break,
And Anger burn, Dejection chill,
And Joy distract, and Sorrow kill.
'Till arm'd by *Care* and taught to Mow,                   95
*Time* draws the long destructive Blow;
And wasted *Man,* whose quick decay
Comes hurrying on before his Day,
Shall only find, by this Decree,
The *Soul* flies sooner back to *Me.*                      100

## An Imitation of some FRENCH Verses.

Relentless *Time!* destroying Pow'r
  Whom Stone and Brass obey,
Who giv'st to ev'ry flying Hour
  To work some new Decay;
Unheard, unheeded, and unseen,                             5
  Thy secret Saps prevail,
And ruin Man, a nice Machine
  By Nature form'd to fail.
My Change arrives; the Change I meet,
  Before I thought it nigh.                          10
My *Spring,* my Years of Pleasure fleet,
  And all their Beauties dye.
In *Age* I search, and only find
  A poor unfruitful Gain,
Grave *Wisdom* stalking slow behind,                       15
  Oppress'd with loads of Pain.
My Ignorance cou'd once beguile,
  And fancy'd Joys inspire;
My Errors cherish'd *Hope* to smile
  On newly-born *Desire.*                            20
But now Experience shews, the Bliss
  For which I fondly sought,
Not worth the long impatient Wish,
  And Ardour of the Thought.
My Youth met *Fortune* fair array'd,                       25
  (In all her Pomp she shone)

And might, perhaps, have well essay'd
  To make her Gifts my own:
But when I saw the Blessings show'r
  On some unworthy Mind,                30
I left the Chace, and own'd the *Pow'r*
  Was justly painted blind.
I pass'd the Glories which adorn
  The splendid Courts of Kings,
And while the Persons mov'd my Scorn,        35
  I rose to scorn the Things.
My Manhood felt a vig'rous Fire
  By Love encreas'd the more;
But Years with coming Years conspire
  To break the Chains I wore.            40
In Weakness safe, the *Sex* I see
  With idle Lustre shine;
For what are all their Joys to me,
  Which cannot now be mine?
But hold—I feel my *Gout* decrease,        45
  My Troubles laid to rest,
And Truths which wou'd disturb my Peace
  Are painful Truths at best.
Vainly the Time I have to roll
  In sad Reflection flies;            50
Ye fondling Passions of my Soul!
  Ye sweet Deceits! arise.
I wisely change the Scene within,
  To Things that us'd to please;
In *Pain, Philosophy* is *Spleen,*        55
  In *Health,* 'tis only *Ease.*

## *A* NIGHT-PIECE *on* DEATH.

B Y the blue Tapers trembling Light,
  No more I waste the wakeful Night,
Intent with endless view to pore
The Schoolmen and the Sages o'er:
Their Books from Wisdom widely stray,      5
Or point at best the longest Way.
I'll seek a readier Path, and go
Where Wisdom's surely taught *below.*

How deep yon Azure dies the Sky!
Where Orbs of Gold unnumber'd lye,      10
While thro' their Ranks in silver pride
The nether Crescent seems to glide.
The slumb'ring Breeze forgets to breathe,
The Lake is smooth and clear beneath,
Where once again the spangled Show      15
Descends to meet our Eyes below.
The Grounds which on the right aspire,
In dimness from the View retire:
The Left presents a Place of Graves,
Whose Wall the silent Water laves.      20
That Steeple guides thy doubtful sight
Among the livid gleams of Night.
There pass with melancholy State,
By all the solemn Heaps of Fate,
And think, as softly-sad you tread      25
Above the venerable Dead,
*Time was, like thee they Life possest,*
*And Time shall be, that thou shalt Rest.*

Those Graves, with bending Osier bound,
That nameless heave the crumbled Ground,      30
Quick to the glancing Thought disclose
Where *Toil* and *Poverty* repose.

The flat smooth Stones that bear a Name,
The Chissels slender help to Fame,
(Which e'er our Sett of Friends decay      35
Their frequent Steps may wear away.)
A *middle Race* of Mortals own,
Men, half ambitious, all unknown.

The Marble Tombs that rise on high,
Whose Dead in vaulted Arches lye,      40
Whose Pillars swell with sculptur'd Stones,
Arms, Angels, Epitaphs and Bones,
These (all the poor Remains of State)
Adorn the *Rich,* or praise the *Great;*
Who while on Earth in Fame they live,      45
Are sensless of the Fame they give.

Ha! while I gaze, pale *Cynthia* fades,

The bursting Earth unveils the Shades!
All slow, and wan, and wrap'd with Shrouds,
They rise in visionary Crouds,                                    50
And all with sober Accent cry,
*Think, Mortal, what it is to dye.*

    Now from yon black and fun'ral Yew,
That bathes the Charnel House with Dew,
Methinks I hear a *Voice* begin;                                 55
(Ye Ravens, cease your croaking Din,
Ye tolling Clocks, no Time resound
O'er the long Lake and midnight Ground)
It sends a Peal of hollow Groans,
Thus speaking from among the Bones.                              60

    When Men my Scythe and Darts supply,
How great a *King* of *Fears* am I!
They view me like the last of Things:
They make, and then they dread, my Stings.
Fools! if you less provok'd your Fears,                          65
No more my Spectre-Form appears.
Death's but a Path that must be trod,
If Man wou'd ever pass to God:
A Port of Calms, a State of Ease
From the rough Rage of swelling Seas.                           70

    Why then thy flowing sable Stoles,
Deep pendent Cypress, mourning Poles,
Loose Scarfs to fall athwart thy Weeds,
Long Palls, drawn Herses, cover'd Steeds,
And Plumes of black, that as they tread,                        75
Nod o'er the 'Scutcheons of the Dead?

    Nor can the parted Body know,
Nor wants the Soul, these Forms of Woe:
As men who long in Prison dwell,
With Lamps that glimmer round the Cell,                         80
When e'er their suffering Years are run,
Spring forth to greet the glitt'ring Sun:
Such Joy, tho' far transcending Sense,
Have pious Souls at parting hence.
On Earth, and in the Body plac't,                               85
A few, and evil Years, they wast:

But when their Chains are cast aside,
See the glad Scene unfolding wide,
Clap the glad Wing and tow'r away,
And mingle with the Blaze of Day.                                    90

## *The* HERMIT.

F AR in a Wild, unknown to publick View,
    From Youth to Age a rev'rend *Hermit* grew;
The Moss his Bed, the Cave his humble Cell,
His Food the Fruits, his Drink the chrystal Well:
Remote from Man, with God he pass'd the Days,          5
Pray'r all his Bus'ness, all his Pleasure Praise.

A Life so sacred, such serene Repose,
Seem'd Heav'n it self, 'till one Suggestion rose;
That Vice shou'd triumph, Virtue Vice obey,
This sprung some Doubt of Providence's Sway:          10
His Hopes no more a certain Prospect boast,
And all the Tenour of his Soul is lost:
So when a smooth Expanse receives imprest
Calm Nature's Image on its wat'ry Breast,
Down bend the Banks, the Trees depending grow,          15
And Skies beneath with answ'ring Colours glow:
But if a Stone the gentle Scene divide,
Swift ruffling Circles curl on ev'ry side,
And glimmering Fragments of a broken Sun,
Banks, Trees, and Skies, in thick Disorder run.          20

To clear this Doubt, to know the World by Sight,
To find if Books, or Swains, report it right;
(For yet by Swains alone the World he knew,
Whose Feet came wand'ring o'er the nightly Dew)
He quits his Cell; the Pilgrim-Staff he bore,          25
And fix'd the Scallop in his Hat before;
Then with the Sun a rising Journey went,
Sedate to think, and watching each Event.

The Morn was wasted in the pathless Grass,
And long and lonesome was the Wild to pass;          30
But when the *Southern* Sun had warm'd the Day,

A Youth came posting o'er a crossing Way;
His Rayment decent, his Complexion fair,
And soft in graceful Ringlets wav'd his Hair.
Then near approaching, Father Hail! he cry'd,                    35
And Hail, my Son, the rev'rend Sire reply'd;
Words followed Words, from Question Answer flow'd,
And Talk of various kind deceiv'd the Road;
'Till each with other pleas'd, and loth to part,
While in their Age they differ, joyn in Heart:                   40
Thus stands an aged Elm in Ivy bound,
Thus youthful Ivy clasps an Elm around.

  Now sunk the Sun; the closing Hour of Day
Came onward, mantled o'er with sober gray;
Nature in silence bid the World repose:                          45
When near the Road a stately Palace rose:
There by the Moon thro' Ranks of Trees they pass,
Whose Verdure crown'd their sloping sides of Grass.
It chanc't the noble Master of the Dome,
Still made his House the wand'ring Stranger's home:              50
Yet still the Kindness, from a Thirst of Praise,
Prov'd the vain Flourish of expensive Ease.
The Pair arrive: the Liv'ry'd Servants wait;
Their Lord receives them at the pompous Gate.
The Table groans with costly Piles of Food,                      55
And all is more than Hospitably good.
Then led to rest, the Day's long Toil they drown,
Deep sunk in Sleep, and Silk, and Heaps of Down.

  At length 'tis Morn, and at the Dawn of Day,
Along the wide Canals the *Zephyrs* play;                        60
Fresh o'er the gay Parterres the Breezes creep,
And shake the neighb'ring Wood to banish Sleep.
Up rise the Guests, obedient to the Call,
An early Banquet deck'd the splendid Hall;
Rich luscious Wine a golden Goblet grac't,                       65
Which the kind Master forc'd the Guests to taste.
Then pleas'd and thankful, from the Porch they go,
And, but the Landlord, none had cause of Woe;
His *Cup* was vanish'd; for in secret Guise
The younger Guest purloin'd the glittering Prize.               70

  As one who 'spys a Serpent in his Way,

Glistning and basking in the Summer Ray,
Disorder'd stops to shun the Danger near,
Then walks with Faintness on, and looks with Fear:
So seem'd the Sire; when far upon the Road,                    75
The shining Spoil his wiley Partner show'd.
He stopp'd with Silence, walk'd with trembling Heart,
And much he wish'd, but durst not ask to part:
Murm'ring he lifts his Eyes, and thinks it hard,
That generous Actions meet a base Reward.                    80

While thus they pass, the Sun his Glory shrouds,
The changing Skies hang out their sable Clouds;
A Sound in Air presag'd approaching Rain,
And Beasts to covert scud a cross the Plain.
Warn'd by the Signs, the wand'ring Pair retreat,            85
To seek for Shelter at a neighb'ring Seat.
'Twas built with Turrets, on a rising Ground,
And strong, and large, and unimprov'd around;
Its Owner's Temper, tim'rous and severe,
Unkind and griping, caus'd a Desert there.                    90

As near the *Miser*'s heavy Doors they drew,
Fierce rising Gusts with sudden Fury blew;
The nimble Light'ning mix'd with Show'rs began,
And o'er their Heads loud-rolling Thunder ran.
Here long they knock, but knock or call in vain,            95
Driv'n by the Wind, and battered by the Rain.
At length some Pity warm'd the Master's Breast,
('Twas then, his Threshold first receiv'd a Guest)
Slow creaking turns the Door with jealous Care,
And half he welcomes in the shivering Pair;                 100
One frugal Faggot lights the naked Walls,
And Nature's Fervor thro' their Limbs recals:
Bread of the coursest sort, with eager Wine,
(Each hardly granted) serv'd them both to dine;
And when the Tempest first appear'd to cease,              105
A ready Warning bid them part in Peace.

With still Remark the pond'ring *Hermit* view'd
In one so rich, a Life so poor and rude;
And why shou'd such, (within himself he cry'd,)

Lock the lost Wealth a thousand want beside?     110
But what new Marks of Wonder soon took place,
In ev'ry settling Feature of his Face!
When from his Vest the young Companion bore
That *Cup,* the gen'rous Landlord own'd before,
And paid profusely with the precious Bowl     115
The stinted Kindness of this churlish Soul.

    But now the Clouds in airy Tumult fly,
The Sun emerging opes an azure Sky;
A fresher green the smelling Leaves display,
And glitt'ring as they tremble, cheer the Day:     120
The Weather courts them from the poor Retreat,
And the glad Master bolts the wary Gate.

    While hence they walk, the *Pilgrim*'s Bosom wrought,
With all the Travel of uncertain Thought;
His Partner's Acts without their Cause appear,     125
'Twas there a Vice, and seem'd a Madness here:
Detesting that, and pitying this he goes,
Lost and confounded with the various Shows.

    Now Night's dim Shades again involve the Sky;
Again the Wand'rers want a Place to lye,     130
Again they search, and find a Lodging nigh.
The Soil improv'd around, the Mansion neat,
And neither poorly low, nor idly great:
It seem'd to speak its Master's turn of Mind,
Content, and not for Praise, but Virtue kind.     135

    Hither the Walkers turn with weary Feet
Then bless the Mansion, and the Master greet:
Their greeting fair bestow'd, with modest Guise,
The courteous Master hears, and thus replies:

    Without a vain, without a grudging Heart,     140
To Him who gives us all, I yield a part;
From Him you come, for Him accept it here,
A frank and sober, more than costly Cheer.
He spoke, and bid the welcome Table spread,
Then talk'd of Virtue till the time of Bed,     145
When the grave Houshold round his Hall repair,
Warn'd by a Bell, and close the Hours with Pray'r.

At length the World renew'd by calm Repose
Was strong for Toil, the dappled Morn arose;
Before the Pilgrims part, the Younger crept,                    150
Near the clos'd Cradle where an Infant slept,
And writh'd his Neck: the Landlord's little Pride,
O strange Return! grew black, and gasp'd, and dy'd.
Horrour of Horrours! what! his only Son!
How look'd our Hermit when the Fact was done?                   155
Not Hell, tho' Hell's black Jaws in sunder part,
And breathe blue Fire, cou'd more assault his Heart.

Confus'd, and struck with Silence at the Deed,
He flies, but trembling fails to fly with Speed.
His Steps the Youth pursues; the Country lay                    160
Perplex'd with Roads, a Servant show'd the Way:
A River cross'd the Path; the Passage o'er
Was nice to find; the Servant trod before;
Long arms of Oaks an open Bridge supply'd,
And deep the Waves beneath the bending glide.                   165
The Youth, who seem'd to watch a Time to sin,
Approach'd the careless Guide, and thrust him in;
Plunging he falls, and rising lifts his Head,
Then flashing turns, and sinks among the Dead.

Wild, sparkling Rage inflames the Father's Eyes,               170
He bursts the Bands of Fear, and madly cries,
Detested Wretch—But scarce his Speech began,
When the strange Partner seem'd no longer Man:
His youthful Face grew more serenely sweet;
His Robe turn'd white, and flow'd upon his Feet;               175
Fair rounds of radiant Points invest his Hair;
Celestial Odours breathe thro' purpled Air;
And Wings, whose Colours glitter'd on the Day,
Wide at his Back their gradual Plumes display.
The form Etherial bursts upon his Sight,                        180
And moves in all the Majesty of Light.

Tho' loud at first the Pilgrim's Passion grew,
Sudden he gaz'd, and wist not what to do;
Surprize in secret Chains his words suspends,
And in a Calm his settling Temper ends.                         185
But Silence here the beauteous Angel broke,
(The Voice of Musick ravish'd as he spoke.)

Thy Pray'r, thy Praise, thy Life to Vice unknown,
In sweet Memorial rise before the Throne:
These Charms, Success in our bright Region find,                    190
And force an Angel down, to calm thy Mind;
For this commission'd, I forsook the Sky,
Nay, cease to kneel—Thy fellow Servant I.

Then know the Truth of Government Divine,
And let these Scruples be no longer thine.                          195

The Maker justly claims that World he made,
In this the Right of Providence is laid;
Its sacred Majesty thro' all depends
On using second Means to work his Ends:
'Tis thus, withdrawn in State from human Eye,                       200
The Pow'r exerts his Attributes on high,
Your Actions uses, not controuls your Will,
And bids the doubting Sons of Men be still.

What strange Events can strike with more Surprize,
Than those which lately strook thy wond'ring Eyes?                  205
Yet taught by these, confess th' Almighty Just,
And where you can't unriddle, learn to trust!

The *Great, Vain Man,* who far'd on costly Food,
Whose Life was too luxurious to be good;
Who made his Iv'ry Stands with Goblets shine,                      210
And forc'd his Guests to morning Draughts of Wine,
Has, with the *Cup,* the graceless Custom lost,
And still he welcomes, but with less of Cost.

The mean, suspicious *Wretch,* whose bolted Door,
Ne'er mov'd in Duty to the wand'ring Poor;                         215
With him I left the Cup, to teach his Mind
That Heav'n can bless, if Mortals will be kind.
Conscious of wanting Worth, he views the Bowl,
And feels Compassion touch his grateful Soul.
Thus Artists melt the sullen Oar of Lead,                          220
With heaping Coals of Fire upon its Head;
In the kind Warmth the Metal learns to glow,
And loose from Dross, the Silver runs below.

Long had our *pious Friend* in Virtue trod,

But now the Child half-wean'd his Heart from God;                    225
(Child of his Age) for him he liv'd in Pain,
And measur'd back his Steps to Earth again.
To what Excesses had his Dotage run?
But God, to save the Father, took the Son.
To all but thee, in Fits he seem'd to go,                            230
(And 'twas my Ministry to deal the Blow.)
The poor fond Parent humbled in the Dust,
Now owns in Tears the Punishment was just.

But how had all his Fortune felt a Wrack,
Had that false *Servant* sped in Safety back?                        235
This Night his treasur'd Heaps he meant to steal,
And what a Fund of Charity wou'd fail!

Thus Heav'n instructs thy Mind: This Tryal o'er,
Depart in Peace, resign, and sin no more.

On sounding Pinnions here the Youth withdrew,                        240
The Sage stood wond'ring as the *Seraph* flew.
Thus look'd *Elisha,* when to mount on high,
His Master took the Chariot of the Sky;
The fiery Pomp ascending left the View;
The Prophet gaz'd, and wish'd to follow too.                         245

The bending Hermit here a Pray'r begun,
*Lord! as in Heaven, on Earth thy Will be done.*
Then gladly turning, sought his antient place,
And pass'd a Life of Piety and Peace.

# Biblical Poems
# from British Library Add. MS 31114

## The Gift of Poetry.  [f.1a]

From Realms of never-interrupted peace,
From thy fair station near the throne of Grace,
From Quires of Angells, Joys in endless round,
& endless Harmonys enchanting sound,
Charmd with a zeal the Makers praise to show,                    5
Bright Gift of Verse descend, & here below
My ravishd heart with raisd affection fill,
& warbling ore the Soul incline my will.
Among thy pomp lett rich expression wait,
Lett ranging numbers form thy train compleat,               10
While at thy motions thro' the ravishd sky
Sweet Sounds & Eccho's sweet-resounding fly,
& where thy feet with gliding beauty tread
Lett Fancys flowry spring erect its head.
     It comes it comes with unaccustomd light,               15
The tracts of airy Thought grow wondrous bright,
Its notions ancient Memory reviews,
& Young Invention new design pursues,
To some attempt my will & wishes press,
& pleasure raisd in hope forebodes success.                  20
     My God from whom proceed the Gifts divine
My God the gift I think I feel is thine.
Be this no vain Illusion which I find,
Nor natures Impulse on the passive mind,
But reasons act, producd by good desire,                   [f.1b]
By Grace enlivend with celestiall fire:
While base Conceits like misty sons of night
Before such beams of Glory wing their flight;

178

& frail Affections born of earth decay
Like weeds that wither in the warmer ray.                        30
   I thank thee Father with a gratefull mind,
Man's undeserving & thy mercy kind.
I now perceive I long to sing thy praise,
I now perceive I long to find my lays
The Sweet incentives of anothers love,                          35
& sure such Longings have their rise above.
My resolution stands confirmed within,
My Lines aspiring eagerly begin.
Begin my lines to such a subject due
That aids our Labours & rewards y^m too;                        40
Begin while Canaan opens to mine eyes,
Where Soules & Songs divinely formd arise.
   As one, whom ore y^e Sweetly varyd meads
Intire Recess or Lonely Pleasure leads
To verdurd banks, to paths adornd with flowrs,                  45
To shady trees, to closely-weaving bowrs,
To bubbling fountains, & aside y^e stream
That softly gliding soothes a waking dream,
Or bears y^e thought inspird with heat along,
& with fair images improves a song.                             50
Through sacred Anthems so may Fancy range
So still from beauty still to beauty change
So feel delights in all the radiant way,                        [f.2a]
& with sweet numbers what it feeles repay.
For this I call that Ancient Time appear                        55
& bring his rolls to serve in method here,
His rolls which acts that endless honour claim,
Have rankd in order for y^e voice of Fame.
My call is favour, Time f^m first to last
Unwinds his years, the Present sees y^e Past,                   60
I view their circles as he turns y^m o're,
& fix my footsteps where he went before.

   The Page unfolding woud atop disclose
Where sounds melodious in their birth arose;
Where first the Morning starrs together sung;                   65
Where first their harps the Sons of Glory strung
With Shouts of Joy, while Halelujahs rise
To prove the Chorus of Eternall skys.
Rich sparkling strokes the letters Doubly gild,
& all's with Love & admiration filld.                           70

# Moses.

[f.2a]

To grace those lines w<sup>ch</sup> next appear to sight,
The Pencil shone with more abated light,
Yet still y<sup>e</sup> pencil shone, y<sup>e</sup> lines were fair,
& awfull Moses stands recorded there.
Lett his repleat with flames & praise divine     [f.2b]
Lett his the first-rememberd Song be mine.
Then rise my thought, & in thy Prophet find
What Joy shoud warm thee for y<sup>e</sup> work designd.
To that great act which raisd his heart repair,
& find a portion of his Spirit there.     10
    A Nation helpless & unarmd I view,
Whom strong revengefull troops of warr pursue,
Seas Stop their flight, their camp must prove their grave.
Ah what can Save them? God alone can save.
Gods wondrous voice proclaims his high command,     15
He bids their Leader wave the sacred wand,
& where the billows flowd they flow no more,
A road lyes naked & they march it o're.
Safe may the Sons of Jacob travell through,
But why will Hardend Ægypt venture too?     20
Vain in thy rage to think the waters flee,
& rise like walls on either hand for thee.
The night comes on the Season for surprize,
Yet fear not Israel God directs thine eyes,
A fiery cloud I see thine Angel ride,     25
His Chariot is thy light & he thy guide.
The day comes on & half thy succours fail,
Yet fear not Israel God will still prevail,
I see thine Angel from before thee go,     [f.3a]
To make the wheeles of ventrous Ægypt slow,     30
His rolling cloud inwraps its beams of light,
& what supplyd thy day prolongs their night.
At length the dangers of the deep are run,
The Further brink is past, the bank is won,
The Leader turns to view the foes behind,     35
Then waves his solemn wand within the wind.
O Nation freed by wonders cease thy fear,
& stand & see the Lords salvation here.
    Ye tempests now from ev'ry corner fly,
& wildly rage in all my fancyd Sky.     40

Roll on ye waters as ye rolld before,
Ye billows of my fancyd ocean roar,
Dash high, ride foaming, mingle all yᵉ main.
Tis don— & Pharaoh cant afflict again.
The work the wondrous work of Freedomes don,                     45
The winds abate, the clouds restore yᵉ Sun,
The wreck appears, the threatning army drownd
Floats ore yᵉ waves to strow the Sandy ground.
　Then Place thy Moses near the calming flood,
Majestically mild, serenely good.                                50
Lett Meekness (Lovely virtue) gently Stream
Around his visage like a lambent flame.
Lett gratefull Sentiments, lett Sense of love,
Lett holy zeal within his bosome move.
& while his People gaze yᵉ watry plain,                          [f.3b]
& fears last touches like to doubt remain,
While bright astonishment that seems to raise
A questioning belief, is fond to praise,
Be thus the rapture in the Prophets breast,
Be thus the thankes for freedome gaind expresst.                60

　Ile sing to God, Ile Sing yᵉ songs of praise       [Exodus 15]
To God triumphant in his wondrous ways,
To God whose glorys in the Seas excell,
Where the proud horse & prouder rider fell.
　The Lord in mercy kind in Justice strong                      65
Is now my strength, this Strength be now my song,
This sure salvation, (such he proves to me
from danger rescu'd & from bondage free).
The Lords my God & Ile prepare his seat,
My Fathers God & Ile proclaim him great,                        70
Him Lord of Battles, him renownd in name,
Him ever faithfull, evermore the same.
　His gracious aids avenge his peoples thrall,
They make the pride of boasting Pharaoh fall.
Within the Seas his stately Chariots ly,                        75
Within the Seas his chosen Captains dy.
The rolling deeps have coverd o're the foe,
They sunk like stones they Swiftly sunk below.
There O my God thine hand confessd thy care,        [f.4a]
Thine hand was glorious in thy power there,                     80
It broke their troops unequall for the fight
In all the greatness of excelling might.

Thy wrath Sent forward on y<sup>e</sup> raging Stream,
Swift sure & Sudden their destruction came,
They fell as stubble burns, while driving skys                    85
Provoke & whirl a flame & ruin fly's.
  When blasts dispatchd with wonderfull intent
On soveraign orders from thy nostrills went,
For our accounts the waters were affraid,
Perceivd thy presence & together fled,                           90
In heaps uprightly placd they learnd to stand,
like banks of Christall by y<sup>e</sup> paths of sand.
Then fondly flushd with hope, & swelld with pride,
& filld with rage, the foe prophanely cryd,
Secure of conquest Ile pursue their way,                         95
Ile overtake them, Ile divide the prey,
My lust I'le Satisfy, mine anger cloy,
My sword Ile brandish, & their name destroy.
How wildly threats their anger: hark above
New blasts of wind on new commission move,                       100
To loose the fetters that confind the main,
& make its mighty waters rage again,
Then overwhelmd with irresistless Sway
They Sunk like lead they sunk beneath the Sea.
  O who like thee thou dreaded Lord of Host           [f.4b]
Among the Gods whom all the nations boast
Such acts of wonder & of Strength displays,
O Great! O Glorious in thine holy ways!
Deserving praise, & that thy praise appear
In Signs of reverence & Sence of fear.                           110
With Justice armd thou stretcht thy powrfull hand,
& earth between its gaping Jaws of land,
Receivd its waters of the parted main,
& swallowd up the dark Ægyptian train.
With mercy rising on the weaker Side,                            115
Thy self became the rescud peoples guide,
& in thy strength they past th' amazing road,
To reach thine holy mount thy blessd abode.
  What thou hast don the neighb'ring realms shall hear,
& feel the strange report excite their fear.                     120
What thou hast don shall Edoms Dukes amaze,
& make dispair on Palestina Seize.
Shall make the warlike Sons of Moab Shake,

& all the melting hearts of Canaan weak.
In heavy damps diffusd on ev'ry breast                                125
Shall cold distrust & hopeless Terrour rest.
The matchless greatness which thine hand has shown,
Shall keep their kingdomes as unmovd as stone,
While Jordan Stops above & failes below,                           [f.5a]
& all thy flock across the Channel go.                               130
Thus on thy mercys silver-shining wing
Through seas & streams thou wilt yᵉ nation bring,
& as the rooted trees securely stand,
So firmly plant it in the promisd land,
Where for thy self thou wilt a place prepare,                       135
& after-ages will thine altar rear.
There reign victorious in thy Sacred Seat,
O Lord for ever & for ever great.
   Look where the Tyrant was but lately seen,
The Seas gave backward & he venturd in,                             140
In yonder gulph with haughty pomp he showd,
Here marchd his horsemen, there his chariots rode;
& when our God restord the floods again,
Ah vainly strong they perishd in the main.
But Israel went a dry surprizing way,                               145
Made safe by miracles amidst yᵉ sea.

   Here ceasd the Song, tho' not yᵉ Prophets Joy,
Which others hands & others tongues employ.
For still the lays with warmth divine expresst
Inflamd his hearers to their inmost breast.                         150
Then Miriams notes the Chorus sweetly raise,
& Miriams timbrel gives new life to praise.
The moving sounds, like Soft delicious wind                        [f.5b]
That breathd from Paradise, a passage find,
Shed Sympathys for Odours as they rove,                             155
& fan the risings of enkindled love.
Ore all yᵉ crowd the thought inspiring flew,
The women followd with their timbrells too,
& thus from Moses where his strains arose,
They catchd a rapture to perform the close.                         160
   We'le sing to God, we'le sing yᵉ songs of praise
To God triumphant in his wondrous ways,
To God whose glorys in yᵉ Seas excell,
Where yᵉ proud horse & prouder rider fell.
   Thus Israel rapturd wᵗʰ yᵉ pleasing thought                      165

Of Freedome wishd & wonderfully gott,
Made chearfull thanks from evry bank rebound,
Expressd by songs, improvd in Joy by sound.
   O Sacred Moses, each infusing line
That movd their gratitude was part of thine,            170
& still the Christians in thy numbers view,
The type of Baptism & of Heaven too.
So Soules from water rise to Grace below:
So Saints from toil to praise & glory goe.
   O gratefull Miriam in thy temper wrought       175
too warm for Silence or inventing thought
Thy part of anthem was to warble o're           [f.6a]
In sweet response what Moses sung before.
Thou led the publick voice to Joyn his lays,
& words redoubling well redoubled praise.         180
Receive thy title, Prophetess was thine
When here thy Practice showd y^e form divine.
The Spirit thus approvd, resignd in will
The Church bows down, & hears responses still.
   Nor slightly suffer tunefull Jubals name       185
To miss his place among y^e Sons of Fame,
Whose Sweet infusions coud of old inspire,
The breathing organs & y^e trembling Lyre.
Father of these on earth, whose gentle Soul
By such ingagements coud y^e mind controul,      190
If holy verses ought to Musick owe,
Be that thy large account of thanks below,
Whilst then y^e timbrels lively pleasure gave,
& now whilst organs Sound Sedately grave.

   My first attempt y^e finishd course commends,     195
Now Fancy flagg not as that subject ends,
But charmd with beautys which attend thy way,
Ascend harmonious in the next essay.
So flys y^e Lark, (& learn from her to fly)       [f.6b]
She mounts, she warbles in y^e wind on high,      200
She falls from thence, & seems to drop her wing,
but e're she lights to rest remounts to sing.
   It is not farr the days have rolld their years,
Before the Second brightend work appears.
It is not farr, Alas the faulty cause          205
Which from the Prophet sad reflection draws!
Alas that blessings in possession cloy,

& peevish murmurs are preferrd to Joy,
That favourd Israel coud be faithless still,
& question Gods protecting power or will,                     210
Or dread devoted Canaans warlike men,
& Long for Ægypt & their bonds again.
    Scarce thrice the Sun since hardend Pharaoh dyd
As bridegrooms issue forth with glitt'ring pride
Rejoycing rose, & lett y^e nation See                         215
three Shining days of easy liberty,
Ere the mean fears of want producd within
Vain thought replenishd with rebellious Sin.
O Look not Israel to thy former way,
God cannot fail, & either wait or pray.                       220
Within the borders of thy promisd Lands,
Lots hapless wife a strange example stands,
She turnd her eyes & felt her change begin,                   [f.7a]
& wrath as fierce may meet resembling Sin.
Then forward move thy camp & forward Still,                   225
& lett sweet mercy bend thy Stubborn will.
    At thy complaint a branch in Marah cast
With sweetning virtue mends y^e waters tast.
At thy complaint the Lab'ring Tempest sailes,
& drives afore a wondrous showr of Quailes.                   230
On tender grass the falling Manna lyes,
& Heav'n it self the want of bread supplys.
The rock divided flows upon the plain,
At thy complaint, & still thou wil't complain.
As thus employd thou went y^e desart through,                235
Lo Sinai mount upreard its head to view.
Thine eyes perceivd the darkly-rolling cloud,
Thine ears the trumpet shrill y^e thunder loud,
The forky lightning shot in livid gleam,
The Smoke arose, y^e mountain all aflame                      240
Quak'd to y^e depths, & worked with signs of awe,
While God descended to dispense the law.
Yet neither mercy manifest in might
Nor pow'r in terrour coud preserve thee right.
    Provokt with crimes of such an heinous kind               245
Allmighty Justice sware the doom designd,
That these shoud never reach y^e promisd seat,               [f.7b]
& Moses gently mourns their hastend fate.
    Ile think him now resignd to publick care,
While night on pitchy plumes slides soft in air.              250

Ile think him giving what y^e guilty sleep
To thoughts where Sorrow glides & numbers weep,
Sad thoughts of woes that reign where Sins prevail,
& mans short life, tho' not so short as frail.
Within this circle for his inward eyes                    255
He bids the fading low creation rise,
& streight a train of mimick Senses brings
The dusky shapes of transitory things,
Thro' pensive shades the visions seem to range,
They seem to flourish, & they seem to change;            260
A moon decreasing runs the silent sky,
The sickly birds on molting feathers fly,
Men walking count their days of blessings o're,
The blessings vanish & the tales no more,
Still hours of nightly watches steal away,               265
Big waters roll green blades of grass decay,
Then all y^e Pensive shades by Just degrees
Grows faint confuses & goes off with these.
But while the affecting notions pass along,
He chuses such as best adorn his song,                   270
& thus with God the rising lays began,                   [f.8a]
God ever reigning God, compard with man:
& thus they movd to man beneath his rod;
Man deeply sinning, man chastisd by God.

   O Lord O Saviour, tho' thy chosen band                [Psalm 90]
Have staid like strangers in a forreign land,
Through numberd ages which have run their race,
Still has thy mercy been our dwelling place.
Before the most exalted dust of earth,
The stately mountains had receivd a birth;               280
Before the pillars of the world were laid,
Before its habitable parts were made,
Thou wer't the God, from thee their rise they drew,
Thou great for ages great for ever too.
   Man (mortall creature framd to feel decays)           285
Thine unresisted pow'r at pleasure sways,
Thou sayst return & parting Soules obey,
Thou sayst return & bodys fall to clay.
For whats a thousand fleeting years w^th thee?
Or Time compard with long eternity,                      290
Whose wings expanding infinitely vast,
Orestretch its utmost ends of first & last?

Tis like those hours that lately saw yᵉ Sun,
He rose, & set, & all the day was don.
Or like the watches which dead night divide,                    [f.8b]
& while we slumber unregarded glide,
Where all yᵉ present seems a thing of nought,
& past & future close to waking thought.
 As raging floods, when rivers swell with rain,
Bear down yᵉ groves & overflow yᵉ plain,                    300
So swift & strong thy wondrous might appears,
So Life is carryd down the rolling years.
As heavy sleep pursues the days retreat,
With dark with silent & unactive state,
So lifes attended on by certain doom,                    305
& deaths yᵉ rest, yᵉ resting place a tomb.
It quickly rises & it quickly goes,
& youth its morning, age its evening shows.
Thus tender blades of grass, when beams diffuse,
Rise from the pressure of their early dews,                    310
Point tow'rds yᵉ skys their elevated spires,
& proudly flourish in their green attires,
But soon (ah fading state of things below!)
The Scyth destructive mows yᵉ lovely show,
The rising Sun that Saw their glorys high                    315
That Sun descending sees their glorys dy.
 We still with more than common hast of fate
Are doomd to perish in thy kindled hate.
Our publick sins for publick Justice call,                    [f.9a]
& stand like markes on which thy Judgements fall.                    320
Our secret sins that folly thought conceald
Are in thy light for punishment reveald.
Beneath the terrours of thy wrath divine
Our days unmixd with happiness decline,
Like empty storys tedious, short, & vain,                    325
& never never more recalld again.
 Yet what were Life, if to yᵉ longest date
Which men have namd a life we backned fate?
Alas its most computed length appears
To reach yᵉ limits but of Seav'nty years,                    330
& if by strength to fourscore years we goe,
That strength is labour, & that labour woe.
Then will thy term expire, & thou must fly

O man O Creature surely born to dy.
  But who regards a truth so throughly known?      335
Who dreads a wrath so manifestly shown?
Who seems to fear it tho' y<sup>e</sup> danger vyes
With any pitch to which our fear can rise?
O teach us so to number all our days
That these reflections may correct our ways,      340
That these may lead us from delusive dreams
To walk in heavnly wisdomes golden beams.
  Return O Lord, how Long shall Israels sin      [f.9b]
How Long thine anger be preservd within!
Before our times irrevocably past      345
Be kind be gracious & return at last.
Let Favour soon-dispensd our soules employ,
& long endure to make enduring Joy.
Send years of comforts for our years of woes,
Send these at least of equall length with those.      350
Shine on thy flock & on their offspring shine
With tender mercy (sweetest act divine).
Bright rays of Majesty serenely shed,
To rest in Glorys on the nations head.
Our future deeds with approbation bless,      355
& in the giving them give us success.

  Thus with forgiveness earnestly desird,
Thus in the raptures of a bliss requird,
The man of God concludes his Sacred Strain,
Now sitt & see y<sup>e</sup> subject once again.      360
  See Ghastly Death where Desarts all around
Spread forth their barren undelightfull ground:
There stalks the silent melancholly shade,
His naked bones reclining on a spade,
& thrice the spade with solemn sadness heaves,      365
& thrice earth opens in the form of graves,
His gates of darkness gape to take him in,      [f.10a]
Then where he soon woud Sink he's pushed by sin.
  Poor Mortalls here your common picture know,
& with your Selves in this acquainted grow.      370
Through life with airy thoughtless pride you range
& vainly glitter in the Sphear of change,
A sphear where all things but for time remain,
Where no fixd starrs with endless glory reign,
But Meteors onely short-lived Meteors rise      375

To shine shoot down & dy beneath y<sup>e</sup> skys.
  There is an hour, Ah who y<sup>t</sup> hour attends!
When man y<sup>e</sup> guilded vanity descends.
When forreign force or wast of inward heat
Constrain y<sup>e</sup> soul to leave its ancient seat;          380
When banishd Beauty from her empire flyes,
& with a languish leaves y<sup>e</sup> Sparkling eyes;
When softning Musick & Persuasion fail,
& all the charms that in y<sup>e</sup> tongue prevail,
When Spirits stop their course, when nerves unbrace,      385
& outward action & perception cease.
'Tis then the poor deformd remains shall be
That naked Skeleton we seem to see.
  Make this thy mirrour if thou woudst have bliss,      [f.10b]
No flattring image shows it self in this;          390
But such as lays the lofty lookes of pride,
& makes cool thought in humble channel glide;
But such as clears y<sup>e</sup> cheats of Errours den,
Whence magick mists surround y<sup>e</sup> soules of men,
Whence Self-Delusions trains adorn their flight,      395
As Snows fair feathers fleet to darken sight,
Then rest, & in the work of Fancy spread
To gay-wavd plumes for ev'ry mortals head.
These empty Forms when Death appears disperse,
Or melt in tears upon its mournfull hearse,          400
The sad reflection forces men to know,
"Life surely failes & swiftly flys below.
  O Least thy folly loose y<sup>e</sup> proffit sought
O never touch it with a glancing thought,
As men to glasses come, & straight w<sup>th</sup>draw,      405
& straight forgett what sort of face they saw:
But fix intently fix thine inward eyes,
& in the strength of this great truth be wise.
"If on y<sup>e</sup> globes dim Side our sences Stray,
"Not usd to perfect light we think it day:          410
"Death seems long sleep, & hopes of heavnly beams
"Deceitfull wishes big with distant dreams.
"But if our reason purge y<sup>e</sup> carnal sight,      [f.11a]
"& place its objects in their Juster light,
"We change y<sup>e</sup> side, from Dreams on earth we move,      415
"& wake through death to rise in life above.

  Here ore my soul a solemn silence reigns,

Preparing thought for new celestial strains.
The former vanish off, yᵉ new begin,
The solemn silence stands like night between,                    420
In whose dark bosome day departing lyes,
& day succeeding takes a lovely rise.
But tho' yᵉ song be changd, be still yᵉ flame,
& Still yᵉ prophet in my lines yᵉ Same,
With care renewd upon the children dwell,                        425
Whose sinfull Fathers in the desart fell,
With care renewd (if any care can do)
Ah least they sin & least they perish too.
   Go seek for Moses at yon Sacred tent
On which yᵉ Presence makes a bright descent.                     430
Behold yᵉ cloud with radiant glory fair
Like a wreathd pillar curl its gold in air.
Behold it hovering Just above the door,
& Moses meekely kneeling on the floor.
But if the gazing turn thine edge of sight,            [f.11b]
& darkness Spring from unsupported light,
Then change yᵉ Sense, be sight in hearing drownd,
While these strange accents from the vision sound.
      The time my Servant is approaching nigh
      When thou shall't gatherd with thy Fathers ly,           440
      & soon thy nation quite forgetfull grown
      Of all the glorys which mine arm has shown,
      Shall through my covenant perversely break,
      Despise my worship & my name forsake,
      By customes conquerd where to rule they go,              445
      & Serving Gods that cant protect yᵉ foe.
      Displeasd at this Ile turn my face aside
      Till sharp Afflictions rod reduce their pride
      Till brought to better mind they seek relief,
      by good confessions in the midst of grief.               450
      Then write thy song to stand a witness still
      Of favours past & of my future will,
      For I their vain conceits before discern,
      Then write thy Song which Israels sons shall learn.
   As thus yᵉ wondrous voice its charge repeats               455
The Prophet musing deep within retreats.
He Seems to feel it on a streaming ray
Pierce through yᵉ Soul enlightning all its way.
& much Obedient will & free desire,                    [f.12a]
& much his Love of Jacobs Seed inspire,                         460

& much O much above y<sup>e</sup> warmth of those
The Sacred Spirit in his bosome glows,
Majestick Notion Seems Decrees to nod,
& Holy Transport speakes y<sup>e</sup> words of God.
 Returnd at length, the finishd roll he brings,   465
Enrichd with Strains of past & future things.
The Priests in order to y<sup>e</sup> tent repair,
The Gatherd Tribes attend their Elders there:
O Sacred Mercys inexhausted Store!
Shall these have warning of their faults before,   470
Shall these be told y<sup>e</sup> recompenses due,
Shall Heavn & Earth be calld to witness too!
Then still y<sup>e</sup> tumult if it will be so,
Its Fear to loose a word lett caution Show,
Lett close Attention in dead calm appear,   475
& softly softly steal with silence near,
While Moses raisd above y<sup>e</sup> listning throng,
Pronounces thus in all their ears the Song.

Hear O ye Heav'ns Creations lofty show,   [Deuteronomy 32]
Hear O thou heavn-encompassd Earth below.   480
As Silver Showrs of gently-dropping rain,   [f.12b]
As Honyd Dews distilling on y<sup>e</sup> plain,
As rain as Dews for tender grass designd,
So shall my speeches sink within y<sup>e</sup> mind,
So sweetly turn y<sup>e</sup> Soules enlivening food,   485
So fill & cherish hopefull seeds of good.
For now my Numbers to the world Abroad,
Will lowdly celebrate y<sup>e</sup> name of God.
 Ascribe thou nation, evry favourd tribe
Excelling greatness to y<sup>e</sup> Lord ascribe,   490
The Lord, the Rock on whom we safely trust,
Whose work is perfect, & whose ways are Just,
The Lord whose promise stands for ever true,
The Lord most righteous & most holy too.
 Ah worse Election! Ah the bonds of sin!   495
They chuse themselves to take corruption in.
They stain their soules with vices deepest blots,
When onely frailtys are his childrens spots.
Their thoughts words actions all are run astray,
& none more crooked more perverse than they.   500
 Say rebell Nation O unwisely light,
Say will thy folly thus thy God requite?

Or is He not the God who made thee free,
Whose mercy purchasd & establishd thee?
   Remember well yᵉ wondrous days of old,         [f.13a]
The years of ages long before thee told,
Ask all thy fathers who the truth will show,
Or ask thine elders for thine elders know.
   When yᵉ most high with scepter pointed down
Describd yᵉ Realms of each beginning Crown,         510
When Adams offspring Providentiall care
to people countrys scatterd here & there,
He so yᵉ limits of their lands confind,
That favourd Israel has its part assignd,
For Israel is yᵉ Lords, & gaines yᵉ place         515
Reservd for those whom he woud chuse to grace.
   Him in yᵉ desart him his mercy found
where famine dwells & howling deafs yᵉ ground,
Where dread is felt by savage noise encreast,
Where solitude erects its seat on wast.         520
& there he led him, & he taught him there,
& safely kept him with a watchfull care,
The tender apples of our heedfull eye
Not more in guard nor more securely ly.
& as an eagle that attempts to bring         525
Her unexperiencd young to trust the wing,
Stirrs up her nest, & flutters ore their heads,
& all yᵉ forces of her pinnions spreads,
& takes & bears yᵐ on her plumes above,         [f.13b]
To give peculiar proof of royall love,         530
Twas so yᵉ Lord, the gracious Lord alone,
With kindness most peculiar led his own,
As no strange God concurrd to make him free,
So none had powr to lead him through but he.
To lands excelling lands & planted high         535
That boast yᵉ kindlyest-influencing sky
He brought, he bore him on yᵉ wings of Grace,
To tast yᵉ plentys of yᵉ grounds encrease,
Sweet-dropping hony from the rocky soil,
from flinty rocks yᵉ smoothly-flowing oyl,         540
The guilded butter from the stately kine,
The milk with which yᵉ duggs of sheep decline,
The marrow-fatness of the tender lambs,
The bulky breed of Basans goats & rams,
The finest flowry wheat that crowns the plain         545

Distends its husk & loads the blade with grain,
& still he drank from ripe delicious heaps
Of clusters pressd the purest blood of grapes.
   But thou art waxen fatt & kickest now,
O Well-Directed O Jesurun thou.                                        550
Thou soon w'ert fatt, thy sides were thickly grown,
Thy fattness deeply coverd evry bone
Then wanton fullness vain oblivion brought,            [f.14a]
& God that made & savd thee was forgott,
While Gods of forreign lands & rites abhorrd,                      555
To Jealousys & anger movd yᵉ Lord;
While Gods thy fathers never knew were ownd;
& Hell ev'n Hell with sacrifice attond.
Oh fooles unmindfull whence your orderd frame
& whence your life-infusing spirit came!                           560
Such strange corruptions his revenge provoke,
& thus their fate his indignation spoke.
   It is decreed. Ile hide my face & see
When I forsake them what their end shall be.
For they're a froward very froward strain,                         565
That promisd duty but returnd disdain.
In my grievd soul they raise a Jealous flame
By new-namd Gods & onely Gods in name,
They make the burnings of mine anger glow
By guilty vanitys displeasing show:                                570
Ile also teach their Jealousy to frett
At people not formd a people yet,
Ile make their anger vex their inward breast
When such as have not known my laws are blesst.
A fire a fire that nothing can asswage                             575
Is kindled in the fierceness of my rage,
To burn the deeps, consume yᵉ lands increase,
& on the mountains strong foundations seize.
Thick heaps of mischief on their heads I send,        [f.14b]
& all mine arrows wingd with fury spend.                           580
Slow-parching dearth & pestilentiall heat,
Shall bring the bitter pangs of lingring fate.
Sharp teeth of beasts shall swift destruction bring,
Dire serpents wound them with invenomd sting,
The sword without & dread within consume                           585
The youth the virgin in their lovely bloom,
Weak tender Infancy by suckling fed,
& helpless age with hoary-frosted head.

I said Ide scatter all the sinfull race,
I said Ide make its meer remembrance cease,                    590
But much I feard the foes unruly pride,
Their glory vaunted & my powr denyd,
While thus they boast, our arm has shown us brave,
& God did nothing, for he could not Save.
So fond their thought, so farr remote of sense,               595
& blind in every course of Providence.
O knew they rightly where my Judgements tend,
O woud they ponder on their latter end!
Soon woud they find, that when upon y^e field
One makes a thousand two ten thousand yield,                  600
The Lord of Hosts has Sold a rebel state,
The Lord inclosd it in y^e netts of fate.
For whats anothers rock compard with ours,            [f.15a]
Lett them be Judges that have provd their powrs,
That on their own have vainly calld for aid,                  605
While ours to freedome & to glory led.
Their vine may seem indeed to flourish fair,
But yet it grows in Sodoms tainted air,
It sucks corruption from Gomorrahs fields,
Rank Galls for grapes in bitter clusters yields,             610
& poison sheds for wine, like y^t which comes
from asps & Dragons death-infected gums;
& are not these their hatefull sins reveald,
& in my treasures for my Justice seald?
To me the province of revenge belongs,                        615
To me the certain recompense of wrongs,
Their feet shall totter in appointed time,
& threatning danger overtake their crime,
For wingd with featherd hast y^e minutes fly,
To bring those things that must afflict them nigh.            620
The Lord will Judge his own & bring y^m low,
& then repent & turn upon y^e foe,
& when the Judgements from his own remove,
Will thus the foe convincingly reprove.
Where are y^e Gods y^e rock to whom in vain                   625
Your offrings have been made your victims slain?
Lett them arise, lett them afford their aid,          [f.15b]
& with Protections shield surround your head.
Know then your maker, I the Lord am he,
Nor ever was there any God with me,                           630
& death or life & wounds or health I give,

Nor can another from my powr reprieve.
With Solemn state I lift mine arm on high
Ore y<sup>e</sup> rich glorys of the lofty sky,
& by my self majestically swear,                                     635
I live for ever & for ever there.
If in my rage y<sup>e</sup> glitt'ring sword I whet,
& sternly sitting take y<sup>e</sup> Judgement seat,
My Just-awarding sentence dooms my foe,
& vengeance wields y<sup>e</sup> blade & gives y<sup>e</sup> blow,               640
& Deep in flesh y<sup>e</sup> blade of Fury bites,
& deadly-deep my bearded arrow lightes,
& both grow drunk with blood defild in sin,
When executions of revenge begin.
   Then lett his nation in a common voice,              645
& with his nation lett y<sup>e</sup> world rejoyce.
For whether God for crimes or tryalls spill
His Servants blood, he will avenge it still.
He'le break y<sup>e</sup> troops, he'le scatter all afarr
Who vex our realm with desolating warr.                              650
& on y<sup>e</sup> favourd tribes & on their land
Shed Victorys & peace from Mercys hand.

   Here ceasd y<sup>e</sup> song, & Israel lookd behind       [f.16a]
& gazd before with unconfining mind,
& fixd in silence & amazement saw                                    655
The strokes of all their state beneath y<sup>e</sup> law.
Their Recollection does its light present
To show y<sup>e</sup> mountain blessd with Gods descent,
To show their wandrings, their unfixd abode,
& all their guidance in the desart road.                             660
Then where the beams of Recollection goe
To leave y<sup>e</sup> fancy dispossessd of show,
The fairer light of Prophecy's begun
Which opening future days supplys their sun.
By such a sun (& fancy needs no more)                                665
They see the coming times & walk y<sup>m</sup> o're,
& now they gain that rest their travel sought,
Now milk & hony stream along the thought,
Anon they fill their soules, y<sup>e</sup> blessings cloy,
& God's forgot in full excess of Joy.                                670
& oft they sin, & oft his anger burns
& ev'ry nations made their scourge by turns,
Till oft repenting they convert to God,

& he repenting too destroys the rod.
    O nation timely warnd in sacred strain,          675
O never lett thy Moses sing in vain.
Dare to be good & happiness prolong          [f.16b]
Or if thy folly will fullfill the song,
At least be found the seldomer in ill,
& still repent & soon repent thee still.          680
When such fair paths thou shalt avoid to tread,
Thy blood will rest upon thy sinfull head,
Thy crime by lasting long secure thy foe,
The gracious warning to the Gentiles goe,
& all the world thats calld to witness here          685
convincd by thine example learn to fear.
The gentil world a mystick Israel grown
Will in thy first condition find their own,
A Gods descent, a Pilgrimage below,
& Promisd rest where living waters flow.          690
They'le see the pen describe in ev'ry trace,
The frowns of Anger, or the Smiles of Grace,
Why mercy turns aside & leaves to shine,
What cause provokes the Jealousy divine,
Why Justice kindles dire-avenging flames,          695
What endless powr $y^e$ Lifted Arm proclaims,
Why Mercy shines again with chearfull ray,
& Glory double-gilds $y^e$ lightsome day.
Tho Nations change & Israels empire dyes,
Yet still $y^e$ case which rose before may rise,          700
Eternall Providence its rule retains,          [f.17a]
& still preserves, & still applys $y^e$ strains.
    Twas such a gift $y^e$ Prophets sacred pen
On his departure left $y^e$ sons of men.
Thus he, & thus $y^e$ Swan her breath resigns          705
(Within $y^e$ beautys of Poetick lines,)
He white with innocence, his figure she,
& both harmonious, but the sweeter he.
Death learns to charm, & while it leads to bliss
Has found a lovely circumstance in this          710
To suit the meekest turn of easy mind,
& actions chearfull in an air resignd.
    Thou flock whom Moses to thy freedome led
How will't thou lay the venerable dead?
Go (if thy Fathers taught a work they knew)          715

Go build a Pyramid to Glory due,
Square y^e broad base, with sloping sides arise,
& lett the point diminish in the skys.
There leave the corps, suspending ore his head
The wand whose motion winds & waves obeyd.                    720
On Sabled Banners to y^e sight describe
The painted arms of evry mourning tribe,
& thus may publick grief adorn y^e tomb
Deep-streaming downwards through y^e vaulted room.
On the black stone à fair inscription raise        [f.17b]
That Sums his Government to speak his praise,
& may the style as brightly worth proclaim,
As if Affection with a pointed beam
Engravd or fird y^e words, or Honour due
Had with its self inlaid y^e tablet through.                 730
    But stop y^e pomp that is not mans to pay,
For God will grace him in a nobler way.
Mine eyes perceive an orb of heavnly state
With splendid forms & light serene repleat,
I hear the Sound of fluttring wings in air,                  735
I hear the tunefull tongues of Angels there,
They fly, they bear, they rest on Nebo's head,
& in thick glory wrap the rev'rend dead.
This errand crowns his songs, & tends to prove
His near communion with y^e quire above.                     740
Now swiftly down the Steepy mount they go,
Now swiftly glides their shining orb below,
& now moves off where rising grounds deny
To spread their vally to the distant eye.
Ye blessd inhabitants of glitt'ring air                      745
You've born y^e prophet but we know not where.
Perhaps least Israel overfondly led
In rating worth when envy leaves y^e dead,
Might plant a grove, invent new rites divine,
Make him their Idol, & his grave y^e shrine.                 750
    But what disorder? what repells y^e light       [f.18a]
& ere its season forces up y^e night?
Why sweep the spectres ore y^e blasted ground?
What shakes y^e mount with hollow-roaring sound?
Hell rolls beneath it, Terrour stalkes before               755
With shriekes & groans, & Horrour bursts a door,
& Satan rises in infernall state

Drawn up by Malice Envy Rage & Hate.
A darkning Vapour with sulphureous steam,
In pitchy curlings, edgd by sullen flame,                    760
& framd a chariot for yᵉ dreadfull Form,
drives whirling up on mad Confusions storm.
    Then fiercely turning where yᵉ Prophet dyd,
Nor shall thy nation scape my wrath he cry'd;
This corps Ile enter & thy flock mislead,                    765
& all thy Miracles my lyes shall aid.
But where?—Hes gon, & by yᵉ scented sky
The fav'rite courtiers have been lately nigh.
O slow to buisness, cursd in mischiefs hour,
Track on their Odours, & if Hell has powr—                   770
This said with spight & with a bent for ill
He shot in fury from yᵉ trembling hill.
    In vain Proud Fiend thy threats are half exprest,
& half ly choaking in thy scornfull breast,
His shining bearers have performd yᵉ rite,                   [f.18b]
& laid him softly down in shades of night.
A Warriour heads yᵉ band, Great Michael he,
Renownd for conquest in yᵉ warr with thee,
A sword of flame to stop thy course he bears,
Nor has thy rage availd, nor can thy snares,                 780
The Lord rebuke thy pride he meekly cryes:
The Lord has heard him & thy project dyes.
    Here Moses leaves my song, yᵉ tribes retire,
The desart flyes, & fourty years expire.
& now my fancy for awhile be still,                          785
& think of coming down from Nebo's hill.
Go Search among thy forms, & thence prepare
A cloud in folds of Soft-surrounding air,
Go find a breeze to lift thy cloud on high,
To waft thee gently rockd in open sky,                       790
Then stealing back to leave a silent calm,
& thee reposing in a grove of palm.
The place will suit my next-succeeding strain,
& Ile awake thee soon to sing again.

# Deborah.                                                    [f.19a]


*Time* Sire of *years* unwind thy leaf anew,
& still the past recall to present view,

Spread forth its circles, swiftly gaze y<sup>m</sup> ore,
But where an action's nobly sung before
There stop & stay for me whose thoughts design                    5
To make anothers song resound in mine.
Pass where y<sup>e</sup> priests procession bore the law,
When Jourdans parted waters fixd with awe,
While Israel marchd upon y<sup>e</sup> naked Sand,
Admird y<sup>e</sup> wonder, & obtaind the land.                       10
Slide through the num'rous fates of Canaans kings,
While conquest rode on *Expeditions* wings.
Glance over Israel at a single view
In bondage oft, & oft unbound anew,
Till Jabin rise, & Deborah stand enrolld                         15
On the broad guilded leafs revolving fold.
  O King subdu'd! O Woman born to fame!
O Wake my *fancy* for the glorious theme,
O wake my *fancy* with the sense of praise,
O wake with warblings of triumphant lays.                        20
The Land you rise in sultry suns invade,
But where you rise to sing you'le find a shade.
  Those trees in order & with verdure crownd,          [f.19b]
The Sacred *Prophetesses* tent surround.
& that fair palm afront exactly plact                            25
That overtops & overspreads the rest,
Near y<sup>e</sup> broad root a mossy bank supports,
Where *Justice* opens unexpensive courts.
There Deb'rah sits, the willing tribes repair,
Referr their causes, & she Judges there.                         30
Nor needs a guard to bring her subjects in,
Each *Grace* each *Virtue* proves a guard unseen.
Nor wants the penaltys enforcing law,
While *Great Opinion* gives effectuall awe.
  Now twenty years that rolld in heavy pain                      35
Saw Jabin gall them with *Oppressions* chain,
When she submissive to divine command,
Proclaims a warr for freedome o're y<sup>e</sup> land,
& bids young Barack with those men descend,
Whom in the mountains he for battle traind.                      40
Go, says the *Prophetess,* thy foes assail,
Go make ten thousand over all prevail,
Make Jabins captains feel thy glittering sword,
Make all his army: *God* has spoke the word.
He fitt for warr & *Israels* hope in sight                       45

Yet doubts y^e number & by that the fight,
Then thus replys with wish to stand secure,                    [f.20a]
Or eager thought to know the conquest sure:
Belovd of God, lend thou thy presence too
& I with gladness lead th' appointed few,                        50
But if thou wil't not lett thy son deny,
For whats ten thousand men or what am I?
If so, she crys, a share of toil be mine,
Another share & some dishonour thine,
For God to punish doubt resolves to show                         55
That less than numbers can suppress his foe;
You'le move to conquer, & the foes to yield,
But 'tis a womans act assures the field.
    Now seem the warriours in their ranks assignd,
Now furling banners flutter in the wind,                         60
Her words encourage, & his actions lead,
*Hope* spurrs them forward, *valour* draws y^e blade,
& *Freedome* like a fair reward for all
Stands reaching forth her hand & seems to call.
    On T'other side & allmost ore y^e plain                       65
Proud Sis'ra Jabins captain brings his men,
As thick as locusts on the vintage fly,
As thick as scatterd leaves in Autumn ly,
Bold with success against a nation tryd,
& proud of numbers, & secure in pride.                           70
    Now sound the trumpets, now my fancy warms,                   [f.20b]
& now methinks I view their toiles in arms,
The lively *Phantomes* tread my boundless mind
With no faint colours or weak strokes designd.
See where in distant conflict from afarr                         75
The pointed arrows bring the wounds of warr.
See where the lines with closer force engage,
& thrust the spear & whirl y^e sword of *rage*.
Here break the files & vainly strive to close,
There on their own repelld assist their foes.                    80
Here Deb'rah calls & Jabins souldiers fly,
There Barack fights & Jabins souldiers dy.
But now nine hundred chariots roll along,
Expert their guiders & their horses strong,
& *Terrour* rattling in their fierce array                        85
Bears down on Israel to restore the day.
O Lord of battles, O the dangers near,
Assist thine Israel or they perish here.

How swift is *Mercys* aid, behold it fly
On rushing tempests through yᵉ troubled sky,                              90
With dashing rain with pelting hail they blow,
& sharply drive them on the facing foe,
Thus blessd with help & onely touchd behind,
The fav'rite Nation presses in the wind.
But heat of action now disturbs yᵉ sight,                              [f.21a]
& wild *confusion* mingles all yᵉ fight,
Cold-whistling winds & shriekes of dying men
& groans & armour sound in all yᵉ plain.
The bands of Canaan fate no longer dare,
Oppressd by weather & destroyd by warr,                              100
& from his chariot whence he ruld yᵉ fight,
Their haughty Leader leaps to Joyn yᵉ flight.
See where he flys, & see the Victour near,
See rapid *Conquest* in pursuit of *Fear*,
See See they both make off, yᵉ work is ore,                              105
& *fancy* cleard of vision as before.
    Thus (if yᵉ mind of man may seem to move
With some resemblance of yᵉ skyes above)
When warrs are gath'ring in our hearts below
We've seen their battles in Ætheriall show:                              110
The Long-distended tracts of opening sky
The Phantoms Azure field of fight supply;
The whitish clouds an argent armour yield;
A radiant blazon guilds their argent shield;
Young glittring comets point yᵉ leveld spear,                              115
Which for the pennons hang their flaming hair;
& ore their helms for gallant glory dresst
Sit curles of air & nod upon the crest.
Thus armd they seem to march & seem to fight,                              [f.21b]
& seeming wounds & deaths delude yᵉ sight,                              120
The ruddy thunder-clouds look staind with gore,
& for yᵉ din of warr within they roar.
Then flys a side, & then a side pursues,
Till in the motion all their shapes they loose,
Dispersing air concludes yᵉ mimick scene,                              125
The sky shuts up & swiftly clears again.
    But does their Sis'ra share yᵉ common fate,
Or mourn his humbled pride in dark retreat?
With such enquiry near the palm repair,

Victorious *Honour* knows & tells it there.                          130
   To that fair type of Israels late success
Which nobly rises as its weights depress,
To that fair type returns yᵉ Joyfull band,
Whose courage rose to free their groaning land,
There stands yᵉ Leader in the pomp of arms,                          135
There stands the Judge in beautys awfull charms.
& whilst reclind upon the resting spear
He pants with chace & breaths in calmer air,
Her thoughts are working with a backward view,
& woud in song the great exploit renew.                              140
   She sees an armd *Oppressions* hundred hands
impose its fetters on the promisd lands.
She sees her nation struggling in the chains,                        [f.22a]
& warrs arising with unequall trains.
She sees their feats in arms, the field embru'd,                     145
The foe disorderd, & the foe pursud.
Till *Conquest* dressd in rays of Glory come
With *Peace* & *Freedome* brought in triumph home.
Then round her heart a beamy *gladness* plays,
Which darting forward thus converts to *praise*.                     150

   For Israels late avengings on yᵉ foe                [Judges 5]
When led by no compelling powr below,
When each sprung forward of their own accord,
For this, for all the mercy praise the Lord.
   Hear O ye Kings, ye neighbring Princes hear,        155
My song triumphant shall instruct your fear,
My song triumphant bids your glory bow
To God confessd the God of Jacob now.
   O Glorious Lord when with thy sov'raign hand
Thou led thy nation off from Edoms Land,                             160
Then trembled Earth, & shook yᵉ Heav'ns on high,
& clouds in drops forsook yᵉ melted sky,
With tumbling waters hills were heard to roar,
& felt such shocks as Sinai felt before.
   But fear abating which by time decays,             165
The Kings of Canaan rose in Shamgars days,
& still continud into Jaels times                                    [f.22b]
Their empire fixing with succesfull crimes.
*Oppression* ravagd all our lost abodes,
Nor durst yᵉ people trust yᵉ common roads,                           170
But paths perplexd & unfrequented chose

To shun the dangers of insulting foes.
Thus direfull *wast* deformd y<sup>e</sup> country round,
Unpeopled towns & disimprovd the ground.
Till I resolving in the gap to stand                              175
I *Deb'rah* rose a Mother of the Land,
Where others slaves by settled custome grown
Coud serve & chuse to serve the Gods unknown,
Where others sufferd with a tame regrett
Destruction spilling blood in ev'ry gate,                        180
& fourty thousand had not for the field
One spear offensive or defensive shield.
    O towrds y<sup>e</sup> Leaders of my nation move
O beat my warming heart with sense of love,
Commend th' Assertours on their own accord,                      185
& bless y<sup>e</sup> Sovreign causer, bless the Lord.
    Speak ye that ride with powr returnd in state,
Speak ye the praise that rule y<sup>e</sup> Judgement seat,
Speak ye the praise to God that walk y<sup>e</sup> roads,
While *Safety* brings you to restord abodes.                     190
    The rescud villagers no more affraid          [f.23a]
Of Archers lurking in the faithless Shade,
& sudden death conveyd from sounding strings,
Shall safe-approach y<sup>e</sup> waters rising springs,
& while their turns of drawing there they wait,                  195
Loytring in ease upon a grassy Seat,
Call all y<sup>e</sup> blessing of y<sup>e</sup> Lord to mind,
& sing the Lord in all y<sup>e</sup> blessing kind.
The townsmen rescud from y<sup>e</sup> tyrants reign
Shall flock with Joy to fill their walls again,                  200
See *Justice* in y<sup>e</sup> gates her ballance bear,
& none but her unsheath a weapon there.
    Awake O *Deb'rah*, O Awake to praise,
Awake & utter forth triumphant lays,
Arise O *Barack*, be thy pomp begun,                             205
Lead on thy triumph thou *Abinoams* Son,
Thy captives bound in chains when Gods Decree
Made humbled Princes stoop their necks to thee,
When He the Giver of Success in fight
Advancd a Woman Ore y<sup>e</sup> Sons of *Might*.                210
    Against this *Amalek* of banded foes
I *Deb'rah* root of All y<sup>e</sup> warr arose,
From *Ephraim* sprung, & leading Ephraims line,
The next in rising *Benjamin* was thine.

The ruling heads of half *Manassehs* land                    [f.23b]
To serve in danger left their safe command.
The tribe of *Zebuluns* unactive men
For Glorious arms forsook yᵉ peacefull pen.
The Lords of *Issachar* with Deb'rah went,
The tribe with *Barack* to yᵉ vale was sent,                    220
Where he on foot performd the gen'ralls part,
& shard yᵉ souldiers toil to raise their heart.

But *Reubens* strange divisions Justly wrought
Amongst his brethren deep concern of thought.
Ah while yᵉ nation in affliction lay,                          225
How coudst thou Reuben by yᵉ sheepfold stay?
& lett thy bleating flock divert yᵉ days
That idely passd thee with inglorious ease.
Divided Tribe, without thy danger free,
Deep were the Searchings of our hearts for thee.              230
Our *Gilead* too by such example swayd
With unconcern beyond yᵉ river staid,
& *Dan* in ships at sea for safety rode,
& frighted *Asher* in its rocks abode.

Now Sing yᵉ field, yᵉ feats of warr begun,                    235
& Praise thy *Nepthali* with *Zebulun*.
To deaths exposd, in posts advancd they stood,                [f.24a]
With soules resolvd & gallant rage of blood.
Then came yᵉ Kings & fought, yᵉ Gatherd Kings
By waters streaming from *Megiddo's* springs,                 240
In *Tanaach* vale sustaind yᵉ daring toil,
Yet neither fought for pay, nor won yᵉ spoil.
The skys indulgent to the cause of right
On Israels side against their army fight;
In evil aspects starrs & Planets range,                       245
& by the weather in tempestuous change
Promote their dire distress, & make it known
That God has hosts above to save his own.
The *Kishon* swelld, grew rapid as they fled,
& rolld them sinking down its sandy bed.                      250
O River *Kishon*, River of renown!
& O my soul that trod their glory down!
The stony paths by which disorderd flight
Conveyd their troops & chariots from yᵉ fight
With rugged points their horses hoofs distresst,              255
& broke them prancing in impetuous hast.

Curse curse ye *Meroz*, curse yᵉ town abhorrd,

(So spake y<sup>e</sup> glorious *Angel* of y<sup>e</sup> Lord.)
For *Meroz* came not into field prepard
To Joyn that side on which the *Lord* declard.　　　260
　But bless ye *Jael,* be y<sup>e</sup> *Kenites* name　　　[f.24b]
Above our womens blessd in endless fame.
The Captain faint with sore fatigue of flight,
Implord for water to support his might,
& milk she powrd him while he water sought,　　　265
& in a lordly dish her butter brought.
With courage well deserving to prevail
One hand her hammer held & one y<sup>e</sup> nail,
& him reclind to sleep she boldly slew,
She Smote, she piercd, she struck y<sup>e</sup> temples through,　　　270
Before her feet reluctant on the clay
He bowd he fell, he bowd he fell he lay,
He bowd he fell he dyd. by such degrees
As thrice she struck each strokes effect she sees.
　His mother gazd with long-expecting eyes,　　　275
& grown impatient through y<sup>e</sup> lattice cryes;
Why moves y<sup>e</sup> chariot of my son so slow?
Or what affairs retard his coming so?
Her Ladys answerd.— but she woud not stay,
(For Pride had taught what Flattry meant to say)　　　280
They've sped she says, & now y<sup>e</sup> prey they share,
For each a damsel or a lovely pair,
For *Sis'ras* part a robe of gallant grace
Where diverse colours rich embroid'ry trace,
Meet for y<sup>e</sup> necks of those who win y<sup>e</sup> spoil　　　[f.25a]
When triumph offers its reward for toil.
　Thus perish all who Gods decrees oppose,
Thus like y<sup>e</sup> vanquishd perish all thy foes.
But lett y<sup>e</sup> men that in thy name delight
Be like y<sup>e</sup> Sun in heavnly glory bright,　　　290
When mounted on y<sup>e</sup> dawn he posts away,
& with full strength encreases on the day.

　Twas here y<sup>e</sup> *Prophetess* respird f<sup>m</sup> song.
Then loudly shouted all y<sup>e</sup> chearfull throng,
By freedome gaind, by victory compleat,　　　295
Prepard for mirth irregularly great.
The frowns of sorrow gave their ancient place
To pleasure drawn in smiles on ev'ry face.
The groans of slav'ry were no longer wrung,

But thoughts of comfort from y^e blessing sprung.                    300
& as they shouted in y^e breezy west,
Amongst y^e plumes that deckt y^e singers crest
The Spirit of *Applause* it self conveyd
On waving air, & lightly wanton plaid.
Such was y^e case, (or such Ideas flow                               305
From thought replenishd with triumphant show.)
   What raisd their Joy their love coud also raise,          [f.25b]
& each contended in the words of praise,
& evry word proclaimd the wonders past,
& God was still y^e first & still y^e last,                         310
Deep in their soules y^e fair impression lay,
Deep-tracd & never to be worn away.
   From hence y^e rescud generation still
Abhorrd the practice of rebellious ill,
& feard the punishment for ill abhorrd,                             315
& lovd repentance & adord y^e Lord.
   From hence in all their day y^e Lord was kind,
His face serene with settled favour shind,
Fair banishd *Order* was recalld in state,
The Laws revivd, the princes ruld y^e gate,                         320
*Peace* cheard y^e vales, *Contentment* laughd w^th Peace,
Gay-blooming *Plenty* rose with large encrease,
Sweet *Mercy* those who thought on mercy blesst,
& so for fourty years y^e land had rest.
   Rest happy Land awhile, ah longer so                             325
didst thou thine happiness sincerely know!
But soon thy quiet with thy goodness past,
& in the song alone obtaind to last.
   Live song triumphant, live in fair record,
& teach succeeding times to love y^e Lord:                          330
For fancy moves by bright example wood,                     [f.26a]
& wins y^e mind with images of good.
   Touchd with a sacred rage & heavnly flame,
I strive to sing thine universall aim,
To quit y^e subject, & in lays sublime                              335
The morall fitt for any point of time:
Then go my verses with applying strain
Go form a triumph not ascribd to men.
   Lett all y^e clouds of *Grief* impending ly,
& storms of *Trouble* drive along y^e sky,                          340
Then Humble *Piety* thine accents raise,
For prayr will prove y^e powrfull charm of ease.

Lo now thy soul has spoke its best desires,
How blessings answer what y^e prayr requires.
Before thy sighs the cloudes of *Grief* retreat,                    345
The Storms of *trouble* by thy tears abate,
& Radiant *Glory* from her upper sphear
Lookes down & glitters in relented air.
  Rise Lovely *Piety* from earthy bed,
The Parted flame descends upon thine head,                          350
This wondrous Mitre framd by Sacred *Love*,
& for thy triumph sent thee from above,
In two bright points with upper rays aspires,
& rounds thy temples with innocuous fires.
Rise Lovely *Piety*, with Pomp appear,                              [f.26b]
& thou Kind *Mercy* Lend a chariot here,
On either side fair *Fame* & *Honour* place,
Behind lett *Plenty* walk in hand with peace,
While *Irreligion* mutt'ring horrid sound
With fierce & proud *Oppression* backward bound                     360
dragg by the wheeles along y^e dusty plain,
& gnashing lick y^e ground, & curse with pain.
  Now come ye thousands & more thousands yet,
With order Joyn to fill y^e train of state,
Soules tund for praising to y^e temple bring,                       365
& thus amidst y^e Sacred Musick sing.
Hail *Piety!* triumphant Goodness hail!
Hail O prevailing! Ever O prevail!
At thine Entreaty *Justice* leaves to frown,
& *Wrath* appeasing lays y^e Thunder down,                          370
The tender heart of yearning *Mercy* burns,
*Love* asks a blessing & y^e *Lord* returns.
In his great name that heavn & earth has made
In his great name alone we find our aid,
Then bless the Name, & lett y^e world adore                         375
From this time forward & for evermore.


# Hannah.                                                           [f.27a]


  Now Crowds move off, retiring trumpetts sound
On Eccho's dying in their last rebound,
The notes of fancy seem no longer strong,
But sweetning closes fitt a private song.

So when the storms forsake ye seas command     5
To break their forces in the winding land,
No more their blasts tumultuous rage proclaim,
But sweep in murmurs ore a murm'ring stream.
    Then Seek ye Subject & its song be mine
Whose numbers next in Sacred story shine;     10
Go brightly-working thought, prepard to fly
Above ye page on hov'ring pinnions ly,
& beat with stronger force to make thee rise
Where beautious Hannah meets ye searching eyes.
    There frame a town & fix a tent with cords,     15
The town be Shiloh calld, the tent ye Lords.
Carvd pillars filleted with silver rear
To close ye curtains in an outward square,
But those within it which ye porch uphold
Be finely wrought & overlaid with gold.     20
    Here Eli comes to take ye resting Seat,     [f.27b]
Slow-moving forward with a revrend gate,
Sacred in office, venerably sage
& venerably great in silverd age.
    Here Hannah comes, a melancholly wife     25
Reproachd for barren in ye marriage life.
Like summer-mornings she to sight appears,
Bedewd & shining in the midst of tears.
Her heart in bitterness of grief she bowd,
& thus her wishes to the Lord she vowd.     30
If thou thine handmaid with compassion see,
If I my God am not forgott by thee,
If in mine offspring thou prolong my line,
The Child I wish for all his days be thine,
His life devoted in thy courts be led,     35
& not a rasour come upon his head.
    So from recesses of her inmost soul
Through moving lips her still devotion stole:
As silent waters glide through parted trees
Whose branches tremble with a rising breeze.     40
The words were lost because her heart was low,
But free desire had taught ye mouth to go.
This Eli markd, & with a voice severe,
While yet she multiplyd her thoughts in prayr,
How long shall wine he crys distract thy breast,     45
Begon & lay ye drunken fitt by rest.
Ah says ye mourner count not this for sin,     [f.28a]

It is not wine but grief that workes within,
The spirit of thy wretched handmaid know,
Her prayr's complaint, & her condition woe.                    50
Then spake ye Sacred Priest, in peace depart,
& with thy comfort God fullfill thine heart.
His blessing thus pronouncd with awfull sound,
The Vot'ry bending leaves ye solemn ground,
She seems confirmd the Lord has heard her crys,               55
& Chearfull Hope the tears of trouble drys,
& makes her alterd eyes irradiate roll
With Joy that dawns in thought upon ye soul.
  Now lett ye Town & Tent & court remain,
& leap the time till Hannah comes again.                      60
As painted prospects skip along ye green
from hills to mountains eminently seen,
& leave their intervalls that sink below
In deep retirement unexpressd to show.
  Behold she comes (but not as once she came                  65
To grieve to sigh & teach her eyes to stream.)
Content adorns her with a lively face,
An open look, & smiling kind of grace.
Her little Samuel in her arms she bears
The wish of long desire & Child of prayrs,                    70
& as ye sacrifice she brought begun,
To rev'rend Eli she presents her son.
Here, crys ye Mother, here my Lord may see         [f.28b]
The woman come who prayd in grief by thee,
The Child I su'd for God with bounty gave,                    75
& what he granted let him now receive.
  But still ye Vot'ry feeles her temper move
With all ye tender violence of Love.
That still enjoys ye gift, & inly burns
To search for larger or for more returns.                     80
Then filld with blessings which allure to praise,
& raisd by Joy to soul-enchanting lays,
Thus thankes ye Lord beneficently-kind
In sweet effusions of ye gratefull mind.


  My lifting heart with more than common heat      [1 Samuel 2]
Sends up its thankes to God on ev'ry beat.
My glory raisd above ye reach of scorn
In God exalts its highly-planted horn.
My mouth enlargd mine enemy defys,

& finds in Gods salvation full replys.                        90
O Bright in holy beautys, Powr divine,
Theres none whose glory can compare w<sup>th</sup> thine,
None share thine honours, nay theres none beside,
No rock on which thy creatures can confide.
     Ye proud in spirit who your gifts adore,            95
Unlearn the fault & speak with pride no more:
No more in words your arrogance be shown,        [f.29a]
Nor call y<sup>e</sup> workes of Providence your own,
Since he that rules us infinitely knows,
& as he will his acts of Powr dispose.              100
     The strong whose sinewy forces archd y<sup>e</sup> bow
Have seen it shatterd by y<sup>e</sup> conqu'ring foe.
The weak have felt their nerves more firmly brace,
& new-sprung vigour in the limbs encrease.
The full whom varyd tasts of plenty fed           105
Have lett their labour out to gain their bread.
The poor that languishd in a starving state
Content & full have ceased to beg their meat.
The barren womb, no longer barren now,
(O be my thankes accepted with my vow)         110
In pleasure wonders at a mothers pain,
& sees her offspring & conceives again,
While she that gloryd in her numerous heirs,
Now broke by feebleness no longer bears.
     Such turns their rising from y<sup>e</sup> Lord derive,      115
The Lord that kills the Lord y<sup>t</sup> makes alive.
He brings by sickness down to gaping graves,
& by restoring health from sickness saves;
He makes y<sup>e</sup> poor by keeping back his store,     [f.29b]
& makes y<sup>e</sup> rich by blessing men with more;      120
He sinking hearts with bitter grief annoys,
Or lifts them bounding with enlivend Joys.
     He takes y<sup>e</sup> beggar from his humble clay
From off y<sup>e</sup> dunghill where despisd he lay
To mix with Princes in a rank supream,          125
Fill thrones of Honour & inherit fame.
For all the pillars of exalted state
So nobly firm so beautifully great,
Whose various orders bear y<sup>e</sup> rounded ball
Which woud without them to confusion fall,      130
All are y<sup>e</sup> Lords, at his disposure stand,
& prop y<sup>e</sup> governd world at his command.

His mercy still more wonderfully sweet
Shall guard y^e righteous & uphold their feet.
While through y^e darkness of y^e wicked soul                135
Amazement Dread & Desperation roll,
While envy stops their tongues, & hopeless grief
that sees their fears but not their fears relief,
& they their strength as unavailing view,
Since none shall trust in that & safely too.               140
   The foes of Israel for his Israels sake
God will to pieces in his anger break.
His bolts of thunder from an opend sky                     [f.30a]
Shall on their heads with force unerring fly.
His voice shall call, & all y^e world shall hear,          145
& all for sentence at his Seat appear.
   But mount to gentler praises, mount again
My thought prophetick of Messiahs reign,
Perceive the glorys which around him shine,
& thus thine hymn be crownd with grace divine.             150
"Strength to y^e King for mans salvation born,
"& honours rising like y^e lifted horn.


   Tis here y^e numbers find a bright repose,
The vows accepted & the Vot'ry goes.
But thou my soul upon her accents hung,                    155
& sweetly pleasd with what she sweetly sung,
Prolong the pleasure with thine inward eyes,
Turn back thy thought, & see y^e subject rise.
   In her peculiar case y^e song begun,
& for awhile through private blessings run,                160
As through their banks the curling waters play,
& soft in murmurs kiss y^e flowry way.
With force encreasing then she leaps y^e bounds,
& largely flows on more extended grounds,
Spreads wide & wider, till vast seas appear,               165
& boundless views of Providence are here.
   How Swift these views along her Anthem glide,           [f.30b]
As waves on waves pushd forward in y^e tide!
How swift thy wonders ore my fancy sweep,
O Providence thou great unfathomd deep,                    170
Where Resignation gently dips y^e wing,
& learns to love & thank, admire & sing,
But bold presumptious Reasnings diving down
To reach y^e bottom, in their diving drown.

Neglecting man forgetfull of thy ways    175
Nor owns thy care, nor thinkes of giving praise,
But from himself his happiness derives,
& thankes his wisdome when by thine he thrives.
His limbs at ease in soft repose he spreads,
Bewitchd with vain delights on flowry beds,   180
& while his sense y^e fragrant breezes kiss,
He meditates a waking dream of bliss.
He thinks of Kingdomes & their crowns are near;
He thinkes of glorys & their rays appear;
He thinks of beautys & a lovely face    185
Serenely smiles in evry taking grace;
He thinks of riches & their heaps arise
Display their glittring forms & fix his eyes;
Thus drawn with pleasures in a charming view
Rising he reaches & woud faign pursue.   190
But still y^e fleeting shadows mock his care,  [f.31a]
& still his fingers grasp at yielding air,
What ere our tempers as their comforts want
It is not mans to take but Gods to grant.
 If then persisting in the vain design   195
We seek true bliss unblessd with help divine,
Still may we search, still search without relief,
Nor onely want a bliss but find a grief.
That such conviction may to sight appear
Sitt down ye Sons of men spectatours here,  200
Behold a scene upon your folly wrought,
& lett this lively scene instruct y^e thought.
 Boy blow thy pipe untill y^e bubble rise,
Then cast it off to float upon y^e skys,
Still swell its sides with breath. O beautious frame! 205
It grows, it shines, be now the world thy name.
Methinks Creation forms itself within,
The men, the towns, y^e birds, y^e trees are seen,
The skys above present an Azure show,
& lovely Verdure paints an earth below.   210
Ile wind my self in this delightfull sphere,
& live a thousand years of pleasure there,
Rolld up in blisses which around me close,
& now regald with these & now with those.
False hope, but falser words of Joy farewell,  [f.31b]
You've rent the lodging where I meant to dwell,

My bubble's burst, my prospects disappear,
& leave behind a moral & a tear.
    If at the type our dreaming soules awake,
& Hannahs strains their Just impression make,                        220
The boundless powr of Providence we know,
& fix our trust on nothing here below.
Then He grown pleasd that men his greatness own,
Lookes down Serenely from his starry throne,
& bids y^e blessed days our prayrs have won                          225
Put on their glorys & prepare to run.
For which our thanks be Justly sent above,
Enlargd by gladness, & inspird with Love:
For which his praises be for ever sung,
Oh Sweet employments of y^e gratefull tongue!                       230
    Burst forth my temper in a godly flame,
For all his blessings laud his holy name:
That ere mine eyes saluted chearfull day
A gift devoted in y^e womb I lay,
like Samuel vowd before my breath I drew,                           235
O coud I prove in life like Samuel too!
That all my frame is exquisitely wrought,
The world enjoyd by sense, & God by thought;
That living streams through living Channels glide      [f.32a]
To make this frame by natures course abide;                         240
That for its good by Providences care
Fire Joyns with water, earth concurrs w^th air;
That Mercys ever-inexhausted store
Is pleasd to proffer & to promise more,
& all y^e proffers stream with grace divine,                        245
& all y^e promises with glory shine.
O praise the Lord my Soul, in one accord
Lett all that is within me praise y^e Lord;
O praise y^e Lord my soul, & ever strive
To keep the sweet remembrances alive:                               250
Still raise y^e kind affections of thine heart,
Raise evry gratefull word to bear a part,
With ev'ry word the strains of love devise,
Awake thine harp, & thou thy self arise,
Then if his Mercy be not half expresst,                             255
Lett wondring silence magnify y^e rest.

# Biblical Poems
## from *Posthumous Works* (1758)

## *DAVID.*

MY thought, on views of admiration hung,
Intently ravish'd and depriv'd of tongue,
Now darts a while on earth, a while in air,
Here mov'd with praise and mov'd with glory there;
The joys entrancing and the mute surprize                    5
Half fix the blood, and dim the moist'ning eyes;
Pleasure and praise on one another break,
And Exclamation longs at heart to speak;
When thus my Genius, on the work design'd
Awaiting closely, guides the wand'ring mind.                 10
   If while thy thanks wou'd in thy lays be wrought,
A bright astonishment involve the thought,
If yet thy temper wou'd attempt to sing,
Another's quill shall imp thy feebler wing;
Behold the name of royal David near,                         15
Behold his musick and his measures here,
Whose harp Devotion in a rapture strung,
And left no state of pious souls unsung.
   Him to the wond'ring world but newly shewn,
Celestial poetry pronounc'd her own;                         20
A thousand hopes, on clouds adorn'd with rays,
Bent down their little beauteous forms to gaze;
Fair-blooming Innocence with tender years,
And native Sweetness for the ravish'd ears,
Prepar'd to smile within his early song,                     25
And brought their rivers, groves, and plains along;
Majestick Honour at the palace bred,
Enrob'd in white, embroider'd o'er with red,

214

Reach'd forth the scepter of her royal state,
His forehead touch'd, and bid his lays be great;          30
Undaunted Courage deck'd with manly charms,
With waving-azure plumes, and gilded arms,
Displaid the glories, and the toils of fight,
Demanded fame, and call'd him forth to write.
To perfect these the sacred spirit came,          35
By mild infusion of celestial flame,
And mov'd with dove-like candour in his breast,
And breath'd his graces over all the rest.
Ah! where the daring flights of men aspire
To match his numbers with an equal fire;          40
In vain they strive to make proud Babel rise,
And with an earth-born labour touch the skies.
While I the glitt'ring page resolve to view,
That will the subject of my lines renew;
The Laurel wreath, my fames imagin'd shade,          45
Around my beating temples fears to fade;
My fainting fancy trembles on the brink,
And David's God must help or else I sink.
   As rolling rivers in their channels flow,
Swift from aloft, but on the level slow;          50
Or rage in rocks, or glide along the plains,
So, just so copious, move the Psalmist's strains;
So sweetly vary'd with proportion'd heat,
So gently clear or so sublimely great,
While nature's seen in all her forms to shine,          55
And mix with beauties drawn from truth divine;
Sweet beauties (sweet affections endless rill,)
That in the soul like honey drops distil.
   Hail holy spirit, hail supremely kind,
Whose inspirations thus enlarg'd the mind;          60
Who taught him what the gentle shepherd sings,
What rich expressions suit the port of kings;
What daring words describe the soldiers heat,
And what the prophet's extasies relate;
Nor let his worst condition be forgot,          65
In all this splendour of exulted thought.
On one thy diff'rent sorts of graces fall,
Still made for each, of equall force in all,
And while from heav'nly courts he feels a flame,
He sings the place from whence the blessing came;          70
And makes his inspirations sweetly prove

The tuneful subject of the mind they move.
   Immortal spirit, light of life instil'd,
Who thus the bosom of a mortal fill'd,
Tho' weak my voice and tho' my light be dim,          75
Yet fain I'd praise thy wond'rous gifts in him;
Then since thine aid's attracted by desire,
And they that speak thee right must feel thy fire;
Vouchsafe a portion of thy grace divine,
And raise my voice and in my numbers shine;         80
I sing of David, David sings of thee,
Assist the Psalmist, and his work in me.
   But now my verse, arising on the wing,
What part of all thy subject wilt thou sing?
How fire thy first attempt, in what resort         85
Of Palestina's plains, or Salem's court?
Where, as his hands the solemn measure play'd,
Curs'd fiends with torment and confusion fled;
Where, at the rosy spring of chearful light
(If pious fame record tradition right)         90
A soft Efflation of celestial fire
Came like a rushing breeze and shook the Lyre;
Still sweetly giving ev'ry trembling string
So much of sound as made him wake to sing.
   Within my view the country first appears,         95
The country first enjoy'd his youthful years;
Then frame thy shady Landscapes in my strain,
Some conscious mountain or accustom'd plain;
Where by the waters, on the grass reclin'd,
With notes he rais'd, with notes he calm'd his mind;         100
For through the paths of rural life I'll stray,
And in his pleasures paint a shepherds day.
   With grateful sentiments, with active will,
With voice exerted, and enliv'ning skill,
His free return of thanks he duely paid,         105
And each new day new beams of bounty shed.
Awake my tuneful harp, awake he crys,
Awake my lute, the sun begins to rise;
My God, I'm ready now! then takes a flight,
To purest Piety's exalted height;         110
From thence his soul, with heav'n itself in view,
On humble prayers and humble praises flew.
The praise as pleasing and as sweet the prayer,
As incense curling up thro' morning air.

When t'wards the field with early steps he trod,     115
And gaz'd around and own'd the works of God,
Perhaps in sweet melodious words of praise
He drew the prospect which adorn'd his ways;
The soil but newly visited with rain,
The river of the Lord with springing grain     120
Inlarge, encrease the soft'ned furrow blest,
The year with goodness crown'd, with beauty drest,
And still to pow'r divine ascribe it all,
From whose high paths the drops of fatness fall;
Then in the song the smiling sights rejoyce,     125
And all the mute creation finds a voice;
With thick returns delightful Ecchos fill
The pastur'd green, or soft ascending hill,
Rais'd by the bleatings of unnumb'red sheep,
To boast their glories in the crowds they keep;     130
And corn that's waving in the western gale,
With joyful sound proclaims the cover'd vale.
    When e'er his flocks the lovely shepherd drove
To neighb'ring waters, to the neighb'ring grove;
To Jordan's flood refresh'd by cooling wind,     135
Or Cedron's brook to mossy banks confin'd,
In easy notes and guise of lowly swain,
'Twas thus he charm'd and taught the listning train.
    The Lord's my Shepherd bountiful and good,
I cannot want since he provides me food;     140
Me for his sheep along the verdant meads,
Me all too mean his tender mercy leads;
To taste the springs of life and taste repose
Wherever living pasture sweetly grows.
And as I cannot want I need not fear,     145
For still the presence of my shepherd's near;
Through darksome vales where beasts of prey resort,
Where death appears with all his dreadful court,
His rod and hook direct me when I stray,
He calls to Fold, and they direct my way.     150
    Perhaps when seated on the river's brink,
He saw the tender sheep at noon-day drink,
He sung the land where milk and honey glide
And fat'ning plenty rolls upon the tide.
    Or fix'd within the freshness of a shade,     155
Whose boughs diffuse their leaves around his head,
He borrow'd notions from the kind retreat,

Then sung the righteous in their happy state,
And how by providential care, success
Shall all their actions in due season bless.                           160
So firm they stand, so beautiful they look,
As planted trees aside the purling brook:
Not faded by the rays that parch the plain,
Nor careful for the want of dropping rain:
The leaves sprout forth, the rising branches shoot,        165
And summer crowns them with the ripen'd fruit.
    But if the flow'ry field with vari'd hue
And native sweetness entertain'd his view;
The flow'ry field with all the glorious throng
Of lively colours, rose to paint his song;                            170
Its pride and fall within the numbers ran
And spake the life of transitory man.
    As grass arises by degrees unseen
To deck the breast of earth with lovely green,
'Till Nature's order brings the with'ring days,               175
And all the summer's beauteous pomp decays;
So by degrees unseen doth man arise,
So blooms by course and so by course he dies.
Or as her head the gawdy flowret heaves,
Spreads to the sun and boasts her silken leaves;            180
'Till accidental winds their glory shed,
And then they fall before the time to fade;
So man appears, so falls in all his prime,
'Ere age approaches on the steps of time.
But thee, my God! thee still the same we find,              185
Thy glory lasting, and thy mercy kind;
That still the just and all his race may know
No cause to mourn their swift account below.
    When from beneath he saw the wand'ring sheep
That graz'd the level range along the steep,                   190
Then rose, the wanton straglers home to call,
Before the pearly dews at ev'ning fall;
Perhaps new thoughts the rising ground supply,
And that employs his mind, which fills his eye.
From pointed hills, he crys, my wishes tend,                195
To that great hill from whence supports descend:
The Lord's that hill, that place of sure defence,
My wants obtain their certain help from thence.

And as large hills projected shadows throw,
To ward the sun from off the vales below,                    200
Or for their safety stop the blasts above,
That with raw vapours loaded, nightly rove;
So shall protection o'er his servants spread,
And I repose beneath the sacred shade,
Unhurt by rage, that like a summer's day,                    205
Destroys and scorches with impetuous ray;
By wasting sorrows undepriv'd of rest
That fall like damps by moon-shine, on the breast.
Here from the mind the prospects seem to wear,
And leave the couch'd design appearing bare;                 210
And now no more the Shepherd sings his Hill,
But sings the sovereign Lord's protection still.
For as he sees the night prepar'd to come
On wings of ev'ning, he prepares for home,
And in the song thus adds a blessing more,                   215
To what the thought within the figure bore:
Eternal goodness manifestly still
Preserves my soul from each approach of ill:
Ends all my days, as all my days begin,
And keeps my goings and my comings in.                       220
    Here think the sinking sun descends apace,
And from thy first attempt, my fancy, cease;
Here bid the ruddy shepherd quit the plain,
And to the fold return his flocks again.
Go, least the lyon or the shagged bear,                      225
Thy tender lambs with savage hunger tear;
Tho' neither bear nor lyon match thy might,
When in their rage they stood reveal'd to sight;
Go, least thy wanton sheep returning home,
Shou'd as they pass thro' doubtful darkness roam.            230
Go ruddy youth, to Beth'lem turn thy way,
On Beth'lem's road conclude the parting day.
    Methinks he goes as twilight leads the night,
And sees the Crescent rise with silver light;
His words consider all the sparkling show,                   235
With which the stars in golden order glow.
And what is man, he crys, that thus thy kind,
Thy wond'rous love, has lodg'd him in thy mind?
For him they glitter; him the beasts of prey,

That scare my sheep, and these my sheep, obey.                        240
O Lord, our Lord, with how deserv'd a fame,
Do's earth record the glories of thy name.
Then as he thus devoutly walks along,
And finds the road as finish'd with the song;
He sings with lifted hands and lifted eyes,                           245
Be this, my God, an ev'ning sacrifice.
    But now, the lowly dales, the trembling groves,
O'er which the whisper'd breeze serenely roves,
Leave all the course of working fancy clear,
Or only grace another subject here;                                   250
For in my purpose new designs arise,
Whose brightning images engage mine eyes.
Then here my verse thy louder accents raise,
Thy theme thro' lofty paths of glory trace,
Call forth his honours in imperial throngs                            255
And strive to touch his more exalted songs.
    While yet in humble vales his harp he strung,
While yet he follow'd after Ewes with young;
Eternal wisdom chose him for his own,
And from the flock advanc'd him to the throne;                       260
That there his upright heart and prudent hand,
With more distinguish'd skill and high command,
Might act the shepherd in a noble sphere,
And take his nation into regal care.
He cou'd of mercy then and justice sing,                              265
Those radiant virtues that adorn a king,
That make his reign blaze forth with bright renown,
Beyond those Gems whose splendour decks a crown:
That fixing peace, by temper'd love and fear,
Make plains abound, and barren mountains bear.                       270
To thee to whom these attributes belong,
To thee my God, he cry'd, I send my song,
To thee from whom my regal glory came,
I sing the forms in which my court I frame;
Assist the models of imperfect skill,                                275
O come with sacred aid, and fix my will.
A wise behaviour in my private ways,
And all my soul dispos'd to publick peace,
Shall daily strive to let my subjects see
A perfect pattern how to live in me.                                 280
Still will I think as still my glories rise,
To set no wicked thing before mine eyes.

Nor will I choose the favourites of state ⎫
Among those men that have incur'd thine hate, ⎬
Whose vice but makes 'em scandalously great; ⎭ 285
'Tis time, that all whose froward rage of heart
Wou'd vex my realm, shall from my realm depart;
'Tis time that all whose private sland'ring lye
Leads judgment falsly, shall by judgment dye;
And time the Great who loose the reins to pride, 290
Shall with neglect and scorn be laid aside.
But o'er the tracts that my commands obey,
I'll send my light with sharp disarming ray,
Thro' dark retreats where humble minds abide,
Thro' shades of peace where modest tempers hide; 295
To find the good that may support my state,
And having found them, then to make them great.
My voice shall raise them from the lonely cell,
With me to govern and with me to dwell.
My voice shall flatt'ry and deceit disgrace, 300
And in their room exulted virtue place;
That with an early care and stedfast hand,
The wicked perish from the faithful land.
    When on the throne he sat in calm repose,
And with a royal hope his Offspring rose, 305
His prayers, anticipating time, reveal
Their deep concernment for the publick weal;
Upon a good forecasted thought they run,
For common blessings in the king begun:
For righteousness and judgment strictly fair, 310
Which from the king descends upon his heir.
So when his life and all his labour cease,
The reign succeeding brings succeeding peace;
So still the poor shall find impartial laws,
And Orphans still a guardian of their cause: 315
And stern oppression have its galling yoke,
And rabid teeth of prey to pieces broke.
Then wond'ring at the glories of his way,
His friends shall love, his daunted foes obey;
For peaceful Commerce neighb'ring kings apply 320
And with great presents court the grand ally.
For him rich gums shall sweet Arabia bear,
For him rich Sheba, mines of gold prepare,
Him Tharsis, him the foreign isles shall greet,
And ev'ry nation bend beneath his feet. 325

And thus his honours far extended grow,
The type of great Messiah's reign below.
  But worldly realms that in his accents shine,
Are left beneath the full advanc'd design,
When thoughts of empire in the mind encrease                330
O'er all the limits that determine place,
If thus the monarch's rising fancy move
To search for more unbounded realms above,
In which celestial courts the king maintains
And o'er the vast extent of nature reigns;                  335
He then describes in elevated words,
His Israel's shepherd, as the Lord of Lords:
How bright between the Cherubims he sits,
What dazling lustre all his throne emits,
How righteousness with judgment join'd, support            340
The regal seat, and dignify the court.
How fairest honour and majestick state
The presence grace, and strength and beauty wait;
What glitt'ring ministers around him stand,
To fly like winds or flames at his command.                345
How sure the beams on which his palace rise
Are set in waters rais'd above the skies,
How wide the skies like outspread curtains fly
To vail majestick light from humane eye,
Or form'd the wide expanded vaults above,                  350
Where storms are bounded tho' they seem to rove,
Where fire and hail and vapour so fulfil
The wise intentions of their makers will,
How well 'tis seen the great eternal mind
Rides on the clouds and walks upon the wind.               355
  O wond'rous Lord! how bright thy glories shine,
The heav'ns declare, for what they boast is thine:
And yon blew tract, enrich'd with orbs of light,
In all its handy work displays thy might!
  Again the monarch touch'd another strain,                360
Another province claim'd his verse again,
Where goodness infinite has fix'd a Sway,
Whose outstretch'd limits are the bounds of day.
Beneath this empire of extended air,
Yet still in reach of Providences care,                    365
God plac'd the rounded earth with stedfast hand
And bid the basis ever firmly stand;
He bid the mountains from confusion's heaps

Exalt their summits, and assume their shapes.
He bid the waters like a garment spread,                           370
To form large seas, and as he spake, they fled;
His voice, his thunder made the waves obey,
And forward hasten, 'till they form'd the sea;
Then least with lawless rage the surges roar,
He mark'd their bounds, and girt them in with shoar;               375
He fill'd the land with brooks that trembling steal
Through winding hills along the flow'ry vale,
To which the beasts that graze the vale, retreat
For cool refreshings in the summers heat;
While perch'd in leaves upon the tender sprays                     380
The birds around their singing voices raise.
He makes the vapours which he taught to fly,
Forsake the chambers of the clouds on high,
And golden harvest rich with ears of grain,
And Spiry blades of grass adorn the plain,                         385
And grapes luxuriant chear the soul with wine,
And ointment shed, to make the visage shine.
Through trunks of trees, fermenting sap proceeds,
To feed, and tinge the living boughs it feeds:
So shoots the firr, where airy storks abide,                       390
So cedar, Lebanon's aspiring pride,
Whose birds by God's appointment in their nest,
With green surrounded, lye secure of rest.
Where small encrease the barren mountains give,
There kine adapted to the feeding live,                            395
There flocks of goats in healthy pastures browse,
And in their rocky entrails rabbits house.
Where forrests thick with shrub entangled stand,
Untrod the roads and desolate the land;
There close in coverts hide the beasts of prey                     400
'Till heavy darkness creeps upon the day,
Then roar with hunger's voice, and range abroad
And in their method seek their meat from God;
And when the dawning edge of eastern air
Begins to purple, to their dens repair.                            405
Man next succeeding, from the sweet repose
Of downy beds, to work appointed goes;
When first the morning sees the rising sun,
He sees their labours both at once begun,
And night returning with its starry train,                         410
Perceives their labours done at once again.

O manifold in works supremely wise,
How well thy gracious store the world supplies!
How all thy creatures on thy goodness call,
And that bestows a due support for all!                           415
When from an open hand thy favours flow,
Rich bounty stoops to visit us below;
When from thy hand no more thy favours stream,
Back to the dust we turn from whence we came;
And when thy spirit gives the vital heat,                         420
A sure succession keeps the kinds compleat;
The propagated seeds their forms retain,
And all the face of earth's renew'd again.
Thus, as you've seen th' effect reveal the cause,
Is nature's ruler known in nature's laws;                         425
Thus still his pow'r is o'er the world display'd
And still rejoices in the world he made.
The Lord he reigns, the king of kings is king,
Let nations praise, and praises learn to sing.
    My verses here may change their stile again,                  430
And trace the Psalmist in another strain;
Where all his soul the soldiers spirit warms,
And to the musick fits the sound of arms,
Where brave disorder does in numbers dwell,
And artful number speaks disorder well.                           435
Arise my genius and attempt the praise
Of dreaded pow'r and perilous essays,
And where his accents are too nobly great,
Like distant ecchos give the faint repeat.
For who like him with enterprizing pen,                           440
Can paint the Lord of Hosts in wrath with men,
Or with just images of tuneful lay
Set all his terrors in their fierce array?
He comes! The tumult of discording spheres,
The quiv'ring shocks of earth, confess their fears;              445
Thick smoaks precede, and blasts of angry breath
That kindle dread devouring flames of death.
He comes! the firmament with dismal night
Bows down, and seems to fall upon the light,
The darkling mists inwrap his head around,                        450
The waters deluge and the tempests sound,
While on the cherub's purple wings he flys,
And plants his black pavilion in the skies.
He comes! the clouds remove, the rattling hail

Descending, bounds and scatters o'er the vale;                              455
His voice is heard, his thunder speaks his ire,
His light'ning blasts with blue sulphurious fire,
His brandish'd bolts with swift commission go
To punish man's rebellious acts below.
His stern rebukes lay deepest ocean bare,                                   460
And solid earth by wide eruption tear;
Then glares the naked gulph with dismal ray,
And then the dark foundations see the day.
O God! let mercy this thy war asswage,
Alas! no mortal can sustain thy rage.                                       465
   While I but strive the dire effects to tell,
And on another's words attentive dwell,
Confusing passions in my bosom roll,
And all in tumult work the troubled soul:
Remorse with pity, fear with sorrow blend,                                  470
And I but strive in vain; my verse, descend,
To less aspiring paths direct thy flight,
Tho' still the less may more than match thy might,
While I to second agents tune the strings,
And Israel's warrior, Israel's battles sings;                              475
Great warrior he, and great to sing of war,
Whose lines (if ever lines prevail'd so far)
Might pitch the tents, compose the ranks anew,
To combat sound, and bring the toil to view.
O nation most securely rais'd in name,                                      480
Whose fair records he wrote for endless fame;
O nation oft victorious o'er thy foes,
At once thy conquests and thy thanks he shews;
For thus he sung the realms that must be thine
And made thee thus confess an aid divine.                                   485
When mercy look'd, the waves perceiv'd its sway,
And Israel pass'd the deep divided sea.
When mercy spake it, haughty Pharoah's host
And haughty Pharoah by the waves were tost.
When mercy led us through the desart sand,                                  490
We reach'd the borders of the promis'd land:
Then all the kings their gather'd armies brought,
And all those kings by mercy's help we fought:
There with their monarch Amor's people bleed,
For God was gracious, and the tribes succeed.                              495
There monst'rous Ogg was fell'd on Basan's plain,
For God was gracious to the tribes again.

At length their yoke the realms of Canaan feel,
And Israel sings that God is gracious still.
    Nor has the warlike prince alone enroll'd          500
The wond'rous feats their fathers did of old;
His own emblazon'd acts adorn his lays,
These too may challenge just returns of praise.
My God! he crys, my surest rock of might,
My trust in dangers and my shield in fight,          505
Thy matchless bounties I with gladness own,
Nor find assistance but from thee alone;
Thy strength is armour, and my path success,
No pow'r like thee can thus securely bless;
When troops united wou'd arrest my course,          510
I break their files, and through their order force;
When in their towns they keep, my seige I form,
And leap the battlements, and lead the storm;
And when in camps abroad intrench'd they lye,
As swift as hinds in chace I bound on high;          515
My strenuous arms thou teachest how to kill,
And snap in sunder temper'd bows of steel;
My moving footsteps are enlarg'd by thee,
And kept from snares of planned ambush free;
And when my foes forsake the field of fight,         520
Then flush'd with conquest I pursue their flight;
In vain their fears that almost reach despair,
The trembling wretches from mine anger bear;
As swift as fear brisk warmth of conquest goes,
And at my feet dejects the wounded foes;         525
For help they call, but find their helper's gone,
For God's against them, and I drive them on:
As whirling dust in airy tumult fly
Before the tempest that involves the sky;
And in my rage's unavoided sway,         530
I tread their necks like abject heaps of clay.
    The warriour thus in song his deeds express'd,
Nor vainly boasted what he but confess'd,
While warlike actions were proclaim'd abroad,
That all their praises, shou'd refer to God.        535
    And here to make this bright design arise
In fairer splendor to the nation's eyes,
From private valour he converts his lays,
For yet the publick claim'd attempts of praise,
And publick conquests where they jointly fought,        540

Thus stand recorded by reflecting thought;
God sent his Samuel from his holy seat
To bear the promise of my future state,
And I rejoicing see the tribes fulfil
The promis'd purpose of almighty will;                    545
Subjected Sichem, sweet Samaria's plain,
And Succoth's valleys have confess'd my reign;
Remoter Gilead's hilly tracts obey,
Manasseh's parted sands accept my sway;
Strong Ephraim's sons, and Ephraim's ports are mine,      550
And mine the throne of princely Judah's line;
Then since my people with my standard go,
To bring the strength of adverse empire low:
Let Moab's soil, to vile subjection brought,
With groans declare how well our ranks have fought;       555
Let vanquish'd Edom bow its humbled head,
And tell how pompous on its pride I tread;
And now Philistia with thy conqu'ring host,
Dismaid and broke, of conquer'd Israel boast;
But if a Seir or Rabbah yet remain                        560
On Johemaan's Hill, or Ammon's plain,
Lead forth our armies Lord, regard our prayer,
Lead Lord of battles and we'll conquer there.
As this the warrior spake, his heart arose,
And thus with grateful turn perform'd the close;          565
Though men to men their best assistance lend,
Yet men alone will but in vain befriend,
Through God we work exploits of high renown,
'Tis God that treads our great opposers down.
　　Hear now the praise of well disputed fields,          570
The best return victorious honour yields;
'Tis common good restor'd, when lovely peace
Is join'd with righteousness in strict embrace;
Hear all ye victors what your sword secures,
Hear all you nations for the cause is yours;              575
And when the joyful trumpets loudly sound,
When groaning captives in their ranks are bound;
When pillars lift the bloody plumes in air,
And broken shafts and batter'd armour bear,
When painted arches acts of war relate,                   580
When slow procession's pomps augment the state,
When fame relates their worth among the throng,
Thus take from David their triumphant song;

Oh clap your hands together, Oh rejoice
In God with melody's exalted voice,                              585
Your sacred Psalm within his dwelling raise,
And for a pure oblation offer praise,
For the rich goodness plentifully shews,
He prospers our design upon our foes.
Then hither all ye nations hither run,                          590
Behold the wonders which the Lord has done,
Behold with what a mind, the heap of slain,
He spreads the sanguine surface of the plain,
He makes the wars that mad confusion hurl'd,
Be spent in victories, and leave the world.                     595
He breaks the bended bows, the spears of Ire,
And burns the shatter'd chariots in the Fire,
And bids the realms be still, the tumult cease,
And know the Lord of war, for Lord of peace;
Now may the tender youth in goodness rise,                      600
Beneath the guidance of their parents eyes,
As tall young poplars when the rangers nigh,
To watch their risings least they shoot awry.
Now may the beauteous Daughters bred with care,
In modest rules and pious acts of fear,                         605
Like polish'd corners of the Temple be,
So bright, so spotless, and so fit for thee.
Now may the various seasons bless the soil,
And plenteous Garners pay the Ploughman's toil;
Now sheep and kine upon the flow'ry meads,                      610
Encrease in thousands and ten thousand heads,
And now no more the sound of grief complains,
For those that fall in fight, or live in chains;
Here when the blessings are proclaim'd aloud,
Join all the voices of the thankful crowd,                      615
Let all that feel them thus confess their part,
Thus own their worth with one united heart;
Happy the realm which God vouchsafes to bless
With all the glories of a bright success!
And happy thrice the realm if thus he please,                   620
To crown those glories with the sweets of ease.
    From warfare finish'd, on a chain of thought
To bright attempts of future rapture wrought;
Yet stronger, yet thy pinnions stronger raise,
Oh fancy, reigning in the pow'r of lays.                        625

For Sion's Hill thine airy courses hold,
'Twas there thy David Prophecy'd of old,
And there devout in contemplation sit,
In holy vision and extatick fit.
  Methinks I seem to feel the charm begin,        630
Now sweet contentment tunes my soul within,
Now wond'rous soft arising musick plays,
And now full sounds upon the sense encrease;
Tis David's Lyre, his artful fingers move,
To court the spirit from the realms above,        635
And pleas'd to come where holiness attends,
The courted spirit from above descends.
Hence on the Lyre and voice new graces rest,
And bright Prophetick forms enlarge the breast;
Hence firm decrees his mystick Hymns relate,        640
Affix'd in Heav'ns adamantine gate,
The glories of the most important age,
And Christ's blest empire seen by sure presage.
  When in a distant view with inward eyes,
He sees the Son descending from the skies,        645
To take the form of Man for Mankind's sake,
Tis thus he makes the great Messiah speak:
It is not, Father, blood of bullocks slain
Can cleanse the World from universal stain,
Such Off'rings are not here requir'd by thee,        650
But point at mine, and leave the work for me;
To perfect which, as Servants ears they drill,
In sign of op'ning to their Masters will,
Thy will wou'd open mine, and have me bear,
My sign of Ministry, the body there.        655
Prophetick volumes of our state assign
The worlds redemption as an act of mine,
And lo, with chearful and obedient heart,
I come, my father, to perform my part.
So spake the Son, and left his throne above,        660
When wings to bear him were prepar'd by love,
When with their Monarch on the great descent,
Sweet humbleness and gentle patience went,
Fair sisters both, both bless'd in his esteem,
And both appointed here to wait on him.        665
  But now before the Prophet's ravish'd eyes,
Succeeding Prospects of his Life arise,

And here he teaches all the world to sing,
Those strains in which the nation own'd him King.
When boughs as at an holy feast they bear,                    670
To shew the Godhead manifested there;
And garments as a mark of glory strow'd,
Declar'd a Prince proclaim'd upon the road;
This day the Lord hath made we will employ
In songs, he crys, and consecrate to joy.                     675
Hosannah, Lord, Hosannah, shed thy peace,
Hosannah, long expecting nations grace,
Oh, bless'd in honour's height triumphant, thou
That wast to come, Oh bless thy people now.
    Twere easy dwelling here with fix'd delight,               680
And much the sweet engagement of the sight;
But fleeting visions each on other throng,
And change the musick and demand the song.
Ah! musick chang'd by sadly moving show,
Ah! song demanded in excess of woe!                           685
For what was all the gracious Saviour's stay,
Whilst here he trod in Life's encumber'd way,
But troubled patience, persecuted breath,
Neglected sorrows, and afflicting death?
Approach ye sinners, think the garden shews                   690
His bloody sweat of full arising throes,
Approach his grief, and hear him thus complain
Through David's person, and in David's strain.
    Oh save me God, thy floods about me roll,
Thy wrath divine hath overflow'd my soul,                     695
I come at length where rising waters drown,
And sink in deep affliction deeply down.
Deceitful snares to bring me to the dead,
Lye ready plac'd in ev'ry path I tread;
And Hell itself, with all that Hell contains,                 700
Of fiends accurs'd, and dreadful change of pains;
To daunt firm will, and cross the good design'd,
With strong temptations fasten on the mind;
Such grief such sorrows in amazing view,
Distracted fears and heaviness pursue.                        705
Ye sages deeply read in human frame,
The passions causes, and their wild extream,
Where mov'd an object more oppos'd to bliss,
What other agony cou'd equal his?
    The musick still proceeds with mournful airs,             710

And speaks the dangers, as it speaks the fears.
Oh sacred Presence from the son withdrawn,
Oh God my father wither art thou gone?
Oh must my soul bewail tormenting pain,
And all my words of anguish fall in vain?                    715
The trouble's near in which my life will end,
But none is near that will assistance lend;
Like Basan's bulls my foes against me throng
So proud, inhuman, numberless, and strong.
Like desart lyons on their prey they go,                    720
So much their fierce desire of blood they shew:
As ploughers wound the ground, they tore my back
And long deep furrows manifest the track.
They pierc'd my tender hands, my tender feet,
And caus'd sharp pangs, where nerves in numbers meet;        725
Rich streams of life forsake my rended veins
And fall like water spill'd upon the plains;
My bones that us'd in hollow seats to close,
Disjoint with anguish of convulsive throes;
My mourning heart is melted in my frame                     730
As wax dissolving runs before a flame,
My strength dries up, my flesh the moisture leaves,
And on my tongue my clammy palate cleaves.
Alass! I thirst, alass! for drink I call,
For drink they give me vinegar and gall.                    735
To sportful game the savage soldiers go
And for my vesture on my vesture throw;
While all deride who see me thus forlorn
And shoot their lips and shake their heads in scorn.
And with despiteful jest, behold, they cry,                 740
The great peculiar darling of the sky,
He trusted God wou'd save his soul from woe,
Now God may have him if he loves him so.
But to the dust of death by quick decay
I come, O Father, be not long away.                         745
And was it thus the prince of life was slain?
And was it thus he dy'd for worthless men?
Yes blessed Jesus! thus in ev'ry line
These suff'rings which the Prophet spake were thine.
  Come christian to the corps, in spirit come,              750
And with true signs of grief surround the tomb.
Upon the threshold stone let sin be slain,
Such sacrifice will best avenge his pain.

Bring thither then repentance, sighs and tears,
Bring mortify'd desires, bring holy fears;                      755
And earnest pray'r express'd from thoughts that roll
Through broken mind, and groanings of the soul;
These scatter on his hearse, and so prepare
Those obsequies the Jews deny'd him there,
While in your hearts the flames of love may burn,              760
To dress the vault, like lamps in sacred urn.
There oft my soul in such a grateful way,
Thine humblest homage with the godly pay.
    But David strikes the sounding chords anew,
And to thy first design recalls thy view;                      765
From life to death, from death to life he flies
And still pursues his object in his eyes.
And here recounts in more enliven'd song
The sacred Presence, not absented long.
The flesh not suffer'd in the grave to dwell,                  770
The soul not suffer'd to remain in hell;
But as the conqueror fatigu'd in war,
With hot pursuit of enemies afar,
Reclines to drink the torrent gliding by,
Then lifts his looks to repossess the sky,                     775
So bow'd the Son in life's uneasy road,
With anxious toil, and thorny danger strew'd;
So bow'd the son, but not to find relief,
But taste the deep imbitter'd floods of grief;
So when he tasted these he rais'd his head,                    780
And left the sabled mansions of the dead,
Ere mould'ring time consum'd the bones away,
Or slow corruption's worms had work'd decay;
Here faith's foundations, all the soul employ
With springing graces, springing beams of joy,                785
Then paus'd the voice where nature's seen to pause,
And for a time suspend her ancient laws.
    From hence arising as the glories rise,
That must advance above the lofty skies,
He runs with sprightly fingers o'er the Lyre,                  790
And fills new songs with new celestial fire:
In which he shews by fair description's ray,
The Christ's Ascension, to the realms of day;
When Justice, pleas'd with life already paid,
Unbends her brows, and sheaths her angry blade;                795

And meditates rewards, and will restore
What mercy woo'd him to forsake before,
When on a cloud with gilded edge of light,
He rose above the reach of human sight,
And met the pomp that hung aloft in air                    800
To make his honours more exceeding fair.
See, cries the prophet, how the chariots wait
To bear him upwards in triumphant state,
By twenty thousands in unnumber'd throng,
And Angels draw the glitt'ring ranks along.                805
The Lord amongst them sits in glory dress'd,
Nor more the Presence Sinai mount confest.
And now the chariots have begun to fly,
The triumph moves, the Lord ascends on high,
And Sin and Satan, us'd to captive men,                    810
Are dragg'd for captives in his ample train;
While as he goes seraphick circles sing
The wond'rous conquest of their wond'rous king,
With shouts of joy their heav'nly voices raise,
And with shrill trumpets manifest his praise.              815
From such a point of such exceeding height
A while my verses stoop their airy flight,
And seem for rest on Olivet to breath,
And charge the two that stand in white beneath,
That as they move and join the moving rear,                820
Within their honour'd hands aloft they bear
The crown of thorns, the cross on which he dy'd,
The nails that pierc'd his limbs, the spear his side;
Then where kind mercy lays the thunder by,
Where Peace has hung great Michael's arms on high,         825
Let these adorn his magazine above,
And hang the trophies of victorious love,
Least man by superstitious mind entic'd,
Shou'd idolize whatever touch'd the Christ.
   But still the Prophet in the spirit soars               830
To new Jerusalem's imperial doors;
There sees and hears the bless'd angelick throng,
There feels their musick, and records their song:
Or with the vision warm'd, attempts to write
For those inhabitants of native light,                     835
And teaches harmony's distinguish'd parts,
In sweet respondence of united hearts;

For thus without might warbling angels sing,
Their course containing on the flutter'd wing;
Eternal gates! your stately portals rear,                    840
Eternal gates! your ways of joy prepare,
The king of glory for admittance stays,
He comes, he'll enter, O prepare your ways;
Then bright arch-angels that attend the wall,
Might thus upon the beauteous order call;                    845
Ye fellow ministers that now proclaim
Your king of glory, tell his awful name.
At which the beauteous order will accord,
And sound of solemn notes pronounce the Lord,
The Lord endew'd with strength, renown'd for might,          850
With spoils returning from the finish'd fight.
Again with Lays they charm the sacred gates,
And graces double while the song repeats,
Again within the sacred guardians sing,
And ask the name of their victorious king,                   855
And then again the Lord's the name rebounds
From tongue to tongue, catch'd up in frequent rounds.
   New thrones and pow'rs appear, to lift the gate,
And David still pursues their enter'd state;
Oh prophet! father! whither woudst thou fly?                 860
Oh mystick Israel's chariot for the sky,
Thou sacred spirit! what a wond'rous height,
By thee supported, soars his airy flight!
For glimpse of Majesty divine is brought,
Among the shifted prospects of the thought;                  865
Dread sacred sight! I dare not gaze for fear,
But sit beneath the singers feet and hear,
And hold each sound that interrupts the mind,
Thus in a calm by pow'r of verse confin'd.
   Ye dreadful ministers of God, displeas'd,                 870
Loud blasting tempests, be no longer rais'd!
Ye deep mouth'd thunders leave your direful groan,
Nor roll in hollow clouds around the throne,
The still small voice more justly will express
How great Jehovah did the Lord address.                      875
And you bright feather'd choirs of endless peace,
A while from tuneful Hallelujahs cease,
A while stand fix'd with deep attentive care,
You'll have the time to sing for ever there.
The royal prophet will the silence break,                    880

And in his words almighty goodness speak.
He spake (and smil'd to see the business done,)
Thou art my first, my great begotten son;
Here on the right of Majesty sit down,
Enjoy thy conquest and receive thy crown,                    885
While I thy worship and renown compleat,
And make thy foes the foot-stool of thy feet,
For I'll pronounce the long resolv'd decree,
My sacred Sion be reserv'd for thee.
From thence thy peaceful rod of pow'r extend,                890
From thence thy messenger of mercy send,
And teach thy vanquish'd enemies to bow,
And rule where Hell has fix'd an empire now.
Then ready nations to their rightful king,
The free-will off'rings of their hearts shall bring,         895
In holy beauties for acceptance dress'd,
And ready nations be with pardon bless'd;
Mean while thy dawn of truth begins the day,
Enlightened subjects shall encrease thy sway,
With such a splendid and unnumber'd train,                   900
As dews in morning fill the grassy plain.
This by myself I swore; the great intent
Has past my sanction and I can't repent;
Thou art a king and priest of peace below,
Like Salem's monarch and for ever so.                        905
Ask what thou wilt, 'tis thine; the gentiles claim,
For thy possession take the world's extream,
The kings shall rage, the parties strive in vain,
By persecuting rage to break thy reign;
Thou art my Christ and they that still can be                910
Rebellious subjects, be destroy'd by thee.
Bring like the Potter to severe decay,
Thy worthless creatures, found in humble clay.
Then hear ye monarchs, and ye judges hear,
Rejoice with trembling, serve the Lord with fear,            915
In his commands with signs of homage move,
And kiss the gracious offers of his love;
Ye surely perish if his anger flame,
And only they be bless'd that bless his name.
Thus does the Christ in David's anthems shine,               920
With full magnificence of art divine,
Then on his subjects gifts of grace bestow,
And spread his Image on their hearts below,

As when our earthly kings receive the globe,
The sacred unction and the purple robe,                              925
And mount the throne with golden glory crown'd,
They scatter medals of themselves around;
There heav'nly singers clap their vary'd wings,
And lead the choir of all created things,
Relate his glory's everlasting prime,                                930
His fame continu'd with the length of time,
While e're the Sun shall dart a gilded beam,
Or changing Moons diffuse the silver'd gleam,
Where e're the waves of rolling ocean sent,
Encompass land with arms of wide extent.                             935
Hail, full of mercy, ready nations cry!
Hail, for ever, ever bless'd on high!
Hail, Oh for ever on thy beauteous throne!
Thou Lord that workest wond'rous things alone,
Still let thy glory to the world appear,                             940
And all the riches of thy goodness hear.
    But thou fair Church in whom he fixes love,
Thou queen accepted of the prince above;
Behold him fairer than the sons of men,
Embrace his offer'd heart, and share his reign;                     945
In Moses's laws they bred thy tender years,
But now to new commands incline thine ears,
Forget thy people, bear no more in mind
Thy Father's houshold, for thy spouse is kind.
Within thy soul let vain affections dye,                            950
Him only worship, and with him comply.
So shall thy spouse's heart with thine agree,
So shall his fervour still encrease for thee.
Come while he calls, supremely favour'd queen,
In heav'nly glories dress thy soul within;                          955
With pious actions to the throne be brought,
In close connection of the virtues wrought,
Let these around thee for a garment shine,
And be the work to make them pleasing, thine:
Come, lovely queen, advance with stately port,                      960
Thy good companions shall compleat thy court,
With joyful souls their joyful entrance sing,
And fill the palace of your gracious king.
What tho' thy Moses and the prophets cease,
What tho' the Priesthood leaves the settled race,                   965
The Father's place their offspring well supplies,

When at thy spouse's Ministry they rise,
When thy bless'd houshold on his orders go,
And rule for him where'er he reigns below.
Come, Queen exalted, come, my lasting song          970
To future ages shall thy fame prolong.
The joyful nations shall thy praise proclaim,
And for their safety crowd beneath thy name.
Oh bounteous Saviour! still thy mercy kind,
Still what thy David sung, thy servants find,          975
Still why thy David sung thy servants see,
From thee sent down, and sent again to thee.
They see the words of thanks and love divine,
In strains mysterious intermingl'd shine,
As sweet and rich unite in costly waves,          980
When purling gold the purpled webb receives,
And still the Church he shadow'd hears the lays,
In daily service as an aid to praise.
At these her temper good devotion warms,
And mounts aloft with more engaging charms.          985
Then as she strives to reach the lofty sky,
Bids gratitude assist her will to fly;
In these our gratitude becomes on fire,
Then feels its flames improv'd by strong desire,
Then feels desirē in eager wishes move,          990
And wish determine in the point of love.
   Such hymns to regulate and such to raise,
Approach, ye sounding instruments of praise.
Tis fit you tune for him whose holy love,
In wish aspiring to the choir above,          995
And fond to practice e're his time to go,
Devoutly call'd you to the choir below;
There where he plac'd you, with your solemn sound,
For Gods high glory fill the sacred ground,
And there and ev'ry where his wond'rous name,          1000
Within his firmament of pow'r proclaim.
Soft pleasing lutes with easy sweetness move,
To touch the sentiments of Heav'nly love,
Assist the Lyre and voice to tell the charms
That gently stole him from the Father's arms;          1005
Gay trembling Timbrels us'd with airs of mirth,
Assist the loud Hosannah rais'd on earth,

When on an Ass he meekly rides along,
And multitudes are heard within the song.
Full-tenor'd Psalt'ry, join the doleful part,                    1010
In which his agony possest his heart;
And seem to feel thyself, and seem to shew,
Arising heaviness and signs of woe.
Sonorous organ at his passion moan,
And utter forth thy sympathizing groan,                         1015
In big slow murmurs anxious sorrow speak,
While melancholy winds thine entrails shake,
As when he suffer'd, with complaining sound,
The storms in vaulted caverns shook the ground;
Swift chearful cymbals give an airy strain,                     1020
When having bravely broke the doubled chain,
Of Death and Hell, he left the conquer'd grave,
And rose to visit those he dy'd to save.
And as he mounts in song and Angels sing
With grand procession their returning king,                     1025
Triumphant trumpets raise their notes on high,
And make them seem to mount, and seem to fly.
Then all at once conspire to praise the Lord,
In musick's full consent, and just accord:
Ye sons of art, in such melodious way                           1030
Conclude the service which you join to pay,
While nations sing Amen, and yet again,
Hold forth the note and sing aloud Amen.
    Here has my fancy gone where David leads,
Now softly pacing o'er the grassy meads,                        1035
Now nobly mounting where the monarchs rear
The gilded spires of palaces in air,
Now shooting thence upon the level flight,
To dreadful dangers and the toils of fight,
Anon with utmost stretch ascending far,                         1040
Beyond the region of the farthest star;
As sharpest sighted eagles tow'ring fly,
To weather their broad sails in open sky,
At length on wings half clos'd slide gently down,
And one attempt shall all my labours crown.                     1045
In other's verse the rest be better shewn,
But this is more, or should be more, thine own.
    If then the spirit that supports my lines,
Have prov'd unequal to my large designs,
Let others rise from earthly passion's dream,                   1050

By me provok'd to vindicate the theme.
Let others round the world in rapture rove,
Or with strong feathers fan the breeze above,
Or walk the dusky shades of death, and dive
Down Hell's abyss, and mount again alive.                          1055
But Oh my God! may these unartful rhimes,
In sober words of woe bemoan my crimes.
Tis fit the sorrows I for ever vent,
For what I never can enough repent;
Tis fit, and David shews the moving way,                           1060
And with his pray'r instructs my soul to pray.
Then since thy guilt is more than match'd by me,
And since my troubles shou'd with thine agree,
O Muse to glories in affliction born!
May thine humility my soul adorn.                                  1065
For humblest prayers are most affecting strains,
As Mines lye rich in lowly planted veins;
Such aid I want to render mercy kind,
And such an aid as here I want I find:
Thy weeping accents in my numbers run,                             1070
Ah thought! ah voice of inward dole begun!
   My God, whose anger is appeas'd by tears,
Bow gently down thy mercy's gracious ears;
With many tongues my sins for justice call,
But mercy's ears are manifold for all.                             1075
Those sweet celestial windows open wide,
And in full streams let soft compassion glide,
There wash my soul and cleanse it yet again,
O th'roughly cleanse it from the guilty stain,
For I my life with inward anguish see,                             1080
And all its wretchedness confess to thee.
The large Inditement stands before my view,
Drawn forth by conscience, most amazing true,
And fill'd with secrets hid from human eye,
When foolish man, thy God stood witness by.                        1085
Then Oh, thou majesty divinely great,
Accept the sad confessions I repeat,
Which clear thy justice to the world below,
Shou'd dismal sentence doom my soul to woe.
When in the silent womb my shape was made,                         1090
And from the womb to lightsome life convey'd,
Curs'd sin began to take unhappy root,
And thro' my veins its early fibres shoot;

And then what goodness did'st thou shew, to kill
The rising weeds, and principles of ill;                          1095
When to my breast in fair celestial flame,
Eternal truth and lovely wisdom came,
Bright gift by simple nature never got,
But here reveal'd to change the antient blot.
This wond'rous help which mercy pleas'd to grant,                1100
Continue still, for still thine aid I want,
And as the men whom leprosies invade,
Or they that touch the carcase of the dead,
With Hysop sprinkled and by water clean'd,
Their former pureness in the law regain'd;                       1105
So purge my soul diseas'd alas! within,
And much polluted with dead works of sin.
For such bless'd favours at thine hand I sue,
Be grace thine Hysop and thy water too.
Then shall my whiteness for perfection vie                       1110
With blanching snows that newly leave the sky.
Thus through my mind thy voice of gladness send,
Thus speak the joyful word, I will be clean'd;
That all my strength consum'd with mournful pain,
May by thy saving health rejoice again:                          1115
And now no more my foul offences see,
Oh turn from these, but turn thee not from me,
Or least they make me too deform'd a sight,
Oh, blot them with oblivion's endless night.
Then further pureness to thy servant grant,                      1120
Another heart, or change in this, I want.
Create another, or the change create,
For now my vile corruption is so great,
It seems a new creation to restore
Its fall'n estate to what it was before.                         1125
Renew my spirit, raging in my breast,
And all its passions in their course arrest,
Or turn their motions, widely gone astray,
And fix their footsteps in thy righteous way.
When this is granted, when again I'm whole,                      1130
Oh ne'er withdraw thy presence from my soul:
There let it shine, so let me be restor'd
To present joy which conscious hopes afford.
There let it sweetly shine, and o'er my breast
Diffuse the dawning of eternal rest;                             1135
Then shall the wicked this compassion see,

And learn thy worship and thy works from me.
For I to such occasions of thy praise
Will tune my lyre, and consecrate my lays.
Unseal my lips, where guilt and shame have hung          1140
To stop the passage of my grateful tongue,
And let my prayer and song ascend, my prayer
Here join'd with saints, my song with angels there;
Yet neither prayer I'd give, nor songs alone,
If other off'rings were as much thy own:          1145
But thine's the contrite spirit, thine's an heart
Oppress'd with sorrow, broke with inward smart;
That at thy footstool in confession shews
How well its faults, how well the judge it knows;
That sin with sober resolution flies,          1150
This gift thy mercy never will despise.
Then in my soul a mystick altar rear,
And such a sacrifice I'll offer there;
There shall it stand in vows of virtue bound,
There falling tears shall wash it all around;          1155
And sharp remorse, yet sharper edg'd by woe,
Deserv'd and fear'd, inflict the bleeding blow;
There shall my thoughts to holy breathings fly
Instead of incense to perfume the sky,
And thence my willing heart aspires above,          1160
A victim panting in the flames of love.


## SOLOMON.


As thro' the Psalms from theme to theme I chang'd,
Methinks like Eve in Paradice I rang'd;
And ev'ry grace of song I seem'd to see,
As the gay pride of ev'ry season, she.
She gently treading all the walks around,          5
Admir'd the springing beauties of the ground,
The lilly glist'ring with the morning dew,
The rose in red, the violet in blew,
The pink in pale, the bells in purple rows,
And tulips colour'd in a thousand shows:          10
Then here and there perhaps she pull'd a flow'r
To strew with moss, and paint her leafy bow'r;
And here and there, like her I went along,

Chose a bright strain, and bid it deck my song.
But now the sacred Singer leaves mine eye,                    15
Crown'd as he was, I think he mounts on high;
Ere this Devotion bore his heav'nly psalms,
And now himself bears up his harp and palms.
Go, saint triumphant, leave the changing sight,
So fitted out, you suit the realms of light;                 20
But let thy glorious robe at parting go,
Those realms have robes of more effulgent show;
It flies, it falls, the flutt'ring silk I see,
Thy son has caught it and he sings like thee,
With such election of a theme divine,                        25
And such sweet grace, as conquers all but thine.
    Hence, ev'ry writer o'er the fabled streams,
Where frolick fancies sport with idle dreams,
Or round the sight enchanted clouds dispose,
Whence wanton cupids shoot with gilded bows;                 30
A nobler writer, strains more brightly wrought,
Themes more exulted, fill my wond'ring thought:
The parted skies are track'd with flames above,
As love descends to meet ascending love;
The seasons flourish where the spouses meet,                 35
And earth in gardens spreads beneath their feet.
This fresh-bloom prospect in the bosom throngs,
When Solomon begins his song of songs,
Bids the rap'd soul to Lebanon repair,
And lays the scenes of all his action there,                 40
Where as he wrote, and from the bow'r survey'd
The scenting groves, or answ'ring knots he made,
His sacred art the sights of nature brings,
Beyond their use, to figure heav'nly things.
    Great son of God! whose gospel pleas'd to throw          45
Round thy rich glory, veils of earthly show,
Who made the vineyard oft thy church design,
Who made the marriage-feast a type of thine,
Assist my verses which attempt to trace
The shadow'd beauties of celestial grace,                    50
And with illapses of seraphick fire
The work which pleas'd thee once, once more inspire.
    Look, or illusion's airy visions draw,
Or now I walk the gardens which I saw,
Where silver waters feed a flow'ring spring,                 55
And winds salute it with a balmy wing.

There on a bank, whose shades directly rise
To screen the sun, and not exclude the skies,
There sits the sacred church; methinks I view
The spouse's aspect and her ensigns too.                    60
Her face has features where the virtues reign,
Her hands the book of sacred love contain,
A light (truth's emblem) on her bosom shines
And at her side the meekest lamb reclines:
And oft on heav'nly lectures in the book,                   65
And oft on heav'n itself, she cast a look;
Sweet, humble, fervent zeal that works within
At length bursts forth, and raptures thus begin.
    Let Him, that Him my soul adores above,
In close communions breath his holy love;                   70
For these bless'd words his pleasing lips impart,
Beyond all cordials, chear the fainting heart.
As rich and sweet, the precious ointments stream,
So rich thy graces flow, so sweet thy name
Diffuses sacred joy; tis hence we find                      75
Affection rais'd in ev'ry virgin mind;
For this we come, the daughters here and I,
Still draw we forward, and behold I fly,
I fly through mercy, when my king invites,
To tread his chambers of sincere delights;                  80
There, join'd by mystick union, I rejoice,
Exalt my temper, and enlarge my voice,
And celebrate thy joys, supremely more
Than earthly bliss; thus upright hearts adore.
Nor you ye maids, who breath of Salem's air,                85
Nor you refuse that I conduct you there;
Tho' clouding darkness hath eclips'd my face,
Dark as I am, I shine with beams of grace,
As the black tents, where Ishmael's line abides,
With glitt'ring trophies dress their inward sides;          90
Or as thy curtains, Solomon, are seen,
Whose plaits conceal a golden throne within.
'Twere wrong to judge me by the carnal sight,
And yet my visage was by nature white,
But fiery suns which persecute the meek,                    95
Found me abroad, and scorch'd my rosy cheek.
The world, my brethren, they were angry grown,
They made me dress a vineyard not my own,
Among their rites, (their vines) I learn'd to dwell,

And in the mean employ my beauty fell;                      100
By frailty lost, I gave my labour o'er
And my own vineyard grew deform'd the more.
Behold I turn, O say my soul's desire,
Where do'st thou feed thy flock and where retire
To rest that flock, when noon-tide heats arise?            105
Shepherd of Israel, teach my dubious eyes
To guide me right, for why shou'd thine abide
Where wand'ring shepherds turn their flocks aside?
    So spake the church and sigh'd, a purple light
Sprung forth, the Godhead stood reveal'd to sight,         110
And heav'n and nature smil'd; as white as snow
His seamless vesture loosely fell below;
Sedate and pleas'd he nodded, round his head
The pointed glory shook, and thus he said:
If thou the loveliest of the beauteous kind,               115
If thou canst want thy shepherd's walk to find,
Go by the foot-steps where my flocks have trod,
My saints obedient to the laws of God,
Go where their tents my teaching servants rear,
And feed the kids, thy young believers there.              120
Shou'd thus my flocks increase, my fair delight,
I view their numbers, and compare the sight
To Pharaoh's Horses, when they take the field,
Beat plains to dust, and make the nations yield.
With rows of gems, thy comely cheeks I deck,               125
And chains of pendant gold o'erflow thy neck,
For so like gems the riches of my grace,
And so descending glory, chears thy face:
Gay bridal robes a flow'ring silver strows,
Bright gold engrailing on the border glows.                130
    He spake, the spouse admiring heard the sound,
Then meekly bending on the sacred ground,
She cries, Oh present to my ravish'd breast,
This sweet communion is an inward feast;
There sits the king, while all around our heads,           135
His grace, my Spikenard, pleasing odours sheds;
About my soul his holy comfort flies,
So closely treasur'd in the bosom lies
The bundled myrrhe, so sweet the scented gale
Breaths all En-gedi's aromatick vale.                      140
Now says the king, my love, I see thee fair,

Thine eyes for mildness with the dove's compare.
  No, thou, belov'd, art fair, the church replies,
(Since all my beauties but from thee arise,)
All fair, all pleasant, these communions shew          145
Thy councels pleasant, and thy comforts so.
And as at marriage feasts they strow the flow'rs,
With nuptial chaplets hang the summer bow'rs,
And make the rooms of smelling cedars fine,
Where the fond bridegroom and the bride recline;       150
I dress my soul, with such exceeding care,
With such, with more, to court thy presence there.
  Well hast thou prais'd, he says; the Sharon rose
Through flow'ry fields a pleasing odour throws,
The valley-lillies ravish'd sense regale,              155
And with pure whiteness paint their humble vale;
Such names of sweetness are thy lover's due,
And thou my love, be thou a lilly too,
A lilly set in thorns; for all I see,
All other daughters are as thorns to thee.             160
  Then she; the trees that pleasing apples yield,
Surpass the barren trees that cloath the field,
So you surpass the sons with worth divine,
So shade, and fruit as well as shade, is thine.
I sat me down, and saw thy branches spread,            165
And green protection flourish o'er my head,
I saw thy fruit, the soul's celestial food,
I pull'd, I tasted, and I found it good.
Hence in the spirit to the blissful seats,
Where love, to feast, mysteriously retreats,           170
He led me forth; I saw the banner rear,
And love was pencil'd for the motto there.
Prophets and teachers, in your care combine,
Stay me with apples, comfort me with wine,
The cordial promises of joys above,                    175
For hope deferr'd has made me sick with love.
Ah! while my tongue reveals my fond desire,
His hands support me, least my life expire;
As round a child the parent's arms are plac'd,
This holds the head, and that enfolds the waist.       180
  Here ceas'd the church, and lean'd her languid head
Bent down with joy, when thus the lover said:
Behold, ye daughters of the realm of peace,

She sleeps, at least her thoughts of sorrow cease.
Now, by the bounding roes, the skipping fawns,                              185
Near the cool brooks, or o'er the grassy lawns,
By all the tender innocents that rove,
Your hourly charges in my sacred grove,
Guard the dear charge from each approach of ill,
I wou'd not have her wake, but when she will.                               190
   So rest the church and spouse, my verses so
Appear to languish with the flames you shew,
And pausing rest; but not the pause be long,
For still thy Solomon pursues the song.
Then keep the place in view; let sweets more rare                           195
Than earth produces, fill the purpled air;
Let something solemn overspread the green
Which seems to tell us, here the Lord has been:
But let the virgin still in prospect shine,
And other strains of hers, enliven mine.                                    200
She wakes, she rises; bid the whisp'ring breeze
More softly whisper in the waving trees,
Or fall with silent awe; bid all around,
Before the church's voice, abate their sound,
While thus her shadowy strains attempt to shew                             205
A future advent of the spouse below.
   Hark! my beloved's voice! behold him too!
Behold him coming in the distant view,
No clamb'ring mountains make my lover stay,
(For what are mountains, in a lover's way?)                                 210
Leaping he comes, how like the nimble roe
He runs the paths his prophets us'd to shew!
And now he looks from yon partition wall,
Built till he comes—'tis only then to fall,
And now he's nearer in the promise seen,                                   215
Too faint the sight—tis with a glass between;
From hence I hear him as a lover speak,
Who near a window, calls a fair to wake.
   Attend ye virgins, while the words that trace
An opening spring, design the day of grace.                                220
Hark! or I dream, or else I hear him say,
Arise my love, my fair one, come away,
For now the tempests of thy winter end,
Thick rains no more in heavy drops descend,
Sweet painted flow'rs their silken leaves unclose,                         225
And dress the face of earth with vari'd shows;

In the green wood the singing birds renew
Their chirping notes, the silver turtles coo:
The trees that yield the fig, already shoot,
And knit their blossoms for their early fruit;                    230
With fragrant scents the vines refresh the day,
Arise my love, my fair one come away.
O come my dove, forsake thy close retreat,
For close in safety hast thou fix'd thy seat,
As fearful pidgeons in dark clefts abide,                         235
And safe the clefts their tender charges hide.
Now let thy looks with modest guise appear,
Now let thy voice salute my longing ear,
For in thy looks an humble mind I see,
Prayer forms thy voice, and both are sweet to me.                 240
To save the bloomings of my vineyard, haste,
Which foxes, (false deluding teachers) waste;
Watch well their haunts, and catch the foxes there,
Our grapes are tender and demand the care.
Thus speaks my love: surprizing love divine!                     245
I thus am his, he thus for ever mine.
And 'till he comes, I find a presence still,
Where souls attentive serve his holy will,
Where down in vales unspotted lillies grow,
White types of innocence, in humble show.                        250
O 'till the spicy breath of heav'nly day,
Till all thy shadows fleet before thy ray,
Turn my beloved with thy comforts here,
Turn in thy promise, in thy grace appear,
Nor let such swiftness in the roes be shown                      255
To save themselves, as thou to chear thine own;
Turn like the nimble harts that lightly bound
Before the stretches of the fleetest hound,
Skim the plain chace of lofty Bether's head,
And make the mountain wonder if they tread.                      260
　　But long expectance of a bliss delay'd
Breeds anxious doubt, and tempts the sacred maid;
Then mists arising strait repel the light,
The colour'd garden lies disguis'd with night,
A pale-horn'd crescent leads a glimm'ring throng,                265
And groans of absence jarr within the song.
　　By night, she cries, a night which blots the mind,
I seek the lover, whom I fail to find;
When on my couch compos'd to thought I lie,

I search, and vainly search with reason's eye;          270
Rise fondly rise, thy present search give o'er
And ask if others know thy lover more.
Dark as it is, I rise, the moon that shines,
Shows by the gleam, the city's outward lines,
I range the wand'ring road, the winding street,          275
And ask, but ask in vain, of all I meet,
'Till, toil'd with ev'ry disappointing place
My steps the guardians of the temple trace,
Whom thus my wish accosts, ye sacred guides,
Ye prophets, tell me where my love resides?          280
'Twas well I question'd, scarce I pass'd them by,
Ere my rais'd soul perceives my lover nigh:
And have I found thee, found my joy divine?
How fast I'll hold thee, 'till I make thee mine.
My mother waits thee, thither thou repair,          285
Long waiting Israel wants thy presence there.
The lover smiles to see the virgin's pain,
The mists roll off, and quit the flow'ry plain.
  Yes, here I come, he says, thy sorrow cease,
And guard her, daughters of the realms of peace,          290
By all the bounding roes and skipping fawns,
Near the cool brooks, or o'er the grassy lawns,
By all the tender innocents that rove,
Your hourly charges, in my sacred grove;
Guard the dear charge from each approach of ill,          295
I'll have her feel my comforts, while she will.
  Here hand in hand with chearful heart they go,
When wand'ring Salem sees the solemn show,
Dreams the rich pomp of Solomon again,
And thus her daughters sing the approaching scene.          300
  Who from the desart, where the waving clouds
High Sinai pierces, comes involv'd with crowds?
For Sion's hill her sober pace she bends,
As grateful incense from the Dome ascends.
It seems the sweets from all Arabia shed,          305
Curl at her side, and hover o'er her head.
For her the king prepares a bed of state,
Round the rich bed her guards in order wait,
All mystick Israel's sons, 'tis there they quell
The foes within, the foes without repel.          310
The guard his ministry, their swords of fight
His sacred laws, her present state of night.

He forms a chariot too to bring her there,
Not the carv'd frame of Solomon's so fair;
Sweet smells the chariot as the temple stood,          315
The fragrant cedar lent them both the wood,
High wreaths of silver'd columns prop the door,
Fine gold entrail'd, adorns the figur'd floor,
Deep fringing purple hangs the roof above,
And silk embroid'ry paints the midst with love.        320
   Go forth ye daughters, Sion's daughters go,
A greater Solomon exalts the show,
If crown'd with gold, and by the queen bestow'd,
To grace his nuptials, Jacob's monarch rode;
A crown of glory from the king divine,                 325
To grace these nuptials, makes the Saviour shine;
While the bless'd pair, express'd in emblem ride,
Messiah Solomon, his church the bride.
   Ye kind attendants who with wond'ring eyes
Saw the grand entry, what you said suffice,            330
You sung the lover with a loud acclaim,
The lover's fondness longs to sing the dame.
He speaks, admiring nature stands around
And learns new musick, while it hears the sound.
   Behold, my love, how fair thy beauties show,    335
Behold how more, how most extremely so!
How still to me thy constant eyes incline,
I see the turtle's when I gaze on thine,
Sweet through the lids they shine with modest care,
And sweet and modest is a virgin's air.                340
How bright thy locks! how well their number paints
The great assemblies of my lovely saints!
So bright the kids, so numerously fed,
Graze the green top of lofty Gilead's head;
All Gilead's head a fleecy whiteness clouds,           345
And the rich master glorys in the crowds.
   How pure thy teeth! for equal order made,
Each answ'ring each, whilst all the publick aid,
These lovely graces in my church I find,
This candour, order, and accorded mind:                350
Thus when the season bids the shepherd lave
His sheep new shorn, within the chrystal wave,
Wash'd they return, in such unsully'd white,
Thus march by pairs, and in the flock unite.
How please thy lips adorn'd with native red!           355

Art vainly mocks them in the scarlet thread!
But if they part, what musick wafts the air!
So sweet thy praises, and so soft thy Prayer.
If through thy loosen'd curls with honest shame
Thy lovely temples fine complexion flame,                          360
Whatever crimson Granate blossoms show,
'Twas never theirs, so much to please, and glow.
But what's thy neck, the polish'd form I see!
Whose Iv'ry strength supports thine eyes to me;
Fair type of firmness when my saints aspire,                       365
The sacred confidence that lifts desire,
As David's turret on the stately frame
Upheld its thousand conqu'ring shields of fame.
And what thy breasts! they still demand my lays,
What image wakes to charm me whilst I gaze?                        370
Two lovely mountains each exactly round,
Two lovely mountains with the lilly crown'd,
While two twin roes, and each on either bred,
Feed in the lillies of the mountain's head.
Let this resemblance, spotless virtues show,                       375
And in such lillies feed my young below.
But now farewel 'till night's dark shades decay,
Farewel my virgin, 'till the break of day,
Swift for the hills of spice and gums I fly,
To breath such sweets as scent a purer sky,                       380
Yet as I leave thee, still above compare,
My Love, my spotless, still I find thee fair.
　　Here rest celestial maid, for if he go,
Nor will he part, nor is the promise slow,
Nor slow my fancy move; dispel the shade,                         385
Charm forth the morning and relieve the maid.
Arise fair sun, the church attends to see
The sun of righteousness arise in thee;
Arise fair Sun, and bid the church adore,
'Tis then he'll court her, whom he prais'd before.                390
As thus I sing, it shines, there seems a sound
Of plumes in air, and feet upon the ground;
I see their meeting, see the flow'ry scene
And hear the mystick love pursu'd again.
　　Now to the mount whose spice perfumes the day,                 395
'Tis I invite thee, come my spouse away,
Come, leave thy Lebanon, is ought we see

In all thy Lebanon, compared to me?
Nor tow'rd thy Canaan turn with wishful sight,
From Hermon's, Shenir's, and Amana's height;                    400
There dwells the leopard, there assaults the bear,
This world has ills, and such may find thee there.
   My spouse, my sister, O thy wond'rous art,
Which through my bosom drew my ravish'd heart!
Won by one eye, my ravish'd heart is gone,                      405
For all thy seeing guides consent as one,
Drawn by one chain which round thy body plies,
For all thy members one bless'd union ties.
My spouse, my sister, O the charm to please,
When love repaid, returns my bosom ease!                        410
Strongly thy love, and strongly wines restore,
But wines must yield, thy love enflames me more.
Sweetly thine ointments, (all thy virtues) smell,
Not altar spices please thy king so well.
How soft thy doctrine on thy lips resides!                      415
From those two combs the dropping honey glides,
All pure without as all within sincere,
Beneath thy tongue—I find it honey there.
Ah while thy graces thus around thee shine,
The charms of Lebanon must yield to thine!                      420
His spring, his garden, ev'ry scented tree,
My spouse, my sister, all I find in thee.
Thee for myself I fence, I shut, I seal,
Mysterious spring, mysterious garden, hail!
A spring, a font, where heav'nly waters flow,                   425
A grove, a garden, where the graces grow.
There rise my fruits, my cyprus, and my firr,
My saffron, spikenard, Cinnamon and Myrrhe;
Perpetual fountains for their use abound,
And streams of favour feed the living ground.                   430
   Scarce spake the Christ, when thus the church replies
(And spread her arms where e'er the spirit flies.)
Ye cooling northern gales, who freshly shake
My balmy reeds, ye northern gales awake.
And thou the regent of the southern sky,                        435
O soft inspiring o'er my garden fly,
Unlock and waft my sweets, that ev'ry grace
In all its heav'nly life regale the place.
If thus a paradice thy garden prove,

'Twere best prepar'd to entertain my love,                                     440
And that the pleasing fruits may please the more,
O think my proffer, was thy gift before.
   At this, the Saviour cries, behold me near,
My spouse, my sister, O behold me here,
To gather fruits, I come at thy request,                                       445
And pleas'd my soul accepts the solemn feast;
I gather myrrhe with spice to scent the treat,
My virgin-honey with the combs I eat,
I drink my sweet'ning milk, my lively wine,
(These words of pleasure mean thy gifts divine)                                450
To share my bliss, my good elect I call,
The church (my garden) must include them all;
Now sit and banquet, now belov'd you see
What gifts I love, and prove these fruits with me;
O might this sweet communion ever last!                                        455
But with the sun the sweet communion past,
The Saviour parts, and on oblivion's breast
Benumb'd and slumb'ring lies the church to rest,
Pass the sweet allies while the dusk abides,
Seek the fair lodge in which the maid resides,                                 460
Then, fancy, seek the maid, at night again
The Christ will come, but comes, alas in vain.
   I sleep, she says, and yet my heart awakes,
(There's still some feeling while the lover speaks)
With what fond fervour from without he cries!                                  465
Arise my love, my undefil'd arise,
My dove, my sister, cold the dews alight,
And fill my tresses with the drops of night;
Alas I'm all unrob'd, I wash'd my feet,
I tasted slumber, and I find it sweet.                                         470
   As thus my words refuse, he slips his hands
Where the clos'd latch my cruel door commands.
What, tho' deny'd, so persevering kind!
Who long denies a persevering mind?
From my wak'd soul my slothful temper flies,                                   475
My bowels yearn, I rise, my love, I rise,
I find the latch thy fingers touch'd before,
Thy smelling myrrhe comes dropping off the door.
Now where's my love?—what! hast thou left the place?
O, to my soul, repeat thy words of grace,                                      480
Speak in the dark, my love; I seek thee round
And vainly seek thee 'till thou wilt be found.

What no return? I own my folly past,
I lay too listless; speak my love at last.
The guards have found me—are ye guards indeed,                485
Who smite the sad, who make the feeble bleed?
Dividing teachers these; who wrong my name,
Rend my long veil, and cast me bare to shame.
But you, ye daughters of the realm of rest,
If ever pity mov'd a virgin breast,                           490
Tell my belov'd how languishing I lie,
How love has brought me near the point to dye.
   And what belov'd is this you wou'd have found,
Say Salem's daughters, as they flock'd around?
What wond'rous thing? what charm beyond compare?              495
Say what's thy lover, fairest o'er the fair?
His face is white and ruddy, she replies,
So mercy join'd to justice, tempers dyes;
His lofty stature, where a Myriad shine,
O'ertops, and speaks a majesty divine.                        500
Fair honour crowns his head, the raven-black
In bushy curlings flows adown his back.
Sparkling his eyes, with full proportion plac'd,
White like the milk, and with a mildness grac'd;
As the sweet doves, when e'er they fondly play              505
By running waters in a glitt'ring day.
Within his breath, what pleasing sweetness grows!
'Tis spice exhal'd, and mingl'd on the rose.
Within his words, what grace with goodness meets!
So beds of lillies drop with balmy sweets.                    510
What rings of eastern price his finger hold!
Gold decks the fingers, Beryl decks the gold!
His Iv'ry shape adorns a costly vest,
Work paints the skirts, and gems inrich the breast;
His limbs beneath, his shining sandals case                   515
Like marble columns on a golden base.
   Nor boasts that mountain, where the cedar tree
Perfumes our realm, such num'rous sweets as he.
O lovely all! what cou'd my king require
To make his presence more the world's desire?                 520
And now ye maids if such a friend you know,
'Tis such my longings look to find below.
   While thus her friend, the spouse's Anthems sing,
Deck'd with the Thummim, crown'd a sacred king,
The Daughter's hearts, the fine description drew,             525

And that which rais'd their wonder, ask'd their view.
   Then where, they cry, thou fairest o'er the fair,
Where goes thy lover, tell the virgins where?
What flow'ring walks invite his steps aside?
We'll help to seek him, let those walks be try'd.                     530
   The spouse revolving here the grand descent,
'Twas that he promis'd, there, she cries, he went,
He keeps a garden where the spices breath,
Its bow'ring borders kiss the vale beneath,
'Tis there he gathers lillies, there he dwells,                       535
And binds his flow'rets to unite their smells.
O 'tis my height of love, that I am his!
O he is mine, and that's my height of bliss!
Descend my virgins, well I know the place,
He feeds in lillies, that's a spotless race.                         540
   At dawning day, the bridegroom leaves a bow'r,
And here he waters, there he props a flow'r,
When the kind damsel, spring of heav'nly flame,
With Salem's daughters to the garden came.
Then thus his love the bridegroom's words repeat                     545
(The smelling borders lent them both a seat.)
O great as Tirzah! 'twas a regal place,
O fair as Salem! 'tis the realm of peace,
Whose aspect, awful to the wond'ring eye,
Appears like armies when the banners fly;                            550
O turn my sister, O my beauteous bride,
Thy face o'ercomes me, turn that face aside,
How bright thy locks, how well their number paints
The great assemblies of my lovely saints,
So bright the kids, so numerously fed,                               555
Graze the green wealth of lofty Gilead's head.
How pure thy teeth! for equal order made,
Each answ'ring each, while all the publick aid;
As when the season bids the shepherd lave
His sheep new shorn within the silver wave,                          560
Wash'd they return in such unsully'd white,
So march by pairs, and in the flock unite.
How sweet thy temples! not pomegranates know
With equal modest look to please and glow.
If Solomon his life of pleasure leads,                               565
With wives in numbers, and unnumbered maids,
In other paths, my life of pleasure shewn,

Admits my love, my undefil'd alone;
Thy mother Israel, she the dame who bore
Her choice, my dove, my spotless owns no more;                       570
The Gentile queens at thy appearance cry,
Hail queen of nations! hail, the maids reply,
And thus they sing thy praise: what heav'nly dame
Springs like the morning with a purple flame?
What rises like the morn with silver light?                          575
What like the sun assists the world with sight?
Yet awful still, tho' thus serenely kind,
Like hosts with ensigns rattling in the wind.
I grant I left thy sight, I seem'd to go,
But was I absent when you fancy'd so?                                580
Down to my garden, all my planted vale,
Where nuts their ground in underwood conceal,
Where blow pomegranates, there I went to see
What knitting blossoms white the bearing tree,
View the green buds, recall the wand'ring shoots,                    585
Smell my gay flow'rets, taste my flavour'd fruits,
Raise the curl'd vine, refresh the spicy beds,
And joy for ev'ry grace my garden sheds.
    The Saviour here, and here the church arise,
And am I thus respected, thus she cries!                             590
I mount for heav'n transported on the winds,
My flying chariot's drawn by willing minds.
    As rap'd with comfort thus the maid withdrew,
The waiting daughters wonder'd where she flew,
And O! return, they cry, for thee we burn,                          595
O maid of Salem, Salem's self return.
And what's in Salem's maid we covet so?
Here all ye nations—'tis your bliss below;
That glorious vision by the patriarch seen,
When sky-born beauties march'd the scented green,                   600
There the met saints, and meeting angels came,
Two lamps of God, Mahanaim was the name.
    Again the maid reviews her sacred ground,
Solemn she sits, the damsels sing around.
    O princes daughter! how with shining show                       605
Thy golden shoes prepare thy feet below!
How firm thy joints! what temple-work can be
With all its gems and art preferr'd to thee?
In thee, to feed thy lover's faithful race,

Still flow the riches of abounding grace,                          610
Pure, large, refreshing, as the waters fall
From the carv'd navels of the cistern-wall.
In thee the lover finds his race divine,
You teem with numbers, they with virtues shine;
So wheat with lillies, if their heaps unite,                       615
The wheat's unnumb'red and the lillies white;
Like tender roes thy breasts appear above,
Two types of innocence and twins of love.
Like Iv'ry turrets seems thy neck to rear,
O sacred emblem, upright, firm and fair!                           620
As Heshbon pools, which with a silver state
Diffuse their waters at their city gate,
For ever so thy virgin eyes remain,
So clear within, and so without serene.
As thro' sweet Firr the royal turret shews,                        625
Whence Lebanon surveys a realm of foes,
So thro' thy lovely curls appear thy face
To watch thy foes, and guard thy faithful race.
The richest colours flow'ry Carmel wears,
Red fillets cross'd with purple braid thy hairs;                   630
Yet not more strictly these thy locks restrain
Than thou thy king with strong affections chain,
When from his palace he enjoys thy sight,
O love, O beauty, form'd for all delight!
Strait is thy goodly stature, firm, and high,                      635
As palms aspiring in the brighter sky;
Thy breasts the cluster, (if those breasts we view
As late for beauty, now for profit too.)
Woo'd to thine arms, those arms that oft extend
In the kind posture of a waiting friend,                           640
Each maid of Salem cries, I'll mount the tree,
Hold the broad branches, and depend on thee.
O more than grapes, thy fruit delights the maids,
Thy pleasing breath excels the Citron shades,
Thy mouth exceeds rich wine, the words that go                     645
From those sweet lips, with more refreshment flow,
Their pow'rful graces slumb'ring souls awake
And cause the dead that hear thy voice to speak.
    This anthem sung, the glorious spouse arose,
Yet thus instructs the daughters ere she goes.                     650
If ought, my damsels, in the spouse ye find
Deserving praises, think the lover kind:

To my belov'd these marriage robes I owe,
I'm his desire, and he wou'd have it so.
   Scarce spake the spouse, but see the lover near,      655
Her humble temper brought the Presence here;
Then rais'd by grace, and strongly warm'd by love,
No second Languor lets her Lord remove,
She flies to meet him, zeal supplies the wings,
And thus her haste to work his will she sings;      660
Come my beloved, to the fields repair,
Come where another spot demands our care,
There in the village we'll to rest recline,
Mean as it is I try to make it thine.
When the first rays their chearing crimson shed,      665
We'll rise betimes to see the Vineyard spread,
See Vines luxuriant verdur'd leaves display,
Supporting Tendrils curling all the way,
See young unpurpled Grapes in clusters grow,
And smell Pomegranate blossoms as they blow;      670
There will I give my loves, employ my care,
And as my labours thrive, approve me there.
Scarce have we pass'd my gate, the scent we meet;
My covering Jessamines diffuse a sweet,
My spicy flow'rets mingled as they fly,      675
With doubling odours crowd a balmy sky.
Now all the fruits which crown the season view,
These nearer Fruits are old, and those are new,
And these, and all of ev'ry loaded tree,
My love I gather and reserve for thee.      680
If then thy spouse's labour please thee well,
 Oh! like my brethren with thy Sister dwell;
No blameless maid, whose fond caresses meet
An Infant-brother in the publick street,
Clings to its lips with less reserve than I      685
Wou'd hang on thine where'er I found thee nigh:
No shame wou'd make me from thy side remove,
No danger make me not confess thy love.
Strait to my Mother's house, thine Israel she,
(And thou my Monarch wou'dst arrive with me,)      690
'Tis there I'd lead thee, where I mean to stay,
'Till thou, by her, instruct my Soul to pray;
There shal't thou prove my virtues, drink my Wine,
And feel my joy to find me wholly thine.
Oh! while my soul were sick thro' fond desire,      695

Thine hands shou'd hold me least my life expire;
As round a child the Parent's arms are plac'd,
This holds the head, and that enfolds the waist.
   So cast thy cares on me, the lover cry'd,
Lean to my bosom, lean my lovely Bride,                          700
And now ye daughters of the realm of bliss,
Let nothing discompose a love like this;
But guard her rest from each approach of ill,
I caus'd her Languor, guard her while she will.
   Here pause the lines, but soon the lines renew,              705
Once more the pair celestial come to view;
Ah! seek them once, my ravish'd fancy, more,
And then thy songs of Solomon are o'er:
By yon green bank pursue their orb of light,
The Sun shines out, but shines not half so bright.             710
See Salem's maids in white attend the King,
They greet the Spouses— hark to what they sing.
   Who from the Desert, where the wand'ring clouds
High Sinai pierces, comes involv'd with crowds?
'Tis she, the Spouse, Oh! favour'd o'er the rest!              715
Who walks reclin'd by such a lover's breast.
   The Spouse rejoicing heard the kind salute,
And thus address'd him— all the rest were mute.
Beneath the law, our goodly parent tree,
I went my much belov'd in search of thee,                       720
For thee, like one in pangs of travail strove,
Hence, none may wonder if I gain thy love.
As seals their pictures to the wax impart,
So let my picture stamp thy gentle heart,
As fix'd the Signets on our hands remain,                       725
So fix me thine, and ne'er to part again;
For love is strong as Death, whene'er they strike,
Alike imperious, vainly check'd alike;
But dread to loose, love mix'd with jealous dread!
As soon the marble Tomb resign the dead.                        730
Its fatal arrows fiery-pointed fall,
The fire intense, and thine the most of all;
To slack the points no chilling floods are found,
Nay shou'd afflictions roll like floods around,
Were wealth of nations offer'd, all wou'd prove                 735
Too small a danger, or a price for love.
If then with love this world of worth agree,
With soft regard our little Sister see,

How far unapt as yet, like maids that own
No Breasts at all, or Breasts but hardly grown,                740
Her part of Proselyte is scarce a part,
Too much a Gentile at her erring heart,
Her day draws nearer, what have we to do,
Least she be ask'd, and prove unworthy too?
   Despair not Spouse, he cries, we'll find the means,      745
Her good beginnings ask the greater pains.
Let her but stand, she thrives; a wall too low
Is not rejected for the standing so;
What falls is only lost, we'll build her high,
'Till the rich palace glitters in the sky.                     750
The Door that's weak, (what need we spare the cost?)
If tis a door, we need not think it lost;
The Leaves she brings us, if those Leaves be good,
We'll close in Cedar's uncorrupting wood.
   Rap'd with the news, the spouse converts her eyes,        755
And Oh! companions, to the maids she cries;
What joys are ours to hail the nuptial day
Which calls our Sister?—Hark I hear her say,
Yes I'm a wall; lo! she that boasted none,
Now boasts of Breasts unmeasurably grown,                      760
Large tow'ry buildings, where securely rest
A thousand thousand of my lovers guests;
The vast increase affords his heart delight,
And I find favour in his Heav'nly sight.
The Lover here, to make her rapture last,                      765
Thus adds assurance to the promise past.
  A spacious Vineyard in Baal-Hamon vale,
The vintage set, by Solomon, to sale,
His keepers took; and ev'ry keeper paid
A thousand Purses for the gains he made.                       770
And I've a vintage too; his vintage bleeds
A large increase, but my return exceeds.
Let Solomon receive his keepers pay,
He gains his thousand, their two hundred they;
Mine is mine own, 'tis in my presence still,                   775
And shall increase the more, the more she will.
My love my Vineyard, Oh the future shoots,
Which fill my garden rows with sacred fruits!
I saw the list'ning maids attend thy voice,
And in their list'ning saw their eyes rejoice,                 780
A due success thy words of comfort met,

Now turn to me—'tis I wou'd hear thee yet.
Say dove and spotless, for I must away,
Say Spouse and Sister, all you wish to say.
He spake, the place was bright with lambent fire,     785
(But what is brightness if the Christ retire?)
Gold bord'ring purple mark'd his road in air,
And kneeling all, the Spouse address'd the pray'r.
    Desire of nations! if thou must be gone,
Accept our wishes, all compriz'd in one;     790
We wait thine advent, Oh we long to see,
I and my Sister, both as one in thee.
Then leave thy Heav'n, and come and dwell below,
Why said I leave?—'tis Heav'n where ere you go.
Haste my belov'd, thy promise haste to crown,     795
The form thou'lt honour waits thy coming down,
Nor let such swiftness in the Roes be shewn
To save themselves, as thine to save thine own.
Haste like the nimblest Harts, that lightly bound
Before the stretches of the swiftest Hound,     800
With reaching feet devour a level way,
Across their backs their branching antlers lay,
In the cool dews their bending body ply,
And brush the spicy mountains as they fly.

## JONAH.

Thus sung the king—some angel reach a bough
From Eden's tree to crown the wisest brow;
And now thou fairest garden ever made,
Broad banks of spices, blossom'd walks of shade,
O Lebanon! where much I love to dwell,     5
Since I must leave thee Lebanon, farewel!
    Swift from my soul the fair Idea flies,
A wilder sight the changing scene supplies,
Wide seas come rolling to my future page,
And storms stand ready when I call, to rage.     10
Then go where Joppa crowns the winding shore,
The prophet Jonah just arrives before,
He sees a ship unmooring, soft the gales,
He pays, and enters, and the vessel sails.
    Ah wou'dst thou fly thy God? rash man forbear,     15

What land so distant but thy God is there?
Weak reason, cease thy voice.—They run the deep,
And the tir'd prophet lays his limbs to sleep.
Here God speaks louder, sends a storm to sea,
The clouds remove to give the vengeance way;                    20
Strong blasts come whistling, by degrees they roar
And shove big surges tumbling on to shore;
The vessel bounds, then rolls, and ev'ry blast
Works hard to tear her by the groaning mast;
The sailors doubling all their shouts and cares                 25
Furl the white canvas, and cast forth the wares,
Each seek the God their native regions own,
In vain they seek them, for those Gods were none.
Yet Jonah slept the while, who solely knew,
In all that number, where to find the true.                     30
To whom the pilot: sleeper, rise and pray,
Our Gods are deaf; may thine do more than they.
　　But thus the rest: perhaps we waft a foe
To heav'n itself, and that's our cause of woe;
Let's seek by lots, if heav'n be pleas'd to tell;              35
And what they sought by lots, on Jonah fell:
Then whence he came, and who, and what, and why
Thus rag'd the tempest, all confus'dly cry,
Each press'd in haste to get his question heard,
When Jonah stops them with a grave regard.                      40
　　An Hebrew man you see, who God revere,
He made this world, and makes this world his care,
His the whirl'd sky, these waves that lift their head,
And his yon land, on which you long to tread.
He charg'd me late, to Nineveh repair,                          45
And to their face denounce his sentence there:
Go, said the vision, prophet, preach to all,
Yet forty days and Nineveh shall fall.
But well I knew him gracious to forgive,
And much my zeal abhor'd the bad shou'd live,                   50
And if they turn they live; then what were I
But some false prophet when they fail to die?
Or what I fanci'd had the Gentiles too
With Hebrew prophets, and their God to do?
Drawn by the wilful thoughts, my soil I run,                    55
I fled his presence and the work's undone.
　　The storm increases as the prophet speaks,
O'er the toss'd ship a foaming billow breaks,

She rises pendant on the lifted waves
And thence descries a thousand watry graves,                    60
Then downward rushing, watry mountains hide
Her hulk beneath in deaths on ev'ry side.
O, cry the sailors all, thy fact was ill,
Yet, if a prophet, speak thy master's will,
What part is ours with thee? can ought remain               65
To bring the blessings of a calm again?
    Then Jonah—mine's the death will best atone
(And God is pleas'd that I pronounce my own)
Arise and cast me forth, the wind will cease,
The sea subsiding wear the looks of peace,                     70
And you securely steer. For well I see
Myself the criminal, the storm for me.
    Yet pity moves for one that owns a blame,
And awe resulting from a prophet's name;
Love pleads, he kindly meant for them to die,               75
Fear pleads against him, lest they pow'r defy:
If then to aid the flight abets the sin,
They think to land him, where they took him in.
Perhaps to quit the cause might end the woe,
And God appeasing, let the vessel go.                          80
For this they fix their oars and strike the main,
But God withstands them, and they strike in vain.
    The storm increases more with want of light,
Low black'ning clouds involve the ship in night,
Thick batt'ring rains fly thro' the driving skies,          85
Loud thunder bellows, darted light'ning flies,
A dreadful picture night-born horrour drew,
And his, or theirs, or both their fates, they view.
    Then thus to God they cry; Almighty pow'r,
Whom we ne'er knew 'till this despairing hour,             90
From this devoted blood thy servants free,
To us he's innocent, if so to thee;
In all the past we see thy wond'rous hand,
And that he perish, think it thy command.
    This pray'r perform'd, they cast the prophet o'er,     95
A surge receives him and he mounts no more;
Then stills the thunder, cease the flames of blue,
The rains abated and the winds withdrew,
The clouds ride off, and as they march away,
Thro' ev'ry breaking shoots a chearful day;                  100
The sea, which rag'd so loud, accepts the prize,

A while it rolls, then all the tempest dies,
By gradual sinking, flat the surface grows,
And safe the vessel with the sailors goes.
The Lion thus, that bounds the fences o'er,                    105
And makes the Mountain-Ecchoes learn to roar,
If on the lawn a branching deer he rend,
Then falls his hunger, all his roarings end,
Murm'ring a while, to rest his limbs he lays,
And the freed lawn enjoys its herd at ease.                   110
   Bless'd with the sudden calm, the sailors own
That wretched Jonah worship'd right alone,
Then make their vows, the victim sheep prepare,
Bemoan the prophet, and the God revere.
   Now tho' you fear to loose the pow'r to breath,            115
Now tho' you tremble, Fancy, dive beneath;
What world of wonders in the deep are seen;
But this the greatest—Jonah lives within!
The man who fondly fled the Maker's view,
Strange as the crime has found a dungeon too.                 120
God sent a monster of the frothing sea,
Fit by the bulk to gorge the living prey,
And lodge him still alive; this hulk receives
The falling prophet as he dash'd the waves.
There newly wak'd, from fanci'd death he lies,                125
And oft again in apprehension dies:
While three long days and nights depriv'd of sleep,
He turn'd and toss'd him up and down the deep.
He thinks the judgment of the strangest kind,
And much he wonders what the Lord design'd;                   130
Yet since he lives, the gift of life he weighs,
That's time for pray'r, and thus a ground for praise;
From the dark entrails of the whale to thee,
(This new contrivance of a hell to me)
To thee my God I cry'd, my full distress                      135
Pierc'd thy kind ear, and brought my soul redress.
Cast to the deep I fell, by thy command,
Cast in the midst beyond the reach of land;
Then to the midst brought down, the seas abide
Beneath my feet, the seas on ev'ry side;                      140
In storms the billow, and in calms the wave,
Are moving cov'rings to my wand'ring grave;
Forc'd by despair I cry'd; how to my cost
I fled thy presence, Oh for ever lost!

But hope revives my soul, and makes me say, 145
Yet tow'rds thy temple shall I turn and pray,
Or if I know not here, where Salem lies,
Thy temple's heav'n, and faith has inward eyes.
Alas the waters which my whale surround,
Have thro' my sorr'wing soul a passage found; 150
And now the dungeon moves, new depths I try,
New thoughts of danger all his paths supply.
The last of Deeps affords the last of dread,
And wraps its funeral weeds around my head:
Now o'er the sand his rollings seem to go 155
Where the big mountains root their base below;
And now to rocks and clefts their course they take,
Earth's endless bars, too strong for me to break;
Yet from th' Abyss, my God! thy grace divine
Hath call'd him upward, and my life is mine. 160
Still as I toss'd, I scarce retain'd my breath,
My soul was sick within, and faint to death.
'Twas then I thought of thee, for pity pray'd,
And to thy temple flew the pray'rs I made.
The men whom lying vanity insnares 165
Forsake thy mercy, that which might be theirs.
But I will pay—my God! my King! receive
The solemn vows my full affection give,
When in thy temple, for a psalm, I sing
Salvation only from my God my king. 170
    Thus ends the prophet, first from Canaan sent,
To let the Gentiles know they must repent:
God hears, and speaks; the Whale at God's command,
Heaves to the light, and casts him forth to land.
    With long fatigue, with unexpected ease, 175
Oppress'd a while, he lies aside the seas,
His eyes tho' glad, in strange astonish'd way
Stare at the golden front of chearful day;
Then slowly rais'd he sees the wonder plain,
And what he pray'd, he wrote to sing again. 180
    The song recorded brings his vow to mind,
He must be thankful, for the Lord was kind;
Strait to the work he shun'd, he flies in haste,
(That seems his vow, or seems a part at least,)
Preaching he comes, and thus denounc'd to all, 185
Yet forty days and Nineveh shall fall,
Fear seiz'd the Gentiles, Nineveh believes,

All fast with Penitence, and God forgives.
  Nor yet of use the prophet's suff'ring fails,
Hell's deep black bosom more than shews the Whales,          190
But some resemblance brings a type to view,
The place was dark, the time proportion'd too.
A race, the Saviour cries, a sinful race,
Tempts for a sign, the pow'rs of Heav'nly grace,
And let them take the sign, as Jonah lay,          195
Three days and nights within the fish of prey;
So shall the Son of Man descend below,
Earth's op'ning Entrails shall retain him so.
  My soul now seek the song, and find me there,
What Heav'n has shewn thee to repel despair;          200
See where from Hell she breaks the crumbling ground,
Her hairs stand upright, and they stare around;
Her horrid front, deep-trenching wrinkles trace,
Lean sharp'ning looks deform her livid face;
Bent lie the brows, and at the bend below,          205
With fire and blood, two wand'ring eye-balls glow;
Fill'd are her arms with num'rous aids to kill,
And God she fancies but the judge of ill;
Oh fair-ey'd Hope! thou see'st the passion nigh,
Daughter of Promise, Oh forbear to fly!          210
Assurance holds thee, fear would have thee go,
Close thy blue wings and stand thy deadly foe;
The judge of ill is still the Lord of grace,
As such behold him in the Prophet's case;
Cast to be drown'd, devour'd within the sea,          215
Sunk to the deep, and yet restor'd to day.
  Oh love the Lord my soul, whose present care
So rules the world, he punishes to spare.
If heavy grief my downcast heart oppress,
My body danger, or my state distress,          220
With low submission in thy temper bow,
Like Jonah pray, like Jonah make thy vow,
With hopes of comfort kiss the chast'ning rod,
And shunning mad despair, repose in God;
Then whatsoe'er the Prophet's vow design,          225
Repentance, Thanks, and Charity be mine.

## *HEZEKIAH.*

FROM the bleak Beach and broad expanse of sea,
To lofty Salem, Thought direct thy way;
Mount thy light chariot, move along the plains,
And end thy flight where Hezekiah reigns.
    How swiftly thought has pass'd from land to land,                    5
And quite outrun Time's meas'ring glass of sand,
Great Salem's walls appear and I resort
To view the state of Hezekiah's court.
    Well may that king a pious verse inspire,
Who cleans'd the temple, who reviv'd the choir,                          10
Pleas'd with the service David fix'd before,
That heav'nly musick might on earth adore.
Deep-rob'd in white, he made the Levites stand
With Cymbals, Harps, and Psaltries in their hand;
He gave the Priests their trumpets, prompt to raise                     15
The tuneful soul, by force of sound to praise.
A skilful master for the song he chose,
The songs were David's these, and Asaph's those.
Then burns their off'ring, all around rejoice,
Each tunes his instrument to join the voice;                            20
The trumpets sounded, and the singers sung,
The People worship'd and the temple rung.
Each while the victim burns presents his heart,
Then the Priest blesses, and the People part.
    Hail sacred musick! since you know to draw                          25
The soul to Heav'n, the spirit to the law,
I come to prove thy force, thy warbling string
May tune my soul to write what others sing.
    But is this Salem? this the proms'd bliss,
These sighs and groans? what means the realm by this?                   30
What solemn sorrow dwells in ev'ry street?
What fear confounds the downcast looks I meet?
Alas the King! whole nations sink with woe,
When righteous Kings are summon'd hence to go;
The King lies sick, and thus to speak his doom,                         35
The Prophet, grave Isaiah, stalks the room:
Oh Prince thy servant sent from God, believe,
Set all in order for thou can'st not live.
Solemn he said, and sighing left the place,
Deep prints of horror furrow'd ev'ry face,                              40

Within their minds appear eternal glooms,
Black gaping marbles of their monarchs tombs,
A King belov'd deceas'd, his offspring none,
And wars destructive e'er they fix the throne.
Strait to the wall he turn'd with dark despair,                    45
('Twas tow'rds the temple, or for private pray'r,)
And thus to God the pious monarch spoke,
Who burn'd the groves, the brazen serpent broke:
Remember Lord with what a heart for right,
What care for truth, I walk'd within thy sight.                    50
    'Twas thus with terror, pray'rs and tears he toss'd,
When the mid-court the grave Isaiah cross'd,
Whom in the cedar columns of the square,
Meets a sweet Angel hung in glitt'ring air.
Seiz'd with a trance he stop'd, before his eye                    55
Clears a rais'd arch of visionary sky,
Where as a minute pass'd, the greater light
Purpling appear'd, and south'd and set in night;
A Moon succeeding leads the starry train,
She glides, and sinks her silver horns again:                    60
A second fanci'd morning drives the shades;
Clos'd by the dark the second ev'ning fades;
The third bright dawn awakes, and strait he sees
The temple rise, the monarch on his knees.
Pleas'd with the scene, his inward thoughts rejoice,                    65
When thus the Guardian angel form'd a voice.
Now tow'rds the captain of my people go,
And, Seer, relate him what thy visions show,
The Lord has heard his words, and seen his tears,
And through fifteen extends his future years.                    70
    Here to the room prepar'd with dismal black,
The Prophet turning, brought the comfort back.
Oh monarch hail, he cry'd, thy words are heard,
Thy virtuous actions meet a kind regard,
God gives thee fifteen years, when thrice a day,                    75
Shews the round Sun, within the temple pray.
    When thrice the day! surpriz'd the monarch cries,
When thrice the Sun! what pow'r have I to rise!
But if thy comfort's human or divine,
'Tis short to prove it—give thy prince a sign.                    80
    Behold, the Prophet cry'd, (and stretch'd his hands)
Against yon lattice where the dial stands,
Now shall the Sun a backward journey go

Through ten drawn lines, or leap to ten below.
'Tis easier posting nature's airy track,                                85
Replies the monarch, let the Sun go back.
Attentive here he gaz'd, the prophet pray'd,
Back went the Sun, and back pursu'd the shade.
    Chear'd by the sign, and by the Prophet heal'd,
What sacred thanks his gratitude reveal'd?                              90
As sickly Swallows when a summer ends,
Who miss'd the passage with their flying friends,
Take to a wall, there lean the languid head,
While all who find them think the sleepers dead;
If yet their warmth new days of summer bring,                          95
They wake and joyful flutter up to sing;
So far'd the monarch, sick to death he lay,
His court despair'd, and watch'd the last decay;
At length new favour shines, new life he gains,
And rais'd he sings; 'tis thus the song remains.                       100
    I said, my God, when in the loath'd disease
Thy Prophet's words cut off my future days,
Now to the grave with mournful haste I go,
Now death unbars his sable gates below.
How might my years by course of nature last?                           105
But thou pronounc'd it, and the prospect pass'd.
I said, my God, thy servant now no more
Shall in thy Temple's sacred courts adore,
No more on earth with living man converse,
Shrunk in a cold uncomfortable hearse.                                 110
My life, like tents which wand'ring shepherds raise,
Proves a short dwelling and removes at ease.
My sins pursue me, see the deadly band,
My God, who sees them, cuts me from the land;
As when a weaver finds his labour sped,                                115
Swift from the beam he parts the fast'ning thread.
With pining sickness all from night to day,
From day to night, he makes my strength decay:
Reck'ning the time, I roll with restless groans,
'Till with a lion's force, he crush my bones,                          120
New-morning dawns, but like the morning past,
'Tis day, 'tis night, and still my sorrows last.
Now screaming like the Crane my words I spoke,
Now like the swallow, chatt'ring quick and broke,
Now like the doleful dove, when on the plains                          125
Her mourning tone affects the list'ning swains.

To heav'n for aid my wearying eyes I throw,
At length they're weary'd quite, and sink with woe.
From death's arrest for some delays I sue,
Thou Lord who judg'd me, thou reprieve me too.　　　130
　　Rapture of joy! what can thy servant say?
He sent his Prophet to prolong my day;
Through my glad Limbs I feel the wonder run,
Thus said the Lord, and this Himself has done.
Soft shall I walk, and well secur'd from fears　　　135
Possess the comforts of my future years.
Keep soft my heart, keep humble while they roll,
Nor e'er forget my bitterness of soul.
'Tis by the means thy sacred words supply
That mankind live, but in peculiar I;　　　140
A second grant thy mercy pleas'd to give,
And my rais'd spirits doubly seem to live.
Behold the time! when peace adorn'd my reign,
'Twas then I felt my stroke of humbling pain;
Corruption dug her pit, I fear'd to sink,　　　145
God lov'd my soul, and snatch'd me from the brink.
He turn'd my follies from his gracious eye,
As men who pass accounts and cast them by.
　　What mouth has death which can thy praise proclaim?
What tongue the grave to speak thy glorious name?　　　150
Or will the senseless dead exult with mirth,
Mov'd to their hope by promises on earth?
The living Lord, the living only praise,
The living only fit to sing thy lays,
These feel thy favours, these thy temple see,　　　155
These raise the song, as I this day to thee.
Nor will thy truth the present only reach,
This the good fathers shall their offspring teach,
Report the blessings which adorn my page,
And hand their own with mine from age to age.　　　160
　　So when the Maker heard his creature crave,
So kindly rose his ready Will to save.
Then march we solemn tow'rds the Temple door,
While all our joyful musick sounds before,
There on this day through all my life appear,　　　165
When this comes round in each returning year,
There strike the strings, our voices jointly raise,
And let his dwellings hear my songs of praise.
　　Thus wrote the monarch, and I'll think the lay

Design'd for publick when he went to pray;                          170
I'll think the perfect composition runs,
Perform'd by Heman's or Jeduthun's sons.
 Then since the time arrives the Seer foretold,
And the third morning rolls an orb of gold,
With thankful zeal recover'd prince prepare                         175
To lead thy nation to the Dome of pray'r.
 My fancy takes her chariot once again,
Moves the rich wheels, and mingles in thy train;
She sees the singers reach Moriah's hill,
The minstrels follow, then the porches fill,                        180
She wakes the num'rous instruments of art,
That each perform its own adapted part,
Seeks airs expressive of thy grateful strains,
And list'ning hears the vary'd tune she feigns.
 From a grave pitch, to speak the Monarch's woe,                185
The notes flow down and deeply sound below,
All long-continuing, while depriv'd of ease
He rolls for tedious nights and heavy days.
Here intermix'd with discord, when the Crane
Screams in the notes through sharper sense of pain;                 190
There run with descant on, and taught to shake
When pangs repeated force the voice to break;
Now like the dove they murmur, 'till in sighs
They fall, and languish with the failing eyes.
Then slowly slack'ning, to surprize the more,                      195
From a dead pause, his exclamations soar,
To meet brisk health the notes ascending fly,
Live with the living, and exult on high.
Yet still distinct in parts the musick plays,
'Till prince and people both are call'd to praise,                 200
Then all uniting strongly strike the string,
Put forth their utmost breath, and loudly sing;
The wide spread chorus fills the sacred ground,
And holy transport scales the clouds with sound.
 Or thus, or livelier, if their hand and voice                 205
Join'd the good anthem, might the realm rejoice.
 This story known, the learn'd Chaldeans came,
Drawn by the sign observ'd, or mov'd by fame;
These ask the fact for Hezekiah done,
And much they wonder at their God the sun,                          210
That thrice he drove through one extent of day
His gold-shod horses in etherial way:

Then vainly ground their guess on nature's laws,
The soundest knowledge owns a greater cause.
    Faith knows the fact transcends, and bids me find          215
What help for practice here incites the mind;
Strait to the song, the thankful song I move,
May such the voice of ev'ry creature prove,
If ev'ry creature meets its share of woe,
And for kind rescues ev'ry creature owe;                       220
In publick so thy Maker's praise proclaim,
Nor what you beg'd with tears, conceal with shame.
    'Tis there the ministry thy name repeat
And tell what mercies were vouchsaf'd of late,
Then joins the church, and begs through all our days           225
Not only with our lips, but lives to praise.
    'Tis there our Sov'reigns for a signal day,
The feast proclaim'd, their signal thanks repay.
O'er the long streets we see the chariots wheel,
And, following, think of Hezekiah still;                       230
In the bless'd Dome we meet the white-rob'd Choir,
In whose sweet notes our ravish'd souls aspire;
Side answ'ring side we hear and bear a part,
All warm'd with language from the grateful heart,
Or raise the song where meeting keys rejoice,                  235
And teach the Base to wed the treble voice;
Arts soft'ning ecchos in the musick sound,
And answ'ring natures from the roof rebound.
    Here close my verse, the service asks no more,
Bless thy good God, and give the transport o'er.               240


## HABAKKUK.


N ow leave the Porch, to vision now retreat,
    Where the next rapture glows with varying heat;
Now change the time, and change the Temple scene,
The following Seer forewarns a future reign.
To some retirement, where the Prophets sons                    5
Indulge their holy flight, my fancy runs,
Some sacred College built for praise and pray'r
And heav'nly dream, she seeks Habakkuk there.
Perhaps 'tis there he moans the nation's sin,
Hears the word come, or feels the fit within,                  10

Or sees the vision fram'd with Angels hands,
And dreads the judgments of revolted lands,
Or holds a converse if the Lord appear,
And, like Elijah, wraps his face for fear.
This deep recess portends an act of weight,                          15
A message lab'ring with the work of fate.
   Methinks the Skies have lost their lovely blue,
A storm rides fiery, thick the clouds ensue.
Fall'n to the ground with prostrate face I lye,
Oh! 'twere the same in this to gaze and dye!                         20
But hark the Prophet's voice: my pray'rs complain
Of labour spent, of Preaching urg'd in vain;
And must, my God, thy sorrowing servant still
Quit my lone joys to walk this world of ill?
Where spoiling rages, strife and wrong command,                     25
And the slack'd laws no longer curb the land?
   At this a strange and more than human sound
Thus breaks the cloud and daunts the trembling ground.
Behold the Gentiles, wond'ring all behold,
What scarce ye credit tho' the work be told,                        30
For lo the proud Chaldean troops I raise,
To march the breadth and all the region seize,
Fierce as the proling wolves at close of day,
And swift as eagles in pursuit of prey.
As eastern winds to blast the season blow,                          35
For blood and rapine flies the dreadful foe;
Leads the sad captives countless as the sand,
Derides the princes and destroys the land.
Yet these triumphant grown offend me more,
And only thank the Gods they chose before.                          40
   Art thou not holiest, here the prophet cries,
Supream, Eternal, of the purest eyes?
And shall those eyes the wicked realms regard,
Their crimes be great yet vict'ry their reward?
Shall these still ravage more and more to reign,                    45
Draw the full net, and cast to fill again?
As watch-men silent sit, I wait to see
How solves my doubt, what speaks the Lord to me.
   Then go, the Lord replys, suspend thy fears,
And write the vision for a term of years.                           50
Thy foes will feel their turn when those are past,
Wait tho' it tarry, sure it comes at last.
'Tis for their rapine, lusts and thirst of blood

And all their unprotecting Gods of wood.
The Lord is present on his sacred hill,                          55
Cease thy weak doubts, and let the world be still.
    Here terrour leaves me with exalted head,
I breath fine air, and find the vision fled,
The Seer withdrawn, inspir'd, and urg'd to write,
By the warm influence of the sacred sight.                      60
    His writing finish'd, Prophet-like array'd,
He brings the burthen on the region laid;
His hands a tablet and a volume bear,
The tablet threatnings, and the volume pray'r,
Both for the temple, where to shun decay,                       65
Enroll'd the works of inspiration lay.
And awful oft he stops, or marches slow,
While the dull'd nation hears him preach their woe.
    Arriv'd at length, with grave concern for all,
He fix'd his table on the sacred wall.                           70
'Twas large inscrib'd that those who run might read,
"Habakkuk's burthen by the Lord decreed,
"For Judah's sins, her empire is no more,
"The fierce Chaldeans bath her ralm in gore".
    Next to the priest his volume he resign'd,                   75
'Twas pray'r with praises mix'd to raise the mind,
'Twas facts recounted which their fathers knew,
'Twas pow'r in wonders manifest to view.
'Twas comfort rais'd on love already past,
And hope that former love returns at last.                       80
    The priests within the prophecy convey'd,
The singers tunes to join his anthem made.
Here and attend the words. And holy thou
That help'd the prophet, help the Poet now.
    O Lord who rules the world, with mortal ear                  85
I've heard thy judgments, and I shake for fear.
O Lord by whom their number'd years we find,
E'en in the midst receive the drooping mind;
E'en in the midst thou canst—then make it known
Thy love, thy will, thy power, to save thine own.                90
Remember mercy tho' thine anger burn,
And soon to Salem bid thy flock return.
O Lord who gav'st it with an outstretch'd hand,
We well remember how thou gav'st the land.
    God came from Teman, southward sprung the flame,             95
From Paron-mount the one that's Holy came,

A glitt'ring glory made the desart blaze,
High Heav'n was cover'd, earth was fill'd with praise.
Dazzling the brightness, not the sun so bright,
'Twas here the pure substantial Fount of Light                    100
Shot from his hand and side in golden streams,
Came forward effluent horny-pointed beams:
Thus shone his coming, as sublimely fair
As bounded nature has been fram'd to bear,
But all his further marks of grandeur hid,                        105
Nor what he cou'd was known, but what he did.
Dire plagues before him ran at his command,
To waste the nations in the promis'd land.
A scorching flame went forth where'er he trod,
And burning Fevers were the coals of God.                         110
Fix'd on the mount he stood, his meas'ring reed
Marks the rich realms for Jacob's seed decreed:
He looks with anger and the nations fly
From the fierce sparklings of his dreadful eye.
He turns, the mountain shakes its awful brow,                     115
Awful he turns, and hills eternal bow.
How glory there, how terrour here, displays
His great unknown yet everlasting ways.
    I see the Sable tents along the strand
Where Cushan wander'd, desolately stand,                          120
And Midian's high pavilions shake with dread,
While the tam'd seas thy rescu'd nation tread.
What burst the path? what made the Lord engage?
Cou'd waters anger? seas incite thy rage?
That thus thine horses force the foaming tide                     125
And all the chariots of salvation ride.
Thy bow was bare for what thy mercy swore,
Those oaths, that promise Israel had before.
    The rock that felt thee cleav'd, the rivers flow,
The wond'ring desart lends them beds below.                       130
Thy Might the mountain's heaving shocks confess'd,
High shatter'd Horeb trembled o'er the rest.
Great Jordan pass'd its nether waters by,
Its upper waters rais'd the voice on high,
Safe in the deep we went, the liquid wall                         135
Curling arose, and had no leave to fall.
The sun effulgent and the moon serene,
Stop'd by thy will, their heav'nly course refrain;
The voice was Man's, yet both the voice obey,

'Till wars compleated close the lengthen'd day.                140
Thy glitt'ring spears, thy ratling darts prevail,
Thy spears of lightning and thy darts of hail.
'Twas thou that march'd against their heathen band,
Rage in thy visage, and thy flail in hand;
'Twas thou that went before to wound their head,             145
The captain follow'd where the Saviour led;
Torn from their earth they feel the desp'rate wound,
And pow'r unfounded fails for want of ground.
With village-war thy tribes where'er they go
Distress the remnant of the scatter'd foe;                   150
Yet mad they rush'd, as whirling wind descends,
And deem'd for friendless those the Lord befriends.
Thy trampling horse from sea to sea subdue,
The bounding ocean left no more to do.
   O when I heard what thou vouchsaf'st to win               155
With works of wonder, must be lost for sin,
I quak'd thro' fear, the voice forsook my tongue,
Or at my lips with quiv'ring accent hung;
Dry leanness ent'ring to my marrow came,
And ev'ry loos'ning nerve unstrung my frame.                 160
How shall I rest, in what protecting shade,
When the day comes, and hostile troops invade?
   Tho' neither blossoms on the Fig appear,
Nor vines with clusters deck the purpling year,
Tho' all our labours olive-trees belie,                      165
Tho' fields the substance of the bread deny,
Tho' flocks are sever'd from the silent Fold,
And the rais'd stalls no lowing cattle hold,
Yet shall my soul be glad, in God rejoice,
Yet to my Saviour will I lift my voice,                      170
Yet to my Saviour still my temper sings,
What David set to instruments of strings:
The Lord's my strength, like Hinds he makes my feet,
Yon mount's my refuge, as I safely fleet,
Or (if the song's apply'd) he makes me still                 175
Expect returning to Moriah's hill.
   In all this hymn what daring grandeur shines,
What darting glory rays among the lines,
What mountains, earthquakes, clouds, and smokes are seen,
What ambient fires conceal the Lord within,                  180
What working wonders give the promis'd place
And load the conduct of a stubborn race!

In all the work a lively fancy flows,
O'er all the work sincere affection glows,
While Truth's firm Rein the course of fancy guides          185
And o'er affection Zeal divine presides.
  Borne on the prophet's wings, methinks I fly
Amongst eternal Attributes on high,
And here I touch at love supremely fair,
And now at pow'r, anon at mercy there;          190
So like a warbling bird my tunes I raise
On those green boughs the Tree of life displays,
Whose twelve fair fruits each month by turns receives
And for the nations healing ope their leaves.
Then be the nations heal'd, for this I sing          195
Descending softly from the prophet's wing.
  Thou world attend, the case of Israel see,
'Twill thus at large refer to God and thee.
If love be shewn thee, turn thine eyes above
And pay the duties relative to love;          200
If pow'r be shewn, and wonderfully so,
Wonder and thank, adore and bow below.
If pow'r that led thee now no longer lead,
But brow-bent Justice draws the flaming blade,
When love is scorn'd, when sin the sword provokes,          205
Let tears and pray'rs avert or heal the strokes;
If justice leaves to wound, and thou to groan
Beneath new Lords in countries not thine own,
Know this for Mercy's act, and let your lays
Grateful in all, recount the cause of praise:          210
Then love returns, and while no sins divide
The firm alliance, pow'r will shield thy side.
  See the grand round of providence's care,
See realms assisted here, and punish'd there,
O'er the just circle cast thy wond'ring eyes,          215
Thank while you gaze, and study to be wise.

# The Affections of Divine Poetry

## A Hymn for Morning.

S<small>EE</small> the star that leads the day
  Rising shoots a golden ray,
To make the shades of darkness go
From heav'n above and earth below;
And warn us early with the sight                      5
To leave the beds of silent night,
From an heart sincere and sound
From its very deepest ground,
Send Devotion up on high
Wing'd with heat to reach the sky.                    10
See the time for sleep has run,
Rise before, or with the sun,
Lift thine hands and humbly pray
The fountain of eternal day,
That as the light serenely fair                       15
Illustrates all the tracts of air,
The sacred spirit so may rest
With quick'ning beams upon thy breast,
And kindly clean it all within
From darker blemishes of sin,                         20
And shine with grace until we view
The realm it gilds with glory too.
See the day that dawns in air,
Brings along its toil and care,
From the lap of night it springs                      25
With heaps of business on its wings;
Prepare to meet them in a mind
That bows submissively resign'd,

That wou'd to works appointed fall,
And knows that God has order'd all.                          30
And whether with a small repast
We break the sober morning fast,
Or in our thoughts and houses lay
The future methods of the day,
Or early walk abroad to meet                                35
Our business, with industr'ous feet,
Whate'er we think whate'er we do,
His glory still be kept in view.
O Giver of eternal bliss,
Heav'nly Father grant me this,                              40
Grant it all as well as me,
All whose hearts are fix'd on thee,
Who revere thy son above
Who thy sacred spirit love.


## A Hymn for Noon.


THE sun is swiftly mounted high,
It glitters in the southern sky,
Its beams with force and glory beat,
And fruitful earth is fill'd with heat.
Father, also with thy fire                                  5
Warm the cold the dead desire,
And make the sacred love of thee,
Within my soul a sun to me.
Let it shine so fairly bright,
That nothing else be took for light;                        10
That worldly charms be seen to fade,
And in its lustre find a shade.
Let it strongly shine within
To scatter all the clouds of sin,
That drive when gusts of passion rise                       15
And intercept it from our eyes.
Let its glory more than vie
With the sun that lights the sky,
Let it swiftly mount in air,
Mount with that, and leave it there,                        20
And soar with more aspiring flight
To realms of everlasting Light.

Thus while here I'm forc'd to be,
I daily wish to live with thee,
And feel that union which thy love                    25
Will, after death, compleat above.
From my soul I send my pray'r,
Great Creator bow thine ear;
Thou for whose propitious sway
The world was taught to see the day,                  30
Who spake the word and earth begun
And shew'd its beauties in the sun,
With pleasure I thy creatures view,
And wou'd with good affection too,
Good affection sweetly free,                          35
Loose from them and move to thee;
O teach me due returns to give,
And to thy glory let me live,
And then my days shall shine the more
Or pass more blessed than before.                     40

## A Hymn for Evening.

T HE beam-repelling mists arise,
  And ev'ning spreads obscurer skies:
The twilight will the night forerun,
And night itself be soon begun.
Upon thy knees devoutly bow,                           5
And pray the Lord of glory now
To fill thy breast, or deadly sin
May cause a blinder night within.
And whether pleasing vapours rise,
Which gently dim the closing eyes,                    10
Which make the weary members bless'd
With sweet refreshment in their rest;
Or whether spirits in the brain
Dispel their soft embrace again,
And on my watchful bed I stay,                        15
Forsook by sleep and waiting day;
Be God for ever in my view
And never he forsake me too;
But still as day concludes in night,
To break again with new born light,                   20

His wond'rous bounty let me find
With still a more enlighten'd mind,
When grace and love in one agree,
Grace from God, and love from me,
Grace that will from heav'n inspire,                           25
Love that seals it in desire,
Grace and love that mingle beams,
And fill me with encreasing flames.
Thou that hast thy palace far
Above the moon and ev'ry star,                                 30
Thou that sittest on a throne
To which the night was never known,
Regard my voice and make me bless'd,
By kindly granting its request.
If thoughts on thee my soul employ,                            35
My darkness will afford me joy,
'Till thou shalt call, and I shall soar,
And part with darkness evermore.

## The Soul in Sorrow.

WITH kind compassion hear my cry
O Jesu, Lord of life, on high!
As when the Summer's seasons beat
With scorching flame and parching heat,
The trees are burnt, the flowers fade,                         5
And thirsty gaps in earth are made,
My thoughts of comfort languish so,
And so my soul is broke by woe.
Then on thy servant's drooping head,
Thy dews of blessing sweetly shed;                             10
Let those a quick refreshment give
And raise my mind, and bid me live.
My fears of danger while I breath,
My dread of endless hell beneath,
My sense of sorrow for my sin,                                 15
To springing comfort, change within,
Change all my sad complaints for ease,
To chearful notes of endless praise;
Nor let a tear mine eyes employ
But such as owe their birth to joy:                            20

Joy transporting sweet and strong,
Fit to fill and raise my song,
Joy that shall resounded be
While days and nights succeed for me:
Be not as a Judge severe,                                    25
For so thy presence who may bear?
On all my words and actions look,
(I know they're written in thy book)
But then regard my mournful cry
And look with Mercy's gracious eye,                          30
What needs my blood since thine will do
To pay the debt to justice due.
O tender mercy's art divine!
Thy sorrow proves the cure of mine,
Thy dropping wounds, thy woful smart,                        35
Allay the bleedings of my heart:
Thy death, in death's extreme of pain,
Restores my soul to life again.
Guide me then for here I burn
To make my Saviour some return.                              40
I'll rise, (if that will please him still
And sure I've heard him own it will)
I'll trace his steps and bear my cross
Despising ev'ry grief and loss;
Since he despising pain and shame,                           45
First took up his, and did the same.


## The Happy Man.


How bless'd the man, how fully so,
As far as man is bless'd below,
Who taking up his cross essays
To follow Jesus all his days,
With resolution to obey,                                     5
And steps enlarging in his way.
The Father of the saints above
Adopts him with a Father's love,
And makes his bosom throughly shine
With wond'rous stores of grace divine;                       10
Sweet grace divine the pledge of joy
That will his soul above employ;

Full joy, that when his time is done
Becomes his portion as a son.
Ah me! the sweet infus'd desires                    15
The fervid wishes, holy fires,
Which thus a melted heart refine,
Such are his and such be mine.
From hence, despising all besides
That earth reveals or ocean hides,                  20
All that men in either prize,
On God alone he sets his eyes.
From hence his hope is on the wings,
His health renews, his safety springs,
His glory blazes up below,                          25
And all the streams of comfort flow.
　　He calls his Saviour, King above,
Lord of mercy, Lord of love,
And finds a kingly care defend,
And mercy smile, and love descend,                  30
To chear, to guide him in the ways
Of this vain world's deceitful maze:
And tho' the wicked earth display
Its terrors in their fierce array,
Or gape so wide that horrour shews                  35
Its hell replete with endless woes;
Such succour keeps him clear of Ill
Still firm to good and dauntless still.
So fix'd, by Providence's hands
A rock amidst an ocean stands;                      40
So bears without a trembling dread
The tempest beating round its head,
And with its side repels the wave
Whose hollow seems a coming grave;
The skies the deeps are heard to roar               45
The rock stands settled as before.
　　I, all with whom he has to do,
Admire the life which blesses you,
That feeds a foe, that aids a friend,
Without a bye designing end;                        50
Its knowing real int'rest lies
On the bright side of yonder skies,
Where having made a title fair
It mounts and leaves the world to care.
While he that seeks for pleasing days               55

In earthly joys and evil ways,
Is but the fool of toil or fame,
(Tho' happy be the specious name)
And made by wealth, which makes him great,
A more conspicuous wretch of state.                    60

## The Way to Happiness.

How long ye miserable blind
    Shall idle dreams engage your mind,
How long the passions make their flight
At empty shadows of delight?
No more in paths of error stray,                       5
The Lord thy Jesus is the way,
The spring of happiness, and where
Shou'd men seek happiness but there?
Then run to meet him at your need,
Run with boldness, run with speed,                     10
For he forsook his own abode
To meet thee more than half the road.
He laid aside his radiant crown
And love for mankind brought him down
To thirst and hunger, pain and woe,                    15
To wounds, to death it self below,
And he that suffer'd these alone
For all the World, despises none.
To bid the soul that's sick be clean,
To bring the lost to life again,                       20
To comfort those that grieve for ill,
Is his peculiar goodness still.
And as the thoughts of parents run
Upon a dear and only son,
So kind a love his mercies shew,                       25
So kind and more extreamly so.
    Thrice happy men (or find a phrase
That speaks your bliss with greater praise)
Who most obedient to thy call
Leaving pleasures leaving all,                         30
With heart with soul, with strength incline
O sweetest Jesu! to be thine;
Who know thy will, observe thy ways,

And in thy service spend their days:
E'en death that seems to set them free                    35
But brings them closer still to thee.


## The Convert's Love.


B LESSED Light of saints on high
   Who fill the mansions of the sky,
Sure defence, whose mercy still
Preserves thy subjects here from ill,
O my Jesus! make me know                                  5
How to pay the thanks I owe.
  As the fond sheep that id'ly strays
With wanton play thro' winding ways,
Which never hits the road of home,
O'er Wilds of danger learns to roam,                      10
'Till weari'd out with idle fear
And passing there and turning here,
He will for rest to covert run
And meet the wolf he wish'd to shun;
Thus wretched I, thro' wanton will                        15
Run blind and headlong on in ill:
'Twas thus from sin to sin I flew
And thus I might have perish'd too;
But mercy dropt the likeness here
And shew'd and sav'd me from my fear;                     20
While o'er the darkness of my mind
The sacred spirit purely shin'd,
And mark'd and bright'ned all the way
Which leads to everlasting day,
And broke the thick'ning clouds of sin                    25
And fix'd the light of love within.
  From hence my ravish'd soul aspires
And dates the rise of its desires.
From hence to thee my God! I turn,
And fervent wishes say I burn,                            30
I burn thy glorious face to see
And live in endless joy with thee.
  There's no such ardent kind of flame
Between the lover and the dame,
Nor such affection parents bear                           35
To their young and only heir,

Tho' join'd together both conspire
And boast a doubled force of fire.
My tender heart within its seat
Dissolves before the scorching heat,                40
As soft'ning wax is taught to run
Before the warmness of the sun.
  O my flame my pleasing pain
Burn and purify my stain,
Warm me, burn me, day by day                45
'Till you purge my earth away,
'Till at the last I throughly shine
And turn a torch of love divine.

## A Desire to Praise.

Propitious Son of God to thee
  With all my soul I bend my knee,
My wish I send my want impart,
And dedicate my mind and heart,
For as an absent parent's son                5
Whose second year is only run,
When no protecting friend is near,
Void of wit and void of fear,
With things that hurt him fondly plays,
Or here he falls, or there he strays;                10
So shou'd my soul's eternal guide
The sacred spirit be deny'd,
Thy servant soon the loss wou'd know,
And sink in sin, or run to woe.
  O spirit bountifully kind,                15
Warm, possess, and fill my mind,
Disperse my sins with light divine
And raise the flames of love with thine,
Before thy pleasures rightly priz'd
Let wealth and honour be despis'd,                20
And let the Father's glory be
More dear itself than life to me.
  Sing of Jesus! virgins sing
Him your everlasting King;
Sing of Jesus! chearful youth,                25
Him the God of love and truth:
Write and raise a song divine

Or come and hear, and borrow mine.
Son Eternal, word supreme,
Who made the universal frame, 30
Heav'n and all its shining show,
Earth and all it holds below;
Bow with mercy bow thine ear
While we sing thy praises here;
Son Eternal ever bless'd, 35
Resting on the Father's breast,
Whose tender love for all provides,
Whose power over all presides;
Bow with pity, bow thine ear
While we sing thy praises, hear. 40
    Thou, by pity's soft extream,
Mov'd, and won, and set on flame,
Assum'd the form of man, and fell
In pains, to rescue man from hell;
How bright thine humble glories rise 45
And match the lustre of the skies,
From death and hell's dejected state
Arising, thou resum'd thy seat,
And golden thrones of bliss prepar'd
Above, to be thy saints reward. 50
    How bright thy glorious honours rise,
And with new lustre grace the skies.
For thee, the sweet seraphick Choir
Raise the voice and tune the Lyre,
And praises with harmonious sounds 55
Through all the highest heav'n rebounds.
    O make our notes with theirs agree
And bless the souls that sing of thee:
To thee, the churches here rejoice,
The solemn organs aid the voice: 60
To sacred roofs the sound we raise,
The sacred roofs resound thy praise:
And while our notes in one agree,
O! bless the church that sings to thee.

## On Happiness in this Life.

THE morning opens very freshly gay
And life itself is in the month of May.

With green my fancy paints an arbour o'er
And flowrets with a thousand colours more;
Then falls to weaving that, and spreading these                5
And softly shakes them with an easy breeze,
With golden fruit adorns the bending shade,
Or trails a silver water o'er its bed.
Glide, gentle water, still more gently by
While in this summer-bower of bliss I lye                10
And sweetly sing of sense delighting flames,
And nymphs and shepherds soft invented names,
Or view the branches which around me twine
And praise their fruit, diffusing sprightly wine,
Or find new pleasures in the world to praise                15
And still with this return adorn my lays;
"Range round your gardens of eternal spring,
"Go range my senses while I sweetly sing."
    In vain, in vain alas, seduc'd by ill
And acted wildly by the force of will!                20
I tell my soul it will be constant May,
And Charm a season never made to stay,
My beauteous arbour will not stand a storm,
The world but promises, and can't perform:
Then fade ye leaves and wither all ye flow'rs,                25
I'll doat no longer in enchanted bow'rs;
But sadly mourn in melancholy song,
The vain conceits that held my soul so long.
The lusts that tempt us with delusive show,
And sin brought forth for everlasting woe.                30
Thus shall the notes to sorrow's object rise,
While frequent rests procure a place for sighs;
And as I moan upon the naked plain,
Be this the burthen closing ev'ry strain;
Return my senses, range no more abroad,                35
He'll only find his bliss, who seeks for God.


## On Divine Love by Meditating on the Wounds of Christ.


H OLY Jesus! God of Love!
    Look with pity from above,
Shed the precious purple tide
From thine hands, thy feet, thy side,
Let thy streams of comfort roll,                5

Let them please and fill my soul.
Let me thus for ever be
Full of gladness, full of thee,
This for which my wishes pine
Is the cup of love divine,                          10
Sweet affections flow from hence,
Sweet above the joys of sense;
Blessed Philtre! how we find
Its sacred worships, how the mind
Of all the world forgetful grown,                   15
Can despise an earthly throne,
Raise its thoughts to Realms above,
Think of God, and sing of love.
    Love Celestial, wond'rous heat
O beyond expression great!                          20
What resistless charms were thine
In thy good thy best design!
When God was hated, Sin obey'd,
And man undone without thy aid.
From the seats of endless peace                     25
They brought the son, the Lord of grace,
They taught him to receive a birth,
To cloath in flesh, to live on earth,
And after lifted him on high,
And taught him on the Cross to die.                 30
    Love Celestial ardent fire,
O extreme of sweet desire!
Spread thy brightly raging flame
Thro' and over all my frame;
Let it warm me let it burn,                          35
Let my corps to ashes turn,
And might thy flame thus act with me
To set the soul from body free,
I next wou'd use thy wings and fly
To meet my Jesus in the sky.                         40

# THE

# WORKS,

## IN

## VERSE AND PROSE,

### OF

# D^{R.} THOMAS PARNELL,

### LATE ARCH-DEACON OF CLOGHER.

ENLARGED WITH VARIATIONS AND POEMS,
NOT BEFORE PUBLISH'D.

GLASGOW,

PRINTED AND SOLD BY R. AND A. FOULIS
MDCCLV.

*The Works in Verse and Prose, 1755.*

# Poems from *Works in Verse and Prose,* 1755

## BACCHUS: OR, THE VINES OF LESBOS.

As Bacchus ranging at his leisure,
(Io Bacchus! king of pleasure)
Charm'd the wide world with drink and dances,
And all his thousand airy fancies;
Alas! he quite forgot the while                                    5
His fav'rite vines in Lesbos isle.
   The God returning ere they died,
Ah! see my jolly Fawns, he cried,
The leaves but hardly born are red,
And the bare arms for pity spread;                                 10
The beasts afford a rich manure,
Fly, my boys, and bring the cure,
Up the mountains, down the vales;
Thro' the woods, and o'er the dales;
For this, if full the clusters grow,                               15
Your bowls shall doubly overflow.
   So chear'd, with more officious haste
They bring the dung of ev'ry beast,
The loads they wheel, the roots they bare,
They lay the rich manure with care,                                20
While oft he calls to labour hard,
And names as oft the red reward.
   The plants revive, new leaves appear,
The thick'ning clusters load the year;
The season swiftly purple grew,                                    25
The grapes hung dangling deep with blue.
   A vineyard ripe a day serene
Now calls them all to work again;

The Fawns thro' ev'ry furrow shoot
To load their flaskets with the fruit;                        30
And now the vintage early trod,
The wines invite the jovial God.
   Strow the roses, raise the song,
See the master comes along!
Lusty Revel join'd with Laughter,                            35
Whim and Frolic follow after.
The Fawns beside the vatts remain
To shew the work, and reap the gain.
   All around, and all around
They sit to riot on the ground,                              40
A vessel stands amidst the ring,
And here they laugh, and there they sing;
Or rise a jolly jolly band,
And dance about it hand in hand;
Dance about, and shout amain,                                45
Then sit to laugh and sing again.
   But, as an antient author sung,
The vine manur'd with ev'ry dung,
From ev'ry creature strangely drew,
A tang of brutal nature too;                                 50
'Twas hence in drinking on the lawns
New turns of humour seiz'd the Fawns.
   Here one was crying out, by Jove!
Another, fight me in the grove;
This wounds a friend, and that the trees;                    55
The Lion's temper reign'd in these.
   Another grins and leaps about,
And keeps a merry world of rout,
And talks impertinently free;
And twenty talk the same as he:                              60
Chatt'ring, airy, idle, kind:
These take the Monkey-turn of mind.
   Here one who saw the nymphs that stood
To peep upon them from the wood,
Steals off, to try if any maid                               65
Be lagging late beneath the shade;
While loose discourse another raises
In naked Nature's plainest phrases;
And ev'ry glass he drinks enjoys
With change of nonsense, lust and noise;                     70
Mad and careless, hot and vain,

Such as these the Goat retain.
   Another drinks and casts it up,
And drinks and wants another cup,
Solemn, silent, and sedate, 75
Ever long and ever late,
Full of meats and full of wine;
This takes his temper from the swine.
   Here some who hardly seem to breathe,
Drink and hang the jaw beneath, 80
Gaping, tender, apt to weep;
Their natures alter'd by the sheep.
   'Twas thus one autumn all the crew
(If what the Poets sing be true)
While Bacchus made the merry feast 85
Inclin'd to one or other beast;
And since 'tis said for many a mile
He spread the vines of Lesbos isle.

## PIETY: OR, THE VISION.

'TWAS when the night in silent sable fled,
    When chearful morning sprung with rising red,
When dreams and vapours leave to crowd the brain,
And best the Vision draws its heav'nly scene;
'Twas then, as slumb'ring on my couch I lay, 5
A sudden splendor seem'd to kindle day,
A breeze came breathing in a sweet perfume,
Blown from eternal gardens, fill'd the room;
And in a void of blue, that clouds invest,
Appear'd a daughter of the realms of rest; 10
Her head a ring of golden glory wore,
Her honour'd hand the sacred volume bore,
Her rayment glitt'ring seem'd a silver white,
And all her sweet companions sons of light.
   Strait as I gaz'd my fear and wonder grew, 15
Fear barr'd my voice, and wonder fix'd my view,
When lo! a cherub of the shining crowd
That sail'd as guardians in her azure cloud,
Fann'd the soft air and downward seem'd to glide,
And to my lips a living coal applied; 20
Then while the warmth on all my pulses ran,

Diffusing comfort, thus the maid began.
 'Where glorious mansions are prepar'd above,
'The seats of Music, and the seats of Love,
'Thence I descend, and PIETY my name,     25
'To warm thy bosom with celestial flame,
'To teach thee praises mix'd with humble pray'rs,
'And tune thy soul to sing seraphic airs;
'Be thou my bard.' A vial here she caught,
(An angel's hand the chrystal vial brought)   30
And as with awful sound the word was said,
She pour'd a sacred unction on my head,
Then thus proceeded. 'Be thy muse thy zeal,
'Dare to be good, and all my joys reveal;
'While other pencils flatt'ring forms create,   35
'And paint the gawdy plumes that deck the great;
'While other pens exalt the vain delight,
'Whose wasteful revel wakes the depth of night;
'Or others softly sing in idle lines,
'How Damon courts, or Amaryllis shines;    40
'More wisely thou select a theme divine;
''Tis Fame's their recompence, 'tis Heav'n is thine.
 'Despise the fervours of unhallow'd fire,
'Where wine, or passion, or applause inspire,
'Low restless life, and ravings born of earth,   45
'Whose meaner subjects speak their humble birth;
'Like working seas, that when loud Winters blow,
'Not made for rising, only rage below:
'Mine is a great, and yet a lasting heat,
'More lasting still, as more intensely great,   50
'Produc'd where pray'r, and praise, and pleasure breathe,
'And ever mounting whence it shot beneath.
 'Unpaint the Love that hov'ring over beds,
'From glitt'ring pinions guilty pleasure sheds,
'Restore the colour to the golden mines    55
'With which behind the feather'd idol shines;
'To flow'ring greens give back their native care,
'The rose and lily never his to wear;
'To sweet Arabia send the balmy breath,
'Strip the fair flesh, and call the phantom Death;  60
'His bow be sabled o'er, his shafts the same,
'And fork and point them with eternal flame.
 'But urge thy pow'rs, thine utmost voice advance,
'Make the loud strings against thy fingers dance,

''Tis Love that angels praise, and men adore,     65
''Tis Love Divine that asks it all and more:
'Fling back the gates of ever-blazing day,
'Pour floods of liquid light to gild the way,
'And all in glory wrapt, thro' paths untrod,
'Pursue the great unseen descent of GOD!     70
'Hail the meek VIRGIN, bid the CHILD appear,
'The CHILD is GOD! and call him JESUS here;
'He comes; but where to rest? a manger's nigh,
'Make the GREAT BEING in a manger lye;
'Fill the wide skies with angels on the wing,     75
'Make thousands gaze, and make ten thousand sing:
'Let men afflict him, men he came to save,
'And still afflict him, 'till he reach the grave;
'Make him resign'd, his loads of sorrow meet,
'And me, like Mary, weep beneath his feet;     80
'I'll bathe my tresses there, my pray'rs rehearse,
'And glide in flames of love along thy verse.
   'Hah! while I speak, I feel my bosom swell,
'My raptures smother what I long to tell!
''Tis GOD! a present GOD! thro' cleaving air     85
'I see the throne! I see the JESUS there!
'Plac'd on the right; he shows the wounds he bore!
'(My fervours oft have won him thus before)
'How pleas'd he looks! my words have reach'd his ear,
'He bids the gates unbar, and calls me near.'     90
   She ceas'd. The cloud on which she seem'd to tread,
Its curls unfolded, and around her spread;
Bright angels waft their wings to raise the cloud,
And sweep their iv'ry lutes, and sing aloud;
The scene moves off, while all its ambient sky     95
Is tun'd to wond'rous music, as they fly;
And soft the swelling sounds of music grow,
And faint their softness, till they fail below.
   My downy sleep the warmth of Phoebus broke,
And while my thoughts were settling, thus I spoke;     100
Thou beauteous Vision on the soul imprest,
When most my reason wou'd appear to rest!
'Twas sure with pencils dipt in various lights
Some curious angel limn'd thy sacred sights;
From blazing suns his radiant gold he drew,     105
White moons the silver gave, and air the blue.
I'll mount the roving wind's expanded wing,

And seek the sacred hill, and light to sing;
('Tis known in Jewry well) I'll make my lays,
Obedient to thy summons, sound with praise.                    110
   But still I fear, unwarm'd with holy flame,
I take for truth the flatt'ries of a dream;
And barely wish the wond'rous gift I boast,
And faintly practise what deserves it most.
   "Indulgent LORD! whose gracious love displays        115
Joys in the light, and fills the dark with ease;
Be this, to bless my days, no dream of bliss,
Or be, to bless my nights, my dreams like this.

# THE
# Poſthumous Works

OF

## Dr. *THOMAS PARNELL,*

LATE

*Arch-Deacon* of *Clogher*;

CONTAINING

# P O E M S

## MORAL and DIVINE:

AND

## On Various other Subjects:

*Dignum laude virum Muſa vetat mori.*       Hor.

---

### D U B L I N:

Printed for Benjamin Gunne, Bookſeller in *Caple-ſtreet,*
M,DCC,LVIII.

*The Posthumous Works,* Dublin, 1758.

# Miscellaneous Poems From *Posthumous Works* (1758)

## On Queen Anne's Peace, Anno 1713.

M OTHER of plenty, daughter of the skies,
  Sweet Peace, the troubl'd world's desire, arise;
Around thy poet weave thy summer shades,
Within my fancy spread thy flow'ry meads,
Amongst thy train soft ease and pleasure bring,      5
And thus indulgent sooth me whilst I sing.
  Great ANNA claims the song; no brighter name
Adorns the list of never-dying fame,
No fairer soul was ever form'd above,
None e'er was more the grateful nation's love      10
Nor lov'd the nation more. I fly with speed
To sing such lines as BOLINGBROKE may read,
On war dispers'd, on faction trampled down,
On all the peaceful glories of the crown.
And if I fail in too confin'd a flight,      15
May the kind world upon my labours write;
"So fell the lines which strove for endless fame,
"Yet fell attempting on the noblest theme.
  Now twelve revolving years has Britain stood
With loss of wealth and vast expence of blood      20
Europa's Guardian; still her gallant arms
Secur'd Europa from impending harms.
Fair honour, full success, and just applause,
Pursu'd her marches, and adorn'd her cause;
Whilst Gaul, aspiring to erect a throne      25
O'er other empires, trembled for her own,

Bemoan'd her cities won, her armies slain,
And sunk the thought of universal reign.
    When thus reduc'd the world's Invaders lie,
The fears which rack'd the nations, justly die:                     30
Pow'r finds its balance, giddy motions cease
In both the scales, and each inclines to peace.
This fair occasion Providence prepares,
To answer pious ANNA's hourly pray'rs,
Which still on warm Devotion's wings arose,                         35
And reaching Heav'n obtain'd the world's repose.
    Within the vast expansion of the sky,
Where Orbs of gold in fields of Azure lie,
A glorious palace shines, whose silver ray
Serenely flowing lights the milky way,                             40
The road of angels. Here with speedy care
The summon'd Guardians of the world repair.
When Britain's Angel on the message sent
Speaks ANNA's pray'rs and Heaven's supream intent,
That war's destructive arm shou'd humble Gaul,                     45
Spain's parted realms to diff'rent monarchs fall,
The grand alliance crown'd with glory cease,
And joyful Europe find the sweets of peace.
He spoke: the smiling hopes of man's repose,
The joy that springs from certain hopes arose                      50
Diffusive o'er the place; complacent airs
Sedately sweet were heard within the spheres;
And bowing all adore the sovereign mind,
And fly to execute the work design'd.
    This done, the Guardian on the wing repairs                    55
Where ANNA sat revolving publick cares
With deep concern of thought. Unseen he stood
Presenting peaceful images of good
On Fancy's airy stage; returning Trade,
A sunk Exchequer fill'd, an Army paid,                             60
The fields with men, the men with plenty bless'd,
The towns with riches, and the world with rest.
Such pleasing objects on her bosom play,
And give the dawn of glory's golden day,
When all her labours at their harvest shewn                        65
Shall in her subjects joy compleat her own.
Then breaking silence, 'tis enough, she cries,
That war has rag'd to make the nations wise.
Heav'n prospers armies whilst they fight to save,

And thirst of further fame destroys the brave;     70
The vanquish'd Gauls are humbly pleas'd to live,
And but escap'd the chains they meant to give.
Now let the pow'rs be still'd and each possess'd
Of what secures the common safety best.
   So spake the Queen, then fill'd with warmth divine     75
She call'd her OXFORD to the grand design;
Her OXFORD prudent in affairs of state,
Profoundly thoughtful, manifestly great
In ev'ry turn, whose steddy temper steers
Above the reach of gold or shock of fears;     80
Whom no blind chance, but merit understood
By frequent tryals, pow'r of doing good,
And will to execute, advanc'd on high,
O soul created to deserve the sky!
And make the nation, crown'd with glory, see     85
How much it rais'd itself by raising thee!
Now let the schemes which labour in thy breast
The long Alliance bless with lasting rest:
Weigh all pretences with impartial laws,
And fix the sep'rate Int'rests of the cause.     90
   These toils the graceful BOLINGBROKE attends,
A Genius fashion'd for the greatest ends,
Whose strong perception takes the swiftest flight,
And yet its swiftness ne'er obscures its sight:
When schemes are fix'd, and each assign'd a part,     95
None serves his country with a nobler heart,
Just thoughts of honour all his mind controul,
And Expedition wings his lively soul.
On such a Patriot to confer the Trust,
The Monarch knows it safe as well as just.     100
   Then next proceeding in her Agents choice
And ever pleas'd that worth obtain the voice,
She from the list of high-distinguish'd fames
With pious BRISTOW gallant STRAFFORD names:
One form'd to stand a church's firm support,     105
The other fitted to adorn a court,
Both vers'd in business, both of fine address,
By which experience leads to great success:
And both to distant lands the Monarch sends,
And to their conduct Europe's peace commends.     110
   Now ships unmoor'd to waft her Agents o'er
Spread all their sail, and quit the flying shore.

The foreign Agents reach th' appointed place,
The Congress opens, and it will be peace.
Methinks the war like stormy winter flies,  115
When fairer months unveil the blueish skies,
A flow'ry world the sweetest season spreads,
And doves with branches flutter round their heads.
 Half-peopled Gaul whom num'rous ills destroy
With wishful heart attends the promis'd joy.  120
For this prepares the Duke—ah sadly slain
'Tis grief to name him whom we mourn in vain:
No warmth of verse repairs the vital flame,
For verse can only grant a life in fame,
Yet cou'd my praise like spicy odours shed  125
In everlasting song embalm the dead,
To realms that weeping heard the loss I'd tell,
What courage, sense, and faith, with BRANDON fell.
 But Britain more than one for glory breeds,
And polish'd TALBOT to the charge succeeds,  130
Whose far-projecting thoughts maturely clear
Like glasses draw their distant objects near.
Good Parts by gentle breeding much refin'd,
And stores of learning grace his ample mind,
A cautious virtue regulates his ways,  135
And Honour gilds them with a thousand rays.
To serve his nation at his Queen's command,
He parts commission'd for the Gallick land:
With pleasure Gaul beholds him on her shore
And learns to love a name she fear'd before.  140
 Once more aloft there meet for new debates
The Guardian Angels of Europa's states:
And mutual concord shines in ev'ry face
And ev'ry bosom glows with hopes of peace,
While Britain's steps in one consent they praise,  145
Then gravely mourn their other realms delays,
Their doubtful claims through seas of blood pursu'd,
Their fears that Gallia fell but half subdu'd,
And all the reas'nings which attempt to shew
That war shou'd ravage in the world below.  150
"Ah fall'n estate of man! can rage delight!
"Wounds please the touch, or ruin charm the sight!
"Ambition make unlovely mischief fair!
"Or ever Pride be Providence's care!

"When stern Oppressors range the bloody field,        155
" 'Tis just to conquer and unsafe to yield:
"There save the nations; but no more pursue
"Nor in thy turn become Oppressor too."
Our rebel angels for Ambition fell,
And war in Heav'n produc'd a Fiend in hell.        160
Thus with a soft concern for man's repose
The tender Guardians join to moan our woes,
Then awful rise, combin'd with all their might,
To find what Fury 'scap'd the den of night
The pleasing labours of their love withstands,        165
And spreads a wild distraction o'er the lands.
Their glitt'ring pinnions sound in yielding air,
And watchful Providence approves the care.
    In Flandria's soil where Camps have mark'd the plain,
The Fiend, impetuous Discord, fix'd her reign;        170
A tent her royal seat. With full resort
Stern shapes of Horrour throng'd her buisy court,
Blind Mischief, Ambush close concealing Ire,
Loud Threat'nings, Ruin arm'd with sword and fire,
Assaulting Fierceness, Anger wanting breath,        175
High Red'ning Rage, and Various Forms of death,
Dire Imps of darkness, whom with Gore she feeds
When war beyond its point of Good proceeds.
In Gallick armour, call'd with alter'd name
Great love of Empire, to the field she came;        180
Now, still supporting Feud, she strives to hide
Beneath that name, and only change the side:
But as she whirl'd the rapid wheels around
Where mangl'd limbs in heaps pollute the ground,
(A sullen Joyless Sport,) with searching eye        185
The shining Chiefs regard her as they fly,
Then hov'ring, dart their beams of heav'nly light,
She starts, the Fury stands confess'd to sight,
And grieves to leave the soil, and yells aloud,
Her Yells are answer'd by the Sable Crowd,        190
And all on Bat-like wings (if Fame be true)
From Christian lands to Northern climates flew.
    But rising murmours from Britannia's shore
With speed recal her watchful Guardian o'er.
He spreads his pinnions, and approaching near,        195
These hints in scatter'd words assault his ear,

The People's Pow'r—The Grand Alliance cross'd
The Peace is sep'rate—Our Religion's lost.
Led by the Blatant voice along the skies,
He comes where Faction over cities flies;          200
A talking Fiend whom snaky locks disgrace,
And num'rous mouths deform her dusky face,
Whence Lies are utter'd, Whisper softly sounds,
Sly Doubts amaze, or Innuendo wounds.
Within her arms are heaps of Pamphlets seen,     205
And these blaspheme the Saviour, those the Queen;
Associate Vices: thus with tongue and hand
She shed her venom o'er the troubled land.
Now vex'd that Discord and the Baneful Train
That tends on Discord, fled the neighb'ring plain,    210
She rag'd to madness: when the Guardian came,
And downwards drove her with a sword of flame.
A mountain gaping to the Nether Hell
Receiv'd the Fury railing as she fell:
The mountain closing o'er the Fury lies,       215
And stops her passage where she means to rise,
And when she strives, or shifts her side for ease,
All Britain rocks amidst her circling seas.
   Now Peace returning after tedious woes
Restores the comforts of a calm repose:       220
Then bid the Warriors sheath their sanguin'd arms,
Bid Angry Trumpets cease to sound Alarms,
Guns leave to thunder in the tortur'd air,
Red streaming colours furl around the spear,
And each contending realm no longer jarr,      225
But pleas'd with rest unharness all the war.
   She comes the Blessing comes, where'er she moves
New springing Beauty all the land improves:
More heaps of fragrant flow'rs the field adorn,
More sweet the Birds salute the Rosy Morn,     230
More lively Green refreshes all the leaves,
And in the Breeze the corn more thickly waves.
She comes the Blessing comes in easy state,
And Forms of Brightness all around her wait:
Here smiling Safety with her bosom bare      235
Securely walks, and chearful Plenty there;
Here wond'rous Sciences with Eagles sight,
There Liberal Arts which make the world polite,
And open Traffick joining hand in hand

With honest Industry, approach the land.                    240
   O welcome long desir'd and lately found!
Here fix thy seat upon the British ground,
Thy Shining Train around the Nation send,
While by degrees the loading Taxes end:
While Caution, calm yet still prepar'd for arms,            245
And Foreign Treaties, guard from foreign harms:
While equal Justice hearing ev'ry cause
Makes ev'ry Subject join to love the laws.
   Where Britain's Patriots in Council meet
Let publick safety rest at ANNA's feet:                     250
Let OXFORD's schemes the Path to Plenty shew
And through the realm increasing Plenty go.
Let Arts and Sciences in glory rise,
And pleas'd the world has leisure to be wise,
Around their OXFORD and their ST. JOHN stand,               255
Like Plants that flourish by the Master's hand:
And safe in hope the sons of Learning wait
Where Learning's Self has fix'd her fair retreat.
Let Traffick cherish'd by the Senate's care
On all the seas employ the wafting air:                     260
And Industry with circulating wing
Through all the land the goods of Traffick bring.
The Blessings so dispos'd will long abide,
Since ANNA reigns, and HARLEY's thoughts preside;
Great ORMOND's arms the sword of Caution wield,             265
And hold Britannia's broad-protecting Shield;
Bright BOLINGBROKE and worthy DARTMOUTH treat
By fair dispatch with ev'ry foreign State;
And HARCOURT's knowledge equitably shewn
Makes Justice call his firm Decrees her own.                270
   Thus all that Poets fanci'd Heav'n of old
May for the nation's present Emblem hold:
There Jove imperial sway'd; Minerva wise,
And Phœbus eloquent, adorn'd the skies;
On Arts Cyllenius fix'd his full delight,                   275
Mars rein'd the War, and Themis judg'd the Right:
All mortals once beneficently great,
(As Fame reports) and rais'd in Heav'nly State;
Yet sharing labours, still they shun'd repose,
To shed the blessings down by which they rose.             280
   Illustrious Queen, how Heav'n hath heard thy pray'rs,
What stores of Happiness attend thy Cares!

A Church in safety fix'd, a State in rest,
A Faithful Ministry, a People bless'd,
And Kings submissive at thy foot-stool thrown,                    285
That others Rights restore, or beg their own.
Now rais'd with thankful mind, and rolling slow,
In grand Procession to the temple go,
By snow-white Horses drawn; while sounding Fame
Proclaims thy coming, Praise exalts thy name,                     290
Fair Honour dress'd in robes adorns thy state,
And on thy Train the crowded Nations wait,
Who pressing view with what a temper'd grace
The looks of Majesty compose thy face,
And mingling Sweetness shines, or how thy dress                   295
And how thy Pomp an inward Joy confess,
Then fill'd with Pleasures to thy glory due
With Shouts the Chariot moving on pursue.
　　As when the Phœnix from Arabia flown,
(If any Phœnix were like ANNA known,)                             300
His spice at Phœbus Shrine prepar'd to lay,
Where'er their Monarch cut his airy way
The gath'ring Birds around the Wonder flew,
And much admir'd his Shape and much his Hue,
The tuft of Gold that glow'd above his head,                     305
His spacious Train with golden feathers spread,
His gilded Bosom speck'd with purple pride,
And both his Wings in glossy purple dy'd:
He still pursues his way, with wond'ring eyes
The Birds attend, and follow where he flies.                     310
　　Thrice happy Britons, if at last you know,
'Tis less to conquer than to want a foe;
That Triumphs still are made for War's decrease,
When Men by Conquest rise to views of Peace;
That over Toils for Peace in view we run,                        315
Which gain'd, the World is pleas'd, and War is done.
Fam'd BLENHEIM's field, RAMILLIES noble seat,
BLAREGNI's desperate act of gallant heat,
Or wond'rous WINENDALE, are war pursu'd
By wounds and deaths through plains with blood embru'd;          320
But good Design to make the world be still,
With human Grace adorns the needful Ill;
This end obtain'd, we close the Scenes of rage
And gentler Glories deck the rising age.
　　Such gentler Glories, such reviving days,                    325

The Nation's wishes, and the Statesman's praise,
Now pleas'd to shine in golden Order throng,
Demand our Annals and enrich our Song.
Then go where Albion's Cliffs approach the skies,
(The Fame of Albion so deserves to rise)     330
And deep engrav'd for Time 'till Time shall cease,
Upon the Stones their fair Inscription place.
Iberia rent, the Pow'r of Gallia broke,
Batavia rescu'd from the threat'ned Yoke,
The royal Austrian rais'd, his Realms restor'd,     335
Great Britain arm'd, triumphant and ador'd,
Its State enlarg'd, its Peace restor'd again,
Are Blessings all adorning ANNA's Reign.

## The Judgment of Paris.

W HERE waving Pines the brows of Ida shade,
   The swain young Paris half supinely laid,
Saw the loose Flocks thro' shrubs unnumber'd rove
And Piping call'd them to the gladded grove.
'Twas there he met the Message of the skies,     5
That he the Judge of Beauty deal the prize.
   The Message known, one Love with anxious mind,
To make his Mother guard the time assign'd,
Drew forth her proud white Swans, and trac'd the pair
That wheel her Chariot in the purple air:     10
A golden Bow behind his shoulder bends,
A golden Quiver at his side depends,
Pointing to these he nods, with fearless State,
And bids her safely meet the grand Debate.
Another Love proceeds with anxious care     15
To make his Iv'ry sleek the shining hair,
Moves the loose Curls and bids the Forehead shew
In full Expansion all its native snow.
A third enclasps the many colour'd Cest
And rul'd by Fancy sets the silver Vest,     20
When to her Sons with intermingl'd sighs
The Goddess of the rosy lips applies.
   'Tis now my darling boys a time to shew
The love you feel, the filial aids you owe:
Yet would we think that any dar'd to strive     25

For Charms, when Venus and her Loves alive?
Or should the prize of beauty be deni'd,
Has Beauty's Empress ought to boast beside?
And ting'd with Poison, pleasing while it harms,
My Darts I trusted to your infant arms;                          30
If, when your hands have arch'd the golden Bow,
The World's great Ruler bending owns the blow,
Let no contending Form invade my due,
Tall Juno's Mein, nor Pallas Eyes of blew.
But grac'd with Triumph, to the Paphian shore,                   35
Your Venus bears the Palms of Conquest o'er,
And joyful see my hundred Altars there
With costly Gums perfume the wanton air.
    While thus the Cupids hear the Cyprian Dame,
The groves resounded where a Goddess came.                       40
The warlike Pallas march'd with mighty stride,
Her Shield forgot, her Helmet laid aside.
Her Hair unbound, in curls and order flow'd,
And Peace, or something like, her Visage shew'd;
So with her eyes serene and hopeful haste,                       45
The long stretch'd Allys of the Wood she trac'd.
But where the Woods a second Entrance found,
With Scepter'd Pomp, and Golden Glory crown'd
The stately Juno stalk'd, to reach the Seat,
And hear the Sentence in the last Debate,                        50
And long, severely long resent the Grove;
In this, what boots it, she's the wife of Jove.
    Arm'd with a Grace, at length, secure to win,
The lovely Venus smiling enters in;
All sweet and shining near the Youth she drew,                   55
Her rosy Neck ambrosial odours threw;
The sacred Scents diffus'd among the leaves,
Ran down the Woods and fill'd their hoary Caves;
The Charms, so am'rous all, and each so great,
The conquer'd Judge no longer keeps his Seat;                    60
Oppress'd with Light, he drops his weary'd eyes
And fears he should be thought to doubt the Prize.

# A RIDDLE.

UPON a Bed of humble clay
   In all her Garments loose
A Prostitute my Mother lay
   To ev'ry Comer's use.

'Till one Gallant in heat of love                          5
   His Own Peculiar made her
And to a Region far above
   And softer Beds convey'd her.

But in his Absence, to his Place
   His rougher Rival came                          10
And with a cold constrain'd Embrace
   Begat me on the Dame.

I then appear'd to Publick View
   A Creature wondrous bright
But shortly perishable too                                 15
   Inconstant, nice and light.

On Feathers not together fast
   I wildly flew about
And from my Father's country past
   To find my Mother out.                          20

Where her Gallant of her beguil'd
   With me enamour'd grew
And I that was my Mother's Child
   Brought forth my Mother too.

# On Mrs. Ar: F: Leaving London.

FROM Town fair Arabella flies,
   The Beaux unpowder'd grieve,
The Rivers play before her eyes,
The Breezes softly breathing rise
   The Spring begins to live.                          5

Her Lovers swore they must expire
   Yet quickly find their Ease,
For as she goes, their Flames retire
Love thrives before a nearer fire
   Esteem by distant Rays.

                    10

Yet soon the Fair one will return
   When Summer quits the Plain
Ye Rivers pour the weeping Urn,
Ye Breezes sadly sighing mourn,
   Ye Lovers burn again.

                    15

'Tis constancy enough in Love
   That Nature's fairly shewn
To search for more will fruitless prove
Romances and the Turtle Dove
   The Virtue boast alone.

                    20

# From Pope's *Works*, Volume 2, Part 2, 1738

---

## THE THIRD SATIRE OF Dr. *JOHN DONNE*.

K IND *pity checks my spleen; brave scorn forbids*
   *Those tears to issue, which swell my eye-lids.*
*I must not laugh, nor weep sins, but be wise,*
*Can* railing *then cure these worn maladies?*
*Is not our Mistress, fair Religion,*           5
*As worthy all our Souls devotion,*
*As Virtue was to the first blinded Age?*
*Are not heavens joyes as valiant to asswage*
*Lusts; as earths honour was to them? Alas,*
*As we do them in means, shall they surpass*     10
*Us in the end? and shall thy fathers spirit*
*Meet blind Philosophers in heaven, whose merit*
*Of strict life may be imputed faith, and hear*
*Thee, whom he taught so easie wayes and near*
*To follow, damn'd? Oh, if thou dar'st, fear this:*    15
*This fear great courage, and high valour is.*
*Dar'st thou ayd mutinous Dutch? and dar'st thou lay*
*Thee in ships wooden Sepulchres, a prey*
*To leaders rage, to storms, to shot, to dearth?*

# The Third Satire of Dr. *John Donne*.

COMPASSION checks my spleen, yet Scorn denies
   The tears a passage thro' my swelling eyes;
To *laugh* or *weep* at sins, might idly show,
Unheedful passion, or unfruitful woe.
*Satyr!* arise, and try thy sharper ways,          5
If ever Satyr cur'd an old disease.
  Is not *Religion* (Heav'n-descended dame)
As worthy all our soul's devoutest flame,
As Moral Virtue in her early sway,
When the best Heathens saw by doubtful day?      10
Are not the joys, the promis'd joys above,
As great and strong to vanquish earthly love,
As earthly glory, fame, respect and show,
As all rewards their virtue found below?
Alas! Religion proper means prepares,        15
These means are ours, and must its *End* be theirs?
And shall thy Father's spirit meet the sight
Of Heathen Sages cloath'd in heavenly light,
Whose Merit of strict life, severely suited
To Reason's dictates, may be *faith* imputed?    20
Whilst thou, to whom he taught the nearer road,
Art ever banish'd from the bless'd abode.
  Oh! if thy temper such a fear can find,
This fear were valour of the noblest kind.
  Dar'st thou provoke, when rebel souls aspire,    25
Thy *Maker*'s Vengeance, and thy *Monarch*'s Ire?
Or live entomb'd in ships, thy leader's prey,
Spoil of the war, the famine, or the sea?

Dar'st thou dive seas, and dungeons of the earth?                    20
Hast thou courageous fire to thaw the ice
Of frozen North discoveries, and thrice
Colder than Salamanders? like divine
Children in th' Oven, fires of Spain, and th' line
Whose Countries limbecks to our bodies be,                          25
Canst thou for gain bear? and must every he
Which cries not Goddess to thy Mistress, draw,
Or eat thy poysonous words? courage of straw!
O desperate coward, wilt thou seem bold, and
To thy foes and his, (who made thee to stand                         30
Sentinel in this worlds Garrison) thus yield,
And for forbid warres leave th' appointed field?
Know thy foes: The foul devil (he, whom thou
Striv'st to please) for hate, not love, would allow
Thee fain his whole Realm to be quit; and as                         35
The worlds all parts wither away and pass,
So the worlds self, thy other lov'd foe, is
In her decrepit wane, thou loving this,
Dost love a withered and worn strumpet; last,
Flesh (it self's death) and joyes which flesh can tast,              40
Thou lov'st; and thy fair goodly soul which doth
Give this flesh power to tast joy, thou dost loath.
   Seek true Religion, O where? Mirreus
Thinking her unhous'd here, and fled from us,
Seeks her at Rome; there, because he doth know                       45
That she was there a thousand years agoe,
He loves the raggs so, as we here obey
The State-cloth where the Prince sate yesterday.
   Grants to such brave Loves will not be inthral'd,
But loves her only, who at Geneva is call'd                          50
Religion, plain, simple, sullen, young,
Contemptuous yet unhandsome: As among
Lecherous humours, there is one that judges
No wenches wholesome, but coarse country drudges.
   Grajus stayes still at home here, and because             55
Some Preachers, vile ambitious bawds, and Laws
Still new like fashions, bids him think that she
Which dwells with us, is only perfect, he
Imbraceth her, whom his Godfathers will

In search of *pearl*, in depth of ocean breathe,
Or live, exil'd the sun, in mines beneath?                                    30
Or, where in tempests icy mountains roll,
Attempt a passage by the Northern pole?
Or dar'st thou parch within the fires of *Spain*,
Or burn beneath the line, for Indian gain?
Or for some *Idol* of thy *Fancy* draw,                                       35
Some loose-gown'd dame; O courage made of straw!
Thus, desp'rate Coward! would'st thou bold appear,
Yet when thy God has plac'd thee Centry here,
To thy own foes, to *his,* ignobly yield,
And leave, for wars forbid, the appointed field?                             40
    Know thy own foes; th' *Apostate Angel,* he
You strive to please, the foremost of the Three;
He makes the pleasures of his realm the bait,
But can *he* give for *Love,* that acts in *Hate?*
The *World's* thy second Love, thy second Foe,                               45
The *World,* whose beauties perish as they blow,
They fly, she fades herself, and at the best
You grasp a wither'd strumpet to your breast.
The *Flesh* is next, which in fruition wasts,
High flush'd with all the sensual joys it tasts,                             50
While men the fair, the goodly *Soul* destroy,
From whence the *flesh* has pow'r to tast a joy.
    Seek thou Religion, primitively sound—
Well, gentle friend, but where may she be found?
    By Faith *Implicite* blind *Ignaro* led,                                 55
Thinks the bright Seraph from *his* Country fled,
And seeks her seat at Rome, because we know
She there was seen a thousand years ago;
And loves her Relick rags, as men obey
The *foot-cloth* where the Prince sat yesterday.                            60
    These pageant Forms are whining *Obed's* scorn,
Who seeks Religion at *Geneva* born,
A sullen thing, whose coarsness suits the crowd,
Tho' young, unhandsome; tho' unhandsome, proud:
Thus, with the wanton, some perversely judge                                 65
All girls unhealthy but the Country drudge.
    No foreign schemes make easy *Cæpio* roam,
The man contented takes his Church at home;
Nay should some Preachers, servile bawds of gain,
Shou'd some new Laws, which like new-fashions reign,                        70
Command his faith to count *Salvation* ty'd

*Tender'd to him, being tender; as Wards still*          60
*Take such wives as their Guardians offer, or*
*Pay valews. Careless* Phrygius *doth abhorr*
*All, because all cannot be good; as one*
*Knowing some women whores, dares marry none.*
Gracchus *loves all as one, and thinks that so*          65
*As women do in divers Countries go*
*In divers habits, yet are still one kind;*
*So doth, so is Religion; and this blind-*
*ness too much light breeds. But unmoved thou*
*Of force must one, and forc'd but one allow;*          70
*And the right; ask thy Father which is she,*
*Let him ask his. Though truth and falshood be*
*Near twins, yet truth a little elder is.*
*Be busie to seek her; believe me this,*
*He's not of none, nor worst, that seeks the best.*          75
*To adore, or scorn an Image, or protest,*
*May all be bad. Doubt wisely: in strange way*
*To stand inquiring right, is not to stray:*
*To sleep, or run wrong, is. On a huge hill,*
*Cragged, and steep, Truth stands, and he that will*          80
*Reach her, about must, and about it goe:*
*And what the hills suddenness resists, win so,*
*Yet strive so, that before age, deaths twilight,*
*Thy Soul rest, for none can work in that night.*

To visit *his,* and visit *none* beside,
He grants Salvation centers in his own,
And grants it centers but in his *alone:*
From youth to age he grasps the proffer'd dame,                    75
And *they* confer his *Faith,* who give his *Name:*
So from the Guardian's hands, the Wards who live
Enthral'd to Guardians, take the wives they give.
    From all professions careless *Airy* flies,
For, *all* professions can't be good, he cries,                    80
And here a fault, and there another views,
And lives unfix'd for want to heart to chuse:
So men, who know what *some* loose girls have done,
For fear of marrying *such,* will marry *none.*
    The Charms of *all,* obsequious *Courtly* strike;              85
On each he doats, on each attends alike;
And thinks, as diff'rent countrys deck the dame,
The dresses altering, and the sex the same;
So fares Religion, chang'd in outward show,
But 'tis Religion still, where'er we go:                           90
This blindness springs from an excess of light,
And men embrace the *wrong* to chuse the *right.*
    But *thou* of force must *one* Religion own,
And only *one,* and that the *Right* alone.
To find that *Right one,* ask thy Reverend Sire;                   95
Let him of his, and him of *his* enquire;
Tho' *Truth* and *Falshood* seem as twins ally'd,
There's Eldership on *Truth*'s delightful side,
*Her* seek with heed— who seeks the soundest *First*
Is not of *No* Religion, nor the *worst.*                          100
T' *adore,* or *scorn* an Image, or *protest,*
May *all* be bad: doubt wisely for the best;
'Twere wrong to sleep, or headlong run astray;
It is not wandring, to inquire the way.
    On a large mountain, at the Basis wide,                        105
Steep to the top, and craggy at the side,
Sits sacred *Truth* enthron'd; and he, who means
To reach the summit, mounts with weary pains,
Winds round and round, and every turn essays
Where sudden breaks resist the shorter ways.                       110
    Yet labour so, that, e're faint age arrive,
Thy searching soul possess her Rest alive;
To work by twilight were to work too late,
And *Age* is twilight to the night of *fate.*

*To will implyes delay, therefore now do:*                                    85
*Hard deeds, the bodie's pain; hard knowledge too*
*The mind's indeavours reach; and mysteries*
*Are like the Sun dazling, yet plain to all eyes.*
*Keep the truth thou hast found; men do not stand*
*In so ill case, that God hath with his hand*                                 90
*Sign'd Kings blank-charters to kill whom they hate,*
*Nor are they Vicars, but hangmen to Fate.*
*Fool and wretch, wilt thou let thy soul be tyed*
*To mans laws, by which she shall not be tryed*
*At the last day? Or will it then boot thee*                                  95
*To say a* Philip *or a* Gregory,
*A* Harry *or a* Martin *taught me this?*
*Is not this excuse for meer contraries,*
*Equally strong, cannot both sides say so?*
*That thou mayest rightly obey power, her bounds know;*                        100
*Those past, her nature, and name are chang'd; to be*
*Then humble to her is Idolatry.*
*As streams are, Power is; those blest flowers that dwell*
*At the rough streams calm head, thrive and do well,*
*But having left their roots, and themselves given*                           105
*To the streams tyrannous rage, alas, are driven*
*Through Mills, Rocks, and Woods, and at last, almost*
*Consum'd in going, in the sea are lost:*
*So perish Souls, which more chuse mens unjust*
*Power, from God claim'd, then God himself to trust.*                         110

To *will* alone, is but to mean delay;                    115
To work at *present* is the use of day:
For man's employ much thought and deed remain,
High *Thoughts* the *Soul,* hard *deeds* the *body* strain:
And *Myst'ries* ask believing, which to View
Like the fair *Sun,* are plain, but dazling too.          120
    Be *Truth,* so found, with sacred heed possest,
Not *Kings* have pow'r to tear it from thy breast,
By no blank Charters harm they where they hate,
Nor are they *Vicars,* but the *hands* of Fate.
Ah! fool and wretch, who let'st thy soul be ty'd          125
To *human* Laws! Or must it *so* be try'd?
Or will it boot thee, at the latest day,
When Judgment sits, and Justice asks thy plea,
That *Philip* that, or *Greg'ry* taught thee this,
Or *John* or *Martin? All* may teach amiss:              130
For, every contrary in each Extream
*This* holds alike, and each may plead the same.
    Wou'dst thou to *Pow'r* a proper duty shew?
'Tis thy first task the bounds of pow'r to know;
The *bounds* once past, it holds the name no more,        135
Its nature alters, which it own'd before,
Nor were submission humbleness exprest,
But all a low *Idolatry* at best.
    Pow'r, from above subordinately spread,
Streams like a fountain from th' eternal head;           140
*There,* calm and pure the living waters flow,
But roar a Torrent or a Flood *below;*
Each flow'r, ordain'd the Margins to adorn,
Each native Beauty, from its roots is torn,
And left on Deserts, Rocks and Sands, or tost            145
All the long travel, and in Ocean lost:
So fares the soul, which more that Pow'r reveres
Man claims from God, than what in God inheres.

# Poems from Swift's *Works*, Volume 8, 1765

## Dr. Parnel to Dr. Swift, on His Birth-day, November 30th, MDCCXIII.

Urg'd by the warmth of Friendship's sacred flame,
  But more by all the glories of thy fame;
By all those offsprings of thy learned mind,
In judgment solid, as in wit refin'd,
Resolv'd I sing: Tho' lab'ring up the way      5
To reach my theme, O Swift, accept my lay.
  Rapt by the force of thought, and rais'd above,
Thro' Contemplation's airy fields I rove;
Where pow'rful Fancy purifies my eye,
And lights the beauties of a brighter sky;      10
Fresh paints the meadows, bids green shades ascend,
Clear rivers wind, and op'ning plains extend;
Then fills its landscape thro' the vary'd parts
With Virtues, Graces, Sciences, and Arts:
Superiour Forms, of more than mortal air,      15
More large than mortals, more serenely fair.
Of these two Chiefs, the guardians of thy name,
Conspire to raise thee to the point of fame.
Ye Future Times, I heard the silver sound!
I saw the Graces form a circle round!      20
Each, where she fix'd, attentive seem'd to root,
And all, but Eloquence herself, was mute.
  High o'er the rest I see the Goddess rise,
Loose to the breeze her upper garment flies:
By turns, within her eyes the Passions burn,      25

And softer Passions languish in their turn:
Upon her tongue Persuasion, or Command;
And decent Action dwells upon her hand.
    From out her breast ('twas there the treasure lay)
She drew thy labours to the blaze of day. 30
Then gaz'd, and read the charms she could inspire,
And taught the list'ning audience to admire,
How strong thy flight, how large thy grasp of thought,
How just thy schemes, how regularly wrought;
How sure you wound when Ironies deride, 35
Which must be seen, and feign to turn aside.
'Twas thus exploring she rejoic'd to see
Her brightest features drawn so near by thee:
Then here, she cries, let future ages dwell,
And learn to copy where they can't excel. 40
    She spake. Applause attended on the close:
Then Poesy, her sister-art, arose;
Her fairer sister, born in deeper ease,
Not made so much for bus'ness, more to please.
Upon her cheek sits Beauty, ever young; 45
The Soul of Music warbles on her tongue;
Bright in her eyes a pleasing Ardour glows,
And from her heart the sweetest Temper flows:
A laurel-wreath adorns her curls of hair,
And binds their order to the dancing air: 50
She shakes the colours of her radiant wing,
And, from the Spheres, she takes a pitch to sing.
    Thrice happy Genius his, whose Works have hit
The lucky point of bus'ness and of wit.
They seem like show'rs, which April months prepare 55
To call their flow'ry glories up to air:
The drops descending, take the painted bow,
And dress with sunshine, while for good they flow.
To me retiring oft, he finds relief
In slowly-wasting care, and biting grief: 60
From me retreating oft, he gives to view
What eases care and grief in others too.
Ye fondly grave, be wise enough to know,
"Life ne'er unbent were but a life of woe."
Some full in stretch for greatness, some for gain, 65
On his own rack each puts himself to pain.
I'll gently steal you from your toils away,

Where balmy winds with scents ambrosial play;
Where, on the banks as crystal rivers flow,
They teach immortal amarants to grow:                    70
Then, from the mild indulgence of the scene,
Restore your tempers strong for toils again.
    She ceas'd: Soft music trembled in the wind,
And sweet delight diffus'd thro' ev'ry mind:
The little Smiles, which still the Goddess grace,        75
Sportive arose, and ran from face to face.
But chief (and in that place the Virtues bless)
A gentle band their eager joys express:
Here Friendship asks, and Love of Merit longs
To hear the Goddesses renew their songs;                 80
Here great Benevolence to Man is pleas'd;
These own their Swift, and grateful hear him prais'd.
You gentle band, you well may bear your part,
You reign Superior Graces in his heart.
    O SWIFT! if fame be life, (as well we know            85
That Bards and Heroes have esteem'd it so)
Thou canst not wholly die; thy works will shine
To future times, and Life in Fame be thine.


# On Bishop BURNET's being set on Fire in his Closet.


F ROM that dire æra, bane to Sarum's pride,
    Which broke his schemes and laid his friends aside,
He talks and writes that Pop'ry will return,
And we, and he, and all his works will burn.
What touch'd himself was almost fairly prov'd,           5
(Oh, far from Britain be the rest remov'd!)
For, as of late he meant to bless the age
With flagrant Prefaces of party-rage,
O'er-wrought with passion and the subject's weight,
Lolling, he nodded in his elbow-seat,                    10
Down fell the candle; Grease and Zeal conspire,
Heat meets with heat, and Pamphlets burn their Sire.
Here crawls a Preface on its half-burn'd maggots,
And there an Introduction brings its faggots;
Then roars the Prophet of the Northern Nation,           15
Scorch'd by a flaming speech on Moderation.

Unwarn'd by this, go on the realm to fright,
Thou Briton, vaunting in thy second-sight;
In such a Ministry you safely tell,
How much you'd suffer, if Religion fell.          20

# From *A Miscellaneous Collection of Poems,* 1721

## On the Death of Mr. *Viner.*

I s *Viner* Dead? and shall each Muse become
  Silent as Death, and as his Musick Dumb?
Shall he depart without a POET's Praise,
Who oft to Harmony has tun'd their Lays?
Shall he, who knew the Elegance of Sound, 5
Find no one VOICE to sing him to the Ground?
MUSICK and POETRY are Sister-Arts,
Shew a like Genius, and consenting Hearts:
My Soul with his is secretly ally'd,
And I am forc'd to speak, since VINER dy'd. 10
Oh that my Muse, as once his Notes, could swell!
That I might all his Praises fully tell;
That I might say with how much SKILL he play'd,
How nimbly four extended Strings survey'd;
How Bow and Fingers, with a noble Strife, 15
Did raise the VOCAL FIDDLE into Life;
How various Sounds, in various Order rang'd,
By unobserv'd Degrees minutely chang'd;
Thro' a vast Space could in Divisions run,
Be all distinct, yet all agree in One: 20
And how the fleeter Notes could swiftly pass,
And skip alternately from Place to Place;
The Strings could with a sudden Impulse bound,
Speak every Touch, and tremble into Sound.

The liquid Harmony, a tuneful Tide, 25
Now seem'd to rage, anon wou'd gently glide;
By Turns would ebb and flow, would rise and fall,

Be loudly daring, or be softly small:
While all was blended in one common Name,
Wave push'd on Wave, and all compos'd a Stream.

                                30

    The diff'rent TONES melodiously combin'd,
Temper'd with Art, in sweet Confusion join'd;
The Soft, the Strong, the Clear, the Shrill, the Deep,
Would sometimes soar aloft, and sometimes creep;
While ev'ry Soul upon his Motions hung,         35
As tho' it were in tuneful Concert strung.
His Touch did strike the Fibres of the Heart,
And a like Trembling secretly impart;
Where various Passions did by Turns succeed,
He made it chearful, and he made it bleed;     40
Could wind it up into a glowing Fire,
Then shift the Scene, and teach it to expire.

    Oft have I seen him on a Publick Stage,
Alone the gaping Multitude engage;
The Eyes and Ears of each Spectator draw,     45
Command their Thoughts, and give their Passions Law;
While other Musick in Oblivion drown'd,
Seem'd a dead Pulse, or a neglected Sound.

    Alas! he's gone, our *Great Apollo*'s dead,
And all that's sweet and tuneful with him fled.     50
HIBERNIA—with one universal Cry,
Laments its Loss, and speaks his ELEGY.
Farewel, thou Author of refin'd Delight,
Too little known, too soon remov'd from Sight;
Those Fingers, which such Pleasure did convey,     55
Must now become to stupid Worms a PREY:
Thy grateful FIDDLE will for ever stand
A silent Mourner for its MASTER's Hand:
Thy ART is only to be match'd Above,
Where Musick reigns, and in that Musick Love:     60
Where Thou wilt with the happy CHORUS join, ⎫
And quickly Thy melodious SOUL refine     ⎬
To the exalted PITCH of *Harmony Divine.* ⎭

# Poems from *Pancharis, Queen of Love*, 1721

---

## CHLORIS *appearing in a* LOOKING GLASS.

### I.

Oft have I seen a Piece of Art,
  Of Light and Shade, the Mixture fine,
Speak all the Passions of the Heart,
  And shew true Life in every Line.

### II.

But what is this before my Eyes,                               5
  With every Feature, every Grace,
That strikes with Love and with Surprize,
  And gives me all the Vital Face.

### III.

It is not *Chloris,* for behold
  The shifting Phantom comes and goes;                        10
And when 'tis here 'tis pale and cold,
  Nor any Female Softness knows.

### IV.

But 'tis her Image, for I feel
  The very Pains that *Chloris* gives;

Her Charms are there, I know 'em well,                    15
  I see what in my Bosom lives.


                        V.


Oh cou'd I but the Picture save!
  'Tis drawn by her own matchless Skill;
Nature the lively Colours gave,
  And she need only *Look* to *Kill.*                     20


                        VI.


Ah! Fair-one, will it not suffice,
  That I shou'd once, your Victim lye;
Unless you multiply your Eyes,
  And strive to make me doubly Dye.


## *On the* CASTLE *of* Dublin, Anno 1715.

T HIS House and Inhabitants both well agree,
    And resemble each other as near can be;
One half is decay'd, and in want of a Prop,
The other new built, but not finish'd a-top.


## LOVE *in Disguise.*

T o stifle Passion is no easy Thing,
    A Heart in Love is always on the Wing;
  The bold Betrayer flutters still,
  And fans the Breath prepar'd to tell:
  It melts the Tongue, and tunes the Throat,            5
  And moves the Lips to form the Note;
    And when the Speech is lost,
    It then sends out its Ghost,
      A little Sigh,
      To say we dye.                                    10
'Tis strange the *Air* that *Cools,* a *Flame* shou'd prove,
But wonder not, it is the *Air of Love.*

II.

Yet *Chloris* I can make my Love look well,
And cover bleeding Wounds I can't conceal,
  My Words such artful Accents break,                    15
  You think I rather act than speak:
  My Sighs enliven'd thro' a Smile,
  Your unsuspecting Thoughts beguile;
    My Eyes are vary'd so,
    You can't their Wishes know:                        20
      And I'm so gay,
      You think I play.
Happy Contrivance! such as can't be priz'd,
To *Live in Love*, and yet to *Live disguis'd*.


# On a LADY *with a foul Breath.*


A RT thou alive? It cannot be,
  There's so much Rottenness in Thee,
*Corruption* only is in Death;
And what's more Putrid than thy Breath?
Think not you Live, because you Speak,                         5
For Graves such hollow Sounds can make;
And Respiration can't suffice,
For *Vapours* do from *Caverns* rise:
From Thee such noisom *Stenches* come,
Thy *Mouth* betrays thy *Breast* a *Tomb*.                     10
Thy *Body* is a *Corpse* that goes,
By Magick rais'd from its Repose:
A *Pestilence* that walks by Day,
But falls at Night to Worms and Clay.
But I will to my *Chloris* run,                                15
Who will not let me be undone:
The *Sweets* her *Virgin-Breath* contains,
Are fitted to remove my Pains;
There will I healing *Nectar* sip,
And to be sav'd, approach her Lip,                             20
Tho' if I touch the matchless Dame,
I'm sure to burn with inward Flame.
Thus when I wou'd one Danger shun,
I'm strait upon another thrown:

I seek a Cure one Sore to ease,    25
Yet in that *Cure*'s a *New Disease*.
But Love, tho' fatal, still can bless,
And greater Dangers hide the less;
I'll go where Passion bids me fly,
And chuse my Death, since I must Dye;    30
As *Doves* pursu'd by Birds of Prey,
Venture with milder Man to stay.

## *On the Number* THREE.

B *Eauty* rests not in *one* fix'd Place,
  But seems to reign in every Face;
'Tis nothing sure, but *Fancy* then,
In various Forms bewitching Men;
Or is it *Shape* and *Colour* fram'd,    5
Proportion just, and WOMAN nam'd?
If *Fancy* only rul'd in *Love*,
Why shou'd it then so strongly move?
Or why shou'd all that Look, agree
To own its mighty Pow'r in THREE?    10
In *Three* it shews a different Face,
Each shining with peculiar Grace;
*Kindred* a Native Likeness gives,
Which pleases, as in All it lives;
And where the Features disagree,    15
We praise the *dear Variety*.
Then *Beauty* surely ne'er was yet,
So much unlike it self and so complete.

## EPIGRAM.

*Haud facile emergunt, quorum virtutibus obstat*
*Res angusta Domi—*

T HE *greatest Gifts* that *Nature* does bestow,
  Can't *unassisted* to *Perfection* grow:
A *scanty Fortune* clips the *Wings of Fame*,
And checks the *Progress* of a *rising Name*;
Each *dastard Vertue* drags a *Captive*'s *Chain*,    5

And moves but *slowly,* for it moves with *Pain.*
*Domestick Cares* sit hard upon the Mind,
And *cramp those Thoughts* which shou'd be *unconfin'd;*
The *Cries of Poverty* alarm the *Soul,*
Abate its *Vigour,* its *Designs* controul:                    10
The *Stings of Want* inflict the *Wounds of Death,*
And *Motion* always *ceases* with the *Breath.*
The *Love of Friends* is found a *languid Fire,*
That *glares* but faintly, and will soon *expire;*
*Weak* is its *Force,* nor can its *Warmth* be *great,*          15
A *feeble Light* begets a *feeble Heat.*
*Wealth* is the *Fuel* that must *feed* the *Flame,*
It *dyes* in *Rags,* and scarce deserves a *Name.*

# Poems from the "Schoedinger" Notebook

## Ps 67

1  Have mercy mercy Lord on us           [f.2a]
     & grant thy blessed grace
  Direct us in yᵉ way of life
     By th' sunshine of thy face

2  So all the nations on the earth          5
     Shall praise my god & king
  & when they see thy saving health
     Shall in a chorus sing.

3  Let all thy people praise thy name
     & lift their voice on high          10
  Let yᵐ extoll it so with shouts
     That heav'n may ring with Joy

4  Rejoyce o earth thy gods thy Judge
     Be glad who righteous are
  He'le rule yᵉ world with equity      15
     & govern it with fear

5  Let all thy people praise thy name
     & lift their voice on high
  Let yᵐ extoll it so with shouts
     that heav'n may ring with Joy     20

  Then god shall open heavens gates
     & pour down all his store
  he shall you bless with great encrease
     & you shall him adore.

# On y^e queens Death.

The Persians us'd at setting of y^e sunn
To howl, as if he nere again should runn
They onely acted it but we indeed ⎫
Must doot for all that lovely was is fled ⎬
all that was great good Just & vertuous Dead. ⎭    5
The poets of y^e graces do relate    [f.2b]
that they did upon none but Venus wait
'Tis false or this was she for in each eye
of hers ten thousand graces you might spy
So many her vertues were Death heard y^m told    10
Mistook y^e for her dayes & thought her old
yet she is gone all that was lovely fled,
all that was great good Just & vertuous dead
When Romulus was taken to y^e gods
& Ceesar mounted to y^e blest abodes    15
in floods & earth-quakes nature Largely grievd
for these her Heroes heaven had receivd
She wept indeed then now she cannot weep ⎫
the stillness of y^e waves but shows y^e deep ⎬
the greatness of y^e Loss putts all her faculties asleep. ⎭    20

# 51 Psalm

1   Look mercyfully down O Lord
     & wash us from our sinn
2   Cleanse us from wicked deeds without
     from wicked thoughts within
3   Lord I Confess my many sinns    5
     that I against thee doe
     Each minute they're before my face
     & wound my soul anew
4   So Great my god my ills have been
     Gainst thee & onely thee    10
     Thy Justice tho' I were Condemnd
     would good & righteous bee
5   For att my birth I wickedness    [f.3a]
     Did with my breath suck in

6  But thou shalt teach me in thy ways                    15
  & keep me pure from sinn
7  Thoult me with hyssopp purge who am
  all over soil's & stain's
 Thou with thy sanctifiyng grace
  shalt wash & make me clean                      20
8  Thoult bless my days with peace no sound
  But Joy shall reach mine ear
 That where thy Justice wounded Lord
  There Gladness may appear
9  Blott from thy thoughts past faults & from             25
  The present turn thy face
10 O make my spirit right & good
  Confirm my heart with grace
11 thy Presence & thy mercy lett
  Me ever L$^d$ possess                            30
12 Me with the comfort of thy help
  & with thy love still bless
13 Then shall the wicked know thy pow'r
  & turn y$^m$ from theyr wayes
14 Deliver me from blood my god                           35
  & I will sing thy praise.
15 Unseal my lips & to y$^e$ Bad                      [f.3b]
  I will thy mercy shew
16 For since thou lovest not sacrifice
  Tis all that I can doo                           40
17 A heart that is with sorrow pierct
  My God thou wilt receive
 this is y$^e$ sweetest offering
  that we to thee can give
18 On Sion Graciously look down                           45
  Preserve us still we pray
19 & hearts upon thine altars Lord
  Instead of beasts we'el Lay.


# Meditation Before sacrament.     [f.3b]


Arise my soul & hast away
Thy god doth call & canst thou stay
Thee to his table he invites

To tast of heavenly delights
He sufferd death to sett thee free                                    5
From sin; & canst thou slothfull be
To serve him should he for it call
Thy life would be a gift too small
But he desires to make it Blest
And now Invites thee to a feast                                      10
A feast of the divinest food                                        [f.4a]
A feast of our own saviours flesh & blood
For shame dull sluggish soul arise
Wilt thou so great a good despise
You'de earthly kings obey with pride                                 15
& is y<sup>e</sup> king of heav'n deni'de
Thou know'st not what this act doth mean
Or would'st not sure be Backward then
The god who all has made tis he            ⎫
Invites so base a worm as thee             ⎬                        20
& wilt thou then ungratefull be            ⎭
No L<sup>d</sup> I come & be thou kind
In mercy to me wretchd & blind
The way thou must not onely shew
But give me eyes to find it too                                     25
Each step I take y<sup>n</sup> to thy holy place
Ile utter Halelujahs to thy praise


# On y<sup>e</sup> Plott against King William.        [f.4a]


Rome when she could King Pyrrhus Life have bought
She scornd a triumph So ignobly gott,
The treason & y<sup>e</sup> traitor both disdaind,
& ever Justly conquerd ever Justly reignd.
But (Like an Affrick) England serpents bears                         5
Which would their parent country's bowels teare,
Our better Genius tumble Headlong down,                             [f.4b]
& sett our evil one upon y<sup>e</sup> throne.
The Titans wickedness nere reacht so high,      ⎫
They fought but for y<sup>e</sup> empire of y<sup>e</sup> sky,       ⎬   10
When Jove unjustly held the soveraignity.       ⎭
That Godlike soul which doth inform our state
Gerion-like, ye'de conquer by deceit.
Ye in one stroke would make three kingdomes bleed,

& Leave our Iles as nile without a head.                    15
Cease fooles with Hellish plotts to wrack your brain,
Ye Cannot wound a God, ye strive in vain;
Ixions fate again is acted here,
He for a Deity imbrac't, ye wounded, air.

## Ps: 113                                    [f.4b]

1    ye who y<sup>e</sup> L<sup>d</sup> of host adore
          O praise his name alone
       O send his praises to y<sup>e</sup> skyes
          Untill they reach his throne
2    his throne who's ever ever blest                    5
          Whose great whose holy name
       still great still holy will endure
          Who ever is y<sup>e</sup> same
3    Morning & night letts praise y<sup>t</sup> god
          Who gave us morn & night.                    10
4    Above all thinges y<sup>t</sup> are he is              [f.5a]
          Above y<sup>e</sup> heav'ns his might
5    tell of his mercy humbleness
          y<sup>t</sup> tho so high he be
       yet he will stoop to mind such poor              15
          such wretched things as we
6    Tell of his Justice too y<sup>t</sup> from
          A mean & lowly state
7    y<sup>e</sup> poor & innocent he does
          among ev'n princes sett                        20
       Those who with barreness were curst
          he blesses w<sup>th</sup> increase,
       That happy thus in all they wish
          They might his goodness praise.

## On S<sup>r</sup> Charles porter the chancellours death
[f.5a]

& tis too true alass! we find, he's gonn,
Virtue from earth a second time is flown,
She onely then with her two sisters flew,

But now since he, what ere were good withdrew;  
Uncertain where to fix, in him they lost their seat,      5  
& had But Heaven as a sure retreat.  
He Held y^e scales when Justice Hand did shake:  
When He, youd think that wisdomes self did speak.  
He was with Honour blest, with Honesty, & praise,  
ev'n Blest with all we could desire but dayes:      10  
& those were much too few, for he is gon      [f.5b]  
(Not for himself but for y^e world) too soon.  
In him we found, & with him buried lies  
What ever poets gave their deity's,  
Joves Brow, Minervas learning, Hermes tongue      15  
Apollo's wisdom, yeares, & his still seeming young;  
The same sweet temper he to all did shew,  
& as his face his mind no wrinkle knew.  
He when with foes opprest was still y^e same,  
Pittying forgave, & smiling overcame.      20  
this glorious sunn, like Heavens, was o're cast   ⎫  
By enymies, as that By clouds opprest,    ⎬  
That keepes his lookes compos'd, & this his breast. ⎭  
Both do in glory sett, as both in glory reign,  
But this for ever, that to rise again.      25  
Perfections here as to their centre flowd,  
He was tho great, yet farr from being proud.  
Was gentle, liberall, & tho modest free,  
Gold has allay, nay ev'ry thing but he.  
yet is he tak'n away snatcht hence by heaven      30  
as if it seemd to envy what 't had given.  
But when we've such a loss—  
How can y^e planetts shine y^e cloudes not melt to rain  
But ev'ry thing their wonted course retain.  
Heav'n in our sorrow cannot have a share      [f.6a]  
We've lost a god on earth 't has got a saint a starr  

# On Content      [f.6a]

Grant heav'n that I may chuse my bliss  
If you design me worldly Happiness  
   Tis not Honour thats but air  
   Glory has but fancied light  
   Fame as oft speak's false as right      5

Riches have wings & ever dwell with care
 Give me an undistemperd mind
As y^e third region undisturbd by wind
 Content from passions ever free
to rule ones selfs indeed a monarchy       10
 this I request of thee

Tho all we see are fortunes apes
& change as oft as she their shapes
 Tho my kinder fortune leave me
 Tho my dearest friends deceive me      15
 I in this universall tide
 firm on heav'ns mercy would abide
& 'mongst y^e giddy waves securely ride
  Tho they should die
 Who never did my love abuse       20
Perhaps in tears I would my passion vent
 But straight again I'de be content
Remembring 'twas th' almighty's deed tho I
 should my best relations loose
 Ide sighing cry Heav'ns will be done     [f.6b]
It did but lend them now it has its own.
     Fortune should never be
Adored as a deity by me
She onely makes them fooles who make her great
But still content on earth intent on heav'n I'de be   30
an equall temper keep in ev'ry state
 nor Care nor fear my destiny
 Death when most dreadfull should not fright
W^n ere he comes Ide patiently submitt
Content thus in my soul should build its halcyons nest   35
As did thy spirit on y^e waters rest
& keep an everlasting calm with in my breast.

# On y^e Bishop of meaths death     [f.6b]

Mourn widdowd Iland, Mourn, your Pan is dead.
Mourn ye unhappy flocks your Sheapherd Pan is fled;
Around your grief in dolefull straines convey,
& Lett y^m in sad Eccho's dy away,
As sympathising w^th their masters care,      5

As if they felt th' unlucky newes they bear,
Of this so true a saint heav'n seem'd to send him here.
To shew how good in innocence we were:
So true a saint.—
We thought he was no man, but from y^e skyes          10
(as there were oft of old) some angell in disguise,
But see to undeceive us to our grief, he dies.
He was with so good thoughts so freely springing blest,
y^e divine garden so few briars did molest,
As if a Paradise were in his breast.                 [f.7a]
Serene his mind as heaven did appear;
His lookes serene as mercy's self might wear;
His actions might in Justice scales be try'd;
When ere he speak & heav'n a theam suppli'd,
Hed melt y^e rockiest hearts like Moses to a tide.   20
But now he setts, his paines & toiles are o're,
& heav'n rewards y^e seer with all his store:
He's spent w^th doing good, & now lies down at ease
Stretcht on y^e Pillows of æternall peace.
So y^e fam'd Pithian Priestess when her soul          25
With y^e demanded Oracle is full,
Vext with y^e God y^t rages in her breast,
Nature is tir'd, her spirits are opprest,
She flyes to sacred groves, & sinkes away to rest.

# The penitent sinner.          [f.7a]


Ah that my eyes were fountaines & could poar
Eternall streams from inexhausted stores
Enough but ah enough there cannot be
to drown th' innumerable ills are done by me
  Not all my breath t attone y^m would suffice          5
  Tho' all were turnd to penitentiall sighs
    Ive sinnd my heart & tongue are vain
  Ive sinnd my eyes to vice too pronely rove
Slowly to good my limbs to ill they promptly move
Ive sinnd & all my soul's but one continu'd stain      10
My crimes beyond all number like my hairs are grown
I sink beneath the weight they press they bend me down
    W^t Charming looks did ill in acting wear         [f.7b]
      how lovely ruin did appear

Now but ah I fear too late     15
Conscience unmasques the guilded cheat
stript of their borrowd rays the horrid forms I see
& y$^e$ gross daub no more deludes my eye
I see I know my wickedness & misery
fancys too exquisite & nicely paints     20
my horrid & deserved punishments
no comfortable glympse my eye or thought presents
All all things speak dispair to poor unhappy me


But stay what heavn'ly light
Breakes thro' this black Egyptian night     25
It strikes my heartstrings w$^{th}$ unusuall bliss
& tunes y$^m$ to delight & happiness
It tells me hope remains
& gives me hope to sooth my raging pains
W$^{th}$in my breast it plays I feel the sacred flame     30
I know it tis my saviours name
his suffrings onely can my troubles calm
His blood alones my balm
In him alone I must confide
In him alone who for me di'd     35
In him who kindly does on sinners call
Who kindly does receive & welcome all
Come come to me his sacred voice has said
Repent ye of your sinns & come to me he cryes
Tho' nere so great & nere so bad     [f.8a]
Ile ease you of your load & calm your miseries
Come take my yoak upon you & my burthens bear
Easy my yoak & light my burthens are
Nor need you a hard master fear
Since he who is my servant is my son     45
a son & servant is w$^{th}$ me all one


Yes I will come my god to thee
I know thou wilt not turn me back
thou'lt not refuse the offering I make
Altho' so bad so late so mean a one it be     50
No flood can drown my sinn but one of tears
No arms can conquer sinn but prayers
Behold in tears & pray'rs & sighs I turn
See how unfeignedly I mourn
See in w$^t$ pain what grief of soul I ly     55

Have mercy mercy lord & hear my cry
Oh save me from this deluge of iniquity
  Save me my god oh rid me from my fear
        Oh save me from dispair
  look on a wounded & repenting heart        60
        Oh ease it of its smart

  W$^n$ to my soul thou'st spoken peace
When from its bonds thou wilt my soul release
  all my mourning then shall cease
then all my sorrow shall be turnd to Joy        65
& then thy mercyes onely shall my soul employ
        Oh hear my god my saviour hear    [f.8b]
  & lett thy goodness towr'ds me soon appear
  arm me w$^{th}$ heavn'ly temperd arms my Lord
Give for my buckler faith & for a sword thy word    70
  Girt up my loins w$^{th}$ truth & on my breast
        lett righteousness be plac't
  thus thus I safely shall oppose
  & safely triumph o're my foes
thus shall I break the force of hell & flee        75
  With a glad heart to thee
  to thee who (all my dangers past)
Wilt give thy self to me thy self & heav'n at last
  theres the continuall treasury of bliss
    the magazine of happiness        80
  Pleasure there does never Cease
  & in æternall Joy I shall remain
  Where in æternall glory thou doest reign.

## To M$^r$ Brown on his book against T——    [f.8b]

  Giddy w$^{th}$ fond ambition, mad w$^{th}$ pride,
Apostate angells once ev'n heavn defi'de;
Avenging heavn its hottest bolts prepard,
And hell and thunder provd their sad reward.
  Yet foolish man by no example won,        5
perverse in ill, dare rashly venture on,
Wildly rebells, calls reason to his aid,
And uses it on him who reason made.
For crimes like this what vengeance is in store?

What but the same w<sup>ch</sup> heaven showrd down on fiends before?     10
What milder could wee hope wee should receive?     [f.9a]
But god is kindly willing to forgive,
He usd his Justice then, but mercy now,
Was then w<sup>th</sup> thunder armd, but now w<sup>th</sup> you:
He bid you rise truths champion, & oppose     15
W<sup>th</sup> their own arms w<sup>th</sup> reason his audacious foes.
You take y<sup>e</sup> lists, & in your gods defence,
Unravell all their specious arguments,
Who lull their hearers with a show of sense,
In artfull words their best objections place,     20
and in fair terms their sly delusions dress;
this guilding you remove, & streight we see
What nothings all their demonstrations be.
   Thus when a fiend upon their sabbats cheats
The witches he has made w<sup>th</sup> fancyd treats,     25
The air condenses round to costly meates:
But if a stranger who by chance has viewd
their rites, dares venture to be boldly good,
No more the pleasing Phantome does remain,
But to its former air dissolves again.     30

## On M<sup>r</sup> Colliers essay on the stage     [f.9a]

Some ages has the stage triumphant stood,
and vice in masquerade debauchd the crowd;
In charming numbers, all bewitching arts,
has the gay syren drest to steal our hearts:
like undesigning pleasure she appears,     5
at once delights & unperceivd insnares,
long has she found th' unhappy pow'r to please,     [f.9b]
& wantond in a luxury of success.
But you unmasque the fashionable cheat,
Draw off the curtain, & dissect the bait,     10
Expose to view the hook so closely hid,
Break down her altars, & her priests deride.
thus, when to painted Idols Israel bowd,
the good Elijah Zealous for his god
Against the blocks, and all their prophets rose,     15
Alone attackd and overthrew his foes.
   Hail man of god, all hail, whose pious quill

Dares check a world thats so perversly ill,
Dares ev'n its darling vanities abuse,
and in its full Carreer arrest the looser muse.    20
You like some angell guide conduct us on,
& shew the sodom w<sup>ch</sup> you teach to shun;
You spoil the varnisht ill of all its rays, ⎫
of all its beauty's, evry borrowd grace, ⎬
& shew w<sup>t</sup> lurks beneath so smooth a face. ⎭    25
    Thus (say the bards) some worthy knight maintains
A warr w<sup>th</sup> fairy states, enchanted scenes,
When he moves on the bright delusion fly's,
& dismall dungeons gape before his eyes

# Ps: 116     [f.10a]

Ime Pleasd that Heaven hears my cry,
    Regards me when I pray,
Ime pleasd, & in a gratefull Joy,
    Will worship every day.
God heard my voice, & I escapd,    5
    Tho death had spread his snare,
Tho hell with horrid pleasure gapd
    to be my sepulchre.
& when with troubles Ime besett
    again Ile call on thee,    10
Ah help the wretch that cry's for aid,
    My God deliver me.
How Just how gratious is the Lord,
    How mercyfull is he?
He to the simple help affords,    15
    Yes, he has succourd me.
Then rest my soul secure from fear,
    Since he so kind has been,
Since he has kept my eyes from tears,
    My sliding feet from sin.    20
Tis he who keeps me living still,
    & when sore vext I cryd;
Since mankind is as weak as ill,
    In him I must confide.
How shall I then the God reward    [f.10b]
    Who did my all bestow?

To pray, & thank, & praise thee Lord,
  Is all that I can do.
In publick will I pay my vows,
  & tell thy mercy's ore,                        30
Tell how our lives are precious
  to thee, whom we adore.
Behold me Lord, for I am thine,
  My parents so have been;
Behold me Lord, for thou art mine,              35
  By thee I'me freed from sin.
Then all shall hear my ready tongue,
  Extoll thy name on high,
That all by my example won,
  May praise as well as I.                      40

# Poems from the "Satires" Notebook

## In Librum hunc/ 1702. [f.1a]

Forte nuper Nostro Certârunt Numina Libro,
   Hic Meus est inquit Vesta, Minerva meus.
Ipse erit, aiebant, discriminis arbiter author,
   & dixi, in causis arbiter ipse Meis:
Hæc tibi dum Vivo do carmina Docta Minerva,
   Hæc Dabo cum Moriar carmina Vesta tibi.

Tho Parnell.

## A Letter to a friend. On poets Satyr 1<sup>st</sup> [f.2a]

Poets are bound by y<sup>e</sup> severest rules,
the great ones must be mad, y<sup>e</sup> little all are fools,
thus w<sup>n</sup> I rime 'tis at my own expence,
to please my friend, I drop my claim to sence.
but now y<sup>e</sup> greater sway w<sup>ch</sup> custome bears,     5
to forfeit souls in oaths, or sence in verse?
the using of an ill has so much power,
stamp it a fashion, & its ill no more.
since then y<sup>e</sup> humour so extremely reigns,
that y<sup>e</sup> gay folly every brest unbends,     10
let me beneath y<sup>e</sup> common shadow hide
the fault's not mine thats all y<sup>e</sup> worlds beside.
say then if passion, discontent, or ease
sho'd e're your friend w<sup>th</sup> poetry possess,

for these, and want, y$^e$ muses setters seeme,     15
to draw in cullies to their loosing game,
how may I know y$^e$ path I ought to tread, ⎤
for 'tis in all mens natures to succeed    ⎬
some one way more than any else beside. ⎦
fancy the reigning planet of y$^{er}$ mind     20
guides poets, & like her they're unconfin'd;
a bounded genius will attempt to prove,
the stings of satyr, & y$^e$ flames of love,
Jear folly, virtue by example praise,
& move our passions & o$^r$ language raise     25
happy one way but one he'l scorn to chuse    [f.2b]
so much o$^r$ wilder hopes our parts abuse.
Durfy more luckily employs his quill
weak as he is he knows his talent still.
W$^n$ C——r taught how plays debaucht y$^e$ age     30
he left to V——ke to defend the stage,
in rufull ballad humbly pleas'd to rage.
how great & undisturb'd by censuring foes
might eithers fame beneath thier wreaths repose
had B——l nere written verse nor C——ve prose.     35
B——r in Epicks may be still inspir'd,
by men of sence approv'd by all y$^e$ rest admir'd
let him of Williams thickned lawrells sing ⎤
while for himself from every page they spring  ⎬
& that shall crowne y$^e$ poet w$^{ch}$ adorns y$^e$ King ⎦     40
but nere to tread in scandalls rougher ways
again depart y$^e$ peacefull realms of praise.
we read his satyr & his wit allow,
we read & own the blended malice too.
but oft his muse shows an unpointed tooth     45
W$^n$ a just turn of verse don't raise y$^e$ illnaturd truth
low puns for wit his lines do often fill
& oft he rambles in too loose a stile;
the biting satyr fights in closer file.
laborious T—te has many methods try'd,     50
to know w$^t$ happy way he may succeed,
A play or two employ'd his hopes at first,    [F.3a]
far from y$^e$ best, a little from y$^e$ worst,
then bits of foreign poets to o$^r$ tongue,
more happily he brought, more sweetly sung,     55
flush'd with success, he rises up from hence,
to rescue David at his own expence.

so have I known some painters w.<sup>n</sup> a face ⎫
in spight of all their touches wants to please ⎬
turn up its eys & alter all its dress ⎭    60
the auction piece a flowing glory wears,
& where the syren fail'd; y<sup>e</sup> saint appears.
Now I, who proudly authors thus arraign,
am, may be, envious thought, & may be vain,
but if my lines can gain one friends esteem, ⎫    65
or my diversion be, 'tis all my aim, ⎬
I never bid perhaps nere shall for fame. ⎭
Nay sho'd I find my censures too severe, ⎫
Ide in my changing prove my temper fair, ⎬
and see with joy an error disappear; ⎭    70
let Dennis rules for writing well lay downe,
believe w<sup>t</sup> he prescribes his play has done,
a preface write to shew he dos not faile,
Till Hypers to himself y<sup>e</sup> fop reveale.

---

## On the Adresses. 1701    [f.3a]

Quam bene whilhelmo coeunt concordia vota,
   Credo, velut regem, gens velit esse deum.
Sed si posse datur Wilhelmum numen haberi,
   Ut rex est nobis, sic deus esse velit.

---

## On D<sup>r</sup> Brown's death.    [f.3b]

   Alas will nothing do,
Nothing arrest the arm of Death
Must learning, sence, nay virtue too,
  Must these o<sup>r</sup> real blessings go
    like all things else beneath?    5
  Must these best guifts while here y<sup>ey</sup> shine
Like y<sup>e</sup> great Stagyrites stars in solid spheres
A common power w<sup>th</sup> worthless meteors share
    To guild the orbs they're in?
  Yes now we find it so since he is gone    10

In whom enough of goodness shone
T'adorn an age, a second Sodom save
but not himself from the devouring grave
   He's gone & that prodigious store
     Of piety w$^{ch}$ here he bore          15
Sat on him onely like the Summers pride
Which crown'd y$^e$ ancients victims 'ere they dy'd

2.

   He's gon far far on high
Born on y$^e$ wings of virtue to his skye
   for sure this world was lesse y$^n$ t'other, his,      20
So much he courted that, so little this,
Besides had he been hers y$^e$ earth had mourn'd his loss
In dreadfull heavings & unwonted flows
   But silently he stole away
     Like some celestial ray        25
W$^{ch}$ plays awhile upon y$^e$ wings of day
   Then soft retiring off y$^e$ Air      [f.4a]
Do's without troubling nature disappear.

3.

   Sure (but avert y$^e$ omen fate)
   Sure a decay of learning's state,      30
   Is now just now a pressing on
W$^n$ thus her great good pillar tumbles down
W$^n$ the light's gone w$^{ch}$ show'd us to advance
Thro y$^e$ Ægyptian night of ignorance      35
   For why, why mayn't we fear
   'Twill y$^e$ same course w$^{th}$ nature run?
W$^{ch}$ when y$^e$ generall dissolution's near,
Shall see a genuine night Ecclypse her sun.
   How well, how too too well does death,
   The cause of ignorance maintain,      40
Robbing her rivalls leader of his breath,
   To fix his Tyrant sisters reign.
How too, too well he mocks o$^r$ blooming joys
   & him & all o$^r$ hopes destroys
Him of the tree of life depriving thus     45
   & of the tree of knowledge us
Thus have his arms disabled at a blow
Both learnings Monarch & its empire too
   Just so y$^e$ Epick muse indites

Ending w<sup>th</sup> some great life y<sup>e</sup> enterprise                                    50
Nor longer toyles she ore her pageant fights
The work is ended w<sup>n</sup> an Heroe dyes.


4.

Curst be the Hour, y<sup>e</sup> Day, y<sup>e</sup> Year,
Curst y<sup>e</sup> disease that ravish'd hence o<sup>r</sup> seer,
Whose sacrilegious dart cou'd show,                              [f.4b]
That one so good was not immortall too;
Yet w<sup>t</sup> alas can this avail?
Why all this mad distemper'd Zeal
As w<sup>t</sup> it did were the effects of chance,
& not of providence.                                            60
No the impatient heavens thought long to want
In their blest choirs so true a saint,
And sent a ministring sickness from above,
his earthy fetters to remove.
It came y<sup>e</sup> call he knew,                            65
& streight obey'd & streight w<sup>th</sup>drew,
Loos'd from y<sup>e</sup> chains of flesh his freer mind
Rose up to sacred love,
To perfect saint or seraphim refin'd,
Quitting his lump of clay,                                       70
As subtle spirits fume away
Loos'd from their earth they upward mount, they flye,
They light, they shine, & blaze along the skye.

---

# In statuam Regis a Civitate Dubliniense Erectam

[f.4b]


Dummodo Rex nostras sub numine protegis oras,
& Duce religio te rediviva viget;
Quas potuit pietas cum numine divide gratos,
Huic surgunt Ædes, surgit imago tibi.

---

# 2 To T:—— M.——y. on Law Satyr     [f.5a]

Health & advice an old acquaintance sends,
Health & advice, the wish & debt of friends,
Tis fitt I teach the templar how to thrive,
Who teaches me with temperance to live.
Be still then murmuring Clients for a while,     5
Ye noisy four Court walls awhile be still,
Splitt with hard banter, & the Lawyers tongue,
Now Give a gentler Eccho to my song.
Of Law I sing, inspire my weaker pen,
Lost Suits, & pleaders little usd to gain.     10
    That angry Justice to her heaven went
There seems not so confessd an argument,
As Lawyers thriving in her name below,
When were she here again, again she'd go.
Thus courtiers, if a Kings from care w$^{th}$drawn,     15
Rise without meritt, & with fraud rule on.
    All Law was conscience once, unmixd w$^{th}$ tricks,
Found out by interest, or for politicks:
To his award each happy village stands,
Whose awfull virtue most respect commands,     20
Nor bribes, nor favour swayd the rigid man,
But all his acts in golden order ran;
Till love of gain, or fame, found out y$^e$ croud,
& rose by seeming good, above the good.
From this gross error to relieve their lands     25
Projecting patriots gave their helping hands:
Then Laws were putt in writing, courts were reard,
& Men for forehead, & strong lungs preferrd,
A friend or whore became a heightning clause,     [f.5b]
& mony grew the meritt of the cause.     30
    Woud you be taught your paths of gain to tread,
But man wants little teaching to be bad,
Gett impudence, each nation has its share,
Or something which does wondrous like appear,
Scotch confidence, the vanity of France,   ⎫     35
The surly English air, the Irish ignorance,   ⎬
All stand for this, or up to this advance.   ⎭
Letts hear the other side, the Judge commands,
& Tully rises with his brief in hand,
Tully so known, so little heard of late,     40

But bauling Matho wont give over yet,
Forbid & shameless still he quotes y<sup>e</sup> lawes
Till want of time & his unceasing noise,
Staves of a Judgement or obtains the cause.
Thus what the first of every term he gaines,                45
So great a family so well maintaines.
Poor modesty, as old records declare,
Was starvd to death behind the foremost barr.
Have many words, nor spare y<sup>e</sup> breath you sell,
Your Clients pleasd you labour, tho' you fail;            50
Hence fluent Nevolus his great success,
Smoothly he utters, finds his words with ease,
his reasons places in the clearest light,
& pleads with humour, where he has not right.
Livy, whose country talks upon his words,                55
Shows reason, reason if the cause affords,
& by his happy fault of speaking long
Makes some believe he shows it in y<sup>e</sup> wrong.
Your terms are too of wondrous consequence,             [f.6a]
To dazzle ignorance, & puzzle sence.                     60
& many private tricks besides are known,
Which practise finds, or custom has sett down.
Young Brutus, who so quickly came in play,
To gainfull fame found this effectuall way,
In formâ pauperis much he undertook,                     65
As men who fish take worm upon y<sup>e</sup> hook,
& to be often heard, for nothing often spoke.
With this last rule I close my whole advice,
Take all you can, he looses who deny's,
Who by one side is usd may honest be,                    70
But he is rich who takes of both his fee.
& least you want a story of your art,
Hear how began this double-dealing part.
    In times of yore, & Æsops vocall grove,
When fingers talkd of something else then Love,          75
The hands fell out, the plaintiff, left maintaind,
The right in all things tho unjustly reignd.
Then this her plea, that had her answer heard,
This brought deponents, that Cross bills preferrd.
After a Long debate to make them pay,                    80
(for you as well may hope to gett away,
for nought, as allmost nought) the Judges say,

What ere the world in other things intends,
To shew how much we wish relations friends,
As often as we can, the court decrees,                    85
To use you both alike in taking fees

[the men namd are of yᵉ Irish barr.]

----

# On The Trust.                    [f.6b]

Think England what it is to shake,
   & better use your King,
His power raisd the frozen snake,
& Must he when he hears it speak,
   find how the tongue can sting?                    5

Trustees you make in long debates,
   Which he is forcd to give;
While by your trust the rebell getts,
The subject looses bought estates,
   & the oppressors live.                    10

Pitty us heaven, & lend your aid,
Anothers intrest sett us free,
& now it gives us slavery,
Thus weakness is a property,
   & Greatness still obeyd.                    15

The men whose heavy arms we feel
By Politicks are good or ill,
   Deceiving, or deceivd;
Their law is founded on their will,
   & our's by that inslavd.                    20

Against their princes acts they rise,
   & in their princes name;
The sly intreaguing factions choice,
   & erring patriots shame.
So Dunghill foggs by fiery rays                    25
   To saucy empire scale,

Obscure the royall planetts face,
With pride supply a lofty place,
   & with out pitty fall.

---

# A Divine Pastorall. [f.7a]

   Strephon & I upon a bank were laid,
Where the gay spring in varied colours playd, ⎫
& her rich odours lavish nature shed. ⎭
When thus the Youth, while this we wondring view
Can we but wonder at its maker too,           5
Amintas, if I know him, did not use
Shoud such a subject call, to want a muse,
Oh sing the great, the wise creating powr,
While silent I admire, & in your words adore.
Then I, for long before the thought was mine,    10
Did thus to meet the good demand begin.
   Ye Mountains, & ye hills which lower rise,
Ye humble vallies, & ye spreading trees,
Ye pleasant meadows, & thou easy stream,
O praise the Lord, O magnify his name!        15
Yes, as you can you tell his name abroad,
The wondrous work proclaims the worker God.
Gently awhile sweet Breezes move along,
Then swiftly bear aloft my finisht song.
   Ye tame & savage beasts in one accord,     20
Joyn with all these to Glorify the Lord;
Ye Birds, Ye tunefull birds in him rejoyce,
Give him your musick, who gave you your voice,
Hark how the cheerfull labour of their throats,
returns the tribute of their pretty notes.     25
Gently awhile sweet Breezes move along,
Then swiftly bear aloft my rising song.
   But still the earth, & still the seas are mute, ⎫  [f.7b]
The Birds are speechless, speechless is the Brute, ⎬
Man that alone can speak his praise must doo't. ⎭  30
Praise him O man with a transported heart,
Let the melodious hand confess its art,
Let the raisd voice his bounteous glory's sing,
Shoud less be joynd to praise so great a King?

Gently awhile sweet Breezes move along, 35
Then swiftly bear aloft my rising song.
   For thee the seasons run the circling year,
The clouds drop fatness, & the fruits appear,
Thee as the Lord of all below he plac'd,
Free in thy choice, & by thy chusing bless'd, 40
Tis true we must account for all we do,
But to a God alone th' account is due.
Gently awhile sweet Breezes move along,
Then swiftly bear aloft my rising song.
   The Seraphim, & all the Heavenly pow'r, 45
Bright in their shapes, but in their virtues more,
Came to the shade where our first parents lay,
They heard him reason, & they heard her pray,
Then struck their Golden harps, & as they flew,
Cry'd, Halelujah, man is made for heaven too. 50
Go on, my Muse, Go on, & Gratefully express,
The Creatures thanks, in the Creators praise.
   To see this pair the fallen powrs came in,
Torturd with malice, & deformd by sin,
They saw this happy pair designd to fill 55
The realms, from whence they fell by doing ill,
They heard their Joyfull anthems to their God, [f.8a]
& faign they woud have harmd y$^m$ if they coud,
Whom they woud harm they impotently curse,
Their strength indeed was great but God was ours. 60
Go on, My Muse, Go on, & Gratefully express.
The Creatures thanks, in the Creators praise.
   I know I cannot speak his mercy's through,
Yet what I can, of what I ought Ile do,
Mean as they are, my notes to him belong, 65
Mean as it is, he will reward my song.
Go on, my Muse go on, & gratefully express
The Creatures thanks, in the Creators praise.
   On such a theam I coud for ever dwell,
Thus lett my voice when I must perish fail 70
& thus my monument my story tell;
Here lyes a Youth—stay passenger & pray,
Nor pitty him who di'd no common way,
But when his breath was all in hymns bestowd
Sent up his soul to bear 'em to his God. 75
   So lett me end, the twilight does appear,
The heat has left to rarify the air,

The winds it broke grow strong enough to fly,
Yes swiftly fly ye winds, & bear my Lays on high.

---

## To ——— [f.8b]

    Thanks to the friend whose happy lines coud cheer
In Derry's oaten soil & frozen air
When to the Citty late I bid farewell
Beneath my firm resolves my scribling fell
The Ghost of my departed Muse you raise         5
& tune her tongue to long forgotten layes
Thus a poor girl by passion overrun
Tires with the folly & forsakes the town
But if her shades present a powrfull swain
She feels y^e woman stirr & loves again         10
    Your thoughts are Just your words fall in w^th ease
Who woud not be abused in lines like these
Mindless of all the ill they say of me
I read them & admire their poetry
So when a Charming beauty strikes y^e heart         15
We slight the wound to gaze upon y^e dart
But oh My friend of writing much beware
If once you're charmd youre fixd for ever there
Fame all abroad & loose desires with in
Intice a giddy creature to the pen         20
A Cælia soon he getts to whom to write
& the brisk bottle must compleat y^e witt
Then every minute of succeeding time   ⎫
Invents a frolick or creates a whim      ⎬
Which his leud absent friend must hear in rime ⎭   25
You'll think (& others have been thus undone)  ⎫ [f.9a]
Your reason can the growing passion shun    ⎬
But did you know its strength youd doubt your own ⎭
    Your best endeavours on y^e law bestow
Rough as it is 'tis proffitable too         30
Cowel & Blunt have words & Cook y^e way  ⎫
to keep the wrangling sons of earth in play  ⎬
then if your books you use your Clients pay  ⎭
    Stay Muse in paths you never trod you rove ⎫
My lean advice does my presumption prove   ⎬
But Can it shew my fault & not my love     ⎭   35

Kindly accept what I in kindness send
& think me as I think my self your friend.

---

# [Untitled poem]                    [f.9a]

Thou Gaudy Idle world adieu,
   & all thy tinsell Joys;
I lovd thee dearly once tis true,
But since a better choice I knew,
   Ive made that better choice.                    5

My wishes mount above the sky
   Upon the wings of faith,
My soul shall follow when I dy,
For much I doubt if bodys fly,
   What ever Asgill saith.                    10

All things are fickle here below,                    [f.9b]
   How ere above they be,
& If I had not left thee now,
   Thy pleasures had left me.

Count but the changes Memory                    15
   Which your short time has known,
This is the third King which you see
   Upon the English throne.

The Irish who by Williams reign
   Were run so much aground,                    20
Do by the Trust (confound it) Gain
   three hundred thousand pound.

& My acquaintance wonder not
   When you my change discover
Ev'n Methwin has a prayr book bought                    25
   'Gainst Rochester comes over.

---

# [Untitled poem]

A Beavy of the fair & Gay,
Such as are daily Smoakt in tea,
   & toasted over wine,
Vext to be made so long the Jeast
Of tongues & pens, to go in quest        5
   Of reputation Joyn.

To K——d's house they first repair,        [f.10a]
But scarce find any footsteps there,
   to keep them off cold scent;
Long had she fled his slavery,        10
Her gallants stabbd him first, & she
   Woud bury him in paint.

To O——y's they next advance,
But he was vanishd on a glance
   to Make some conquest shott;        15
One who so many loves as she,
& one who loves fooles company,
   Must love for you know what.

Of T——n newes in vain they sought,
Scarce M——ws covets to be thought        20
   So ignorant in dressing;
For scandall had like Cr——fts appeard,
He urgd his suit, the God retird,
   & left the Nymph unlacing.

No longer on your search remain,        25
For since your labour must be vain,
   What need you make it long:
Believe me fairs, that every one
preserves him for her self alone,
   Upon her proper tongue.        30

# 3 Satyr Virtue [f.10b]

Is virtue something reall here below
Or but an Idle name & empty show
While on this head I take my thoughts to task
Methinks young Freedom answers w$^t$ I ask
In his own moralls thus the Spark goes on     5
Or thus if he were here he might have don
  In what wild hill or unfrequented plain  ⎫
hast thou been bred so ignorant of men  ⎬
Such doubts in such a world to entertain  ⎭
Or has thy father had an hopefull son  ⎫    10
by Colledge education quite undon  ⎬
& therefore wisely gave his others none ⎭
Believe me S$^r$ that what you faign woud know
is but a word to signify a show
Often it is 'tis often not designd     15
& still it makes a riddle of the mind.
Now see how evidently this appears
in the clear language of particulars.
  All men do *Sporus* very chast esteem
But does he rule his will or nature him     20
What he might be himself he little knows
Who never had a passion to oppose
he must be chast with out a world of pains
for all his virtue is his impotence.
*Damon* the hottest rakell of the town     [f.11a]
has his cast misses on the common thrown
No signs of great repentance does he show
But the mans bound his wife's his virtue now
  Nor friends nor glorious wine nor sparkling witt
Makes *Codrus* ere beyond a bottle sitt     30
this is his temperance his acquaintance say
& att the barr they give him leave to pay
But they forgett that Codrus is so poor
& all his virtue may be want of more
  A sexton scarcely can resolve to ring     35
But *Cotta* flyes as on devotions wing
tows his old aunt in black to every prayer
Whines as he goes & prayes aloud when there
thus to be Guardian when she dies he'le gett
his virtue is the hopes of pow'r to cheat     40

thus various mankind cou'd I quickly trace
& show how fondly we mistake their wayes
how something which they are not oft they seem
& how that something brings them in esteem
but to be short with in my self I feel                                45
too deepely rooted all the seeds of ill
Mad passions reason not invincible                                 [f.11b]
& chance to be misguided in my will
Why shoud I think another has not these
is he more perfect man or am I less.                                50
    To such a loose harangue on t'other side
My honest Trueman woud have thus replyd
While by y$^r$ own you blame anothers soul ⎫
You must go wrong & y$^e$ illbiassd bowl      ⎬
bear on a falser ground at every roul   ⎭                          55
tis granted where the moralls run awry
there your reflections very justly ly
but think you there are none to good inclind
from the meer sway of reason on their mind
think you that every one woud rather be                            60
Slave to his passions then from passion free
for such they are who have no powr to stay
When every weak temptation calls away
*Curio* is summond to *Corinna*'s house
Cross is his father cruell is her spouse                           65
the dangers great but Curio must be gon
a pleasure tempts a passion hurry's on
Nor are the troubles which pursue it all
for you may feel the very fetters gall
Dispair & hope with lingring pangs remain ⎫                        70
Sorrow & Joy give much a quicker pain     ⎬                       [f.12a]
& love & hate in wild convulsions reign.  ⎭
When with their proper objects these attack ⎫
tis to be virtuous then to drive 'em back   ⎬
entrenchd with in y$^e$ rules w$^{ch}$ prudence makes ⎭           75
tis virtue still an æquall mind to bear
Nor swoln w$^{th}$ hope nor too depressed w$^{th}$ fear
to lett the Man secure from passion move
in reasons orb serenely plac'd above
tis Virtue to maintain your country's cause                        80
Support your king while he supports her laws
nor in th' oppressing of a kingdom share ⎫
for fifteen hundred English pounds a year ⎬
paid down by order of y$^e$ Commons here  ⎭

tis virtue & the highest mentiond yet                                          85
to think religion not a trick of state
   Nature has fooles who know not of this way
& fooles alone have priviledge to stray
But if a Competence of Sense she give
& the receivers do not upright live                                            90
their different failures do such words create
as Atheist traytor villain rakehell cheat
defamer pander whore knight of y^e post
& hypocrites a Common name for most
Most strive to varnish their prevailing vice   ⎫                     [f.12b]
& grant with ease when they succeed in this   ⎬
the Case the same where the appearance is   ⎭
but goodness ever has the same appeard
While no design is still upon its guard
the best is onely but y^e best begun                                          100
Sooner or later by its self undon
   Ore peaceful citts the hectring bullys reign
But while they hector so they know their men
Shoud they vex one at last to Cudgells bred   ⎫
the masque of valour wont protect y^e head   ⎬                       105
While the tough cane insults the shining blade ⎭
   I scorn in verity old *Gripus* cry's
this swearing this unprofitable vice
but mony mollifys the wretches scorn
& he who hates to swear will be forsworn                                       110
   thus ill men never fail of being known
how sly so e're a vizard they put on
but still the good both seem & are y^e same
unmovd by passion, int'rest, humour, fame
tis thus that they deserve y^e name of men   ⎫                       115
by ruling of themselves they empires gain   ⎬
& laugh at fortune raisd above her reign.   ⎭

––––––––––

# A dream                                                                     [f.13a]

  Just when y^e dead of night began to fail
& boding visions senceless dreams expell
Methought a matron stood beside my bed   ⎫
Upon her face a wondrous sweetness playd   ⎬
& pointed Glorys dressd the modest visions head ⎭                               5

my tongue grew speechless & my eyes were fixt
by silent fear with admiration mixt
She to my lips a living coal apply's
perhaps from some well pleasing sacrifice
then thus she said while I more courage found            10
to bear her sight & hear y<sup>e</sup> heav'nly sound
from the bright realms my vot'ries have I came
saints are my vot'ries Piety my name
Oft do I come but often am dispisd
happy were all if all my favour prizd                    15
now my best offers to y<sup>r</sup> soul I give
Accept these offers O be mine & live
Ile teach you how to pray for w<sup>t</sup> you want
& when I teach you God y<sup>r</sup> prayr will grant
Ile teach you your redeemer to rehearse                  20
& glide in flames of love along y<sup>r</sup> verse
Lett other men describe w<sup>th</sup> flowing lines       [f.13b]
How Damon courts or Amarillis shines
But for your subject chuse a theme divine
fames their reward while heaven it self is thine          25
& then since Angells sing of nought below
they'le sing like men but like an angell you
Be thou my bard (& as these words she said
She powrd a sacred unction on my head
then thus proceeded) Be thy muse thy Zeal                 30
dare to be good & all my Joys reveal
if Drunkards to their Deity apply
A short contentment & a fleeting Joy
Apply to me true peace & lasting bliss
I should not dress in weaker charms y<sup>n</sup> his      35
New-paint y<sup>e</sup> love y<sup>t</sup> hov'ring over beds
from purple wings his guilty pleasures sheds
his bow be sable sable be the darts
but tingd with endless flame to scorch our hearts
his bones without the sanguin stream or vital parts      40
But above all employ thy utmost powr
on love Divine twill need it all & more
Oh boundless Goodness to poor mankind shown ⎤
tell but the fact, lett rhetorick alone,          ⎟
no colours can become it like its own.            ⎦    45
Draw a Descending Jesus from y<sup>e</sup> sky          [f.14a]
Make the great being in a manger ly
Of men despisd of men he came to save
pursu'd afflicted to y<sup>e</sup> very grave

Make y^e great being cheerfully submitt                               50
& me like Mary weeping at his feet
Much have I said & more woud tell you yet
but raptures smother what I woud repeat
My thoughts grow giddy while I strive to sound
the height & depth of love w^thout a bound            55
My God I cannot comprehend thy wayes
but what I cannot comprehend Ile prayse
   & then With raptures in her mouth she fled
the Cloud (for on a cloud she seemd to tread)
its curles unfolded & around her spread               60
My downy rest the warmth of fancy broke
& when my thoughts grew settled thus I spoke
   Ah Gracious Lord make all my dreams like this
& make mine innocence compose my bliss
When reason lyes Asleep & leaves to reign            [f.14b]
May my good Angell my passions restrain
Or I must wake to find upon my breast
the gaudy forms more deep y^n ere imprest
they'le make my reason's victorys in vain
& make my former habits mine again                    70
Thus if the snake w^ch hardly moves the tail
to shun the conqu'ring season takes a cell
if nature in a sleep a skin prepare
give him more strength & make him look more fair
He finds his robe is changd f^m what he wore ⎫        75
He proudly shoots along y^e sunny shore       ⎬
& hunts the man f^m whom he fled before.     ⎭

----

## Satyr. 4 The Pretty Gentleman            [f.14b]


   Where Creditors their bankrupt debtors stow ⎫
Where men for want of coin to durance go       ⎬
& are for being wretched made more so          ⎭
Where poor W—— G—— could 3 months abide ⎫
When all his creditt would not him provide       ⎬      5
with one nights lodging any where beside        ⎭
there on a bed by moths half eat away    ⎫
Damon y^e witt y^e generous y^e gay      ⎬
the heir of Eighteen hundred sterling lay ⎭
Sullen with grief impatient to endure                [f.15a]

& yet oppressd with what he coud not cure
Long did his thoughts upon his Sorrows dwell
then they on generall reflections fell
for still the mind by private ills aggrievd
Is by the thought of common ills relieved                    15
this soths y^e spleen while that creates dispair
One you ingross in 'tother others share
    Alass he crys how many have I known
by giddy pleasures & y^mselves undon
We hunt for happiness on eager speed                        20
& have a chance that we may all succeed
reason & passion draw y^e diffrent views
& we're all blessd according as we chuse
but to our reason seldom we attend
tho' all our hopes upon that choice depend              25
see y^e degrees thou heedless creature man
by which the passions on y^e mind obtain
as in y^e pretty Gentleman suppose           ⎫
for instance how in him y^r empire grows     ⎬
up from his swadling to his beauish clothes ⎭          30
    Scarce can his tongue in tripping accents rove
but the nurse lulls him w^th wild tales of love
Where a kings son as many such have been          [f.15b]
dyes for y^e youngest daughter of a queen
these mold his temper till he learns to read           35
& then romantick authors fill his head
Where honour in enamelld armour bleeds
for love thats errant on y^e milk white steed
how his eyes dance when magick Castles fly      ⎫
When beautyes freed how pants his heart for Joy ⎬   40
how much what ere he reads he longs to try       ⎭
When he can Nature more distinctly see
he finds such things as these coud never be
Yet still the prejudice is on his Soul
& love & honour must his actions rule                       45
then that he may their due proportions trace  ⎫
playes following nature he will follow playes   ⎬
at these he dresses talkes fightes loves from these ⎭
he railes at buisness w^ch he does not know
because y^e poett who had none did so                       50
In wine & whores & games his guinnys run   ⎫
because the like in such a part is don        ⎬
thats drawn with art to please y^e lookers on ⎭

to repeat verse & with a grace be leud
is gay is Dorimant & must be good                           55
But when his fullgrown witt a figure makes ⎫               [f.16a]
Without a guide agreably he rakes              ⎬
Nor the stage longer for a pattern takes     ⎭
himself a mode a man of airs a beau
Nay poet too—as far as songs will go                        60
thus with a world of pains the work is past
& he's an entertaining fool at last
he does the men of buisness pitty move        ⎫
the men of Moralls soberly reprove             ⎬
the tradesmen cheat him—but the Ladies love. ⎭        65
    As on this head he woud have spoken more
the Jailour happend to unlock the door
to lett him know his creditors did wait         ⎫
to make him sell if he woud freedom gett     ⎬
At least three quarters of his whole estate    ⎭          70

———————

# Satyr 5 Verse.                                          [f.16a]


    Thou soft Engager of my tender years
Divertive verse now come & ease my cares
The Rake has wine the aged knave ye view    ⎫
Of what his death bed Charity will do          ⎬
to lay his cares & mine are layd by you        ⎭            5
You give my mind when I unbend relief
Raise ev'ry Joy & lessen ev'ry grief
Nor do I onely these thy comforts find
thy comforts are diffusive to mankind
The men of sense of buisness or of whims ⎫            [f.16b]
half witts or lovers ev'ry one sometimes     ⎬
Will toy away a vacant hour in rimes          ⎭
    & they give all but lovers troubles ease
the Muses fires the flames of love encrease
Yet the fond fooles write more yn all ye rest               15
as if they studyd to be more unblest
of Moving things they speak in moving strains
& moan & beg a cure of all their pains
till at the last theyre workd to a belief
that what they said has been their reall grief              20

As strong as fate they call the chains they wear ⎫
To starrs & Angells ev'ry nymph compare ⎬
Then think their chains as strong, their nymphs as fair ⎭
thus our loves more & more the womens pride
so the wounds deeper & the cure denyd                          25
Long may you gentle souls your fetters wear ⎫
if still you write upon yᵉ pangs you bear ⎬
Yet know that writing makes them more severe ⎭
If Celia or Aminta scornfull grow ⎫
On the great praises which your lines bestow ⎬               30
Long may you feel them since you make yᵐ so ⎭
    Verse is on other subjects less unkind
& with its transports brightens up yᵉ mind
the Drunkards catch is half the rogues delight
Where noise & briskness do their charms unite              35
The drawers calld & ink & paper brought ⎫        [f.17a]
& so extempore the work is wrought ⎬
While wine inspires they never stay for thought ⎭
the Jolly words are roard in tunefull sound ⎫
While the full bottles run the tables round ⎬               40
& Ecchoes from the Empty ones rebound ⎭
Raisd to the Joyes above the cares of kings
their singing makes yᵐ drink their drinking sing
O happy men if twere not for the curse ⎫
of qualms repentance & an empty purse ⎬                     45
but happy men at least for some few hours ⎭
Who force the Muse to nothing else but rime
& when your sense is drownd sing off yʳ time
    Verse has another powr on other men
When the vexd thoughts by writing grow serene             50
full of the spleen & rage & scorn to see ⎫
the tide of vice & folly run so high ⎬
some from the world retire to poetry ⎭
& when their pens what grieves their bosoms speak
how honesty's a cully witt a rake                           55
fair Virtue beggerd beauty grown a baud
Religion made a masque & gold a God
their breasts find ease by laying down their load
so Prophetts usd inspird of old to swell
& when they spoke their Oracles grew well                   60
    For me who never have a drinker been       [f.17b]
Nor provd the witty forces of the spleen

for me who be it chance or carelessness ⎫
(forgive me half the world when I confess) ⎬
have never been in love in all my dayes ⎭    65
On other principles my pen I take
for meer disintrested diversions sake
I onely write as many lovers woo ⎫
but just when I have nothing else to do ⎬
& then to please my self as well as you ⎭    70
I seek no praise & keep me safe from shame
Not known to many & unknown to fame
I woud not bluntly rail a folly down
Nor with undecent rage on vices run
Our master Horace wisely sung of old    75
that satyrs better if it Jear then scold
the Gall too much prevailing spoils the ink
Nor woud I frett mankind but make y$^m$ think
tis farr more human thus to show y$^e$ place
Where you ly open then throw in y$^e$ pass    80

---

# Satyr: 6   the Spleen    [f.17b]

   Hail to the sacred silence of this Grove
Hail to the greens below the greens above
Oft have I found beneath these shady trees
A reall in imaginary bliss    [f.18a]
for they my fancy sooth & she's a cheat    5
Which can agreably adorn deceit
some state of life she draws with pleasing art
& brings Enchanted reason to her part
Reason awhile is captive by consent
& acts from all its rigid rules unbent    10
from our own selves conceales our reall case
Nor shows us what may be but what may please
When I by these am from my self with drawn
I straight become what ere I think upon
   Now do I turn a statesman of the rate    15
that furnishes the world beside with chat
I many use I make a friend of none
& if I flatter tis my prince alone

Mankind well versd in various villany ⎫
Misrepresent each study'd Case to me ⎬     20
in long petitions & a present fee ⎭
sayes one your Lordship has y^e royall ear ⎫
& I some articles against me fear ⎬
for sinking publick funds in such a year ⎭
Then on my chair he layes a bag of coin     25
Nor dares to offer what he woud have mine
Another cryes I want a place at Court ⎫
Your L:^dships word woud make y^e buisness short ⎬
& I present two hundred guinnys for't ⎭
This as I take it is a life of state          [f.18b]
& when I think of this I think Ime great
But now a leaf is noisy by my head
My chain is broke & all my greatness fled
In vain I woud recall the vanishd thought
Something I know did please I cant tell what     35
& as I hunt the traces of my mind
In a new whim a new delight I find
   Now among books my chief diversion lyes ⎫
& I affect to be thought wondrous wise ⎬
in strange experiment discovery's ⎭          40
On All y^e sorts & shapes of flyes I read
Or print a book of shells as Lister did
& when I meet a thing unknown till y^n
I write for Holland to y^e Learned men
the subtiltys of schooles with ease I cutt     45
Where learnings nothing but a meer dispute
With Ipse Dixit's fixd for arguments
& quibbles formd by rules & hid with pains
Waging a warr of words in spight of sense
My skill in many languages is shown          50
Altho' I gracefully can speak in none
No Cares no business do my brain molest ⎫
the world admires the treasures of my breast ⎬
& I in barren satisfaction rest ⎭
   Here do I change Insensibly again          [f.19a]
& my gay fancy paints another scene
Heark or a pleasing madness charms my sense
Or I hear songs & well tund instruments
Yes tis a ball where I with airs & cloths
Engage the Ladys & outshine the beaus          60
I chuse a creature beautious as the light

Of her I beg & she denys a night
Scorn with the fair does still attendant go
they're proud because their outward charms they know ⎫
& fondly think them reasons to be so                          ⎭          65
But passion hearts of any temper moves
Anon shes complaisant anon she loves
When sated with the bliss their arms I quitt
I boast my triumph to each friend I meet
for men are now so scandalously vain       ⎫                          70
They think it less of pleasure to obtain     ⎬
their Joys then tell 'em or'e to other men ⎭
& more of grief to hide the ripe amour
then twas to smother infant love before
I drink I dance I swear I shake y^e dice                          75
& try each path of pleasurable vice
till at y^e last my wild unsettled life
like Comedys is finishd in a wife
    by Just degrees the breezes louder grow
& the same breast they sooth they roughen too                 80
Methinks Ime strangely alterd in a trice          [f.19b]
All soft unmanly pleasures I despise
Warr is my buisness honour is my prize
I grasp it in my thoughts & push along
Nor mind the toiles by which it must be won                 85
With such bewitching powr the walking light
leads men thro' all the dangers of the night
Ore hills & vales they hunt the dazzling game
Nor feel the trouble while they see the flame
Strange force of Glory what a world are slain                 90
to please the pride of two or three great men
how towns have fed on ratts y^t scornd to yield
how dear y^e hardy soldier buys y^e field
Warm without anger to their arms they crowd
& for anothers quarrell wast their blood                         95
some fight & curse while others run & pray
In Camps they rook each other at their play
& then the loosers mutiny for pay
are my brave followers slain why lett y^m dy
false musterd companys my purse supply                         100
Thus summers fraud feeds winters luxury
When in warm quarters nature craves a punk
& for the Queen I loyally get drunk
    Give ore my wanton fancy now give ore

the clouds are gath'ring & anon they'le powr                    105
the pleasures of my groves are fled away
the sacred silence & y<sup>e</sup> shiny day
what have you then to lull you in your play

---

# 7 The Isle of Wight.                    [f.20a]


In noble deeds our valiant fathers shone
We'le shine in all their glory's & our own
So Or——d does & O——d Leads us on
    Thus say y<sup>e</sup> Gallant youth who bravely dare
Not to expect— tis more— to meet the warr                    5
    Ye Men of pleasure be like these, awake,
Your Country calls consider whats at stake
our wealths decaying while our trading stands
& Europes Ballance shakes within our hands
This is a Cause thats greater nobler farr                    10
then wanton loves on beds of feathers are
    Abroad your wounds meet plunder & renown
While infamy pursues your Jarrs in town
Where the whole acts a breach upon y<sup>e</sup> laws
perhaps a stew y<sup>e</sup> scene a whore y<sup>e</sup> cause                    15
    If here at home you stay & rack your brains
to find out fashions then to dress with pains
Vain is the humour, Idle the expence
The garb appears Phantastick which we see
Before 'tis grown familiar to the eye                    20
& when it is then half its beauty's dy
    If you would stay that Lady's shoud not want
A gay Mirtillo for a smooth Courant
Alas you need not speak to show your soul
Your bounds Coupees & sinks betray the fool                    25
Men find a jest in evry diffrent step                    [f.20b]
for postures are the buisness of an ape
    In short if you woud stay at home to run
thro' all the lawless pleasures of the town
How vile the means how guilty is the end                    30
How many troubles your designs attend
You live a life that merits infamy
& live to be forgotten when you dy

For shame arise & in this cause appear
It is not for our selves alone we're here                        35
Your country Justly claims her share in you
& honour does her rightfull claim allow
Honour a courage still imployd in good
Unshockd by passions & above the croud
the soul in this Heroick beauty deckt                           40
Stands over these triumphant & erect
Dares for its country any fate defy
& mounts a brave deserver of the sky
   Some men of pleasure have been drawn so farr
by such like reasons as to think on warr                        45
Straight in a heat their Horses they provide⎤
& to the Ile of wight like warriors ride    }
before them pistolls placd & swords aside ⎦
but with what arms the mock campaign is made
With inlaid pistolls & a guilded blade                          50
Thus at a distance each the foe defy's          [f.21a]
Who fears to meet a toil or leave a bliss
But for the ending of their great design
they light they see his grace in publick dine
they view the ships they talk among the men                     55
& when a gale blows fair are gone again
the world believd they nobly did intend   ⎤
their Country by their going to defend    }
& now it wonders at the trifling end     ⎦
   Some Indians thus the town a gazing ore⎤    60
Saw a white vizard hanging at a door     }
& wonderd at the fighting face it wore   ⎦
But that soon turning with the change of wind⎤
They wonderd more the counterfeit to find   }
So like a man before & nought behind.    ⎦    65

----

# 8 The Picture of Time          [f.21a]

Well he designd & well deserves our praise
Whose pencill first a drafft of time coud trace
He knew how fast the flowing moments glide
& to the figure airy wings applyd
He knew how all things have their proper date       5

& drew a scyth to do the work of fate
His right hand this his left hand held a glass                    [f.21b]
thro which by sand an emblem of our dayes
Life ever ever ebbing seemd to pass
    Methinkes the picture thus instructs my mind                  10
Our hours are fleeting & the last assignd
Soon will it Come too soon alas for most
& all the time we use not well is lost
    This all allow but many disagree
In settling what the use of time shoud be                         15
The disagreement I with ease espyd
& to an old experiencd friend applyd
Who thus when he had heard my question cryd
    Believe my son your fathers friend in this
Whom sixty teaches how to give advice                             20
When mankind with a serious thought I read
I found the most by various follys led
these think their own because they are so best
& much of life to gratify y$^m$ wast
for still the reigning folly is the end                           25
to which the actions of the man will tend
When reason at the Helm no longer steers
She onely means to help it on prepares
thus goes their present time their past has gon
& at this rate their future will go on                            30
The man for Conversation onely fitt                               [f.22a]
Will evry night be drunk to speak his witt
if thus his minutes indolently glide
he knows no cause to lay the course aside
the Miser allwayes is of this belief                              35
that to heap riches is the use of life
tis a sure maxim few or none gett ore
that who loves mony much will love it more
    In short such instances as these youle find
As numerous as the passions in our mind                          40
If so the way by which we safest tread
Is to quitt passions & lett reason lead
lett her the offices of man define
& then your hours to what she says resign
She'le teach you what devotions sacred flame                      45
Your country what & what your friends may claim
Nor is she in prescribing too severe
Since pleasure wisely mingled eases care

To buisness diligently now attend
Anon in innocent delights unbend                          50
this course our nature has by tiring shewd
nor does our reason speak against her good
But why shoud man intirely life employ
On idle humours & forbidden Joy
Why shoud the beau but onely mind his dress ⎤      [f.22b]
the whore her wantonness the rake excess    ⎬
& Courtiers nothing but what gains a place   ⎦
The noble Titus when a setting sun
Had seen by him no virtuous action don
(Be still his name preservd) was heard to say           60
With sighs Alas—my friends Ive lost a day
We thank you Heathen Christians thank you now
Your words have taught us what we ought to do
twas wisdom this and well becoming grief
Who ever feels it knows the use of life                  65
    He Ceasd—Contentment shone upon my face
for knowledge ever has a charm to please
My tongue my satisfaction then exprest
& Ime convincd he told me for the best
but for the picture by whose sight my thought ⎤         70
Was sett a work & then to knowledge brought  ⎬
that I may nere forgett the truths he taught  ⎦
With in my closett will I hang the piece
& underneath it write such lines as these
Fly swiftly Time bear off our numberd dayes             75
Yet if man will you cannot win yᵉ race
He who lives well outlives your scanty space
By virtuous actions is a fame bestowd                   [f.23a]
& fames the least reward of doing good.

---

# 9 The state of Love imitated fᵐ an Elegy of Mons:ʳ
## Desportes.                                            [f.23a]


    In the 1ˢᵗ season of the infant earth
When all from Chaos took their orderd birth
When mankind from the hand of heaven came
All pure & white ere vice had gott a name

But evry act with innocence indu'd                                      5
Was more by nature then from knowledge good
Love mighty powr did graciously descend
grew fond of man & here w<sup>th</sup> man remaind
In their unsullyd hearts he chose to stay
their bliss anights their buisness all the day                         10
Nor wonder if in such he made abode
No temples better can befitt a god
His gentle influence did their soules inspire ⎫
Each found a mate nor wanted amorous fire ⎬
Evn when injoyment had allayd desire          ⎭                        15
Secure of sweet content they daily livd
Content unmixd with fears to be deceivd
their tongues their reall sentiments disclosd
Nor studyd language on the ears imposd
their eyes an undissembling flame expresst                             20
& they who felt it most coud speak it least
desert & softness love or beauty were                           [f.23b]
their onely arts to make a yielding fair
Plain undesigning love that never knew
to practise crueltys as Empire grew                                    25
to fashion smiles with managd airs to court
& wound a tender breast in barb'rous sport
twas more then riches riches coud not move
the meanest thought them not a price for love
   But when the vices to a head increast                              30
& all this age of downy pleasure ceast
when gold by glistring showd its dark abode
& fickleness began to be the mode
When feigning was by way of breeding taught
& onely worth his wealth the lover thought                             35
When first to speak the mind was reckond shame
& masqd hypocrisy took honours name
the fatall change with anger Cupid saw
& thus bespoke y<sup>m</sup> ready to withdraw
   Hence lett us hence with Just abhorrence go                         40
for ill their happyness these mortalls know
Who slight the mighty favours I bestow
   then darting upwards soon y<sup>e</sup> clouds he gaind
& hung in air his purpose thus explaind
   You shall repent ungratefull race you shall                        45
& know too late the Joyes from whence you fall

the loss regretting by your selves undon      }
who true contentments heavnly blisses shun   }
& after false appearing pleasures run        }
Since all in common do my Godhead slight                 50
On all in common shall my fury light
   & first on men who wont their hours employ
In my soft paths of simple artless Joy
Who woud be free tho for the worse you change
My powr shall thus my slighted gifts revenge             55
Henceforth your charmers shall be versd in arts
Not loving faithless & designing hearts
the tend'rest shall their pitty least obtain    }
they'le feel a pride ore many slaves to reign   }
to make believing fooles then give y^m pain     }       60
their look their smile their action their intent
Shall all against your peace of Soul be bent
Now hope restraining when it forward bears
Now quickning hope when you're restraind by fears
Oft seeming kind then scrupulously nice                  65
& mixing as it were their flames with Ice
to keep confusd irresolute & rackt
those bosoms they by various wayes distract
What pains you then shall feel w^t rage express
How many purposes to love y^m less                       70
How many oaths to shun their sight you'le swear
Which never shall be kept against the fair
A tear a word thats feignd shall soon restore            [f.24b]
their empire & enslave their rebells more
No matter what you saw you must believe                  75
for strange enchantments may the sight deceive
   Nay more Ile change my quiver bow & darts
to make mad work within your alterd hearts
Nor ever give the pleasing wounds I usd
Ere you my empire scornd my laws refusd                  80
Here one a nymph that is deformd shall fire
another one to honour lost admire
& while all night by others she's embracd
The wretch shall doat because she acts the chast
Some shall be prodigall their end to gain                85
Nor know that who gives most shall least obtain
their hopes will still be fed but never don
to keep them still in play & loving on

In short Ile make them feel & own it pain     ⎫
to live beneath inconstant womans chain    ⎬   90
& know their folly when they scornd my reign  ⎭
   & You ye women shall confess it too
repenting that you ere from me withdrew
You who have given wealth its powr to move
& triumph ore the sacred rites of love             95
Who vice to virtue ignorance to parts
& mony can prefer to faithfull hearts
Who think to sell your selves is nothing mean    [f.25a]
& from the prostituted bed reap gain
You never never shall again perceive          100
the wondrous sweets that mutuall passions have
but for their mighty riches love the great
While even they shall win you by deceit
their purpose in inveagling flattrys hide
& the lost creatures whom they gain deride     105
then leaving those that can be new no more
the self same arts to others practise ore
by such poor victorys to boast adress
& the faint glorys of their fame increase
   As Huntsmen when they have a hare in view     110
Fird & impatient eagerly pursue
Now ore the mountains now across the plains
& for a little take a world of pains
Unweari'd still they follow with delight
fond of the hunting tho the game they slight     115
Just so the great their amorous chace shall run
Nor ought to gain you shall be left undon
With oaths & sighs & tears they will assail
but love no more when ever these prevail
Unmindfull then of what had causd their cares    120
for other beautys they display their snares
   While you who soon perceive their broken faith    [f.25b]
their oaths no more esteemd then common breath
tho never by my flame divine inspird
Shall inly with a rage of soul be fird           125
All spight to find your flatterd charms contemnd
& mad to see another more esteemd
for Justly thus my anger does ordain
that you shoud each create $y^e$ others pain
   When Cupid thus had spoke his wings he spread    130
& with redoubled springs to heaven fled

Nor were in Idle air his curses lost
Succeeding ages found them to their cost
   Ah Madam you alas have found them true
The prophesy is made too good on you                    135
You've had the great become your beautys slave
& by experience know the great deceive
& tho' those starrs of love your charming eyes  ⎫
Outshine the brightness of the midday skys   ⎬
tho' your complexion with the morning vies   ⎭     140
tho all the Graces which around you wait
Dwell on each part & fill up beautys state
Tho the bright virtues which within remain              [f.26a]
Might promise you an everlasting reign
You see the heart was givn to you before                145
at a new shrine anothers charms adore
But cease my lovely weeper cease to mourn
The fair that triumphs now will have her turn
No charm against inconstancy secures    ⎫
You know the lovers fire but short endures  ⎬       150
& she'le forsaken meet a fate like yours   ⎭

------------

# 10 Colin                                              [f.26a]

   Ye tender virgins listen to the strains
With which our skillfull Colin charmd the plains
tis true the rivers did not cease to run   ⎫
the winds still blew tho still the shepheard sung  ⎬
But greater strangely greater things were don  ⎭    5
the younger nymphs woud give no lover ear
the older even left their talk to hear    ⎫
   Twas thus if I remember he begun    ⎬
Fly charming beauty fly the lovers tongue   ⎭
tis not in beauty to resist it long                     10
Be very cautious whom you chuse to hear
Your hearts are tender shepheards know they are
Not that of sacred love my layes complain              [f.26b]
Perish the layes that dare its fires prophane,
But men shoud never in feignd passions rave,            15
Or women know how much they can deceive,
Believe me virgins, for I tell you true,
Believe your Colin the sincere are few.

    A hope of pleasure or a pride to gain
brings to a fair some well-dissembling swain        20
thus urgd along he practises to move
thro' each ingaging path of reall love
If e're he lookes his passions in his eyes
If ere he sighes tis heard upon his sighes
In all his words a soft enchantment reigns  ⎫      25
Ah shepheardess beware his words are chains  ⎬
& their design is on your innocence         ⎭
You must not lett him conquer tho he swear
Nor longer than he talks of Hymen hear
Oaths without Hymen never bind till death        30
The lovers oaths but go for so much breath
Believe me fairs he best deserves a heart
Who gives you proof that he can never part
    A gratitude or pitty well designd
Oft unawares has made a woman kind        35
she sees she pittys by degrees she burns
& all the youth perhaps but acts returns
Ah shepheards leave in this to show y$^r$ skill    [f.27a]
The more success you meet the more you're ill
deceive those women who design on you  ⎫      40
But why shoud harmless virgins suffer too  ⎬
Methinks they shoud not—yet Alas they do  ⎭
Believe ye fairs what faithfull Colin speakes
He who dissembles no distinction makes.
    By easy numbers some obtain a love        45
By presents some, by dressing others move
by singing this by dancing that insnares
Inconstancy is often in its airs
thus by a thousand slights to love you're drawn  ⎫
While he who draws you may be touchd by none  ⎬  50
Or if he chance to be so maynt be long       ⎭
Believe ye Virgins what the poet sings
Loves darts have feathers & himself has wings
    Yet have I seen & read of happy pairs
Who with a mutuall kindness past their years    55
Hang up your garlands Beautys to their fame
& ever in your songs preserve their name
Nay I have seen a lover hereto fore
Who dy'd to show how much he did adore
He might to lust or pride a martyr prove    [f.27b]
But since tis said Alexis dy'd for love

give up a tear to his uncommon doom      ⎫
still when at each full moon the shepheards come   ⎬
With Hellebore to strow along his tomb    ⎭
These are the rights the shepheards think are due        65
to him whom they call mad to dy for you
Believe their actions & tis quickly known    ⎫
Men think their constancy is fairly shown    ⎬
In loving allwayes not in loving one      ⎭
   Take not a perjurd lover for you know        70
He may be false because he has been so
Take not a fool for fear you may esteem
Another more to be belovd than him
Take not a man thats but a man of airs     ⎫
for the nymphs qualitys he little cares      ⎬        75
Who likes his own too well to value hers    ⎭
In ages humours riches or in bloods
Unequall matches make eternall feuds
Believe me virgins if you woud be blest     ⎫
You must how ere you manage for the rest    ⎬        80
Take one thats near your temper to your breast  ⎭
Thus without quarrells will your hours run on
While your opinions still unite in one
Thus when the thing will please y^rself you know    [f.28a]
You know what pleases one another too.        85
   Divine Orinda now my labours crown
& if my voice or harp have glory won
Thine was the influence thine the glory be
Thee Colin loves & loves thy sex for thee
   He ceasd his voice was rather sweet than loud        90
The mountains coud not as the nymphs applaud
but every fair of that admiring throng     ⎫
Warbling a part on't as she went along    ⎬
Raisd a shrill Eccho to resound his Song.   ⎭

---

# 11 The Court       [f.28a]

   Now see the port lett winds & waters warr
You madam triumph in your happy starr
& as the Pilot safe arrivd from shore
With pleasure hears tumultuous billows roar

With pleasure sees the tempest toss the seas                          5
for even dangers in a prospect please
so now look back & view with such delight
Your great deliv'rance when the court you quitt
While your retirements give you certain ease               [f.28b]
& calmer hours to spend in virtues wayes                            10
    Believe me nymph no common grace inspires
When any from this dang'rous place retires
Where the small boats or ships that proudly ride
Meet the same wracking winds & driving tide
The courts involvd in errors endless night,                         15
You see, but with a false deceiving light,
Its splendour cheats & does at once surprize
Nor less your Judgement suffers than your eyes
None there the lookes of simple nature wears
theres none without disguise & art appears                          20
the fault is publick & a custom grown
that scarce a soul without its masque is shown
The young the old the little & the great
With miens affected & feignd colours cheat
Now gay now sad & never long the same,                              25
they change to suit the time or serve their aim.
Friendship unsound, caresses unsincere,
& praises with a faint malicious air,
Low flattrys, oaths on purpose made to cheat, ⎫
& all the glossy varnish of deceit              ⎬       [f.29a]
the supple courtiers masquing dress compleat ⎭
    What greater dangers can be mett with there
Where lions rage & dragons poison air
With open forces to destroy they run
& can be shunnd because they can be known                           35
But at yᵉ court the Lions like the deer
& dragons like the gentle lambs appear
    Assist us heavn where such disguisements reign
Or human wisdom will assist in vain
When borrowed Manners all our fears remove                          40
& feather out the vultur like the dove
Where as in woods in which the robbers live
We're lost by innocence by rapin thrive
& all around us scarce we hear a noise
but of the robd or of the robbers voice                             45
there by a strange but often tryd device
On wrecks of houses greater houses rise

Which suffring in their turn make others great
& raise them high in view for marks to fate.
   Thus nothing stands at court on stable ground     50
Not you your self have always favour found
Yet wonder not that while your beautys reign     [f.29b]
While the bright Loves & Graces form y^r train
the winds are high bring envy on their wing
& ruffle all the glorys of your spring     55
Evn on the breast of Flora where it grows    ⎫
Spight of its charms rude blasts will discompose    ⎬
the sweet carnation or the lovely rose    ⎭
   Nor think you've lost y^r freedoms rather savd
for to be there you must have been enslavd     60
All courts are gallys painted dazzling fair
Where the great slaves their chains w^th glory wear
In golden chains at polishd oars they sweat
thus undergoing drudgerys of state
But what availes this mighty pomp & shine     65
No yoak is less a yoak for being fine
those abject slaves who to their oar confind
With heavy pains supply the want of wind
Whose arm the badge whose feet the fetters wear
Are less inthralld then fortunes prisoners here     70
   These suffer deeper in a better part
& tho the legs unbound enslave the heart
their words when words are free in all beside
Or to their close or known designs are ty'd
Dependance is the common servile case     [f.30a]
& the free-will a stranger to the place
the tyrant passions tread fair meritt down
& their proud thrones erect above the crown
their wretched captives many bonds secure
for love ambition avarice make y^m sure     80
   But we may yet much greater ills declare
for much impiety infects its air
The blessed Gospell courtiers can believe
A sett of fables minted to deceive
That canopys of state where monarchs reign     85
Are Heav'ns on earth & Heav'n a Fairy scene
   The courts no ground where virtues often grow
Their proper soil is less exposd & low
Retirement means the tempting world to shun
& when thats quitted virtues workes begun     90

To fly with safety is to conquer here
& scaping triumphs ore a baffled snare
Tis true the pow'r above in ev'ry place
Dispenses flames divine & heav'nly grace
That Lillys may have grown on thorny ground                95
& there a Glorious Anna may be found
but yet the priviledge is rarely known                    [f.30b]
Like Arethusa's fabled stream to run
tis hard to roll along the briny sea
With pure untainted waters all the way                    100
Your life has made the common fable true
& few I fear at court will follow you
How few coud ever keep themselves from blame
If the great gifts that crown you tempted them
The bright enchantments of unbounded witt                 105
With charms adornd in easy nature sweet
The rank you held besett with ev'ry vice
Which follow pleasures or from grandeur rise.

---

# 12 The Test of Poetry                                   [f.30b]


　　Much have I writt, says Bavius, Mankind knows
By my quick printing how my fancy flows:
Yet Thyrsis (& they say the youth's inspird)
Mindless of mine, your Genius has admird;
When have you ere, or in what paper been,                 5
Where the news faild, among our authors, seen?
In what collection do we meet y$^r$ name?  ⎫
No, what you write, you can your self condemn ⎬           [f.31a]
& lett the private closett hide from fame.  ⎭
Here, ink & paper, lett us lock the door,  ⎫             10
The Muses flames are quick, weel write an hour, ⎬
Then count whose lines are fewer, whose are more. ⎭
What shoud I do? The challenge I decline,
& own his readier knack to master mine.
　　Is witt thus tryd? is this its onely test?           15
Or is it but the newest, not the best?
You Mighty Bards, whose memorys remain,
& ore oblivion, time, & envy reign,
With your long-labourd works in hand, appear,

Raise your pale conscious lamps, tell ore y$^r$ care, 20
& fright the sudden writers of our times,
from giddy flights & undigested rimes:
Those hardend Browns, that Plague a Judging age, ⎤
That scribble fast, & many a thoughtless page, ⎬
To prove their title to poetick rage. ⎦ 25
How distant are the Beautys from their sight,
Which come by years, & keep a Poem bright.
These catch the little flashes of their witt,
They teach them how to move w$^{th}$ numberd feet,
Then hasty to supply a craving dun, 30
Or warm from Taverns, to the Press they runn:
No length of Judgement ripens every line, [f.31b]
They own no chain of thought, no great design,
But to succeed, to spurious arts descend,
Which sooth our follys, or our vice defend; 35
Brisk drunken Catches on the Sober Jest;
Soft luscious Elegys debauch the chast;
Lampoon will rage upon unspotted fame;
& Panegyrick daub a worthless name;
So plants unapt to bear the wintry skys 40
If dunghill warmth the distant sun supplys
To seasons not their own appear with hast
And while they boast a colour want a tast.
  Tis hence the proffit which accrues from all
May now be nothing, & anon be small; 45
Perhaps the sellers (ventrous race of men) ⎤
While their lost pains the writers mourn in vain, ⎬
May reap a silver harvest from their pen; ⎦
Or both at last (for both a hazzard run)
By the same labours find themselves undon. 50
they woud be known, tis thats the Poets aim,
Yet few shall have, since few deserve a name,
The rest shall find their hopes at dying fled,
Or ere they dy themselves in fame be dead.
  The world woud verse with love & warmth admire, [f.32a]
But the wild managers put out the fire;
For shoud not man respect the sacred thing
Which prophets write, which saints & angells sing?
Be then our poetry, (to make it please,)
Fair sense & virtue, in a charming dress, 60
Nor publishd soon, it will the more endure,
By being kept for years, of years secure.

The Justest may be partial to his strains,
While the fresh subject on his mind remains,
himself applaud, & evry line approve,                          65
With all the blindness of a fathers love;
Till in cool temper, as at ebb of tide,
He sees those shallows which before coud hide,
Waits till his heat by Just degrees expires,    ⎫
The Parents dotage by the same retires,         ⎬           70
& then hele censure what he now admires;        ⎭
Hele look his labours ore & ore w<sup>th</sup> care,    ⎫
Appeal to Judgement, & consult his ear,         ⎬
While here he dashes out, & changes there:      ⎭
He'le figures when they are not proper quit,                  75
& lop rank branches off luxuriant witt
Hele give the swelling verse a sober pace,                 [f.32b]
He'le smooth the rugged, & the flatt he'le raise;
Then Bid the Polishd lines securely thrive;
and the great founder of their fame survive.                 80

---

# The Ecstasy.                                             [f.32b]


    The fleeting Joy that all things have beneath
Goes off like snow while Zephirs warmly breath
The happy wish that makes our bliss compleat
it is not wealth it is not to be great
To glide along on pleasures easy floud                        5
Or in fames wreaths to shine above the croud
Weak man who charms in these alone can see
Hear what I ask & learn to ask of me.
    Send to my breast Allmighty King send down
A beam of brightness from thy starry throne                   10
Break on my mind drive errors cloud away
& make a calm in passions troubled sea
that the poor banishd Soul serene & free
May rise from earth to visit heav'n & thee.
Come peace Divine shed gently from above    ⎫             [f.33a]
Inspire my willing bosome wondrous love      ⎬
& lend thy wings & teach me how to move      ⎭
    But Whither whither now? what wondrous fire
With this blest influence equalls my desire?

I rise or love the kind deluder reigns                    20
& acts in fancy such inchanted scenes
The earth retires, the parting skyes give way
& now I view the native realms of day
I mount above the starrs above the sun
& still methinks the spirit bears me on.                  25
O strange enjoyment of a bliss unseen!
O ravishment! o sacred rage within!
Tumultuous pleasure raisd on peace of mind
Which he thats good & onely he can find!
I hear (it must be so) Ime sure I hear                    30
Seraphick musick strike my rapturd ear
I see the light that veiles the throne on high
A light too glorious for the dazzled eye
look how around this great mysterious place
The Angells fly & as they fly they praise                35
Look how Apostles prophets martyrs Joyn ⎫    [f.33b]
& all their tongues & all their harps combine ⎬
to celebrate the Majesty divine ⎭
to please heav'ns King their heav'nly lays are sung
No voice is silent not a harp unstrung                    40
   Pure & immortall quire allow me now
Since faign my heart woud pay its tribute too
Allow my Zeal to bear a part w^th you
Assist my words and as they move along
With Halelujah's crown the burthend song                 45
   Father Eternall, God of truth & light
Great above all beyond expression bright
No bounds thy knowledge none thy powr confine
For powr & knowledge in their source are thine
Around thee Glory spreads her golden wing                50
Sing Glittering Angells Halelujah sing.
   Son of the Father, blest, begotten Son
Ere the short measuring line of time begun
In thee his perfect Essence makes abode
the world has seen thy workes & owns thee God            55
The world must own thee loves unfathomd spring.  [f.34a]
Sing Glittering Angells Halelujah Sing.
   Proceeding Spirit, Equally divine
In whom the Godheads true perfections shine
You fill our bosomes with celestiall fire                60
& tis a bliss to burn when you inspire
O Lord Of Grace for Grace on earth you bring.

sing glittering Angells Halelujah sing
  But Ah whats this? & where is all my heat
What interruption makes my Joy retreat        65
the worlds gott in my meditation crost
& the gay pictures in my fancy lost
How willingly Alas our soules woud rise
& be fixd starrs inserted in the skyes
But our attempts these chains of earth restrain    70
Deride our toiles & dragg us down again
Thus meteors mounting with the planets vie
But their own bodys sink them in the Sky
When the warmths gon that taught y^m how to fly.

---

# Concerning Resolution.    [f.34b]


  Happy the man whose firm resolves obtain
Assisting Grace to burst his sinfull chain
For him the Days with golden minutes glow
Tis his the Land where milk & hony flow
Justice & mercy piety & peace        5
Attend his workes & crown them with success
He hopes the best that is for heavn prepard
& wants no bliss while virtue can reward
That purpled hour which ushers in the light ⎫
& that which shuts its beautys up in night  ⎬  10
Still hears him pray still sees his actions right ⎭
For him they still on easy minutes speed
& as they move for him the rest succeed
  But most Alas by vain opinion lead
Ore the wild maze of erring passions tread    15
& now to this & now to that we go
& each desire & neither rightly know
& act irresolute in all we do
& seldom stay to search our objects through
Desire is vain & wanton free to range    20
Fond of a Chace & fond the Chace to Change
By turns a thousand inclinations rise
& each by turns as impotently dies
Now thought grows wild if loose Aminta's kind  [f.35a]
Shee spreads her Charms & captivates the mind  25
Anon Aminta leaves the thought at ease

No more her aires & soft Allurements please
We love reclining in y<sup>e</sup> shady bowers
by running waters near sweet banks of flowrs
To surfeit nature with full bowles of wine                    30
& with forcd appetites on bliss refine
Then buisy then fantastically wise
Then to be some thing else we streight devise
For Fancy still undreind affors supplys
tis thus if reason from the throne be gon                      35
The madd affections bear their master on
His life proves restless & his labour vain
By hurrying after Phantomes of the brain
So the brave Falcon when its glorys fade
When its strong wings their generous forces shed               40
The vacant holds ignobler birds supply        ⎫
With Ravens feathers impd she mounts on high  ⎬
& weak or giddy strayes along the sky          ⎭
   In Every Change indeed resolves we make
But those resolves to settle newer break                       45
By contradictions thus we seem to live
Nor want the colour of a cause to give
Kind heav'n forgive us when for what we do            [f.35b]
We woud debauch our knack of reasning too
When int'rest does on thought its force dispence               50
When pleasure beats upon the dazzled sence
Our resolutions oft in vain are made
Kind heavn forgive the fault & lend thine aid.
If by thy law we must temptations find
If these must try the temper of the mind                       55
We begg thee not to change thy good decree
We begg for pardon or support from thee
Our wisdome never shoud thy ways confine
but thus confess & humbly rest in thine
Tis well theres tryalls since the mans so proud                60
& since he's weak tis well theres Grace allowd.

---

# To <sup>+</sup><sub>+</sub><sup>+</sup> on the various Styles of Poetry        [f.35b]

At modern Rome an easy Nymph was bred
In tender tales & soft Romances read
These on the brain a wild impression brought

& made her sure she saw what ere she thought
Within her Fancy shady groves were reard     5
& Dancing nymphs & piping swains appeard
Complaints were heard rewarded passions glowd     [f.36a]
A plain extended & a river flowd
But Soon Alas her friends successfull care
from the sweet frenzy disengagd y<sup>e</sup> fair     10
Untimely friends restore my Joys again ⎞
Restore my grove my river & my plain  ⎬
She often cryd & often cryd in vain   ⎠
Till a bright youth with skill to manage came
Who while he fed her fancy raisd her flame     15
Then the fond creature lost her heedless heart
In making Celia's answer Damons part.
    Change but y<sup>e</sup> sex make poetry y<sup>e</sup> thing
& the whole story to my case you bring
When first to think with order I began     20
& dawning reason aimd to show the man
Pleasd with the flowing graces of a line ⎞
Methought I wishd y<sup>e</sup> name of poet mine  ⎬
The wish grew stronger & became design  ⎠
Strange modells in my fancy then were reard     25
& y<sup>e</sup> thin shades of different styles appeard
My pastorall enervate movd along
My rough was Satyr & my smooth was song
Ah cruell world thou foe to calm repose     [f.36b]
from thee the knowledge of this errour rose     30
I thought I coud have taught the birds to love
& wakt the tunefull Ecchoes of y<sup>e</sup> grove
What made your truths my pleasing cheat destroy
Tho' twas opinion twas a reall Joy
But see the fetters of your wisdome loose     35
A friend once more provokes y<sup>e</sup> silent muse
the magick charms which in his numbers reign
Strike on y<sup>e</sup> tender part that turnd my brain
buisness & verse he calls consistent things
& Ile believe that 'tis a truth he sings     40
I yield I yield unusuall heats arise
twere now resisting pleasure to be wise
    I hate y<sup>e</sup> vulgar with untunefull ears
Soules uninspird & negligent of verse
Hence ye prophane be farr removd away     45
While to my powr I woud my friend repay

When Greece did truth in mystick fables shroud
& with delight instruct the listning croud
An ancient bard (I need not tell his name)
These strains deliverd down to future fame                          50
Still as he sung he touchd the trembling lyre ⎫        [f.37a]
& felt the notes his rising song inspire      ⎬
Forgive my Genius where I want his fire       ⎭
   Witt is the Muses horse & bears on high
The daring rider to the muses Sky                                   55
Who while his strength to mount aloft he trys
By regions varying in their nature flyes
   By the poor trifling region first he goes
Where words inverted anagrams compose
Where Jingling puns the meagre couplets raise                       60
That do the pointed Epigram debase
Where mean Acrosticks labourd in a frame    ⎫
On scatterd letters raise a painfull scheme ⎬
Whose scanty bounds exclude yᵉ sprightly flame ⎭
Ah sacred verse within my thoughts adord ⎫                          65
Ah be for ever in my lines deplord       ⎬
If men get fame by tricks upon a word     ⎭
Can such as these to character pretend
Can any muse the worthless toil befriend
At this awhile yᵉ poet held his peace        ⎫                      70
& scornfull smiles were spread upon his face ⎬
Which moving off he thus resumd the layes   ⎭
   By a cold country next yᵉ rider goes ⎫       [f.37b]
Where all is coverd with eternall snows     ⎬
Ore which the shining Genius never rose     ⎭                       75
Bleak level realm where frigid styles abound
Where never yet a mounting thought was found
But starvd conceits that chill the readers mind
& counted feet is poetry defind
Ah sacred verse replete with heavnly flame ⎫                        80
If such a frozen piece invade thy name      ⎬
The name of man may breathless statues claim ⎭
Here grief awhile delayd his hand & tongue
But then again he playd again he sung.
   Pass the next region which appears to show           85
Tis very open very green & low
No noble flight no strength of sence is there
Its turns are common childish is their air
On callow wings & like a plague of flyes

The little fancys through a poem rise                                      90
The Jaded reader every where to strike
& move his passions every where alike
There the best beautys which y^e brightest write
are copy'd ill or flourishd out of sight
There metaphors on metaphors abound                             [f.38a]
& sence with differing images confound
Strange injudicious management of fire    ⎫
Ah sacred verse from such a realm retire  ⎬
Tis credit lost no better to inspire       ⎭
Here a soft pitty rolld within his breast                                100
& soon his voice the following strains exprest
    Mount higher still, still keep thy faithfull seat
Mind the firm reins & curb thy coursers heat
Nor lett him touch the realms y^t next appear  ⎫
They're all composd of castles in y^e air      ⎬            105
Whose threatning turrets seem a fall to fear   ⎭
Thoughts for extravagance & words for noise
are here the reasons that conclude their choice
The swelling lines with stalking strutt proceed
& in the clouds terrifick rumblings breed                                110
The reader scard with sounds does plainly see
Tyrannick port mistook for majesty
While the loud Bard does on Apollo call
he bids him enter to possess him all
& makes his flames afford a wild pretence                       [f.38b]
to keep him unrestraind by common sence
Ah sacred verse least reason quitt thy state
Give none to such or give a gentler heat
The poet here awhile collected stood
Within himself & thus his track pursud.                                  120
    Above y^e beautys farr above y^e show
in which weak nature dresses here below
Stands the great Palace of y^e bright & fine
That does around with fair Ideas shine
Eternall modells of unbounded parts                                     125
The pride of minds & conquerours of hearts
Tis here that guided by the muses fire
& full of warmth divine her friends retire
To tast repose & elevated Joys
Which in a deep untroubled leisure rise                                  130
from hence the charms that most engage they chuse
& as they please the glittering objects use

While to their genius more than art they trust
Yet art acknowledges their labours Just
from hence they look from this exalted place    }    135
On the low world sublimely rich in layes
to crown a victour w<sup>th</sup> rewarding praise    }
The Soul with knowledge gently to improve    }    [f.39a]
to knitt a friendship or obtain a love
& but to speak of heaven look above    }    140
Hail sacred verse ye sacred muses hail
Coud I your pleasures with your fire reveal
The world might then be brought to know you right
& court your rage & envy my delight
But time may bring a genius on his wings—    }    145
With admiration stoppd no more he sings    }
No more his flying fingers shake y<sup>e</sup> strings    }
   To this recess do you my friend retreat
From thence report the pleasures of the seat
Describe the raptures which a writer knows    150
When in his breast a vein of fancy glows
say what he feeles while op'ning of y<sup>e</sup> mine
& what he feeles when first he sees it shine
say when a reader views a beauteous piece
How much the writers mind can act on his    155
How images in charming numbers sett
a sort of likeness in the soul begett
What various things y<sup>e</sup> softned swiming eye
Believes it sees & onely seems to see
Pierce further still thro' natures maze to find    160
How passions drawn give passions to y<sup>e</sup> mind
Is verse a Soveraign regent of the soul    [f.39b]
& fitted all its motions to controul
Or are they sisters tund at once above
& shake like unisons if either move    165
For at a fine description of a fight    }
Ive heard a souldiers voice confess delight    }
Ive seen his eyes with crowding spirits bright    }
When from his fair the fickle Trojan flyes    }
& in enchanting lines Eliza cryes    }    170
Ive seen y<sup>e</sup> tears stand in y<sup>e</sup> virgins eyes    }
Ive seen y<sup>m</sup> blush at soft Corinnas name
& in red Characters confess a flame
say tender maids (to such my lays appeal)
If here the powr of verse my verses tell    175

Oft does a nymph by sweet experience prove ⎫
the passions well describd her passions move ⎬
& longs to meet a swain & longs to love ⎭
Then if by chance the sighing youth arrives ⎫
In pleasure lost her melted heart she gives ⎬ 180
& the raisd lover by the poet lives ⎭

## Metr: Boetius 1ˢ 1 Quisquis comp: [f.40a]

    The Man whose mind & actions still Sedate
Can bravely triumph ore yᵉ thoughts of fate
He who unaltered fortunes Changes brookes
Without elated or dejected lookes
With a fixd carriage & undaunted soul 5
Shall see yᵉ oceans boiling surges roll
Vesuvius flames in smoaky pillars rise
& bolts of thunder dart from opening skys
Why dread we wretched mankind tell me why
When the vain threats of tyrants idely fly 10
Weigh all things right as in themselves they are
Unlearn your minds to move by hope & fear
With in yʳ breast lett resolution reign
& all their baffled forces act in vain
But he who servily can wish or grieve 15
For that which is not in his powr to give
Casts off the firmness wᶜʰ shoud make him great
the strongest shield we can oppose to fate
letts inclinations grow & thus he weaves
Those very bonds which keep us passions slaves. 20

## A Tavern feast [f.40b]

Gay Bacchus liking B——s wine
    A noble meal bespoke
& for yᵉ guests that were to dine
    Brought Comus Love & Joke

The God near Cupid drew his chair                              5
  & Joke by Comus plact
Thus wine makes Love forget his care
  & Mirth exalts a feast
To make it more deserve y<sup>e</sup> God
  Each sweet engaging Grace                          10
Put on some cloaths to come abroad
  & took a waiters place
Then Cupid namd for ev'ry glass
  A Lady of y<sup>e</sup> sky
& Bacchus swore he'd drink y<sup>e</sup> Lass              15
  & had it bumper high
Fat Comus tossd his brimmers o're
  & allways gott y<sup>e</sup> most
For Joke took care to fill him more
  When ere he missd y<sup>e</sup> toast          20
They calld & drunk at evry touch                          [f.41a]
  & calld & drunk again
& if y<sup>e</sup> Gods can take too much
  Tis said they did so then
Free Jests ran all the table round                          25
  & with y<sup>e</sup> wine conspire
While they by sly reflections wound
  To Set their heads afire
Plump Bacchus little Cupid stung
  By reckning his deceits                           30
& Cupid mockd his stammring tongue
  & all his stagg'ring gates
Joke drolld on Comus Greedy ways
  & tales without a Jest
& Comus calld his witty plays                               35
  But waggerys at best
such talking sett them all at odds
  & had I Homers pen
Ide sing you how they drunk like Gods
  & how they fought like men                        40
To part y<sup>e</sup> fray the Graces fly                 [f.41b]
  Who make them soon agree
& had y<sup>e</sup> furys selves been nigh
  They still were three to three
Bacchus appeasd letts Cupid up                              45
  & gave him back his bow
But kept some darts to stirr y<sup>e</sup> Cup

Where Sack & Sugar flow
Joke taking Comus rosy crown
   In triumph wore y<sup>e</sup> prize              50
& thrice in mirth he pushd him down
   As thrice he strove to rise
Then Cupid sought y<sup>e</sup> mirtle grove
   Where Venus did recline
& Beauty close embracing Love           55
   They Joyn to rail at Wine
& Comus loudly cursing witt
   Rolld off to some retreat
Where boon companions gravely sitt
   In dull unwieldy state            60
Bacchus & Joke who stay behind        [f.42a]
   For one fresh glass prepare
& kiss & are exceeding kind
   & vow to be sincere
But part in time whoever here          65
   Are couchd within my song
For tho the friendship may be dear
   It cant continue long.

---

# The Ecstasy.        [f.43a]

The fleeting Joys which all affords below
Work the fond heart with unperforming show
And vanish off as snows that swiftly fail
Thawd by the breathings of a Vernall gale
The Wish that makes our happier life compleat     5
Nor grasps the wealth nor honours of the great
Nor loosely sailes on Pleasures easy stream
Nor crops for Lawrels all y<sup>e</sup> groves of Fame
Weak man who charms to these alone confine
Attend my prayr & learn to make it thine     10
   From thy rich throne where circling trains of light
Make day that's endless infinitely bright
Thence heavnly Father thence with pitty dart
One beam of brightness to my longing heart
Dawn through the mind drive Errors clouds away     15
And still the rage in Passions troubled sea
That the poor banishd soul serene and free

May rise from Earth to visit heavn & thee
Come Peace Divine shed gently from above                    [f.43b]
Inspire my willing bosome wondrous Love                          20
Thy Purple pinnions to my shoulders ty
And point the passage where I want to fly.
   But whither whither now what powrfull fire
With this blest influence equals my desire
I rise (or love the kind Deluder reigns                          25
and acts in fancy such enchanted scenes)
Earth lessning flys the parting skys retreat
The fleecy clouds my waving feathers beat
And now the sun and now the starrs are gon
And still methinks the spirit bears me on                        30
Where Tracts of Æther purer blue display
And edge the golden realm of native day
   Oh strange Enjoyment of a bliss unseen
Oh ravishment Oh sacred rage within
Tumultuous Pleasure raisd on peace of mind                       35
Sincere excessive from the world refind
I see the light that veiles the throne on high
A light unpiercd by mans impurer eye
I hear the words which issuing thence proclaim
That Gods attendants praise his awfull name                      40
Then heads unnumberd bend before the shrine             [f.44a]
Mysterious seat of Majesty divine
And hands unnumberd strike the silver String
And tongues unnumberd Halelujah sing
See where the shining seraphims appear                           45
And sink their decent eyes with holy fear
See flights of Angels all their feathers raise
Range the vast heigths and as they range they praise
Behold the great Apostles sweetly met
And high on Curles of Azure Æther sett                           50
Behold the Prophets full of Heavnly fire
With wandring fingers wake the tunefull lyre
And hear the Martyrs sing and all around
The Church Triumphant make the region sound
With harps with Crowns of Gold with boughs of green             55
With robes of white the pious throngs are seen
Exalted Anthems all their hours employ
And all is musick and excess of Joy
   Charmd with the sight I long to bear my part
The pleasure flutters at my ravishd heart                        60

Sweet saints and Angels Heavns immortall Quire
If Love have warmd me with celestial fire
Assist my words and as they move along                    [f.44b]
With Halelujah crown the burthend Song
    Father of all above and all below                      65
O great and farr beyond expression so
No bounds thy knowledge none thy powr confine
For powr and knowledge in their source are thine
Around thee glory spreads her golden wing
Sing glittering Angels Halelujah sing                         70
    Son of the Father first begotten son
Ere the short measuring line of Time begun
The world has seen thy workes & Joyd to see
His bright Effulgence manifest in thee
The world must own thee Loves unfathomd spring               75
Sing glittering Angels Halelujah sing
    Proceeding Spirit equally divine
In whom the Godheads full perfections shine
With various grace with comfort unexprest
With Holy transport you refine the breast                     80
And Earth grows heavnly where your gifts you bring
Sing Glittering Angels Halelujah sing
    But wheres my rapture where my wondrous heat        [f.45a]
What interruption makes my bliss retreat
This worlds got in the thoughts of T'other crosst            85
And the fair pictures in my fancy Lost
With what an eager zeal the Conscious Soul
Woud seek its home & soaring pass the Pole
But our attempts these chains of earth restrain
Deride the toil and drag us down again                        90
So from the ground aspiring Meteors goe
And rankd with Planets light the world below
But their own bodys sink them in the Sky
When the warmths gon by which they learnd to fly.

---

## The Horse & Olive or Warr & Peace     [f.46a]

With Moral tale let Ancient wisdome move
    Which thus I sing to make yᵉ moderns wise
Strong Neptune once with sage Minerva strove
    And rising Athens was the Victors prize

By Neptune Plutus guardian Powr of gain                                  5
  By great Minerva Bright Apollo stood
But Jove superiour Bad y^e side obtain
  Which best contrivd to do y^e nation good

Then Neptune striking from the parted ground
  The Warlike horse came pawing on y^e plain                    10
And as it tossd its main & prancd around
  By this he crys Ile make the people reign

The Goddess smiling gently bowd y^e spear
  And rather thus they shall be blessd she said
Then upwards shooting in y^e Vernal air                                 15
  With loaded boughs y^e fruitfull Olive spread

Jove saw what gifts y^e rival Powrs designd
  Then took th' impartial scales resolvd to show
If greater bliss in warlike pomp we find
  Or in y^e calm which peacefull times bestow                     20

On Neptunes part he placd victorious days                        [f.46b]
  Gay trophys won & fame extending wide
But plenty safety science arts & ease
  Minerva's scale with greater weight supplyd

Fierce warr devours whom gentle Peace woud save                        25
  Sweet peace restores w^t angry warr destroys
Warr made for peace with that rewards y^e brave
  While Peace its pleasures from it self enjoys

Hence Vanquishd Neptune to y^e Sea withdrew
  Hence Wise Minerva ruld Athenian lands                         30
Her Athens hence in arts & honour grew
  And still her Olives deck pacifick hands

From fables thus disclosd a Monarchs mind
  May form Just rules to chuse y^e truly great
And subjects wearyd with distresses find                               35
  Whose kind endeavours most befriend a state

Evn Britain here may learn to place her love
  If Citys won her kingdomes wealth have cost
If Anna's thoughts y^e Patriot soules approve
  Whose cares restore y^t wealth y^e wars had lost               40

But if we ask yᵉ Moral to disclose
   Whom best Europa's patroness it calls
Great Anna's title no exception knows
   And unapplyd in this yᵉ fable falls

With her no Neptune or Minerva vyes         [f.47a]
   When ere she pleasd her troops to conquest flew
When ere she pleases peaceful times arise
   She gave the horse & gives yᵉ Olive too.

-------

# A Parody of Donec Gratus Eram in A dialogue Between M—— & his Wife.   [f.47a]

He.  When first my Biddy love profest
     My rapture ran so high
    Not Gentle S——s fondly prest
    To beautious G——s panting breast
     Was half so blest as I         5

She.  When first my bard you taught my name
     To sound in Song divine
    Not S——s exalted fame
    Tho S——s a P—— aim
     I wishd instead of mine        10

He.  But now the Muse thy late delight
     You See thy rival prove
    For night & day & day & night
    To write & read & read & write
     Is all yᵉ life I love        15

She  Forlorn yet senceless of yᵉ pain    [f.47b]
     I to the Mirrour fly
    Survey my self am Justly vain
    And but I know my self again
     For that dear face coud dy        20

He.  But shoud thy Bard no longer pore
     Wilt thou forsake thy glass
    If I admire my works no more
    Wilt thou to court thy shade give o're

And all be as it was                                          25

She  Since none but we our rivals are
         And none the lovers too
      Be fond or void of am'rous care
      I fond or vain of being fair
         Yet both are ever true.                              30

---

# Epigram. On a Ladys lace shown for a favour

[f.47b]

As Nelly to a chamber got
   To take her leave of Ned
She loosd her lace & Cast a knot
   (Ah why unlacd the maid.).

Now pull the further end she cryd                         [f.48a]
   The Youth obeyd commands
And still the knot y^e faster tyd
   The more they parted hands

This fancy by the lover seen
   She gave the silken braid                                   10
And with a kiss or two between
   The parting posy said

When this you see remember me
   And love me more & more
This knot when you at distance drew                           15
   Came closer than before.

---

# An Allegory on Man.                          [f.48a]

A thoughtfull *Being,* long and spare,
Our race of Mortals call him *Care,*
(Were *Homer* living well he knew
What Name the *Gods* woud call him too)
With fine Mechanick Genius wrought,                            5

And lovd to work tho no one bought.
   This *Being* by a Model bred
In *Joves* eternal sable head,
Contrivd a Shape impowrd to breath
And be the *worldling* here beneath.                    10
   The *Man* rose staring, like a stake,
Wondring to see himself awake;
Then lookd so wise before he knew                    [f.48b]
The buisness he was made to do,
That pleasd to see with what a grace,                 15
He gravely showd his forward face,
*Jove* talkd of breeding him on high
An *under-something* of the Sky.
   But ere he gave the mighty nod,
Which ever binds a Poets *God,*                          20
For which his curles *Ambrosial* shake,
And Parent *Earth's* oblidgd to quake,
He felt her move, he saw her rise,
She stood confessd before his eyes.
But not with what we read she wore,                  25
A Castle for a crown before,
Or lengthning streets and longer roads;
Dangling behind her like Commodes:
As yet with onely wreaths She drest,
She traild a landskip-painted vest;                     30
And thrice she raisd, as *Ovid* said,
And thrice she bowd her weighty head.
   Her honours made, great *Jove,* she cryd,
The man was fashiond from my side,
His hands, his heart, his head are mine,              35
Then what hast thou to call him thine?
Nay rather ask, yᵉ Monarch said,
What boots his hand, his heart, his head,
Were what I gave removd away,                         [f.49a]
Thy part's an Idle shape of clay.                         40
To shares apiece, says artfull Care,
Your pleas woud make your titles fair,
You claim The body, you the soul;
But I who Joynd them claim the whole.
   Thus with the *Gods* debate began,                45
On such a trivial cause as *man.*
And can Celestial tempers rage!
(Quoth *Virgil* in a later age.)

As thus they wrangled *Time* came by;
(Theres none who paints him such as I;                          50
For what the Fabling Ancients sung,
Makes *Saturn* old when *Time* was young)
As yet his winters had not shed
Their silver honours on his head,
He Just had got his pinions free,                              55
From his old sire *Eternity*.
A serpent Girdled round he wore,
The tail within the mouth before,
By which our *Almanacks* are clear,
That learned *Ægypt* meant the Year.                           60
A staff he carryd, where on high                               [f.49b]
He fixd a glass to Measure by;
As Amber boxes made a show
For heads of Canes an age agoe.
His Vest for day and night was pyd;                            65
A bending Sickle arms his side;
And *Springs* new months his train adorn;
(The Other *Seasons* were unborn)
    Known by the *Gods* as near he draws
They make him Umpire of the Cause.                             70
Ore a low trunk his arm he layd,
Where since his *Hours* a Dial made.
Then leaning heard the nice debate,
And thus pronouncd the words of *Fate*.
    Since *Body* from the Parent *Earth*,                      75
And *Soul* from *Jove* receivd a Birth,
Return they where they first began,
But since their Union makes the *man*,
Till *Jove* & *Earth* shall Part the two,
To *Care* who Joynd them *Man* be due.                         80
    He said, & sprung with swift career
To trace a Circle for the year,
Where since the seasons ever wheel,
And tread on one anothers heel.
    Tis well, says Jove, & for Consent                         85
Thundring he shook the firmament.
Our Umpire *Time* shall have his way,                          [f.50a]
With *Care* I lett the *Creature* stay.
But thou for whom he seems to breath
Shall half defeat thy grant beneath:                           90
For *Time* whose forces shoud be shown,

When *Natures* harvest fully grown
Bows with the Mellowd ears of grain,
And longs to Prostrate on y<sup>e</sup> plain,
Will *Natures* bended *Sickle* bear                    95
But till he gets y<sup>e</sup> *Scythes* of *Care*.
Then Toil shall rise from fond desire,
And Idleness & buisness tire,
Bright Glory strain for Shades of Joy,
Soft Pleasure but to Pains decoy,                      100
Ambition Vex, or Av'rice blind,
And doubt & knowledge rack y<sup>e</sup> Mind,
Mad Errour act, Opinion speak,
Low want afflict, & Sickness break,
Wild Anger burn, dejection chill,                      105
And Joy distract, & Sorrow kill.
Thus armd by *Care* & taught to mow,
*Time* Draws the long promiscuous blow,
And wasted *Man*, whose quick decay
Comes hurrying on before the day,                      110
Will onely find by this decree,
The *Soul* flys sooner back to me.

# Epigram

Kate counts her years on ev'ry finger ten             [f.50b]
And counts them over & begins again
For a whole cent'ry passd she lovd to ly
For which the creature well deservd to dy
She railes & scolds in one eternall strain            5
For which the Creature ought to dy again
Pin on her back a paper where tis said
Since Kate still lives the Devil must be dead

# Martial                                              [f.50b]

For Nothing Lucy never plays y<sup>e</sup> whore
Thats true—for Lucy ever pays before

# An Eclogue                    [f.51a]


Now early shepheards ore y^e meadow pass,
And print long foot-steps in the glittering grass;
The Cows unfeeding near the cottage stand,
By turns obedient to the Milkers hand,
Or loytring stretch beneath an Oaken shade,                    5
Or lett the suckling Calf defraud the maid.
    When Harry softly trod the shaven lawn,
Harry a youth from Citty care with drawn,
Unlike the lowly swains Arcadia bore,
Their Pipes but sounded in the days of yore:                    10
Now Gales regardless range the Vaults above,
And No fond swain believes they sigh for love,
No more the Waters sympathising weep;
Our Lads unskilld in musick tend the sheep;
For Tom and Will our Yellow Ceres waves,                    15
And Kate instead of Chloris binds y^e sheaves.
Sicilian Muse thy higher strains explore,
Thy higher strains may suit with nature more.
    Long was the pleasing Walk he wanderd through;
A Coverd arbour closd y^e distant View:                    20
Cross-sloping railes a lattice front supplyd,
And twind the flowring woodbine crept aside.
There rests the Youth, and while the featherd throng
Raise their wild Musick, thus contrives a song.
    Here wafted o're by mild Etesian air                    [f.51b]
Thou Country Goddess Beautious Health repair;
Here lett my breast thro' quiv'ring trees inhale,
Thy rosy blessings with the Morning gale.
The Months that wake y^e fragrant year renew,
The Sun is golden and the skys are blue,                    30
Fair silver sprinklings fill y^e walk with light,
The boughs are verdant and the blossoms white;
Yet what are these, or those, or all I see,
Ah Joyless all! if not enjoyd with thee.
    Come Country Goddess come, nor thou suffice,                    35
But bring thy Mountain Sister Exercise.
Calld by thy lively voice she turns her pace,
Her winding horn proclaims a finishd chace,
She bounds the rocks, she skims y^e level plain,
Dogs hawks and horses croud her early train,                    40
Her hardy face repells the tanning wind,

And lines and meshes loosely float behind.
These all as means of toil the feeble see,
But these are helps of pleasure all w<sup>th</sup> thee.
   O come the Goddess of my rural Song,       45
And bring thy daughter calm content along,
Dame of the ruddy cheek & laughing eye,
From whose bright presence clouds of trouble fly;
For her I mow my walks, I platt my bowrs,      [f.52a]
Clip my low hedges & support my flowrs.      50
To wellcome her this summer seat I drest;
And here Ile court her when she comes to rest.
She'le lead from exercise to learned Ease,
And Change again, & teach y<sup>e</sup> change to please.
   Joy to my soul! I feel the Goddess nigh,     55
The face of Nature cheers as well as I.
Ore the flat Green refreshing Breezes run
To make young Dazys blow beneath the sun;
While limpid waters to the bottom seen
Lave the soft margin of the lovely Green,      60
Brisk chirping birds from all the compass rove
To tempt y<sup>e</sup> warbling Ecchoes of y<sup>e</sup> grove,
High sunny summits, deeply-shaded dales,
Thick mossy banks, and flowry winding vales,
With Various prospect gratify the sight,      65
And scatter fixd attention with delight.
Till the raisd soul by gay confusion wrought
Within a sphear of pleasure rolls on thought.
     Here beautious Health for all y<sup>e</sup> year remain,
     When y<sup>e</sup> next comes I'le charm thee thus again.   70
   But rustling boughs y<sup>t</sup> round my temples play,   [f.52b]
Drive the deep doze of Vision swift away.
Lett sloth ly softning till the noon in down,
Or lolling fan her in the sultry town,
Unnerve with rest & turn her own disease,     75
Or foster others in luxurious ease.
I mount the Courser, call y<sup>e</sup> deep'ning hounds,
The fox unkennelld flys to covert grounds.
I lead where stags through cumbrous thickets tread,
And shake the saplings with their branching head.   80
I make the falcons wing their airy way,
And soar to seize, or stooping, strike y<sup>e</sup> prey.
To snare y<sup>e</sup> fish I fix y<sup>e</sup> luring bait.
To Wound y<sup>e</sup> fowl I load y<sup>e</sup> gun with fate.

Tis thus through changing shows of toil I range,                                    85
And strength & pleasure rise in ev'ry change.
    Here beautious Health for all y^e year remain,
     When the next comes Ile charm thee thus again.
   Now friends my life with usefull talk refine,
And Tullys Tusculum revives in mine.                                                90
Now to grave books I bid y^e mind retreat,
And such as make me rather good than great.
Or o're the works of easy fancy rove,
Where pipes and innocence amuse y^e grove:
The Native Bard that on Sicilian plains                                             95
Best sung the lowly manners of the Swains;
Great Maro's Muse, that in the finest light                                    [f.53a]
Paints Country prospects and the charms of sight;
Strong Spencers Calender, whose Moons appear
To trace their Changes in the rural year;                                          100
Sweet Pope whose lays along with Nature run
Through all the seasons which divide y^e sun;
The tender Philips lines, who lately tryd
To plant Arcadia by the Severn side;
And Gentle Gays that happily explore                                              105
Those British Shepheards Spencer sought before.
The Soft Amusements bring content Along,
And Fancy, void of sorrow, runs to song.
    Here Beautious Health for all y^e year remain,
     When the next comes Ile charm thee thus again.                110
   So sung the Youth. But now y^e cool w^thdrew;
The sun had dryd the shaking drops of dew,
Then ragd with flames insufferably bright,
& shot the lattice with a checq'ring light;
The Zephirs fall, tho' not to hear his lay,                                        115
And in his shade the Flyes offensive play.

---

# The Heroins or Cupid Punishd Transl: from Ausonius.
[f.53b]

  In airy fields y^e fields of bliss below
Where woods of Myrtle sett by Maro grow
Where grass beneath & shade diffusd above
Refresh the feavour of distracted Love

There at a solemn tide y^e Beautys slain                                    5
By tender passion act their fates again
   Through gloomy light that Just betrays y^e grove
In orgys all disconsolately rove
They range the reeds & ore y^e poppys Sweep
That nodding bend beneath their load of Sleep                               10
By lakes subsiding with an easy face
By rivers stealing with a silent pace
Where kings & swains of ancient Authors sung
Now changd to flowrets ore y^e margin hung
The self-admirer white Narcissus so                                        15
Fades at y^e brink his picture fades below
In Bells of Azure Hyacynth arose
In crimson painted young Adonis glows
The Fragrant Crocus shines with golden flame
And leaves inscribe with Ajax haughty name                                 20
   A sad remembrance brings their lives to view
And with their passion makes their tears renew
Unwinds y^e years & lays y^e former scene
Where after death they live for deaths again
   Deluded Semele bewailes her fate                           [f.54a]
Lost by the glorys of her Lovers state
She runs & seems to burn the flames arise
And fan with Idle furys as she flys
The lovely Cænis whose transforming shape
Securd her honour from a second rape                                       30
Now moans y^e first with ruffled garb appears
Feeles her whole sex return & baths with tears
The Jealous Procris wipes a seeming wound
Whose trickling Crimson dyes y^e bushy ground
Knows the sad shaft & calls before she goe                                 35
To kiss y^e favrite hand that gave y^e blow
Ore well-dissembled waves y^e Sestian fair
Holds forth a taper from a towr of air
A noiseless wind assaults y^e wav'ring light
The Damsel tumbling mingles with y^e night                                 40
Where Curling shades for rough Leucate rose
With love distracted tunefull Sappho goes
Sings to mock cliffs a melancholy lay
And with a Lovers leap affrights y^e Sea
The sad Eryphile retreats to moan                                          45
What wrought her husbands death & causd her own

Surveys y<sup>e</sup> glitt'ring Vail y<sup>e</sup> bribe of fate
& tears y<sup>e</sup> shadow but she tears too late
Here three that brand y<sup>e</sup> royal house of Crete                [f.54b]
In thin design & airy picture fleet.                                    50
To court a bull the mad Pasiphae flys
The snowy Phantome feeds before her eyes
Left Ariadne raves the thread she bore
Trailes on unwinding as she walks y<sup>e</sup> shore
And desp'rate Phædra seeks y<sup>e</sup> lonely groves               55
To read her guilty letter while she roves
Red shame confounds y<sup>e</sup> first y<sup>e</sup> second wears
A starry crown the third a halter bears.
Here Laodamia mourns her nuptial night
Of Love defrauded by the thirst of fight                                60
Yet for another as delusive crys
And dauntless sees her Heroes ghost arise
There Thisbe Canace & Dido stand
All armd with swords a fair but angry band
This sword a Lover ownd A Father gave                                   65
The next a stranger chancd y<sup>e</sup> last to leave
And there evn she the Goddess of y<sup>e</sup> grove
Joynd with the Phantome fairs affects to rove
As once for Latmos she forsook y<sup>e</sup> plain
To steal the Kisses of a slumbring swain                                70
Around her head a starry fillet twines
And at y<sup>e</sup> front a silver Crescent shines
These & a thousand & a thousand more                                    [f.55a]
With sacred rage recall y<sup>e</sup> pangs they bore
Strike y<sup>e</sup> deep dart afresh & ask relief                      75
Or sooth the wound with softning words of grief.
   At Such a tide Unheedfull Love invades
The dark recesses of the Madding shades
Through long descent he fans y<sup>e</sup> foggs around
His purple feathers as he flyes resound                                 80
The Phrantick Beautys thickning all to gaze
Perceive the common troubler of their ease
Tho Dulling Mists & dubious day destroy
The fine appearance of y<sup>e</sup> fluttering Boy
Tho all y<sup>e</sup> Pomp that glitters at his Side                    85
The golden belt y<sup>e</sup> clasp & quiver hide
& tho the torch appear a gleam of white
That faintly spots & moves in haizy night

Yet still they know y<sup>e</sup> Boy y<sup>e</sup> gen'rall foe
& threatning lift their airy hands below                    90
As mindless of their rage he slowly sailes
On pinnions cumberd in y<sup>e</sup> misty vales.
Ah fool to light, the nymphs no more obey,
Nor was this region ever his to sway
Cast in the deepend ring they close y<sup>e</sup> plain          95
& seize the God reluctant all in vain
     From hence they lead him where a myrtle stood      [f.55b]
The saddest Myrtle in y<sup>e</sup> darkling wood
Devote to vex y<sup>e</sup> Gods. To this before
Hells awfull Empress soft Adonis bore                     100
When the Young Hunter scornd her graver air
And onely Venus warmd his shadow there
     Fixd to y<sup>e</sup> trunk y<sup>e</sup> tender Boy they bind
They cord his feet beneath his hands behind
He mourns but Vainly mourns his angry fate               105
For Beauty still relentless acts in hate
Tho no offence be don No Judge be nigh
Love must be guilty by y<sup>e</sup> common cry
For all are pleasd by partial passion led
To shift their follys on anothers head                   110
     Now Sharp reproaches ring their shrill alarms
And all the Heroins brandish all their arms
And evry Heroin makes it her decree
That Cupid suffer Just the same as she
To fix the desp'rate halter one essaid                   115
One Seekes to wound him with an empty blade
Some headlong hang the nodding rocks of air
They fall in fancy & he feels despair
Some toss their hollow seas around his head              [f.56a]
The seas that want a wave afford a dread                 120
Or shake y<sup>e</sup> torch y<sup>e</sup> sparkling fury flys
And flames that never burnd afflict his eyes
The Mournfull Myrrha bursts her rinded womb
& drowns his Visage in y<sup>e</sup> moist perfume
While others Seeming mild advise to wound                125
With hum'rous pains by sly derision found
That prickling bodkins teach y<sup>e</sup> blood to flow
From whence the roses first began to glow
Or when their flames to singe y<sup>e</sup> boy prepare
That all shoud chuse by wanton fancy where               130
     The lovely Venus with a bleeding breast

She too Securely through y<sup>e</sup> Circle presst
Forgot y<sup>e</sup> Mother urgd his hasty fate
& spurrd the female rage beyond debate
Ore all her scenes of frailty swift she runs                    135
Absolves her self & makes y<sup>e</sup> crime her sons
That claspd in chains with Mars she chanc'd to ly
A noted fable of the laughing sky
That from her loves intemp'rate heat began
Sicanian Eryx born a savage man                                140
The loose Priapus & y<sup>e</sup> monster wight          [f.56b]
In whom the sexes shamefully unite
    Nor words suffice y<sup>e</sup> Goddess of y<sup>e</sup> fair
She snaps the rosy wreath y<sup>t</sup> binds her hair
Then on the God who feard a fiercer woe                        145
Her hands upittying dealt the frequent blow
    From all his tender skin a purple dew
The dreadfull Scourges of y<sup>e</sup> Chaplet drew
From whence the rose by Cupid tingd before
Now doubly tinging flames with lustre more                     150
    Here ends their wrath y<sup>e</sup> Parent seems severe
The strokes unfit for little love to bear
To Save their foe the melting Beautys fly
& Cruel Mother spare thy Child they cry
To loves account they placd their deaths of late              155
& now transferr the sad account to fate
The Mother pleasd beheld y<sup>e</sup> storm aswage
Thankd y<sup>e</sup> calmd mourners & dismissd her rage
    Thus Fancy once in dusky shade expresst
With empty terrours workd y<sup>e</sup> time of rest            160
Where wretched Love endurd a world of woe
For all a winters length of night below
Then soard as sleep dissolvd unchaind away
& through y<sup>e</sup> port of Iv'ry reachd y<sup>e</sup> day.

----

# [Untitled poem]                                    [f.57a / f.1a]


Ye Wives who scold & fishes sell,
    Or sing & sell your fruit,
I want a wondrous thing to tell,
    Then (if you can) be mute.

From some of You one Homer came,                    5
   Who wrote a ballad first,
For He knew neither Parents name
   Nor livd where he was nurst

His verse in length exceeds us all
   So when a crowd he drew,                  10
Like you he got him to a stall,
   & spoke as long as you.

Some tatterd *Mermaid* gave him birth
   Who crys her oyster wares
Or Else some ragged *nymph of earth*               15
   Who sings her Mellow pears

If 'twas the *nymph of fruit* was prest,          [f.1b]
   *Apollo* was y^e Lover:
With tunefull cry he filld her breast,
   & got a singing Rover.                     20

A Man, tho blind, yet usd to ply                  [f.57b]
   Where 'ere he heard of Chear;
His dog it seems preserved an eye,
   Its Master livd by ear.

Or if Apollo chancd to Love                         25
   The *Mermaid* near y^e sea,
Whose shriller voice he taught to move
   With *buy my oysters pray.*

Her shriller voice when raised to Ire
   Woud thunder on y^e crew,                  30
So from y^e Mother & y^e Sire
   Old *Homers Iliad* grew.

& then (as big with child she stood)              [f.2a]
   The place she sold her fishes
Might in his fancy form a floud                     35
   To rage in all th' Odysses.

# Poems from the "Lyrics" Notebook

## [Fragmentary ending of a poem] [f.1a]

To the kind powr who taught me how to sing
Thus with the first of all w<sup>ch</sup> he bestowd
Did ancient piety approach the God.
   Defended long by prejudice & pride
Ive fancyd love a cant its god defyd         5
but bravely you assert y<sup>r</sup> monarchs reign
wound with a look & w<sup>th</sup> a word inchain
I feel th' enchanting pain w<sup>th</sup> pleasure bow ⎞
& surely fair Aminta none but you           ⎬
Can slav'ry give yet make it lovely too    ⎠    10

## [Untitled poem] [f.1a]

Now kind now coy w<sup>th</sup> how much change
   You feed my fierce desire
As if to more extravagance
   Youd manage up the fire
In vain if this your meaning be        5
   In vain you use these wayes
Tis æqually as hard for me
   To love you more as less
To other nymphs bequeath y<sup>r</sup> arts
   Whose eyes more faintly shine      10
Or practise them at least on hearts
   Which love you not like mine.

# [Untitled poem] [f.1b]

Phillis I long y<sup>r</sup> powr have ownd
  & you still gently swayd
Now nature has y<sup>r</sup> charms dethrond
  & time your chain decayd
Both are w<sup>th</sup> such perversness curst                5
  they still would bliss destroy
this change approves tho' for y<sup>e</sup> worst
  that makes the best things cloy
try then the forces of disdain
  Since kindness wins not me                10
for know you must to rule again
  another woman be.

———

# The hint f<sup>m</sup> french. [f.1b].

How nicely fair Phillis you manage y<sup>r</sup> slave
  You neither reproach nor approve him
Just keep him in play w<sup>th</sup> y<sup>e</sup> hopes w<sup>ch</sup> you leave
  Not give him enough that you'le love him
Tis tyrrany ruling in love w<sup>th</sup> such art                5
  Own rather the cruellest meaning
If I cant have the pleasure to conquer y<sup>r</sup> heart
  I shall have some at least in complaining

———

# On——— Embroydring [f.2a]

How justly art when Cælia aids so well
Contends her m<sup>s</sup> nature to excell
The slender needles in that hand create
Such forms as hers but of a better date
The silk is placd the winding traces laid                5
& the gay scene with rising figures spread
here springing lillies opening roses dress ⎫
in such sweet colours & so fixd a grace ⎬
they outdoe all but those w<sup>th</sup>in her face ⎭

the well turnd leaves if by the natrall shown 10
You'd think they both were workd or both had grown
So strange yet beautious birds are here designd
as if she had increasd the Phœnix kind
Sure had she livd w$^n$ poets tho below
Where meritt pleaded cou'd a heavn bestow 15
the wondrows product of her needle here
had made her self a goddess it a starr.
   Oh may no moth so rare a piece approach
May nought corrupt it with unhallowd touch
May nothing—but alas I wast my prayr 20
My wishes rise to loose themselves in air.
This work w$^{ch}$ angells wou'd not blush to own [f.2b]
Must once the common road of ruin run
then quickly fairest on y$^r$ life reflect
Nor all your downy hours of youth neglect 25
think you behold this lovely piece decayd
think you are brighter yet must sooner fade
then quitt your folly be no more severe ⎫
Why woud you have no difference appear ⎬
In how the ugly live & how the fair ⎭ 30
& tell me Celie where the diffrence lyes ⎫
'twixt those who Cant & those who wont possess ⎬
When both alike are distanc't f$^m$ their bliss. ⎭

---

# [Early version of first stanza of "A Song"] [f.2b]

Thirsis a young & amorous swain
lovd two the glory's of the plain
the charms of each prepare a chain
   & both at once subdue
Celia's eyes appeard so fair 5
they dazzeld where they did insnare
Saphella's easy shape & air
   W$^{th}$ softer Magick drew
he languishd dy'd for either maid
doted on all they did or said 10

# [Fragmentary ending of a poem]          [f.3a]

Then do not Cloe do not more
Boast what success youve found
Tis pride to tell your conquests ore
   Tis cruelty to wound.
These are the ills which Beauty breeds          5
   its blisses woud you give
With pitty all your slaves besides
   & me with love relieve.

---

# Prop: 2, L: 11 E: Quicunque &c          [f.3a]

Vast was his soul some favorite above
Whose bolder pencil made a boy of love
A boy he thought him lovers less then boyes
Who barter all things for a crop of toyes
He wisely too his roving pow'r bestowd—          5
& in unconstant feathers drest the God
for now we love anon we hate y^e same
Fantastick passion varyes all extreams
Justly he drew him for his play things darts
The little wanton sports with bleeding hearts          10
Justly he drew them to my cost Ive found
Unseen they fly & still secure to wound
his arms & younger follys fill my heart
But he has lost or hid his better part
His wings no more their heav'nly burthen bear          [f.3b]
He sitts an everlasting trouble here
My bloud he fires torments my wretched breast
Drains all my bones & robs my soul of rest
Cease cruell master fly to fuller veines
Your slave is wasted with incessant pains          20
Imploy your force on something I alas
Am but the shadow of the man I was
Why shoud I dy who live but for your use
& to your part debauch the virgin muse
Who write of nought but arrows flames & eyes          25
& sing your brightest servants to the skyes.

---

# [Untitled poem] [f.3b]

I lookd & in a moment run
   The poison thro' my veins
Nor Celia think your self too young
   to give me amorous pains
When heaven did the Sun create        5
   He shone as bright as now
& w^th the fires which guild them yet
   The infant starrs did glow.

---

# [Untitled poem] [f.4a]

O Tell if any fate you see
   Can more unhappy prove
Than where the nymph will cruell be
   & still the swain must love
Twere Joy to sigh & serve a fair      5
   Coud sighs & service gain
But if they not availing are
   they grow the lovers pain
Damon as thus he spoke his grief
   Thought all around him pind      10
But Celia bringing no relief
   He Car'd not what was kind

---

# [Untitled poem] [f.4a]

Young Philomela's powrfull dart
   Two gentle shepheard's hitt
With Beauty touchd Amintors heart
   & Celadons with witt
The Rivall swains on either side      5
   Their am'rous pangs expressd
Till young Amintor she denyd
   & Celadon she blessd

The youth who mett a mutuall fire                              [f.4b]
 In pleasure lost his pain                                     10
The others hopeless flames expire
 Beneath a cold disdain
Ye Priests of love ye Poets tell
 What Cupids forces are
If when the suit goes ill or well                              15
 No more we serve a fair.

---

# [Untitled Poem]                                       [f.4b]

Since bearing of a Gentle mind
 Woud make you perfect be
Dear Celia to your self be kind
 By being so to me
Hast to be happy while you can                                5
 Time flys and pleasures flow
Nor ere will have the Chance again
 To be so long as now
Give me a kiss now give me more
 And now another bliss                                     10
For Love has such a world in store
 We need not dy on this
Twas thus Amintor Celia wood                                 [f.5a]
 the Fair expecting lay
He took the hint his point pursud                            15
 And blessd the lucky day.

---

# [Early version of "Song"]                             [f.5a]

When my Nancy Appears
 In her graces and airs
Inviting as pleasure and soft as a sigh
I think her divine and am checkd by my fears
 So strangely she dazzles the eye                          5

But if she impart
  The kind thoughts of her heart
And her love rise in blushes from every vein
If she heave up her breast as it longd to be prest
  Then I know she's a woman again          10

Ah my Nancy said I
  Shoud you slight me I dy
Yet you suffer by being too kind to your swain
Now I think you an Angel, but if you comply
  Then I know you're a woman again        15

Theres a passion and pride          [f.5b]
  In our sex she replyd
And thus might I gratify both I woud do
Still an Angel appear to each lover beside
  And still be a woman to you.        20

---

# [Untitled poem]     [f.5b]

Hark the thundring Drums inviting
  All our forward youth to arms
Hark the trumpets sounds exciting
  Manly Soules with fierce alarms
Peace affords an Idle pleasure        5
  Glory shines an active flame
Life has but too short a Measure
  Strive to make it long by fame.
See the brave by boldly daring
  Raises trophys of the slain        10
See the brave by nothing fearing
  Comes in triumph back again
The Men admire the Women love him
  Fortune favours all he does
The Powrs that bless the great approve him    15
  Praise & Lawrell crown his brows.

---

# [Untitled poem]

As Celia with her Sparrow playd
　　She took a glass unseen
　　　　Her mouth she filld
　　　　& while he billd
She spirts y<sup>e</sup> liquor in                                    5

Usd to such sweet such rosy lips
　　He feard no treach'ry there
　　　　But love & such
　　　　Were too too much
For one poor bird to bear                                   10

Against y<sup>e</sup> Pretty fluttring fool
　　The Mighty foes combine
　　　　So down he Sunk
　　　　Bewitchd or drunk
By Beauty or w<sup>th</sup> wine                                   15

But ere he left y<sup>e</sup> Chirping cup                      [f.6b]
　　& dropp'd the little head,
　　　　The folks who guess
　　　　What Birds express
have told me thus he said,                                  20

How use the various scenes of joy
　　at various times to reign?
　　　　Men kiss'd in one
　　　　They drunk anon
Then after kiss'd again.                                    25

But Celia shews short life to grasp
　　A double store of blisses,
　　　　While by her Means
　　　　A Bird obtains
At once both Drink & kisses.                                30

———————

# Scriblerian Epigrams

---

Our Carys a Delicate Poet; for What?
For having writt? No: but for having writ not.

---

## On M^r Pope drawing D: Swifts Picture.

One authour has anothers head begun
Lett no man say it might be better don
For since they both are Witts Ime very glad
To find he has not drawn him twice as bad.

---

## After the French Manner

As Pope who gathers mony to translate
With Gay the Shepheard Writer mett of late.
Says Pope, your Ecclogues wont come out w^th speed
For Phillips to reprieve him Tonson feed.
Indeed the story may be true, says Gay,                    5
For Your Subscriptions give him powr to pay.

---

## A Impromptu like Martial.

Gays gon out early, how comes it to pass?
Not that he has buisness, but thinks that he has

---

## On a certain Poets Judgement between M<sup>r</sup> Pope & M<sup>r</sup> Philips don in an Italian air

Upon a time, and in a place,
  With Pan Apollo playd,
Grave Midas sat to Judge y<sup>e</sup> case,
  And Pan y<sup>e</sup> Victour made.
The Rustick to his Fauns withdrew;                    5
  Whilst on y<sup>e</sup> silver wing
Sweet Phœbus for Parnassus flew
  To hear his Homer sing.
Yet ere he went to Midas said,
  Ile fitt you for your Jears,                        10
So took two leaves from off his head,
  And stuck them in his ears.
Tis hence he thinks the bays his own,
  And hence it comes to pass
That as we think his ears are grown                   15
  We sooner find the Ass.

---

## To Mistress ———.

Hadst thou but livd before y<sup>e</sup> Gods were dead
That Heathens ownd y<sup>e</sup> world might thus have said.
"If any settled seat y<sup>e</sup> Muses use
"Thou art that seat or art thy self a Muse.

---

## On Platina    Prosperus Spiriteus

The Man whose Judgement Joynd with force of Witt
The lives of Popes & lives of Heroes writt
Who sung true Pleasure showd y<sup>e</sup> Golden mean
And taught Wild Youth to shun y<sup>e</sup> Lovers pain
Who wrote all this—Who more than this designd        5
All fine impressions of Celestial mind
That Man that Platina so lately fled

From earth to silent Darkness is not dead
Evn Death is here restraind y^e stroke he gives
has killd the man y^e Writer ever lives.                              10

---

## Jac: Faber Stapul: by J: Scaliger.

[space has been left in the manuscript for two lines]
a Nations praise thine ample glory be
or let the Nation find its praise in thee.

---

## By Simon Vallambert. Erasmus

Here Great Erasmus resteth all of thine
That Death can touch or Monument confine
Thy Hope and Virtue soard y^e lofty sky
Round y^e wide world thy Fame & Knowledge fly
Those meet rewards above and these below.                             5
Thus seek Erasmus. What has Death to show?

---

Once Pope under Jevais resolvd to adventure
& from a Good Poet Pope turnd an ill painter
So from a Good Painter Charles Jervais we hope
May turn an ill Poet by living with Pope
Then Each may perform the true parts of a friend            5
While each will have something to blame or commend

---

## out of Greek

The things that Mortals love are mortal too
& swiftly transient fleet before the view
Or if with man a longer while they stay
Man swiftly transient fleets himself away.

# An Epitaph desird on one Wheeler

My name is Wheeler here I ly
Because I happend for to dy
life wheeld me in death wheeld me out
how strangely things are wheeld about.

---

# Miscellaneous Poems

## [Untitled poem]

In Biddy's Cheeks y<sup>e</sup> roses blow
   In Cattys nose they rise
From Biddys lips soft accents flow
   And streams from Catty's Eyes

The jet that Biddy's brows display            5
   To Catty's teeth repairs
And Biddy's Lillies bleachd to grey
   Appear in Catty's hairs

Yet all y<sup>e</sup> world sweet Biddy toast
   neglected Catty lyes            10
While she deserves y<sup>e</sup> Bumper most
   who most attracts our Eyes

---

## [Untitled poem]

Oft have I read that Innocence retreats
Where cooling streams salute y<sup>e</sup> summer Seats
Singing at ease she roves y<sup>e</sup> field of flowrs
Or safe with shepheards lys among the bowrs
But late alas I crossd a country fare         5
And found No Strephon nor Dorinda there
There Hodge & William Joynd to cully ned
While Ned was drinking Hodge & William dead

There Cicely Jeard by day the slips of Nell
& ere y^e night was ended Cicely fell                          10
Are these the Virtues which adorn the plain
Ye bards forsake your old Arcadian Vein
To sheep those tender Innocents resign
The place where swains & nymphs are said to shine
Swains twice as Wicked Nymphs but half as sage                 15
Tis sheep alone retrieve y^e golden age.

———————

# For Philip Ridgate Esq.

To friend with fingers quick & limber,
I send this piece of tunefull timber:
that, as 'tis said in Orpheus story,
He may teach trees to dance a Bory;
Or else in modern Phrase more knavish,                          5
He may the heart of broomstick ravish.
The man whose parts in Taverns shine,
Doates on the merry pipe of wine;
& he who late has got his pate full,
perceives the water pipe is gratefull;                          10
But these are pipes that still are mute,
there is some musick in a flute.
Which since I as a present send,
the presents worth to recommend,
Ile in soft words its praises warble,                           15
translated from Italian marble.
    "When ere we hear its strains & closes,
    "Enchanted reason sweetly dozes,
    "on laps of nymphs, & beds of roses;
    "the Soul that all its charms admires,                      20
    "for lodgings in the ear enquires;
    "Gay pictures do the Fancy store;
    "& passions felt but heard no more.
All that my author says is true,
When th' instrument is playd by you.                            25
& least you think I came by this ill,
Splut her was preed her from a whistle.
                    T P.

# [Untitled poem]

When Haizy clouds obscure the night
No more the starrs afford us light
When ruffling winds arise at sea
tho smooth as glass & clear as day
the mudd workes up the ocean frys                    5
& thickend waters stopp the eyes,
The brook which from the mountain flows
oft runs astray if rocks oppose
then woud you with the piercing sight
of reason see the truth aright                       10
still woud you tread in virtues way
remove the hindrance & you may
Banish Joy & banish love
Banish hope & banish fear
the mind has clouds we run astray                    15
& reason's captive when they sway

---

# Caius Rubrius Urbanus Romae in domo Lud: Matthæi.
# E Grutero.

The Father lying in Bed hugging in his left arm a pot of Mony & laying
severall pieces out of it before him. the son sitts at his feet in the habit of
a souldier taking with his right hand some pieces that drop. A three
footstool stands near him on which three other pots: this written.

Qui dum Vita fuit Semper vivebat avarus
   Hæredi parcens invidus ipse sibi
Hic accumbentem sisti genialiter arte
   Se Jussit docta post sua fata manu
Ut saltem recubans in Morte quiescere posset         5
   Securaque Jacens ille quiete frui
Filius a dextra residet qui castra secutus
   Occidit ante Patris funera mœsta sui
Sed quid defunctis prodest genialis imago
   Hoc potius ritu vivere debuerant.                10

The case something near it in English

The Man who livd with avaritious care
Who starvd the growing virtues of his heir
Who bound to slav'ry by the vice he chose                    [f.1b]
Coud envy to himself his own respose
Woud have his latest image here exprest                         5
Thus lolling on y<sup>e</sup> Genial bed of rest
That since with death his long vexations cease
His Stone might speak him with an air of peace
Beneath his feet the son a Souldier leans
Compelld by want to warr in forreign plains                    10
There fell the Youth by deaths unerring dart
& with fresh sorrows broke y<sup>e</sup> misers heart
Here both seem pleasd but what avails y<sup>e</sup> sight
No Picturd kindness gives y<sup>e</sup> dead delight
The Father Never thus supplyd the son                          15
But thus to bless them both he shoud have don

# Latin Verses on Set Themes

## Ex otio Negotium

Vestra cur Antoni dissolvit in otia virtus:
  Mollia cur patitur mens tua vincla thori
Erige dum possis contendere viribus æquis,
  Erige dum neutri palma petita favet.
Ecce instat Cæsar, sequitur victoria currum,                    5
  Urbes deficiunt, deficiuntque viri.
Dimidium terræ socordia perdidit, et Jam
  Vincere habes totum si diadema cupis.

## Gratia ab officio quod mora tardat abest

Dum Trojam tendunt, Helenæ vindicta, Pelasgi,
  Atque agitata frequens æquora puppis arat;
Heu cito Troja ruat, ruat heu cito, quæque precatur
  Fæmina, et assiduis Thuribus ara calet.
Nono anno volvente, nec adsunt Troica fata,                     5
  Græcia ad antiquos nec reditura domos;
Mitte viros sine honore, viros sine honore, precantur
  Mutatis precibus, Jupiter alma viros,
Displicet empta moris tot tantis gloria, vendis
  tempore nunc urbes? en sat et orbe damus.                    10

# Labor omnia vincit.

Phœbus adest, et adest magni certamen Olympi,
    Et fronti nectit præmia quisque suo.
Intenti expectant, sonat en tuba, finibus omnes
    Haud mora prosiliunt, pulvere Apollo latet,
Fetibus ingeminat tellus, atque ocior alis              5
    fulminis hic metam transit, et ille tenet;
Applaudunt victorem omnes, donantque corona,
    Lauras et ad superos evehit usque deos.
Tertius est currus latis affixus inhæret,
    Numina in auxilium, nec Juvat ipse, vocat,          10
Invocat Herculeum sed frustra auriga Juvamen
    Invocet usque pigras negligit ille preces.

----

# In vitium ducit culpæ fuga si caret arte

Corpora dum rigide Zenonis turba lacessat
    Affectuque gravi dum negat illa premi
Mollior irridet propriis Epicurus ab hortis
    tantus ait vester grex malesane furor?
Furte rosas socii Thain properare Jubete           5
    Optimus, hoc cætu qui mage distat, erit
sed non in stoam male caute Epicure triumphas
    Hic dolor hæ crapulæ sunt tolerand[a]

----

# — natura beatis
# omnibus esse dedit si quis cognoverit uti

Fare age Phœbe pater cur sic natura novercat
    Cur sua non æquâ pignora forte fovet
Pande q$^d$ hunc opibus titulis et honoribus ornat
    Pande quid hunc fatis damnat iniqua malis
Sic quondam infælix vexavit limina Templi          5
    Cum tali numen concutit antra sono
Vane vir ingrato naturam murmure damnas

Hæc sed diverso munere q<sup>m</sup>que beat
Q<sup>m</sup> fortuna levat possit fortuna nocere
  Quem bona non decorant nec sua tela nocent          10

---

# Mors sola fatetur Quantula &c

Postq<sup>m</sup> Narcissus correptus Imaginis umbra
  per fontis vitreas attenuavit aquas
Fertur ahuc malesanus adhuc non immemor oris
  In stigiâ faciem sollicitasse lacu
Ast ubi mutatos sensit sine numine vultus          5
  dicitur his primum pœnituisse necis
Hosne putem adspectus ad quos heu stulte peribam
  Hosne putem quorum surripit hora decus
Rebar in Elysiis talem remanere figuram
  posse arvis viguit tanta per ora Venus         10
Hoc nymphæ et speculum nympharum dixit, et amnis
  His negat hic cunctos tingit honore pari.

---

# In Cameram ubi anatomia perag:

Membra viri quondam finxisse promethea fertur
  Pectus et æthereis incaluisse focis
Nec Mora sævit ubique acies inimica dolorum
  Mille valens homines excruciare modis
Nos hic dissictos scrutamur corporis artus         5
  Sis pote cœlestem sit reperire facem
Protinus ut sese divina scientia pandit
  Vanescit macies et redit alma salus
sanguinis enarrat currus exsangue cadaver
  Organa quæ sensus cum periere refert.         10
Sic quæ sit nostra hæc natura quibusve Juventu[r]
  Vulnera quæ cepit hoc tot velut ora docent
Euge q<sup>d</sup> est mortale times q<sup>d</sup> fallet acumen
  Cum vel ad hanc vitam mors feret ipsa viam.

# Fragments

## [Three verse passages from a prose meditation]

On verdurd trees y<sup>e</sup> silver blossoms grow  ⎫
Whose leaves atop their perfect whiteness show ⎬
& faintly streak with stains of red below  ⎭
The western breeze steales ore y<sup>e</sup> shady grove
to sigh near roses as insnard by love.                                    5

*

The waves pushed on by waves in mountains ly  ⎫
Mixd with y<sup>e</sup> clouds y<sup>e</sup> Parent waters fly ⎬
& the cross'd winds roar hideous in y<sup>e</sup> sky  ⎭
The east & west the south & north contend
While the vexd sea beneath is neithers friend                            10
Above y<sup>e</sup> winds below the billows Jarr
& nature is become the seat of warr

*

Look how y<sup>e</sup> silent waters stealing by  ⎫
With such smooth motions as deceive our eye ⎬
Returns y<sup>e</sup> pleasing pictures of y<sup>e</sup> sky  ⎭                         15
There shines y<sup>e</sup> sun with imitated rayes  ⎫
her borrowd light y<sup>e</sup> paler moon displays ⎬
& y<sup>e</sup> cleare heavens wear an azure face  ⎭
So lett thy temper due composure find
By all the modest rules that bound y<sup>e</sup> mind                          20
That Whether fortune with a storm assails
Or Courts thy wishes with indulgent gales
No passion interpose a cloud between  ⎫
But on thy bosome undisturbd within ⎬
May natures God & natures form [be seen]  ⎭                              25

# [Untitled, unfinished poem]

The first who lovd me turnd w<sup>th</sup> tender eyes
Since y<sup>e</sup> rogue will why lett us sail she cryes
Her kind consent was sure for Love is kind
& Woman's Love when Love has won her mind
The second stopd then with a careless moan—     5
Tis well— tis dang'rous to be left alone
   The grant obtaind y<sup>e</sup> lovely creatures plact
I loosd— No reader— broke y<sup>e</sup> rope for hast
Bending I plyd the oar to me twas rare
A new mean labour— but y<sup>e</sup> dear was there     10
Yet far from Shore I never meant to rove
Fond to divert but not to risque my Love.
No means were here to shun y<sup>e</sup> Lovers view
& I woud gaze & she must bear it too
But as I gazd (the maid sat Just before)     15
how faint I drew y<sup>e</sup> Long forgetfull oar
How my tird balls with fixd attention strain
Still feel y<sup>e</sup> pleasure & forget y<sup>e</sup> pain
In my soft words I made my soul appear
& tund my voice to melt them in her ear     20
She sits & heares yet hears with no regard
I thought the rocks we passd not half as hard
The second maid the more unhappy she
With eager glances bent her eyes on me
Whilst I regardless from her rival dame     25
Still took y<sup>e</sup> fewel which increasd my flame
Yet not to kill her as a lovers cares
Are oft dissembled I grew brisk in airs
Then both grew brisk & as they saild along
first softly warbling raisd a syren song     30
Through seas & air the trembling Musick flew
& charmd y<sup>e</sup> powers that wear y<sup>e</sup> watry blew
Drawn by the notes around them Dolphins play
& wave soft circles in the glassy Sea

# [Untitled fragment]

When ore my temples balmy vapours rise
Whose soft suffusion dims the sinking eyes
Gay dreams in troops fantastically light
On silent plumes wave down through sable night
Nights sable curtains draw before my eye                    5
& gently clears a visionary Sky
the running darkness draws its dusky shade
from off the beautys of a flowry mead
More & still more forsakes the lengthening plain
Mounts gray & ends it in a sylvan scene.                   10
    Poizd & aloft I sail in glittring air
& Joy to view my newborn earth so fair

———————

# [Untitled fragment]

When Pop'ry s arbitrary yoak
    Britannia feard of late
To liberty Religion spoke
    To save yᵉ sinking state
Joy of the World the Goddess said                          5
    Can no great soul be found
To move for this
    Ore
Joy of both worlds the nymph replyd

———————

# Commentary

The following abbreviated citations are used:

Aitken      Thomas Parnell. *Poetical Works*. Edited by George A. Aitken. London: George Bell and Sons, 1894.

Case      Arthur E. Case. *Bibliography of English Poetical Miscellanies, 1521–1750*. Oxford: Oxford University Press, 1935.

Foxon      D. F. Foxon. *English Verse, 1701–1750*. 2 vols. Cambridge: Cambridge University Press, 1975.

Goldsmith      Oliver Goldsmith. *Collected Works*. Edited by Arthur Friedman. 5 vols. Oxford: Clarendon Press, 1966.

*J.S.*      Jonathan Swift. *Journal to Stella*. Edited by Harold Williams. 2 vols. Oxford: Clarendon Press, 1948.

*Pope Corr.*      Alexander Pope. *Correspondence*. Edited by George Sherburn. 5 vols. Oxford: Clarendon Press, 1956.

Rothschild      *The Rothschild Library*. 2 vols. Cambridge: Privately Printed, 1954.

*Spectator*      *The Spectator*. Edited by Donald F. Bond. 5 vols. Oxford: Clarendon Press, 1965.

*Swift Corr.*      Jonathan Swift. *Correspondence*. Edited by Harold Williams. 5 vols. Oxford: Clarendon Press, 1963–65.

Swift, *Tale*      Jonathan Swift. *A Tale of a Tub etc*. Edited by A. C. Guthkelch and D. Nichol Smith. 2d ed. Oxford: Clarendon Press, 1958.

TE      Alexander Pope. *Poems*. Twickenham Edition. Edited by John Butt et al. 12 vols. London: Methuen, 1939–69.

Woodman      Thomas M. Woodman. *Thomas Parnell*. Boston: Twayne, 1985.

Latin quotations have been slightly normalized as follows: *u* and *v* are distinguished, but *i* and *j* are both treated as *i*; accents are ignored; and contractions (such as "&" for "et" and "q;" for "que") are expanded.

# An Essay on the Different Stiles of Poetry (1713)

TP's poem is in the tradition of Horace's *Ars Poetica*, a tradition that had most recently been embodied in Pope's *An Essay on Criticism* (1711). Although TP's poem was published after Pope's (and has inevitably been overshadowed by it), it may have been conceived before Pope's appeared. An early, less ambitious version appears in the "Satires" Notebook (ff. 35b–39b), under the title "To ——— on the Various Styles of Poetry." This consists of only 180 lines, including an opening passage of 42 lines rejected before publication, so that only 138 lines of "To ———" correspond to the 520 lines of the *Essay* as published. In this edition, the early version is printed separately as part of the "Satires" Notebook.

Another Congleton manuscript contains a text of the *Essay* substantially as published. This manuscript, which we have called the "Essay" Notebook, consists of ten leaves folded and sewn to make a gathering of thirty-eight pages, folded size 159 × 94 mm. Presumably the notebook was once enclosed in a protective cover or wrapping, but if so it has now been lost. The text of the poem is written on the rectos only, with about twenty-six lines to the page. There are some corrections, and some readings are underlined (TP's usual way of indicating his intention to rewrite). For most of the underlined readings, alternatives are written on the facing verso. The versos also contain several longer passages written out in revised versions, and a number of short notes.

At the time he transcribed the poem into this notebook, TP evidently still intended to use the original opening; but a note against what became line 1 of the published poem reads "Here yᵉ beginning." It may have been in this very manuscript that Swift and Bolingbroke read the poem before publication. Several references in the *Journal to Stella* allow us to follow the immediate prepublication history. On 22 December 1712 Swift wrote, "I gave Ld Bolinbroke a Poem of Parnels, I made Parnel insert some Complimts in it to His Ldship; He is extreamly pleasd with it" (*J.S.* 586). These compliments to Bolingbroke do not appear in the poem as originally written in the "Essay" Notebook. The compliments (lines 4 and 435–51) are written on the versos, suggesting that Swift saw the poem in this manuscript before making TP insert the compliments. Other evidence suggests that Bolingbroke, too, may have done so. At six points in the notebook there are short notes on the versos: "strengthen a little" (line 102), "Change" (line 134), "move that he" (line 140), "very difficult" (line 149), "Clear these lines up" (lines 172–76), and "Array active" (line 290). Taken together, these notes do not read like an author's notes to himself, but rather his record of another's objections. They seem to be in TP's hand and are perhaps his record of Bolingbroke's comments. On 31 December Swift wrote to Stella that he and TP had dined with Bolingbroke, and that he had made Bolingbroke show TP "all the Places he disliked" (*J.S.* 591). On 19 February 1713, Swift again noted that Bolingbroke had shown TP "3 or 4 more Places to alter a little" (623). Apart from the six comments already noted, there are a number of marginal crosses (not all of which are against passages that have actually been revised), and some of these, too, may indicate lines against which Bolingbroke had objected. In other manuscripts, however, TP uses the marginal cross to indicate dissatisfaction with a line, so these may be only notes to himself.

The "Essay" Notebook was probably not sent to the printer. The alterations and corrections are not marked clearly enough for that, and there are no printers' marks. Most likely, TP wrote out a fair copy, making some of the revisions that are found in the printed text but not in the manuscript even as corrected. On 19 February Swift wrote to Stella that TP's poem would "be printed in a few days" (*J.S.* 623). On 20 March he wrote that it would "be published on Monday" (642), and on 27 March that "Parnels Poem is mightily esteemed, but Poetry sells ill" (646). It is advertised ("This Day is Published") in the *London Gazette* for 21–24 March, and George Berkeley slightly misquotes lines 453–56 in *Guardian*, No. 35, 21 April. See *The Guardian*, ed. John Calhoun Stephens (Lexington: University Press of Kentucky, 1982), 145, 637.

The *Essay* was published by Swift's friend Benjamin Tooke as an octavo pamphlet (Foxon P70; Bibliography A1). A presentation copy inscribed by TP to "Edw: Smyth Esq" is now at Trinity College, Cambridge (Rothschild 1512), and another, "For Benj: Everard Esq", is at the University of Illinois at Urbana-Champaign. Some copies were issued on fine paper (Foxon P71). The text of the poem occupies thirty-six pages, and the preface (for which we have no manuscript; it may therefore be a late addition) four.

With two small exceptions (in lines 139 and 201) the poem is here printed as it appeared in the 1713 edition. Variations between the printed edition and the "Essay" Notebook are recorded in the textual notes, except that for the rejected opening passage the readings of the "Essay" Notebook are given in the textual notes to the early version, which in this edition is printed in its place in the "Satires" Notebook. In the "Essay" Notebook, TP usually makes smaller corrections on the page of text itself, longer ones on the facing verso; but small corrections are occasionally made on the verso. In a few instances (e.g., line 218) the printed edition reverts to the earlier manuscript reading.

The *Essay* was reprinted in Dublin in 1715, with John Philips's poem *Cyder* (Foxon P241.5). Although the text of TP's poem occupies signatures E–G, indicating that it was planned as part of the composite volume, TP's poem is sometimes found apart from Philips's. This may mean that it was also issued separately at the time of publication. It is a close reprint of the London edition. The odd double hyphen in line 139 of the London printing was evidently misinterpreted as a dash and printed in the Dublin edition as a triple hyphen; and there are a few other small changes to spelling, capitalization, and punctuation. There is no evidence that TP corrected the text in any way, and it has no authority.

Pope, however, excluded the *Essay* from his edition of TP's *Poems on Several Occasions* (1722). Swift was surprised at this omission, attributing it (probably wrongly) to the malign influence of TP's "Booby Brother who is endeavoring to be a Judge" (Letter to Daniel Jackson, 28(?) March 1722; *Swift Corr.* 2 : 424).

The *Essay* was next reprinted (without the preface) in *Miscellaneous Poems, Original and Translated* (1724), edited by Matthew Concanen (Case 332); TP's poem is on pp. 277–307. The poem was apparently first printed in a collected edition of TP's poems in the Dublin, 1735 edition (although it may have appeared in the 1727 edition, which we have been unable to trace); it was subsequently regularly reprinted in the Dublin (but not in the London or Scottish) editions.

The *Essay* has recently been reprinted (with Roscommon's *Essay on Translated Verse* and Swift's *On Poetry*) in *Different Styles of Poetry*, edited by Robert Mahony (Dublin: Cadenus Press, 1978).

Our copy-text is the London 1713 edition.

## Textual Notes

Readings enclosed within angle brackets are canceled in the MS. A note in the typical form:

77    arm their]    ⟨arms its its⟩    MS

means that "arm their", the reading of the printed edition, is also the corrected reading of the "Essay" Notebook, where, however, an earlier reading ("arm its its") has been canceled.

94    Which] 13, MSb; That MSa

means that "That" is the uncanceled reading of the MS, as originally written on the recto; "Which" is 1713's reading, and is also found (the same word; not necessarily spelled or capitalized in the same way) in the MS, as an alternative reading, written on the verso.

| | |
|---|---|
| 3–4 | These lines originally read, "Hence ye Prophane, I touch no common lay, / While to my powr I woud my friend repay." On the facing verso, TP wrote first, "prophane I raise yᵉ sounding string / & deathless [?] B—— shall hear me sing". He then deleted "deathless" (if that was the word) and "shall", replacing them with "descends to", thus arriving at the wording of 13. |
| 5 | Fable] 13; fables MS |
| 13–14 | These lines are not in the MS. |
| 19–22 | This passage is found on the verso in the MS, worded as in 13 (with "yet" in line 22 written over "still"). It replaces the following couplet on the recto, around which a half-box has been drawn to indicate its omission: "By that poor Region with disdain he goes / Where words inverted Anagrams compose." |
| 24 | Whose] ⟨&⟩ MS |
| 25 | There is no asterisk in the MS; the note was originally to have been attached to line 26, opposite which TP has written, "A Note to explain Hatchets &c". |
| 31 | And by Confinement] In the MS TP originally wrote, "Confine the flames"; there is a marginal cross against the line, and 13's reading is found on the verso. |
| 33–38 | In the MS this passage is an insertion on the verso. |
| 39 | This line originally began "Where"; when he inserted lines 33–38, TP changed it to begin "&". |
| 44 | In the MS this line originally read, "Shall voice with voices fond reflection talk"; there is a marginal cross against it, and the line as it appears in 13 is written on the verso. |
| 45 | This line is marked with a marginal cross in the MS, but no alternative reading is given and the line appears unchanged in 13. |
| 47 | Resound] ⟨Shall range⟩ MS |
| 49 | The MS has a marginal cross against this line. |
| | lasting Praise] 13, MSb; character MSa |
| 58 | his] ⟨the⟩ MS |
| 60 | The MS has a line count ("100") under this line. |
| 61 | a cold *Region*] cold⟨er⟩[?] Region MS |
| 75–76 | In the MS TP wrote first, "Here fair Exploits Historick Order |

trace, / Confind to measures destitute of Grace", then
changed the second line to end, "measures void of evry
Grace". TP may have deleted the final *s* in "measures". 13's
version is not found in the MS.

77          arm their] ⟨arms its its⟩ MS
78          paint] ⟨paints⟩ MS
92          The MS has a marginal cross against this line.
            cold] 13, MSb; cool MSa
93          *Writer*] 13; Writers MS
94          The MS has a marginal cross against this line.
            Which] 13, MSb; That MSa
            never] 13; have not MS
95          *Applause* or *Fame*] 13, MSb; a fame or praise MSa
            his] 13; their MS
102–6       In the MS this passage originally read: "Tis very open, very
            green, & low, / No Noble flights, no strength of sence is there,
            / Its turns are common, Childish is their air." There is a note
            in TP's hand against line 102, "strengthen a little"; and the
            passage is rewritten on the verso as it appears in 13, except
            that the MS has "springing green" for "unimprov'd" in line
            102.
119         The MS has a marginal cross against this line.
            the teiz'd *Hearer,* vexed at last] 13, MSb; at the last the Reader
            vexd MSa
120         constant] 13; frequent MS
122         hastes] 13, MSb; loves MSa (where the word is underlined but
            not canceled)
133–36      In the MS this passage originally read: "Ah sacred Verse from
            such a realm retire, / Tis credit lost no better to inspire." TP
            has underlined "credit lost", and a note in his hand against
            line 134 reads "Change". The passage is expanded on the
            verso as follows: "Ah sacred Muse from such a realm retire /
            Nor Idly play with flashes of thy fire / On Vain attempts which
            Judgment will condemn / & thou prove slighted while it
            censures them". TP further revised the passage for 13.
139         loud-resounding] MS; loud--resounding 13
140         In the MS the line originally read: "While he with stronger
            tones of Musick sings"; "he" is underlined, and there is a note
            on the verso "move that he". TP subsequently rewrote the
            line on the verso, worded as in 13.
144         hanging] 13; threatning MS
149–50      This couplet originally read as follows: "Are here elected by
            the Publick voice, / & have their natures as their cause of

choice." There is a marginal cross against the second line, with the comment opposite, "very difficult". On the verso TP rewrote the couplet as it appears in 13, except that the MS has "or" for "and" in line 149.

| | |
|---|---|
| 151 | All] 13; The MS |
| | attempt] ⟨appear⟩ MS |
| 153 | a mean Conceit] 13; an humble flight MS |
| 164 | The MS has a line count ("200") against this line. |
| 171–76 | There is a wavy line in the margin against this passage, with the comment opposite, "Clear these Lines up". |
| 172 | the] 13; their MS |
| 173 | So will] In the MS TP first wrote, "So may"; subsequently he underlined this and on the verso wrote a note, "Then will th [for "they"] or so will". He selected the second alternative for 13. |
| 174 | *Sally*] 13; venture MS |
| 175 | find] 13; in the MS TP first wrote "know", then underlined it and wrote on the facing verso, "Learn or find", selecting the second reading for 13. |
| 181 | Seat] ⟨state⟩ MS |
| 185 | And] 13; Then MS |
| 192 | fair Ideas in full Glory] ⟨all around with fair Ideas⟩ MS |
| 193 | exalted] 13; unbounded MS |
| 198 | circling] 13; circled MS |
| | *Poet's*] 13; tunefull MS |
| 201 | Breeze] 13 has "Breze", which is a possible spelling, but we have emended it to the more usual form since the MS has "breeze" in this line, as does 13 in line 355. |
| 204 | Shore] 13; shoars MS |
| 215 | see] In the MS TP wrote "feel" before erasing the *l* and converting the *f* into an extralong *s*. |
| 216 | *Realm*] ⟨place⟩ 13 |
| 218 | And *Judgment* likes] This is the original reading of the MS, where it is revised to "Judgement approves". This reading remains uncanceled in the MS, but TP evidently reverted to his original wording for 13. |
| 219 | its] 13; it MS |
| 220 | This is the last line on f. 9a of the MS; on f. 10a TP began by copying again lines 193–94 (the first lines on f. 9a in the "Essay" Notebook) before canceling them. |
| 229 | gently-breathing] 13; scarcely-breathing MS |
| 233–36 | This passage is expanded from a single couplet in the MS: "The Shades whom Fame has thus enthrond above, / For ages |

conquer, or for ages love."

238    Her] 13; Its MS

255    Fine] ⟨Great⟩ MS

259–60    This couplet is written as an insertion on the verso in the MS, its wording the same as 13 except "its" for "her" in line 260.

261    with sprightly] 13; & sprightly MS

262    her] 13; it MS

263    She] 13; It MS

266    The MS has a line count ("300") against this line.

283    that rose] 13; compose MS

284–86    These lines are 13's expansion of the following single line in the MS: "While thus the sober Voice their morall shows".

287    *its Enemies*] 13; the lives of foes MS

288    *it self*] 13; its own MS

290    TP first wrote "In moving pomp & powr of words array". A marginal cross is against the line, with the comment opposite, "Array active", under which TP wrote, "In pomp & powr of words themselves array" before canceling "pomp &" in favor of "all the", thus arriving at the wording of 13.

301–2    This couplet, identically worded, appears three times in the MS: after line 298 (where it is canceled); after line 300 (where it is again canceled); and after a couplet that in the MS follows line 300 but that (though uncanceled in the MS) does not appear in 13. The omitted couplet reads: "Fell hatred seems to fling her snakes aside / & to the thought on verse attempts to glide." There is a marginal cross against the second line, and on the verso TP has rewritten it with "yᵉ Soul" replacing "the thought". TP allowed lines 301–2 to stand after this third attempt, so that with the omission of the couplet they follow line 300.

308    arm'd] 13; arm MS

        they] 13; to MS

311    This line is marked with a marginal cross in the MS, but no alternative reading is given.

314    'tis] 13; its MS

324    her] 13; its MS

325    beauteous] 13; ranging MS

327–28    In the MS the couplet reads: "Of likeness fond, for likeness ownd a Grace, / They frame their features on anothers face,".

329–30    In the MS TP first wrote, "With close approach, on near expression flow, / & imitate yᵉ turn it loves to show:", then on the verso revised the couplet to read, "with close approaches in expression flow / & take that turn their Patterns love to show". He later canceled "close" in favor of "near", and changed "their Patterns love" to "the Pattern loves". The second line was further revised for 13.

333     doth] ⟨does⟩ MS
        her] 13; its MS
340     Which] 13; That MS
351     she] 13; it MS
352     she] 13; it MS
355     that hopes] 13; in Hope MS
357–58  In the MS the couplet reads: "There wondrous Fiction of a Person stands, / & offers Phantomes to the Poets hands,".
365     ⟨Tis hence that over urns the Rivers moan⟩ MS
366     The MS has a line count ("400") against this line.
378     And] ⟨Which⟩ MS
379     There] ⟨Here⟩ MS
384     Sense] ⟨thought⟩ MS
385     He freely] 13; With leave MS
395     And . . . and] ⟨Be . . . be⟩ MS
397     Fire] In the MS "fire" is written first over, and then above, a now-illegible deletion.
403     that most engage] 13, MSa; the most engaging MSb. (Here TP has rejected the second reading and reverted in 13 to his earlier wording.)
408     Subject] 13; subjects MS
416     on fire] ⟨afire⟩ MS
427     Appearance dazzles] 13; engagements dazzle MS
432     the] In the MS "the" is canceled and replaced with "his"; but for 13, TP evidently reverted to the original word, as he did in line 403 (where, however, the original reading was not canceled, as it was here).
435–51  This entire passage is an insertion in the MS, added on f. 17b.
440     Nation's] ⟨kingdomes⟩ MS
451–52  In the MS, before the insertion of the compliment to Bolingbroke, line 451 began a new paragraph and read, "To this Recess do you my Friend retreat," and line 452 began, "From thence". These readings stand uncanceled.
456     When] ⟨Where⟩ MS
457     Or say when] 13, MSb; Say when the MSa
463     Or further pierce] 13, MSb; Pierce further still MSa (where the line begins a new paragraph)
465–68  These lines are written as an insertion on the verso in the MS, with no indication that they were to begin a new paragraph.
476     The MS has a line count ("500") against this line.

round] 13; on MS

478     poor] This is the original reading of the MS, underlined but
not canceled: "fond" is written on the verso as an alternative,
which TP seems to have rejected.

480     Eyes] 13; eye MS

484     gave the World] 13, MSb; scornd a world MSa (where the
reading is underlined)

506     like *Hector* in the] The original reading of the MS is "an
Hector of a"; "an" and "of a" have been underlined and "like"
and "in the" written above the line. This is an exceptional
example of TP making a change on the recto without cancel-
ing the original reading.

520     The MS has a line count ("44"; i.e., 544) against this line.


### Explanatory Notes

Epigraph     Horace *Epistles* 2.1.217–18: "to stimulate poets to greater
efforts."

Preface      This imagery of the horse and charioteer or rider (lines 9–10,
and poem, lines 15–16) is in its broad sense traditional and
goes back to Plato, *Phaedrus*, 246a-ff. See Pope, *Essay on Crit-
icism,* lines 84–87, and commentary at TE 1:248–49, with
citations from Longinus, Quintilian, Jonson, and Waller. The
most famous recent satirical examples are in Swift, *Tale of a
Tub,* 9: "when a Man's Fancy gets *astride* on his Reason . . ."; "a
Person, whose Imaginations are hard-mouth'd, and exceed-
ingly disposed to run away with his *Reason,* which I have
observed from long Experience, to be a very light Rider . . ."
(Swift, *Tale,* 171, 180; cf. also section 11, p. 203). For pre-
Swiftian examples in English of wit or imagination as a horse
riding too fast or without proper control, see *Love's Labour's
Lost,* 2.1.119–21; Webster, *Duchess of Malfi,* 2.1.92–93; and cf.
Dryden, Preface to *Troilus and Cressida* (1679), in *Of Dramatic
Poesy and Other Critical Essays,* ed. George Watson (London:
Dent, 1962), 1.255; and Thomas Tryon, *A Discourse of the
Causes, Natures, and Cure of Phrensie, Madness, or Distraction*
(1689), ed. Michael V. DePorte (Los Angeles: William An-
drews Clark Memorial Library, 1973; Augustan Reprint So-
ciety, No. 160), 255–56.

1–3     An allusion to Horace *Odes* 3.1.1, "Odi profanum vulgus et
arceo." This Horatian declaration was not uncommon in
poems about poetry: see Rochester, "An Allusion to Horace,"

line 120, "I loathe the rabble" (*Complete Poems,* ed. David M. Veith [New Haven: Yale University Press, 1974], 126).

4      BOLINGBROKE] Henry St. John (1678–1751), created Viscount Bolingbroke in 1712; at this time he was secretary of state and a leading member of the government. The idea of dedicating to him seems to have been Swift's; for Bolingbroke's pre-publication reading and criticism of the poem see the head-note.

19      *Land* of Toil] The best commentary on this paragraph is Addison's series of *Spectator* papers on false wit, Nos. 58–63 (7–12 May 1711; ed. Bond, 1:244–74).

61–96      Mahony (p. 66) refers to some similarities with Pope's *Essay on Criticism,* lines 289–373.

70      Mahony (p. 67) cites *Essay on Criticism,* line 357, "drags its slow length along."

129–30      Cf. *Dunciad,* 1.63–65 ("A" version) on "motley Images" and the "Mob of Metaphors"; *Dunciad* 1.61ff addresses some of the themes of TP's poem.

156      TP's wording contains a more or less punning allusion to the famous *deus ex machina,* against whose use in drama Horace warned, though without using the full phrase (*Ars Poetica,* lines 191–92; the idea goes back to Plato *Cratylus* 425d and Aristotle *Poetics* 1454a-b), but TP's main object of censure is a poetic extravagance that resembles, or exploits, excesses of stage presentation (cf. the "Angels in Machines" in *Rape of the Lock,* 4.46; and 4.43ff, TE 2:187 and n.).

202      Cf. Pope, *Temple of Fame* ("Written in 1711," though not published until 1715): "And a low Murmur runs along the Field" (line 287).

335–48      Mahony (p. 75) compares this with lines 42–48 above, on echoes.

336      Cf. *Essay on Criticism,* line 359: "What's *roundly smooth,* or *languishingly slow.*"

435–46      TP here idealizes the harmony of the Tory government, ignoring the bitter quarrel between Oxford and Bolingbroke that was tearing the ministry apart.

477      the fickle *Trojan*] Aeneas, when in Book 4 of the *Aeneid* he abandons Dido (or "Elissa," as in *Aeneid* 4.610; "Eliza" in line 478 below, as in Dryden's translation of the *Aeneid* 1.932 and 4.968) to seek his new home in Italy. Mahony (p. 79) is surely mistaken in seeing an allusion to *Iliad* 3.

518      *Septimius . . . Acme*] The lovers in Catullus 45.

# Homer's Battle of the Frogs and Mice (1717)

*Occasion.* TP's decision to translate the *Batrachomyomachia* may well have been the result of his association with Pope, who was engaged on his own translation of the *Iliad.* The extensive "Zoilus" material that surrounded the *Battle* on its first publication was certainly inspired by TP's desire to take arms on Pope's behalf against the detraction and abuse that Pope and his translation encountered. The best general account of Pope's Homer and its context is the Twickenham editors' Introduction (TE 7). The pamphlets attacking Pope and his translation are described in J. V. Guerinot, *Pamphlet Attacks on Alexander Pope, 1711–1744* (London: Methuen, 1969).

*The poem.* The *Batrachomyomachia* or "Battle of the Frogs and Mice" is an anonymous Greek poem of uncertain date. Aristotle does not mention it in the *Poetics,* but he does attribute to Homer the *Margites,* a lost poem that (he says) bore the same relation to comedy as the serious epics did to tragedy, and he assigns to Homer as important a place in the development of the comic as in serious modes (4.12). There was thus some plausibility to the popular attribution of the "Battle" to Homer. Suidas attributes the poem (and also the *Margites*) to Pigres, brother of Artemisia (*Lexicon,* ed. Ada Adler [Leipzig: B.G. Teubner, 1935], 4 : 127). Evelyn White, the Loeb editor, suggests that Suidas is confusing Artemisia the wife of Mausolus with the earlier Artemisia who fought under Xerxes at Salamis, but that a date about 480 may be correct (p. xli). The poem is now regarded as a pastiche or parody of Homer. Its text is in a confused state. The most elaborate edition is by Arthur Ludwich (Königsberg, 1894), which presents a critical text and textual notes but no commentary. The most accessible text (with English translation) is in the Loeb edition of *Hesiod, the Homeric Hymns, and Homerica,* ed. H. G. Evelyn White (1914), pp. 542–63. Evelyn White did not think highly of the poem and gave it little attention in his introduction (p. xli). Although the poem was accepted as Homer's by Statius and Chapman, among others, TP himself seems to have regarded the attribution with

442

some scepticism. Although, naturally enough, in *Homer's Battle* itself he pretends to accept it as Homer's, his real views are more probably represented by the comments in his "Essay on Homer" prefixed to Pope's translation, where he says:

> The *Batrachomyomachia* or *Battle of the Frogs and Mice*, has been disputed, but it is however allow'd for his by many authors; amongst whom *Statius* has reckon'd it like the *Culex* of *Virgil*, a Trial of Force before his greater Performances. It is indeed a beautifull Piece of Raillery, in which a great Writer might delight to unbend himself; an Instance of that *agreeable Trifling*, which has been at some time or other indulg'd by the *finest Genius*'s, and the Offspring of that amusing and chearful Humour, which generally accompanies the Character of a rich Imagination, like a Vein of *Mercury* running mingled with a Mine of *Gold*. (TE 7:52)

TP is here perhaps more concerned with an implied defense of Pope's "agreeable Trifling" than with asserting the poem's Homeric authorship.

The poem was printed in many editions of Homer. One contemporary edition of the poem that TP certainly used was that in Joshua Barnes's edition of Homer (Cambridge, 1711), for part of his "Preface" is clearly based on a passage from Barnes (see explanatory note to line 129). TP's "Essay" shows that he was well versed in Homeric scholarship; many of his sources are indicated in our notes, others have eluded us.

*Previous translations.* The first translation of the poem into English was by "W.F." (William Fowldes?), *The Strange, Wonderful, and Bloody Battle between Frogs and Mice* (1603; STC 13626). Fowldes translated into 135 eight-line stanzas rhyming *ababccdd;* he did not translate the names, but usually glossed them with an epithet (as *"Eat-cheese Tyroglyphus"*) or by incorporating an explanatory phrase. George Chapman included a translation of the poem in *The Crowne of All Homers Workes* (1624?); this is reprinted in *Chapman's Homer,* ed. Allardyce Nicoll (London: Routledge, 1957), 2:513–24. Chapman uses rhymed pentameter couplets, but does not divide the poem into books, nor does he translate the names (although he does provide marginal glosses). The next translation was by Samuel Parker, *Homer in a Nutshell: or, His War between the Frogs and Mice, Paraphrastically Translated* (1700). Parker (1681–1730) was a nonjuror and theological writer, son of James II's bishop of Oxford. He divided the poem into three cantos: Canto I (176 lines) corresponds to TP's Book I, lines 1–131, and ends before Lycopinax sees Psycarpax; Canto II (179 lines) ends at the same point as TP's Book II; Canto III (146 lines) corresponds to TP's Book III. Parker translates the names (as Crambeef, Lapcustard, Groggle, Bisketto, and so on); his style is burlesque rather than mock-heroic, and he adds passages (printed in italic) of his own. The first translation to be published after TP's was *The Iliad in a Nutshell*

(1726), by Samuel Wesley the younger (1691–1739). This is in seventy-five ten-line stanzas *(ababcdcdee),* and is bulked out with feeble notes in a would-be humorous style. TP's translation is certainly the best of these. For a brief listing of the poem in English, see Richmond P. Bond, *English Burlesque Poetry 1700–1750* (Cambridge: Harvard University Press, 1932), 176–88. For a more detailed survey up to about 1800, see Friedrich Wild, *Die Batrachomyomachia in England* (Vienna, 1918; Wiener Beiträge zur Englischen Philologie, vol. 48); Wild discusses TP's version on pp. 49–61.

*Zoilus.* The most important classical sources that refer to Zoilus are: Vitruvius 7, preface; Aelian *Varia Historia* 11.10 (ed. Mervin R. Dilts [Leipzig: B. G. Teubner, 1974], 123); and Suidas *(Lexicon,* ed. Adler, 2:512; also 1:179, 2:45). In numerous incidental references he usually appears as the type of the carping critic (as often in Martial, and in Ovid *Remedia Amoris,* lines 365–66). The fullest collection of classical references to Zoilus appears in Udalricus Friedlaender, *De Zoilo Aliisque Homeri Obtrectatoribus* (Königsberg, 1895). TP follows the classical sources in making Zoilus a contemporary of Ptolemy Philadelphus; Zoilus the critic is now usually identified with Zoilus the rhetorician (fl. 365–336; J. E. Sandys, *A History of Classical Scholarship,* 3d ed. [Cambridge: Cambridge University Press, 1920], 1:108–10). Through the historical Zoilus, TP seems to have been attacking three contemporaries in particular: Sir Richard Blackmore, Richard Bentley, and John Dennis. In Section 3 of *A Tale of a Tub,* Bentley and Dennis are described as among the descendants of Zoilus (Swift, *Tale,* 94). Blackmore is coupled with Zoilus against Homer and Dryden in the *Essay on Criticism* (lines 462–65; TE 1:291). As early as 1700, in the preface to his *Paraphrase upon the Book of Job,* Blackmore had denied the morality of the pagan epics, and he had returned to the attack in his "Essay on the Nature and Constitution of Epic Poetry" *(Essays upon Several Subjects,* 1716). The purpose of this essay was to redefine epic against Homer and Virgil and in favor of his own practice. In a later essay in the same volume Blackmore attacked Swift as an "impious Buffoon" (p. 217); in a second volume (1717) he reviled Pope himself as a "godless Author" (p. 270; for further details of the Pope-Blackmore quarrel, see Norman Ault, *New Light on Pope* [London: Methuen, 1949], 248–58). Several particular attacks on Blackmore's ideas are noted in the commentary; but more generally, Blackmore earned his place as a Zoilus through the arrogant and condescending attitude to Homer revealed throughout his "Essay." Bentley had been notorious since the controversy over Phalaris as the type of the presumptuous modern critic. Bentley, too, thought Homer (and especially his moral seriousness, an essential component of Pope's interpretation) much overrated: "Take my word for it, poor Homer, in those circum-

stances and early times, had never such aspiring thoughts. He wrote a
sequel of songs and rhapsodies, to be sung by himself for small earnings
and good cheer, at festivals and other days of merriment; the *Ilias* he
made for the men, and the *Odysseis* for the other sex" (*Remarks upon a
Late Discourse of Free-Thinking*, 1713; *Works*, ed. Alexander Dyce [London,
1838], 3:304). TP presents a burlesque version of this view in his poem
"Ye Wives Who Scold" ("Satires" Notebook, ff. 57a-b). Dennis had been
an enemy of Pope's since his intemperate attack on the *Essay on Criticism;*
he is clearly aimed at in several parts of the "Remarks of Zoilus." There is
a brief survey of the poem in relation to Pope's Homer in Richard J.
Dircks, "Parnell's 'Batrachomoumachia' [*sic*] and the Homer Translation
Controversy," *Notes and Queries* 201 (1956): 339–42.

*Publication.* Although it was not published until 1717, the genesis of
the work can probably be traced to 1714, when TP and Pope were
working on Homer together at Binfield. Writing to TP on 18 March
1715, Pope asked him for the "Life of Zoilus" and the "Battle." Replying
on 27 June, TP referred to the "Zoilus" as "finished last spring" and
offered it to Pope; but in February 1716 Pope had to repeat his earlier
request in another letter. By early 1717, however, Pope had received the
work and was arranging publication. He told TP in a letter that:

> I have put it into the press, beginning with the poem *Batrachom:* for
> you seem by the first paragraph of the dedication to it, to design to
> prefix the name of some particular person. I beg therefore to know
> for whom you intend it, that the publication may not be delayed on
> this account, and this as soon as possible. Inform me also upon what
> terms I am to deal with the bookseller, and whether you design the
> copy-money for Gay, as you formerly talk'd, what number of books
> you would have yourself, &c. I scarce see any thing to be altered in the
> whole piece . . . (*Pope Corr.* 1:395–96).

TP carried out his generous intention with regard to Gay. Lintot's ac-
counts show a payment to Gay of £16 2s 6d for the "Battle of the Frogs"
on 4 May 1717 (John Nichols, *Literary Anecdotes of the Eighteenth Century*
[1812–15], 8:296). There are several other references to the poem in
the letters of Pope and Gay: see *Pope Corr.* 1:253, 284–85, 292, 299, 322–
23, 347, 371, 377, 395–96, 415; John Gay, *Letters*, ed. C. F. Burgess
(Oxford: Clarendon Press, 1966), 17, 29; and C. J. Rawson, *Review of
English Studies* 10 (1959): 377.

The work finally appeared as an octavo pamphlet on 16 May 1717.
There were two issues: one on ordinary paper and one on fine paper
(Foxon P73-74; see Bibliography, A4). For the fine-paper issue, engraved
headpieces were substituted for woodblocks as follows: (1) using the
same setting of type, leaf A3 was printed with an engraved headpiece
and initial *H;* (2) leaf B1 was canceled and reset with an engraved

headpiece and initial *T;* the resetting resulted in one minor variant (see textual note to "Life," line 4); B1b seems to have been reset as far as "of Mankind" (line 13); (3) leaf C6 was canceled and reprinted with an engraved headpiece and initial *T;* lines 1–28 were thus reset, but with no variants; (4) leaf E5 was canceled and reprinted with an engraved initial *I* and with the text reset. A presentation copy from Parnell to Swift is in the library of the Victoria & Albert Museum (Dyce 4914). It has an autograph presentation inscription on the half-title, and is signed on the title page "Es: Johnson," which suggests that Swift may in turn have given it to Stella. Pope's copy (also a gift from Parnell) is at Harvard: see Maynard Mack, *Collected in Himself* (Newark: University of Delaware Press, 1982), 434, and a copy inscribed "For Benj: Everard Esq" is at the University of Illinois at Urbana-Champaign.

Pope included the poem, but not the accompanying prose pieces, in his edition of TP's *Poems.* The 1722 text contains very few alterations, but this is hardly surprising since Pope evidently corrected the poem before its appearance in 1717. The "Zoilus" prose was restored to the 1737 edition of *Poems on Several Occasions,* apparently as an afterthought. The original title page does not mention it, but a second title page was printed with the additions, which are separately signed and paged. The text of the prose in 1737 is a careful and close reprinting of the text of 1717, though with a very few accidental omissions, some apparent corrections, and numerous changes to spelling and capitalization and rather fewer to punctuation. For later printings, reference should be made to the Bibliography.

*Manuscripts.* No manuscript of the poem is extant, nor of the "Remarks of Zoilus," but there are manuscripts of the "Preface" and "Life of Zoilus" among the Congleton papers. One of these, which we have called the "Homer" MS, is an autograph manuscript, with corrections, of the "Dedication" (which was never published, and which is here printed for the first time) and the "Preface" only; the other, which we have called the "Zoilus" MS, contains "Dedication," "Preface," and "Life," but is mainly nonautograph. (It is written in TP's hand from the end of line 10 on f. 17b; but some evident miscopyings, as well as the very tidy appearance of the MS, suggest that here TP was himself transcribing from a MS that is no longer extant.) In this transcript the "Dedication" and "Preface" were evidently copied from the "Homer" MS by an intelligent copyist— someone who was able to supply a word accidentally omitted as the result of revision and to decipher correctly much-revised passages. The evidence that the transcript copied from the particular MS we have is not only that its corrected text is followed, but that in two passages where the "Homer" MS is very heavily revised the transcriber has left spaces, and these have been filled in by TP himself. The only passage unique to the transcript is part of one of these longer passages in TP's hand. The most likely reason for TP to have taken over at this point in the transcript is that the insertion existed only in a much-corrected draft on a separate slip of paper, and that it was as easy for him to transcribe it himself directly into the transcript as to make a legible copy for his amanuensis. It should be noted that, although an intelligent copyist, TP's scribe paid little attention to conventions of presentation and regularly began a sentence, for example, with a lower-case letter. TP seems to have made a few corrections in the "Homer" MS itself after it had been transcribed and also in the transcript itself. In addition, there is a small inserted slip in the "Zoilus" MS, apparently an idea for an addition that was never actually incorporated into the text. But these slight anomalies do not seriously affect the relationship between the two manuscripts, of which more detailed descriptions follow.

The "Homer" MS consists of four sheets, folded and stitched to form a sixteen-page gathering (page size $158 \times 102$ mm). F. 1a is a title page, headed "Dedication or Preface.", below which is the epigraph from Seneca. Lower down the page "pervigilium Veneris" has been crossed out. F. 1b is blank; ff. 2a-b contain the dedication. The preface begins on f. 2b a little below the end of the dedication and ends on f. 7b; f. 8 is blank.

The "Zoilus" MS consists of sixteen sheets, folded and gathered into four-sheet signatures to make a sixty-four-page notebook (page size $190 \times 125$ mm.) The notebook is side-stitched in a marbled paper cover, of which only the front is now preserved; this has the inscription "Parnells Poems &c". F. 1 is blank; f. 2 has been removed. On f. 3a is what seems to be the beginning of a list: "Glauberi Tractatus Chimicus / Martial / Statius". This list is probably not in TP's hand, and has been canceled. Below it there is a title in TP's hand: "The Life of Zoilus with ⟨the⟩ Homers / Battle of the Frogs & Mice / To Which is added the ⟨Notae⟩ Notes / of Zoilus upon it". F. 3b is blank. The transcript of the dedication and preface occupy ff. 4a–10b; f. 11a has the title "The Life of Zoilus" and the epigraph from Martial; f. 11b is blank. "The Life of Zoilus" begins on f. 12a; from "made him appear" (line 10 on f. 17b) it is in TP's hand. There are some short passages in TP's hand before this point. The "Life" ends on f. 26a; f. 26b is blank. On f. 27a appears the single word "The" in TP's hand; perhaps it would have begun the poem's title, but the remainder of the MS is blank, except that at the foot of f. 32b (upside-down from the point of view of the main text) there is the inscription "Miscellaneous / Writings of/ D$^r$ Parnell".

*The text of this edition.* Pope evidently worked from a manuscript very similar to the extant "Homer" and "Zoilus" MSS, which both begin with a dedicatory "To" followed by a blank space, just as is implied in Pope's

letter to TP quoted above. In his reply TP probably told Pope that the
dedication was to be omitted; just possibly this was Pope's own decision.
Since we do not have the manuscript from which Pope worked, it is
impossible to say whether the differences between the 1717 text and our
manuscripts were TP's latest thoughts, or whether Pope was responsible
for them. A number of the small additions are references to sources and
authorities. In any case, it seems clear that Pope had TP's permission to
revise and polish the work, and we have followed the 1717 text here. In
the poem, we have in a few instances emended its punctuation to follow
the 1722 text, but 1722's verbal variants are most likely to be Pope's and
we have excluded them from the text. The prose is unchanged except for
the correction of occasional slips in the 1717 text. The textual notes
record all departures from the 1717 text, the variant readings of the
manuscripts where they affect the wording, and the changes made to the
poem in 1722.

## Textual Notes

### DEDICATION

The final text of the "Dedication" is as follows; the original readings
are recorded in the textual notes below:

To [a space has been left for the insertion of a name in large
letters]

Sir.
    I had no sooner placd your name at the Head of this work, but
I drew a *new* reason for not subscribing my own, from a belief that
I was not able to speak in the manner I ought of the affability          5
benevolence good sense and good learning which are justly as-
cribd to you, and which qualify a man with candour and ability, at
once to accept and defend the performances of others. Yet while I
fail of doing you Justice, I contrive that you shoud feed my vanity,
by making you appear along with me to the Publick: a                     10
Vanity, as I have orderd matters, something like that of a stranger
at court, who fixes on a person of the most oblidging carriage to
ask a question, that he may do himself honour by their being seen
to talk together, tho' he be neither known there before nor after.
But in an affair of this nature, where the world expects your            15
praises, your own modesty excuses them, & I dread least I shoud
injure my subject, I ease my self as I imagine by complying with
you rather than others, & turning the discourse to an account of
the following translation, which I begin at the Occasion that not
only made me first think of it but also directed my thoughts as I        20
proceeded.

| 11–12 | stranger] strangers "Homer" and "Zoilus" MSS |
| 12 | a person of the most oblidging carriage] ⟨the most affable person in appearance⟩ |
| 13 | that] ⟨&⟩ |
| 13–14 | their being seen to talk together] ⟨being seen to talk with him⟩ |
| 14 | there] The word is deleted, an illegible insertion in turn deleted, and "there" rewritten. |
| 15 | But in] "But" is an insertion; we have made the consequential change of "In" to "in". |
| | this] ⟨this nice⟩ |
| 16 | your own] TP first wrote "while your", then changed "while" to "&" before deleting "&" in turn and inserting "own". |
| | &] ⟨where⟩ |
| 17 | subject,] A canceled clause follows: "and woud not force him to slight in publick what he must not be thought to pride in"; "must" is written over a word that is probably "woud". |
| 19 | translation,] ⟨performances⟩ |
| | begin at the Occasion] This awkward phrase is underlined to indicate TP's dissatisfaction, but no revision has been made. |
| 19–20 | that not only] ⟨which⟩ ? |
| 20 | first] The word is canceled, then rewritten above. |
| | my thoughts] TP wrote and deleted "my [ ? ]"; the illegible portion seems to read "the", so it may be that he was writing "theme". |

PREFACE

| 2 | *attempted*] 17; attempted, and being concerned for its success "Homer" MS |
| 3 | *him*] ⟨him to be⟩ "Homer" MS |
| | *Presence*] In the "Homer" MS, "presence" is underlined, but no alternative reading is given. |
| 7 | *the Character*] 17; its Characters "Homer" MS |
| 8 | *him*] 17; him pleasantly "Homer" MS |
| 12 | *continued*] 17; continues "Homer" MS |
| 13 | *knew*] 17; know "Homer" MS |
| 14 | *Manhood*] 17; earth "Homer" MS |
| 26 | *The First*] 17; first "Homer" MS |
| 27–28 | *He might . . . with*] In the "Homer" MS TP first wrote, "As for the names of things or places which are retaind, he may preserve their Greek manner: as Creech says Bouprasium, or adhere to what the world is least acquainted with". He then deleted everything as far as "adhere to". He then added, "He |

may retain ⟨names⟩ some names"; "which" is formed from "what" with the last two letters altered.

28      *his old Translator*] This phrase is an insertion in the "Homer" MS.

        *uses*] 17; in the "Homer" MS, "say" (for "says") is canceled in favor of "keeps"

29      Baratrum *for* Hell] 17; not in "Homer" MS

30      Greek] 17; the Greek "Homer" MS

32      *very different*] ⟨which differd⟩ "Homer" MS (where "very different" is possibly not in TP's hand)
        *Reason, he thought,*] 17; Reason he thought "Homer" MS; reasons he thought "Zoilus" MS (In the "Homer" MS, "Reason" is inserted above the line between "which" and "he", perhaps in the same hand as "very different" at line 32 above.)

36      *even they*] 17; they "Homer" MS

41      *Freedom*] ⟨unfetterd freedome⟩ "Homer" MS

42      *sounds*] 17; sound "Homer" MS

45      *Want*] 17; the want "Homer" MS

50      *succeeds*] ⟨thrives⟩ "Homer" MS

51–52   *are to be . . . introduced*] In the "Homer" MS, the original reading is "ruin it". This has been underlined to indicate TP's dissatisfaction, and the following longer passage inserted: "are to be fairly derided least they ruin it by being frequently imitated". The transcriber of the "Zoilus" MS evidently had difficulty with the passage, and left part of a line blank, transcribing only "by being frequently imitated". TP did not insert the reading of the "Homer" MS, but instead canceled "by being frequently imitated" and inserted "when they are imitated by weak or unskillfull hands will end in a corruption of it". He further revised the passage for 17.

54      *often*] The word is an insertion in the "Homer" MS.
        *Ridicule*] ⟨derision⟩ "Homer" MS

55      *exceeds*] 17; outnumbers "Homer" MS

56      *Copiousness of Words*] 17; words "Homer" MS

58      *Monosyllables*] 17 reads *"Monysyllables"*; "Homer" MS has "monosyllables"

60      *Version*] ⟨longlegd Version⟩ "Homer" MS

67      *unintelligible Pomp*] 17; unintelligibleness "Homer" MS

70      *whether*] ⟨if⟩ "Homer" MS

71      *or ty'd up*] 17; in the "Homer" MS TP first wrote, "like Hobbs who allmost tyes himself up" and then changed this to "& allmost tyd up".

| | |
|---|---|
| 72 | *wherein*] 17; as "Homer" MS |
| 72–73 | *to express in one Language*] 17; any language can express "Homer" MS |
| 74 | *or*] ⟨and⟩ "Homer" MS |
| 76 | *Author*] ⟨Author also, by taking him upon you⟩ "Homer" MS |
| 78 | *we ought to*] ⟨continues he⟩ "Homer" MS (?; the "inues" of "continues" is uncertain) |
| 79 | *but*] ⟨but as⟩ "Homer" MS |
| 82 | *you began with*] ⟨which introduced this discourse⟩ "Homer" MS |
| 84–85 | *All I remember further was, that*] 17; replaces a longer passage in the "Homer" MS: "What followd was but ⟨pleasantry such as⟩ advice to him that he shoud gett his eyes put out, in Order to be like his Author while he translated him, & sing darkling as Milton has it.ˣ Onely this much I remember further in behalf of any Critick who may think it worth his while to challenge the Promise, that I". The cross after the reference to Milton marks where the loose slip should have been inserted. The slip reads: "+ & a little laughter at Hobbes his unlitteral translation which when the Author makes Telemachus sail in a Ship puts him aboard a tub for yᵉ rimes sake". |
| 84 | *further*] The word is omitted from the "Zoilus" MS. |
| 87 | *was*] The "Homer" MS has "is", canceled; the "Zoilus" MS "is", uncanceled. The corrected reading "was", found in 17, was presumably inadvertently omitted in the "Homer" MS. |
| 88 | *Bargain of them*] 17; bargain "Homer" MS |
| 89 | *translate*] ⟨thought of translating⟩ "Homer" MS ("resolvd to try what it was to" is an interlined addition) |
| 90 | *Spirit*] ⟨Spirit and Genius⟩ "Homer" MS |
| | *chose*] ⟨Chosen⟩ "Homer" MS |
| 93 | *Poems*] 17; Works "Homer" MS |
| 95 | *and Fame*] 17; the "Homer" MS has "&c", deleted but with no replacement, making the passage read rather oddly. In the "Zoilus" MS, the transcriber has copied the "&c", so its deletion in the "Homer" MS was probably a late (and unfinished) revision on TP's part. |
| 97 | *himself at last*] 17; himself "Homer" MS |
| 97–98 | *Reason . . . than*] ⟨reasoning may be onely⟩ "Homer" MS |
| 99 | *Conjecture that this Poem was*] 17; in the "Homer" MS TP first wrote "assertion of ⟨the⟩ this Poems being" before canceling it in favor of the wording of 17, except that he accidentally omitted "was". |
| 100 | *after the* Iliad] 17; last "Homer" MS |
| | *probable*] ⟨true⟩ "Homer" MS |

101   *that Poem*] 17; the *Iliad* "Homer" MS
    *or a*] 17; nor "Homer" MS
102   *there*] 17; in the "Homer" MS, "there" follows "not".
102–3  *Warrior or other*] 17; Warriour "Homer" MS
104   *Action*] In the "Homer" MS, "near" is written above as an insertion, but canceled.
105   *or ridiculous*] These words are deleted in the "Zoilus" MS.
108   *this always*] The "Zoilus" MS has an insertion (probably in TP's hand), "on the other hand", between these words.
    *the Subject*] In the "Zoilus" MS, "the" is changed to "its".
111   *nearer*] ⟨a Poem nearer⟩ "Homer" MS
    *or*] ⟨and⟩ "Homer" MS
112   *a Poem*] ⟨a Ludicrous Poem⟩ "Homer" MS
113   *own*] The word is an insertion in the "Homer" MS.
    *to its Honour*] ⟨for it⟩ "Homer" MS
114   *cries out in an Apostrophe to*] ⟨thus addresses⟩ "Homer" MS
117   *indeed*] 17; indeed for my own part "Homer" MS
118   *talk*] 17; ask "Homer" MS
    *learn*] ⟨think⟩ "Homer" MS
119   *observ'd*] 17; proposd "Homer" MS
120   *that a* ] 17; a "Homer" MS
121   *think of*] 17; imagine over "Homer" MS
122–23  *the Battle . . . before me*] In the "Homer" MS TP first wrote: "Jove smile at their Combatants, our struggles for Glory and empire appear a battle of frogs and mice to me". He changed "their" to "the" and "Glory" to "Honour", before canceling the whole passage and rewriting it as it appears in 17, except that the "Homer" MS has the phrase "in [ ? ]" after "glorious". The "in" has been left to stand, presumably in error, but the rest of the phrase is canceled and illegible. In the margin against this passage TP has written "Raise" (?), enclosed in a rough circle, apparently a note rather than an alternative reading. The transcriber of the "Zoilus" MS had difficulty deciphering this passage, and left a blank in which TP wrote out the passage as he meant it to stand (and as it appears in 17), without the phrase beginning "in".
124   No new paragraph in the "Homer" MS.
    *Imitations*] ⟨translations⟩ "Homer" MS
126   *find it.*] After this phrase the "Zoilus" MS has an insertion written in TP's hand: "Nay so fond have the Grecians been of preserving it that even after their language sufferd [illegible word of about five letters beginning "th"] it was translated into the Barbarous Greek by Demetrius Zenus." TP con-

tinued transcribing himself (beginning a new paragraph at "I have taken") as far as "framd as follows", following the wording of the "Homer" MS except that he added "of it" after "translation". For Demetrius Zenos, see the explanatory note to line 113.

126–28    *I have . . . Original*)] ⟨The translation I have divided into books⟩ "Homer" MS

132–33    *in Imitation . . .* Iliad] 17; not in either "Homer" or "Zoilus" MS

134    BOOK I.] 17; L.1. "Homer" MS

137    BOOK II.] 17; L.2. "Homer" MS

139    *Council*] 17; Councils "Homer" MS

140    BOOK III.] 17; L.3. "Homer" MS

143    *am averse from all*] ⟨hate the⟩ "Homer" MS
       *lessens*] ⟨takes off from⟩ "Homer" MS

144    *only*] "onely" is an insertion in the "Homer" MS
       *long*] ⟨even longer⟩ "Homer" MS

145    *before a Poem*] The phrase is an insertion in the "Homer" MS.
       *be*] ⟨perhaps be⟩ "Homer" MS

146    *abstruse*] 17; abundant "Homer" MS
       *an Epitome*] ⟨a sort of contraction⟩ "Homer" MS ("contraction" is underlined in the "Homer" MS, probably indicating TP's intention to rework the phrase rather than for emphasis)

147–48    *a previous Account of*] ⟨telling⟩ "Homer" MS

149    *Thoughts*] 17; thought "Homer" MS

149–50    *It might . . . from*] ⟨I must certainly have destroyd⟩ "Homer" MS

150    *Poem*] Poem ⟨& given it too burlesque an air⟩ "Homer" MS
       In the "Zoilus" MS, "Physignathus" was omitted by the transcriber and added in TP's hand.

152    Bluffcheek] 17; Pluff cheek "Homer" MS (a slip, or indecision between "Puff" and "Bluff"?—the transcriber of the "Zoilus" MS wrote "Pluff")

154    *I place*] 17; I both place "Homer" MS

156    *some*] 17; a "Homer" MS
       *sight*] sight "Homer" MS; *Light* 17 (an easy misreading of TP's hand)
       *Humour*] 17; both MSS read "humour", but in the "Zoilus" MS the word is changed (in TP's hand) to "propriety".

158–59    *was . . . Poet*] In the "Homer" MS TP first wrote "was that the Poet", then inserted "to see" before "that". He then deleted "to see that", inserting in its place "how I shoud follow".

159    *when he inserted*] ⟨inserting⟩ "Homer" MS (the change was consequent upon the revision in lines 158–59 above)

160       *Application*] A canceled passage follows in the "Homer" MS: "when I had no Iliad in English to practise the same beauty."

160–61     *To supply this in my Translation, I have*] The "Homer" MS originally read: "I therefore once or twice have taken some". TP canceled this, then wrote above what appears to be "For this", evidently intending to begin the new sentence with these words; he then deleted "For this" and wrote "To supply this" before the canceled "For this".

161       *Particularities*] 17; little appearing particularitys "Homer" MS

162       English] The word is an insertion in the "Homer" MS.
         *most resemble*] ⟨are nearest⟩ "Homer" MS

163       *some Image*] 17; a representation "Homer" MS
         *with*] 17; in "Homer" MS
         *an equivalent Beauty*] 17; this is also the original reading of the "Homer" MS, where it was changed to "equivalent beautys" before being changed back again.

164       *rather*] 17; more "Homer" MS

165       *to*] 17; with "Homer" MS

167       *go to*] ⟨go for the knowledge of this to⟩ "Homer" MS
         *Painter's*] 17; in the "Homer" MS TP first wrote "picture shop", then altered "picture" to "painters".
         *apply*] 17; transfer "Homer" MS

170       *sets*] 17; puts "Homer" MS

175–76     *believe . . . Characters*] 17; in the "Homer" MS TP wrote first, "apply to me in those Characters: which writers give of their own performances even while their friends object to them", then canceled this in favor of "believe writers their own Characters". This is the original reading of the "Zoilus" MS, where "in" has been inserted before "their", probably by TP.

176       *answer*] ⟨answer in our generall style⟩ "Homer" MS

177       *as follows*] 17; that "Homer" MS

178       No new paragraph in "Homer" MS

180       *When*] In the "Homer" MS TP first wrote "If", then changed it to "Where". In the "Zoilus" MS, the original reading is "if", changed (probably in TP's hand) to "where". This evidence suggests that TP continued to correct the "Homer" MS after the transcript had been made.

181       *when*] 17; where "Homer" MS
         *a Point of*] ⟨the⟩ "Homer" MS

181–85     *As for . . . Faculties*] 17; in the "Homer" MS TP first wrote, "What ever fault you can find it is rather the affect of fancy or Judgement than the trans", then canceled from "fancy" and wrote, "too unbounded fancy or too nice Judgement than the transgression of either faculty, &." He then canceled the whole passage, rewriting it as follows: "as for beautys there never can be one ⟨beauty⟩ found in me which was not really intended; & for any fault whose excuse may have slipd me, it ⟨rather⟩ proceeded from too unbounded fancy or too nice Judgement rather than from a transgression of either faculty on the side of defect." The passage was further revised in 17.

THE LIFE OF ZOILUS

| | |
|---|---|
| 1 | They] 17; Those "Zoilus" MS |
| 2–3 | Interpretations] 17; interpretation "Zoilus" MS |
| 4 | the Art] 17; this art "Zoilus" MS |
| | itself.] 17 (ordinary paper); it selfe "Zoilus" MS; —, 17 (fine paper) |
| 5–6 | to prepare us] 17; we come the better provided "Zoilus" MS |
| 11 | that] 17; which "Zoilus" MS |
| 23 | *Designs*] 17; dessign "Zoilus" MS |
| 27 | since] 17; ever since "Zoilus" MS |
| 30 | oppos'd] 17; sett "Zoilus" MS |
| 36–37 | and I think . . . is not] 17; nor that . . . is "Zoilus" MS |
| 38 | when] 17; "Zoilus" MS has canceled "since" replaced by "where" |
| 40 | and is] 17; or to be "Zoilus" MS |
| 41 | when] 17; where "Zoilus" MS |
| 50 | before him] 17; before "Zoilus" MS |
| 52 | Accusation or Invective] 17; in the "Zoilus" MS, the transcriber's "accusation" is canceled (possibly in TP's hand) in favor of "invective". |
| 57–58 | by *Ælian*] 17; not in "Zoilus" MS |
| 64 | or] 17; and "Zoilus" MS |
| 73 | Men] 17; them "Zoilus" MS |
| 74 | with the Creature] 17; what "Zoilus" MS |
| 79 | Sophists] 17; the Sophists "Zoilus" MS |
| 80 | Oratory] ⟨Poetry⟩ "Zoilus" MS (the revision is in TP's hand) (says *Dionisius Halicarnassensis*)] 17; not in "Zoilus" MS |
| 83 | upon the] 17; upon "Zoilus" MS |
| 88 | *Aristotle*] ⟨and Aristotle⟩ "Zoilus" MS |
| 89 | with him . . . Cause] 17; in the "Zoilus" MS, the transcriber first wrote "sufficient cause with him" before he (or possibly TP himself) canceled "with him" and inserted the phrase before "sufficient". |
| 98 | went] 17; goes "Zoilus" MS |

98–99     voluminous Work] 17; in the "Zoilus" MS, the transcriber first
          wrote "voluminous work" before he or TP canceled it in favor
          of "work of nine volumes".
99        *The* Ψόγος, *or*] 17; Ψογοσ or the "Zoilus" MS (where "the" is an
          insertion)
103       In the "Zoilus" MS this title is not set apart, but is run on as
          part of the text.
108       fond] ⟨found⟩ "Zoilus" MS
111       apply] 17; use "Zoilus" MS
116       *Il.* 5] 17; Iliad Ibid: "Zoilus" MS
117       the Poet] 17; he says the Poet "Zoilus" MS
118       have run] 17; ran "Zoilus" MS
125       *Od.* 10] 17; in the "Zoilus" MS, a space has been left for the
          insertion of the number of the book.
          who were] 17; whom Circe "Zoilus" MS
126–27    The first . . . *Didymus,*] 17; not in "Zoilus" MS
127       the last] 17; This last remark is "Zoilus" MS
128       No new paragraph in the "Zoilus" MS.
141       Thither] 17; thither then "Zoilus" MS
142       recited] 17; recited before him "Zoilus" MS
145       found] 17; finds "Zoilus" MS
148       dart] ⟨toss⟩ "Zoilus" MS
149       Kind] 17; sort "Zoilus" MS
151       did] 17; dos "Zoilus" MS
          forward] 17; along "Zoilus" MS
158       Ring,] 17; ring, which grew even beyond the strength of his
          voice "Zoilus" MS
160       It] ⟨and⟩ "Zoilus" MS
165       undertook] 17; went on "Zoilus" MS
167       impertinent] The word is an insertion in the "Zoilus" MS,
          probably in TP's hand.
169       mean or] 17; mean and "Zoilus" MS
171       to be a] 17; a "Zoilus" MS
          they that] 17; they who "Zoilus" MS
172       those] 17; the "Zoilus" MS
175       up to]17; to "Zoilus" MS
176       There was] 17; the phrase is not in the "Zoilus" MS
177       who being] 17; he being "Zoilus" MS
192       or] 17; or probably "Zoilus" MS
193       he set] 17; sett "Zoilus" MS
195       *Ægypt*] 17; Now Ægypt "Zoilus" MS
202       we hear] 17; we there hear "Zoilus" MS

| 204–05 | courteous] 17; courtly "Zoilus" MS |
|---|---|
| 206 | so much] 17; so "Zoilus" MS |
| 209 | Writing; And] 17; writing; Lycophron whose works have bin found worthy to be preserved through every age; and "Zoilus" MS |
| 212 | No new paragraph in the "Zoilus" MS. |
| 218–19 | of the] 17; concerning the "Zoilus" MS |
| 223 | foretold] 17; foretold the Condition "Zoilus" MS |
| 225 | which] 17; in a place which "Zoilus" MS |
| 232 | turning] 17; twining "Zoilus" MS |
| 245–46 | the same Name] 17; it "Zoilus" MS |
| 250 | dead Bays] 17; bay dead & with their points reversd "Zoilus" MS |
| 251 | they] "Zoilus" MS; he 17 |
| 256 | write] 17; write also "Zoilus" MS |
| 262 | how] 17; now how "Zoilus" MS |
| 264 | it] 17; that it "Zoilus" MS |
| 265 | that they] 17; this is the original reading of the "Zoilus" MS, where "that" has been deleted. |
| 267 | that] 17; as that "Zoilus" MS |
|  | lost] 17; lost to them "Zoilus" MS |
| 269 | My] 17; O my "Zoilus" MS |
| 278 | No new paragraph in the "Zoilus" MS. |
| 282 | born] 17; ⟨from⟩ "Zoilus" MS (presumably a slip) |
| 286–90 | The Day . . . himself] This passage is written in TP's hand in the "Zoilus" MS, presumably because the original was heavily corrected and the transcriber was unable to follow it. |
| 291 | was] 17; were "Zoilus" MS |
| 292–93 | which . . . *Vitruvius*] 17; not in "Zoilus" MS |
| 296 | a Person] 17; him "Zoilus" MS |
| 297 | made him] From this point on, the "Zoilus" MS is in TP's hand. |
| 301 | had been] 17; had "Zoilus" MS |
| 306 | to the] 17; to "Zoilus" MS |
| 307 | name] 17; mention "Zoilus" MS |
| 319 | (as *Vitruvius* words it)] 17; not in "Zoilus" MS |
| 322 | from the] 17; from "Zoilus" MS |
|  | hooted] 17; in the "Zoilus" MS, TP first wrote "Hooted" but then canceled it in favor of "drove". |
|  | away] 17; off "Zoilus" MS |
| 323 | at] 17; in "Zoilus" MS |
| 329 | but] 17; & "Zoilus" MS |

330        renew'd] 17; renews "Zoilus" MS
331        Petitions] 17; petitions upon the back of one another "Zoilus"
           MS
           Persecution] 17; persecutions "Zoilus" MS
332        these] 17; this "Zoilus" MS
333        has] 17; has all along "Zoilus" MS
334        than he] 17; than Homer "Zoilus" MS
335        but many] 17; but "Zoilus" MS
336        His] 17; As for his "Zoilus" MS
           thrown carelessly] 17; carelessly thrown "Zoilus" MS
           were] 17; they were "Zoilus" MS
337        Men] 17; the men "Zoilus" MS
339        than to] 17; than "Zoilus" MS
345        Expressions] ⟨insinuations⟩ "Zoilus" MS
350        the Ways] 17; ways "Zoilus" MS
355        he did what he cou'd] 17; what he coud do that he did
           "Zoilus" MS
356        envy'd] 17; suspected "Zoilus" MS
358–59     consisted . . . Sciences] 17; ran onely over the Surface of
           sciences "Zoilus" MS
361        have made] 17; make "Zoilus" MS
365        his constant] 17; his "Zoilus" MS
368        No new paragraph in the "Zoilus" MS.
370        even what] 17; what "Zoilus" MS
371        grew more and more] 17; became more "Zoilus" MS
372        Derision] 17; derisions "Zoilus" MS
374        Poverty] 17; and Poverty "Zoilus" MS
           had] 17; had had "Zoilus" MS (evidently a slip; the word is
           repeated at the end of one line and the beginning of the next)
378        'twas the whole Business of his Life] 17; he but livd "Zoilus"
           MS
379        subsisted] 17; was subsisted "Zoilus" MS
382        Children] ⟨little children⟩ "Zoilus" MS
385        being ston'd] 17; in the "Zoilus" MS, TP wrote and canceled
           "taken up for dead" before "stond", evidently a copying er-
           ror.
386–87     wherever he coud meet it] 17; out of bookes "Zoilus" MS
389        Place] In the "Zoilus" MS there is an illegible deletion before
           "place"; it may possibly be "Parish".
393        some] 17; and some "Zoilus" MS
395        his fixing an Eye] 17; the fixing of his eyes "Zoilus" MS
401        on this] 17; in this "Zoilus" MS
419        Wreaths] 17; wreaths on their heads "Zoilus" MS

Lawrel] 17; Lawrel in their hands "Zoilus" MS
424    born, as led] 17; led "Zoilus" MS
427    and was] 17; it was "Zoilus" MS
428    The Hands were manacled behind,] 17; not in "Zoilus" MS
       arm'd] 17; were armd "Zoilus" MS
431    *ZOILUS the HOMERO-MASTIX*] 17; Zoilus the Scourge of Homer
       "Zoilus" MS (TP has written the phrase in larger letters, but
       not all in capitals)
434–35  King and his Court were] 17; Court was "Zoilus" MS
436    upon] 17; up upon "Zoilus" MS
439    Statue] 17; Image "Zoilus" MS
446    believ'd] 17; believd here "Zoilus" MS
449    Unworthiness] 17; Worthlessness "Zoilus" MS
454    and which . . . Birth] 17; not in "Zoilus" MS
461    him]17; him with his stick "Zoilus" MS
464    leave] 17; forsake "Zoilus" MS
465    for it is certainly true] 17; & showd the world "Zoilus" MS
467    from] 17; from a "Zoilus" MS
469    Street] 17; streets "Zoilus" MS
470    concerning] 17; in the "Zoilus" MS, TP wrote and canceled,
       "which informed him" before "concerning", apparently a
       copying error.
476    to] 17; for "Zoilus" MS
479    about his Commentators] 17; his commentatours about
       "Zoilus" MS
480    that were cast of] 17; which were cast for "Zoilus" MS
482    Priests] 17; Priest "Zoilus" MS
486    to] 17; for "Zoilus" MS
488    a long]17; of a long "Zoilus" MS
489    bore] 17; it bore "Zoilus" MS
490–92  This made . . . ZOILUS;] 17; not in "Zoilus" MS
495–96  Sentence] ⟨adress⟩ "Zoilus" MS
497    the Stake] 17; a stake "Zoilus" MS
499–500 a Language] 17; a living language "Zoilus" MS
502    lighted] ⟨set on fire⟩ "Zoilus" MS (the phrase was first under-
       lined, presumably to indicate TP's dissatisfaction with the
       repetition of "set")
503    more than] 17; not in "Zoilus" MS
507    of whom] 17; concerning whom "Zoilus" MS
508    of the] ⟨of this⟩ "Zoilus" MS
508–09  the Honour] 17; in the "Zoilus" MS, TP wrote and canceled
       "birth of Homer so" after "the", apparently a copying error.
510    likewise] ⟨also⟩ "Zoilus" MS

511–12  we observe also] ⟨also we observe⟩ "Zoilus" MS
523  both hinder] 17; hinder "Zoilus" MS
525  at once to] 17; to "Zoilus" MS
526  hinder] 17; spoil "Zoilus" MS
526–27  from producing any Thing] 17; for productions of "Zoilus" MS
527  ZOILUS] 17; his steps "Zoilus" MS
533  hitherto felt] ⟨mett with⟩ "Zoilus" MS
  who has] 17; who "Zoilus" MS
534–35  as long as] 17; while ever "Zoilus" MS

NAMES OF THE FROGS AND MICE

Pternophagus] Pternophogus 17, 22; corrected as in the poem, 3.59
In 17, there are (for lack of space) no periods after "Water" or "Mud" in the entries "Hydrocharis" and "Borborocates."

HOMER'S BATTLE OF THE FROGS AND MICE: BOOK I

16  Flies] 17; Fled 22
17  Hangs] 17; Hung 22
18  dips] 17; dipt 22
32  *Hydromeduse'*] 17; *Hydromede*'s 22 (Pope, however, omitted to make the change in the list of "Names of the Frogs".)
57  Offspring] 22; Ofspring 17 (The last example of 17's spelling in the *OED* is dated 1666. TP has "Offspring" in the MS of "Hannah", line 33.)
89  leant] 17; bent 22
92  dissemble] 17; resembling 22
123  flings] Wakefield says that the first edition has " 'Fling'st' . . . very properly"; but all the copies examined read "flings", as does the 1722 edition.

BOOK II.

3  Monarch] 17; Sov'reign 22
15  *Country*'s] 22; *Country*'s 17 (Although we have, in general, not attempted to impose consistency of conventions on the texts, we have here accepted 22's reading in order to achieve consistency within a single line.)
59  and] 17; clad 22
66  Waters; ecchoing] 17; Waters; and the 22

| | |
|---|---|
| 73 | their] 22; theit 17 |
| 104 | When] 17; But 22 |
| 118 | And] 17; The 22 |
| 118–20 | These lines are within parentheses in 22. |
| 120 | gets] 17; gains 22 |
| 121 | gain] 17; win 22 |
| 124 | Fight,] 22; —. 17 |
| 135 | Who, wildly rushing,] 17; Some daring Mouse may 22 |

## Book III.

| | |
|---|---|
| 4 | Sign to loose] 17; Signal to 22 |
| 9 | flew,] 17, 22; but some ordinary paper copies (Bodley, Yale) appear to have a semi-colon (see also line 24 below). |
| 10 | slew.] 22; —, 17 |
| 12 | Fame;] 22; —. 17 |
| 13 | hung;] 22; —, 17 |
| 17 | New paragraph in 22 but not in 17 (as also at lines 29, 41, 51, 55, 69, 73, 83, 93, 99, 105, and 113). |
| 24 | Plain,] 17, 22; but some ordinary paper copies appear to have a semi-colon (see line 9 above). |
| 34 | Yet] 17; But 22 |
| 59 | The] 17; But 22 |
| 84 | Lifts] 17; Heav'd 22 |
| 85 | Warrior] 17; Hero 22 |
| 91 | to] 17; on 22 |
| 96 | runs] 17; run 22 (where the spacing suggests that an *s* may have broken or otherwise failed to print) |
| 100 | Plain;] 22; —.17 |
| 103 | of]17; from 22 |
| 107 | Then]17; But 22 |
| 128 | Threats all its Nations with] 17; To all its Nations threats 22 |
| 136 | *Mouse*] 17; *Mice* 22 |
| 153 | Nor] 17; Not 22 |
| 154 | And] 17; Or 22 |
| 182 | the Bones] 17; their Bones 22 |
| 191 | depend,] Some copies of 17 lack the comma. In the Bodleian ordinary-paper copy the comma has dropped slightly below the line; during the course of printing the edition it probably dropped out altogether. |

## Preface to Zoilus's Remarks

| | |
|---|---|
| 26 | *Carvilius*] *Carbilius* 17 (see explanatory note) |

The Remarks of Zoilus

263      *Reed*] The correct reading of the poem is "Reeds".
398      Phœbus] Phæbus 17
410      Pallas, Jove] *Pallas, Jove* 17

## Explanatory Notes

Preface

Epigraph      Seneca *De Beneficiis* 2.24 (the Loeb text has "et" for "etiam"): "See how unjust men are in appraising the gifts of the gods, even those who profess to be philosophers."

6      Cedrenus] Georgius Cedrenus, a Greek monk of the eleventh century, compiled a universal history (up to 1057). He describes a statue of Homer that was destroyed in a fire at the Baths of Severus at the time of Hypatius's revolt against Justinian (*Compendium Historiarum;* in *Patrologia Graeca,* ed. J.-P. Migne [Paris, 1844–1905], 121:706–7). TP may have found the reference in Chapman's preface to his translation of Homer, since his description echoes Chapman's: "thoughtfull and musing, his hands folded beneath his bosome, his beard untrimmed and hanging downe . . . his eyes fixt or turned up to his eyebrowes, like one blind" (*Chapman's Homer,* ed. Nicoll, 1.19–20). In his "Essay on Homer," TP speaks of conventional portraits of Homer, though "purely notional", as agreeing in "representing him with a short curl'd Beard, and distinct Marks of Age in his Forehead. That which is prefix'd to this Book . . . is taken from an ancient Marble Bust, in the Palace of *Farnese* at *Rome*" (TE 7:54). The Farnese bust is reproduced in TE 9, following 256. There is an interesting section on Homeric portraiture in Gisela M. A. Richter, *The Portraits of the Greeks* (London: Phaidon Press, 1965), 1:45–56 (see 46 for Cedrenus).

9      *the secret History of* HOMER] At the opening of his (lost) *Annals,* the Roman poet Ennius (239–169) told how Homer appeared to him in a dream and revealed that his soul had migrated into Ennius's body (*Remains of Old Latin,* Loeb edition, 1:5–7). This story (in which one of Homer's reincarnations is a Peacock) is referred to by Lucretius (1.124), Horace (*Epistles* 2.1.52), and Persius (6.9). None of these sources mention "*the Camel of* Bactria", however; if not TP's addition (as, of course,

is the compliment to Pope with which the "secret history" ends), this must come from a source we have not traced.

28    Ephaistus] Chapman sometimes uses "Ephaistus" for Homer's "Ηφαιστος" in his translation (e.g. *Iliad* 1.554 and 574); elsewhere, however, he uses the more usual Latinized form "Vulcan" (e.g., *Iliad* 18.329 and 340).

29    Baratrum] Chapman uses "Barathrum" in *Iliad* 7.11, but elsewhere he uses "Hell". "Barathrum" was not (in Chapman's time) so obscure a word as TP implies; the *OED* cites uses from Dekker and Massinger; the Greek word "βάραθρον" is not Homeric.

41    *Blank Verse*] The respective merits of rhyme and blank verse were an old subject of controversy. Dennis was a great champion of blank verse. In his *Remarks upon Mr. Pope's Translation of Homer* (1717), he apostrophizes: "O wicked, wicked Rhyme! what Errors, what Blunders art not thou the Occasion of, in lazy and ignorant Poetasters!" (*Critical Works*, ed. E. N. Hooker [Baltimore: Johns Hopkins Press, 1939–43], 2:129.)

54–58    The idea that French was a less copious language than English was a commonplace.

60    Chapman] Chapman published *Seven Books* in 1598, and the complete *Iliad* in 1611; the *Odyssey* followed in 1614. His translation of the "Battle of the Frogs and Mice" was published, with the Homeric "Hymns" and "Epigrams," as *The Crowne of All Homer's Workes* about 1624.
La Motte] Antoine Houdar de la Motte (1672–1731), French poet and dramatist, published a prose contraction of the *Iliad*, with a "Discours sur Homère," in 1714. Madame Dacier replied to La Motte's criticisms of Homer in *Des Causes de la Corruption du Goust* (Paris, 1714).

61–69    For the commonplace comparison between poetry and painting, see note on lines 173–81 below.

62–69    In the *Essay on Criticism*, Pope makes a similar comparison between fashion and diction: "In *Words*, as *Fashions*, the same Rule will hold, / Alike Fantastick, if *too New*, or *Old*" (lines 333–34).

70–78    In his preface to *Ovid's Epistles Translated* (1680), Dryden had distinguished between metaphrase, paraphrase, and imitation (*Works*, ed. E. N. Hooker and H. T. Swedenberg [Berkeley and Los Angeles: University of California Press, 1956–    ], 1:114–19), and these are the three kinds of translation that TP seems to have in mind here. For Dryden's comments on literal as against freer forms of translation (a matter of active debate in the seventeenth century), see John M. Aden, *Critical Opinions of John Dryden* (Nashville: University of Tennessee Press, 1963), 254–61. TP's comments should also be compared with those in Pope's preface to the *Iliad* (TE 7:17–18). An influential classical statement against slavishly literal translations is Horace *Ars Poetica*, lines 133–34.

78     *had it been in ours*] The principle of aiming at what an ancient author would have written if he had written in the modern author's language, country, and period was a commonplace of imitation-theory as well as of translation-theory; see H. F. Brooks, *Review of English Studies* 25 (1949): 124–40; Aden, *Critical Opinions of John Dryden*, esp. 255–57; and TE 4:xxvi–xxvii. For a more recent version, see Robert Lowell's introduction to his *Imitations* (1962), p. xi.

79     *seek for* HOMER *in a Version of* HOMER] Cf. Aden, *Critical Opinions of John Dryden*, 259; and *Critical Essays of the Seventeenth Century*, ed. J. E. Spingarn (Oxford, 1908–9), 1:53–54.

80     *such as* Ovid *tells us*] This seems to be a general reference; for examples of persons or things retaining their names after changing their nature, see e.g. *Metamorphoses* 1.410, 8.254–55, 10.501–2.

82     *Transmigration*] For Homer's supposed transmigration into Ennius, see note to line 9 above.

92     Culex] The "Culex" (Gnat) is one of the poems in the *Appendix Virgiliana*, poems formerly thought to have been the work of Virgil's youth. Statius (prose preface to *Sylvae* 1; Loeb i.3) links it to the *Batrachomyomachia* and accepts both as the juvenilia of great poets. TP's words recall his own "Essay on Homer" (TE 7:52), and are echoed in a letter of Pope (*Pope Corr.* 1:376).

94–97     Chapman . . . *Hymns.*] Paraphrased from Chapman's prefatory "The Occasion of this Impos'd Crowne"; *Chapman's Homer*, ed. Nicoll, 2:511.

104–110     This distinction between two kinds of epic parody was standard: see Boileau, *Le Lutrin*, "Au Lecteur"; Addison, *Spectator*, No. 249; and TE 2:107–8.

110     Gaddius] Jacobus Gaddius (Jacopo Gaddi), Italian scholar and bibliophile (d. 1677?). His major work was *De Scriptoribus Non Ecclesiasticis* (Florence, 1648–49), in which he praises the *Batrachomyomachia* in these terms: "Paradoxum dicere volo, licet verear nasutos censores, vel Momos, Batrachomyoma-

chia videtur mihi nobilior, propriorque perfectioni, quam
Odyssea, et Ilias, imo utraque superat iudicio, ac ingenio, et
praestantia texturae, cum sit Poema ludicrum excellens" ([Flo-
rence, 1648], 1:208–9). TP could have read these remarks in
the "Tractatus" prefaced to the *Batrachomyomachia* in Barnes's
edition, where they are quoted (p. 6).

113      Crusius] Martinus Crusius (1526–1607), German classical
scholar and specialist in demotic Greek. He edited Demetrius
Zenos's translation of the *Batrachomyomachia* into "the Barba-
rous Greek" (TP's phrase in a portion of the "Preface" can-
celed in the MS; see the textual note to line 126). The remark
TP translates comes from Crusius's "Praefatio": "Noli tu, quis-
quis es, curare Nomina Animalculorum, sed ipsas res inspice;
quae nihil refert, sive sub λογικοῖς Animalibus, sive sub
ἀλόγοις innuantur. Finge esse Homines, esse Reges, esse
Consiliarios, esse Πολιτείαν Humane. Invenies ibi Ἠθικὰς
Doctrinas, Οἰκονομικὰς et Πολιτικάς." TP's next remark,
down to "Friendship," although placed outside the quotation
marks, is also based on Crusius: "Ubi inter Ranam et murem
hospitalitas initur, docemur, inaequalium amicitias non bene
cedere." Both remarks are on p. 55 in the edition appended
to J. M. Lange's *Philologia Barbaro-Graecae* (Altdorf, 1707–8).
TP perhaps more probably read them in Barnes's "Trac-
tatus," where they are quoted on p. 7. TP's following com-
ments are not based closely on Crusius, although he may have
taken some hints. Presumably TP ended the marked quota-
tion at the point he did in order to avoid the awkwardness of
his next, elaborately structured sentence being partly in
quotation marks.

124      *many Imitations*] TP's list derives from Barnes, who mentions
"Ludicrum quoddam Poema scenicum, *Graecis* Jambis do-
natum, extare, ex Imitatione nimirum hujus *Batracho-
myomachiae*, cui nomen Γαλεομαχία, quod & Impressum vidi
olim, & MS. *Oxoniae* conservari accepi." This poem is the
*Galeomyomachia* now attributed to Theodore Prodromus (a
monk of the twelfth century); this was first printed about
1494 and subsequently included in many editions of Aesop.
The manuscript to which Barnes refers is probably Bodley
Baroccianus 64, a fifteenth-century manuscript that includes
both the *Galeomyomachia* and the *Batrachomyomachia*. The
other poems are not stated by Barnes to be imitations of the
*Batrachomyomachia;* he says "*Suidas* etiam inter *Homeri* ponit
Ἀραχνομαχίαν, & Γερανομαχίαν, necnon Ψαρομαχίαν." Ad-

dison wrote a Latin poem, "Praelium inter Pygmaeos et Grues Commissum" (*Miscellaneous Works,* ed. A. C. Guthkelch [London, 1914], 1:257–62); this was later translated by Samuel Johnson (*Poems,* ed. E. L. McAdam [New Haven: Yale University Press, 1964], 21–27).

130     Aristarchus *and* Zenodotus] Zenodotus of Ephesus (c. 325–c. 234), first librarian of the Alexandrian Library, is described by Suidas as the first editor of Homer, and he was probably the first to divide the Homeric poems into books, in his edition of c.274 (Sandys 1.119–20); on Aristarchus as an editor of Homer, see Sandys 1.131–35. See also TP's "Essay on Homer," TE 7:60–61.

132–33     Greek Inscriptions] The early editions of Homer have both long and short arguments prefixed to each book. TP is here parodying the short arguments, of which Chapman's translation of that to *Iliad* 1 will serve as an example: "Alpha, *the prayer of Chryses, sings: | The Armie's plague: the strife of Kings.*" (ed. Nicoll, 1:23).

144–45     *long Arguments*] Pope's translation in fact contains such "arguments."

149     *the Heroes Names*] Goldsmith seems to have approved TP's decision, but regarded it as a regrettable though necessary "defect in the translation, which sinks it below the original" (3:425). On the names, see note on "The Names of the Frogs and Mice," below.

161–63     The practice of alluding to other poets in the course of translation was familiar to Pope, who spoke in his "Postscript" to the *Odyssey* of having made use of Milton's style "to dignify and solemnize" the plainer parts of Homer (TE 10:390), and had indeed touched on the question more hesitantly in his preface to the *Iliad* (TE 7:19, 23; 10:437). Milton, who is called "the best and greatest imitator of *Homer*" in the note to Pope's *Odyssey* 2.341 (TE 9:77), particularly fits TP's reference to "*our* English *Poets who most resemble him.*" The TE editors point out that Dryden had echoed Milton in translating "The First Book of Homer's Ilias" (TE 7:xcii). Pope's use of other poets, including Milton, in translating Homer is discussed in the TE introduction (especially 7:lxvii–lxx, xcff, ci, ccxxxvi). Parallels with several poets and other translators are tabulated in Appendix F (TE 10:492–586).

166–72     For the commonplace of poetry and painting as "sister arts," see Jean H. Hagstrum, *The Sister Arts* (Chicago: University of Chicago Press, 1958); the idea had achieved currency in

England through Dryden's translation of Dufresnoy's *De Arte Graphica* (1695), published with a prefatory "Parallel betwixt Painting and Poetry" by Dryden himself. For a specific comparison between translation and painting, see Dryden, preface to *Sylvae* (1685), in *Works*, California ed., 3:4.

178–85     Perhaps a friendly parody of Pope's preface and its discussion of the places where "a Version almost literal" is appropriate, and of the "Liberties one ought to take . . . for transfusing the Spirit of the Original." TP's whole paragraph contains several verbal echoes of Pope's paragraph (TE 7:17–18).

## THE LIFE OF ZOILUS

Epigraph     Martial 4.75.5: "I wish to see Zoilus hanging by the neck" (the poet has asked for wealth, to have the satisfaction of seeing Zoilus hang himself from envy).

6     *Bacon*] TP's division of criticism into three branches follows Bacon's in *De Augmentis Scientiarum* (1623) 6.4 (*Works*, ed. Spedding, Ellis, and Heath [London, 1857–74] 1:708–9). In the earlier *Advancement of Learning* (1605; *Works*, 3:414), Bacon had divided criticism into five branches, alloting no preeminence to the branch he would later regard as "Criticorum tanquam cathedra."

8–9     TP here lists the major critics of classical antiquity. Demetrius of Phalerum (fourth century B.C.), Athenian philosopher and politician, was the traditionally ascribed author of the treatise (now regarded as much later) *On Style*. Dionysius of Halicarnassus (first century B.C.), historian and critic, makes several references to Zoilus, not all of them unfavorable. Quintilian (first century A.D.) wrote the influential *Institutio Oratoria*. "Longinus" is the supposed author of the treatise *On the Sublime;* in TP's time he was identified with Cassius Longinus (213–73), the rhetorician and philosopher.

44–77     These two paragraphs are derived mainly from Aelian *Varia Historia* 11.10; ed. Dilts, p. 123.

49     *Polycrates*] Polycrates, a radical democrat, was chiefly remembered for his attack on Socrates (published c. 393; not extant); see Anton-Hermann Chroust, *Socrates, Man and Myth* (London: Routledge and Kegan Paul, 1957), 69–100.

80     *Dionisius*] In his "Isaeus," 20, Dionysius lists Zoilus among "those who preferred factual discourses and practical rhetoric designed for the law courts"; *Critical Essays*, Loeb ed., 1:229.

106        five or six] It seems odd that TP does not refer to one of
           Zoilus's objections extant in so obvious a source as Plutarch
           (*Questiones Conviviales* 5.4; *Moralia*, Loeb ed., 8:401–5); this is
           the criticism of the "stronger drink" that Achilles orders for
           his guests (*Iliad* 9.203). Pope cites this objection in his note to
           9.268 in his translation (TE 7:445–46).

110–27     All six of the objections of Zoilus that TP mentions here are
           referred to at least indirectly by Pope (see the following
           notes), though he does not always mention Zoilus by name.
           In the case of the *Iliad* passages especially, TP may have
           actually supplied the materials for Pope's notes, though the
           notes themselves were "entirely composed" by Pope (TE
           7:xviii). For example, at TE 7:265, Pope refutes Zoilus by
           citing Eustathius on the passage referred to in the "Life of
           Zoilus" (lines 102–7); TP read Eustathius and extracted mate-
           rial for Pope (TE 7:xxxix; *Pope Corr.* 1:225).

110–12     The reference is to *Iliad* 1.50; Aristotle *Poetics* 25 defends
           Homer against this criticism, though without mentioning
           Zoilus. Pope has a note (to 1.69 in his translation; TE 7:89)
           explaining, on medical grounds, why the dogs and mules
           should die first, but with no reference to Zoilus.

113–15     The reference is to *Iliad* 5.7. Pope has a note (to 5.5 in his
           translation; TE 7:265) justifying the passage explicitly
           against Zoilus's "insipid Piece of Raillery."

116–19     The reference is to *Iliad* 5.20. Pope has a note (to 5.27 in his
           translation; TE 7:266) explicitly justifying Homer against
           Zoilus's "Cavil."

120–22     The reference is to *Iliad* 24.649. Pope's note (to 24.816 in his
           translation; TE 8:570) does not mention Zoilus or his objec-
           tion, but quotes Eustathius's defense of "ἐπικερτομέων" as
           meaning not (as usual) "insultingly" but rather "soothingly."
           Pope does not translate the word.

123–24     The reference is to *Odyssey* 9.60. Pope has a note (to 9.69 in
           his translation; TE 9:305) quoting Eustathius's explanation of
           the passage against Zoilus's objection.

125–27     The reference is to *Odyssey* 10.241, a passage discussed by
           "Longinus," who, as an instance of the absurdities with which
           he thought the *Odyssey* abounded, quoted Zoilus's objection
           with evident approval (*On the Sublime*, ed. D. A. Russell [Ox-
           ford: Oxford University Press, 1964], 9.14). Russell com-
           ments: "Does κλάιοντες here mean squealing or weeping? Is
           Zoilus complaining of the vulgarity of the description or the
           improbability of pigs shedding tears?" (p. 98). Pope translates

"groan," and his note (to 10.281 in his translation; TE 9:356) quotes Longinus and gives (which he had not done in any of his previous notes cited above) details about Zoilus, quoting Dionysius of Halicarnassus and Vitruvius.

127      Didymus] Didymus (c. 80–10), a prolific scholar, edited a commentary on Homer among his many other works. Scholia attributed to Didymus were printed in many editions of Homer's works.

138–88    The source of the incident at Olympus is (as TP cites at line 178) Suidas; *Lexicon*, ed. Adler, 2:512.

195      *Ptolomy Philadelphus*] Ptolemy II Philadelphus (308–246), joint ruler from 285 and sole ruler from 283–282; he founded the Museum and completed the Alexandrian Library. His reign was especially noted for its flourishing cultural life, but the historical Zoilus (fl. 365–336) did not belong to his period. Schoedinger (p. 117) suggests that TP may have intended some contemporary references in his account of Ptolemy's court. He identifies Ptolemy with Lord Oxford, Callimachus with Pope, and Apollonius with TP himself; and more doubtfully, Eratosthenes with Bolingbroke, Aristophanes with Arbuthnot, and Aristarchus with Broome. All these identifications seem fanciful.

202      *Eratosthenes*] Eratosthenes (c. 275–194) was the most versatile scholar of his time, and librarian from c. 234.

203      *Aristophanes*] Aristophanes of Byzantium (c. 257–180), best known as a textual scholar. He edited Homer, and was librarian from c. 194.

204      *Callimachus*] Callimachus (c. 305–240); his poem on the hair of Berenice survives only in the Latin translation by Catullus (66).

206–8    The translation from Ovid is from *Amores* 2.4.19–20: "est quae Callimachi prae nostris rustica dicat / carmina—cui placeo, protinus ipsa placet."

208      *Theocritus*] Theocritus (c. 300–260?), the pastoral poet.

209      *Aristarchus*] Aristarchus of Samothrace (c. 217–145); primarily a textual critic, and head of the library from c. 153.

210      *Apollonius Rhodius*] Apollonius of Rhodes (c. 295–?), author of the *Argonautica;* probably librarian from c. 260.

224–85    Zoilus's dream seems to be TP's invention. It is a satirical variant of the kind of periodical-essay "vision" of which TP himself wrote at least five (published in his *Poems on Several Occasions*, 1722; two had previously appeared in the *Spectator* and two in the *Guardian*). The introductory formula, "He found himself sitting . . ." occurs also in "Vision II" (1722 edition, p. 192; originally published in the *Spectator* No. 501). Zoilus's vision also derives in part from the set-pieces of prophecy in epic poems; the "Monster . . . surrounded with Snakes" (line 213) may derive from such epic and mock-epic monsters as Milton's Sin (*Paradise Lost*, 2.651–53, 794–800) and, more immediately, the goddess Criticism in Swift's *Battle of the Books* (Swift, *Tale*, 240).

285  *Canopus*] There was a famous temple of Serapis at Canobus, used to record events of significance; see Strabo, 17.1.17 (Loeb ed., 8:63–65).

293–307 This incident is taken from Vitruvius 7. Preface. 4–7.

309–35  TP's account is expanded from Vitruvius 7. Preface. 8 (in Vitruvius it is placed some years after the anecdote about Aristophanes).

336–67  The petitions are not in Vitruvius, and are apparently TP's addition.

339–44  With the account of the bee given here, compare that in Swift's *Battle of the Books* (Swift, *Tale*, 231, 234–35).

366  *Antiochus*] Since the historical setting is the court of Ptolemy II Philadelphus, this must be Antiochus II, king of Syria 261?–247, who fought against Ptolemy until a peace was confirmed by his marriage to Ptolemy's daughter Berenice. The more famous Antiochus III fought against Ptolemies IV and V. The contemporary application is the tendency of Whig writers (Bentley, Blackmore, and Dennis were all Whigs) to accuse the Tories of leanings towards popery and arbitrary power (symbolized by Louis XIV, who is meant by Antiochus). Dennis insinuated this charge in his attack on Pope's Homer (*Critical Works*, ed. Hooker, 2:119).

385  ston'd to Death] Vitruvius 7. Preface. 8 records a report that Zoilus was stoned in Chios.

396  that splendid Temple] The Temple of Homer was the work of Ptolemy Philopator (222–205); it is mentioned in Aelian *Varia Historia* 13.22; ed. Dilts, p. 162. Aelian does not connect Zoilus with it.

414  *Calliope*] The muse of epic poetry.

430  Paper of *Nilus*] Papyrus.

431  *HOMERO-MASTIX*] "Scourge of Homer"; see textual note to this line, and see line 103 above. It may have been one of the titles of Zoilus's work against Homer, and it became the critic's nickname.

454        pretended to his Birth] TP discusses the contenders in his "Essay" on Homer (TE 7:43–45).

462        *Ælian*] Aelian says this in *Varia Historia* 1.11; ed. Dilts, 3–4.

475        the *Homereum*] This is described by Strabo: "There is also [at Smyrna] a library; and the Homereium, a quadrangular portico containing a shrine and wooden statue of Homer; for the Smyrnaeans also lay especial claim to the poet; and indeed a bronze coin of theirs is called Homereium" (14.1.37; Loeb ed., 6:245–47).

493        by Fire] This is one of the alternative deaths mentioned in Vitruvius 7. Preface. 8.

508        several Cities] See above, line 454.

THE NAMES OF THE FROGS AND MICE

See Preface, lines 155ff. These satirically or comically descriptive names belong to an old tradition, of which the *Batrachomyomachia* must be one of the earliest examples. There are many examples in Lucian (e.g., *True Story,* 1.11–21 passim, 35, 42; 2.37, 44). More's *Utopia* contains several such terms or names, derived from the Greek: see for example *Traniborus* (bench-eater), *Anemolius* (windy one, windbag), and of course Hythlodaeus himself (learned in nonsense). On these and others, see *Utopia,* ed. Edward Surtz and J. H. Hexter (New Haven: Yale University Press, 1965), 301–2, 398–99, 430; and the glossary to Paul Turner's Penguin translation (Harmondsworth, 1965), 153–54 (Turner's translations are in the same spirit as TP's table of English equivalents, although TP does not carry these English equivalents into the translation proper). Rabelais is still closer to the spirit of the *Batrachomyomachia's* list, since many of his comic terms and names concern eating and digestive functions: Grangousier, crotenotaire, crocquenotaire, Happe mousche, Bolivorax, Maschefain (1.3; 2.Prol.; 2.1), and especially the long list of such names at 4.40. At least one of Rabelais' names, Rodilardus (4.67; 1.3), appears to derive from a Latin imitation of the *Batrachomyomachia* (*Oeuvres,* ed. Abel Lefranc et al. [Paris, 1912–   ], 1:43n).

HOMER'S BATTLE OF THE FROGS AND MICE
BOOK I

5        write] In his "Essay on Homer," TP noted that Homer studied under one Pronapides: "From him he might learn to preserve his Poetry by committing it to Writing; which we mention, because it is generally believ'd no Poems before him

were so preserv'd; and he himself in the third line [fifth in
TP's translation] of his *Batrachomyomachia* (if this Piece be
allow'd to be his) expressly speaks of writing his Works in his
Tablets" (*Iliad* [Pope's translation, 1715], 1:21–22; TE 7:46–
47, textual note).

10          Earth-born Giants] The story is not mentioned in the *Iliad* or
the *Odyssey*, although it is found in Hesiod, *Theogony*, lines
147–210. TP is here probably recalling Virgil *Aeneid* 6.577–
79.

18          Gilbert Wakefield, who included the poem at the end of his
edition of Pope's Homer (*Odyssey*, new ed., vol. 5, 1796; subse-
quently cited as Wakefield), suggested that Pope might have
borrowed from this line in his imitation of the *Sixth Satire of
the Second Book of Horace*, line 203 (TE 4:263).

34          *Eridanus*] A mythical river, mentioned in Hesiod (*Theogony*,
line 338) but not in the Homeric poems.

103         So pass'd *Europa*] Homer barely alludes to Europa (*Iliad*
14.321–22); TP's description of her fright is probably a re-
collection of Ovid *Metamorphoses* 2.873–75 and 6.105–7.

105         With oary Feet . . . rode] Wakefield, whose text reads "row'd"
for "rode", cites *Paradise Lost*, 7.439–40, "rows . . . with oary
feet", which he in turn derives from Silius Italicus *Punica*
14.191 ("pedibus . . . eremigat undas").

## BOOK II

1           rosy-finger'd Morn] A frequent Homeric formula.

81–140      In the *Iliad* (e.g., 4.1–72, 7.443–63), the gods frequently meet
to discuss the state of the war and whether and how they
should intervene.

133         Let heav'nly Blood] In *Iliad* 5, Diomede wounds Venus, and
(in Pope's translation), "From the clear Vein a Stream immor-
tal flow'd, / Such Stream as issues from a wounded God"
(lines 421–22). Pope has a long note on the passage, in which
he quotes Milton's imitation of Homer, Michael's wounding
of Satan (*Paradise Lost*, 6.330–34). In the 1726 edition of TP's
*Poems on Several Occasions*, "Let" is emended to "Lest". Al-
though the change is a plausible one, we have retained "Let",
not only because it is the reading of both 17 and 22, but also
because it makes a more extravagantly mock-heroic point: the
gods had better stick to fights with men, for the mice will be
more than a match for them. This is in keeping with the
hyperbole in the speech of Mars in Book III (lines 149–60).

## Book III

48      Silver Flood] The epithet was common in descriptions of rivers, streams, and so on, as far back as Homer (e.g., *Iliad* 2.753: 2.912 in Pope's translation, "silver Surface"). For lists of early occurrences in Greek, Latin, and earlier English poets, see Spenser, *Works,* Variorum Edition (Baltimore: Johns Hopkins Press, 1933–49), 6:246; and Ian Donaldson, *Essays in Criticism* 25 (1975): 116–19, 122nn. The phrase "silver Flood" occurs in Pope (*Pastorals,* "Winter," line 64; *Dunciad,* "A" version, 2.262; *Iliad* translation, 18.604, 617; 20.14; *Odyssey* translation 6.146). Pope frequently uses such common phrases as "silver *Thames*" and "silver Streams." See also *Mac-Flecknoe,* line 38; *Dispensary* (1699), 6.77; Prior, *An Ode, Humbly Inscribed to the Queen* (1706), line 234; Gay *Rural Sports,* 1.172; and *Poems on Affairs of State,* ed. George deF. Lord et al. (New Haven: Yale University Press, 1963–75), 5:285. Dryden's commentators sometimes cite an early poem by Waller, "Of the Danger His Majesty . . . Escaped in the Road at Saint Anderes," lines 61–62.

86      Wakefield pointed out that Curll's "brown dishonours" in *Dunciad* 2.100 ("A" version; TE 5:109) recall this line; TP may have had in mind *Aeneid* 5.357–58. See also Gay, *Trivia* (1716), 2.534: "And Mud enwraps the Honours of his Face." TP had been in correspondence with Gay during the composition of *Trivia,* which is mentioned in their letters (John Gay, *Poetry and Prose,* ed. Vinton A. Dearing and Charles E. Beckwith [Oxford: Clarendon Press, 1974], 2:546).

88      Cf. *Iliad* 5.302ff, 12.380ff, 20.285ff, and *Aeneid* 12.896ff; and see Jasper Griffin, *Homer on Life and Death* (Oxford: Clarendon Press, 1980), 81. At *Iliad* 5.302ff, Homer makes Diomede lift a stone that would be too heavy for two modern men. Pope points out in a note to his translation (5.371, TE 7:284–85) that Virgil, with a keener sense of modern degeneration, imitates Homer by making Turnus lift a stone that twelve modern men could hardly lift (*Aeneid* 12.896ff). Swift imitated Virgil's passage in "scarce a dozen *Cavaliers* . . . in our degenerate Days" (*Battle of the Books,* in Swift, *Tale,* 249), and Pope followed Swift ("Twelve starveling bards of these degen'rate days"; *Dunciad,* "A" version, 2.36; TE 5:100). The best-known early satiric example, which alludes to both Homer and Virgil, is Juvenal 15.65–71 (see the commentary by J. C. B. Mayor, *Thirteen Satires of Juvenal* [London, 1900],

2:374–76, and E. Courtney, *A Commentary on the Satires of Juvenal* [London: Athlone Press, 1980], 601, for further references).

117     Wakefield pointed out the allusion to Dryden's translation of the *Aeneid* 2.745: "And faintly tinckl'd on the Brazen Shield" (*Poems*, ed. James Kinsley [Oxford: Clarendon Press, 1958], 3.1111).

134     Wakefield comments: "This entire verse is borrowed from one of the translators of the *Iliad:* but my memory cannot specify the author or the passage."

137–38     An allusion to Addison's *Campaign* (1705; published December 1704): "Rivers of blood I see, and hills of slain, / An Iliad rising out of One Campaign" (lines 11–12; *Miscellaneous Works*, ed. Guthkelch, 1:157).

189–90     The original Greek (lines 298–99, Loeb ed., 562–63) does not mention the gods having a different name for crabs. The distinction between the gods' and men's names for things goes back to the *Iliad*, e.g., 1.403–4, 2.813–14, 14.291, 20.74; see Pope's notes to his translation, 1.523, 14.328–30 (TE 8:113, 178–79). It became very common in satire and mock-heroic: see Rabelais, *Quart Livre*, prologue (ed. Jean Plattard [Paris: Société Les Belles Lettres, 1959], 14; *Battle of the Books*, in Swift, *Tale*, 239; *Rape of the Lock*, 1.177–78 (TE 2:151); *Dunciad*, 4.361–62 (TE 5:378). See also Dryden, *The Hind and the Panther*, 3.823–24; and TP's own "Allegory on Man," lines 2–4.

## PREFACE TO ZOILUS'S REMARKS

Epigraph     Ovid *Remedia Amoris* 365–66, (adapted?; the Loeb text has "Homeri" for "Amici" and "es" for "&"); "Envy disparages the great genius of a friend, and whoever does this deserves to be called Zoilus" (translating TP's text).

20     *Maevius*] Bavius and Maevius are the bad poets contemptuously referred to by Virgil in *Eclogues* 3.90. Horace's *Epode* 10 is, as TP says, addressed to Maevius and wishes him a bad sea-journey; see especially lines 11–14.

26     *Carvilius Pictor*] Donatus cites "adversus Aeneida liber Carvilii Pictoris, titulo Aeneidomastix" in his *Vita Virgilii; Vitae Virgilianae Antiquae*, ed. Colin Hardie, 2d ed. (Oxford: Clarendon Press, 1966), 17.

34–35     *Scaliger*] Julius Caesar Scaliger (1484–1558), philosopher and scientist, whose *Exercitationes* (1557), directed against the *De*

*Subtilitate* (1550) of Girolamo Cardano (1501–76), the Italian mathematician and scientist, was a famous example of bitter scholarly invective.

35–36   *Le Clerc*] The reference is to "De Judicio de Stylo et Charactere Scriptoris Ferendo" (of which the running title is "Judicium de Q Curtio"), published in Le Clerc's *Ars Critica* (3 vols., Amsterdam, 1697; 2:535–716).

## The Remarks of Zoilus

1       Protagoras] This objection is recorded (and rejected) by Aristotle in *Poetics* 19.8. TP may have aimed this remark particularly at Dennis. Discussing *Iliad* 1.138 in Pope's translation in his *Remarks upon Mr. Pope's Homer,* Dennis considers his own interpretation of the line and Madame Dacier's, concluding that, whoever is right, "it must absolutely condemn the English Translator" (*Critical Works,* ed. Hooker, 2:151; see also 2:153 for another example of Dennis's either-way-you-lose reasoning).

7       Aristotle] Blackmore impugned the authority of Aristotle: "It's clear, that *Aristotle* form'd all his Axioms and Doctrines in Poetry, from the Patterns of *Homer* and other *Greek* Writers; and, without assigning any Reason of his Positions, relies for the Truth of them on his own, or the Authority of those Authors" (*Essays,* 1716, 11–12). See also Dennis, ed. Hooker, 2:lxxxii. It was a common view that Aristotle's precepts were derived from the practice of Homer and other writers. This was not normally held to his discredit; for examples from Dryden, Pope, and others see Aden, *Critical Opinions,* 217, 250; Pope, *Essay on Criticism,* line 68 and commentary at TE 1:249.

19–20   *What I have written in my Tablets*] This is a translation of line 3 in the Greek text (Loeb ed., p. 542). The remark is probably intended as a thrust against Bentley, who was famous for declaring passages spurious.

33      *Perizonius*] Jacobus Perizonius (or Accinctus); Jakob Voorbroek (1651–1715), Dutch classical scholar. The reference is perhaps to his *Animadversiones Historicae* (1685). Perizonius edited Aelian's *Varia Historia* (Leyden, 1701), and in the course of his commentary discusses the date of Zoilus (p. 648), but this does not help to explain the remark.

42–48   Both Bentley and Blackmore denied Homer's moral intention. In his preface to his *Paraphrase upon the Book of Job*

(1700), Blackmore admitted that there were "indeed some few *Moral Sentences* interspers'd in these *Poets*" (the classical epics), but he agreed with Le Clerc's view that modern moral interpretations of the poets' intentions were critical inventions (sig. d2a). In his *Essays* (1716) he repeated the view that "since *Homer* and *Virgil* do not expresly draw any Doctrine from their Fables, it is uncertain whether they design'd any" (p. 77). Blackmore's intention was to draw favorable attention to the undoubted and explicit morals of his own epics. Bentley's low opinion of Homer's "moral" is quoted above in the headnote to *Homer's Battle*.

52      they write *Prefaces*] Dennis is meant here; for example, his prefaces to *Rinaldo and Armida* (1696), to *Liberty Asserted* (1704), and to *Gibraltar* (1705). TP had earlier criticized this foible in Dennis in the "Letter to a Friend: On Poets" ("Satires" Notebook, ff. 2a–3a, lines 71–74).

56      they write *Remarks*] Dennis is again meant here; for example, his *Remarks upon a Book Entituled Prince Arthur* (1696); *Remarks upon Cato* (1713); and *Remarks upon Mr. Pope's Translation of Homer* (1717).

63      *Scaliger*] Julius Caesar Scaliger, mentioned above (in the preface to the "Remarks," lines 34–35) as an example of Zoilus-like scholarly ill-humor; the reference here is to his *Poetices Libri Septem* (posthumously published in 1561), which was notorious for its partisanship of Virgil against Homer.

66–73   TP's reference is correct; the passage is from 3.112 and is found on p. 162 in the 1561 edition. TP's text is verbally identical with that of 1561, except that he has omitted a sentence after "duximus": "Deum vero filium Dominum nostrum Iesum Christum tanquam humani generis servatorem." Scaliger is not being so egotistical as TP implies. The chapter is about hymns, and Scaliger's point is that divine subjects are particularly inspiring. In context (Scaliger is speaking of celebrating each of the persons of the Trinity separately) the passage may be paraphrased: "Writing a hymn to God brought the creator of the world immediately into my presence. [Writing a hymn to our Saviour] was a transcendent experience that freed my mind from its bodily prison. But when I wrote in praise of the Holy Spirit, though the poem was feeble and unpolished, suddenly it blazed with divine fire." Scaliger attributes the inspiration to his subject, not to himself.

76–77   *opprobious Names*] The reference is to Achilles' abuse of

Agamemnon; Pope has a note (to *Iliad* 1.298 in his translation; TE 7:101) defending its propriety. TP's "*below the Dignity of the* Epick" probably alludes to Dennis's *Remarks upon Mr. Pope's . . . Homer,* which had dealt in some detail with the opening of Book I, finding Pope's renderings "low" (*Critical Works,* 2:127ff, e.g., 129, 133).

92    *Ridiculousness*] Dennis repeatedly called Pope's translation "ridiculous" (*Critical Works,* 2:128, 148, etc.).

96    Burlesque] Another of Dennis's frequent terms for Pope's translation (*Critical Works,* 2:128, 130–31, 133).

112    Polycrates] Zoilus's teacher; see note above to "Life," line 49. The attack on Socrates is not extant, although it can be partially reconstructed from the replies of Xenophon and Libanius. That verse-making was one of the charges seems to be TP's joke.

113    Socrates] For the poems Socrates wrote shortly before his death, see Plato's *Phaedo,* 60c–61b.

150–54    Pope's note on *Iliad* 22.449 in his translation (TE 8:474) defends Hector's dying prophecies.

161    Men who quote themselves] In his *Essays* (1716), Blackmore quotes himself on the subject of the character of an hero (49–50).

169–71    The irrelevance of Books 23 and 24 of the *Iliad* was a commonplace; the point is made, for example by Blackmore in his *Essays,* where he calls them "superfluous" (48). In his prefatory note to *Iliad* 23 in his translation (TE 8:485–86), Pope defends them while admitting that "Many judicious Criticks" have condemned them.

177    *Ajax*] In Sophocles' play (which has 1,421 lines in the Loeb edition) Ajax kills himself at line 865.

187    Stall to Stall] That is, from one secondhand bookstall to another.

196    *an ample Digression*] Either Bentley or Dennis might be aimed at here.

214    *let* Phœbus *explain*] We have been unable to find an example of the use of this expression.

245–47    The critic who attacks whatever is approved is certainly Dennis, who had attacked such popular and critical successes as the *Essay on Criticism,* Addison's *Cato,* and Pope's Homer.

257–60    The reference is perhaps to La Motte's contraction of the *Iliad* in twelve books (1714), referred to above (TP's "Preface," line 62–63).

271–75    Aelian *Varia Historia* 1.3; ed. Dilts, p. 2.

277–88     For an example of his practice, see Blackmore's *Essays* (1716), where he refers to Addison as "a judicious Critick, in his Discourses on *Milton*" (p. vi); later he refers to "A Superior Critick of our own Nation" (p. 68).

314        the Apotheosis of HOMER] The passage in Cuperus is as follows: "Adscribitur quoque ab auctore huius marmoris Homeri illud obscuri argumenti poematium Batrachyomachia [*sic*] (dubitantibus sane vitae Homeri scriptoribus, hoc est, tam Proclo, quam Auctore anonymo apud Allatium de Patria Homeri in fine suae praefationis) ut ex muribus in imo solio volumen hinc inde arrodentibus infertur; quod nec pariter Kircherius advertit, Aegyptiis mysteriis, in Graeco quamvis poeta et statuario evolvendis intentus." (Gisbertus Cuperus, *Apotheosis vel Consecratio Homeri* [Amsterdam, 1683], 197.) The "Apotheosis" is mentioned in TP's "Essay on Homer" (TE 7:55) and was illustrated in Pope's edition (it is reproduced in TE, facing 7:81).

341        *Trumpets*] See Pope's note to *Iliad* 21.259 in his translation (TE 8:334).

376–82     The reference to Homer's impure Greek alludes to Dennis's charges against Pope's bad English (*Critical Works*, 2:124, 127, 129, 157), lapsing into Irish at times (2:125, 126).

397        *Lipsius*] Justus Lipsius (1547–1606), Dutch classical scholar. Lipsius made the remark quoted while congratulating himself on an emendation to the text of the *Pervigilium Veneris:* "Aut ego me amo, aut Phoebus me amavit, cum correxi, *explicant agni latus:* Nec sane significantius exprimi potuit decubitus ille ovium in latus, quasi apricantium. Id enim solent super genistas, myricas et humiliores fructices." TP probably read the remark (which was first published in Lipsius's *Electiones*) in the edition of the *Pervigilium Veneris* edited by Jean le Clerc (Amsterdam, 1712), 16. In his translation of the poem, TP rejected Lipsius's emendation; see the headnote to "The Vigil of Venus" below, and the textual note to line 80 of the Latin text.

401–02     *regundi . . . perdidit*] The reference seems to be to Bentley's edition of Horace (Cambridge, 1711), where he makes a point of restoring antique spellings: "Porro autem Orthographiae rationem institui ad Augusti saeculi normam, quae ex Inscriptionibus, Numis, Vetustioribusque Membranis abunde constat, quamque et alii et praesertim *Nic. Heinsius* in *Virgilio* suo secutus est" (preface, C3b). Examples are "volgus," "divom," "inpius," and "conpesco." Of TP's examples, however, "regendi" does not occur in Horace; "perdidit" occurs twice, but in *Epistles* 1.1.67 Bentley emends to "prodidit" and in *Epistles* 2.2.40 he retains "perdidit." There may be some further reference that we have missed.

413      Pythagoras] This anecdote, which is from Diogenes Laertius 8.21, is cited by Pope in his note to *Iliad* 5.422 in his translation (TE 7:287).

# The Horse and the Olive (1713)

The story of the contest between Athena and Poseidon for the city of Athens is of great antiquity. It was depicted on the rear pediment of the Parthenon (Pausanias 1.24.5) and is mentioned by Herodotus (8.55). In the Greek sources, however, Poseidon's gift is not the horse but water in the form of a spring or pool on the Acropolis (Apollodorus 3.14.1, where many references are collected in the Loeb edition). Ovid follows this tradition (*Metamorphoses* 6.70–82). An alternative version is represented in Servius's commentary on *Georgics* 1.12–13, where Virgil addresses Neptune as "cui prima frementem / fudit equum magno tellus percussa tridenti", without, however, explicitly referring to the contest for Athens. Servius glosses the passage with the following story: "cum Neptunus et Minerva de Athenarum nomine contenderunt, placuit diis, ut eius nomine civitas appellaretur, qui munus melius mortalibus obtulissit. tunc Neptunus percusso litore equum, animal bellis aptum, produxit; Minerva iacta hasta olivam creavit, quae res melior conprobata et pacis insigne" (ed. G. Thilo [Leipzig, 1887], 3.1.133). This version is substantially repeated by later Latin mythographers (First Vatican Mythographer, 1.2; Second, 2.119; Third, 5.4; in *Scriptores Rerum Mythicarum Latini Tres Romae Nuper Reperti*, ed. G.H. Bode [Celle, 1854]).

In the classical sources cited, the contest is usually judged by the twelve gods, never by Jupiter weighing the gifts in a balance. This may have been TP's own variation, or he may have read a version of the story that already included it. The source of the balance motif is surely *Iliad* 8.68–74 and 22.208–13. Pope has a long note on the first of these passages (8.87–94 in his translation; TE 7:399–400), where he cites *Iliad* 22 and other parallels from the Bible, Virgil, and Milton. In Homer and Virgil it is the heavier scale that portends defeat and death. Belshazzar's soul, however, is "found wanting" (Daniel 5:27), and Milton in turn makes the lighter scale portend defeat (*Paradise Lost* 4.995–1000). In the iconography of the Last Judgment, souls about to be damned are similarly shown outweighed by their sins. TP follows the biblical tradition in this respect.

Pope, in his parody of the device in *The Rape of the Lock* (5.71–74), makes the hairs of the belles outweighing the wits of the beaux portend Belinda's defeat of the Baron.

*The Horse and the Olive* was published in a folio half-sheet, the usual format for separately published poems of its length, by Swift's friend and publisher Benjamin Tooke. It was advertised as published "yesterday" in the *Examiner* for 10 April 1713.

An autograph manuscript of the poem in practically its published state appears in the Congleton "Satires" Notebook (ff. 46a–47a), and we have chosen to print this text in its proper place to illustrate the extent to which authorial manuscripts underwent styling at this period. There is another manuscript of the poem among the Congleton papers, a non-autograph transcript on a single sheet (303 × 185 mm). Its variants are probable miscopyings. There is also a transcript of the poem in an eighteenth-century poetical commonplace book in the Brotherton Library, Leeds (Accession No. B 7104); its text (pp. 173–74) is verbally the same as the 1713 edition except for "when" for "whom" in line 25. A further transcript appears in a small group of Parnell's poems copied in the late eighteenth or early nineteenth century and headed "Some Additional Peice's of Dean Parnell's not Publish'd with his Works". This is preserved in the Osborn Collection in the Beinecke Rare Book and Manuscript Library at Yale. It includes transcripts of "The Third Satire of D^r John Donne," "On Bishop Burnet's being set on Fire in his Closet," "Piety, Or the Vision," "Bacchus," "The Horse & the Olive," "D^r Parnel to D^r Swift, on his Birth-Day." *The Horse and the Olive* is given in a text which derives from 1713 but which reads "honours" for "Honour" at line 31.

The later textual history of the poem is curious. It was twice reprinted in 1762: in the *London Magazine* (31 [December 1762]: 671) and the *Annual Register* (5 [1762]: 183–84). Both these printings follow the text of the poem as published in 1713. In the *Annual Register* the poem was later printed a second time (13 [1770]: 226–27, second pagination). This volume also reprinted TP's "Bacchus." In the text in the *Annual Register* for 1770, *The Horse and the Olive* is printed from a text independent of the 1762 printing. It is just possible that it was printed from an autograph MS, for one of the variants ("rural" for *"Rival"* in line 17) is a plausible misreading of TP's hand. The other variants are "Whilst" for "Which" (line 2); "her" for "the" (line 13); "nor" for "no" (line 45); and, most interestingly, "Whom her best patroness Europa calls" in line 42. But the poem was not collected in any edition of TP's works until 1773.

The poem is here reprinted from the rare original half-sheet. Our text is taken from the copy in the Clark Library; Foxon (P77) records another copy at Harvard.

# Poems from Steele's *Poetical Miscellanies* (1714)

TP contributed four poems to Steele's *Poetical Miscellanies*. Steele requested contributions for this anthology in the *Guardian*, No. 50 (8 May 1713). It was published at the end of December 1713, although the title page was dated ahead (and also in error, "MDDCXIV" for "MDC-CXIV"). The volume was the first printing of some minor pieces by Pope: "The Wife of Bath her Prologue" (TE 2:57–78); "Prologue, Designed for Mr. Durfey's Last Play" (if this is indeed Pope's; see TE 6:101–2); and "The Arrival of Ulysses in Ithaca" (TE 1:465-74). In this first printing of the anthology, one of the leaves containing TP's "Hymn on Contentment" (E4) is a cancel. We have not been able to find a copy of the volume with E4 in its uncanceled state. The leaf may have been canceled to revise either the beginning of TP's "Hymn" or the end of the previous poem. The volume was reprinted, presumably soon after publication, with the date of the title page corrected. Although this edition is sometimes described as a variant or a reissue, it is a complete resetting of the type. TP's poems, however, are textually identical in both printings. The collection was reprinted again in 1727; and there was a partial reprint in Dublin in 1726 (containing, however, none of TP's poems). Further details and bibliographical references to this collection are given in our Bibliography (A3).

## A Hymn on Contentment

This poem was first published in *Poetical Miscellanies* (pp. 56–60). It was reprinted in *The Bee: A Collection of Choice Poems* (1715; Part I, pp. 9–12), and (with a few slight changes) in Pope's edition.

There is some evidence that it may have been written in two parts. In the Congleton inventory of TP's works, the group called "The Affections of Divine Poetry" ends with the entry "On Contentment," against which two line counts are given, 48 and 32. This "On Contentment" is probably the same as the "Hymn," the first forty-eight lines of which form a self-contained unit with its own conclusion. The remainder of the poem consists of only thirty lines in the texts we have; probably TP canceled a couplet in revision.

There is further evidence of the poem being composed in two separate halves in that lines 1–48 have a fairly close direct source, "Metrum XXII" in the *De Divina Psalmodia* of Cardinal Giovanni Bona (1609–74). Bona's poem (here taken from the Cologne, 1677, edition of *De Divina Psalmodia*, pp. 275–76) is as follows:

> O sincera parens beatitatis,
> Coeli delitium, Deique proles,
> Pax terrae columen, decusque morum,
> Pax cunctis potior ducum triumphis,
> Quos mundi colis abditos recessus?
> Hic te sollicito requiret aestu,
> Urbanos fugiens procul tumultus.
> Hic inter scopulos, vagosque fluctus,
> Spumantis pelagi latere credit.
> Hic deserta petit loca, et per antra
> Te quaerens varias peragrat oras,
> Qua lucens oritur, caditque Titan.
> Hic ut te celer assequatur, aurum
> Congestum colit, atque dignitatum
> Regalem sibi praeparat decorem.
> Hic demens iuga scandit, et remotos
> Perscrutatur agros: tamen supernae
> Hi pacis nequeunt bonis potiri.
> Cur sic ergo tuum benigna Numen
> Caelans implacidum relinquis Orbem?
> Pacem sic ego scisitabar: illa
> Respondit. Proprio imperare cordi
> Si nosti, tibi cognitumque Numen,
> Possessumque meum est: sinu receptam
> Sic me perpetuo coles amore.

The theme of TP's poem is too commonplace to make it worthwhile citing parallels from seventeenth-century English poems on the subject. But see Woodman, 67–71, for some references.

Transcripts of the poem at the University of Chicago (MS 551, pages 26–29) and in BL Add. MS 4456 (ff. 155b–57a), the latter a collection of poems made by Thomas Birch, follow Pope's text, except for obvious errors. Another, at Yale (Osborn shelves C163, pages 5–8) derives from *Miscellanies*. A more interesting transcript is found in Trinity College Dublin (R.8.109); this generally agrees with the *Miscellanies* text but has some unique variants that may possibly derive at some remove from an authorial manuscript. These are "Threads" for "Treads" in line 20; "on" for "o'er" in line 26; "the" for "thy" in line 44; and "raise" for "lift" in line 61. These could all be corruptions, of course, and we have therefore excluded them from the textual notes in the absence of any evidence linking them or the MS with TP.

The "Hymn" is here printed from the 1714 edition, with the 1722 variants recorded in the textual notes.

## Textual Notes

| | |
|---|---|
| Title | In 22 the poem is called "A Hymn to Contentment." |
| 12 | find] 14; meet 22 |
| 19 | whom] 14; which 22 |
| 24 | a] 14; the 22 |
| 41 | if] 14; all 22 |
| 56 | In 22, the line ends with a colon and line 57 does not begin a new paragraph. |
| 72 | Wou'd] 14; Shou'd 22 |

## *Song* ("My days have been")

This poem was first printed in Steele's *Poetical Miscellanies* (pp. 61–63) and reprinted (with a few slight revisions) in Pope's edition. It was subsequently reprinted in numerous eighteenth-century miscellanies and song books.

Three contemporary transcripts are known. Two are in BL Stowe MS 972 (ff. 28b and 32a) and follow Pope's text, from which they were probably copied. More interesting is the transcript in Bodleian Library Ballard MS 50 (f. 110a), which seems to preserve an early form of the text. It includes the stanza printed in 1714 but omitted in Pope's edition (lines 13–16) and is addressed to a "Celia" instead of to "Nancy." Since some of the poems in the Congleton "Lyrics" Notebook ("On———Embroydring," "I looked and in a moment," "O tell if any fate," and "Since bearing of a gentle mind"; ff. 2a–5a) are addressed to a "Celia," this poem too may have been written before TP's marriage and subsequently transferred to his wife. On the other hand, "Celia" is a conventional name for a woman in a poem, and since the "Lyrics" Notebook contains on the same page (f. 5a) poems addressed to Celia and to Nancy, this may not be a justifiable inference. Since this creates a presumption that the Ballard transcript may preserve authorial readings from a pre-1714 form of the text, we have here included its variants in the textual notes. In the Ballard transcript, the poem is divided into four numbered, eight-line stanzas; in both printed texts it is divided into unnumbered, four-line stanzas.

There is a further transcript, described as nineteenth-century, in Bodleian MS Eng. poet. e.8 (ff. 3b–4a), headed "To the Tune of the Broom," and also addressed to Celia. This version consists of eight quatrains, as in Steele's text, but grouped into four eight-line stanzas and in a different order, with lines 25–32 appearing before lines 17–24. This may be a simple mistranscription or else may derive from a song-book adaptation (as the heading perhaps suggests).

The poem is here reprinted from the text in the *Poetical Miscellanies* and the textual notes record the verbal variants in Pope's edition (22) and the Ballard transcript (TS).

## Textual Notes

| | |
|---|---|
| 1 | have been] 14, 22; were once TS |
| 3 | careless] 14, 22; chearful TS |
| 4 | but as] 14, 22; not so TS |
| 7 | flying] 14, 22; fleeting TS |
| 8 | a] 14; one TS, 22 |
| 11 | sweet] 14, 22; soft TS |
| 13–16 | This stanza appears in TS (with, however, the variants "And" for "An" in line 13 and "Celia" for "*Nancy*" in line 15) and in 14, but is omitted in 22. |
| 23 | a] 14, 22; her TS |
| 24 | Her ever] 14, TS; my *Nancy* 22 |
| 27 | And hardly] 14, TS; Nor ever 22 |
| 28 | be] 14, 22; were TS |
| 31 | while] 14, 22; whilst TS |

## To a Young Lady

This poem was first published in Steele's *Poetical Miscellanies* (pp. 63–64); Pope, however, did not include it in his edition, so that there is only the one authoritative text and no variants. The poem was, however, reprinted in a volume of *Poetical Miscellanies* "Publish'd by Mr. J. Gay" (Dublin, 1729; Case 355). This book seems not connected at all with John Gay. The text of TP's poem (on p. 18) is verbally identical with Steele's.

The Congleton inventory of TP's works (for which see Appendix), listing the four poems that appeared in Steele's *Miscellanies*, described it as "To a young Lady / ⟨Lady⟩ Miss [?]". The name is almost illegible, and could be "Tollet" or "Joliet". In either case, it is a piece of evidence that there was a real "young lady."

The story of Phoebus and Daphne comes from Ovid's *Metamorphoses* 1.452–567.

## *Anacreontick* ("Gay Bacchus")

This poem is textually the most complicated of the group of four first published in Steele's *Poetical Miscellanies* (where it appears on pp. 64–68). There is an autograph text in the Congleton "Satires" Notebook (ff. 40b–42a) that agrees in the main with the 1714 text. When the poem was reprinted in Pope's edition, however, numerous changes were made. Apart from stylistic revisions, the scene of the poem was changed from Button's Tavern to Estcourt's. We do not know whether TP himself or Pope was responsible for these changes.

There is a transcript of the poem in BL Lansdowne MS 852 (ff. 66b–67b). This is of interest since in several passages it agrees with the Congleton manuscript against 1714, and in two places it preserves what seems to be an intermediate reading (lines 9 and 18). We have therefore recorded its variants in the textual notes.

The poem is here reprinted from the 1714 text, with variants from the "Satires" Notebook (MS), the Lansdowne transcript (TS), and Pope's edition (22) recorded in the textual notes. The "MS" readings refer to the latest readings of the MS; the corrections made to the MS itself are recorded in the textual notes to the "Satires" Notebook. The poem was included in many eighteenth-century poetical miscellanies.

The poem can be dated within narrow limits. Estcourt opened his Bumper Tavern on 1 January 1712 and died in August 1712. But TP's poem evidently began as a compliment to Daniel Button, Addison's ex-servant, whom he set up in a tavern early in 1712, so the change of name does not materially affect the question of the date of the poem. Goldsmith claimed that TP "applied the characters to some of his friends" (3:424), but this seems most unlikely.

As Goldsmith pointed out (3:424), the poem is in part an adaptation of a Latin poem, the "Gratiarum Convivium" of Aurelius Augurellus (c. 1440–1524). TP could have read this poem in a collection of neo-Latin poems, the editing of which is often attributed to Francis Atterbury: Ἀνθολογία, *seu Selecta quaedam Poemata Italorum qui Latine Scripserunt* (1684; Wing A3476). This was the anthology that Pope subsequently

enlarged as *Selecta Poemata Italorum* (1740). The poem is here reprinted
from the 1684 edition, pp. 135–36:

Invitat olim Bacchus ad coenam suos
    Comon, Jocum, Cupidinem.
Discumbit una Liber, atque Amor; Jocus
    Comosque contra proxime;
Illis decentes subministrant Gratiae
    Grati saporis pocula:
Succosque miscent, et venena temperant
    Multi vicissim palmitis.
Inusitato proluunt se nectare
    Plene sodales uvidi,
Ac forte iusto plus parum dulcedine
    Lactante capti ingurgitant.
Hic inter aegros incipit verbis Deos
    Ridenda primum rixula.
Graves Amori Bacchus obiectat dolos,
    Quibus frequenter utitur.
Illi Cupido vana ludens gaudia
    Blaesasque voces exprobrat.
Como Iocus risus leves, Comus Ioco
    Sales ineptos obiicit.
Mox in capillos, atque ocellos advolant,
    Manusque nectunt parvuli
Adsunt sorores illico tres perditis,
    Pacemque suadent optimae.
Tandem sagittas, et pharetram clanculum
    Bacchus Cupidini involat.
At vi nitentem florida Iocus coma
    Como coronam diripit.
Sic inde scissis crinibus cedens Amor
    Matri fit obviam ebrius.
Comus facetos ad viros se proripit
    Per angiportum devium.
Bacchus, Iocusque contrahunt foedus, brevi
    Mox desiturum tempore.
Ast ut propinquans sordidum natum mero
    Venus madentem conspicit:
Irata secum, limpidum ad fontem manu
    Apprensum et haerens attrahit.
Huic rore puro protinus lavat sacri
    Crines solutos verticis.
Pectitque, et aegre extricat, ac dat undique
    Collo nitenti pendulos.
Sed forte oberrans roscidam manus cutim
    Contingit acri pectine.
Tum laesus ille subdit accensam pio

Facem parentis pectori.
Ambusta at ipsa (ut erat) in undas prosilit
 Secum trahens Cupidinem.
Fons unus ergo sic levatos dispari
 Ambos calore liberat.

## Textual Notes

| | |
|---|---|
| 1 | *Estcourt's*] 14, TS, 22; B——s MS |
| 2 | bespoke] 14, MS, TS; bespoke us 22 |
| 4 | *Joke*] 14, MS, TS; *Jocus* 22 |
| 6 | MS and TS agree with 14 in this line, except that they have "by" for "near"; 22 reads "Near *Comus, Jocus* plac'd". |
| 7 | Thus] 14, MS, TS; For 22 |
| | its] 14, 22; his MS, TS |
| 9 | In the MS this line reads, "To make it more deserve the God"; TS has the intermediate reading, "To make it better please the God"; 22 follows 14. |
| 13 | at] 14, 22; for MS, TS |
| 15 | While] 14, 22; And MS, TS |
| 18 | always got] 14, MS, 22; Chanc'd to get TS |
| 19 | For *Joke*] 14, MS, TS; *Jocus* 22 |
| | him] 14, MS, 22; them TS |
| 21 | call'd] 14, MS, 22; fill'd TS |
| | drank] 14, TS, 22; drunk MS |
| 22 | MS reads "& calld & drunk again"; TS and 22 agree with 14, except that 22 has "He" for "Then". |
| 25–28 | This stanza is found in 14, MS, and TS; it is omitted in 22 |
| 25 | run] 14; ran MS, TS |
| 26 | And] 14, MS; Which TS |
| 27 | Reflection] 14, TS; reflections MS |
| 28 | on Fire] 14, TS, 22; afire MS |
| 29 | Gay] 14, TS, 22; Plump MS |
| 31 | And] 14, MS, 22; While TS |
| 32 | With] 14, 22; & MS, TS |
| 33 | 22 reads "And *Jocus* droll'd on *Comus*' Ways"; MS and TS agree with 14. |
| 35 | While] 14, 22; & MS, TS |
| 37 | Talk soon] 14, 22; talking sett MS, TS |
| 39 | ye] 14, 22; you MS, TS |
| | drunk] 14, MS, 22; drank TS |
| 43 | And] 14, MS, TS; Nay 22 |
| 45 | rais'd] 14, 22; letts MS, TS |

| | |
|---|---|
| 49 | *Joke* taking] 14, MS, TS; *Jocus* took 22 |
| 50 | In Triumph] 14, MS, TS; And gayly 22 |
| 51 | in] 14, MS, 22; for TS |
| | pusht] 14, MS, 22; pulld TS |
| 52 | strove] 14, MS, 22; meant TS |
| 55 | *Beauty*] 14, MS, TS; *Venus* 22 |
| 56 | join'd] 14, 22; Joyn MS, TS |
| 60 | fat] 14, TS, 22; dull MS |
| 61 | MS and TS agree with 14, but 22 reads "*Bacchus* and *Jocus*, still behind,". |
| 66 | MS and TS read "Are couchd within my song"; 22 follows 14. |
| 67–68 | MS and TS read, "For tho the friendship may be dear / It cant continue long"; 22 follows 14. |

## Explanatory Notes

| | |
|---|---|
| Title | The poem is an "anacreontic" in the loose sense of a drinking song or a song celebrating the pleasures of drinking. |
| 1 | Gay] Possibly a slang term for drunk; Dearing and Beckwith so gloss it in Gay's *Wine* (line 62; *Poetry and Prose* [Oxford: Clarendon Press, 1972], 1:23; 2:477n), but cite no other examples or authority. |
| | *Estcourt*] Richard Estcourt (1668–1712), actor and dramatist; see the account in Philip H. Highfill et al., *A Biographical Dictionary of the London Stage* (Carbondale: Southern Illinois University Press, 1978), 5:97–102. Estcourt opened his Bumper Tavern in James Street, Covent Garden, early in 1712 (it was advertised as opening on 1 January in the *Spectator* No. 260 (28 December 1711; quoted, ed. Bond 1:42, n. 2). He died in August 1712; Steele wrote an obituary tribute to him in the *Spectator* No. 468 (27 August 1712; ed. Bond, 4:154–58). In the earlier version of the poem in the "Satires" Notebook, the tavern-keeper is "B——" (presumably Daniel Button). |
| 4 | *Comus*] The god of festive mirth and joy in later classical mythology; Milton ("Comus," lines 46–58) makes him the son of Bacchus and the enchantress Circe. |
| 65–68 | TP's moralizing conclusion departs from Augurellus's ending of his poem. |

# From Pope's *Works* (1717)

## To Mr. Pope

This poem was first printed among the commendatory verse prefixed to the collected edition of Pope's *Works* (1717; published early in June). The other tributes were from the duke of Buckingham, Lady Winchelsea, Wycherley, Francis Knapp, Elijah Fenton, and Simon Harcourt. Pope naturally reprinted the poem in his edition of TP's poems. It is here reprinted from the text of 1717, with the variants of 1722 recorded in the textual notes; in line 21 we have accepted 22's reading as a correction.

### Textual Notes

| | |
|---|---|
| 1 | and still with just] 17; yet still with due 22 |
| 21 | set] 22; sets 17 |
| 28 | Peeps o'er their head, and laughs] 17; Peep o'er their Heads, and laugh 22 |
| 45 | ye] 17; thy 22 |
| 80 | very far from thee.] 17; far, oh far from thee! 22 |
| 84 | sides] 17; Side 22 |
| 89 | when] 17; while 22 |

### Explanatory Notes

| | |
|---|---|
| 12 | play the Critic] The reference is to Pope's *Essay on Criticism* (1711). |
| 13 | the Dame] Lodona, the nymph who is turned into a tributary of the Thames in an Ovidian episode in *Windsor-Forest* (1713), lines 171–218. |
| 17 | *Belinda*] The heroine of *The Rape of the Lock* (1712), to which TP makes further references in lines 20–26. |
| 19 | *Ægypt's* Princess] Berenice; Callimachus's poem on her hair is referred to by TP in the "Life of Zoilus" (lines 204–6). Pope |

compares Belinda's hair to Berenice's in *The Rape of the Lock* 5.129.

27      a Satyr-train] Earl Wasserman, "The Limits of Allusion in *The Rape of the Lock*," *JEGP* 65 (1966): 441, n. 41, thought TP might here have taken a hint from the frontispiece of the 1714 edition of *The Rape of the Lock*. That, however, shows a single satyr, looking up rather than peeping over, and no graces. More probably TP was thinking of the serious and even grotesque elements in the poem itself. In the 1717 *Works,* the engraved headpiece to *The Rape of the Lock* has two masked satyrs in its border, suggesting this grotesque element. These illustrations are reproduced in Robert Halsband, *"The Rape of the Lock" and Its Illustrations* (Oxford: Clarendon Press, 1980).

29      Fame's fair Temple] In Pope's *Temple of Fame* (1715), Virgil's fame is described in lines 196–209.

34      *Strephon . . . Daphnis*] The competing swains in Pope's first *Pastoral* ("Spring"); Damon (referred to by TP in line 35) judges their contest.

48      *Homer*] The first volume of Pope's translation of the *Iliad* was published in 1715; the third volume (containing Books 9–12) appeared at about the same time (June 1717) as the edition of Pope's *Works* in which TP's poem was published.

65      new designs] This reference is unclear, although it must be to the projects that Pope intended to move on to after he had completed the translation of Homer. It is tempting to see here a reference to Pope's later plans for a moral epic; he may have discussed with TP some early version of this scheme.

70      *Windsor*] Probably a reference to TP's staying with Pope at his home at Binfield, near Windsor, helping him with his translation of Homer, in 1714; see *Pope Corr.* 1:222–23, 225–26.

78–86      Johnson thought these lines ("the description of barrenness") "borrowed from Secundus; but lately searching for the passage which I had formerly read I could not find it" (2.53). Johannes Secundus (Jan Everaerts, 1511–36) was a Dutch poet writing in Latin who was most famous for his Catullus-like *Basia* (written about 1533, but published posthumously in 1539). Secundus spent some time in Spain, employed as a secretary by the archbishop of Toledo. Many of his poems and letters addressed to the friends he had left behind speak of his exile in a harsh land. Two particular passages have been cited, but as neither is very close to TP's description it is perhaps safer to conclude that Johnson remembered the resemblance as closer than it actually was. Birkbeck Hill, in his edition of the *Lives of the Poets* (2:53, n. 3) cited the following lines from *Epistles* 1.1:

> Me retinet salsis infausta Valachria terris,
>     Oceanus tumidis quam vagus ambit aquis.
> Nulla ubi vox avium, pelagi strepit undique murmur,
>     Caelum etiam larga desuper urguet aqua.
> Flat Boreas, dubiusque Notus, flat frigidus Eurus:
>     Felices Zephyri nil ubi iuris habent.
> Proque tuis ubi carminibus, philomela canora,
>     Turpis in obscoena rana coaxat aqua.

Apparently independently of Hill, Dougald Crane, in *Joannes Secundus: His Life, Work, and Influence on English Literature* (Leipzig, 1931), 73, cited the following passage from Secundus's *Elegies* 3.12:

> Rara comes ubi luxuriat frondentibus arbor,
>     Rara stat artifici marmore fulta domus.
> Sed miser excisis in rupibus incola vivit,
>     Et crescit toto nil nisi spina solo,
> Et paucae ficus, et, non hic grata Minervae
>     Arida liventi languet oliva coma.

The poem of which these are lines 7–12 is reprinted in *Renaissance Latin Verse,* ed. Alessandro Perosa and John Sparrow (London: Duckworth, 1979), 485–86, from which we have taken our text.

85     unconscious of a flood] Pope may be echoing this line in his phrase "unconscious flood" in the *Dunciad* ("A" version, 2.292; TE 5:138).

# From Pope's *Poems on Several Occasions* (1717)

## A Translation of Part of *The Rape of the Lock*

This "Translation" was first published in *Poems on Several Occasions*, a poetical miscellany edited by Pope that was published on 13 July 1717 and that is now best known as *Pope's Own Miscellany*, the title under which it was edited by Norman Ault (1935). The poem was subsequently included in Pope's edition of TP's poems. In 1717 the "Translation" was printed in italic, with the original passage from *The Rape of the Lock* in roman on the facing page. In 1722 the "Translation" and the original were both printed in roman. We have followed 1717 in this respect. We have, however, accepted two corrections made to the text in Pope's edition. In line 3, the terminal punctuation is a comma in 1717 and a semicolon in 1722. In line 21, "reparant" in 1717 is corrected to "reparat" in 1722. Otherwise the two texts are verbally identical.

A transcript of the "Translation" in BL Stowe MS 973 (f. 28a) has three variants. Two are evident errors: "Hîc" for "Hâc" in line 6; and "qua" for "quae" in line 9. But "reparat" for "reparant" in line 21 is the corrected reading; unless the transcriber was able to make this correction himself, it suggests that the transcript was copied from Pope's edition, as seems likely with the other TP poems included in the manuscript.

Goldsmith tells an anecdote about the origin of this poem:

> I am assured that it was written upon the following occasion. Before the Rape of the Lock was yet completed, Pope was reading it to his friend Swift, who sat very attentively, while Parnell, who happened to be in the house, went in and out without seeming to take any notice. However he was very diligently employed in listening, and was able, from the strength of his memory, to bring away the whole description of the toilet pretty exactly. This he versified in the manner now published in his works, and the next day when Pope was reading the poem to some friends, Parnell insisted that he had stolen that part of the description from an old monkish manuscript. An old paper with the Latin verses was soon brought forth, and it was not till after some time that Pope was delivered from the confusion which it at first produced (3:425–26).

This story is too evidently apocryphal to require critical examination; the genesis of the poem was surely as a Scriblerian jest in 1713–14. The description of Belinda's toilet is from *The Rape of the Lock*, canto 1, lines 121–48.

"Leonine" verse (so-called either from Leoninus, a canon of Saint Victor's in Paris, or from Pope Leo II) is a term used for various kinds of rhyming Latin hexameters or elegiac couplets. Such rhymes occur occasionally in classical writers (in Ovid, for example), but whole poems written in such forms are postclassical. It was particularly popular in the twelfth century, hence TP's description of it as "the manner of the ancient monks." We do not know which particular poems of this kind TP had read.

# Poems from *Poems on Several Occasions*

For a general discussion of Pope's edition of TP's poems, see the Introduction to this edition, section 2; and for bibliographical details, see the Bibliography (A10 and B1). The poems that follow are those that were first printed in Pope's edition, and Pope's order has been retained. Pope's edition serves as the copy-text in each case, and any departures from it are recorded in the textual notes to the individual poem.

When Pope's edition was reprinted in 1726, numerous changes were made to spelling (most of which were presumably compositorial), and some to punctuation (for some at least of which Pope was probably responsible), and there are also a few verbal variants. While these changes have a certain interest for the light they might throw on Pope as tinkering editor, they also mark the beginning of the gradual process of modernization that TP's poems underwent during the course of their numerous eighteenth-century reprintings. We have not, therefore, recorded them in the textual notes, since their interest is historical rather than textual. Only in a few cases where the punctuation of 1722 clearly required emendation have we had recourse to the 1726 edition to supply a correction.

## Hesiod

According to Goldsmith, this "very fine illustration of an hint from Hesiod . . . was one of his earliest productions, and first appeared in a miscellany, published by Tonson" (3:424). So far as is known, however, the poem's first appearance was in the 1722 *Poems on Several Occasions*. Goldsmith may possibly have been confusing "Hesiod" with one of the poems that appeared in Steele's *Poetical Miscellanies* (which was published by Tonson). Alternatively, he may have seen the poem reprinted in volume 2 of *Miscellany Poems* (5th ed., London, 1727, 217–18) and assumed that the poem had appeared in earlier editions of this miscellany (which it had not), and confused it with the Dryden *Miscellany Poems* collections that were indeed published by Tonson. The first reference that we have to the poem is in Pope's letter to Parnell of March or April 1717, where he speaks of "the story of Pandora, and the Eclogue upon Health" as "two of the most beautiful things I ever read" (*Pope Corr.* 1:396). While Pope's remarks need not mean that he had not seen the poems before, it seems unlikely on general stylistic grounds that "Hesiod" was an early poem. It is much more likely to date between 1714 and 1716.

A longer text of this poem was contained in the MS used by the editor of the 1755 *Works.* The 1755 "Variations" (pp. 203–4) give seven additional passages amounting to twenty lines in all; together with the repetitions of the refrain (see textual note to lines 117–18), which would add another eight lines, this would have made the earlier text consist of 284 lines against 256 in Pope's text. In the same letter as quoted above, Pope spoke of his intention to "take the liberty you allow me" with the poems TP has sent. But we have no way of knowing to what extent, if at all, Pope rather than TP was responsible for the differences between the 1722 text and that in the manuscript used by the 1755 editor. For the reasons outlined in the Introduction, we have decided to reprint Pope's text and to record the 1755 "Variations" in the textual notes.

"Hesiod" belongs to a tradition of antifeminist writing that can be traced back to the famous poem on women by Semonides, which Addison had lately popularized through a prose translation in the *Spectator* No. 209 (30 October 1711). Because of the commonplace nature of the antifeminist material, it is hardly profitable to look for specific parallels between TP's poem and (for example) *The Rape of the Lock,* although there are obviously some general resemblances. TP's major sources for the story of Pandora are Hesiod, *Works and Days,* lines 47–105, and *Theogony,* lines 535–616; specific parallels and notable differences are cited in the explanatory notes. TP's poem is a skillful conflation of his Hesiodic sources, combining the more detailed account of the *Works and Days* with the more misogynistic slant of the *Theogony.* TP also expands the "machinery" of the poem, giving the gods (whom he Latinizes) more prominent roles. TP has added to his Hesiodic sources an account of the death of Hesiod that is partly his own invention and partly drawn from classical sources.

**Textual Notes**

44      mingled . . . softer] 22; lovely . . . mingling 55
88      +55:

Whatever shining gemms the Nymphs by land,
What orient pearl the Nymphs by sea command.

94 +55:
Fine links in golden chains for bracelets hung,
Gay buckles sparkling round about the tongue,
And brazen pins, a num'rous aid on earth,
From whence new turns of fashion find a birth;

95 And] 22; But 55
104 +55:
On which dissembl'd Nature seem'd to yield
Her painted gardens in a silken field,)

117–18 In 55 the editor noted that "In the manuscript, at the end of
every six lines thro' the whole Song of the Fates, the two first
lines of it come in as a burthen."

126 *Women* have Time, to sacrifice] 22; Not born to labour
Women live 55

168 +55:
For Women pain'd to conquer when they yield,
But keep from empire while they keep the field:

174 fatal . . . tempting] 22; faithless . . . faithless 55
180 +55:
What rocks, what shelves within her bosom hide,
Ah! where the wrecks are frequent leave to ride.

199 whining, and of] 22; whining court, the 55
204 +55:
Expence on fashions tho' the wealth decay,
Tho' still we see the danger, fret, and pay;

205 Expence, and] 22; the curse of 55
210 +55:
As men who failing touch on Libyan land,
See brinded Panthers scour the desart sand,
Fierce Wolves and Tigers wand'ring swains engage,
And scaly Dragons fill the realm with rage;
If still the distant breaks are heard to roar,
Much what they view they dread, and fear for more.

250 inscribes the Moral on] 22; the point reversing graves 55

### Explanatory Notes

10 to vindicate the Fair] By causing the death of Hesiod (lines
233–44). Although partly based on traditional sources, TP's
interpretation of the death seems to be his own addition. The

poet Stesichorus is said to have been blinded for writing a lampoon on Helen, and others were punished for anti-feminist activities, but not (in the classical sources) Hesiod.

15      no matter where or when] Compare Pope: "This Phoebus promis'd (I forget the year)" (*To a Lady*, line 283; TE 3.2:73).

19–30    Based on *Works and Days*, lines 47–58, and *Theogony*, lines 535–69 (which gives a more detailed account of the origin of the quarrel).

31–146   Considerably expanded from *Works and Days*, lines 59–82, and *Theogony*, lines 570–84. The "Song of the Fates" (lines 117–42) is not in Hesiod, and many of the satiric touches (e.g., lines 35, 68, 76, and 95–96) are TP's additions.

69–76    On the role of Hermes in the myth of Pandora, see Norman O. Brown, *Hermes the Thief* (Madison: University of Wisconsin Press, 1947), 52–65.

87      decent *Graces*] Possibly a recollection of the "decentes . . . Gratiae" of Augurellus's *Gratiarum Convivium*, line 5, which TP translated as "Each sweet engaging *Grace*" in his "Anacreontick" ("Gay Bacchus"), line 10.

117–42   The "Song of the Fates" is not in Hesiod, though its substance is based on *Theogony*, lines 590–612.

131–36   Cf. *Theogony*, lines 594–602.

145     *Pandora*] TP omits Hesiod's explanation (*Works and Days*, lines 81–82) of the meaning of Pandora's name.

147–80   Cf. *Works and Days*, lines 83–89. TP departs from Hesiod's account in several respects. In Hesiod, it is Hermes and not "the Winds" (line 147) who brings Pandora to Man.

151     golden Coffer] In line 191 it is called a "Box"; in Hesiod, Pandora carries a πίθος or jar (*Works and Days*, line 94). Pandora's box is a Renaissance invention; Dora and Erwin Panofsky trace it to Erasmus's confusion of πίθος with "pyxis"; *Pandora's Box: The Changing Aspects of a Mythical Symbol*, 2d ed. (Princeton: Princeton University Press, 1962), 13–19.

155     the Man] Unnamed; in Hesiod, it is Epimetheus who, receiving Pandora, ignores his brother Prometheus's warning not to accept a gift from Zeus.

155–68   TP's account of this encounter has an erotic element that is not in Hesiod.

176     the flatt'ring Deep] TP's phrase may have been influenced by Lucretius's "placidi pellacia ponti" (2.559 and 5.1004).

181–90   Expanded from *Works and Days*, lines 90–93.

190     golden Age] A familiar idea, mentioned in Hesiod (*Works and*

*Days,* lines 109–20); but TP may have had in mind Ovid's description, in *Metamorphoses* 1.89–112.

191–210 Cf. *Works and Days,* lines 94–101; in Hesiod, Pandora is made responsible for opening the jar and bringing the miseries it contained upon mankind. In Hesiod, only Hope remained in the jar; TP significantly omits any reference to this.

216 In the *Theogony* (lines 22–34) Hesiod describes his receiving an olive branch from the Muses themselves; in "The Contest of Homer and Hesiod" he is supposed to have won a tripod (Loeb ed., p. 587). The linking of the prize with his telling of the Pandora story seems to be TP's own.

217–44 Apart from the addition of Love's revengeful plot against Hesiod for satirizing women, TP's account of the death of Hesiod broadly follows the classical sources. These are conveniently collected in A. W. Mair's translation of Hesiod's *Poems and Fragments* (Oxford, 1908), xxx–xxxv. TP omits the oracle that warns Hesiod that he would die in the grove of Nemean Zeus to introduce his idea of the revenge of Love. In the traditional sources Hesiod stays with two brothers, who kill him because they suspect him of seducing their sister; their names vary, as does whether Hesiod is guilty or not. In TP's version, Hesiod seems not to have met the girl and is not staying with the brothers; this emphasizes the chance nature of the means that Love uses to take revenge. In the traditional sources, Hesiod's body is cast into the sea, carried ashore by dolphins after three days, and given a handsome burial. TP retains only the dolphins from this account.

227–28 The names of the lovers seem to be TP's invention. In the traditional accounts the girl lives at Locris and the seducer is a stranger. Plutarch (*Septem Sapientium Convivium* 19) makes the stranger a Milesian; TP perhaps misremembered Plutarch here.

251–56 This epitaph seems to be TP's invention. In "The Contest of Homer and Hesiod" an inscription supposed to have been placed on the poet's tomb is given (Loeb ed., p. 589) and the *Greek Anthology* contains other sepulchral epigrams, but TP seems to have used none of these.

# Song ("When thy beauty")

There is an autograph manuscript of a longer (four-stanza) and ear-
lier version of this poem in the Congleton "Lyrics" Notebook (ff. 5a–b).
This manuscript establishes TP's authorship of the poem, placed in some
doubt by its attribution to Pope by Lord Peterborough in an undated
letter to Mrs. Howard (BL Add. MS 22625). In this letter Peterborough
quotes the poem as it appears in Pope's edition, except that the last line of
each stanza is lengthened by the repetition of a phrase ("you dazzle", "a
woman", "a woman"). This attribution is discussed in TE 6:436–37,
which concludes that Pope may have reworked the poem sufficiently for
his friends to have regarded it as essentially his own. Although TP's
authorship is now beyond doubt, Pope's share in the differences between
the poem as it appears in the "Lyrics" Notebook and the version that
appeared in 1722 remains, as with the other poems in his edition,
uncertain.

A transcript of the poem in BL Stowe MS 972 follows Pope's text
except for minor variants probably due to miscopying.

The "Song" is here printed as it appears in 1722; for the early version,
see the text in the "Lyrics" Notebook. The poem was frequently re-
printed in eighteenth-century miscellanies and song books.

# Song ("Thyrsis")

This poem can be traced through three stages of composition. The
first, represented by a ten-line version of the first stanza only, is found in
the Congleton "Lyrics" Notebook (f. 2b). The second version, consisting
of three eight-line stanzas, was printed among the 1755 "Variations"; it
ends with an "&c", presumably indicating that the last stanza was the
same as in Pope's text. The third version is the one printed in Pope's
edition, where the poem consists of three stanzas of six lines and a fourth
of eight lines. Since we can be sure that it was TP who cut the first stanza
from ten to eight lines, there is no reason to suppose that he was not also
responsible for the further pared-down version that appeared in 1722.

There is a transcript of the poem in BL Stowe MS 972 (ff. 31b–32a);
its text follows Pope's edition, from which it was probably copied.

We print all three versions. The earliest form of the first stanza will be
found in the "Lyrics" Notebook; the intermediate text given in the 1755
"Variations" is reprinted in the textual note below, while Pope's version
has been accepted as our text above.

## Textual Note

THYRSIS, a young and am'rous swain,
  Saw two, the beauties of the plain,
And both their charms prepar'd a chain,
    And both his heart subdue;
Gay Caelia's eyes appear'd so fair,
They dazzl'd, while she pull'd the snare;
Sabina's easy shape and air
    With softer magic drew.

He haunts the stream, he haunts the grove,
Where-e'er the friendly rivals rove,
Lives in a fond romance of love,
    And seems for each to dye;
'Till each a little spiteful grown,
They make their faults to Thyrsis known,
Sabina Caelia's shape run down,
    And she Sabina's eye.

Their envy made the shepherd find
Those eyes which love cou'd only blind,
Thus both the chains of both unbind,
    And set the lover free:
No more he haunts the grove or stream,
The flow'ry walk of either dame,
Or with a true-love knot and name,
    Engraves a wounded tree, &c.

# *Anacreontick* ("When Spring came on")

Goldsmith says that this poem is "taken from a French poet, whose name I forget, and as far as I am able to judge of the French language, is better than the original" (3:424).

There is a heavily corrected autograph manuscript of this poem among the Congleton papers. The manuscript is far from clear and is TP's most thoroughly worked-over extant manuscript; as such, it is of unusual interest.

In the textual notes, the corrections made in the manuscript are recorded, so far as they can be deciphered, and also the differences between the MS and 1722.

## Textual Notes

The MS is a single folded sheet (folded size $168 \times 106$ mm); the poem is written on ff. 1a–2a, with f. 2b blank. The MS was evidently begun as a fair copy. There is only one heavily revised passage before line 54 (lines 39–40), but the poem's ending has been very thoroughly worked over. We therefore present the textual record in two parts: for lines 1–54 in the conventional way, but from line 55 to the end in the form of a conjecturally reconstructed account of how TP seems to have revised the poem.

| | |
|---|---|
| Title | The MS has "An Anacreontick." |
| 1 | WHEN] ⟨As⟩ MS |
| | Delight] ⟨delights⟩ MS |
| 5 | yonder Piny Grove] The sequence of readings in the MS seems to be: "yonder spiring grove"; "yon aspiring grove"; "yonder poplar grove"; "yonder piny grove". Having settled on the final version, TP wrote it out again more clearly. (The *OED* quotes "aspiring tree" from a 1707 manual of husbandry.) |
| 7 | There is no new paragraph in the MS. |
| | Green was] ⟨All green⟩ MS |
| | Robe] ⟨suit⟩ MS |
| 8 | Where-e'er] ⟨& where⟩ MS |
| | trod] ⟨treads⟩ MS |
| | 'twas] The MS originally read "tis as", which seems to have been successively altered to "tis" and "twas"; but it is unclear how these changes correlate with the other variants in the line. |
| 9 | turn'd] ⟨movd⟩ MS (there is also an illegible intermediate reading) |
| 15 | finds] ⟨found⟩ MS |
| 16 | wait] ⟨stood⟩ MS |
| 17 | Aside] ⟨Beside⟩ MS |
| 18 | wait] 22; yet MS (This is the first substantive reading, apart from the title, where the MS as finally worded does not agree with 22.) |
| 21 | *Smiles*] ⟨mirth⟩ MS |
| 22 | Conspir'd] This is the original reading of the MS, where it has been canceled in favor of "Contend", an interesting example of 22 reverting back to an earlier reading. |
| 25 | The MS originally read "fluttring, hopping"; "hopping" has been underlined and rewritten above the line, before |

|       | "fluttring". This is a clear example of TP's use of underlining to indicate his dissatisfaction with a reading. |
|-------|--------|
| 26    | from] ⟨of⟩ MS |
| 27–28 | In the MS these lines read: "to fledge the darts that learn to fly / for all the year returning by". |
| 29–30 | In the MS this couplet originally read: "Tis thus they meet in evry wood, / When every spring renews yᵉ blood,". TP then replaced "meet" by "Joyn" and altered the second line to begin "As e're[?] the spring". At one point the second line read "springs renew". Finally TP revised the couplet to read as in 22, except that the MS retains "Joyn" for "meet" in line 29. |
| 34    | Which] 22; That MS |
|       | each] 22; a MS |
| 35    | tow'ring] ⟨soaring⟩ MS |
| 36    | Hearts] ⟨Lover⟩ MS |
|       | accept] In the MS the sequence of readings seems to be "takes"; "receives"; "receive" (at which point "Lover" must have been changed to "Hearts"); "accept". |
|       | their] 22; a a MS (the repetition presumably inadvertent) |
| 37    | painted Eye] ⟨hundred eyes⟩ MS |
| 38    | airy] ⟨dazzled⟩ MS |
|       | *Lovers* dye] The successive MS readings seem to be "Lover lyes" and "Lovers lye". |
| 39–40 | In the MS, the following couplet originally came after line 38: "If scornfull arrows wound yᵉ sight / The milky swan supports the flight". TP changed "milky" to "snowy" before deleting the whole couplet and interlining an early version of lines 39–40: "With carefull dames & frugall men / The shafts are speckled by the hen". A further couplet omitted in 22 follows line 40 in the MS. It originally read: "If others fly with kinder Love / They take their silver from yᵉ dove;" and was subsequently revised to read: "while others glide with tender Love / & ⟨fly [followed by a further word, canceled and illegible]⟩ shine in silver from yᵉ dove;". |
| 41–44 | These couplets are written in the MS in reverse order, but are marked in the outer margin with "2" and "1" respectively to indicate that they were to be transposed. |
| 42    | wins] This is the original reading of the MS, where it is canceled in favor of "takes", which is itself deleted. |
| 44    | warbling *Finch*] 22; sweet serene MS |
| 46    | Down fall] 22; Fall down MS |
| 50    | In the MS this line originally read: "This I viewd in yonder |

grove". TP then deleted "This" and wrote first "trembling"
and then "waving grove".

| 52 | deal with] ⟨work by⟩ MS |
| 53 | both support] ⟨each perform⟩ MS |
| 54 | gives the] ⟨gives her⟩ MS |

From this point on, TP's changes are best followed through a con-
jectural narrative. Five stages can be distinguished from the point at
which TP must have written out the poem as far as line 54 (how far he
had already revised the poem to this point is, of course, uncertain).

(1) TP wrote three and a half lines as follows (they are here lettered
for ease of reference):

    *a*  From her y$^e$ powr to speed [?] flee,
    *b*  Its act of speed it gains of me
    *c*  Tis some attraction in the mind
    *d*  That ever helps y$^e$ dart

The last line was presumably to have ended with "find", but at this point
TP must have stopped and gone back to revise *c*, changing "in the mind"
to "still we [?] find"; this allowed him to revise and complete *d* as "helps
on y$^e$ dart from mind to mind". Either now or later *a* was revised to read
"From her it gains the powr to flee" and in *b* "speed" was changed to
"flight". Even as revised these lines are not very satisfactory, and al-
though they are uncanceled in the MS, it is not surprising that they do
not appear in 22.

(2) Having reached at least a provisional form of *a–d*, TP added a
further four lines that are clearly an early version of lines 57–60 in the
published text:

    Unwingd by her it scarcely flys
    It shakes & shuffles in y$^e$ skys.
    But if y$^e$ Soules alike be found
    From both to both I dart y$^e$ wound

In the first of these lines, "her" is apparently written over a word that is
probably "the". At some stage these lines were revised: in line 57 "it
scarcely" was changed to "my weapon"; in line 58 "It shakes & shuffles"
was changed to "To shake & shuffle".

(3) TP seems next to have written an insertion in the inner margin of
f. 1b. These four lines, written vertically up the page, are the germ of
lines 55–56 in the published text:

    *e*  Then why shoud mortalls pine in cares
    *f*  to match with soules averse to theyrs?
    *g*  They fondly court, & Idely sigh,
    *h*  If Nature cross them, so do I.

Two marginal crosses seem to indicate that the insertion was to come after line *b*. This insertion was itself revised at some point: in line *f*, "pair" was written above "match" (which was not, however, canceled); in line *g*, "They fondly" was changed to "fondly they"; and in *h* "cross" was deleted in favor of an almost illegible insertion, probably "hinders", itself subsequently canceled.

(4) The bottom half of f. lb being now in a confused state, TP crossed out everything after line *b* and rewrote the ending of the poem at the top of f. 2a. The first four lines correspond to *e–h*, the next four to lines 57–60, and the last two make their first appearance in the MS:

> Then why shoud Mortalls pine in Cares
> To match with soules averse to theirs?
> Fondly they court, & Idely sigh;
> If Nature Cross them, so do I:
> Unwingd by her my weapon flys
> To shake & shuffle in the Skys.
> But if in common charms I find
> Where Nature joyns you Mind to Mind
> These plume⟨s⟩ my shaft, I fix the darts,
> And wound them both from both their hearts.

Under "hearts" TP has made the characteristic horizontal stroke that he uses in the Congleton notebooks to mark the end of a poem. The absence of this mark at the foot of f. lb is evidence that the poem was not meant to end at that point.

(5) These ten lines on f. 2a were subsequently further revised. Lines *e–f* were rewritten as "Then Mortall⟨s⟩ vainly leave to pine / To match with soules averse to thine"; unhappy with this, TP seems to have wanted to revert to the previous wording (although since he had crossed some words out, this is not clear). No form of this couplet appears in 22. At the beginning of *g* TP tried out various combinations of "you", "fondly", and "they"; and in *h* he tried "you" instead of "them". This couplet is written out again just under the last lines of the poem, where it reads as in 22 except that the MS here has "you" for "ye". Lines 57–58 were revised to read as in 22, except that the MS has "in" for "through" in line 58. Lines 59–60 were similarly revised to read as in 22, except that the MS retains "common" where 22 has *"mutual";* and TP wrote "gifts" above "charms", but deleted it. In line 60, "Where Nature joyns" is not canceled, but TP has written, "By which she suits ⟨them⟩". The remainder of the line is as in 22. In line 61 TP changed "These plumes" to "They plume" before settling on "They wing", which is 22's reading; but the MS retains the singular "shaft", and TP changed "darts" to "dart". In line 62 the final reading of the MS is "And strike through both from both your hearts." The final *s* of "hearts" is crossed out, apparently in response to the

change to "dart" above; but "heart" makes no sense, and TP must have
meant to change "dart" back to "darts" (as he or Pope did in 22).
Underneath the last line TP has written what seems to be an incomplete
alternative: "& strike through both your bosome ["each" written above
"bosome"] through both ["either" written above "both"] your". Under-
neath this is written the final version of lines 55–56. Above "averse to
sigh" (and below "either/both your") are the words "Ye vainly". Finally,
after a space of about 5 mm, "the sweet" is written in a slightly different
hand; if related to the poem, these words may refer to line 44, where the
MS has "The sweet serene".

## A Fairy Tale in the Ancient English Style

This poem is a version of a widely dispersed folktale. It belongs to type
503 ("The Gifts of the Little People: Dwarfs take hump of a man and
place it on another man") in Antti Aarne's *The Types of the Folk-Tale*,
translated and enlarged by Stith Thompson, 2d rev., (Helsinki:
Suomalainen Tiedeakatemia, 1961), 170–71. In TP's version, Edwin
takes part in a dance with fairies; other variants recorded in Aarne-
Thompson are that a wanderer plays for the fairies, adds to their song,
or lets them cut his hair. TP's Edwin loses his hump; a variant reward is a
gift of gold. Sir Topaz in TP's poem is given Edwin's hump; in other
versions the corresponding character is given coal instead of gold.

Numerous references to different versions of the tale are collected in
Stith Thompson, *Motif-Index of Folk-Literature*, rev. ed. (Copenhagen:
Rosenkilde and Bagger, 1955–58), where it is F.344.1. An Irish version,
"The Legend of Knockgrafton," is recorded in T. Crofton Crocker, *Fairy
Legends and Traditions of the South of Ireland*, ed. T. Wright (London, 1870),
14–22. Although it is there claimed to be "the foundation of Parnell's
well-known fairy tale" (20), this version differs in several respects from
TP's. Lusmore ( = Edwin) adds to the fairy's song, and Jack Madden
( = Sir Topaz) is an unpleasant hunchback, not a handsome rival in love.
Nevertheless, it seems probable that TP derived his story from an Irish
oral tradition, possibly from his *"Sybil-Nurse,"* as he himself claims (line
181).

On the contemporary vogue for "fairy" poems, see Woodman, 41.

Pope's edition provides the only substantive text of this poem. There is
a transcript in British Library Add. MS 4456; the few places where it
differs from Pope's text are plainly errors of copying. The same MS also
contains a transcript of "A Night Piece on Death" that is verbally identical
with Pope's text, from which both poems were probably copied.

### Explanatory Notes

71      *Mab*] "Mabh" is the name of an Irish Fairy, though "Mab" is better known from *Romeo and Juliet* (1.4.53); see W. J. Thoms, *Three Notelets on Shakespeare* (London, 1865), 92–108. Mab is Oberon's queen in Drayton's *Nymphidia* (1627).

91      *Robin*] For the background to this figure (Shakespeare's Puck), see *A Midsummer Night's Dream*, ed. H. H. Furness, 8th ed. (Philadelphia: J. P. Lippincott, 1923), 289–93; and Thoms, *Three Notelets on Shakespeare*, 48–59.

100      *Oberon*] Oberon was a traditional name for the king of the fairies before Shakespeare; for a source in *The Boke of Huon of Burdeux*, see *A Midsummer Night's Dream*, ed. Harold Brooks (London: Methuen, 1979), 145–46.

157      *Will*] In *A Midsummer Night's Dream* (2.1.39) it is Puck who plays the part of will-o'-the-wisp. See further Thoms, *Three Notelets*, 59–72.

## The Vigil of Venus

This famous poem was certainly not written in the time of Julius Caesar, nor by Catullus, but its date and authorship remain uncertain. The most recent scholarly opinion places it in the early fourth century and attributes it to Tiberianus (Alan Cameron, as reported in *The Times*, 5 August 1978, 14). For Tiberianus, see *Minor Latin Poets*, Loeb ed., pp. 555–56.

TP's was the second translation into English, the first being by Thomas Stanley and published in his *Poems and Translations* (1647). Translations since TP's have been very numerous. In "Translations of the *Pervigilium Veneris* into English Verse," *Cambridge Journal* 5 (1952): 339–54, Wayland Hilton-Young divides the translators into the pedestrian, the individualist, and the balanced, and awards the palm to Stanley. TP is placed in the second category. Calling him "splendidly slapdash," Hilton-Young links him with Quiller-Couch as among translators who "in the enthusiasm the poem raised at first reading, seem hardly to have had time to look at it again" (p. 344). Although TP's rendering is certainly free at times, Hilton-Young exaggerates its distance from the Latin.

Sir Cecil Clementi's edition of the *Pervigilium Veneris* (3d ed. [Oxford: Basil Blackwell, 1936]) contains an account of the poem's discovery; facsimiles of the three manuscripts, with collations and descriptions; a discussion of the major attempts at rearranging the poem; a critical text and translation; extensive textual and explanatory notes; and an elaborate bibliography of the poem to about 1935.

TP must have shown his translation, perhaps in draft, to Pope before February 1716, when Jervas and Pope wrote urging him to send the poem to them (*Pope Corr.* 1:332–33). Pope seems not to have had available to him the Latin text which TP used, but if, as seems most likely, the translation was made after 1712, the standard edition for him to have used would have been the anonymous edition (usually attributed to Jean Le Clerc) published at Amsterdam in that year. This edition contains (1) a reprint of Rivinus's edition of 1644, with a text of the poem based on the Thuanus MS and copious notes collected from Pithoeus, Lipsius, Weitzius, and Douza (pp. 1–17); (2) a text of the poem based on the "S" MS, with the notes of Salmasius and Scriverius (pp. 18–42); (3) Rivinus's own commentary on the poem, with his conjecturally restored text (pp. 43–166); (4) an edition of Ausonius's *Cupid Crucified* (pp. 167–208; a translation of this poem by TP appears in the "Satires" Notebook); (5) indexes (unpaged).

It seems likely that TP used this edition, although of course he may never have reconstructed his own Latin text from the three available in Le Clerc's edition. Pope's Latin text is certainly based on the 1712 reprint of Rivinus's edition, which it follows very closely in spelling and punctuation. Even if he knew that this was the edition that TP had used, Pope evidently was not sure which emendations to incorporate from the notes. The evidence for his uncertainty is found in the "Errata" to the 1722 edition and in the canceled leaf D8. A copy of the 1722 edition in the Cambridge University Library (Y.21.65(1); probably but not certainly a copyright deposit copy) has leaf D8 in both its original and reprinted states. The uncanceled state of the leaf (so far as we are aware, unique) is here reproduced.

Pope had two reasons for canceling the leaf. The compositor had evidently misunderstood the way in which the Latin text was to face the corresponding portions of the English; since the alignment is correct in the later portion of the poem, the error was probably noticed at once. If it had not been for this, Pope might have left the leaf uncanceled and simply printed a list of errors. When the leaf was reprinted, three changes were made. One ("decidivo" for "decidiro" in line 17) seems to be the correction of a simple misprint. The other two (for which see the textual notes to lines 15 and 21) are changes made to the Latin text to bring it into line with TP's translation. Pope later detected other such errors, but was content to print a list of errata rather than to cancel and reprint the relevant leaves (see the textual notes to lines 15, 17, and 21). TP's translation is sufficiently free for it to be sometimes uncertain which reading he is rendering. Nevertheless, comparison of the translation with Pope's Latin text reveals several instances in which he seems clearly to have been rendering a different reading from Pope's; in these instances we have emended the text. In the textual notes to the Latin we have recorded: (a) our departures from Pope's text, and the source in the 1712 edition from which our reading is taken; (b) the few minor discrepancies between Pope's text and the "T" text of 1712; to show its closeness, we have departed from our usual practice and recorded any variant, however trivial. To have indicated in each case which of the alternative readings TP rejected would, however, have swelled the notes out of proportion. The *Pervigilium Veneris* was (and remains) a much-emended text, and the interested reader can best explore the problems further by consulting the 1712 edition itself. For a full commentary on the Latin poem, Clementi's edition should be consulted; in the textual notes we have referred to it in the case of a few of the most difficult cruxes.

### Textual Notes (Latin text)

| | |
|---|---|
| 1 | In the 1712 reprint of T, this line is printed in italic capitals. |
| 2 | vere] 22, Pithoeus; uer T |
| 5 | amorum] Pithoeus; amorem 22, T |
| 6 | casas] Pithoeus; gazas 22, T. TP's "Bow'rs" in line 11 was surely a translation of "casas", since "Arbours" (line 75, translating line 43 of the Latin) is below. |
| 9 | The line is corrupt in T: "Tuno quiuore de superhuc spumeo pont' de glouo". Pitheous emended as follows: "Tunc liquore de superno, spumeo ponti è globo". Pope's text follows Pithoeus, except that *e* is unaccented and "spumeo" was misprinted "spameo" (though this was corrected in the list of errata). But TP's "celestial Blood" (line 18) shows that he was translating Douza's reading "cruore", not "liquore", and we have emended the text accordingly. T does not indent the first line after the refrain, here or later in the poem. |
| 11 | Dionen] 22, Salmasius; Dione T |
| 14 | turgentes] Weitzius; surgentis 22, T. TP's "turgid Buds" (line 27) was surely a translation of "turgentes papillas", and we have emended accordingly. |
| | Favonî spiritu] 22, Pithoeus; Fabonî paritu T |
| 15 | toros stupentes] In the uncanceled state of D8, the phrase read "totos pentes", which is the reading of T. Pope emended to "toros tepentes" on the cancellans; this is Lipsius's conjecture (though with the spelling "thoros"). However, there is |

nothing in TP's translation to suggest warmth; we have there-
fore adopted Pithoeus's conjecture ("stupentes"), since TP's
lines 27–28 do contain the idea of inert buds being given life.

17      micant lacrymæ] 22, Lipsius; canat lacryme T

decidivo] 22, Weitzius; detadum T. In the uncanceled state of
D8, the word was misprinted "decidiro".

20      noctibus,] T;—. 22

21      virgines papillas] 22, Lipsius, Douza; virgineas papilla T. The
uncanceled state of D8 reads "virgineas".

22      Ipsa jussit] 22, Pithoeus; Ipiussit T.

mane] T; misprinted in 22 as "muae", corrected to "mane" in
the list of errata; the misprint is repeated in some copies of
the 1726 edition.

ut udæ] 22, Douza; tuæ T

23      Fusæ] 22, Lipsius; Fusta T. Lipsius also emended "prius" to
"aprino", seeing an allusion to the story of Narcissus.

osculis] 22, Pithoeus; oculis T

26      pudebit] 22, Pithoeus; pudent T

28      luco] 22, Pithoeus; loco T

myrteo,] T;— 22

32      nudus] 22, Pithoeus; durus T

33      neu quid] 22; quid T (the third "neu" evidently omitted in
error)

44      Poetarum] 22; Poetarum T

45      Decinent] This is a difficult reading. The original reading of
22 is "Detinent", corrected in the errata to "Decinent"; as an
explicit correction, we have felt bound to accept it. "Detinent"
is the reading of T, although most editors emend. It gives
some sense ("they while away the time"). "Decinent" is
Rivinus's reading. In his "Notae" on line 45 (pp. 91–93 in the
1712 edition), Rivinus discusses several possible emendations.
His notes are headed with his preferred reading of the line as
"Decinunt, & tota nox est pervigilata cantibus"; in the notes
themselves, however, he uses the form "Decinent", saying
that it is appropriate to Apollo but neither giving his meaning
nor quoting any authority for the word: "Quid vero speratu
facilius, quid planius, quid aptius, quid proprius Poetarum
Deum insequatur? quid choris tripudiantium, et consuetae
Pervigiliorum laetitiae convenientius, quid ad somnum pel-
lendum fortius, et melius faciat, quam *decinent*?" "Decinent" is
the reading of his reconstructed text (p. 92 in the 1712
edition). We have not been able to find any verb "decino" or

"decineo" in any dictionary of classical Latin. R. E. Latham's *Revised Medieval Latin Word-List* (1965) lists "decino" with the meaning "sing to a close", which would fit the context, but the date given is c. 1160.

50      annus] 22, Pithoeus; annis T

51      T reads (corruptly): "Hibla florum rumperest equant' ethne cāp-". 22 prints the line as emended by Lipsius, except that it adds the comma and has "Ænnæ" for Lipsius's "Ennæ". We have emended to "Ennæ", as required by TP's translation (line 92). Some editors prefer "Ætnæ", and Pope's reading may be the result of a confusion; "Ænnæ" seems not to be an alternative spelling.

53      fontes] Scriverius; montes 22, T. The emendation seems called for by TP's "Waters" in line 96.

55      nudo] 22, Pithoeus; nullo T

57      recentibus virentes] 22, Pithoeus; rigentibus vergentis T

59      pater roris] 22, Pithoeus; pat totis T

        nubibus,] Pithoeus;— 22, T

60      fluxit almæ] 22, Pithoeus; fluctus alma & T

61      fœtus] 22; fetus Pithoeus; fletus T

80      explicant tauri] This is the reading of 22's list of errata, and follows Pithoeus; 22 originally read "explicat aonii", which is T's reading. This is the line corrected by Lipsius in the self-praising way that TP ridicules in "The Remarks of Zoilus" (lines 397–8): "Aut ego me amo, aut Phoebus me amavit, cum correxi, *explicant agni latus:* Nec sane significantius exprimi potuit decubitus ille ovium in latus, quasi apricantium. Id enim solent super genistas, myricas & humiliores frutices." TP's translation follows Pithoeus rather than Lipsius.

81      tutus] Scriverius; tuus 22, T. The emendation seems required by TP's translation "Secure" (line 142).

85      Adsonat Terei puella] This is the reading of 22's list of errata, and follows Salmasius; the text of 22 reads "Adsonant Terei puellæ", following Pithoeus. T reads "Adsonant aërei puellæ".

88      No new paragraph in T.

89      chelidon] Pithoeus; celidon 22, T

        tacere] 22, Pithoeus; taceret T

## Textual Note (English text)

130      always] alwyas 22; corrected in the 1726 edition

## Explanatory Notes

17    that Day] The reference is to the story of the birth of Venus as recorded in Hesiod (*Theogony*, lines 126–206), in which Aphrodite (Venus) arises from the foam where blood from heaven (caused by Kronos's wounding of Ouranos) fell into the sea.

22    *Dione*] Originally the mother of Aphrodite, but often (as here) identified with Aphrodite herself.

25    the purple Year] For this phrase, see Arthur Johnston, " 'The Purple Year' in Pope and Gray," *Review of English Studies* 14 (1963): 389–93.

65    *Delia*] Diana, so called from the legend that she (Artemis) and Apollo were born on Delos.

69    if she cou'd persuade] It is possible that this phrase translates "si pudicam flecteret" from the one line in the poem that is found in the Salmasius MS but not in the Thuanus or Vienna MSS ("Ipsa vellet te rogare, si pudicam flecteret"), and therefore not in Pope's text, which is based on the reprint of the Thuanus MS in the 1712 edition. But the possibility does not seem strong enough to justify restoring the line, which would be out of place in a text based mainly on the Thuanus MS.

86    *Hybla*] For the possible identities of this place, see Clementi, pp. 239–40.

92    *Enna*] For Enna (Henna, in Sicily), and the alternative reading "Aetnae" (which Clementi prefers), see Clementi, p. 243.

120    *Troy*'s Remainder] The reference is to the Trojans who, led by Aeneas (son of Venus), left Troy to found Rome, the story of Virgil's *Aeneid*.

123    the Maid] Rhea Silvia, the vestal virgin who, raped by Mars, gave birth to Romulus and Remus, the traditional founders of Rome.

125    *Sabin* Dames] A reference to the fictitious episode in the early history of Rome (told by Livy, 1.9–10), in which the Romans forcibly carried off brides from among the Sabines.

149    *Philomela*] For the story of Philomela and her rape, see Ovid, *Metamorphoses*, 6.438–674.

163    *Amycle*] For the identity of the town of Amycle and explanations of its fall by silence, see Clementi, pp. 263–69.

# *Health, an Eclogue*

There is an autograph MS of this poem (called "An Eclogue") in the Congleton "Satires" Notebook (ff. 51a–53a). This version is much longer than Pope's text (116 lines against 78), and there are numerous verbal variants as well as omissions and transpositions of many lines. The various corrections made in the MS, as well as a summary of the main differences between the two texts (complete collation being impracticable) are given in the textual notes to the longer version.

Pope refers to this poem in his letter of March or April 1717 to TP, singling out "the story of Pandora, and the Eclogue upon Health" as "two of the most beautiful things I ever read" (*Pope Corr.* 1:396). Whether Pope had seen the longer version of the poem as it appears in the "Satires" Notebook or a text similar to the one he eventually published is uncertain. In either case his particular admiration of the poem seems strange.

The poem belongs to the "Georgic" tradition of poems in praise of country life. The most obvious contemporary example is Gay's *Rural Sports* (1713). The commentary on this poem in Dearing's and Beckwith's edition of Gay's *Poetry and Prose* contains much that is relevant to TP's "Health." The general influence of Milton's "L'Allegro" is also evident in the poem. A hymn to Health by Ariphron of Sicyon, cited by Athenaeus, *Deipnosophists* 15.702, Loeb ed. 7:273, has been mentioned as a source, but the resemblance is only a very general one (Woodman 44, 121n.)

The poem is here printed as it appears in Pope's edition, except that in line 34 "crow'd" has been corrected to "crowd," a correction made in the 1726 edition.

### Explanatory Notes

| | |
|---|---|
| 11 | *Etesian* Air] The "Etesian" winds are the winds that (in Mediterranean countries) blow from the northwest for about forty days every summer; here, they are thought of as giving relief from the heat of the summer. |
| 66 | *Tully's Tusculum*] Cicero's favorite villa, a country retreat near Rome and the scene of his *Tusculan Disputations*, the spirit of which friendly philosophical discussions TP here invokes. |
| 71 | The native *Bard*] Theocritus, the most admired Greek pastoral poet. |
| 73 | *Maro*] Virgil, the most admired Latin pastoral poet. |

## The Flies. An Eclogue

No direct source for this poem has been discovered, but it belongs to a type of Aesopic fable; it is Type 249 in Aarne and Thompson, *Types of the Folktale*, and J.711.1 (The Ant and the Lazy Cricket) in Stith Thompson's *Motif-Index of Folk-Literature*. A classical example is Phaedrus, 4.25 ("The Ant and the Fly").

Pope's edition is the only authority for this poem, from which it is here reprinted with the exception of minor corrections to the punctuation in lines 67 and 68, where we have adopted readings from the 1726 edition.

### Textual Notes

| | |
|---|---|
| 67 | *Love,*] 26; —. 22 |
| 68 | Dove:] 26; —, 22 |

### Explanatory Notes

| | |
|---|---|
| 23–27 | Such behavior was a regular target for contemporary satire; see, for example, the account of "Charles Easy" at the theater in the *Spectator*, No. 240 (5 December 1711; ed. Bond, 2:434–45). |
| 38 | Compare George Granville, Lord Lansdowne, "The Vision," line 31; "Cease, lover, cease, thy tender heart to vex" (Woodman 38, 121n.). |
| 42 | *Zephyretta*] The name of a sylph in *The Rape of the Lock* (2.112; TE 2:166), which TP may have recalled here. |
| 67 | *Trees* and whisp'ring *Breeze*] Pope gives these as examples of poetic clichés in the *Essay on Criticism*, lines 350–51 (TE 1:279); TP himself, however, uses them in the *Essay on the Different Styles of Poetry*, lines 201–2 and 355–56; in "Hannah," lines 39–40; and in "Solomon," lines 201–2. |

## An Elegy, to an Old Beauty

Pope's edition is the only authority for this poem, which Johnson called "perhaps the meanest" of TP's poems (2:53).

The theme of the poem is a commonplace one; it is found in Horace *Odes* 1.25, 3.15 and 4.13. See also Woodman 44 for English analogues. In the *Tatler* No. 52 (9 August 1709; ed. George A. Aitken [London, 1898],

2:20–27), Delamira bequeaths her fan to Virgulta and gives her instruction in the use of it, marking her own retirement from fashionable life. For the association of the fan with female affectation, see also the *Spectator*, No. 102 (27 June 1711; ed. Bond, 1:426–29), and Gay's poem *The Fan* (1714; published December 1713).

### Explanatory Notes

2          Frontlets] A frontlet is "a bandage worn at night to prevent or remove wrinkles" *(OED)*.

60         The wise *Athenian*] Socrates; the anecdote is recorded in Diogenes Laertius 2.25 (Loeb ed. 1:155); the list in line 62 is TP's addition.

## *The Book-Worm*

Two versions of this poem are extant: the longer and earlier ("A") survives in manuscript; the shorter and later ("B") was published in Pope's edition. The "A" version has 136 lines, the "B" version 100. The "A" version contains a number of topical references that help to date it; the changes in the "B" version remove many of these topicalities but do not introduce new ones, making it less easy to date.

The "A" version was probably written or at least completed late in 1714. It refers to Gildon's *New Rehearsal*, published in April 1714, and to Budgell's appointment to a government job, which took place in October 1714. Gay is represented in the poem by *The Shepherd's Week*, published in 1714. The favorable references to Addison and to Tickell would be most unlikely later than 1714, and impossible after Addison's sponsorship of Tickell's rival translation of Homer. Indeed, the absence of any reference to Pope's Homer is an important piece of negative evidence in favor of a date in 1714. There are no external references to the poem from as early as 1714.

The first external evidence is in a letter of Gay to TP of March 1716 in which Gay says, "I am obliged to your Bookworm," meaning presumably for the compliment TP pays him in the poem (*Letters*, ed. Burgess, p. 29). The poem is again referred to in Pope's letter of (?) 14 November 1716 to Charles Jervas, where Pope speaks of it in such a way as to leave it unclear whether he has seen the poem previously or not: "unless *Parnelle* sends me his *Zoilus* and *Bookworm* (which the Bishop of *Clogher*, I hear greatly extols) it will be shortly, *Concurrere Bellum atque Virum*" (*Pope Corr.* 1:371). The date of this letter is uncertain. What does seem clear is that

Pope links the poem with TP's "Zoilus" prose (which attacks Pope's adversaries in the Homer controversy), which suggests that he had seen or was expecting to see the poem in something like the "B" version, with the friendly references to the Addison circle cut out. While this is certainly not conclusive, it is one reason for attributing the changes made to the "B" version to TP himself.

A passage in the "A" version that is hard to explain is the compliment to Marlborough (see textual note to lines 69–74). It seems curious that in 1714 TP would have been prepared to bring in such a compliment where it is hardly called for. He had made favorable reference to Marlborough in "On Queen Anne's Peace" (1713), but in that poem it would hardly be unexpected.

The "A" version survives in two manuscripts from the Congleton papers. One is a probably late transcript of the whole poem, written in a large and rather childish hand, headed "I writ this from y^e original. on a book-worm." The other is an autograph manuscript of the poem from "Ile have my filet flame with red" (see textual note on line 42). The transcript was probably copied from the extant holograph, with which it is verbally identical. The transcript, however, makes no attempt to reproduce the spelling or punctuation of the original, and is particularly sparing in the use of capitals, even at the beginning of lines. With two exceptions (the couplet that followed line 33 of Pope's text, and the compliment to Marlborough replaced by lines 69–74 of Pope's text) the passages found in the MSS but not in 1722 are given in the 1755 "Variations." The manuscript available to the 1755 editor was thus probably very much the same as the extant manuscripts of this poem.

From an artistic point of view, Pope's text is certainly to be preferred. The omissions in 1722 remove many topical references (including the inapposite compliment to Marlborough) and some feeble couplets. Nevertheless, it remains an open question how far it represents TP's intentions rather than Pope's.

As with the other poems, we have decided to let Pope's text stand and to record the variations in the textual notes. "MS" refers to the autograph manuscript; "TS" to the transcript (which is, of course, not referred to after line 42); and "55" to the "Variations."

Goldsmith seems to have been the first to point out that the poem is an adaptation (he calls it an "unacknowledged translation") from a Latin poem by Theodore Beza (3:426). Goldsmith reproved "the wits of the last age" for so concealing their sources, but perhaps as Beza's *Poemata* had been reprinted in London in 1713 Pope expected the adaptation to be recognized. (Pope owned a copy of this edition, now at the Houghton Library at Harvard). Certainly TP's poem is longer, more elaborately and high-spiritedly mock-heroic: his book-worm takes on comic overtones of the dragon slain by Saint George; Satan crushed by Michael; the Hydra slain by Hercules; Antichrist; and the Python slain by Apollo. TP's references to his own contemporaries have no counterpart in Beza's poem. The following text of Beza's poem is taken from the 1713 edition; the closer parallels are recorded in the explanatory notes:

### Ad Musas

Si rogat Cereremque, Liberumque
Vitae sollicitus suae colonus,
Si Mavortis opem petit cruentus
Miles, sollicitus suae salutis:
Quid ni, Calliope, tibi, tuisque                             5
Iure sacra feram, quibus placere
Est unum studium mihi, omnibusque
Qui Vatum e numero volunt haberi?
Vobis ergo ferenda sacra, Musae.
Sed quae victima grata? quae Camoenis              10
Dicata hostia? parcite, o Camoenae,
Nova haec victima sed tamen suavis
Futura arbitror, admodumque grata.
Accede, o tinea, illa quae pussilo
Ventrem corpore tam geris voracem:                     15
Tene Pieridum aggredi ministros?
Tene arrodere tam sacros labores?
Nec factum mihi denega: ecce furti
Tui exempla, tuae et voracitatis.
Tu fere mihi passerem Catulli,                              20
Tu fere mihi Lesbiam abstulisti.
Nunc certe meus ille Martialis
Ima ad viscera rosus usque languet,
Et quaerit medicum suum Triphonem.
Immo et ipse Maro, cui pepercit                           25
Olim flamma, tuum tamen cerebrum
Nuper, o fera ter scelesta, sensit.
Quid dicam innumeros bene eruditos,
Quorum tu monimenta, tu labores
Isto, pessima, ventre devorasti?                             30
Prodi, iam tunicam relinque, prodi.
Vah, ut callida stringit ipsa sese!
Ut mortem simulat scelesta! prodi,
Pro tot criminibus datura poenas.

Age, istum iugulo tuo mucronem,                                        35
Cruenta, excipe, et istum, et istum, et istum.
Vide ut palpitet, ut cruore largo
Aras polluerit prophana sacras!
   At vos, Pierides, banaeque Musae,
Nunc gaudete, iacet fera interempta,                                   40
Iacet sacrilega illa, quae solebat
Sacros Pieridum vorare servos.
Hanc vobis tunicam, has dico, Camoenae,
Vobis exuvias, ut hinc trophaeum
Parnasso in medio locetis, et sit                                      45
Haec inscriptio. De fera interempta,
Bezaeus spolia haec opima Musis.

There are transcripts of TP's poem in British Library Add. MS 4456
(ff. 160a–61a) and Stowe MS 973 (ff. 28b–30a). Both follow Pope's text
with minor variants probably due to miscopying; both also give some of
the proper names in full.

## Textual Notes

| | |
|---|---|
| 9 | and] 22; with TS |
| 20 | + TS, 55 (with "That" for "which"): |
| | the monster issues from the wood |
| | which boasts the gallant Nisus blood, |
| 27 | Teeth] 22; tusks TS |
| 32 | mourns] 22; moans TS |
| 33 | + TS: |
| | the tender Ovid sees thee cut |
| | those strings on Orpheus harp he put |
| | *Ovid*] 22; homer TS |
| 42 | + TS, MS (begins at "Ile have"), 55: |
| | around my temples lawrel bind |
| | but leave that azure silk behind |
| | Ile have my filet flame with red, |
| | To suit a Sacrificers head. |
| 44 | + MS, 55: |
| | Now *Spencer Milton Driden* lift, |
| | *Row Steel Pope Addison* and *Swift*. |
| 45 | thy Hand out-run] 22; thine hand out run MS; thy hand out-runs 55 (The editor of 55 evidently failed to recognize "run" as a regular simple past tense.) |

46        *D——s*] 22; *Dennis* MS, 55
47        *Ph——s*] 22; *Philips* MS, 55
          rustick] 22; rural MS
48        Pray take] ⟨Remove⟩ MS
49        This line in Pope's text is all that remains of the following
          passage, which is found in MS and (with one variant, "his" for
          "its" in the second line) in 55:
          Come bind the Victime, but forbear
          To turn its throat to upper air,
          That posture suits the Gods above,
          This earth the *Muses* often love,
          And now I think they are not Gone,
          They live with *Pope* and *Addison.*
                  So—as I woud the *Savage* lyes,
50        num'rous] ⟨clustring⟩ MS
52        From *Manuscripts* just swept] 22; Just swept from Manuscripts
          MS
54        For] 22; Theres MS
          + MS, 55:
          It foams with wine, upon the Beast
          I pour a drop, & drink the rest.
57        Sense may they seek] 22; Still may they write MS
58        + MS, 55 (with "get" for "have" in the fourth line):
          Heres Fame to *Pope,* and Wealth to *Steel,*
          And all to *Addison* he will,
          May *Garth* have Practice, *Congreve* sight;
          May *Row* have many a full third night;
          Be Gentle *Gays* & *Tickels* lot
          At least as good as *Budgel* got:
          (TP originally wrote "Budgels lot" in the fifth line, probably
          an error of transcription.)
62        + MS, 55:
          *Devoted wretch,* thy mischief past
          Has made this point of time thy last.
64        + MS, 55:
          Beneath the native mail I run,
          He bleeds, he bleeds, the Work is don:
66        And now he dies, and] 22; Now he's dying, MS
          + MS, 55 ("reach thy" for "call a"):
                  Go call a sounding harp, my Boy,
          & *Io Pean* sing for Joy.
67        No new paragraph in MS.
69–74     Instead of these lines, the MS (but not 55) has:

Or thee, the mightier *Heroe* thou,
Who forct the strength of *Gaul* to bow,
While *Blenheim* hills returnd thy name
To teach the various tongues of Fame.
And you my *Bookes,* yᵉ Learned Race,
Possess your lofty shelves in peace;
Uneat for ever hence remain,
The *Beast,* the dreadfull *Beast* is slain.
Lett others run the golden line
Which makes your *Turky* Covers shine,
Or pay to paint your faces ore,
Who saves your lives deserves you more.

| | |
|---|---|
| 77 | *Sh——ll's* 22; *Gildons* MS |
| | Second Bays] The phrase is underlined in the MS. |
| 78 | *T——*] 22; *Ward* MS |
| 83 | these] 22; the MS |
| 84 | *D——y*] 22; *Durfy* MS |
| 87 | studious Morning] 22; morning *Indian* MS |
| 91 | glorying in] 22; coming from MS |
| 92 | Hung on these Shelves] 22; Has hung within MS |

## Explanatory Notes

| | |
|---|---|
| 20 | Cf. Beza, lines 25–27. |
| 20 + | *Nisus* blood] Nisus is a Trojan in the *Aeneid;* he is killed avenging his friend Euryalus (9.440–45). |
| 29–30 | Cf. Beza, line 18. |
| 32 | *Anacreon*] Greek lyric poet (6th century B.C.), better known through the loose imitations of his manner in light amorous or drinking songs (as in TP's own "Anacreontics") than for the small extant remains of his own poems. |
| 33 | *Ovid*] Ovid (43 B.C.–A.D. 17) is here linked with Anacreon and Catullus, as a poet of love. |
| 33 + | For Ovid's telling of the Orpheus legends, see *Metamorphoses* 10 and 11; TP perhaps had in mind Orpheus's song to Pluto and Proserpine (10.17–39), which made the spirits weep. |
| 34 | *Lesbia's Sparrow*] The reference is to Catullus 2; cf. Beza, lines 20–21. |
| 36 | *Biddy Floyd*] A beauty to whom Swift wrote a poem, first published in 1709 (*Poems,* ed. Harold Williams, 2d ed. [Oxford: Clarendon Press, 1958], 1 : 117–18). |

| | |
|---|---|
| 37 | *Belinda*] The heroine of *The Rape of the Lock*. |
| 38 | *Blouzelind*] A maid in Gay's *Shepherd's Week*. |
| 39 | Cf. Beza, lines 33–34. |
| 44 | sacred Altar] TP is here parodying an epic convention, as Pope does in *The Rape of the Lock* (2.37–38) and the *Dunciad* (1.135–42). |
| 44+ | The mixture of Whig wits (Rowe, Steele, and Addison) with the Tory Swift and the uncommitted Pope in this line, like the linking of Pope with Addison in the canceled passage that followed line 49, is an indication of TP's own political neutrality or indifference at the time of writing. |
| 46 | *D——s*] John Dennis (1657–1734), the critic and dramatist. Dennis was a regular target of ridicule and had already been satirized by TP in "A Letter to a Friend: On Poets," lines 71–74. |
| 47 | *Ph——s*] Ambrose Philips (1674–1749), whose pastoral poems had been mocked by Pope in the *Guardian*, No. 40 (27 April 1713), and by Gay in his *Shepherd's Week*. |
| 50 | num'rous Eyes] TP's book-worm is hydra-headed (line 68), and therefore has many eyes. |
| 58 | Party-Rage] This point is made more general by the omission of the list of writers that follows in the "A" version of the poem. In 1722 it would recall not only the pamphleteers of the last years of Queen Anne's reign, but more recent controversies. |
| 58+ | Sir Samuel Garth (1661–1719) was a physician as well as a poet. Congreve suffered from cataracts; Swift reports finding him "almost blind" in October 1710 (*J.S.* 1:69). When a new play was performed, the dramatist received the profits of the third and sixth nights (if the play was performed that number of times); thus a play that received only two performances would be of no financial benefit to the author. Thomas Tickell (1686–1740) and Eustace Budgell (1686–1737) were both members of Addison's circle and both minor writers. |
| 65–66 | Cf. Beza, lines 37–38. |
| 67 | the Son of *Jove*] Hercules slew the Hydra, a monstrous water snake with numerous heads; when one head was cut off, others grew in its place. |
| 69+ | The "mightier *Heroe*" is the duke of Marlborough; the battle of Blenheim (1704) was the greatest of his victories. The "golden line" is presumably a reference to gilding; "*Turky*" is a kind of leather. By "paint your faces" TP may be referring to the practice of fore-edge painting. |

74          *S——*] Probably Richard Steele, offered as a type of the hasty
            journalist.
77          *Sh——ll*] Thomas Shadwell (1642–92), dramatist; the hero of
            Dryden's *MacFlecknoe* and Dryden's successor as poet laure-
            ate.
78          *T——*] Nahum Tate (c. 1652–1715), poet and dramatist;
            Shadwell's successor as poet laureate. TP describes him as
            "laborious T——te" in "A Letter to a Friend: On Poets," line
            50.
84          *D——y*] Thomas D'Urfey (1653–1723), poet and dramatist,
            ridiculed by Swift and Pope.
87          Morning Gown] A garment (something like a modern dress-
            ing gown) that would be worn before dressing to go out;
            either to receive informal morning visits or (as here) while
            reading or studying (hence "studious").
88–92       Cf. Beza, lines 43–47.
89          *Python*] The serpent or monster near Delphi slain by Apollo;
            TP is here playing Apollo to the book-worm's python.

## An Allegory on Man

The ultimate extant source of this fable is the Latin mythographer
Hyginus (second century A.D.). Hyginus's version is here quoted from
the critical edition by H.J. Rose (Leiden: A. W. Sijthoff, 1934). The
portions in square brackets are Rose's conjectural restorations:

### CCXX CURA

Cura cum quendam fluvium transiret, vidit cretosum lutum, sustulit
cogitabunda et coepit fingere hominem. dum deliberat secum quid-
nam fecissit, intervenit Iovis; rogat enim Cura ut ei daret spiritum,
quod facile ab Iove impetravit. cui cum vellet Cura nomen suum
imponere, Iovis prohibuit suumque nomen ei dandum esse dixit. dum
de nomine Cura et Iovis disceptarent, surrexit et Tellus suumque
nomen ei imponi debere dicebat, quandoquidem corpus suum
praebuisset. sumpserunt Saturnum iudicem; quibus Saturnus [secum
contemplatus] videtur iudicasse: Tu Iovis quoniam spiritum dedisti
animam post mortem accipe; Tellus quoniam corpus praebuit recipito.
Cura quoniam prima eum finxit, quamdiu vixerit Cura eum possideat;
sed quoniam de nomine eius controversia est, homo vocetur quoniam
ex humo videtur esse factus. (P. 144)

Rose thinks (p. 145) that the pun on *homo/humus* means that the fable
cannot have been copied from a Greek original; but the pun is not

essential, as TP's version shows. Mary Grant has translated *The Myths of Hyginus* (Lawrence: University Press of Kansas, 1960).

An autograph text of this poem appears in the Congleton "Satires" Notebook (ff. 48a-50a). It is longer than the poem as printed by Pope (112 lines, not counting a four-line deletion in the manuscript itself, against 100 lines in 1722), but for lines 1–88 the differences are minor. The major change in Pope's text is the omission of a passage of twelve lines and the substantial reworking of the last twelve lines of the poem.

The differences between the manuscript and the 1722 text are recorded in the textual notes; however, only the departures from the MS as finally worded are noted. The corrections made to the MS itself will be found in the textual notes to the "Satires" Notebook version. Although this division may seem awkward, in fact it is convenient to separate the final form of the poem that we can be sure was TP's (that found in the "Satires" Notebook) from a record of the differences between that text and Pope's.

## Textual Notes

| | |
|---|---|
| 4 | have call'd] 22; woud call MS |
| 22 | Mother] 22; Parent MS |
| 23 | saw old Mother *Earth* arise] 22; felt her move, he saw her rise MS |
| 27 | Nor with long] 22; Or lengthning MS |
| 29 | Wreaths alone] 22; onely wreaths MS |
| 30 | And] 22; she MS |
| 31 | Then] 22; And MS |
| 34 | This *Thing*] 22; The man MS |
| 41–42 | As finally revised in the MS this couplet reads as follows: "To shares apiece, says artfull Care,/Your pleas would make your titles fair,". |
| 50 | that paint] 22; who paints MS |
| 62 | A Glass was fixd] 22; He fix'd a glass MS |
| 66 | arm'd] 22; arms MS |
| 79 | these] 22; the MS |
| 80 | is] 22; be MS |
| 83 | ever since the *Seasons*] 22; since the seasons ever MS |
| 88–100 | The last twelve lines of the poem differ so much from the ending in the manuscript that collation is impracticable; the earlier ending will be found in the text of the poem as it appears in the "Satires" Notebook. |

**Explanatory Notes**

3–4    For examples of Homer giving the different names used by men and gods, see (in Pope's translation) *Iliad* 2.984–85, 14.329–30, and 20.101–2 (TE 7:170, 8:179, 398). See note to *Battle of the Frogs and Mice,* 3: 189–90, above.

19–22  In *Aeneid* 9.106 Jove's affirming nod shakes the firmament; Dryden imitates the passage in *Absalom and Achitophel,* lines 1026–27.

31     The reference is presumably to the story of Phaethon in Ovid's *Metamorphoses* 2, where Tellus makes an imploring speech to Jupiter (lines 272–300); but it is Neptune who, just before Tellus's speech, tries three times to raise his arms and face to Jupiter.

47–48  The allusion is to *Aeneid* 1.11: "tantaene animis caelestibus irae?" (said of Juno).

49     *Time*] For a note on the iconography of Time, see TP's poem "The Picture of Time" in the "Satires" Notebook.

59     our *Almanacks*] Contemporary almanacs contained certain standard astronomical information; other features (historical, prophetic, and miscellaneous) varied from one to another. TP is here referring to Francis Moore's *Vox Stellarum* (1699–; the ancestor of *Old Moore's Almanack,* which is still being published), the only one to give any attention to hieroglyphics. In 1706 Moore explained that "the *Egyptian* Priests . . . never deliver'd their Doctrines but by some dark representation, and not by many words, and this they imagin'd kept their Mysteries from Profanation" (p. 9), and each year until 1714 his almanack contained an emblematic or hieroglyphic picture in the form of a crude woodcut, together with some explanatory text. There were no woodcuts in the issues of 1715 or 1716, although each of these years contained a brief discussion of hieroglyphics. Since Moore himself died in 1714, it is natural to assume that his successor did not share his interest in the subject. He explained the significance of the snake in 1708, and again in 1715. The latter is here quoted, as more likely to have been seen by TP: "For a Year, they painted a Snake with his Tail in his Mouth, to shew how one succeeding another, kept the World still in an endless Circle" (p. 5).

## *An Imitation of Some French Verses*

Pope's edition is the only authority for this poem. The original is "Sur la Première Attaque de Goutte que j'eus, en 1695" by Guillaume Amfrye, abbé de Chaulieu (1639–1720). Chaulieu's poem is here reprinted from his *Oeuvres* (1774; reprint, Geneva: Slatkine, 1968):

Le destructeur impitoyable
Des marbres & de l'airain,
Le Temps, ce tyran souverain
De la chose la plus durable,
Sappe sans bruit le fondement       5
De notre fragile machine;
Et je ne vis plus un moment
Sans sentir quelque changement
Qui m'avertit de sa ruine.

Je touche aux derniers momens       10
De mes plus belles années;
Et déja de mon printemps
Toutes les fleurs sont fanées.
Je regarde, & n'envisage
Pour mon arriere-saison,       15
Que le malheur d'être sage,
Et l'inutile avantage
De connoître la raison.

Autrefois mon ignorance
Me fournissoit des plaisirs;       20
Les erreurs de l'Espérance
Faisoient naître mes désirs:
A présent l'Expérience
M'apprend que la jouissance
De nos biens les plus parfaits       25
Ne vaut pas l'impatience,
Ni l'ardeur de nos souhaits.

La Fortune à ma jeunesse
Offrit l'éclat des grandeurs:
Comme un autre avec souplesse       30
J'aurois briqué ses faveurs;
Mais, sur le peu de mérite
De ceux qu'elle a bien traités,

J'eus honte de la poursuite
De ses aveugles bontés;                                    35
Et je passai, quoi que donne
D'éclat & pourpre & couronne,
Du mépris de la personne
Aux mépris des dignités.

Aux ardeurs de mon bel âge                                 40
L'Amour joignit son flambeau;
Les Ans, de ce Dieu volage
M'ont arraché le bandeau:
J'ai vu toutes mes foiblesses,
Et connu qu'entre les bras                                 45
Des plus fidelles Maîtresses,
Enivré de leurs caresses,
Je ne les possédois pas.

Mais quoi! ma goutte est passée;
Mes chagrins sont ecartés:                                 50
Pourquoi noircir ma pensée
De ces tristes vérités?
Laissons revenir en foule
Mensonge, erreurs, passions:
Sur ce peu de temps qui coule,                             55
Faut-il des réflexions?
Que sage est qui s'en défie!
J'en connois la vanité:
La bonne ou mauvaise santé
Fait notre philosophie.                                    60

The first collected edition of Chaulieu's poems was published in 1724; TP probably read the poem in a miscellany.

# A Night-Piece on Death

This poem belongs in a tradition that leads from Milton's "Il Penseroso" to Robert Blair's *The Grave* (1743) and Thomas Gray's *Elegy Written in a Country Churchyard* (1751). Today it is probably the most widely read and anthologized of TP's poems. It is reprinted in Charles Peake's anthology *Poetry of Landscape and the Night* (1967), which provides a convenient collection of other eighteenth-century poems on the theme. See also Woodman, 72–77.

The manuscript used by the editor of the 1755 edition contained a text of this poem that differed hardly at all from that printed by Pope. Though only negative evidence, this should be taken into account in assessing how far Pope may have been responsible for the differences between his text and the surviving manuscripts.

There is a transcript of the poem in British Library Add. MS 4456, but it follows Pope's text, from which it was probably copied. The 1755 "Variations" are recorded in the textual notes. We have followed the 1726 edition in making a necessary correction to the punctuation in line 52.

## Textual Notes

| | |
|---|---|
| 28 | And thou like them shalt sink to rest. 55 |
| 52 | *dye.*] 26;—, 22 |
| 78 | +55: |
| | Nor count we death a cause to grieve, |
| | But dying when to vice we live. |
| 85–86 | In 55 the couplet reads, "Confin'd to flesh, and plac'd beneath, / A few, and evil years they breathe." |

## Explanatory Notes

| | |
|---|---|
| 1 | TP may here be echoing the opening lines of Congreve's "To a Candle": "Thou watchful Taper, by whose silent Light, / I lonely pass the melancholy Night" (*The Mourning Bride etc*, ed. Bonamy Dobrée [London, 1928], 290). |
| 4 | Schoolmen and the Sages] TP here invokes two intellectual traditions, the Christian (represented by the medieval scholastic theologians, the "Schoolmen") and the pagan (the "Sages"). |

# The Hermit

TP's poem is based on a theodicy story of great antiquity and probably of Eastern origin. In the 18th Surah of the Koran (verses 59–81), Moses travels with an angel specifically to gain an understanding of God's providence; he is forbidden to ask questions. He sees the angel damage a ship; kill a boy; and repair a wall. His incomprehension finally makes him break the taboo and ask the angel to account for his actions. Here we have the essential elements of the story. For other early and Eastern versions see Haim Schwarezbaum, "The Jewish and Moslem Versions of Some Theodicy Legends," *Fabula* 3 (1959): 119–69, and *Babrius and Phaedrus,* ed. B. E. Perry (Loeb ed., 1965), 554–56. A brief version contemporaneous with TP is found in the *Spectator,* no. 237 (1 December 1711).

Pope told Joseph Spence that "Parnell's 'Pilgrim' is very good. The story was written originally in Spanish" (February or March 1735; recorded in *Anecdotes,* ed. James M. Osborn [Oxford: Clarendon Press, 1966], No. 492). Spence adds from another source (Sir Clement Cotterell, 1685–1758), "whence probably Howell had translated it in prose, and inserted it in one of his letters." There is a puzzle here, because Pope surely knew that (as Thomas Warton pointed out, and as seems most likely) TP's immediate source was Henry More's *Divine Dialogues;* perhaps both he and Spence regarded this as too obvious to note. (Spence can hardly have consulted Howell's book, for Howell names his source as Sir Percy Herbert.) Thomas Warton, in his *History of English Poetry* (ed. W. Carew Hazlitt, 1871) rejected Pope's theory of a Spanish origin and proposed More as TP's chief source (1:256–59). The only Spanish version of the story that we have been able to find is in the *Libro de los Exemplos* of Clemente Sanchez de Vercial (1370?–1425?): "Judicia Dei Justa et Abissus," *Libro,* ed. J. E. Keller (Madrid: Consejo Superior de Investigaciones Científicas, 1961), No. 230 (161), 181–82. Sanchez seems to have taken the story from the *Gesta Romanorum;* his book (which survives in only two manuscripts) was not printed until 1860 (A. H. Krappe, "Les Sources du *Libro de Exemplos,*" *Bulletin Hispanique* 39 [1937]: 5–54). TP can hardly have known it.

It is probably not profitable to trace the history of the story back further than Sir Percy Herbert's *Certaine Conceptions, or Considerations* (1650; Wing H1524a). In Herbert's version, the troubled hermit prays for an explanation of the ways of providence; some weeks later, he is visited by a young man (who reveals himself from the first as a divine messenger) and they go on a journey together. The journey takes five days and comprises seven inexplicable actions. The first four correspond to TP's version: the pair are hospitably entertained, but the young man steals a silver goblet; they are scurvily entertained, and the young man makes a present of the goblet; they are again very sumptuously entertained, but the young man strangles the host's only son and pushes another traveler (who is not, however, connected with the previous host) off a bridge. Herbert's version has three further elements that are not found in TP's poem: the young man misdirects a traveler in a hurry; at an inn, the young man revels all night with a company of thieves; and (arriving at a city) the pair find only one devil asleep at the city gates, but many devils besieging the monastery where they are entertained. Herbert's moralization of the incidents that are common to his and TP's versions is also slightly different; most important, the miserly host is given the cup as his reward in this world, rather than in an effort to convert him (as in TP's lines 214–23).

James Howell's *Epistolae Ho-Elianae* was first published in 1645; book 4 (in which this story appears) was added to the third edition (1655). There is a modern edition by Joseph Jacobs (1892). Howell tells the story in book 4, letter 4, and credits it to Herbert. His version is essentially the same as Herbert's, although he re-arranges the order of the incidents.

Closer to TP's poem is the story as told by Thomas White in *A Treatise of the Power of Godliness* (1658); White tells it as "a famous story of providence in *Bradwardine*" (pp. 376–79). In this version the angel does not initially reveal his true identity. The golden cup is stolen from a holy man (not, as in TP, from someone who is ostentatiously hospitable); the angel kills the child of a second holy man and flings the host's steward (sent to guide them, as in TP) into a river; and the angel gives the cup to a wicked man (whose entertainment of the pair is reluctant but not particularly parsimonious). White's moralizations also differ from TP's. The explanation for the theft of the cup is that it was too large and encouraged the owner to drink too freely, and it is given to the wicked man to make him more intemperate, not in any attempt to convert him to better ways.

Henry More does not give a source for the story when he tells it as "The Parable of the Eremite and the Angel" in his *Divine Dialogues* (1668; book 2, chapter 24; 1.320–27. The story is on pp. 165–68 in the 1713 reprint, which TP may have seen.) More's version is very close to TP's. The main differences are that More has four episodes (the steward thrown into the river is not, as in TP, connected with the man whose child is strangled) and the episodes relating to the cup are explained differently. The angel steals the cup because (being enchanted or bewitched) it made the owner drink too much, and similarly gives it to the niggard to destroy rather than save him.

Assuming, then, that More was TP's immediate source, it is apparent that TP has made two main changes. By connecting the last two episodes he has tightened the structure, making the three nights illustrate the undesirable extremes of hospitality and the moderate ideal. Second, by giving the cup to the miser not (as in the earlier versions) to ruin him but in the hope of turning his thoughts to God, TP makes the theodicy more complete.

"The Hermit" proved a very popular poem. It was frequently reprinted, both in anthologies and in separate editions (of which the first two known to have survived were published in Edinburgh in 1751, one of them with poems by Pope and Addison. For other separate printings,

see Appendix 2 below). Voltaire told the story in chapter 18 of *Zadig;* he
seems to have known TP's poem and to have taken hints from it as well as
from other sources. The fullest modern account of the sources is prob-
ably to be found in the Commentary to Voltaire's *Zadig,* ed. Georges
Ascoli, rev. Jean Fabre, 2 vols. (Paris: Didier, 1962), 1: xxxv, 2: 136–64.
See also W. E. A. Axon, "The Literary History of Parnell's Hermit,"
*Memoirs of the Manchester Literary and Philosophical Society for the Session
1879–80,* 3rd Series, 7 (1881): 144–60, and A. P. Hudson, "The Hermit
and Divine Providence," *Studies in Philology* 28 (1931): 218–34.

The manuscript used in the 1755 edition contained a text of the poem
slightly longer that Pope's; its "Variations" are given in the textual notes.
We have followed the 1726 edition in making a necessary correction to
the punctuation in lines 187 and 231.

## Textual Notes

| | |
|---|---|
| 4 | +55: |
| | His goods a glass to measure human breath, |
| | The books of wisdom, and the spade of death. |
| 61–62 | In 55 the couplet reads "With fresh'ning airs o'er gay par-terres they creep, / And shake the rustling groves to banish sleep." |
| 129 | This line is condensed from two lines in 55: "When dusky twilight bid the night prepare, / To light with radiant drops the dark'ning air;". |
| 156 | black] 22; deep 55 |
| 179 | +55: |
| | So when the sun his dazzling splendour shrowds, |
| | Yet just begins to break the veiling clouds; |
| | A bright effulgence at the first is seen, |
| | But shorn of beams, and with a mist between, |
| | Soon the full glory bursts upon the sight, |
| | And moves in all the majesty of light. |
| | (The last two lines of this passage are an early version of lines 180–81 in Pope's text.) |
| 186 | +55: |
| | So loud thro' rocks the tumbling waters stray, |
| | Then glide beneath the fall unheard away. |
| 187 | spoke.)] 26; —) 22 |
| 196–97 | In 55 this couplet reads: "Eternal God the world's founda-tions laid, / He made what is, and governs what he made,". |
| 198 | Its] 22; His 55 |
| 231 | Blow.)] 26; —) 22 |

## Explanatory Notes

23   by Swains alone] Boswell was worried by the apparent incon-
    sistency between this statement and the "Books, or Swains" in
    line 22, and asked Johnson's opinion in a letter of 28 Febru-
    ary 1778 (*Life of Johnson*, ed. George Birkbeck Hill, rev. L. F.
    Powell [Oxford: Clarendon Press, 1934], 3:220). When he
    finally secured Johnson's opinion, Johnson agreed that it was
    an "inaccuracy" of expression (Hill-Powell, 3:393); but in a
    note on Johnson's opinion Boswell quoted Edmond Malone's
    defense of TP's lines. Briefly, Malone's explanation was that in
    line 23 TP means that the hermit had no direct experience of
    the world, although he had read about it and had derived
    second-hand experience from the passing swains.

26   Scallop] An emblem of pilgrimage, originally particularly
    associated with Saint James and his shrine at Compostella in
    Spain.

43–44  Aitken 225 cites *Paradise Lost*, 4.598–99.

61–62  creep . . . Sleep] Pope gives this rhyme as an example of
    poetic cliché in the *Essay on Criticism*, lines 352–53 (TE
    1:279); see also the explanatory note to "The Flies," line 67.

171ff.  Aitken 225 cites *Aeneid* 2.379ff.

174–81  It has been suggested, questionably, that this passage "comes
    from Cowley's description of Gabriel" near the end of
    *Davideis*, Book 2 (Woodman 81).

242   *Elisha*] In 2 Kings 2:1–12, while the prophet Elijah is talking
    to his disciple Elisha, a chariot and horses of fire appear and
    Elijah is taken up into heaven in a whirlwind.

247   TP here alludes to part of the Lord's Prayer (Matthew 6:10).

# Biblical Poems from British Library Add. MS 31114

British Library Add. MS 31114 consists of thirty-three folios (each 159 × 96 mm), of which f. 32b and f. 33 are blank. The leaves have been individually remounted and rebound, and some cropping indicates that the page size was originally larger. The provenance of the manuscript cannot be traced before its acquisition by the then British Museum. For a general discussion of the relationship between the text of the manuscript and that of the poems as they appear in the 1758 *Posthumous Works,* see the Introduction, section 5.

Our aim has been an exact transcription of the manuscript with the minimum of editorial alteration. In "Moses," line 465, TP's change of "He now returns" to "returnd at length", using the original "returns", results in the line inadvertently beginning with a lowercase letter. We have changed this to a capital in the text. Similar cases occur at "Moses," line 725, "Deborah," lines 16, 27, and 84, and "Hannah," lines 64 and 226. Where TP begins a line with a lowercase letter in the first instance, we have allowed it to stand. Periods have been added at "Moses," line 724, and "Hannah," line 166, where sentences end at the bottom of a recto and where wear to the corner of the page has probably resulted in the loss of TP's terminal punctuation; similarly, a comma has been added to "The Gift of Poetry," line 24. Otherwise, the punctuation of the original has not been altered. The textual notes record the alterations made to the MS and the verbal variants of the 1758 edition, in which the poems were first printed. A note in the form "⟨take⟩ MS, 58" means that "take" is canceled in the MS but is also the reading of 58.

# The Gift of Poetry

## Textual Notes

| | |
|---|---|
| 7 | raisd] ⟨sweet⟩ MS |
| 11 | thro' the ravishd] ⟨over all the⟩ MS, 58 |
| 18 | design] MS; designs 58 |
| 19 | attempt] ⟨great work⟩ MS |
| 22 | the gift I think I feel] MS; I think I feel the Gift 58 |
| 24 | ⟨Nor onely natures Impulse on the mind⟩ MS |
| 28 | wing] ⟨take⟩ MS, 58 |
| 32 | ⟨Man's merits nothing but thy mercy's kind⟩ MS |
| | At the end of this line (as also at the end of line 38 below) the MS seems to have both a period and a comma; either could be an inconsequential mark. In both cases we have accepted the period as preferable. |
| 33 | long] ⟨wish⟩ MS |
| 34 | long] ⟨wish⟩ MS |
| 36 | Longings] ⟨wishes⟩ MS |
| 41 | Canaan] ⟨Eden⟩ MS |
| | to] ⟨in⟩ MS |
| 42 | Where] ⟨&⟩ MS |
| | formd] ⟨tund⟩ MS |
| 44 | or] ⟨&⟩ MS, and 58 |
| 46 | closely-weaving] MS; closely-waving 58 |
| 50 | fair] {its} MS |
| 52 | This line is cropped in the MS. |
| 53 | So] MS; To 58 |
| 55 | Ancient] ⟨Aged⟩ MS |
| 59 | favourd] ⟨heard⟩ MS |
| 62 | where] ⟨as⟩ MS |
| 66 | Where] ⟨&⟩ MS |

## Explanatory Note

| | |
|---|---|
| 41 | Canaan] An old name for an area comprising roughly Palestine and Syria. |

## *Moses*

### Textual Notes

| | |
|---|---|
| 5 | Above this line, at the top of f. 2b, TP began and canceled line 7, apparently an error of transcription. |
| 9 | raisd] ⟨movd⟩ MS |
| 18 | march it] ⟨travell⟩ MS |
| 21 | the] ⟨those⟩ MS, 58 |
| 31 | His rolling cloud inwraps] {He Spoiles his cloud of all} MS |
| 41 | as ye] MS; as they 58 |
| 43 | TP began the line with "Tis", probably an error of transcription, then wrote "Dash" over it. |
| 56 | doubt] MS; doubts 58 |
| 79 | There O my God] MS; Thine hand my God! 58 |
| 83 | on] MS; o'er 58 |
| 90 | The line ends (like "The Gift of Poetry," lines 32 and 38) with both a comma and a period; here, however, we have accepted the comma. |
| 91 | learnd] MS; learn 58 |
| 92 | like banks of Christall by yᵉ] {like Christall banks congeald for} MS |
| 94 | the foe prophanely] ⟨our Adversary⟩ MS |
| 99 | ⟨But while they threatned Idely, from above⟩ MS |
| 103 | irresistless] MS; their resistless 58 |
| 105 | who] MS; who's 58 |
| 111 | stretcht thy powrfull]⟨stretched out thine⟩ MS; stretchedst out thine 58 |
| 118 | TP has underlined "thine holy", probably to indicate an intended revision, and has written "ain of" above "mount"; he may have intended "To reach the mountain of thy blessd abode", but as he did not complete the revision we have let the original wording stand. |
| 121 | Dukes] MS; Duke 58 |
| 127 | greatness] The word is written above the line in the MS, probably an accidental omission during transcription. |
| 128 | A canceled couplet follows in the MS at the foot of f. 4b: "While all thy flock to liberty restord / While all thy Flock the swelling Jordan ford". TP must have canceled this couplet after making the line count, but it is not in 58. |
| 140 | The line ends with both a comma and a period (as line 90 above), of which we have accepted the comma. |

151 ⟨Then Miriam sweetly did the Chorus raise,⟩ MS
152 Miriams] ⟨with her⟩ MS
gives] ⟨gave⟩ MS
153 sounds] {notes} MS
160 close.] 58;— MS
167 rebound] MS; resound 58
187 coud] ⟨did⟩ MS
200 in] MS; on 58
201 Three versions of this line are found in the MS, but we have let the original wording stand (even though "seems to" is actually canceled) because it is not clear which of the alternatives, if either, TP had settled on. Since TP usually wrote his revisions above the line, the alternative written above the line here was presumably his first attempt to rewrite the line: "Thence swiftly drops upon y^e closing wing". Below the line is his second attempt to rework it: "Down she descends she drops upon y^e wing". An apparently isolated revision is "weary", placed below "her wing" in the line as originally written; it may be an alternative to "closing". 58 has "She falls from thence and seems to drop her wing".
203 The number "11" is written and crossed through in the outer margin against this line; its significance is uncertain.
210 &] MS; Or 58
217 Ere the mean] ⟨Before the⟩ MS
219 Look] The word is underlined in the MS, but no alternative is given.
222 hapless] ⟨happless⟩ MS
227 complaint] ⟨request⟩ MS
231 On] MS; In 58
244 terrour] MS; terrours 58
247 these] MS; they 58
248 gently] MS; greatly 58
249 resignd] ⟨retird⟩ MS, 58
250 on] MS; in 58
253 Sins] MS; such 58
257 a] MS; the 58
262 The] ⟨&⟩ MS; And 58
263 blessings] MS; blessing 58
267 shades] In the MS, the word is written above the line, apparently having been omitted in transcription.
268 confuses & goes] MS; in prospect and go 58
269 affecting] {the lively} MS (there is a marginal cross against this line)

273          movd] MS; move 58
282          its] MS; the 58
283          the] MS; their 58
295          dead] MS; dread 58
296          slumber unregarded] {soundly sleep unminded} MS
297          Where] MS; When 58
306          yᵉ . . . yᵉ] MS; their . . . their 58
315          that] MS; thus 58
316          descending] MS; descended 58
327          longest] ⟨furthest⟩ MS
328          men] MS; we 58
333          will] ⟨does⟩ MS
343          Israels] MS; Israel 58
348          TP first wrote, "& still-rememberd Favour live in Joy", and
             this is the wording of 58. In the MS he then wrote above the
             line, "last to bless us with a lasting Joy", retaining the "&" from
             the original line. There are marginal crosses against each of
             these first two versions, and each is scored out with a horizon-
             tal line. TP then wrote, below the line, the version that we
             have accepted as his final intention, which seems clearer here
             than in the similar case of line 201 above. This version may
             have originally begun with "yet".
356          There is a marginal cross against this line, but it has not been
             revised.
362          their] MS; the 58
380          After this line, TP first wrote out lines 385–86 as they appear
             in our text (possibly this was an error of transcription); he
             then canceled them and wrote above them the following early
             version of lines 381–82: "When with a languish from yᵉ
             sparkling eyes / Their thrones of Beauty Banishd beauty flys".
             This version was in turn deleted, and TP wrote out the lines
             as they appear in our text. This revision is evidence that, here
             at least, TP stopped transcribing to revise a couplet, and
             possibly to insert a short passage.
383          TP wrote and canceled "yᵉ sparkling eyes her throne" above
             the first half of this line.
388          seem] MS; seem'd 58
401          sad] ⟨Just⟩ MS
402          failes . . . flys] ⟨flys . . . failes⟩ MS
416          rise in] MS; rising 58
429          yon] {that} MS
431          glory] {beauty} MS
432          its gold] {it self} MS; its-self 58

| | |
|---|---|
| 435 | thine] MS; thy 58 |
| 446 | yᵉ] MS; their 58 |
| 448 | Afflictions] ⟨afflictions⟩ MS. This small alteration, like the parallel one in line 475 below, is worth noting for its evidence that TP was paying some attention to capitalization. |
| 456 | retreats] MS; repeats 58 (picked up from line 455) |
| 465 | Returnd at length] ⟨He now returns⟩ MS, 58 |
| 468 | their] MS; the 58 |
| 474 | Its . . . lett] ⟨Lett . . . its⟩ MS (there is a marginal cross against the line); Let fear, to lose a word, it's caution shew, 58 |
| 475 | Attention] ⟨attention⟩ MS (cf. line 448 above) |
| 476 | softly softly] ⟨very softly⟩ MS |
| 478 | There is a marginal cross against this line; there is no revision, although "thus" is an insertion. |
| 482 | Honyd] MS; honey 58 |
| 491 | we safely] TP wrote "its safe", canceled and replaced this with " 'tis safe", before arriving at "we safely" (the reading of 58). |
| 492 | work is] In the MS, TP probably wrote "works are" and then turned the "e" of "are" into the "i" of "is", then canceled "ar" and scratched out the "s" of "works". 58 reads "work is". |
| 501 | 0] ⟨&⟩ MS; and 58 |
| 502 | thy God] MS; the lord 58 |
| 503–8 | There is a marginal cross against each of lines 503, 504, 507, and 508; but no revisions have been made. |
| 513 | so] MS; to 58 |
| 515–16 | & gaines . . . to grace] ⟨his chosen lott / & in his kindness has its portion gott⟩ MS (The spacing shows that TP made this revision before continuing to transcribe.) |
| 517–18 | him his . . . ground] {unfrequented ground / & howling wilderness his mercy found} MS (TP seems to have tried "pines" and "rages" as verbs for famine before settling on "dwells"; "rages" may have been written, then canceled, then rewritten; but the MS is barely legible at this point.) |
| 536 | boast] MS; boasts 58 |
| | kindlyest-influencing] MS; kindest influencing 58 |
| 549 | waxen] MS; wanton 58 |
| 555 | rites] MS; writes 58 |
| 558 | Hell ev'n Hell] {fiends themselves} MS, 58 |
| 561 | his revenge] ⟨coud his hate⟩ MS, 58 |
| 566 | That promisd] MS; They promise 58 |
| | returnd] MS; return 58 |
| 567 | In my grievd] ⟨Within my⟩ MS, 58 |
| | they raise] ⟨they've rais'd⟩ MS, 58 |

569          They make] ⟨They've made⟩ MS
             mine] MS; my 58
571–74       Each of these lines has a marginal cross against it, but only in
             line 572 is there an alteration. At line 575 there is a small
             stroke in the margin, perhaps meant to be half a cross.
572          people] ⟨such as are⟩ MS, 58 (The revision makes the line
             short, but it is clearly marked and must also have been in the
             MS from which 58 was printed.)
577          deeps] MS; depths 58
             consume] In the MS, TP wrote and canceled "th" before
             "consume".
579          ⟨Upon their heads Ile heaps of mischief send,⟩ MS
581          dearth] MS; death 58
583          Sharp] {The} MS, 58
584          Dire] {The} MS, 58
586          the] {&} MS; and 58
590          its] ⟨their⟩ MS
591          much] ⟨that⟩ MS, 58
             the foes unruly] ⟨its adversarys⟩ MS
594          An incomplete, canceled line follows in the MS: "Thou
             thoughtless nation so fond their thoughts". TP used the sec-
             ond half in line 595.
595          thought, so farr] ⟨thoughts are, so⟩ MS, 58
596          &] ⟨So⟩ MS
597          knew they rightly where] ⟨did they know to what⟩ MS, 58
599          Soon woud they find] ⟨They Soon woud find⟩ MS, 58 (58,
             however, has "The" for "They")
602          The Lord] ⟨& sure⟩ MS, 58
605          own] The word is an insertion in the MS; it seems to have
             been omitted in error, written once and deleted, then rewrit-
             ten.
607          may seem indeed] ⟨may seem awhile⟩ MS; indeed, may seem
             58
610          Rank] {&} MS; And 58
612          TP inserted "livid" between "from" and "asps", but made no
             corresponding deletion; nor is "livid" in 58. We have there-
             fore left the text as it originally stood.
630          ever was there] ⟨was there ever⟩ MS
631          & wounds] MS; or wounds 58
633          mine] MS; my 58
634          Ore yᵉ rich] ⟨Above yᵉ⟩ MS, 58
647          God] {he} MS, 58

| | |
|---|---|
| 649 | all] ⟨yᵉ⟩ MS; them 58 |
| 651 | their] MS; the 58 |
| 660 | road] ⟨rode⟩ MS (a slip apparently influenced by "abode" in line 659) |
| 667 | travel] MS; travail 58 |
| 669 | fill] MS; feel 58 |
| | blessings] MS; blessing 58 |
| 683 | long] ⟨will⟩ MS, 58 |
| 687 | gentil] MS; gentle 58 |
| 692 | Anger] ⟨anger⟩ MS |
| 693 | leaves] MS; leave 58 |
| 699 | change] ⟨alter⟩ MS |
| 700 | which rose before] {again on earth} MS; on earth again 58 |
| 702 | & still] ⟨yet⟩ MS |
| 704 | left yᵉ sons of] ⟨hence bequeathd to⟩ MS |
| 706 | beautys] MS; beauty 58 |
| 711 | ⟨To suit or crown the meekest turn of mind,⟩ MS |
| 719 | suspending ore] {there hang above} MS; impending o'er 58 |
| 721 | Sabled] MS; sable 58 |
| 725 | ⟨Upon the tomb a fair inscription place⟩ MS (TP changed "Upon" to "Above" before settling on "on".) |
| 730 | its] MS; it 58 |
| 731 | yᵉ] ⟨yᵗ⟩ MS |
| 736 | tunefull] {Charming} MS |
| 749 | rites] The word is written over a scraped-off erasure. |
| 752 | up] MS; on 58 |
| 753 | spectres] ⟨Phantomes⟩ MS |
| 756 | Horrour] ⟨horrour⟩ MS |
| 760 | by] ⟨with⟩ MS |
| 762 | drives] ⟨drove⟩ MS |
| 763 | turning] MS; burning 58 (This is a plausible misreading of TP's hand, and is an indication that the MS from which 58 was set was probably autograph.) |
| 770 | Track] MS; Trace 58 |
| 772 | in] MS; with 58 |
| 775 | yᵉ rite] MS; their right 58 |
| 778 | conquest] {Victorys} MS, 58 |
| | yᵉ warr] ⟨warrs⟩ MS, 58 |
| 780 | The MS has a canceled comma after "rage". |
| 793 | suit] ⟨start⟩ (?) MS |

794          Below this line is the figure "866", evidently a line-count
             including "The Gift of Poetry" and the canceled couplet at
             the foot of f. 4b.


## Explanatory Notes

11–44        The crossing of the Red Sea is described in Exodus 14.

61–146       The song of Moses is expanded from Exodus 15:1–19,
             where however it is sung by the Israelites as well, and not by
             Moses alone.

151–64       This passage is expanded from Exodus 15:20–21.

169–74       For the idea of the crossing of the Red Sea as a type of
             baptism, see 1 Corinthians 10:1–2.

185–94       Jubal comes from Genesis 4:21, where he is described as "the
             father of all such as handle the harp and organ".

203–34       The complaints of the Israelites are described in Exodus
             15:23–17:7.

221–24       Lot's wife looked back at Sodom and Gomorrah and was
             turned into a pillar of salt (Genesis 19:26).

227–34       For the waters of Marah, see Exodus 15:23–25; for the
             quails, Exodus 16:13; for manna, Exodus 16:14–16; and for
             the water struck from the rock, Exodus 17:6.

235–44       God gives Moses the laws on Mount Sinai in Exodus 19.

249–74       This account of the dream of Moses seems to be TP's addi-
             tion.

275–356      This passage is expanded from Psalm 90.

361–416      The meditation on death is TP's addition; the theme invites
             comparison with the later poem "A Night-Piece on Death,"
             although there are no close similarities.

373–76       The contrast between meteors and the fixed stars was a
             favorite image of TP's; he uses it also in "On Dr. Brown's
             Death," lines 6–9, and in both versions of "Ecstasy" ("A," lines
             68–74; "B," 89–94); both poems are from the "Satires" Note-
             book.

409–16       The passage is presumably a direct paraphrase, since TP
             placed it in quotation marks; but it seems not to be biblical.
             The idea is related to the myth of the cave used by Plato in
             *Republic* 7.

429–38       God so appears to Moses in Deuteronomy 31:15.

439–54       God's words are closely based on Deuteronomy 31:16–19.

465–78       This passage is loosely based on Deuteronomy 31:22–29.

479–652 The song of Moses is closely based on Deuteronomy 32:1–43.

713–82 This episode is not biblical, but is based on the apocryphal "Assumption of Moses." Since the extant part of the "Assumption" does not include the struggle for the body of Moses, TP must have been drawing on a secondary source, but we have not been able to identify it. In Michael Drayton's poem *Moses his Birth and Miracles* (*Works*, ed. J. W. Hebel, new ed. [Oxford: Basil Blackwell, 1961], 3:357–417), angels keep the burial place of Moses secret for fear of idolatry (book 3, lines 761–64).

# *Deborah*

## Textual Notes

1 unwind] MS; unfold 58

3 its] MS; thy 58

9 TP deleted "upon" and inserted "wandring" before "Israel"; but he then canceled the insertion and we have therefore left the line as it originally stood.

12 conquest] MS; conquests 58

  *Expeditions*] ⟨expeditions⟩ MS

16 On the broad] ⟨Upon the⟩ MS, 58

22 where] MS; when 58

25 plact] ⟨plac'd⟩ MS, 58

27 TP first wrote, "A mossy bank upon its root supports". He then canceled "upon its root" and wrote above "near yᵉ"; this intermediate revision seems incomplete. Finally he erased "near yᵉ" and inserted "near yᵉ broad root" at the beginning of the line. In 58 the line reads: "Near the firm root a mossy bank supports".

32 each] ⟨&⟩ MS

43 feel thy glittering sword] ⟨fall beneath thy sword⟩ MS; feel thine edged sword 58 (In the MS, TP seems first to have deleted "beneath" and altered "fall" to "feel"; then changed "thy" to "thine" (the reading of 58) and begun "edg" for "edged" (again the reading of 58); but he crossed out the "ed" and used the "g" to begin "glittering". Finally he changed "thine" back to "thy". The occurrence of "edged" in 58 is

another small piece of evidence that its variants are authorial, but it creates a difficulty about the exact relationship between Add. MS 31114 and the manuscript behind 58.)

| | |
|---|---|
| 58 | assures] {secures} MS, 58 |
| 60 | furling] {waving} MS |
| 64 | hand] MS; hands 58 |
| 71 | trumpets] MS; trumpet 58 |
| 74 | With] MS; And 58 |
| 75 | conflict] MS; conquest 58 |
| 79 | break] MS; brake 58 |
| 84 | Expert their guiders] ⟨Their guiders expert⟩ MS |
| 102 | Leader] ⟨leader⟩ MS |
| 106 | cleard of vision as] ⟨show-less as it was⟩ MS (this reading is heavily canceled and is conjectural) |
| 114 | guilds] ⟨dyes⟩ MS |
| 116 | the] MS; their 58 |
| 117 | their] MS; the 58 |
| 120 | & deaths] MS; of death 58 |
| 123 | a side . . . a side] MS; aside . . . aside 58 |
| 124 | the] MS; their 58 |
| 142 | fetters on] ⟨chains upon⟩ MS |
| 143 | her] MS; their 58 |
| 145 | feats] MS; fate 58 |
| 149 | round] {on} MS |
| 153 | sprang] MS (or possibly "sprung"); spring 58 |
| 155 | ye] ⟨you⟩ MS |
| 158 | Jacob] {Israel} MS |
| 160 | thy] MS; the 58 |
| 167 | into] MS; in 58 |
| 170 | durst] MS; dare 58 |
| 172 | dangers] MS; danger 58 |
| | insulting] MS; perplexing 58 |
| 173 | *wast*] MS; was 58 |
| 196 | grassy] MS; mossy 58 |
| 197 | blessing] MS; blessings 58 |
| 198 | blessing] MS; blessings 58 |
| 201 | her] MS; the 58 |
| 204 | The line ends with both a comma and a period. We preserve the comma here. See "The Gift of Poetry," lines 32 and 38, and "Moses," lines 90 and 140. |
| 226 | sheepfold] MS; sheepfolds 58 |
| 227 | yᵉ] MS; thy 58 |
| 229 | danger] MS; dangers 58 |

| | |
|---|---|
| 230 | hearts] MS; heart 58 |
| 232 | unconcern] ⟨unconcerns⟩ MS |
| 234 | frighted] MS; frighten'd 58 |
| 243 | to] MS; in 58 |
| 244 | On Israels] ⟨Upon our⟩ MS |
| 245 | starrs &] ⟨all y^e⟩ MS |
| 247 | their] MS; the 58 |
| 259 | into] MS; in the 58 |
| 266 | a] MS; her 58 |
| 268 | her] MS; the 58 |
| 285 | win] MS; in 58 |
| 287 | who Gods decrees] ⟨y^t woud y^e Lord⟩ MS; whom Gods decrees 58. Another word, written above ⟨Lord⟩, is also canceled in the MS; it may be "derees", a deleted misspelling of "decrees". |
| 300 | from y^e blessing] {out of comfort} MS |
| 301 | in] MS; from 58 |
| 302 | deckt] MS; deck 58 |
| 304 | waving] ⟨wafted⟩ MS, 58 |
| | wanton] MS; waving 58 |
| 317 | day] MS; days 58 |
| 319 | Order] ⟨order⟩ MS |
| 324 | years] MS; year 58 |
| 330 | love] MS; fear 58 |
| 335 | sublime] ⟨divine⟩ MS |
| 343 | thy] MS; my 58 |
| 353 | bright] ⟨fair⟩ MS |
| 355 | *Piety*] ⟨*Piety* MS |
| 356 | a] MS; thy 58 |
| 360 | *Oppression*] ⟨*oppression*⟩ MS |
| 376 | The MS has a line count ("374") under this line. |

## Explanatory Notes

| | |
|---|---|
| 7–10 | These events are described in Joshua 3–5. |
| 17–106 | This passage is expanded from Judges 4:1–16. |
| 151–292 | Deborah's song is based on Judges 5, where, however, it is sung by both Deborah and Barak. |
| 293–376 | There is no biblical source for this passage; the apostrophe to Piety suggests a comparison with TP's later poem "Piety: or, The Vision," but there are no close parallels. |

## *Hannah*

### Textual Notes

| | |
|---|---|
| 2 | in] ⟨on⟩ MS |
| 10 | next] MS; mixt 58 |
| 30 | to yᵉ Lord] ⟨as she⟩ MS (TP canceled this while writing the line) |
| 64 | This line is difficult. TP first wrote, "Obscurd in deep retreat from open show". He seems then to have deleted "Obscurd" and "from open", and to have inserted "& unexpressd to". Next he wrote "irement" above "retreat", clearly intending "retirement"; but he failed to take out the now hypermetrical "&". The intermediate reading is preserved in 58, which has "retreat and". We have taken out the "&", printed "retirement", and changed "in" to "In", as most likely to reflect TP's final intentions. |
| 75 | with] MS; in 58 |
| 89 | enemy] MS; enemies 58 |
| 96 | fault] MS; faults 58 |
| 97 | in words your] MS; your words in 58 |
| 98 | A canceled couplet follows this line in the MS: "Since God the God of knowledges reveales / & weighs our actions in impartiall scales". |
| 117 | He] ⟨Who⟩ MS |
| 140 | safely] MS; safety 58 |
| 148 | thought] MS; thoughts 58 |
| 149 | the] ⟨thy⟩ MS |
| 151–52 | These lines are not in 58. |
| 158 | thought] MS; thoughts 58 |
| 168 | pushd] MS; push 58 |
| | in] ⟨by⟩ MS |
| | tide!] MS;—? 58 |
| 190 | Rising he reaches] {He rises reaching} MS |
| 195 | persisting] MS; perishing 58 |
| 196 | seek true] ⟨look for⟩ MS, 58 |
| | unblessd with] ⟨without an⟩ MS, 58 |
| 197 | Still may we] ⟨We still may⟩ MS, 58 |
| | still] ⟨&⟩ MS; and 58 |
| 203 | thy] MS; the 58 |
| 219 | the] ⟨this⟩ MS |

| 226 | TP has written and canceled "Dres" (for "Dress") at the beginning of the line. |
| 228 | with] ⟨by⟩ MS |
| 230 | employments] MS; employment 58 |
| 256 | The MS has a line count ("256") written below this line. |

## Explanatory Notes

| 15–20 | The details of the description of the tent are taken from the account of the building of the tabernacle in Exodus; for the pillars overlaid with gold, see 26:37, and for the pillars filleted with silver, 27:10, 17. |
| 21–84 | This passage is based on 1 Samuel 1. |
| 85–152 | Hannah's prayer is based on 1 Samuel 2:1–10. |
| 147–52 | Lines 147–50 are TP's interpolation, stressing the messianic interpretation of the last part of Hannah's prayer ("And he shall give strength unto his king, And exalt the horn of his annointed"), which he paraphrases in lines 151–52. |
| 153–254 | TP's meditation on providence again anticipates the theme of a later poem (this time "The Hermit"), but again there are no close parallels. |
| 203–18 | For the image of the bubble, see Francis Quarles, *Emblems*, 1.4 (*Complete Works*, ed. A. B. Grosart [1880–81; reprint, New York: AMS Press, 1967], 3:49); and the note to Pope's *Essay on Man*, 1.87–90 in TE 3.i:24–25. |
| 233–36 | An important autobiographical passage, possibly indicating TP's motivation in writing these biblical poems. |
| 247–56 | This passage seems to be largely a cento of phrases from the psalms (e.g., line 247 echoes Psalm 146:1; line 248, Psalm 103:1; and line 254, Psalm 57:8). |

# Biblical Poems from *Posthumous Works* (1758)

For a general account of the 1758 *Posthumous Works,* see the Introduction, section 5. For the reasons given there, the poems for which 1758 is our sole authority need more frequent emendation than any other of TP's poems. All departures from 1758 are, however, recorded in the textual notes, except that we have (by analogy with the poems in Add. MS 31114) omitted the lines between the paragraphs that are found in 1758. The emendations are chiefly to punctuation. The words printed in capitals in 1758 have all been reduced to lowercase, since the printing in capitals is neither itself rational nor has any analogy in the British Library manuscript.

## *David*

### Textual Notes

| | |
|---|---|
| 1 | thought,] — 58 |
| 2 | tongue,] — 58 |
| 6 | eyes;] —, 58 |
| 8 | And] An 58 |
| 9 | Genius,] Genious 58 |
| 11 | wrought,] — 58 |
| 17 | Devotion] DEVOTION 58 |
| 23 | Innocence] INNOSENCE 58 |
| 24 | Sweetness] SWEETNESS 58 |
| | ears,] — 58 |
| 26 | along;] —: 58 |
| 27 | Honour] HONOUR 58 |
| 28 | red,] —; 58 |
| 29 | state] sate 58 |

| | |
|---|---|
| 30 | great;] —, 58 |
| 31 | Courage] COURAGE 58 |
| 32 | arms,] —; 58 |
| 33 | fight,] — 58 |
| 39 | aspire] —, 58 |
| 41 | Babel] BABEL 58 |
| 42 | skies.] —, 58 |
| 47 | brink,] — 58 |
| 48 | David's] DAVID's 58 |
| 52 | So,] — 58 |
| | copious,] — 58 |
| 61 | shepherd] shehperd 58 |
| | sings,] — 58 |
| 71 | prove] —, 58 |
| 73 | spirit,] — 58 |
| | instil'd,] — 58 |
| 83 | verse,] — 58 |
| 86 | Palestina's] PALESTINA's 58 |
| | Salem's] SALEM's 58 |
| 87 | Where,] — 58 |
| | hands] —, 58 |
| 88 | fled;] —. 58 |
| 89 | Where,] — 58 |
| 91 | fire] —, 58 |
| 93 | string] —, 58 |
| 96 | years;] —, 58 |
| 103 | sentiments,] — 58 |
| 107 | harp,] — 58 |
| 108 | lute,] — 58 |
| 109 | God,] — 58 |
| 110 | Piety's] PIETY's 58 |
| 111 | soul,] — 58 |
| 115 | trod,] — 58 |
| 116 | God,] —; 58 |
| 117 | praise] —, 58 |
| 118 | ways;] —, 58 |
| 122 | drest,] —. 58 |
| 127 | fill] —, 58 |
| 130 | keep;] —. 58 |
| 133 | drove] —, 58 |
| 134 | waters,] — 58 |
| 135 | Jordan's] JORDAN's 58 |
| 136 | Cedron's] CEDRON's 58 |

137    swain,] — 58
138    train] rain 58
146    near;] —, 58
150    calls] call's 58
154    rolls] roll's 58
156    head,] —; 58
158    state,] — 58
159    success] —, 58
167    hue] —, 58
169    throng] —, 58
170    colours,] — 58
       rose] —, 58
       song;] —, 58
185    thee,] — 58
187    know] —, 58
189    sheep] —, 58
197    defence,] — 58
201    blasts] blast 58
202    rove;] —. 58
213    come] —, 58
214    ev'ning,] e'vning 58
217    still] —, 58
218    Preserves] Preserve's 58
219    Ends] End's 58
222    attempt,] — 58
       fancy,] — 58
225    Go,] — 58
234    light;] —, 58
237    kind,] — 58
239    glitter;] —, 58
246    this,] — 58
270    bear.] bare, 58
279    see] —, 58
283    state] —, 58
286    heart] —, 58
287    depart;] —, 58
289    dye;] —. 58
290    reins] reigns 58
291    aside.] —; 58
293    ray,] —. 58
306    prayers,] — 58
       time,] — 58
       reveal] —, 58

| | |
|---|---|
| 313 | succeeding brings] —, — 58 |
| | peace;] —, 58 |
| 316 | its] it's 58 |
| 337 | Lords:] —. 58 |
| 338 | sits,] — 58 |
| 340 | righteousness] righteous 58 |
| 342 | majestick] magestick 58 |
| 343 | wait;] — 58 |
| 344 | stand,] — 58 |
| 345 | winds] —, 58 |
| 347 | skies,] — 58 |
| 352 | fulfil] —, 58 |
| 359 | its] it's 58 |
| 371 | fled;] —, 58 |
| 375 | shoar;] — 58 |
| 376 | steal] —, 58 |
| 391 | cedar,] — 58 |
| | pride,] — 58 |
| 393 | rest.] —, 58 |
| 394 | give,] — 58 |
| 395 | kine] kines 58 |
| 396 | browse,] — 58 |
| 400 | There] These 58 |
| 403 | God;] —, 58 |
| 406 | succeeding,] — 58 |
| 407 | goes;] —, 58 |
| 410 | starry] stary 58 |
| 412 | O] O' 58 |
| 414 | call,] — 58 |
| 415 | bestows] —, 58 |
| 418 | stream,] — 58 |
| 419 | came;] — 58 |
| 420 | heat,] — 58 |
| 421 | kinds] KINDS 58 |
| | compleat;] —, 58 |
| 422 | propagated] propogated 58 |
| 424 | cause,] — 58 |
| 425 | Is] —, 58 |
| | ruler] —, 58 |
| | laws;] —, 58 |
| 431 | strain;] —. 58 |
| 434 | dwell,] — 58 |
| 438 | great,] — 58 |

445          earth,] — 58
446          smoaks] smoak 58
450          inwrap] inrap 58 ("inwrap" is the spelling in *Homer's Battle*, 3.167)
454          hail] —, 58
455          Descending,] Discending 58
             vale;] —, 58
460          bare,] — 58
461          tear;] —. 58
463          day.] —, 58
466          No new paragraph in 58
471          verse,] — 58
             descend,] — 58
472          flight,] — 58
473          less] —, 58
480          name,] — 58
481          fame;] —. 58
486          sway,] — 58
488          spake] speak 58
             host] —, 58
494          Amor's] AMOR's 58
496          Ogg] OGG 58
             plain,] — 58
501          feats] fates 58 (In "Deborah," line 145, the MS has "feats" and 58 reads "fate"; the same misreading seems to have occurred here.)
             old;] —, 58
504          might,] — 58
509          bless;] — 58
512          towns] —, 58
528          fly] —, 58
532          express'd,] — 58
544          fulfil] —, 58
554          soil,] — 58
560          Rabbah] —, 58
561          Ammon's] Amon's 58
563          there.] —; 58
572          peace] —, 58
584          rejoice] —, 58
605          fear,] —; 58
609          Garners] Gard'ners 58 (The emendation is confirmed by the text of the first part of Psalm 144:13: "That our garners may be full".)

| | |
|---|---|
| 621 | ease.] —, 58 |
| 622 | No new paragraph in 58 |
| | finish'd,] — 58 |
| | thought] —, 58 |
| 625 | fancy,] — 58 |
| 634 | Tis] Fit 58 (an easy misreading of TP's hand) |
| 645 | descending] decending 58 |
| 647 | speak:] spake, 58 |
| 648 | not, Father,] — — 58 |
| | slain] —, 58 |
| 655 | Ministry,] — 58 |
| 656 | assign] —, 58 |
| 658 | lo,] — 58 |
| 659 | come,] — 58 |
| | father,] — 58 |
| | part.] —, 58 |
| 660 | throne] throng 58 |
| 673 | road;] —, 58 |
| 674 | employ] —, 58 |
| 675 | songs,] — 58 |
| 676 | Hosannah, Lord,] — —, 58 |
| 677 | Hosannah,] — 58 |
| 678 | triumphant,] — 58 |
| | thou] —, 58 |
| 683 | song.] —, 58 |
| 689 | death?] —, 58 |
| 690 | shews] —, 58 |
| 726 | life] —, 58 |
| 734 | call,] — 58 |
| 740 | cry,] — 58 |
| 742 | woe,] — 58 |
| 757 | soul;] —, 58 |
| 763 | with] which 58 (TP probably wrote "w^th" which the compositor mistook for "w^ch") |
| | pay.] —; 58 |
| 765 | recalls] recals 58 |
| 778 | son,] — 58 |
| 782 | time] —, 58 |
| 783 | decay;] —, 58 |
| 793 | Ascention] The *OED* gives this as a sixteenth–seventeenth-century spelling, and it was thus probably current at the time of TP's writing. |
| 794 | Justice,] — 58 |

796      rewards,] — 58
         restore] —, 58
797      before,] —. 58
803      state,] —. 58
806      dress'd,] — 58
815      praise.] —; 58
820      they] the 58
         rear,] — 58
826      above,] — 58
827      love,] —. 58
828      entic'd,] — 58
834      write] —, 58
839      wing;] —, 58
850      endew'd] The *OED* gives this as a regular seventeenth-cen-
         tury spelling.
859      state;] —, 58
871      Loud] Send 58
874      voice] —, 58
         express] —, 58
883      art] —, 58
         first,] — 58
902      swore;] — 58
         intent] —, 58
906      thine;] —, 58
910      be] —, 58
913      clay.] —, 58
922      subjects] subject 58 (In the copies examined, the tail of the *t* is
         broken and there is space for an *s*, which has perhaps
         dropped out.)
929      things,] —. 58
936      Hail,] — 58
         mercy,] — 58
937      Hail,] — 58
945      reign;] —, 58
948      mind] —, 58
954      calls,] — 58
960      Come,] — 58
         queen,] — 58
963      king.] —, 58
970      Come,] — 58
         exalted, come,] — — 58
         song] —, 58
973      crowd] crow'd 58

| 989 | its] it's 58 |
|---|---|
| 993 | Approach,] — 58 |
| 997 | below;] —, 58 |
| 1004 | charms] —, 58 |
| 1010 | Psalt'ry,] — 58 |
| 1017 | shake,] —. 58 |
| 1024 | sing] —, 58 |
| 1030 | art,] — 58 |
| | way] —, 58 |
| 1036 | rear] —, 58 |
| 1067 | veins;] —, 58 |
| 1073 | ears;] —, 58 |
| 1093 | its] it's 58 |
| 1105 | regain'd;] —. 58 |
| 1106 | alas] alass 58 |
| 1110 | vie] —, 58 |
| 1124 | restore] —, 58 |
| 1125 | Its] It's 58 |
| 1127 | its] it's 58 |
| 1132 | restor'd] —, 58 |
| 1134 | breast] —, 58 |
| 1140 | lips,] — 58 |
| | hung] —, 58 |
| 1145 | other] either 58 |
| 1146 | heart] —, 58 |
| 1148 | shews] —, 58 |
| 1152 | altar] alter 58 |

## Explanatory Notes

| 14 | imp] In falconry, feathers are "imped" or engrafted into a bird's wing in order to improve or restore its power of flight; the *OED* cites examples from Spenser, Drayton, and Milton of "imp" used as a metaphor for "taking higher flights". |
|---|---|
| 41–42 | For the building of the tower of Babel, see Genesis 11 : 1–9. |
| 87–88 | In 1 Samuel 16 : 14–23, the evil spirit leaves Saul as the result of David's playing. |
| 106–8 | A conflation of Psalm 57 : 8 and Psalm 108 : 2 (TP's lute is the psalmist's psaltery). |
| 119–32 | Based on Psalm 65 : 9–13. |
| 139–50 | Based on Psalm 23 : 1–4. |
| 153 | In Exodus 3 : 8, God promises Moses that the Israelites will |

enjoy "a land flowing with milk and honey"; the phrase occurs several times later in the Old Testament, but not in the Psalms.

161–66  Based on Psalm 1:3.

173–88  Based on Psalm 103:15–18.

195–208  Based on Psalm 121:1–6.

217–20  Based on Psalm 121:7–8.

225–28  In 1 Samuel 17:34–37, David tells Saul of his killing of the lions and bears that took his sheep.

233–42  Based on Psalm 8:3–9.

245–46  Based on Psalm 141:2.

265–303  Expanded from Psalm 101; lines 266–70 are TP's interpolation, though lines 269–70 perhaps recall Psalm 72:3.

269–70  The sense seems to be: "Mercy and justice, tempering love with fear, establish peace, and in peace the harvests are good and even the normally bare mountains become productive".

310–25  Based on Psalm 72:1–2, 4–17.

326–27  Psalm 72 was traditionally interpreted as one of the "messianic" psalms prophesying the reign of Christ.

338–41  Based on Psalm 99:1–4.

342–55  Based on Psalm 104:1–4.

356–59  Based on Psalm 19:1–2

366–427  Based on Psalm 104:5–18, 20–24, 27–31.

400  There] Although 58's "These" is possible, "There" gives better sense, balancing "Where" (line 398) and making "the beasts" the subject of "hide", as they must be of "roar" (line 402).

428–29  Probably based on a conflation of Psalm 99:1–2 and Psalm 117:1.

444–63  Based on Psalm 18:7–15.

446  smoaks] Psalm 18:8 has "smoke", but in view of the later "blasts" it seems preferable to emend 58's "smoak" rather than "precede".

486–99  Based on Psalm 136:13–20 and Psalm 135:11.

504–31  Based on Psalm 18:2–42.

542–45  TP here recalls 1 Samuel 16, where God sends Samuel to find and anoint David.

546–59  Expanded from Psalm 108:7–9 (Psalm 60:6–8 is very similar).

560–63  This passage is apparently TP's addition. Rabbah was the capital of the Ammonites (inhabitants of "Ammon's plain"; we have emended 1758's "Amon's"). In 2 Samuel 10–12 David makes war on the Ammonites; Joab takes Rabbah. Seir is mentioned in Joshua 15:10 as one of the places marking the boundaries of Israel; here, then, like Rabbah, it is used to indicate the far points of David's rule. We have been unable to identify "Johemaan", which seems not to be biblical. The text is possibly corrupt.

566–69 Based on Psalm 108:12–13 (or on Psalm 60:11–12, which is almost the same).

572–73 Perhaps an echo of Psalm 85:10.

574–83 TP seems to have a modern triumphal procession in mind here.

584–89 Based on Psalm 47:1–6.

592 The sense of "mind" is difficult here; the text may be corrupt, or perhaps TP means "power of mind".

594–99 Based on Psalm 47:9–10.

600–621 Expanded from Psalm 144:12–15.

648–50 Recalls Psalm 50:9–14 and Psalm 51:16–17.

652–55 Piercing the ear is mentioned as a badge of servitude in Exodus 21:6 and Deuteronomy 15:17; for the idea of "opening" the ear, see Psalm 40:6.

670–73 Based on Matthew 21:8–9 and Mark 11:8–10.

674–79 Based on Psalm 118:24–26.

694–99 Based on Psalm 69:1–2, 4.

712–15 Based on Psalm 22:1–2.

716–21 Based on Psalm 22:11–13.

722–23 Based on Psalm 129:3.

724–33 Based on Psalm 22:16, 14–15.

734–35 Based on Psalm 69:21.

736–37 Based on Psalm 22:18 (the soldiers, however, are taken from John 19:23–24).

738–43 Based on Psalm 22:19.

749 The evangelists all recall these anticipations of the sufferings of Christ; see Matthew 27, Mark 15, Luke 23, and John 19–20.

772–75 Based on Psalm 110:5–7, traditionally interpreted as "messianic."

792–801 Christ is received into a cloud in Acts 1:9, but TP is here probably thinking of Elijah's being taken up to heaven in a chariot of fire (2 Kings 2:11–12), often seen as a type of Christ's ascension.

802–11 Based on Psalm 68:17–18.

812–15 Perhaps recalls Psalm 47:5–6.

816–29 The two angels are taken from Acts 1:11, but the theme of their removing the relics to prevent idolatry (which recalls

"Moses," lines 731–50) is either TP's addition or from a nonbiblical source.

840–43　　Based on Psalm 24:7–9.

844–51　　Expanded from Psalm 24:10.

870–75　　This passage seems to be a conflation of phrases from Psalm 104:3–4, 7 with 1 Kings 19:11–13, where God manifests himself to Elijah not in a wind, an earthquake, or a fire but in a "still small voice".

883–911　　Based on Psalm 110:1–6; the application to Christ in line 883 derives from the New Testament (see Matthew 22:44, Mark 12:36, and Luke 20:42–43).

912–19　　Based on Psalm 2:9–12.

930–41　　Expanded from hints in Psalm 72 (especially verses 5, 8, 15, and 18).

942–73　　Based loosely on Psalm 45:2–17.

1002–33　　The passage seems mainly TP's own, but the instruments chosen may reflect Psalm 150, the last psalm.

1072–1161　Despite TP's apparent claim of originality in lines 1045–46, this passage is expanded from Psalm 51.

1103–5　　The idea is in Psalm 51:7, but TP has also drawn on Leviticus 14:1–7 (where, however, the purification prescribed for leprosy is more complicated than TP implies) and on Numbers 19:13–18 (where purification with hyssop and water is prescribed for having touched the dead).

1145　　other] Conjecturally emended from 58's "either"; the sense (following Psalm 51:15–16) seems to be: "I will offer prayer and songs, and I would offer other (material) sacrifices if they would please you; but I know that the kind of sacrifices that you want are spiritual ones."

## Solomon

This poem is a greatly expanded paraphrase of the Song of Solomon, which TP allegorizes in terms of the Church as the bride of Christ. TP's copy of the second edition (London, 1669) of *Clavis Cantici: or, an Exposition of the Song of Solomon* (first published Edinburgh, 1668) by the Scottish covenanting divine James Durham (1622–58) is one of a number of his books now in the Cashel Diocesan Library; see Robert S. Matteson, "Books from the Library of Thomas Parnell," *The Library* 6 (1984): 374, No. 6. Durham prefaced his detailed (478 pages) commentary on the Song with a long general introduction in which he defends the Song's doctrinal value and expounds its allegorical significance.

## Textual Notes

| | |
|---|---|
| 4 | she.] — 58 |
| 16 | high;] —, 58 |
| 19 | Go,] — 58 |
| 27 | Hence,] — 58 |
| 28 | dreams,] —; 58 |
| 30 | bows;] —, 58 |
| 36 | feet.] —; 58 |
| 47 | vineyard] —, 58 |
| 66 | look;] —, 58 |
| 76 | mind;] —, 58 |
| 80 | delights;] —, 58 |
| 86 | their;] —, 58 |
| 87 | face,] — 58 |
| 89 | Ishmael's] Ismael's 58 |
| | abides,] — 58 |
| 104 | do'st] dos't 58 |
| 108 | aside?] —. 58 |
| 112 | below;] —, 58 |
| 114 | said:] — 58 |
| 134 | feast;] —, 58 |
| 136 | sheds;] — 58 |
| 137 | soul] —, 58 |
| 139 | myrrhe,] — 58 |
| 153 | says;] —, 58 |
| 171 | forth;] —, 58 |
| 178 | expire;] —, 58 |
| 179 | plac'd,] — 58 |
| 180 | and] aud 58 |
| 181 | languid] lanquid 58 |
| 182 | said:] — 58 |
| 183 | peace,] — 58 |
| 189 | charge] —, 58 |
| | ill,] — 58 |
| 200 | hers] her's 58 |
| 202 | whisper] —, 58 |
| 225 | flow'rs] —, 58 |
| 226 | shows;] —, 58 |
| 227 | renew] —, 58 |
| 230 | fruit;] —, 58 |
| 231 | scents] —, 58 |
| 256 | own;] —, 58 |

| | |
|---|---|
| 520 | presence] —, 58 |
| 524 | Thummim,] The comma is extremely faint in all copies we have seen. |
| 531 | here] —, 58 |
| 534 | Its] It's 58 |
| 541 | leaves] leave's 58 |
| 542 | waters] water's 58 |
| | props] prop's 58 |
| 547 | place,] — 58 |
| 553 | paints] paint's 58 |
| 555 | fed,] — 58 |
| 557 | made,] — 58 |
| 558 | aid;] —, 58 |
| 561 | such] snch 58 |
| | white,] — 58 |
| 568 | alone;] —, 58 |
| 571 | queens] —, 58 |
| | appearance] —, 58 |
| | cry,] — 58 |
| 577 | kind,] — 58 |
| 583 | blow] blown 58 |
| 584 | blossoms] —, 58 |
| 588 | grace] —, 58 |
| 608 | its] it's 58 |
| 616 | white;] —, 58 |
| 635 | Strait] Srait 58 |
| 651 | damsels,] — 58 |
| 656 | here;] —, 58 |
| 670 | blow;] —, 58 |
| 672 | there.] —: 58 |
| 673 | gate,] — 58 |
| | meet;] —, 58 |
| 674 | Jessamines] Jessamine 58 |
| 683 | meet] —, 58 |
| 685 | its] it's 58 |
| | I] —, 58 |
| 699 | me,] — 58 |
| 701 | bliss,] — 58 |
| 706 | celestial] —, 58 |
| 707 | more,] — 58 |
| 714 | involv'd] invol'd 58 |
| 727 | love] —, 58 |
| 728 | alike;] —, 58 |

| | |
|---|---|
| 731 | Its] It's 58 |
| 735 | prove] —, 58 |
| 737 | love] —, 58 |
| | agree,] — 58 |
| 739 | own] —, 58 |
| 740 | No Breasts] No Breast's 58 |
| 745 | No new paragraph in 58. |
| 759 | wall;] —, 58 |
| 761 | rest] —, 58 |
| 767 | Baal-Hamon] BAAL-HAMON 58 |
| 774 | they;] —, 58 |
| 804 | they] thy 58 |

## Explanatory Notes

| | |
|---|---|
| 12 | TP may have had in mind the bower of Adam and Eve as described in *Paradise Lost* 4.690–702. |
| 27 | o'er] The sense is perhaps "go away to your imaginary scenes, you prophane writers". Possibly "o'er" should be emended to "of", which gives an easier sense. |
| 47 | vineyard] Christ tells parables of vineyards in Matthew 20:1–8, 21:28–31, 21:33–41 (this one is substantially repeated in Mark 12:1–11 and Luke 20:9–18), and Luke 13:6–9. |
| 48 | marriage-feast] For the parable of the unwilling guests invited to the marriage-feast, see Matthew 22:1–14 and Luke 14:7–11. |
| 50 | with illapses of] Suffused or permeated with; "illapse" is used frequently in the seventeenth century in such phrases as "the illapse of the holy spirit" *(OED)*. |
| 59–68 | A standard Christian reading of the Song of Solomon (subsequently cited as "Song") interpreted the groom as Christ and his bride as the Church (Saint Paul uses the image in 2 Corinthians 11:1–4). The book, the light, and the lamb are standard emblems of the Church, but TP may here be recalling Revelation 5. |
| 69–108 | The Church's speech is developed from Song 1:2–7. |
| 112 | Christ's seamless garment is mentioned in John 19:23. |
| 115–30 | Christ's speech is based on Song 1:8–11. |
| 133–40 | The Church's speech is based on Song 1:12–14. |
| 141–42 | Christ's words are based on Song 1:15. |
| 143–52 | The Church's speech is based on Song 1:16–17. |
| 153–60 | Christ's speech is based on Song 2:1–2. |

| | |
|---|---|
| 161–80 | The Church's speech is based on Song 2:3–6. |
| 182–90 | Christ's speech is based on Song 2:7. |
| 207–18 | The Church's speech is based on Song 2:8–9. |
| 221–60 | Christ's speech (as reported by the Church) is based on Song 2:10–17. |
| 267–86 | The Church's speech is based on Song 3:1–4. |
| 301–28 | Based on Song 3:6–11. |
| 355–82 | Christ's speech is based on Song 4:1–7. |
| 361 | Granate] Pomegranate. |
| 395–430 | Based on Song 4:8–15. |
| 433–42 | The Church's speech is based on Song 4:16. |
| 443–54 | Based on Song 5:1. |
| 463–92 | Based on Song 5:2–8. |
| 493–96 | The speech of the Daughters of Jerusalem is based on Song 5:9. |
| 497–522 | Christ's reply is based on Song 5:10–16. |
| 523 | The sense is presumably "the spouse's anthems sing [of] her friend". |
| 524 | Thummin] The Urim and Thummim were objects (of uncertain nature) worn by the Jewish high priest and used by him to cast lots declaratory of God's will. |
| 527–30 | The speech of the Daughters of Jerusalem is based on Song 6:1. |
| 532–40 | The Church's speech is based on Song 6:2–3. |
| 547–88 | The Church repeats Christ's words from Song 6:4–11. |
| 583 | It is the leaves and blossom of the pomegranate tree that "blow". |
| 595–602 | The idea is taken from Song 6:13. |
| 605–48 | The Daughters' song is based on Song 7:1–9. |
| 650–54 | The hint for the Church's speech is taken from Song 7:10. |
| 661–98 | The Church's speech is based on Song 7:11–8:3. |
| 713–16 | The Daughters' song is based on the first part of Song 8:5. |
| 723–44 | The Church's speech is based on Song 8:9. |
| 759–65 | Expanded from Song 8:10. |
| 766–84 | Christ's speech is based on Song 8:11–13. |
| 795–804 | Expanded from Song 8:14. |

# *Jonah*

This poem is a paraphrase of the first three chapters of the Book of Jonah. In order to emphasize Jonah as a type of Christ, sent to mankind, and raised from the dead to save the Gentiles, TP omits chapter 4 (in which Jonah is displeased when God decides to save Nineveh), replacing it with an explicit analogy between Jonah and Christ.

## Textual Notes

| | |
|---|---|
| 2 | brow;] —, 58 |
| 31 | pilot:] —, 58 |
| 33 | the] they 58 |
| | rest:] —, 58 |
| 35 | heav'n] heav'en 58 |
| | tell;] —, 58 |
| 39 | heard,] — 58 |
| 55 | run,] — 58 |
| 58 | ship] —, 58 |
| 63 | O,] — 58 |
| 76 | against] agaiust 58 |
| 79 | cause] —, 58 |
| | woe,] — 58 |
| 81 | main,] — 58 |
| 88 | theirs] their's 58 |
| 95 | o'er,] — 58 |
| 97 | stills] still's 58 |
| 100 | breaking] —, 58 |
| 102 | then] —, 58 |
| 103 | grows,] — 58 |
| 110 | its] it's 58 |
| 119 | view,] — 58 |
| 122 | bulk] —, 58 |
| 123 | alive;] —, 58 |
| 124 | prophet] —, 58 |
| 140 | side;] —, 58 |
| 141 | calms] —, 58 |
| | wave,] — 58 |
| 142 | grave;] —, 58 |
| 147 | lies,] — 58 |
| 149 | Alas] Alass 58 |
| 150 | sorr'wing] sorrow'ng 58 |
| 156 | mountains] —, 58 |
| 165 | men] —, 58 |
| 168 | vows] —, 58 |
| | give] gave 58 |
| 193 | race,] — 58 |

201     Hell] —, 58
209     Hope] HOPE 58
210     Promise] PROMISE 58
212     foe;] —, 58
214     case;] —, 58

### Explanatory Notes

1–6     These lines provide a transition from "Solomon."
7–128     Greatly expanded from Jonah 1.
129–74     Expanded from Jonah 2.
175–88     Based on Jonah 3 (treated much more briefly than 1 and 2).
189–225     This Christian interpretation replaces Jonah 4.

## Hezekiah

There are three major accounts of Hezekiah (king of Judah from about 715 B.C., and a noted religious reformer) in the Old Testament: 2 Kings 18–20, 2 Chronicles 29–32, and Isaiah 36–39. TP's poem uses all three sources.

### Textual Notes

1     Beach] —, 58
4     where] when 58
     Hezekiah] HEZEKIAH 58
7     resort] —, 58
8     Hezekiah's] HEZEKIAH's 58
18     Asaph's] ASAPH's 58
27     string] —, 58
33     Alas] Alass 58
36     Isaiah] ISAIAH 58
44     destructive] —, 58
52     Isaiah] IASIAH 58
68     Seer] SEER 58
94     dead;] —, 58
96     sing;] —. 58
98     despair'd] dispair'd 58
     decay;] —, 58
101     said,] — 58
     God,] — 58

| | |
|---|---|
| 110 | uncomfortable] uncumfortable 58 |
| 142 | seem] seeem 58 |
| 143 | reign,] — 58 |
| 144 | humbling] humbl'ing 58 |
| 167 | raise,] — 58 |
| 178 | train;] —, 58 |
| 201 | string,] — 58 |
| 207 | came,] — 58 |
| 220 | owe;] —, 58 |
| 230 | still;] —, 58 |
| 232 | aspire;] —, 58 |
| 235 | song] —, 58 |
| 237 | ecchos] eccho's 58 |

## Explanatory Notes

| | |
|---|---|
| 1–24 | TP here follows mainly 2 Chronicles 29 (there is a similar account in 2 Kings 18). |
| 29–88 | Here TP follows 2 Kings 20:1–11. |
| 75 | thrice a day] Not the same as "on the third day" of 2 Kings 20:5, 8. Lines 56–64 clearly speak of the sun rising and setting three times in one day in Isaiah's vision. In lines 210–12 TP writes as though the miracle seen in the vision had actually happened. |
| 101–69 | This passage follows Hezekiah's psalm of thanksgiving in Isaiah 38:10–20. |
| 172 | Heman's or Jeduthun's sons] In 1 Chronicles 25:1–7 David establishes three guilds of musicians, the sons respectively of Asaph, Jeduthun, and Heman. Heman is also the attributed author of Psalm 88, and the name of a singer in 1 Chronicles 6:33. "Jeduthun" occurs in the headings of some psalms (39, 62, and 77), but its interpretation there is disputed. |
| 179 | Moriah's hill] The site of Solomon's temple. |
| 207 | Chaldeans] Babylonian ambassadors visit Hezekiah in all three biblical accounts (2 Kings 20:12–13, 2 Chronicles 32:31, and Isaiah 39:1–2), but in each case the point of the incident is that Isaiah rebukes Hezekiah for showing his wealth to them. TP suppresses this theme and changes the moralization of their visit. |
| 210–12 | The actual miracle (as all the biblical accounts agree) performed for Hezekiah was making the sun go back ten degrees; the sun rises and sets three times as a sign of Hezekiah's recovery only in Isaiah's vision (lines 56–64). |

# *Habakkuk*

The prophet Habakkuk, living in evil and troubled times, questions the wisdom of providence; it is revealed to him that the Israelites are soon to be chastised by the Chaldeans, and he prophesies accordingly. TP's poem (especially his added conclusion, lines 177–216) is evidence of his early interest in the theme of God's justice, an interest that finds its best expression in his later poem "The Hermit."

## Textual Notes

| | |
|---|---|
| 8 | Habakkuk] HABAKKUK 58 |
| 19 | Fall'n] Fal'n 58 |
| | prostrate] prostate 58 |
| | lye] Iye 58 |
| 21 | voice:] —, 58 |
| | complain] —, 58 |
| 22 | vain;] —. 58 |
| 23 | still] —, 58 |
| 29 | the] ye 58 |
| 35 | blow,] — 58 |
| 38 | destroys] destroy's 58 |
| 49 | replys] reply's 58 |
| 54 | Gods] God's 58 |
| 59 | Seer] See'r 58 |
| 87 | number'd] numbred 58 |
| 93 | it] —, 58 |
| 100 | Light] —, 58 |
| 109 | where'er] where're 58 |
| 113 | fly] —, 58 |
| 138 | refrain;] —, 58 |
| 143 | band,] — 58 |
| 145 | head,] — 58 |
| 146 | led;] —, 58 |
| 156 | wonder,] — 58 |
| 159 | leanness] leaness 58 |
| 187 | Borne] Born 58 |
| 197 | attend,] — 58 |

## Explanatory Notes

| | |
|---|---|
| 14 | Elijah] In 1 Kings 19:1–3, Elijah "wrapped his face in his mantle" when he heard the "still small voice" of God. |

29–48     Based on Habakkuk 1.
49–55     Based on Habbakuk 2, chiefly verses 2–3, 8, 18–20.
71        Alludes to Habakkuk 2:2.
72–73     Alludes to Habakkuk 1:6.
85–176    Based on Habakkuk 3.
153       horse] Habakkuk 3:15 has "horses", but TP's "horse" seems
          to be used collectively.
176       Moriah's hill] The site of Solomon's temple.

# The Affections of Divine Poetry

The identification of these poems as a group, and their general title, derive from the Congleton inventory of TP's works, where they are listed as follows:

| The Affections of Divine Poetry Containing | |
| --- | --- |
| A Hymn for Morning | 44 |
| Noon | 48 |
| Evening | 38 |
| A Soul in Sorrow | 46 |
| The Happy Man | 60 |
| The Way to Happiness | [3]6 |
| The Convert's Love | 48 |
| On yᵉ Divine Love | 40 |
| A Desire to Praise | 64 |
| On Contentment | 48 |
| | 32 |
| | 504 |

The presumption must be that there was once a manuscript containing these poems, but that it is no longer extant. As we have argued in the Introduction, TP probably adjusted the contents of the group for the "Everard" manuscript by omitting "On Contentment" (which is probably the same as the "Hymn on Contentment" published in Steele's *Poetical Miscellanies*) and by adding others. "Piety" precedes these poems in the 1758 edition, but it does not follow that it was intended as a preface to them. A longer poem in heroic couplets, it seems too weighty for such a purpose. All of the poems listed in the "Affections" group in the inventory are in octosyllabic couplets, and all are short. The only poem in heroic couplets in the group as it appears in 1758 is "On Happiness in this Life"; this was presumably inserted into the group at the time TP prepared the manuscript for Everard. Because the sequence of poems in

567

1758 from "A Hymn to Morning" to "On Divine Love" is so close to the poems as listed in the inventory, we have felt justified in printing them here as a group under the general title of "The Affections of Divine Poetry." The inventory is printed in the Appendix to this edition.

The only text of the poems in this group is 1758, from which they are here reprinted with a few slight modifications mainly in the punctuation, as recorded in the textual notes.

## Textual Notes

### A Hymn for Morning

| | |
|---|---|
| 3 | make] makes 58 |
| 8 | its] it's 58 |
| 24 | its] it's 58 |
| 26 | its] it's 58 |

### A Hymn for Noon

| | |
|---|---|
| 3 | Its] It's 58 |
| 11 | worldly] wordly 58 |
| 12 | its] it's 58 |
| 17 | its] it's 58 |
| | vie] —, 58 |
| 25 | love] —, 58 |
| 27 | pray'r,] — 58 |

### A Hymn for Evening

| | |
|---|---|
| 5 | bow,] — 58 |
| 6 | now] —, 58 |
| 11 | make] makes 58 |
| | bless'd] —, 58 |
| 13 | brain] —, 58 |
| 31 | throne] —, 58 |
| 34 | its] it's 58 |
| 36 | joy,] —. 58 |

## The Soul in Sorrow

| | |
|---|---|
| 6 | made,] —. 58 |
| 35 | smart,] — 58 |

## The Happy Man

| | |
|---|---|
| 19 | hence,] — 58 |
| | besides] —, 58 |
| 27 | Saviour,] — 58 |
| | above,] — 58 |
| 33 | display] —, 58 |
| 34 | Its] It's 58 |
| 36 | Its] It's 58 |
| 42 | its] it's 58 |
| 43 | its] it's 58 |
| 51 | Its] It's 58 |
| 55 | days] —, 58 |
| 58 | specious] spacious 58 |

## The Way to Happiness

| | |
|---|---|
| 4 | delight?] —. 58 |
| 5 | stray,] — 58 |
| 9 | need,] — 58 |
| 19 | clean,] — 58 |
| 20 | again,] — 58 |
| 25 | shew,] — 58 |
| 32 | thine;] —. 58 |

## The Convert's Love

| | |
|---|---|
| 8 | ways,] — 58 |
| 9 | home,] — 58 |
| 14 | shun;] —. 58 |
| 20 | fear;] —. 58 |
| 28 | its] it's 58 |
| 29 | turn,] — 58 |
| 38 | fire.] —, 58 |
| 39 | its] it's 58 |

## A Desire to Praise

| | | |
|---|---|---|
| 6 | run,] — 58 | |
| 7 | near,] — 58 | |
| 15 | kind,] — 58 | |
| 25 | youth,] — 58 | |
| 29 | supreme,] — 58 | |
| 31 | its] it's 58 | |
| | show,] — 58 | |
| 34 | here;] —, 58 | |
| 35 | bless'd,] — 58 | |
| 54 | Lyre,] — 58 | |
| 57 | theirs] their's 58 | |
| 59 | rejoice,] — 58 | |
| 63 | agree,] — 58 | |

## On Happiness in this Life

| | | |
|---|---|---|
| 6 | breeze,] —. 58 | |
| 8 | its] it's 58 | |
| 10 | summer-bower] —, 58 | |
| 14 | wine,] —. 58 | |
| 17 | spring,] — 58 | |
| 18 | sing.] —: 58 | |
| 22 | stay,] — 58 | |
| 33 | plain,] — 58 | |

## On Divine Love

| | | |
|---|---|---|
| 5 | roll,] — 58 | |
| 14 | Its] It's 58 | |
| 17 | its] it's 58 | |
| 27 | birth,] — 58 | |

# Poems from *Works in Verse and Prose* (1755)

"Bacchus" and "Piety" were first printed, as a pair, in the *Dublin Weekly Journal* for 4 June 1726. In the 1755 *Works in Verse and Prose* they were printed among a group of five poems that had not appeared in Pope's edition; and both poems were again printed in the 1758 *Posthumous Works*. Neither in 1755 nor in 1758 were the two poems printed as a pair. Each of the three printings seems to have been from an independent manuscript; and although there is an extant manuscript of an early version of "Piety" ("A Dream," in the "Satires" Notebook, ff. 13a–14b), this manuscript offers little help with the relationships between the printed texts. The variants are few, and mostly of uncertain interpretation; this makes for a difficult editorial problem.

In the *Dublin Weekly Journal* the poems were introduced by the following letter:

*To* HIBERNICUS

SIR,
 YOU have so often obliged me in this Way already, that I begin to think my self entiteled to a Place in your Paper, from a Right of Prescription. What I now send you has a Claim to it for a much better Reason. The following Pieces are the genuine Remains of a Reverend Gentleman, whose Writings have been received with Universal Applause. How these came to miss a Place in the printed Collection of his Works, I do not know, but sure I am, the publick ought not to be deprived of them, nor any other production of so deserving and excellent a person; though I am informed, there are a good many other Pieces of the same Hand, that have never yet seen the Light.

*I am, Sir,*
*Your very Humble Servant.*
MUSOPHILUS

"Musophilus" and "Hibernicus" were the same person, James Arbuckle, a Scot who arrived in Dublin about 1724, and who contributed a series of essays and papers to the *Dublin Weekly Journal* from 1725 to 1727 under the title "Hibernicus's Letters." (For details about Arbuckle, see James Woolley, "Arbuckle's 'Panegyric' and Swift's Scrub Libel," *Contemporary Studies of Swift's Poetry*, ed. John I. Fischer and Donald C. Mell [Newark: University of Delaware Press, 1981], 191–209.) In his last paper (No. 104, 25 March 1727), Arbuckle stated that he had "even sometimes endeavoured, under the Name of *Musophilus*, to divert my Readers with a few Pieces in Poetry," and referred specifically to "the two incomparable Poems in the sixty Second Paper, which were written by the late Reverend Archdeacon *Parnel*, and are no ways unworthy that great and extraordinary Genius." It seems reasonable to infer that Arbuckle's manuscript was not autograph (or he would surely have said so), and that it contained only the two poems (since he does not claim personal knowledge of any other unpublished poems). Most probably, then, this manuscript was a nonauthorial transcript; we know that transcripts of other poems found their way into print in the 1720s.

The poems are very poorly printed (in italic, using roman for emphasis), and in the copies that we have examined many letters have failed to print and many are broken. In "Piety," for example, the final *s* of the first "thousands" in *DWJ*'s version of line 76 has failed to print, though its presence can be inferred from the spacing; and in line 98 the last two letters of "fall" have failed to print. The two poems are very heavily capitalized (many adjectives beginning with a capital), much more so than in any extant TP holograph. The few substantive variants unique to 1726 are mostly probable errors (such as "wakeful" in "Piety", line 38); but "Fame is" ("Piety", line 42) seems likely to be authorial, and "Jolly" ("Bacchus", line 2) may be, although it might be the work of a transcriber unfamiliar with the invocation "Io Bacchus", since TP's capital *I* is virtually identical to his *J*. For all these reasons, the texts of the poems as printed in the *Dublin Weekly Journal* are not suitable as copy-texts.

The manuscript available to the editor of the 1755 *Works in Verse and Prose* seems to have been a "working" notebook rather than a book of "fair copies." Of the five "new" poems printed in the edition, we have later texts of two ("Elysium" and "Ecstasy") in the "Satires" Notebook, and a later text of "To Dr. Swift" was published in Swift's own *Works* (1765). We might, then, expect 1755's texts of "Piety" and "Bacchus" to be early rather than late. In the case of "Elysium," however, 1755's text is later than that of 1758, though earlier than that of the "Satires" Notebook. With "Piety" and "Bacchus" the evidence is inconclusive. With one exception ("lure" in "Bacchus," line 12, a probable misreading of TP's hand), 1755's unique variants are all probably authorial. This need not mean that they are late readings, but it does mean that 1755 probably reflects the wording of its manuscript more faithfully than either 1758 or the *Dublin Weekly Journal*. As the most carefully printed, it is the most reliable text. It is, however, clearly modernized in its spelling and capitalization, and the editor probably tidied up what punctuation he found in the manuscript.

The texts of the two poems in 1758 show the typical features of that volume. Of its unique variants, most are probable errors, and many are the same classes of error that are found by comparison between the poems of British Library Add. MS 31114 as they appear in that MS and in 1758. For example, 1758's frequent confusion between singular and plural is found in "Bacchus," lines 18 and 20, and in "Piety," lines 3, 18, and 76. Nevertheless, a few of 1758's unique variants are probably authorial: "restore", in "Piety," line 57; and "Skulks", in "Bacchus," line 65. As usual, 1758's punctuation is poor, and we may suspect (on the evidence of the poems in Add. MS 31114) that its spelling and capitalization do not closely follow those of the manuscript from which it was printed. It is, however, not "modernized" in the way 1755 is; indeed, 1758, particularly in its capitalization, looks rather old-fashioned for a book of its date.

Although it might seem from the above discussion that 1755 would be excluded as a copy-text by reason of its modernization, we have in fact chosen it as our copy-text in the belief that it is (unexpectedly) probably closer to its manuscript than either of the two other texts. TP himself was an erratic, but not a heavy capitalizer. For example, in the early version of "Piety" ("A Dream," in the "Satires" Notebook, ff. 13a–14b) TP wrote "lips a living coal" (line 8). These words survived into the expanded version of the poem, and appear in exactly the same form in 1755 (where they occur in line 20); 1758, however, prints "Lips a living Coal". It seems less misleading to the reader to have almost all capitals removed than to have a text in which many words are capitalized, but not necessarily those that TP himself would have so spelled. Similarly with the spelling: 1755's "blue" ("Piety," line 9) looks like a modernization compared with 1758's "blew"; but "blue" is a spelling found in TP's manuscripts (e.g., "Ecstasy," "Satires" Notebook, f. 43b, line 31). The use of large and small capitals in 1755, however, has no parallel in TP's extant manuscripts; probably the 1755 editor decided to use small capitals for words underlined in the original manuscript. We have decided to leave the texts of the two poems exactly as they appear in 1755, however (except for the correction of "lure" in "Bacchus," line 12), even at the cost of losing some probable TP spellings. For example, "breath" in "Piety," line 51, is the reading both of the *Dublin Weekly Journal* and of 1758; it is also TP's regular spelling of "breathe".

The superiority of 1755's verbal variants is far from certain. Three main passages can be cited in favor of its readings being more likely to be later than those of the *Dublin Weekly Journal* or of 1758. The first is in

"Piety," line 43, where 1755's "fervours of unhallow'd fire" seems pre-
ferable to the "raptures of discorded fire" found in 1758 and the *Journal:*
"fervours" goes better with "fire" and is a more pejorative word than
"raptures", while "unhallow'd" introduces an appropriately moral and
religious dimension absent from "discorded". The second passage oc-
curs a few lines later, where 1755 has "great" and "lasting" for the
"warm" and "lambent" of 1758 and the *Journal* (line 49). Although one
might suppose that TP had taken out "great" and "lasting" to avoid the
repetition with the following line, it seems more likely that he intended
the chiasmus; while "warm" and "lambent" make a poor antithesis. The
third passage is the couplet found in 1758 and the *Journal* but not in
1755 (see the textual note to "Bacchus," line 46). Its omission might be
due to carelessness, especially as line 46 is the last line on a page in the
1755 edition; but in general 1755 is carefully printed, and such a slip
seems unlikely. Small excisions are characteristic of TP's revisions; for
example, in the manuscript version of "Health" ("An Eclogue," "Satires"
Notebook, ff. 51a–53a), two separate couplets are canceled. (The 1755
"Variations" also contain many examples, but as they may possibly be
Pope's rather than TP's, they can hardly be called in evidence.)

On balance, then, we have accepted 1755's texts of the poems, since, if
not close to the texture of TP's manuscript, they at least do not misrepre-
sent it. In the textual notes we have recorded the verbal variants between
the three texts; in accepting "cure" in line 12 of "Bacchus," we have
modified it from "Cure" to conform with 1755's own capitalization. It
should be noted that the only evidence of these poems being in any sense
a pair is the presumed existence of a manuscript (that behind the *Journal*
printing) containing only them. In the *Journal* "Piety" was printed first
(though this arrangement need not have been authorial). In 1755 the
order of the "new" poems is "Bacchus," "Elysium," "To Dr. Swift,"
"Piety," and "Ecstasy". In 1758 "Piety" was printed before the group of
poems "The Affections of Divine Poetry"; "Bacchus" immediately after
"The Judgment of Paris" among the secular poems headed by "On
Queen Anne's Peace."

TP's two poems were included in the collected reprint of Arbuckle's
essays, *A Collection of Letters and Essays on Several Subjects, Lately Publish'd in
the Dublin Journal* (2 vols., 1729). The few minor changes made in this
reprinting do not suggest that Arbuckle had recourse to the manuscript
from which he had printed the poem in 1726. Most variants suggest
routine correction, either by Arbuckle or the 1729 printer: "Lesbos" for
"Lesbos", in "Bacchus", line 88; "lo" for "low", in "Piety", line 17; and
"thousand" for the second "thousands" in "Piety", line 76. A less intel-
ligent correction, but understandable in view of *DWJ*'s phrasing, gives
"which" for the second "that" in *DWJ*'s version of "Bacchus", line 63. The

reading of that line in 1755 and 1758 is superior in every way. At "Piety", lines 29–30 the 1729 volume reads "Viol" for *DWJ*'s "Vial", a spelling on which *DWJ* agrees with 1755 and 1758. It is clear that 1729 attempted to correct the most obvious printing errors of *DWJ* but has no independent authority of its own and we have not included its readings in the textual commentary. Arbuckle's collection was reissued, without the dedications but with the addition of an index in each volume, as *Hibernicus's Letters: or, a Philosophical Miscellany,* in 1734 (the evidence of the press figures shows that this was not a reprint but a reissue of the 1729 sheets).

There is a transcript of "Piety" in Bodley MS Montagu d.1 (ff. 86–88). The way the scribe has begun each paragraph with a word written in capitals and the presence of variants found only in the 1726 printing suggest that this transcript was copied from the collected reprint of Arbuckle. In line 17, the transcript has "lo", following Arbuckle's correction of *DWJ*'s "low"; and in line 76 it replaces the second "thousands" with "thousand", also corrected by Arbuckle. Another transcript, at Yale (Osborn Collection), of both this poem and "Bacchus," similarly follows Arbuckle's corrected version in these and other details (see headnote to *The Horse and the Olive* for the Yale MS).

# Bacchus

We have not been able to find a source for this poem, or any classical original for the particular story about Bacchus. The closest analogue that we have discovered is a Jewish story told of Noah, that when about to plant a vineyard, Satan offered him his help in return for a share in the produce. Noah agreed, and Satan successively fertilized the ground with the blood of several animals (a lamb, a lion, a pig, and a monkey). The interpretation is that after the first glass of wine, man becomes mild like a sheep, and then after each further glass becomes successively like the other animals (Louis Ginzberg, *Legends of the Jews* [Philadelphia, 1913], 1 : 167–68; and for variants and sources [1925], 5 : 190).

Nor have we been able to find any particular connection between Bacchus and Lesbos (lines 6 and 88). The mention of the island suggests that TP was working from a particular source. Similarly, the reference in line 47 to "an antient author" suggests that TP was translating or adapting rather than inventing.

## Textual Notes

Title    In *DWJ* the title is "ʙᴀᴄᴄʜᴜs"; in 58 it is *Bacchus or the Drunken Metamorphosis.* In the Congleton inventory, the poem is listed

as "Bacchus's Entertainment, or the Drunken Meta-
morphosis."

2        Io] 55, 58; Jolly *DWJ*
9        are] 55, 58; and *DWJ*
12       and] 55; to 58, *DWJ*
         cure] Cure 58, *DWJ;* lure 55
13       down] 55; o'er 58, *DWJ*
14       o'er] 55; down 58, *DWJ*
15       clusters] 55; Cluster 58, *DWJ*
18       dung] 55, *DWJ;* Dungs 58
19       bare] 55; bear 58, *DWJ*
23       revive] 55; refresh'd 58, *DWJ*
28       calls] 55, *DWJ;* call 58
32       jovial] 55, *DWJ;* jolly 58
37       beside] 55; aside 58, *DWJ*
42       here] 55, *DWJ;* there 58
46       An additional couplet follows this line in 58 and *DWJ*, but is
         not found in 55: "Thus they drink and thus they play / The
         Sun and all their Wits away."
50       tang] 55, 58; Twang *DWJ*
52       humour] 55, 58; Humours *DWJ*
61       airy, idle] 55, *DWJ;* Idle, Airy 58
62       Monkey-turn] 55; *Monkey* turn *DWJ;* Monkey's turn 58
63       one who] 55, 58; one, that *DWJ*
65       Steals] 55, *DWJ;* Skulks 58
75       Solemn] 55, *DWJ;* Is very 58
78       the] 55, *DWJ;* a 58
79       Here] 55, *DWJ;* There 58
84       sing] 55; say 58, *DWJ*
88       Lesbos] 55, 58; Lebos *DWJ*

# Piety

There is an early version of this poem under the title "A Dream" in the
"Satires" Notebook.

### Textual Notes

Title    "PIETY: OR, THE VISION" is the title in 55 and *DWJ;* in 58 the
         poem is called *The Vision of Piety,* which is the name under
         which it is listed in the Congleton inventory.

| | |
|---|---|
| 3 | dreams] 55, *DWJ;* dream 58 |
| 13 | glitt'ring] 55; glist'ning 58; glist'ring *DWJ* |
| 17 | lo] 55, 58; low *DWJ* |
| | a cherub] 55, *DWJ;* the Cherub 58 |
| 18 | guardians] 55, *DWJ;* Gaurdian 58 |
| 21–22 | In 58 these lines are separated from the preceding and following paragraphs. |
| 21 | on] 55, *DWJ;* o'er 58 |
| 38 | wasteful] 55, 58; wakeful *DWJ* |
| 42 | 'Tis Fame's] 55; 'Tis flames 58; Fame is *DWJ* |
| | 'tis Heav'n] 55, 58; but Heav'n *DWJ* |
| 43 | fervours of unhallow'd] 55; raptures of discorded 58, *DWJ* |
| 49 | great . . . lasting] 55; warm . . . lambent 58, *DWJ* |
| 57 | flow'ring] 55, 58; flow'ry *DWJ* |
| | give back] 55, *DWJ;* restore 58 |
| 61 | shafts] 55, 58; Shaft *DWJ* |
| 63 | thine] 55, *DWJ;* thy 58 |
| 64 | fingers] 55, *DWJ;* Finger 58 |
| 73 | manger's] 55, 58; Manger *DWJ* |
| 75 | skies] 55, 58; Sky *DWJ* |
| 76 | thousands . . . thousand] 58; thousands . . . thousands 55, *DWJ* (In some copies of *DWJ* the first "thousands" has a space for a final *s* which has apparently failed to print, but the BL copy at Colindale shows the *s*. Arbuckle's reprint corrects *DWJ*'s second "thousands" to "thousand".) |
| 82 | thy] 55, *DWJ;* my 58 |
| 83 | Hah!] 55; Ah! 58, *DWJ* |
| 86 | throne! I] 55; Throne and 58, *DWJ* |
| 96 | tun'd] 55; turn'd 58, *DWJ* |
| 98 | fail] 55, 58; fa[ ] *DWJ* (In the copies of *DWJ* examined, the second half of the word has failed to print; in the collected edition, Arbuckle reprints as "fall", which may be the original reading or may be a conjectural correction.) |
| 106 | White] 55, *DWJ;* While 58 |
| 116 | Joys] 55, 58; Joy *DWJ* |
| 118 | my nights] 55; the nights 58, *DWJ* |

# Miscellaneous Poems from *Posthumous Works* (1758)

Of the nonbiblical poems that probably filled a fourth of the notebooks from which the 1758 edition was printed, "Bacchus" and "Piety" have been printed above from the superior texts in the 1755 edition; "Ecstasy" and "Elysium" (the latter as "The Heroins") are printed below from the manuscript texts in the "Satires" Notebook; and "On the Bishop of Sarum" (as "On Bishop Burnet") is printed below from the superior text in Swift's *Works*. The remaining four poems are the "miscellaneous" group here reprinted from 1758. For three of the poems ("On Queen Anne's Peace," "The Judgment of Paris," and "On Mrs. Arabella Fermor") 1758 provides our only text. "A Riddle" was first printed among a collection of so-called Swiftiana included in the second volume of *Miscellanea*, a miscellany published by Edmund Curll (1727). The differences between the two texts are slight, although in line 23 Curll's text seems to blunt the paradox. We have preferred to base our text on 1758, since it was probably printed directly from a TP autograph, whereas Curll's MS is likely to have been at some removes from TP's original. Curll's text adds notes explaining the riddle; there is no reason to think that TP was responsible for these.

## On Queen Anne's Peace

Numerous poems were written to celebrate the Peace of Utrecht (signed in March–April 1713), and since the peace was a long time negotiating, many poems anticipated it. The first, and initially the most popular, was Thomas Tickell's *On the Prospect of Peace*, published on 28 October 1712, which went through four editions before the end of the year (Foxon T303–07). Tickell's poem had the advantage of being praised by Addison in the *Spectator*, No. 523 (30 October 1712; ed. Bond,

3 : 361). In the same *Spectator* (3 : 363–64), Addison warned others who might be planning poems on the peace to avoid the heathen mythology; TP's poem violates the Spectator's edict. Less popular immediately but the most notable poem produced for the peace was Pope's *Windsor-Forest*, which was published on 7 March 1713. TP's own shorter poem, *The Horse and the Olive*, was published on 9 April, a few days after the news of the actual signing of the treaties had reached London (on 3 April; Swift dined with Bolingbroke that day, *J.S.* 2 : 652).

"On Queen Anne's Peace" must have been written in these months, but since it was not published in TP's lifetime we cannot date it more precisely. The description of the public thanksgiving (lines 287–98) is actually less helpful than it might have been. The service (held at Saint Paul's) was postponed from 16 June to 7 July because of the queen's ill health. But in the event she was unable to attend on 7 July. Thus the poem can hardly be later than that date and was perhaps written for publication in May or June. TP obviously did not abandon his poem after reading Addison's *Spectator* paper; more probably he felt that his poem could not compete with Pope's, or perhaps Swift advised against publication. "On Queen Anne's Peace" is certainly a very unSwiftian poem, whereas *The Horse and the Olive* has affinities with some short poems that Swift wrote (although he did not publish) about this time, especially "Atlas" and "The Faggot" (*Poems*, ed. Williams, 1 : 159–60 and 188–91). It is easy to suppose that Swift advised the publication of *The Horse and the Olive* and the suppression of "On Queen Anne's Peace."

The poem was first published in the 1758 *Posthumous Works.* Our text is based on 1758, although we have corrected its punctuation in a few cases where it is misleading (these instances are recorded in the textual notes). One feature of the 1758 text that is almost certainly not TP's is the printing of most of the proper names in capitals. If the poem had been printed in 1713, these would have been printed in italic; when preparing the poem for the press, TP would probably have underlined them. In the case of the biblical poems printed from 1758, we reduced the words printed in capitals to lower case; but those words seemed chosen arbitrarily. Here, proper names are printed in capitals with reasonable consistency and we have let them stand.

Most of the people mentioned in the poem had long and distinguished careers. We have identified them all, but the notes are largely confined to indicating their positions in 1713; we have not attempted full biographies. TP's attitude to the war and the peace are very similar to Swift's. An account of Swift in these years (such as Irvin Ehrenpreis, *Swift* [Cambridge: Harvard University Press, 1967], vol. 2) thus provides a fuller commentary on the poem.

## Textual Notes

| | |
|---|---|
| Title | *Anne's*] *Ann's* 58 |
| 1 | skies,] — 58 |
| 7 | name] —, 58 |
| 29 | lie,] — 58 |
| 31 | its] it's 58 |
| 59 | stage;] —, 58 |
| 61 | bless'd,] — 58 |
| 67 | enough,] — 58 |
| 85 | see] —, 58 |
| 94 | its . . . its] it's . . . it's 58 |
| 107 | address,] — 58 |
| 113 | place,] — 58 |
| 144 | peace,] — 58 |
| 145 | praise,] — 58 |
| 164 | night] —. 58 |
| 178 | its] it's 58 |
| 193 | Britannia's] Britania's 58 |
| 221 | arms,] arm 58 |
| 226 | with] wirh 58 |
| 245 | Caution,] — 58 |
| | arms,] — 58 |
| 246 | guard] gaurd 58 |
| 266 | Britannia's] Britania's 58 |
| 271 | Poets] Poet's 58 |
| 281 | Queen,] — 58 |
| 287 | mind,] —; 58 |
| | slow,] — 58 |
| 311 | Britons] Britains 58 |
| 317 | seat,] — 58 |
| 321 | still,] — 58 |
| 322 | Ill;] —. 58 |
| 323 | obtain'd,] — 58 |
| 337 | Its . . . its] It's . . . It's 58 |

## Explanatory Notes

| | |
|---|---|
| 7 | ANNA] Queen Anne (1665–1714), queen from 1702. TP pays her a compliment in "The Court," lines 95–96 ("Satires" Notebook). |
| 12 | BOLINGBROKE] Henry St. John (1678–1751), created Viscount |

Bolingbroke in 1712; at this time secretary of state and a principal negotiator of the peace. TP had, at Swift's suggestion, dedicated his *Essay on the Different Styles of Poetry* to him earlier in 1713.

19      twelve revolving years] War had only been declared in 1702; but perhaps TP dates from the death of Charles II of Spain in 1700, and Louis XIV's acceptance of his will, which made a European conflict almost inevitable.

25      Gaul] France, under Louis XIV suspected of designs of European hegemony (TP's "universal reign" in line 28).

46      Spain's parted realms] The point of the war was to prevent the entire Spanish empire falling into the hands of either France or Austria.

47      The grand alliance] The second Grand Alliance, principally between England, the United Provinces, and the emperor, was signed in 1701 to concert opposition to the inheritance by Philip V, Louis XIV's grandson, of the entire Spanish empire.

67–74      This is the Tory view, that France had been sufficiently humbled; the Whigs wished to continue the war until Philip V had been driven out of Spain.

76      OXFORD] Robert Harley (1661–1724), chief minister, 1710–14, created earl of Oxford and appointed Lord Treasurer in 1712.

104      BRISTOW] John Robinson (1650–1723) cleric and diplomat, appointed bishop of Bristol in 1710, and in 1711 Lord Privy Seal and one of the British plenipotentiaries at Utrecht; later bishop of London.

     STRAFFORD] Thomas Wentworth (1672–1739), created earl of Strafford in 1711, ambassador at The Hague, 1711–14, and joint plenipotentiary at the Utrecht conference with Bishop Robinson.

114      The Congress opens] The formal peace conference opened at Utrecht at the end of January 1712.

121      the Duke] James Douglas (1658–1712), fourth duke of Hamilton, crated duke of Brandon in the English peerage in 1711 (TP uses this title in line 128). Appointed ambassador to France, he was killed in a duel with Lord Mohun on 15 November 1712. Hamilton's death was at the time regarded in some Tory circles as a Whig plot.

130      TALBOT] Charles Talbot (1660–1718), twelfth earl and created (1694) first duke of Shrewsbury. He served as Lord Chamberlain in the Tory government and was appointed ambassador to France on Hamilton's death.

140        a name she fear'd before] John Talbot (1388?–1453), first earl
           of Shrewsbury, a hero in the Hundred Years War.

197–98     The factious Whigs try to obstruct the peace with specious
           slogans, accusing the Tory government of breaking the
           Grand Alliance by opening separate talks with France, and of
           plotting to restore the Pretender and thus of undermining
           the security of the Protestant religion. "The People's Pow'r" in
           line 197 probably refers to the ideas of popular sovereignty
           that the Whigs had upheld at the trial of Henry Sacheverell in
           1710.

258        her fair retreat] Oxford, a Tory stronghold.

265        ORMOND] James Butler (1665–1745), second duke of Or-
           monde; appointed commander-in-chief on the dismissal of
           Marlborough in 1712. In the 1712 campaign he was issued
           the "restraining orders" that the Whigs regarded as a betrayal
           of the alliance; TP's "sword of Caution" is probably an allu-
           sion to this.

267        DARTMOUTH] William Legge (1672–1750), second baron, cre-
           ated earl of Dartmouth 1711; at this time secretary of state
           (1710–13) and later Lord Privy Seal (1713–14) in the Tory
           government.

269        HARCOURT] Simon Harcourt (1661?–1727), created Baron
           Harcourt 1711; an eminent Tory lawyer, he took a promi-
           nent part in the defense of Sacheverell in 1710; was Lord
           Keeper (1710–13) and later Lord Chancellor (1713–14) in
           the Tory government.

273–76     TP here particularly offends against the Spectator's edict
           against heathen allegories. Since TP has just mentioned six
           names (in lines 264–69), they must be the six meant here.
           Jove is Anne; Minerva, Oxford, and Phoebus, Bolingbroke.
           Mars must be Ormonde, and Harcourt, Themis. By elimina-
           tion, Dartmouth must be Cyllenius. Swift calls him "a Man of
           Letters" in *Examiner* No. 27 (8 February 1711; *Prose Works,* ed.
           Herbert Davis [Oxford: Blackwell, 1939–68], 3 : 81), but we
           have not been able to find any evidence that would justify
           TP's emphasis on his "full delight" in the arts.

275        Cyllenius] Mercury, so called from his birthplace on Mount
           Cyllene.

277        All mortals once] This theory was first put forward by Eu-
           hemerus of Messene (fl. c. 300 B.C.), after whom it is called
           euhemerism.

283        A Church in safety] The "Church in Danger" was the favorite
           slogan of the Tories.

288   the temple] Saint Paul's Cathedral; the service of thanksgiv-
     ing for the peace was held on 7 July 1713. Because of ill
     health, the queen was in fact unable to attend the service.

299   Phoenix] there are no striking parallels, but TP may have
     taken hints from Ovid *Metamorphoses* 15.391–407, the anony-
     mous Latin poem "The Phoenix" (*Minor Latin Poets*, Loeb ed.,
     643–65), or Claudian's "Phoenix."

317   BLENHEIM] The first and most decisive of Marlborough's
     great victories against the French, fought on 13 August 1704,
     N.S.
     RAMILLIES] The second of Marlborough's major victories,
     fought on 23 May 1706, N.S.

318   BLAREGNI] Blaregnies, the village near the allied encampment
     before the battle usually known as Malplaquet, fought on 11
     September 1709, the last of Marlborough's important battles.
     TP has omitted the battle of Oudenarde (11 July 1708) in
     favor of the minor engagement at Wynendael (line 319 be-
     low).

319   WINENDALE] General Webb's successful repulse of the French
     at Wynendael on 28 September 1708 N.S. Webb was a Tory,
     and TP is here following Tory journalists in elevating this
     relatively minor engagement to the level of Marlborough's
     great battles.

333–37  The achievements of the Utrecht settlement: the division of
     the Spanish empire between the Bourbon and Hapsburg
     claimants; the reduction of the exorbitant power of France;
     the United Provinces (Batavia) secured from the threat of
     French hegemony; and Great Britain's emergence as a major
     power, with enlarged colonial possessions.

# The Judgment of Paris

We have not been able to trace a close source for TP's poem, but the
story of the Judgment of Paris itself goes back at least to the seventh
century B.C. and was a favorite subject in art. Because of a prophecy that
he would be the ruin of his country, Paris was exposed on Mount Ida on
the orders of his parents, Priam and Hecuba. He was, however, saved
and reared as a shepherd (lines 1–2). Later the dispute between Juno,
Venus, and Minerva for the golden apple, thrown by Eris and divisively
labeled "for the most beautiful," was referred to him.

## Textual Notes

| | |
|---|---|
| 5–6 | These lines are indented in 58. |
| 18 | its] it's 58 |
| 29 | harms,] — 58 |
| 30 | arms;] —, 58 |
| 31 | Bow,] — 58 |
| 36 | o'er,] —. 58 |
| 37 | Altars] Alters 58 |
| 41 | stride,] — 58 |
| 50 | Debate,] —. 58 |
| 53 | Grace,] — 58 |
| 60 | Seat;] —, 58 |

# A Riddle

Julius Caesar Scaliger wrote a riddle ("Glacies") on a similar subject. It is here quoted (from *Musae Reduces,* ed. Pierre Laurens [Leiden: E. J. Brill,1975], 2:276) not as a possible "source" but as an example of "that *agreeable Trifling*" that TP in his "Essay on Homer" (TE 7:52) attributed to the best writers:

> Sto, quae currebam; sed non tego, quae tego. Mater
>   Olim, nunc sterilis, rursus eroque parens.
> Quae constat facies, non constitit; horridus illam
>   Iuppiter instabilem sed tamen esse dedit.
> Aufugio tamen, et velles me forte tenere,
>   Aut tota aut sensim subtraho me minuens.

TP's poem is here printed from the 1758 edition, with variants from Curll's 1727 *Miscellanea* recorded in the textual notes. The notes explaining the riddle are found only in Curll's text.

## Textual Notes

| | |
|---|---|
| 2 | Garments] 58; Postures 27 |
| 3 | Prostitute] 27 adds note: * *Water gliding smoothly along a River.* |
| 5 | Gallant] 27 adds note: † *The* Sun *exhales* the *Dew.* |
| 10 | Rival] 27 adds note: ¶ Boreas, *the* North-Wind, *froze the* Water. |
| 11 | cold] 58; close 27 |
| 12 | Begat] 58; Begot 27 |
| 14 | bright] 27 adds note: * *Ice.* |

| 15 | But] 58; And 27 |
|----|----------------|
| 17 | Feathers] 27 adds note: † *Snow.* |
| 18 | wildly] 58; loosely 27 |
| 20 | Mother] 58; *Mother's* 27 |
| 21 | Where] 58; Till 27 |
| 22 | With] 58; Of 27 |
|    | Me] 27 adds note: ‡ The *Frost.* |
| 23 | And I who was my *Father's* Child, 27 |
| 24 | Mother] 27 adds note: § *The* Ice *thawed, returned to* Water. |

## On Mrs. Ar: F:

Arabella Fermor was the "original" of the Belinda who is the heroine of Pope's *Rape of the Lock* (for biographical details about her and her family see TE 2:81–102 and 371–75). She is mentioned in a poem published in 1708 as a prominent beauty, so there is no reason why TP should not have known her independently of Pope (it is uncertain whether Pope knew her before the publication of *The Rape of the Lock*). TP's poem must predate her marriage (which took place in late 1714 or early 1715; *Pope Corr.* 1:269). The probability must be, however, that TP met Arabella through Pope, and that the poem belongs to 1713 or 1714.

In the case of this poem, 1758's punctuation is very light but never actively misleading. It thus approximates to that of a typical TP holograph, and we have allowed it to stand. Thus the poem is here printed exactly as it appears in 1758, the only authority for the text.

# From Pope's *Works,* Volume 2, Part 2 (1738)

## *The Third Satire of Dr. John Donne*

We have no external evidence about this poem except for its bare listing in the Congleton inventory; all that we know must be deduced from its curious publication history, which is bound up with that of Pope's own "versifications" of Donne.

Pope claimed to have "versified" Donne's satires during the latter part of the reign of Queen Anne (TE 4:xli–ii), but his versions were not then published. His *Fourth Satire* was not published until 1733, and the *Second Satire* was first published in the 1735 edition of his *Works.* There is no reason, however, to doubt that Pope indeed wrote early versions of these poems before Queen Anne's death. In British Library Lansdowne MS 852, a poetical compilation put together for the second earl of Oxford, there is a text of Pope's *Second Satire* that differs considerably from the poem as published in 1735. It is much closer to being a simple "versification" of Donne; in the 1730s, Pope made his poem more topical and relevant to the times.

TP's poem, like the early version of Pope's *Second Satire,* keeps very close to Donne's original. It therefore fits in with how Pope evidently saw the enterprise at the time of first writing; and it is natural to assume that TP undertook the poem either at Pope's suggestion, or at least in connection with Pope's own project. The Twickenham editors date the Lansdowne manuscript text of Pope's poem about 1713, and this fits in very well with what we know of TP's activities. In 1713 he was involved in several Popean and Scriblerian projects. It would have been natural for Pope to suggest that TP, a clergyman, should be responsible for the Donne poem that is about religion; while Donne's treatment of Catholicism in the poem would have made it an awkward one for Pope himself to have versified.

For whatever reason, Pope did not proceed with the project in 1713, but he must have retained a copy of TP's poem. Pope evidently passed over TP's "Third Satire" when he chose poems for the 1722 *Poems on Several Occasions.* But in the 1730s, when he came first to publish and then to collect his own versions of Donne, he seems to have felt that TP's poem could usefully fill the gap left between his own two.

Textually and bibliographically, the printing of the volume in which TP's poem first appeared has a very complicated history. Fortunately, only a very summary account as far as relates to TP's poem needs to be given here, as the problems have been treated very fully by Maynard Mack, "Pope's Horatian Poems: Problems of Bibliography and Text," *Modern Philology* 41 (1943): 33–44. This article is reprinted in Mack's *Collected in Himself* (Newark: University of Delaware Press, 1982), 106–21. TP's poem was first printed in vol. 2, part 2, of Pope's *Works,* 1738 (Griffith 507); it was reprinted almost immediately in another edition of the same volume (Mack calls it "Griffith 507x") that was also dated 1738 but which is certainly a later reprint and was probably not published until 1739. There are a few variants (recorded in the textual notes) between the two printings, which we have distinguished as "38" (for 507) and "39" for (507x). Except for the obvious corrections in lines 12, 71 and 79, we have followed the first printing on the assumption that the variants are more likely to be Pope's tinkering than corrections from a TP holograph. In the case of the text of Donne's poem, we have accepted corrections from 39 in lines 12 and 48. Pope omitted the poem from the 1740 and 1743 editions of his *Works;* Warburton restored it in the edition that he edited in 1751.

In 38 the part-title adds "Versifyed by Dr. PARNELL." In 39 this is expanded to "Versifyed by Dr. PARNELLE. In Imitation of Mr. POPE.

A late transcript at Yale (see headnote to *The Horse and the Olive*) follows 38 rather than 39 for both poems, including some errors of 38, while correcting such obvious cases as "Pholosophers" (Donne, line 12) and "vanqnish" (TP, line 12). It also introduces several errors of its own, and in line 148 of TP reads "he fears" for "inheres".

For a commentary on Donne's poem, the edition of Donne's *Satires, Epigrams, and Verse Letters* by W. Milgate (Oxford: Clarendon Press, 1967) should be consulted.

### Textual Notes (Donne's poem)

| | |
|---|---|
| 8 | *as*] 38; *more* 39 |
| 12 | *Philosophers*] 39; *Pholosophers* 38 |
| 48 | *yesterday.*] 39; —, 38 |
| 71 | *she,*] 38; —. 39 |
| 94 | *mans*] 38; *man's* 39 |
| 104 | *well,*] 38; — 39 |

## Textual Notes (TP's version)

| | |
|---|---|
| 12 | vanquish] 39; vanqnish 38 |
| 14 | below?] 38; —! 39 |
| 32 | pole] 38; Poll 39 (errata corrects to "Pole") |
| 71 | Command] 39; Comand 38 |
| 79 | professions] 39; possessions 38 |
| 88 | and] 38; yet 39 |
| 105 | mountain] 38; Mountain 39 |
| 109 | essays] 38; —, 39 |
| 115 | delay;] 38; —: 39 |
| 126 | Or must it *so*] 38; By these can Souls 39 |
| 134 | know;] 38; —: 39 |
| 147 | soul] 38; Soul 39 |
| 148 | than] 38; that 39 |

## Explanatory Note

64      Woodman 28 cites Denham's famous passage, *Coopers Hill*, line 191, "Though deep, yet clear, though gentle, yet not dull." For the vogue of Denham's passage and its many imitators, see *The Poetical Works of Sir John Denham*, ed. T.H. Banks (2nd ed., Hamden: Archon Books, 1969), 343–51. See also Brendan O Hehir, *Expans'd Hieroglyphicks: A Critical Edition of Sir John Denham's Coopers Hill* (Berkeley: University of California Press, 1969), 294–97.

# Poems from Swift's *Works* (1765)

Both poems in this group had been previously printed, but in inferior texts. "To Dr. Swift" was first published in the 1755 edition of TP's *Works*, pp. 221–24. This text evidently represents an earlier stage in the poem's composition; line 77 is incomplete, and in three passages (lines 27–28, 37–40, and 85) the 1765 text is recognizably a reworking of its 1755 counterpart. It is a natural inference that the "working notebook" used by the 1755 editor contained TP's penultimate draft of the poem, while the copy actually sent to Swift by TP survived among Swift's papers to be printed in 1765.

"On Bishop Burnet's Being Set on Fire in his Closet" was first published, under a somewhat different title, in the 1758 *Posthumous Works*, pp. 285–86. In this case the variants are slight, but 1765's are superior.

The poems were printed in Swift's *Works* in 1765 in what Teerink-Scouten distinguishes as the "Third Stage" of the so-called Hawkesworth edition, this stage actually being edited by Deane Swift, Swift's cousin and biographer. It was published in four different formats: quarto (vol. 8, part 2; Teerink-Scouten No. 87, p. 86); large octavo (vol. 16; T-S No. 88, p. 90); small octavo (vol. 17; T-S No. 90, p. 96); and 18mo (vol. 17; T-S No. 92, pp. 101–2). It seems probable that the text was originally set for the quarto format, then reimposed for the large octavo printing. In the octavo, the page looks cramped and there are many turned lines; but the two texts are identical except for variations in spacing. For the small octavo and octodecimo editions the texts were evidently reset. There are no verbal variants, but some changes to spelling, punctuation, and the use of capitals and italic. In the quarto edition, from which we have taken our texts, "To Dr. Swift" appears in vol. 8, part 2, pp. 143–45, and "On Bishop Burnet" on p. 149. Our only changes to these texts are the removal of the misleading "it's" in "To Swift," line 13, and "On Burnet," line 14. Although "it's" was a regular form, TP does not use it in his manuscripts and it seems pointless to retain a feature that is almost certainly compositorial and that is actively misleading to the modern reader. Similarly we have removed compositorial "it's" in some of the poems reprinted from the 1758 *Posthumous Works*. In the textual notes, verbal variants are recorded from the 1755 edition for "To Swift" and from the 1758 edition for "On Burnet."

Both poems are included in a Yale transcript (see headnote to *The Horse and the Olive*) and both follow the text of 65, except for mistranscriptions at lines 83 and 87 of "To Swift."

Deane Swift evidently found TP's poems among such miscellaneous manuscripts as Swift's own "Of Mean and Great Figures" (which he printed for the first time) and poems by other members of the Swift circle, including Atterbury's "Epigram on Mr. Harley being Stabbed by Guiscard," which appears immediately before TP's poem on Burnet.

## To Dr. Swift

### Textual Notes

| | |
|---|---|
| Title | In 55 the title is simply "TO D$^{R.}$ SWIFT". |
| 1 | Friendship's sacred] 65; sacred friendship's 55 |
| 2 | glories] 65; wonders 55 |
| 13 | its] 55; it's 65 |
| 17 | Of these] 65; And there 55 |
| 18 | Conspire] 65; Contend 55 |
| 23 | rest I see] 65; throng I saw 55 |
| 24 | Loose] 65; Free 55 |
| 25 | eyes] 65; eye 55 |
| 26 | And] 65; The 55 |
| 27–28 | This couplet was condensed from a four-line passage that is found in 55: |

> Upon her lips convincing Proof resides,
> Thro' all her speech Persuasion melting glides;
> A golden crown confess'd her high command,
> And waving Action gently grac'd her hand.

| | |
|---|---|
| 29 | Out of her bosom, where the treasure lay 55 |
| 36 | and] 65; yet 55 |
| 37–40 | These lines replace the following passage in 55: |

> How far uncommon, with an air of ease,
> How nicely taking are thy turns of praise!
> Fame wants no words to make the Patriot shine,

> But yet, to chuse the best, must borrow thine:
> What public spirit in thy works appears!
> What rolling language fills the ravish'd ears!
> Where Nature all her force of writing shows,
> Where Art concealing Art with Nature goes.

| | |
|---|---|
| 41 | spake] 65; ceas'd 55 |
| 42 | Poesy] 65; Poetry 55 |
| 43 | deeper] 65; deepest 55 |
| 44 | more] 65; as 55 |
| 45 | cheek] 65; cheeks 55 |
| 49 | curls of] 65; curling 55 |
| 52 | And,] 65; While 55 |
| | a] 65; her 55 |
| 56 | their] 65; the 55 |
| 57 | take the painted] 65; make the varied 55 |
| 58 | And while they fall for profit, dress for show. 55 |
| 60 | From slow consuming care, and pining grief; 55 |
| 64 | were] 65; is 55 |
| 65–66 | These lines are not in 55, and may be a late addition. |
| 68 | with] 65; and 55 |
| 71 | mild] 65; wild 55 |
| 76 | ran] 65; run 55 |
| 77 | This line is incomplete in 55, reading only "But chief". |
| 81 | Here] 65; There 55 |
| | Man] 65; Men 55 |
| 85 | Corresponding to this single line, 55 has the following longer apostrophe: |

> O SWIFT! if Friendship's warm yet lasting flame,
> If Love of Merit have to praise a claim;
> If just esteem from ev'ry temper flows
> To crown a tender sense of human woes;
> These fair returns are thine: nor cou'dst thou lye
> Unknown alive, nor wilt unlovely dye.
>     Or if high fame be life, (and well we know,

| | |
|---|---|
| 87 | wholly die] 65; all expire 55 |

### Explanatory Notes

| | |
|---|---|
| 64 | A common idea, but perhaps recalling Horace's "dulce est desipere in loco" (*Odes* 4.12.28). |
| 70 | amarants] By derivation, the name means "unfading"; hence |

the flower is used as an emblem of immortality.

87          Recalling Horace's "non omnis moriar" (*Odes* 3.30.6).


## *On Bishop Burnet's Being Set on Fire in His Closet*

TP had met Burnet as early as 1702 (Schoedinger, p. 33), as indeed had Swift. We do not, however, know how well TP got to know him. Certainly in this poem we can see the influence of Swift and of Swift's post-1710 attitude to Burnet, a Scot who had been active in promoting the success of the 1688 Revolution and whom William III had promoted to the see of Salisbury. Burnet was a violent Whig and a pathological hater of popery. In 1713 (the obvious date of this poem) he published three pieces of virulent antipopery, increasingly hysterical in their tone and in their warning that the Tory government was plotting to introduce popery and the Pretender: a preface to a new collection of sermons; a preface to a new edition of his *Pastoral Care* (see line 8); and an *Introduction* (see line 14) to the long-awaited third volume of his *History of the Reformation of the Church of England* (the first two volumes of which had appeared in 1679 and 1681). Swift ridiculed Burnet and his fears of popery (which to Swift were nothing more than party-inspired nonsense) in his *Preface to the Bishop of Sarum's Introduction* (published December 1713).

We have been unable to verify whether the incident that TP dramatizes really took place. Reports of it were certainly current, for in a letter of 28 December 1713 a correspondent wrote to Burnet:

> hearing from London that you had mett with some accident by ffire amongst your papers when you was reading or writing, I could not forbear informing myselfe whether you had sustained any personall damnage or not, and caused write to your nephew thereof. But he sent me word he had heard nothing of it; and now that you say nothing thereof yourselfe, I am satisfied with the mistake.

This letter is quoted from Nicholas Pocock's edition of Burnet's *History of the Reformation* (Oxford, 1865), 7:223. It can hardly be from the duke of Hamilton, as Pocock states; James, the fifth duke (1703–43) was only ten in 1713, having succeeded on his father's death in the famous duel with Lord Mohun (to which TP refers in "On Queen Anne's Peace"). In any case, the letter need only imply that Burnet tried to deny or suppress the report, which if untrue was *ben trovato*. The date of the "Hamilton" letter, and the association of the poem with TP's poem on Swift's birthday (30 November 1713) suggests a date late in 1713 for the poem on Burnet.

## Textual Notes

| | |
|---|---|
| Title | In 58 the title is *"On the B——p of S——, who had like to be burnt lately in his* STUDY". |
| 1 | bane to Sarum's] 65; Bane of S—— 58 |
| 2 | broke] 65; lost 58 |
| 4 | And we, and he] 65; And He, and We 58 |
| | will] 65; must 58 |
| 13 | its] 65; it's 58 |
| 14 | its] it's 65, 58 |
| 18 | in] 65; on 58 |

## Explanatory Notes

| | |
|---|---|
| 1 | that dire æra] 1710, when Queen Anne dismantled the Whig government (Burnet's "friends") and gradually replaced it with a predominantly Tory one; the "schemes" are Tory bogeys, such as the Whig threats to the church and monarchy. |
| 16 | speech on Moderation] The reference is probably to Burnet's famous speech in the House of Lords in 1703, published as *The Bishop of Salisbury's Speech in the House of Lords, upon the Bill against Occasional Conformity* (1704). Burnet there claims that he "began the World on a Principle of Moderation" and that he hoped to continue in the same "to my Life's end" (p. 5). "Moderation" here, as usually in the Queen Anne period, is a codeword for firm Whiggishness. TP's joke contrasts the pretended moderation of Burnet's principles with the violence with which he expressed them. |

# From *A Miscellaneous Collection of Poems* (1721)

## *On the Death of Mr. Viner*

We have not been able to determine the priority between the two 1721 printings of "On the Death of Mr. Viner." *The Pleasures of Coition,* in which the poem is printed on pp. 53–56, was advertised as published on 31 January 1721. But *A Miscellaneous Collection of Poems, Songs and Epigrams,* edited by "T. M. GENT" (2 vols., Dublin, 1721; TP's poem appears on 1:55–58), might have been postdated and been published late in 1720. There is a "John Parnel, *Esq;*" among the subscribers to the *Miscellaneous Collection;* he may have been the poet's brother. Our reason for preferring the Dublin edition as our copy-text is that it is more likely to have been printed from an autograph, and it was probably printed from at least an authorized transcript (either might have been supplied by the poet's brother), whereas the manuscript from which the London edition was printed is more likely to have been a transcript at a greater remove from a TP holograph.

"T. M. GENT" is usually identified as Thomas Mosse, for example by Case (No. 320, p. 235). Mosse was admitted to Trinity College, Dublin, in 1681, where he took his B.A. in 1685 and his M.A. in 1688 (*Alumni Dublinenses,* ed. G. D. Burtchaell and T. U. Sadleir [Dublin, 1935], 601). If his politics are to be judged from this anthology he was a Whig; there are numerous copies of verses addressed to George I, Lord Wharton, Addison, and other Whig notables.

There is a transcript of the poem in British Library Add. MS 26877, ff. 173b–74a. The transcriber records that the poem was copied from *The Altar of Love,* Curll's 1727 reprint of *The Pleasures of Coition, Pancharis,* and *Cupid's Bee-Hive.* There is another transcript in a manuscript at the University of Nottingham (Pw V 331); it has "in" in line 61, and it too was probably copied from one of Curll's printings of the poem.

William Viner, violinist and composer, was Master of the State Music in Ireland from 1703 to his death in 1716 (when his will was proved on 30 November; details from *The New Grove Dictionary of Music and Musicians,* ed. Stanley Sadie, 1980, 19:790). Matthew Pilkington (at one time a friend of Swift's) published the following tribute to him in *The Progress of Musick in Ireland* reprinted in Pilkington's *Poems on Several Occasions* (Dublin, 1730):

> The *Muses* now from *Albion's Isle* retreat,
> And here with kind Indulgence fix their Seat:
> Then *Viner* rose, with all their warmth inspir'd,
> A Bard caress'd by all, by all admir'd;
> He Choral strings, in sleepy Silence bound,
> Touch'd into Voice, and waken'd into Sound;
> Then taught those Sounds to flow with easy Art,
> To wooe the Soul, and glide into the Heart,
> In Notes, untry'd before, his Fancy dress't,
> And bid new transports rise in ev'ry Breast.
> While round in Crouds the fair Creation stand,
> The polish'd *Viol* trembling in his Hand,
> While swift as Thought, from note to note he springs,
> Flies o'er th' unerring Tones, and sweeps the sounding Strings,
> The Old, the Young, the Serious, and the Gay,
> With ravish'd Ears devour the 'witching Lay;
> The *Lover's* Eyes now languishingly Roll,
> And speak the Dictates of the raptur'd Soul;
> *Foes,* in whose Breasts the wildest Passion strove,
> Forget their Rage, and soften into Love:
> The prideful *Beauty,* feels with new Surprize
> Her Bosom swell, and wonders why she Sighs,
> Each Passion acts as he affects the Heart,
> And Nature answers ev'ry stroke of Art.
>
> (Pp. 16–18)

### Textual Notes

| | |
|---|---|
| 12 | fully] This word is not found in the Dublin edition; we have supplied it from Curll's text. Although it may only be Curll's conjectural filling of an obvious gap, it may have been in his manuscript (not that this need imply that it has TP's authority). We have thought it better to insert it than to leave the line short. |
| 61 | with] Dublin; in Curll |

### Explanatory Note

| | |
|---|---|
| 53–54 | TP is here perhaps recalling the opening line of Dryden's "To the Memory of Mr. Oldham" (1684): "Farewel, too little and too lately known". |

# Poems from *Pancharis, Queen of Love* (1721)

The attribution of these poems to TP rests solely on Curll, and his is our only text of them. We have seen no reason to reject the attribution, but they were the only poems published as TP's that were excluded from the 1786 Foulis Press folio edition; we do not know the reason for their exclusion, but they should perhaps be regarded as to some extent doubt-fully TP's. They were published in *Pancharis Queen of Love: or, Woman Unveil'd* (1721). This volume was advertised as published in the *Daily Post* for 27 March 1721. The part relating to TP is as follows:

II Original POEMS upon several Occasions. By the late Reverend Mr. Archdeacon PARNELL. Publish'd from his own Manuscripts sent from Ireland, viz. 1. Chloris appearing in a Looking Glass. 2. Love in Disguise. 3. On the Number THREE. 4. On the Castle of Dublin. 5. Ode to Silvia. 6. A luscious Bit for a Lawyer.

We cannot explain the absence from the list of "On a Lady with a Foul Breath" and the "Epigram," except as the result of carelessness on the part of Curll or his copywriter. The "Ode to Silvia" must refer to the "Ode to Sylvia. In Imitation of Mr. Prior," one of the other poems published in *Pancharis* (pp. 32–33). The "luscious Bit for a Lawyer" remains unexplained. A second edition of *Pancharis* was published in 1722.

A clue to the dating of the poems is the epigram "On the Castle of Dublin"; this is dated 1715, but of course it does not follow that the other poems in the same manuscript would have been exactly contemporary.

The poems are here reprinted from the first edition of *Pancharis* with two minor corrections. In "Love in Disguise," line 11 is corrected selec-tively from the list of *errata* on the verso of the title page, which, however, introduces errors of its own (*"Coots"* for *"Cools"*); the original text reads "'Tis strange the *Air,* that *cools a Flame* shou'd prove". In "On a Lady with a Foul Breath", line 17, *"Sweets"* is from the second edition; the first edition reads *"Sweet's"*.

These poems (together with the poem on Viner) were virtually re-discovered by John Nichols and printed in volume 3 of his *Select Collection of Poems* (4 vols., 1780; later extended to 8 vols.). In his "Advertisement" Nichols describes the collection as founded on Dryden's *Miscellany,* but intended as a supplement to Dodsley's collection and the edition of the poets for which Dr. Johnson wrote his *Lives of the Poets.* Nichols probably took the poems from one of the printings of Curll's texts; in the poem on Viner, he has "fully" in line 10 and "in" in line 61.

## On the Castle of Dublin

The new part of the castle to which TP refers was probably the new privy council chamber built to replace the one burned down in a fire on Essex Quay in 1711. The decayed part was probably Bermingham's Tower. These suggestions are taken from the account in James L. J. Hughes, "Dublin Castle in the Seventeenth Century," *Dublin Historical Record* 2 (1940): 81–97 (especially pp. 90, 92). The inhabitants are the two Lords Justices appointed by letters patent dated 6 September 1715 and sworn in on 1 November. The "decay'd" one is Henry de Massue de Ruvigny (1648–1720), earl of Galway; he had previously been a Lord Justice in 1697–1701. A soldier and diplomat, he had served under William III and again in the War of the Spanish Succession. His conduct of the war in Spain was censured by the Tory House of Commons in 1711. The "new built" but unfinished one is Charles Fitzroy (1683–1757), second duke of Grafton; he was later Viceroy at the time of Wood's halfpence. Swift, though hardly an unprejudiced witness, calls him "Almost a Slobber without one good Quality" in his marginalia on John Macky's *Characters* (1733); *Prose Works,* ed. Davis, 5:258.

## On the Number Three

The subject of this poem is possibly a family of three sisters, each beautiful but in very different ways.

## Epigram ("The greatest Gifts")

The epigraph is from Juvenal *Satires* 3.164–65.

# Poems from the "Schoedinger" Notebook

These poems, which are probably the earliest of TP's still extant, survive only in a manuscript that we have called the "Schoedinger" Notebook, after its former owner, P. S. Schoedinger, who bought it in England in 1925. Schoedinger described the manuscript and transcribed the poems in an appendix to his Ph.D. dissertation (Yale University, 1940), but they have not been printed previously. The manuscript is now preserved in the archives of the Columbus Academy, Gahanna, Ohio. It consists of 100 leaves (approximate size of leaf 195 × 150 mm) as follows: three preliminary leaves, with various signatures and some scribbled jottings; ten leaves, numbered (probably by Schoedinger himself), which contain (ff. 2a–10b) TP's poems; sixty-two blank leaves; a leaf containing "A Prayer made by M$^r$ William King minister of S$^t$ Wardours Dublin"; a leaf containing "Maditations"; seventeen blank leaves; a leaf containing an inventory of linen; a leaf containing "The 6 1$^{st}$ verses of y$^e$ 69 psalme", probably the composition of TP's father; and four blank leaves.

TP was admitted to Trinity College, Dublin, in November 1692, graduated B.A. in 1697 and M.A. in 1700; thus the poems in the "Schoedinger" Notebook, which mostly seem to date between 1694 and 1698, can properly be regarded as "student" work.

The poems are here printed from the manuscript as exactly as possible; revisions and corrections are recorded in the notes on each poem. In the manuscript the title of each poem is divided off by lines above and below running the whole width of the page. There is some variation in the hands in which the poems are written, but only "To Mr. Brown" seems definitely not autograph.

## Psalm 67

There are no corrections to this poem. TP has numbered the first five stanzas (each of which corresponds to one of the first five verses of Psalm

598

67), but not the last one. This stanza corresponds to verses 6–7 of the psalm, which may account for its not being numbered.

## On the Queen's Death

There are no corrections to this poem. In line 11, "y$^e$" must be TP's inadvertency for "y$^m$", but we have let it stand. The date "1694" has been penciled against the title, perhaps by Schoedinger himself. Queen Mary II died about 11 P.M. on 27 December 1694 (Stephen B. Baxter, *William III* [London: Longmans, 1966], 320; some accounts, such as Burnet's, put the death early in the morning of the 28th). She was thirty-two at the time of her death, which was lamented in numerous poetic tributes.

### Textual Note

20    asleep] This word is underlined in the MS, perhaps as a stroke indicating the end of the poem rather than as a mark of emphasis.

## Psalm 51

The only correction in this poem is in line 37, where "Bad" is written after an illegible deletion ("B[  ]d"?). Line 12, at the foot of f. 2b, is no longer legible, the bottom of the page having frayed; it has been supplied from Schoedinger's text.

## Meditation before Sacrament

The only corrections in the text are that TP wrote and deleted "to" at the end of line 3, presumably copied in error from the beginning of the next line. In line 27 he originally wrote "Haleleujah" before deleting the second *e* and adding the final *s*.

## On the Plot against King William

The Assassination Plot, to murder William III in order to prepare the way for a Jacobite invasion supported by France, was planned for early 1696; but news of it leaked out and it was prevented (see Baxter, *William*

*III,* 336–67). News of the plot was announced to Parliament on 25 February; an "Association" was formed, pledged to defend William. TP's poem reflects this national mood of hostility to the Jacobites.

## Textual Notes

11      Jove] TP seems to have written, deleted, and then rewritten the word.
13      ye] ⟨you⟩ ? MS
15      as] "Li" (for "Like") is erased before "as".

## Explanatory Notes

1       Pyrrhus] Pyrrhus (319–272 B.C.), king of Epirus, invaded Italy and fought against Rome. Plutarch ("Pyrrhus," 21) tells the story to which TP refers: the Roman general Fabricius received a letter from Pyrrhus's physician, offering to poison the king, but Fabricius magnanimously refused to take advantage of the treachery and informed Pyrrhus of it.
8       our evil one] James II.
9       Titans] For the Titans' assault on Olympus, and Jove's defeat of them, see Ovid *Metamorphoses* 1.151–62.
13      Gerion] Geryon (or Geryones) was a winged, three-bodied giant; capturing his cattle was one of the labors of Hercules. Here, William is "Gerion-like" as king of England, Scotland, and Ireland, the three bodies that would be left headless at "one stroke" (line 14).
18      Ixion] Ixion, purified by Zeus for the murder of a kinsman (in some versions his father-in-law) and admitted to Olympus, nevertheless sought to seduce Hera. He was deceived by a cloud in the shape of Hera, but thrown into hell for his crime and there perpetually bound to a wheel. He is thus a type of the ungrateful men who sought to kill William. Just as Ixion embraced air, so they wounded air instead of the god-like William. There is a further parallel between the plot to ambush William and the version of the story in which Ixion ambushes and murders his father-in-law.

# *Psalm 113*

The only correction to this poem is that in line 5 "who's" originally read "who'se". In line 2, we have spaced the MS's "Opraise". In lines 1–

20, TP's marginal numbers indicate the verses of the psalm to which his lines correspond. TP omitted verse 8 of the psalm; lines 21–24 correspond to verse 9.

## On Sir Charles Porter's Death

Sir Charles Porter, an English lawyer, was twice Lord Chancellor of Ireland, in 1686–87 and from 1690 to his death in 1696. This poem on the Tory Porter, coming shortly after the poem on the Assassination Plot, shows that in 1696 TP could be politically bipartisan.

### Textual Notes

| | |
|---|---|
| 15 | Minervas learning] ⟨& Mars his valour⟩ MS |
| | A canceled line follows in the MS: "Minerva's learning, Saturns living long". Lines 15–16, and this canceled line, are bracketed together as a triplet. |
| 27 | great] ⟨Great⟩ MS (?) |
| 36 | After "earth", the MS has "we've go", canceled; probably TP intended "we've got". |

### Explanatory Note

| | |
|---|---|
| 2–3 | TP may be recalling Ovid's account of the iron age in *Metamorphoses* 1, where first modesty, truth, and faith (line 129) and later Astraea (line 150) flee the earth. |

## On Content

### Textual Notes

| | |
|---|---|
| 12 | see] The word is written above an illegible deletion. |
| 37 | keep] ⟨keeps⟩ MS |

## On the Bishop of Meath's Death

Anthony Dopping (1643–97), bishop of Kildare (1679) and later Meath (1682), was a prominent opponent of the Jacobite regime in Ireland and supporter of the Williamite settlement.

## Textual Notes

| | |
|---|---|
| 4 | echo's] ⟨accents⟩ MS |
| 7 | true] ⟨good⟩ MS |
| 9 | true] ⟨goodness⟩ MS (?) |

# The Penitent Sinner

## Textual Notes

| | |
|---|---|
| 17 | rays] The word is an insertion in the MS. |
| 69 | arm] ⟨arms⟩ MS |

# To Mr. Brown

Peter Browne (1665?–1735) was at this time a fellow of Trinity College, Dublin; he was later (1699) provost, and in 1710 was appointed bishop of Cork. His *Letter in Answer to a Book Entitled "Christianity Not Mysterious"* (1697) was one of the most popular answers to John Toland's deist tract.

This poem is written in a different hand, and is almost certainly not autograph.

# On Mr. Collier's Essay on the Stage

Jeremy Collier (1650–1726), nonjuring divine, best known for his *Short View of the Immorality and Profaneness of the English Stage* (1698), to which TP here refers. Collier is also mentioned as a reformer of the stage in TP's "Letter to a Friend: On Poets," line 30. The reference to Elijah (line 14) is to 1 Kings 18:17–41.

## Textual Notes

| | |
|---|---|
| 19 | its] ⟨th⟩ MS |
| 25 | face.] —, MS (We have made the change since the MS has a period at the end of the second canceled line.) A canceled couplet follows in the MS: "What netts were usd for those entrapd before, / & evry subtler snare prepard for more". |
| 28 | A canceled line follows in the MS: "Where stood the glorious |

work of hell, there ly's". Despite the clear comma after "hell", the sense of this and the following line as originally written must have been: "Where stood the glorious work, of hell there lies / A dismal prospect".

29 &] ⟨a⟩ MS
dungeons] ⟨prospect⟩ MS
gape before] ⟨evry way⟩ MS
Three canceled lines follow in the MS: "Some yet unfilld, some glutted w^th their prey, / Where captivd wretches labour in their chains, / Whom the false vision had deceivd to paines."

## *Psalm 116*

### Textual Notes

11 help] ⟨aid⟩ MS
31 Tell how] ⟨How pr⟩ MS (presumably for "precious")
32 we] ⟨thee⟩ ? MS
38 name] ⟨Will⟩ ? MS

# Poems from the "Satires" Notebook

The "Satires" Notebook is the single most important TP manuscript among the Congleton papers. It is a bound notebook, comprising 161 leaves (average size of leaf 148 × 90 mm) of which 104 are blank. Six leaves have been removed from the notebook, apparently with no loss of text. On the front flyleaf there is an autograph signature "Tho Parnell"; a canceled inscription "Ex do[?] dono S. Hall [or perhaps 'Hill'?]"; and the numeral "2." On the rear pastedown (upside-down from the point of view of the contents of the notebook) "Hobbs" has been written and canceled, and there is the signature "T: Parnell"; the signature "T Parnell" also occurs on the rear free endpaper. The fifty-seven leaves that have been used contain thirty-seven items, of which twenty-eight are poems here printed for the first time. The other nine items are versions of eight published poems (there are two texts of "The Ecstasy"); some of these differ greatly from the published text, others hardly at all. Of particular interest among the "new" poems are a series of twelve satires. Although the material they contain is commonplace, these poems illustrate an aspect of TP's work that is barely represented in his published poems.

Most of the poems are autograph, although at the beginning of the notebook two poems have been copied in by someone else in a careful, copybook hand; and the last poem in the manuscript is written in a very different, rather undisciplined hand.

The first poem, a Latin epigram written as a motto for the notebook, is dated 1702. Some of the poems, however, must be earlier than this. "On the Addresses" is dated 1701, and the poem "On Dr. Brown's Death" must be about 1699, the year of Browne's death. A starting date around 1700 is likely, since the poems in the "Schoedinger" Notebook can mostly be dated between 1695 and 1698. A link between the two notebooks is the use of the pindaric form in the elegies on the bishop of Meath (in "Schoedinger") and on Dr. Browne (in "Satires"); TP seems never to have used such a form again. The poem on "The Isle of Wight" must be contemporary with the events of 1702 to which it refers. Towards the end of the "Satires" Notebook there are several poems for which a date of 1713–14 can be suggested: "The Horse and the Olive" is probably late 1712 or early 1713, while "Ye Wives Who Scold" surely derived from TP's association with Pope's translation of Homer. The middle poems are less easy to date. By the time he wrote "The Test of Poetry" TP had apparently met Pope; and we may suspect Pope's influence in the removal of triplets from the slightly later "Concerning Resolution."

The notebook is not a working manuscript, but a book into which TP transcribed fair copies of his poems. Few poems, however, are entirely without corrections; some are heavily revised. Several of the poems have vertical strokes down the center of the page, apparently an indication that the poem had been recopied elsewhere. The manuscript is also a "private" one in that TP uses many contractions and in many poems hardly punctuates at all. An exception is "An Allegory on Man," which is written out as though for the press.

## *In Librum Hunc* (f. 1a)

This poem was presumably written after some poems had already been copied into the notebook; TP's self-mocking point (consistent with lines 63–67 of "A Letter to a Friend" below) is that, while he would like to be a poet, he has no real hope of achieving immortality and is willing that his poems should be burned after his death (Vesta being the Roman goddess of the hearth).

*Translation.* "Not long ago two goddesses were fighting for possession of my book. 'It belongs to me,' said Vesta; 'No, it is mine,' said Minerva. 'Let the author himself,' they concluded, 'decide the question.' And this is how I judged my own case: these poems I dedicate to you, Minerva, while I live; when I am dead, they shall be Vesta's."

### Textual Notes

| | |
|---|---|
| Title | Written first in letters of ordinary size, then deleted and rewritten in much larger letters. |
| 1 | Certârunt] ⟨Pugnarunt⟩ MS |

## *A Letter to a Friend* (Satire 1) (ff. 2a–3a)

With one exception, the topical literary references are to publications of the years 1696–1700; thus the poem can be no earlier than 1700, and if the reference to Dennis in line 71 is to the *Large Account,* at least the last part of the poem can be no earlier than 1702.

The poem and the first part of the title are written in the hand of an unknown transcriber; "On poets Satyr 1ˢᵗ" has been added in TP's hand. The corrections are possibly autograph. The transcriber almost always wrote a large initial *s,* which we have usually interpreted as lower case. In a few instances (recorded in the textual notes) we have corrected the transcriber's punctuation where it is positively misleading.

## Textual Notes

| | |
|---|---|
| 4 | sence.] —, MS |
| 8 | more.] —, MS |
| 10 | unbends,] —. MS |
| 12 | beside.] — MS (no room in margin) |
| | A canceled couplet follows in the MS: "thus wⁿ we rail at man in generall, / 'tis no mans quarrell, as it touches all,". |
| 16 | their] ⟨a⟩ MS |
| | game,] —. MS |
| 19 | beside.] — MS |
| 20 | yᵉʳ] ⟨yᵉ⟩ MS |
| 26 | one way] ⟨in one⟩ MS |
| 27 | abuse.] — MS |
| 29 | weak] ⟨fool⟩ MS |
| | still.] — MS |
| 32 | rage.] —, MS |
| 33 | undisturb'd] ⟨undisturbed⟩ MS |
| 35 | prose.] — MS |
| 36 | inspir'd,] —. MS |
| 42 | praise.] — MS |
| 49 | file] ⟨files⟩ MS |
| 57 | expence.] —, MS |

## Explanatory Notes

| | |
|---|---|
| 7–12 | Although the idea is a commonplace, in the context of 1696–1700 the idea of the country being overrun with poets may owe something to the opening lines of Blackmore's *Satyr against Wit* (1700; see *Poems on Affairs of State,* Yale ed. 6 : 135), for which see line 36 below. |
| 28 | Durfy] Thomas D'Urfey (1653–1723), prolific songwriter, poet, and dramatist. |

30      C——r] Jeremy Collier (1650–1726), the nonjuring cler-
gyman whose *Short View of the Immorality and Profaneness of the
English Stage* (1698) provoked the "Collier controversy" in
which Congreve, Vanbrugh, and others (but not D'Urfey)
defended the stage against Collier's attack.

31      V——ke] Sir John Vanbrugh (1664–1726), dramatist and ar-
chitect; the reference here is to his *Short Vindication of "The
Relapse" and "The Provoked Wife" from Immorality and Pro-
faneness* (1698).

35      B——l] Presumably Charles Boyle (1676–1731), later fourth
earl of Orrery, nominal author of *Dr. Bentley's Dissertations
Examined* (1698; thought to be mainly the work of Atterbury
and Smalridge), and editor of and contributor to the *Commen-
datory Verses on the Author of the Two Arthurs and the "Satyr
against Wit"* (1700; an attack on Blackmore). The point seems
to be that TP approves of Boyle's attack on Bentley, but not of
his attack on Blackmore (who is praised in lines 36–40 below).
C——ve] William Congreve (1670–1729), now best known
for his prose comedies. TP's point is that if Congreve had
never written these (which had been attacked as immoral and
indecent by Collier), but only such works as his verse tragedy
*The Mourning Bride* (1697) and his verses on the death of
Queen Mary (1695; for TP's poem on the same subject, see
the "Schoedinger" Notebook above), he would have escaped
Collier's censure and earned universal applause. Lines 33–35
may recall Juvenal's comments (*Satires* 10.118–32) on Demos-
thenes and Cicero.

36      B——r] Sir Richard Blackmore (1654–1729), physician and
poet, whose epics *Prince Arthur* (1695) and *King Arthur* (1697)
were intended to glorify William III. These poems had been
ridiculed by the wits, who were in turn attacked by Blackmore
in his *Satyr against Wit*. As lines 41–49 show, TP liked this
poem less than he admired Blackmore's epics. TP's Whiggish
politics (natural enough in a young Irishman) come out
clearly here.

37      Compare Pope, *Essay on Criticism* (1711), line 391: "For Fools
*Admire*, but Men of Sense *Approve*" (TE 1:284).

50      T—te] Nahum Tate (1652–1715), poet and dramatist. His
plays appeared between 1678 and 1687; the *New Version of the
Psalms of David* that he produced with Nicholas Brady was
published in 1696. Tate was involved with numerous transla-
tions, and the exact point of the "bits of foreign poets" is
uncertain.

71      Dennis] John Dennis (1657–1734), whose attack on Black-

more, *Remarks on a Book Entitled "Prince Arthur"* (1696), had already established his reputation as an ill-natured critic. If TP's poem was written as late as 1702, the reference here is almost certainly to the "Large Account of the Taste in Poetry and the Causes in the Degeneration of it" prefixed to the published text of Dennis's *The Comical Gallant* (1702), which had failed on the stage. If TP was writing before the appearance of the "Large Account" in May 1702, the reference is probably to the preface to *Rinaldo and Armida* (1699), which is similarly (if not so garrulously) self-justificatory.

74    Hypers] Presumably a variant on "the Hyp," a slang term for nervous hypochondria; "hypers" is not recorded in the *OED*, where "hyp" is first recorded in 1705.

## *On the Addresses* (f. 3a)

This poem is in TP's hand, and may have been added later in the space left by the transcriber at the foot of f. 3a; there are no corrections.

*Translation.* "What a splendid impression our loyal addresses to King William make; I believe that the people would be as pleased if he were a god as a king! But if he were endowed with divine power, he would use it as responsibly as his royal power."

The poem refers to the series of loyal addresses presented to William III in response to Louis XIV's recognition of the Pretender as king of England. The first, presented by the City of London, was printed in the *London Gazette* on 2 October 1701; numerous others followed over the next three months. TP probably had particularly in mind the Irish addresses. On 10 December 1701 the *London Gazette* printed addresses from the archbishops, bishops, and clergy (undated); from the County of Dublin (dated 23 October); from the City of Dublin (dated 17 October); and from Trinity College, Dublin (dated 28 October).

## *On Dr. Brown's Death* (ff. 3b–4b)

This poem was copied by the same hand that transcribed the "Letter to a Friend" above. Three words evidently omitted in error ("victims", line 17; "earth" and "upward", line 72) have been inserted in a hand that may possibly be TP's; the corrections may also be autograph. We have corrected the transcriber's misleading punctuation in lines 28, 38, and 42.

Dr. George Browne was provost of Trinity College, Dublin, for most of TP's term of residence there. Browne succeeded Swift's friend St.

George Ashe as provost in 1695, holding the position until his death in 1699. The following account, from R. B. McDowell and D. A. Webb, *Trinity College Dublin, 1592–1952: An Academic History* (Cambridge: Cambridge University Press, 1982) helps to explain the apparent extravagance of TP's poem: "He is one of those men, baffling to historians, who evidently made a strong impression on their contemporaries, but have left behind virtually nothing by which that impression can be objectively assessed"; while his epitaph "even by the standards of the day, is remarkably full and laudatory" (p. 31).

### Textual Notes

| | |
|---|---|
| 1 | Alas] ⟨Alass⟩ MS |
| 4 | go] ⟨bow⟩ MS |
| 28 | disappear.] —, MS |
| 38 | sun.] —, MS |
| 40 | maintain] mantain MS |
| 42 | reign.] —, MS |

### Explanatory Notes

| | |
|---|---|
| 6 | TP uses similar images in "Moses," lines 373–76, and in "Ecstasy" ("A" version, lines 68–74; "B" version, lines 89–94). |
| 34 | Ægyptian night] Perhaps referring to Wisdom 16–17, where the Egyptians were haunted by monstrous apparitions while Israel was guided by God's light. |
| 52 | The *Aeneid* and *Orlando Furioso* both end with the death of a hero, but neither Homeric epic does. |

## *In Statuam Regis* (f. 4b)

Like "On the Addresses," these lines are in TP's hand and may be a later insertion.

*Translation.* "While, Sir, your auspicious influence protects our altars, and religion (under your protection) is restored and flourishes, this statue is a tribute both to your piety and your power. The statue is raised to you, as our king; but we are more pleased with it as a representation of the champion of religion."

The statue to which this poem refers was erected on College Green at the expense of the Corporation of Dublin, and inaugurated with an elaborate ceremonial on 1 July 1701 (the anniversary of the Battle of the Boyne). A report of the ceremony and the attendant festivities appeared in the *London Gazette* on 10 July 1701. The statue was so placed that the king's back was turned to Trinity College, and it became the object of student pranks, especially at times when Tory sentiments ran high (as in 1710 and 1714); for further details, see J. T. Gilbert, *A History of the City of Dublin* (Dublin, 1861), 3:40–45.

## Textual Notes

| | |
|---|---|
| Title | statuam] statuā MS |
| 2 | religio] ⟨relligio⟩ MS |
| 3 | potuit] ⟨posuit⟩ MS |

## *To T——— M———y: On Law* (Satire 2) (ff. 5a–6a)

This poem is in TP's hand, as is the remainder of the notebook with the exception of the final poem. Above each of the fictional names (Tully, Matho, Nevolus, Livy, and Brutus) a real name has apparently been written in a very small hand; except in one instance, however, these names have been so thoroughly deleted as to be unrecoverable. Nor, unfortunately, are the classical names much help in seeking for the originals.

The only alteration made to the text of the poem is in line 62, where "practise" replaces canceled "custom".

## Explanatory Notes

| | |
|---|---|
| 39 | Tully] The primary force of the name must be eloquence, but if a secondary reference to Cicero's political career is intended, TP may be referring to a lawyer who was compromised with the Jacobite regime and hence has dropped from prominence since the Revolution. |
| 41 | Matho] Presumably named from the lawyer in Juvenal's *Satires*, who is described as fat (1.32), extravagant (7.129), and loud-mouthed (11.34). |
| 51 | Nevolus] This is the only case where the original name is recoverable; it is "Brodrick," probably Alan Brodrick (1660?–1728), at this time (1695–1707) Solicitor General for Ireland. He was later created Lord Midleton and served as Lord |

Chancellor of Ireland. The classical original is perhaps the poor pimp in Juvenal's ninth satire.

55   Livy] The only Irish lawyer of any note who was also an historian was Sir Richard Cox (1650–1733), author of *Hibernia Anglicana* (1689–90); in 1703 he was appointed Lord Chancellor of Ireland. However, he was not active in Irish affairs at the time TP was writing, and the canceled name does not look like "Cox".

63   Brutus] It is not clear which Brutus TP had in mind here; possibly he meant the name to suggest no more than a patriot (real or supposed).

65   In forma pauperis] "In the character of a pauper"; a poor litigant might be assigned counsel (who would serve without fee) by the judge.

74–79   This story is a variant on the familiar fable of "The Belly and the Members," for which see Thompson, *Motif Index of Folk Literature*, J 461.1; and Babrius, Loeb ed., Appendix, No. 310.

## *On the Trust* (f. 6b)

The background to this poem is familiar to students of Swift, whose first political pamphlet, the *Discourse of the Contests and Dissensions in Athens and Rome* (1701) was written as part of the controversy surrounding the resumption of William's grants. William III had given large grants of forfeited Irish land (forfeited, that is, by James II and his adherents) to some of his personal favorites. The House of Commons in England passed an act to resume these grants, and to vest the forfeited lands in trustees, who were to sell them for the benefit of the government. Much of the land, however, had been bought from William's favorites by Irish purchasers, and the resumptions (though popular in England) were therefore resented in Ireland itself. TP's poem reflects this Irish hostility to the thwarting of the king by the English House of Commons. The poem can probably be dated in 1700; the trustees began their work in June of that year. For the historical background, see J. G. Simms, *The Williamite Confiscation in Ireland, 1690–1703* (London: Faber & Faber, 1956), and the edition of Swift's *Discourse* by Frank H. Ellis (Oxford: Clarendon Press, 1967). TP again refers to the Trust in "Thou gaudy, idle world" (line 21), and in "Virtue" (line 83).

In order to fit the entire poem onto f. 6b, TP wrote lines 11–29 without dividing them into stanzas. We have introduced breaks after lines 15 and 20, as TP must have intended. There are no corrections.

## *A Divine Pastorall* (ff. 7a–8a)

### Textual Notes

| | |
|---|---|
| 7 | Should] ⟨When⟩ MS |
| | call] ⟨calld⟩ MS |
| 15 | his] ⟨him⟩ MS |
| 16 | abroad,] The word is written above a deleted word (which may be the same word) and the comma follows the deleted word. |
| 27 | rising] ⟨finishd⟩ MS |
| 34 | less be joynd] ⟨there less joyn⟩ MS |
| 36 | rising] ⟨finishd⟩ MS |
| 44 | rising] ⟨finishd⟩ MS |
| 68 | praise.] — MS |
| 76 | So] ⟨Here⟩ MS |

## To ———— (ff. 8b–9a)

This is the first of many poems in the notebook written by TP with little or no punctuation.

### Textual Notes

| | |
|---|---|
| Title | The MS has a name illegibly deleted. |
| 4 | firm] ⟨formd⟩ MS |
| 7 | girl] ⟨wench⟩ MS |
| 18 | once you're] ⟨youre once⟩ MS |
| 26 | thus] ⟨so⟩ MS |

### Explanatory Note

| | |
|---|---|
| 31 | "Cowel" is John Cowell (1554–1611), author of *Institutiones Iuris Anglicani* (1605) and other legal works. "Blunt" is Thomas Blount (1618–79), author of *Fragmenta Antiquitatis: Antient Tenures of Land* (1679) and other legal works. "Cook" is Sir Edward Coke (1552–1634), Lord Chief Justice and author of the *Institutes of the Laws of England* (4 parts, 1628–44), of which the first part is the famous legal text popularly known as "Coke upon Littleton." |

# "Thou Gaudy, Idle World, Adieu" (ff. 9a–b)

The division into stanzas is editorial, based on a clear break in the MS after line 4; on f. 9b there are no breaks in the text. There are no corrections. The reference to Rochester (line 26) dates the poem before September 1701, and probably in the spring or summer of that year.

### Explanatory Notes

10     Asgill] John Asgill (1659–1738), religious eccentric; he was most notorious for his idea (expressed in a book published in 1700, and hence very topical at the time this poem was written), that a man might be "translated" from earthly to eternal life without passing through the state of death. He was a major purchaser of land from the trustees of the forfeited estates. According to Simms, *The Williamite Confiscation*, 155, he bought fifteen thousand acres.

21     the Trust] For the Trust, see TP's poem "On the Trust" above. The figure of £300,000 is perhaps the notional sum realized by the trustees at the time TP was writing. The sum eventually realized was £724,501 (Simms, *The Williamite Confiscation*, 168).

25     Methwin] John Methuen (1650–1706), Lord Chancellor of Ireland (1697–1703), but better known as the architect of the "Methuen treaties" with Portugal. In politics he was a violent Whig, hence TP's jibe about his irreligion. A ballad satirizing Methuen (and including a reference to his patronage of the deist John Toland) is printed in A. D. Francis, *The Methuens and Portugal* (Cambridge: Cambridge University Press, 1966), 356–57).

26     Rochester] Laurence Hyde (1641–1711), created earl of Rochester in 1681; he was appointed Lord Lieutenant in December 1700, but delayed his departure for Ireland and did not arrive in Dublin until September 1701. The reference thus dates the poem probably to the spring or summer of 1701.

# "A Bevy of the Fair and Gay" (ff. 9b–10a)

This very topical poem was evidently intended to satirize (with what degree of seriousness it is impossible to say) certain ladies in Dublin society, presumably known at least by repute to TP and his circle. The only one, however, whose identity can be guessed at is "O⟨rr⟩——y" (line 13), presumably "Orrery". In line 20, "M——s" is perhaps "Matthews", and in line 22 "Cr—fts" probably "Crofts".

## Textual Notes

| | |
|---|---|
| 13 | O——y's] TP began to write out the name in full, but deleted the letters (almost certainly *rr*) he wrote after the initial *O*. |
| 18 | you] ⟨I⟩ MS |

## *Virtue* (Satire 3) (ff. 10b–12b)

### Textual Notes

| | |
|---|---|
| Title | ⟨on Virtue⟩ MS |
| 13 | that what you faign] TP wrote "the thing you want" above these words, presumably intending the revised line to end "to know"; but as he did not complete the reworking we have let the original wording stand. |
| 56–57 | ⟨tis granted your reflections Just are found / in men of principles that are not sound⟩ MS |
| 59 | reason] ⟨virtue⟩ MS |
| 72 | wild convulsions] ⟨giddy transports⟩ MS |
| 73 | When] The word is canceled and rewritten in the MS. |
| 94 | a] ⟨the⟩ MS |

### Explanatory Notes

| | |
|---|---|
| 19 | *Sporus*] The classical name is probably taken from Suetonius "Nero" 28. |
| 25 | *Damon*] A conventional name for a character in pastoral; TP also uses it below in "The Pretty Gentleman," line 8, but this need not mean that he had the same person in mind in both cases. |
| 30 | *Codrus*] Probably named after the very poor poet in Juvenal *Satires* 3.203–11. |
| 36 | *Cotta*] Apparently simply a typical classical name. |
| 64 | *Curio*] Like "Cotta" above (and "Corinna" in the same line), apparently a typical classical name. |

| | |
|---|---|
| 83 | fifteen hundred] This was the salary paid to the forfeiture trustees (Simms, *The Williamite Confiscation*, 119); see TP's poem "On the Trust" above. |
| 93 | knight of yᵉ post] A professional perjuror, a familiar figure in contemporary satires. |
| 107 | *Gripus*] A postclassical name for a miser; Pope later used it in the *Essay on Man*, 4.280 (TE 3.1:154). |

## A Dream (ff. 13a–14b)

This poem is an early version of "Piety." In the MS it is marked with a vertical line down the center of pages 13a, 13b, and 14a (though not 14b), an indication that TP had copied it elsewhere. The text of the poem evidently began as a fair copy, but TP subsequently used it at least in part as a working manuscript. Most of his revisions are written above the original readings, which remain uncanceled. Where the later readings are sufficiently clear and complete, we have incorporated them into the text, recording the original readings in the notes. The justification for this is that it is the later readings that reappear in those parts of "Piety" that are closely related to this early form of the poem.

### Textual Notes

| | |
|---|---|
| 3 | beside] ⟨aside⟩ MS |
| 7 | silent] ⟨a dumb⟩ MS ("silent", however, is in turn deleted, but we have retained it since TP did not substitute a third reading.) |
| 15 | all my favour] {I by all were} MS |
| 18–19 | above lines 18 and 19 respectively Parnell wrote, "tune your numbers with seraphick air" and "[          ] of holy praise and humble prayer" (the first two words of the second line are not legible, but may be "When brought") |
| 25 | it self is] {shall be} MS |
| 29 | unction on] {oil upon} MS ("unction" is the reading in "Piety," line 32) |
| 30 | proceeded . . . zeal] {went on) thy muse shall be thy Zeal} MS ("Be thy muse thy zeal" is the reading of "Piety," line 33) |
| 31 | Joys reveal] {comforts tell} MS ("Piety" has "joys reveal" in line 34) |
| 34 | true] ⟨short⟩ MS (this must be an error of transcription) |
| 38–40 | These lines originally read: "Make his bow black his arrows |

still yᵉ same / but headed with ⟨more⟩ an everlasting flame /
his bones all bare & Death his alterd name". In line 38, "black
his arrows still" is underlined, apparently to indicate TP's
dissatisfaction (as in line 70 below); and in line 39, "more"
must have been deleted as soon as written. Apart from
"more", the only word in this original version actually can-
celed is "Make".

40        parts] part MS (TP must have intended this change)

57        A canceled triplet (bracketed as such) follows in the MS:
"Glory be to the great Three One on high / as it has been
from all eternity / as it has been & is so lett it ever bee".

58        & then With] ⟨With these last⟩ MS

61        An incomplete revision is written above the line: "Musick
⟨dying⟩ mounting up till its gon".

63        Gracious] {my dear} MS
Lord] ⟨god⟩ MS
make] {be} MS

64        make] {may} MS
mine innocence] ⟨my hap⟩ MS (presumably the word was to
have been "happiness")

66        my passions restrain] {keep my passions in} MS

70        {& my ill habits be confest again} MS ("ill" and "be confest"
are underlined, presumably indicating TP's intention to re-
work them)

71        Thus {So} MS
the tail] ⟨its tail⟩ MS

76        He proudly] ⟨proudly he⟩ MS

## *The Pretty Gentleman* (Satire 4) (ff. 14b-16a)

Like "A Dream," this poem is marked with vertical strokes as having
been copied elsewhere; in the case of this poem, however, no other text
is known.

As with many topical references in this notebook, the identities of
"W—— G——" and "Damon" remain unknown.

### Textual Notes

9        Eighteen] ⟨fifteen⟩ MS

16       soths yᵉ spleen while] ⟨yᵉ spleen tickles⟩ MS

32       wild] ⟨soft⟩ MS

60 After this line, TP began copying line 63 (as far as "he does the men of buis"), apparently in error.

### Explanatory Note

55 Dorimant] The hero of Sir George Etherege's comedy *The Man of Mode* (1676). One of his mannerisms is quoting scraps of poetry (mainly from Waller); his first lines in the play are such a quotation.

## *Verse* (Satire 5) (ff. 16a–17b)

### Textual Notes

24–25 These lines were either a later addition or were an accidental omission during transcription. TP originally wrote "as fair" (the end of the long line 23) on a separate line, then deleted it (rewriting it on the end of line 23 itself) and in the one-line space thus freed wrote lines 24–25 in a smaller hand.

36 & ink] ⟨the ink⟩ MS

56 fair Virtue beggerd] ⟨Virtue a begger⟩ MS. After "beggerd", TP wrote and then deleted "virtue", probably a slip.

65 Above this line TP has written (in a single line in a tiny hand) a reworking of lines 61–62: "nor am in love no[r] have a drinker been nor provd $y^e$ witty forces of $y^e$ spleen". He may have intended this couplet to replace line 65, so avoiding the triplet. Although we have usually incorporated these interlinear revisions into the text, here we have allowed the original reading to stand. If TP had finally decided on so important a change, he would surely have made some mark against lines 62–63 or crossed out the triplet bracket.

### Explanatory Notes

61 never have a drinker been] This comment, if it is to be taken as a straightforward biographical statement, is interesting in the light of the reputation for excessive drinking that TP later acquired.

75 Horace] The idea of Horace as the type of the gentle, and of

Juvenal as the type of the savage satirist was commonplace. A passage TP may have had in mind is Horace *Satires* 1.10.14–15.

77      Gall . . . ink] A commonplace pairing, exemplified in Sir Toby Belch's advice to Sir Andrew Aguecheek in *Twelfth Night:* "Let there be gall enough in thy ink" (3.2.47). Swift has "*Gall* and *Copperas*" in *The Battle of the Books* (*Tale,* pp. 221, 251).

## *The Spleen* (Satire 6) (ff. 17b–19b)

This poem can be dated within narrow limits. The reference to the queen in line 103 must postdate Queen Anne's accession in March 1702; and the poem is presumably earlier than "The Isle of Wight," the next poem in the manuscript, which can be dated about June 1702.

### Textual Notes

2      below] ⟨beneath⟩ MS

8      her] ⟨his⟩ MS

10      its] ⟨our⟩ MS

11      case] The word may possibly be "ease".

51      in] ⟨of⟩ MS

54      barren] ⟨perfect⟩ MS

60      Engage] ⟨do win⟩ MS

79      ⟨The winds by Just degrees do louder grow⟩ MS (In revising the line, TP forgot to delete the now hypermetrical "do".)

96      pray] ⟨play⟩ MS (an error of transcription)

97      The first two words of this line correct an undecipherable reading.

103      "Queen" was first written "queen" and capitalized as an afterthought.

### Explanatory Notes

42      Lister] Martin Lister (1638?–1712), scientist and author of a major work on shells, *Historia Conchyliorum* (1685–92).

78      finishd in a wife] The heroes of restoration comedy were usually married off to a virtuous lady at the end of the play, no matter how wild and wicked they had been; the con-

vention changed about 1700 (see J. H. Smith, *The Gay Couple in Restoration Comedy* [Cambridge: Harvard University Press, 1949], esp. 193–201).

## *The Isle of Wight* (Satire 7) (ff. 20a–21a)

The occasion of this very topical poem can be quite precisely dated. It refers to an expedition, of which the land forces were commanded by the duke of Ormonde, which assembled at the Isle of Wight in the spring of 1702 with the intention of capturing Cadiz. (The expedition failed in its intended purpose, but on its return managed to ransack and destroy the Spanish plate fleet in the action of Vigo Bay.)

On 2 June 1702 the *Post Boy* reported that troops from Ireland had landed at Cowes on 30 May, and that Prince George of Denmark had set out to view the fleet at Portsmouth and the forces encamped on the Isle of Wight. On 4 June it reported that this encampment now numbered twelve thousand men. On 6 June it reported Ormonde's return from a visit to the Isle of Wight; and on 13 June that Ormonde had finally set out. Of particular interest as providing a gloss on TP's satire on "volunteers" is the following report, which appeared in the *Flying Post* on 4 June: "We hear that about 30 Persons of Quality with fine Equipages, will attend his Grace the Duke of Ormonde as Volunteers on board the Fleet, intended for the Descent."

There are no corrections to the text of this poem.

### Explanatory Notes

3       Or——d] James Butler (1665–1745), second duke of Ormonde, in 1702 appointed to command the land forces that sailed on Sir George Rooke's expedition to Cadiz.

23     Mirtillo . . . Courant] Both are names of dances.

24     speak to show your soul] Proverbial; sometimes quoted in the Latin version "Sermo animi est imago".

25     Coupees . . . sinks] Technical movements in dancing; the *OED*'s first quotation of "sink" in this sense is dated 1706.

34–43   This passage loosely recalls Horace *Odes* 3.2.13–25.

60–65   This anecdote is a variant of a fable found in Phaedrus (1.7; "Vulpis ad personam tragicam"). The date of the poem precludes a reference to the famous Indian kings who visited London in 1710.

# The Picture of Time (Satire 8) (ff. 21a–23a)

## Textual Notes

16      I with ease] ⟨quickly I⟩ MS
22      follys] ⟨passions⟩ MS
33      indolently glide] {do most gayly slide} MS
53      man] ⟨men⟩ MS (the manuscript is unclear, but "whore" in line 56 makes "man" seem more likely to be the later reading)

## Explanatory Notes

1–9      Erwin Panofsky, "Father Time," *Studies in Iconology,* new ed. (New York: Peter Smith, 1962), 69–93, makes the point that the old man with wings, scythe, and hourglass is not a classical but a Renaissance image. TP's "picture of time" is unconventional in one respect, that he does not explicitly make Time an old man (as he always is in Renaissance art). In "An Allegory on Man," lines 49–64, TP draws another "picture of time," and there he is self-consciously unconventional in making Time young.

19      your father's friend] This interlocutor is surely a conventional figure.

25      reigning folly] For a discussion of the traditional idea of a "reigning," "ruling," or "predominant" passion, see Maynard Mack's introduction to the *Essay on Man,* TE 3.1 : xxxvi–xxxix, and his notes on the *Essay,* 2.123–60.

28      If reason loses control, it will actually assist the "reigning folly" with "means to help it on." Pope makes this point in the *Essay on Man* 2.155–56.

45–46      This commonplace can be traced back to Ecclesiastes 3 : 1–8; TP may here be recalling *Henry VIII,* 3.2.144–49.

51      By tiring us when we do one thing for too long, nature teaches us to vary our activities.

58      Titus] Titus Flavius Sabinus Vespasianus (39–81), Roman emperor (79–81); the anecdote is told by Suetonius "Titus" 8.

62      Heathen Christians] Heathens who, like Titus, practised Christian virtues.

# The State of Love (Satire 9) (ff. 23a–26a)

This is a translation of Philippe Desportes (1546–1606), "Élégie IX"; for a critical text, see *Élégies,* ed. Victor E. Graham (Geneva: Librairie Droz, 1961), 70–79.

## Textual Notes

| | |
|---|---|
| 16 | The line originally read, "full of content they daily lovd & livd"; TP seems to have changed this to "full of content & love they daily livd" before arriving at the final version. |
| 20 | expresst] ⟨expressd⟩ MS |
| 22 | desert & softness love] ⟨softness adress desert⟩ MS |
| 25 | Empire] {power} MS |
| 29 | the meanest thought them not a] ⟨Which evn the meanest thought no⟩ MS (where "them" is written, canceled, then rewritten) |
| 31 | ⟨& all this downy age of bliss was past⟩ MS |
| 58 | the tend'rest] ⟨their tender⟩ MS (?) |
| 98 | At the top of f. 25a, above line 98, TP first wrote and then deleted, "You never never shall aga", apparently mis-transcribing from line 100 below. |
| 143 | virtues] ⟨Graces⟩ MS |
| 148 | Below "now will have" TP has added, in the smaller hand in which he usually writes corrections, "Cupid has sworn it". This seems to be a note for an intended revision; but it cannot be a simple alternative to any phrase in the text as we have it. |

# Colin (Satire 10) (ff. 26a–28a)

## Textual Notes

| | |
|---|---|
| Title | ⟨Collin⟩ MS |
| 20 | a] ⟨your⟩ MS |
| 66 | whom they call] ⟨who was so⟩ MS |
| 70 | TP wrote this line flush left before canceling it and writing it again, this time indenting for a new paragraph. |
| 75 | the nymphs] ⟨his wives⟩ MS |

**Explanatory Notes**

2  Colin] Probably named after the shepherd in Spenser's *Shepherd's Calendar*.
61  Alexis] A common pastoral name, as in Virgil's *Eclogue* 2.
86  Orinda] The pseudonym of Katherine Philips (1631–64), but also a typical pastoral name.

# The Court (Satire 11) (ff. 28a–30b)

**Textual Notes**

8  deliv'rance] ⟨deliverance⟩ MS
30  glossy] ⟨tinsell⟩ MS
42  ⟨Where men as in a wood where robbers live⟩ MS
43  We're] ⟨are⟩ MS
61  All] {The} MS
72  legs] ⟨leggs⟩ MS
85  state] ⟨states⟩ MS
86  ⟨Are Heav'ns & Heaven but a Fairy scene⟩ MS

**Explanatory Notes**

3–6  The image perhaps recalls Lucretius 2.1–4.
96  Anna] Queen Anne.
98  Arethusa] Originally a nymph, pursued by the river god Alpheus, and turned by Diana into a fountain; for the story, see Ovid *Metamorphoses* 5.572–641.

# The Test of Poetry (Satire 12) (ff. 30b–32b)

  This poem is notable in several respects. Unlike the several preceding poems in the notebook, it is extensively (if erratically) punctuated, and it is more heavily revised than any of the earlier poems in the manuscript. It is also the first poem in which TP thinks of himself not as an amateur dabbler (as in the "Letter to a Friend" or in "Verse"), but as a poet in the great world of letters. He knows "Thyrsis" (surely Pope is meant here); he is crossquestioned by envious "Bavius." It is also the last poem to be designated one of the series of satires, and in another respect it marks a transition: all five of the poems in the notebook that were printed either by TP himself or by Pope are transcribed after this poem. In "The Test of Poetry," then, we can see TP becoming more aware of a possible audience (and trying to punctuate for it?), and taking himself more seriously as a publishing poet. If we compare the text of this poem with that of "A Dream," the only earlier poem in the notebook that is anything like so heavily revised, two differences stand out. In "A Dream," many of the revisions were simply written above the original readings, and the poem as a whole was marked as having been recopied; here, all the necessary deletions are clearly made, but the poem is not marked as having been copied. This may mark a change in TP's habits of composition.

### Textual Notes

| | |
|---|---|
| Title | Test] ⟨Practise⟩ MS |
| 6 | our] ⟨the⟩ MS |
| 9 | from] ⟨yʳ⟩ MS |
| 14 | knack to master] {vein orepowers} MS |
| 21 | sudden writers] ⟨giddy authors⟩ MS |
| 22 | giddy] ⟨sudden⟩ MS |
| 32 | TP originally wrote this line after line 33, then canceled it and rewrote it above line 33. |
| 35 | follys, or] ⟨folly, &⟩ MS ("sooth" is written above the line, probably an accidental omission, since the meter requires it) |
| 36 | Brisk drunken Catches on] ⟨The drunken Catch does on⟩ MS (TP altered "does" to "will" before arriving at the final version.) |
| 37 | Soft] ⟨The⟩ MS |
| 38 | will] ⟨does⟩ MS |
| | unspotted] ⟨a spotless⟩ MS |
| 39 | worthless] ⟨wretched⟩ MS |
| 40–43 | These four lines replace the following canceled triplet (which is bracketed as such): "So hot-bed Plants, by forreign warmth increast, / Wont wait the kindly Sun, but shooting fast, / Arise with shape, & not with worth or tast." |
| 43 | a . . . a] ⟨the . . . the⟩ MS |
| 51 | they woud] ⟨Say they'd⟩ MS |
| | tis] ⟨for⟩ MS |
| 52 | Yet] ⟨but⟩ MS (?) |
| 58 | sing?] ⟨—;⟩ MS |
| 63 | The Justest may] ⟨An author must⟩ MS |

65 ⟨He will himself applaud, his lines approve,⟩ MS (TP changed "will" to "may" before arriving at the final version; and at one point the line ended "approves", but this may have been a slip.)

71 censure] ⟨[?]⟩ MS

74 changes] ⟨alters⟩ MS

80 This line replaces two canceled lines that, with line 79, formed a triplet (bracketed as such by TP): "Abroad theyle go their author to survive, / & for new times & new editions live." We have changed the terminal punctuation of this line from a comma to a period.

## Explanatory Notes

1 Bavius] The bad poet mentioned in Virgil *Eclogues* 3.90, and subsequently a name for any poetaster.

3 Thyrsis] Presumably Pope.

7 If this line is to be taken to imply that TP's poems had not yet appeared in any collection, the poem would have to be dated before November 1713, when four of his poems appeared (attributed to him by name) in Steele's *Poetical Miscellanies*.

23 Browns] A generic name for prolific hack writers, derived from Tom Brown (1663–1704).

## *The Ecstasy* (ff. 32b–34a: "A" version)

This poem is marked with vertical lines, indicating that it had been recopied. A second text of it appears below (ff. 43a–45a), but it seems likely that an intermediate text intervened. The differences between the two texts are recorded in the textual notes to the second version; here only the corrections made to this version of the poem are recorded. A leaf has been removed from the notebook between ff. 32 and 33, apparently before f. 33 was written on.

## Textual Notes

12 passions] ⟨errors⟩ MS

14 After this line, TP has written (at the foot of f. 32b) and then canceled lines 18–19 (with "powrfull" in line 18), apparently an error of copying.

| | |
|---|---|
| 18 | wondrous] {powrfull} MS |
| 29 | There is a marginal cross against this line; usually such a mark is an indication of TP's intention to revise the line, but here there is no alteration. |
| 61 | Above this line TP has written the following apparently tentative alternative "[?] our [?] & fitt us for heavnly quire". The first and third words are illegible (though the first may be "sweet"), and the third has been deleted; "fitt" is uncertain. |
| 62 | O] ⟨Thou⟩ MS |
| 66 | meditation] ⟨meditations⟩ MS |
| 67 | fancy] ⟨thought are⟩ MS |
| 71 | dragg] ⟨bear⟩ MS |

## *Concerning Resolution* (ff. 34b–35b)

### Textual Notes

| | |
|---|---|
| Title | ⟨The resolution⟩ MS (?) |
| 1–4 | These lines originally read: "Happy the man (may such a fate be mine / Who by resolving breakes the Chains of sin / For him indeed the golden dayes arise / The Land that flows with milk & hony's his". The first line is not canceled, but the original readings of lines 2–4 are. In order to preserve the rhyme TP must have intended line 1 to be canceled as well; this passage shows that TP did not always delete his rejected readings, and supports our general textual policy of accepting his interlined revisions when his intention is reasonably clear. |
| 14 | opinion] ⟨opinions⟩ MS (?) |
| 17 | This line is an interlinear addition, inserted by TP to remove the triplet originally formed by lines 16 and 18–19 (the bracket marking which has been deleted). |
| 18 | &] ⟨We⟩ MS |
| 20 | vain & wanton] ⟨wanton very⟩ MS |
| 23 | each] {then} MS |
| | as impotently] {again the thousand} MS (The original readings in line 23 are underlined but not canceled; as elsewhere, for example, "A Dream," lines 38 and 70, TP seems to have done this to indicate his dissatisfaction with a reading before he had settled on a suitable alternative). |
| 24 | wild] TP first wrote "wild", canceled it in favor of "mad", and then reverted to "wild". |

| 28 | reclining in yᵉ shady bowers] ⟨in shady bowers to recline⟩ MS |
|---|---|
| 29 | This line (like line 17) is an interlinear addition inserted to remove the triplet formed by lines 28 and 30–31; the bracket marking the triplet has been deleted. The reading "near" is doubtful. |
| 34 | Fancy still undreind] ⟨undreind Fancy still⟩ MS |
| 35 | {It must be thus if reason quitt her throne} MS (TP wrote "the" and replaced it by "her" while writing the line.) |
| 37 | labour] {projects} MS |
| 40–41 | TP began reworking these lines, apparently in order to remove the triplet (as he had already done in lines 16–19 and 28–31 above). He wrote "so when yᵉ faulcons plumes" above the first half of line 40, and "ignobler" and "invade" above the second half of line 41. Possibly he intended to compress lines 39–41 into a couplet rhyming "fade / invade". We have accepted "ignobler" for "less noble" into the text, but the other alterations seem only tentative. |
| 53 | thine] ⟨thy⟩ MS |

## To ⁺₊⁺ On the Various Styles of Poetry (ff. 35b– 39b)

This is an early version of the *Essay on the Different Styles of Poetry* and is marked with vertical strokes to indicate its having been recopied. For ease of reference, the textual notes to this poem have been divided into three groups. Below are (a) the alterations made to this early version of the poem and (b) the differences between this version ("S") and the later manuscript in the "Essay" Notebook ("E") in the rejected opening of the poem. A record of the variants between the different versions of the main body of the poem will be found in the textual notes to the *Essay* above.

### (a) Textual Notes

| Title | In E, the title reads, "⟨An Essay on⟩ On the Styles of Poetry ⟨in a letter⟩". In MS the title reads, "To ⁺₊⁺ on ⟨Poetry⟩ the various Styles of Poetry". |
|---|---|
| 10 | sweet] ⟨wild⟩ MS |
| 32 | tunefull] ⟨sleeping⟩ MS |
| 43–50 | These lines (with which the poem as published begins) are marked with an oblique stroke of uncertain significance. |

49          We have closed the parenthesis, which TP forgot.
90          through a] ⟨thro' a⟩ MS
102         TP began writing the line without indenting for a new para-
            graph, probably an error of transcription.
168         crowding] ⟨sparkling⟩ MS


## (b) Variations in the Canceled Opening Lines

1           Nymph] S; maid E
3           the] S, E; but in E "her" is written above as an alternative
            brought] S, E; in E, "wrought" is written above as an alter-
            native
5           shady groves were reard] S; groves of shady green E
6           appeard] S; were seen E
7           rewarded passions glowd] S; or hopefull loves begun E
8           flowd] S; run E
13          E avoids the triplet by expanding line 13 into the following
            couplet: "She often cryd, & cryd but vainly still, / For truth
            repelld the shades & crossd her will."
14–15       Expanded as follows in E:
                    Till one bright youth upon her temper wrought
                    With words expressive of the tender thought
                    With soft description of the lovers cares,
                    Their moving arts & captivating airs,
                    Their lonely forrest or frequented stream,
                    & while he fed her fancy, raisd her flame,
19          the whole] S; all the E
21–23       E again avoids the triplet and expands as follows:
                    & reason strove to show the dawn of man,
                    Much pleasd with verse where sense exalted high
                    On airy raptures woud appear to fly,
                    Where words with native grace or figurd show
                    On easy measures woud appear to flow,
25–26       These lines appear in E as follows: "Then in the warmth a
            faint resembling shade / for ev'ry style my working fancy
            made,". Against the first line, there is a comment on the
            verso, "in the warmth dark". If this was one of Bolingbroke's
            comments, it indicates that TP had not yet decided to reject
            the opening passage when he showed the poem to him.

29        Ah cruell world thou foe to] S; Thou world destructive to my
          E
33        your] S; thy E
          cheat] S; dream E
35–36     In E these lines read, "But now thy cautious maxims disap-
          pear, / & I woud write because a friend woud hear,".
40        the] S; a E
          E adds the following couplet after line 40: "He tells of grief
          decreasd, of comfort raisd, / Of all the breast from care by
          writing easd". TP wrote "lessend grief" before changing it to
          "grief decreasd".

## Boethius, Book I, Metre 4 (f. 40a)

There is another text of this poem on a loose manuscript among the
Congleton papers; this manuscript also contains a second translation
from Boethius (printed below as "When Haizy Clouds"). The two texts of
the present poem are very similar. The "A" text (on the loose sheet) is
earlier and has more corrections; its revised readings are found in the
"B" text (in the notebook), which has a few new readings evidently
introduced during the process of transcription. The "B" text is itself
revised in a few places. Three stages of revision can thus be dis-
tinguished, and although the changes are only minor, they illustrate the
way TP worked on his poems.

Pope translated part of Boethius, 3, metre 9 (TE 6:73–74), and al-
though the translation probably predates 1710, it was first published in
*Poems on Several Occasions (Pope's Own Miscellany)* in 1717. It is therefore
possible that TP's translations were undertaken as a result of, or in
connection with, Pope's revived interest in Boethius some time before
1717.

### Textual Notes

2         Can] A has "can" as an alternative to uncanceled "do".
          triumph] A has "triumphs" canceled in favor of "triumph".
6         Shall see] A has "beholds" canceled in favor of "Shall see".
7         In A, the line originally read: "Vesuvius spouting smoaky
          flames on high". This was subsequently canceled and re-
          placed by the line as it appears in B.
8         & bolts of thunder] A's original wording, "& thunder bolts",
          was canceled and replaced by B's version.
9         In A the line reads, "Why do we dread poor wretched man-

kind why". In B, TP began the line "Why doe we" before
arriving at the final version.

10     idely] B; loudly A

12     minds] A has "selves" canceled in favor of "minds".

13     breast] B; breasts A

15     or] B; & A

17     the] A has "that" canceled in favor of "the".

18     the strongest shield we] In A, TP wrote "the onely shield he"
before writing "his" above "the"; he then canceled "his" and
changed "he" to "we". In B, he wrote first "that onely shield
we"; changed "that" to "the"; canceled "onely" and wrote
"firm" above, probably intending "firmest", before canceling
"firm" in its turn in favor of the final reading, "strongest".

19     he weaves] A has "does weave", which is also the original
reading of B, where it is canceled in favor of "he weaves".

20     keep] In A, TP wrote and canceled "Ma" (probably intending
"Make") before writing "keep".
us passions slaves] B; him passions slave A, ⟨B⟩

# A Tavern Feast (ff. 40b–42a)

This is an early version of the poem published in Steele's *Poetical
Miscellanies* (1714) as "Anacreontick" (with much the same text as here)
and (in a heavily revised version) in Pope's edition. In the "Satires"
Notebook, the poem is marked with vertical lines to indicate that it had
been copied elsewhere. Here only the alterations made to the man-
uscript itself are recorded; a full record of the differences between the
manuscript as finally worded and the printed texts is given in the textual
notes to "Anacreontick" ("Gay Bacchus") above. The poem is written in a
larger hand than TP usually uses; since f. 42b is blank, it may be that TP
inserted the poem after writing one or more subsequent poems, and
found that he had left too much space.

"B——s" in line 1 is "Button's", the tavern opened early in 1712 by
Daniel Button, a former servant of Addison's; see Peter Smithers, *The
Life of Joseph Addison*, 2d ed. (Oxford: Clarendon Press, 1968), 242–43.
When he revised the poem, TP transferred the scene to Estcourt's
tavern.

### Textual Notes

18     allways gott] ⟨seemd to gett⟩ MS (TP wrote and canceled "dr",
probably for "drink", before "gett".)

25      ⟨Rough banters ran about yᵉ place⟩ MS

27      ⟨By taking sly reflections face⟩ MS

32      all his] ⟨drunken⟩ MS

41      TP began this line at the foot of f. 41a, then after writing "To part", canceled it and turned the page to begin again.

54      did recline] ⟨oft reclines⟩ MS

56      ⟨They rail at drinking Wines⟩ MS

60      After this line, the MS has lines 65–68 (with lines 67–68 in the original wording) at the top of f. 42a, canceled; this was probably an error of transcription.

67–68      ⟨For howesoere yᵉ knott appear / Tis not by nature long.⟩ MS

## The Ecstasy ("B" version) (ff. 43a–45a)

We have four texts of this poem: the earliest extant text is the one that appears on ff. 32b–34a above (we have called this the "A" version); the revised (or "B") version that occurs at this point in the notebook; and two printed texts (in the 1755 and 1758 editions, on pp. 229–32 and pp. 241–45 respectively) that evidently derive from manuscripts close to, but not identical with, the "B" version. Where the printed texts differ from the manuscript of the "B" version, they seem to preserve a slightly earlier form of the text since some of their readings are the original, canceled readings of the manuscript. Both printed texts may derive from a "working" manuscript of the poem that preceded the copying of the "B" version into the "Satires" Notebook. The incomplete line 66 in 1755 certainly suggests a "working" manuscript, and 1755's text of "To Dr. Swift" also contains an incomplete line. Possibly TP copied the poem into the "Everard" manuscript from the working notebook that later became available to the 1755 editor.

The differences between the "A" and "B" versions are too extensive to record in textual notes. The following table shows the main correspondences between the two versions:

| "A" (ff. 32b–34a) | "B" (ff. 43a–45a) |
| --- | --- |
| 1–8 | 1–10 (2 and 4 are new) |
| 9–17 | 11–22 (12–13, 21–22 are new) |
| 18–25 | 23–32 (31–32 are new) |
| 26–35 | 33–48 (39–46 are new) |
| 36–40 | 49–58 (mostly new) |
| 41–45 | 59–64 (59–60 are new) |
| 46–51 | 65–70 (broadly similar) |
| 52–57 | 71–76 (broadly similar) |
| 58–63 | 77–82 (79–81 are new) |
| 64–74 | 83–94 (87–88 are new) |

A notable effect of the revisions is to remove all the triplets in the "A" version; in "Concerning Resolution" TP removed some but not all of the triplets, so that we can here observe the development of a stylistic preference.

### Textual Notes

| | |
|---|---|
| 2 | unperforming] unavailing 55 |
| 3–4 | These lines are not in 55 or 58. |
| 6 | grasps the wealth nor honours of] These words are deleted, but so is the insertion "asks the gaudy plumes that deck", written above. Since TP has here definitely rejected his second thoughts, we have retained the first reading, which is found in 55 and 58. |
| 8 | crops for Lawrels] ⟨gathers wreaths from⟩ MS, 55, 58 |
| 9 | who] MS, 55; whose 58 |
| 13 | pitty] MS; mercy 55, 58 |
| 16 | still the rage] ⟨make a calm⟩ MS |
| 21 | Purple] MS; purpl'd 55, 58 |
| 30 | And] MS; Yet 55, 58 |
| 39 | which] MS; that 55, 58 |
| 40 | That] MS; Let 55, 58 |
| 45 | seraphims] MS; Seraphims 58; seraphim 55 |
| 48 | Range the vast heigths] ⟨And range the orbs⟩ MS, 55, 58 (We have made the consequential change of "range" to "Range", since in this poem TP regularly begins a new line with a capital.) |
| 49 | sweetly] MS; 58; joyful 55 |
| 50 | Curles] MS; pearls 55, 58 |
| 52 | tunefull] MS; trembling 55, 58 |
| 53 | sing] MS; tune 55, 58 |
| 54 | make] MS; makes 55, 58 |
| 55 | With harps of gold, with boughs of ever-green, 55, 58 (which has "Bows") |
| 59 | my] MS; a 55, 58 |
| 61 | Heavns immortall] MS; of the heav'nly 55, 58 |
| 62 | have warmed me] MS; has warm'd me 55; has warm'd you 58 |
| 64 | Halelujah] MS, 55; Hallelujahs 58 |
| 66 | 55 has an incomplete line: "O great beyond expression!——". |
| 74 | His] MS, 55; The 58 |
| 79 | grace with comfort] MS; graces, comforts 55, 58 |
| 80 | transport] MS; transports 55, 58 |
| 81 | grows] MS; is 55, 58 |

85          thoughts] MS, 58; thought 55
            T'other] MS; t'other's 55, 58
86          fair] MS; {gay} MS, 55, 58
87          The MS has a canceled "Oh" at the beginning of the line.
88          seek its home] MS; claim its seat 55, 58
90          the] MS; our 55, 58 ("our" is also the reading of the "A" version)
94          by which they learnd] MS; ⟨which taught them where⟩ MS; that taught them how 55, 58 (the printed texts here have the reading of the "A" version)

## The Horse & Olive (ff. 46a–47a)

This poem is marked with vertical strokes as having been recopied; as it was published as a folio half-sheet in 1713, this part of the notebook can thus be roughly dated. Probably TP copied the poem from the notebook onto a separate sheet to send to the printer. There are no corrections in the MS; in line 24 TP wrote and canceled "art" before "weight", evidently an error of copying. The text of the poem as published in 1713 is reprinted above. There are no substantive variants but a comparison between the poem as published and the manuscript text as here printed illustrates the degree of styling, in spelling, capitalization and punctuation, that an author's manuscript underwent.

An unexplained feature of the notebook is that f. 45b is blank, and at the head of f. 46a (above the title to this poem) TP has written "ye maids who when the bards adore", possibly the opening of a lost poem.

## *A Parody of Donec Gratus Eram* (ff. 47a–b)

There are two practically identical texts of this poem, here in the "Satires" Notebook and another in a loose manuscript (a single sheet, 151 × 95 mm, now rather frayed). The variants are too slight to determine which text was copied from which. There are no corrections in either manuscript of the poem. The poem is here printed from the text in the notebook (here called "N"), and the substantive variants between it and the loose manuscript (here called "L") are recorded in the textual notes. "L" is fully punctuated, but we have not recorded its punctuation.

The original poem is Horace's much-translated *Odes* 3.9. TP's version seems to have been written to poke fun at Richard Steele and his second wife, Mary Scurlock ("Prue"), whom he married in 1707; we have not been able to identify the other characters alluded to. The most probable date for the poem is 1713–14.

## Textual Notes

| Title | In L, the title reads, "Donec Gratus &c a Dialogue Between Mʳ S— & His Wife." |
|---|---|
| 1 | Biddy] N; L has "Prue your" written over uncanceled "Biddy". |
| 3 | S——s] N; S—— L |
| 4 | G——s] N; G—— L |
| 9 | S——s a] N; S——'s yᵉ L (where the whole line is placed within parentheses) |
| 18 | self] N; face L |

## *Epigram: On a Ladys Lace* (ff. 47b-48a)

The subtitle is probably a later insertion; the only revisions in the text are in line 1, where "chamber" and "got" probably both began as other words, and in line 3, where "Cast" replaces canceled "tyd". The "lace" referred to is not a piece of lace, but a lace such as was used to fasten a bodice or similar garment.

## *An Allegory on Man* (ff. 48a–50a)

This poem (which was first printed in Pope's edition) is unlike any other in the "Satires" Notebook in that it is written out with great care as though for printing. Punctuation is full, and TP has made a determined effort (not entirely successful) to avoid contractions. The "Allegory" is also one of three poems towards the end of the notebook (the others are "An Eclogue" and "The Heroines") of which the lines have been counted: correctly, in this case, as 112. It seems clear that this poem was being prepared for print; the text in the notebook may have been TP's final fair copy before writing it out on a separate sheet to send to Pope. The verbal differences between this text and Pope's are not great (except at the end of the poem), but this text preserves evidence of TP's own habits in preparing poems for the press. Here we have recorded only the corections made on the manuscript itself; the differences between this text (as finally worded) and Pope's are recorded in the textual notes to Pope's text. In general, it will be seen that Pope's text is practically identical as far as line 88; lines 89–100 are omitted from Pope's text, and lines 101–12 appear there in a substantially revised form.

**Textual Notes**

| | |
|---|---|
| 1 | A thoughtfull] ⟨An aged⟩ MS |
| 24–25 | "She" is written in the outer margin against these lines; its significance is uncertain. |
| 39 | removd] ⟨him once⟩ MS (there is a marginal cross against this line, TP's usual mark indicating dissatisfaction) |
| 40 | part's an Idle shape] ⟨part is but a lum⟩ MS (TP was presumably writing "lump") |
| 41–43 | In the MS these lines originally read as follows: "Let *Care* decide it. I says *Care* / Why both your pleas may claim a share: / The body yours, and yours the soul;". |
| 43 | You] you MS; we have made the change, required by the rewriting of lines 41–43, as TP is here regularly beginning lines with a capital. |
| 44 | Four canceled lines follow in the MS: |
| | Nor think I break on either bound, |
| | Twill in a learned world be found, |
| | When Sages fix their liberall arts, |
| | The whole can differ from its parts. |
| 45 | debate] ⟨dispute⟩ MS |
| 79 | Part] ⟨Joyn⟩ MS (apparently a slip) |
| 90 | This line is interlined, apparently having been omitted in transcription. |
| 99 | Bright] {Gay} MS |

## *Epigram* ("Kate counts her years") (f. 50b)

There are no corrections in the manuscript.

## *Martial* (XI.1xii) (f.50b)

This epigram is translated from Martial 11.62: "Lesbia se iurat gratis numquam esse fututam. / verum est. cum futui vult, numerare solet." In line 1, TP first wrote and canceled a name (possibly "Nancy") that is now hardly legible; then wrote and canceled "Biddy" before settling on "Lucy". In line 2, he wrote and canceled "Biddy" before settling on "Lucy".

# *An Eclogue* (ff. 51a–53a)

Pope printed a shorter version of this poem (78 lines against 116 in this text) as "Health, an Eclogue." "An Eclogue" is one of three poems in the notebook in which the lines have been counted; in this case, correctly, as 116. It is not, however, so carefully prepared for the press as "An Allegory on Man," although it is (unlike "The Heroins") fully punctuated.

The textual notes record the changes made in the manuscript, as well as the differences between the MS and Pope's edition.

### Textual Notes

| | |
|---|---|
| Title | In 22 the poem is called "HEALTH, *an* ECLOGUE." |
| 3 | unfeeding near the cottage] MS; neglectful of their Pasture 22 |
| 5 | an Oaken] ⟨a neighbour⟩ MS |
| 5–6 | These lines are omitted in 22. |
| 7, 8 | Harry] MS; *Damon* 22 |
| 8 | care] MS; Cares 22 |
| 9–18 | These lines are omitted in 22. |
| 21–22 | These lines are omitted in 22. |
| 26 | repair] ⟨appear⟩ MS |
| 29 | fragrant] ⟨springing⟩ MS |
| 29–32 | These lines are omitted in 22. |
| 33 | Yet what are these, or those] MS; What are the Fields, or Flow'rs 22 |
| 34 | Joyless] MS; tastless 22 |
| 38 | a] MS; the 22. In 22, this line is followed by a version of the passage corresponding to lines 55–66 (see note to lines 55–72 below). |
| 39 | bounds] MS; mounts 22 |
| 43 | These all] MS; All these 22 |
| 44 | of pleasure all] MS; to Pleasure join'd 22 (In 22, lines 73–88 of the MS text follow line 44.) |
| 45 | the] MS; thou 22 |
| 48 | trouble] MS; Sorrow 22 |
| 52 | Ile] MS; I 22 |
| | court] ⟨bring⟩ MS |
| 53 | She'le lead] MS; When she 22 |
| 54 | And] MS; Shall 22 |

55–72    In 22, lines 55–66 follow what is line 34 of MS, with variants
as listed below; lines 67–72 are omitted in 22.

59–60    22 reads "The Brooks run purling down with silver Waves, /
The planted Lanes rejoice with dancing Leaves,".

60    lovely] {circled} MS

61    Brisk] MS; The 22

62    warbling] MS; tuneful 22
tempt] ⟨Court⟩ MS

64    Thick] ⟨Smooth⟩ MS

66    with] MS; in 22
Two canceled lines follow in the MS: "Tis wondrous sweet!
how quick my senses range / From bliss to bliss, and hardly
feel the change,".

70    charm] ⟨court⟩ MS
thee] MS has "the", an obvious slip.

73    the] MS; high 22

75    Unnerve] MS; Unnerv'd 22

77    deep'ning] MS; deep mouth'd 22

78    to] ⟨the⟩ MS

79    cumbrous] MS; tangled 22

80    the] The MS has "the" lightly canceled and "high" written
above but more heavily canceled; we have therefore retained
"the", which is the reading of 22.

82    soar to] ⟨soaring⟩ MS
strike] There is a canceled insertion in the MS, illegible but
possibly a word ending in "ass".
yᵉ] MS; their 22

83    luring] TP wrote and canceled "specious" and "tempting" in
turn before arriving at "luring".

85    changing shows of toil] MS; change of Exercise 22

86    in] MS; from 22

88    charm] ⟨court⟩ MS

89    my life with usefull talk] MS; conversing my soft Hours 22

94    pipes] MS; Flutes 22

96    Best] MS; First 22

97    Great] MS; Or 22
finest] MS; fairest 22

98    Country] MS; rural 22

99–106    These lines are omitted in 22.

107    The] MS; These 22

108    runs] MS; turns 22

109–10    Written as an interlinear insertion in the MS.

111–16    These lines are omitted in 22.

111     So] ⟨Thu⟩ MS (TP was probably writing "Thus")
116     And in] There is a canceled insertion in the MS, possibly
        "Against".
        In the MS the poem ends with the following canceled cou-
        plet: "They sting his face they buzz with humming tone / &
        break his musick while they make their own."

## *The Heroins or Cupid Punishd* (ff. 53b–56a)

Apart from the manuscript, we have two other texts of this poem, which was printed in both the 1755 and 1758 editions (on pp. 215–20 and 265–74 respectively). The MS clearly preserves the latest form of the text, for in five passages (lines 12, 27, 38, 81, and 99) the printed editions agree in readings that are canceled in the MS. The exact relationship between the 1755 and 1758 texts is less clear, but the evidence points to 1755 representing the earliest form of the text. There are only a few instances where 55 agrees with the MS against 58 (see notes to lines 4, 28, 43, 55, 123 "rinded," 124, and 155). Most of these fall into one of 58's most typical kinds of error (such as the addition or omission of a final *s*). None are clear cases of authorial revision. Some of the more numerous cases, however, where 58 agrees with the MS against 55, do seem to be likely authorial revisions: examples are "Perceive" in line 82 and "Mournfull" in line 123.

A small piece of evidence that TP was considering this poem for publication is the presence at the end of the poem in the MS of a line count (as with "An Allegory on Man" and "An Eclogue," noted above). In this case the number of lines has been counted (incorrectly) as 166. The text of "The Heroins," however, is much the roughest of the three, and the virtual absence of punctuation shows that TP had not seriously begun to prepare it for print (nor is it marked with vertical strokes to indicate its having been copied elsewhere; this confirms the MS as the latest text of the poem).

The poem is a translation of Ausonius's "Cupid Crucified" (Loeb ed., 2:209–15), a popular poem often printed with the *Pervigilium Veneris*. Ausonius took the hint for his poem from the passage in the *Aeneid* where Aeneas, in the underworld, comes upon a company of unhappy lovers that includes Dido (6.440–50). The women that Aeneas sees (besides Dido) are Phaedra, Procris, Eriphyle, Evadne, Pasiphae, Laodamia, and Caenis. All these (except Evadne) reappear in Ausonius's poem, of which TP's is a close translation. We have not thought it necessary to recount the stories of each of the unhappy lovers, but have given brief references, usually to Ovid's *Metamorphoses* or *Heroides*.

**Textual Notes**

| | |
|---|---|
| Title | In 55 and 58 the poem is called "Elysium." |
| 4 | feavour] MS, 55; Fevers 58 |
| 11 | an easy] MS; a gentle 55, 58 |
| 12 | By] ⟨&⟩ MS; And 55, 58 |
| | stealing] ⟨gliding⟩ MS, 55, 58 |
| | silent] {lazy} MS |
| 13 | Where] ⟨On whose⟩ MS |
| | of] MS; by 55, 58 |
| 19 | shines] MS; shone 55, 58 |
| 20 | inscribe] MS; inscrib'd 55, 58. Either reading is difficult; the sense must be "leaves are inscribed with". |
| 25–26 | These lines appear in the reverse order in 55 and 58. |
| 27 | She] ⟨And⟩ MS, 55, 58 |
| | burn] ⟨burns⟩ MS (a slip) |
| 28 | furys] MS, 55; fury 58 |
| 31 | garb] MS; dress 55, 58 |
| 37 | Ore well-dissembled waves] MS; O'er a feign'd Ocean's rage 55; Where Ocean feigns a rage 58 |
| 38 | forth a taper] ⟨a dim taper⟩ MS, 55, 58 |
| 40 | Damsel] MS; beauty 55, 58 |
| 43 | cliffs] MS, 55; Clifts 58 |
| 49–50 | In 55 this couplet reads: "In thin design and airy picture fleet / The tales that stain the Royal House of Crete:"; 58 agrees with 55 except for differences of punctuation and capitalization. |
| 51 | a bull the mad] MS; a lovely bull 55, 58 |
| 53 | Left] MS; Lost 55, 58 |
| 55 | desp'rate Phædra] MS, 55; Phædra desp'rate 58 |
| 59 | Here] MS; Fair 55, 58 |
| 63 | There] MS; Here 55, 58 |
| 66 | In 55 this line reads "The next, the last a stranger chanced to leave"; 58 agrees with MS. |
| 75 | ask] ⟨find⟩ MS |
| 81 | Phrantick] MS; nimble 55, 58 |
| | thickning] ⟨crowding⟩ MS, 55, 58 |
| 82 | Perceive] MS, 58; Confess 55 |
| 86 | hide] MS, 58; hid 55 |
| 88 | moves] ⟨sailes⟩ MS |
| | in] MS, 58; thro' 55 |
| 89 | Boy] MS; God 55, 58 |
| 90 | threatning] ⟨brandish⟩ MS |

| 91–96 | In 58, these lines are transferred to the end of the poem, possibly as a result of being (in the MS behind 58) omitted and added at the end, without being clearly marked for insertion in their proper place. |
|---|---|
| 92 | On] ⟨With⟩ MS |
| 98 | darkling] MS; mournful 55, 58 |
| 99 | Gods] MS, 58; God 55 |
| | To this] ⟨Twas here⟩ MS, 55, 58 |
| 119 | their] MS; the 55, 58 |
| 123 | Mournfull] MS, 58; groaning 55 |
| | rinded] MS, 55; rended 58 |
| 124 | yᵉ] MS, 55; a 58 |
| 128 | began] MS; begin 55, 58 |
| 129 | when their] MS; in the 55; in their 58 |
| 133 | Mother] MS; parent 55, 58 |
| 135 | swift she] MS; swiftly 55, 58 |
| 136 | her] ⟨his⟩ MS (a slip?) |
| 146 | frequent] ⟨fatal⟩ MS |
| 150 | tinging] MS, 58; tinged 55 |
| | lustre] ⟨beauty⟩ MS |
| 155 | deaths] MS, 55; death 58 |
| 158 | calmd] MS; calm 55, 58 |

### Explanatory Notes

| 2 | sett by Maro] In *Aeneid* 6.440–51, where the despairing lovers wander in a grove of myrtle (sacred to Venus). |
|---|---|
| 15 | Narcissus] See *Metamorphoses* 3.346–510. |
| 17 | Hyacynth] See *Metamorphoses* 10.162–219. |
| 18 | Adonis] See *Metamorphoses* 10.503–739. |
| 19 | Crocus] See *Metamorphoses* 4.283. |
| 20 | Ajax] See *Metamorphoses* 10.207–8, 13.394–98. The flower is the hyacinth, thought to be marked with the Greek letters AI in commemoration both of Hyacinth's cry of woe (α'ιαῖ) and of Ajax's name (A'ίας). |
| 25 | Semele] See *Metamorphoses* 3.259–309. |
| 29 | Cænis] See *Metamorphoses* 12.189–209, 459–535. |
| 33 | Procris] See *Metamorphoses* 7.694–862. |
| 37 | Sestian fair] Hero; see *Heroides* 18–19. |
| 41 | Leucate] Leucas or Leucate was a promontory on the island of Leucas, from which despairing lovers used to throw themselves. |

42        Sappho] See *Heroides* 15.
45        Eryphile] Eriphyle; see *Metamorphoses* 9.407–9.
49        royal house of Crete] Minos, the legendary king of Crete, was
          the husband of Pasiphae and the father of Ariadne and
          Phaedra, the next three women.
51        Pasiphae] See *Metamorphoses* 8.132–37.
53        Ariadne] See *Metamorphoses* 8.169–82; *Heroides* 10. She was
          translated to a constellation, hence the "starry crown."
55        Phædra] See *Metamorphoses* 15.497–546; *Heroides* 4. She
          hanged herself, hence the "halter."
59        Laodamia] See *Heroides* 13.
63        Thisbe] See *Metamorphoses* 4.55–166.
          Canace] See *Heroides* 11.
          Dido] See *Metamorphoses* 14.75–81; *Heroides* 7; *Aeneid* 4.
65–66     Thisbe killed herself with a sword "a Lover ownd"; Canace
          with a sword "A Father gave"; Dido with one left by "a stran-
          ger" (the swords belonged to Pyramus, Aeolus, and Aeneas).
67        the Goddess] Diana.
69        Latmos] The mountain on which Endymion, beloved of Di-
          ana, tended his sheep.
123       Myrrha] See *Metamorphoses* 10.312–502.
140       Eryx] The son of Venus and Butes.
141       Priapus] The son of Venus and Bacchus (in some versions,
          Mercury).
          monster wight] Hermaphroditus, son of Venus and Mercury;
          see *Metamorphoses* 4.285–388.
164       port of Iv'ry] One of the twin gates of sleep in *Aeneid* 6.895;
          false dreams come through the gate of ivory.

# "Ye Wives who Scold" (ff. 57a–58b)

This poem is a humorous ballad probably written in connection either
with TP's assistance to Pope on his translation of Homer, or with TP's
own translation of "The Battle of the Frogs and Mice." A possible clue to
the date and context is provided by a joint letter of Pope and TP to
Charles Ford, sent from Binfield on 19 May 1714 (*Pope Corr.* 1:223–24).
Written in a burlesque style that evidently reflects the two poets' reading
of Homer, part of TP's share is as follows: "Darkness has now spread its
veil over the variety of this terrestriall creation for which rejoyce ye
quarrelling Oyster wenches whom it parts & ye fondling Lovers who are
to meet in it" (p. 224). The reductive view of Homer humorously treated
in the poem had (in 1714) most recently been expressed by Richard

Bentley in his *Remarks upon a Late Discourse of Free-Thinking* (1713); Bentley's remarks have already been quoted above in the head-note to *Homer's Battle*. Thus it is possible that this ballad can be linked to the inception of TP's "Zoilus" project.

The text of this poem, the last in the notebook, is written in a large, sprawling hand, quite unlike TP's own or that of the transcriber of the early poems in the notebook. It is evidently a fair copy; why TP himself did not transcribe it is unclear. The poem's genuineness is attested by two manuscripts among the Congleton papers that contain holograph drafts of the poem with numerous corrections.

The earliest text (which we have called "A") of the poem is found on a single sheet, folded to make four pages (folded size 162 × 105 mm); the poem is written on f. 1a–b. F. 2a is blank, but on f. 2b (upside-down from the point of view of the main text) there is a revised version ("AA") of the first stanza. As finally worded, the "AA" text is almost identical with "B"; but there are two revisions made before this final text is achieved. Line 3 is canceled in favor of "& you who things in printing tell", itself subsequently canceled; and in line 4, "Then if you can" is canceled in favor of "I beg a while".

The "B" text itself is found on a separate sheet, similarly folded (folded size 161 × 105 mm; a piece about 65 × 35 mm has been torn from f. 2, but with no loss of text). It seems to have been copied by TP from the "A" text; in its present state it is rubbed and dirty and not always legible. The unknown transcriber apparently copied the poem into the "Satires" Notebook from the "B" manuscript, making a number of errors in the process.

We have decided not to print from the transcript in the "Satires" Notebook, but to substitute the text of the "B" manuscript, supplemented where that is illegible from "A." In the "B" manuscript, there are no corrections until the last two lines. TP originally wrote, "Might in his fancy form y^e big", then changed "y^e" to "a", before deleting the line and writing instead, "Might in his [space left] Odysses". He then crossed out "Odysses", completing the line "fancy form a floud". In the last line, he wrote, "To rage in his", canceling "in his" first in favor of "[?] then in all th", before deleting this in turn in favor of the final reading, "in all th'".

In addition, the text of the "A" MS is printed below, since together with the "B" text it preserves interesting evidence of TP at work on a poem. To make the evolution clearer, we have printed the "A" version as originally written (that is, with the deleted rather than the final readings), recording the deletions and reworkings in the textual notes. As a further aid to clarity, a few corrections evidently made *currente calamo* have been placed in the text itself within angle brackets. In the textual notes, readings are recorded in sequence. Thus in line 2, TP wrote and

canceled "&"; then wrote "the"; and finally (but without canceling "the")
"your".

Ye ⟨Who⟩ wives that either scold or sing
    Who sell y<sup>e</sup> fish & fruit
I want to tell a wondrous thing
    & beg you to be mute
Perhaps from you his birth he drew        5
    Who wrote my ballad first
For he his parents never knew
    Nor livd where he was nurst
This Jovial fiddler usd to ply
    Where ere he heard of chear        10
His dog it seems preservd an eye
    The Master livd by ear
His verse in length exceeded all
    & when a croud he drew
He daily mounted on a stall        15
    & spoke as long as you
Some tatterd Mermaid gave him birth
    Who crys her oyster wares
Or else a ragged nymph of earth
    Who sings to Mellow pears        20
If twas y<sup>e</sup> Nymph of fruit was prest
    Apollo was y<sup>e</sup> Lover
With Many tunes he fird her breast
    & Gott a singing Rover
A Man who blind yet usd to ply        25
    Where ere he heard of Chear
His dog it seems preservd an eye
    Its Master livd by ear
Or If Apollo chancd to love
    The Maremaid near y<sup>e</sup> Sea        30
Whose shriller voice he taught to Move
    With buy My Oysters pray
Her shriller voice when raisd to Ire
    Woud thunder on y<sup>e</sup> crew
So from y<sup>e</sup> Mother & Sire        35
    ⟨The⟩ Old Homers Iliad grew
& then When big with Child she stood
    The place she sold her ⟨?⟩ fishes
Might in his fancy form ⟨y<sup>e</sup>⟩ a flood
    To trouble poor Odysses.        40

## Textual Notes

| | |
|---|---|
| 1 | ⟨that either⟩ who |
| | ⟨or sing⟩ & fishes sell |
| 2 | ⟨Who⟩ Or sing |
| | ⟨yᵉ fish⟩ |
| | ⟨&⟩ {the} your |
| 3 | ⟨to tell⟩ (written again above "thing" at the end of the line) |
| 4 | ⟨& beg⟩ then if |
| | ⟨to⟩ can |
| 5 | The line (except for "from you") is canceled, and written above as "from one of you ⟨the fidler one⟩ blind Homer came". |
| 6 | ⟨my⟩ a |
| 7 | ⟨his⟩ knew neither |
| | ⟨never knew⟩ name |
| 9–12 | These lines are canceled, but reappear (with minor changes) below as lines 25–28. |
| 9 | ⟨Jovial fiddler⟩ man was blind yet |
| 14 | Above "a" TP has written and canceled "his". |
| 15 | ⟨mounted on⟩ got him to |
| 19 | ⟨a⟩ some |
| 23 | ⟨Many tunes⟩ tunefull cry |
| 24 | The *R* of "Rover" has been changed to make an *L* for "Lover"; this reading is unclear, and it may be that an original *L* has been changed to an *R*. |
| 40 | Above "trouble" TP has inserted and then canceled "Where". |

# Poems from the "Lyrics" Notebook

The "Lyrics" Notebook is signature-sewn and bound in vellum with fold-over flaps (these were once fastened with a strap that has since been lost); at either end of the notebook there is a pocket, and the endpapers are marbled. Originally it probably contained three twelve-leaf gatherings, making seventy-two pages in all; but many pages have been removed. F. la is blank; f. lb has the signature "Tho: Parnell"; probably four leaves have been removed at this point. Three leaves of text follow; since the first leaf begins with what is obviously the ending of a poem, and since some stubs show traces of text, it is evident that some text has been lost. Four further leaves appear to be missing from the first gathering. Probably seven leaves have been removed from the middle gathering, with some stubs again showing traces of lost text, leaving five (of which two are blank). Eleven leaves, all blank, remain of the third gathering; the last leaf has been removed. Thus the notebook contains only six leaves of text. We have called it the "Lyrics" Notebook because of the typically lyric forms of its poems. There is no evidence for the notebook's date, but we have placed it after the "Satires" Notebook since its contents seem clearly later than the earliest poems in that volume.

## Fragment ("To the kind powr") (f. la)

This is evidently the ending of an otherwise lost poem; there are no corrections to the text.

## "Now kind now coy" (f. la)

There are no corrections to the text of this poem.

# "Phillis, I long y^r powr" (f. lb)

There are no corrections to the text of this poem.

## *The Hint f^m French* (f. lb)

There are no corrections to the text. In line 4, the MS has "hī", the contraction being used for lack of space; we have expanded it to "him".

## *On* ——— *Embroydring* (ff. 2a–b)

There are no corrections to the text of this poem. In lines 5–11, TP may have had in mind the story of the contest between Arachne and Minerva in Ovid *Metamorphoses* 6.5–145.

## "Thirsis" (f. 2b)

This is an early version of the first stanza of the "Song" ("Thyrsis") first published in Pope's edition. The stanza is marked with the vertical stroke that TP used to indicate that a poem had been copied elsewhere.

### Textual Note

3      the charms of each prepare] ⟨Each of their charms prepard⟩ MS

# Fragment ("Then do not Cloe") (f. 3a)

Some leaves have been removed from the notebook at this point, since this is obviously the fragmentary ending of an otherwise lost poem.

### Textual Notes

2      what] ⟨of the⟩ MS
7      your slaves] This replaces an almost illegible deletion, which probably read "other men el", the last word perhaps to have been "else"; "men el" is doubtful.

## *Prop:2, L:11 E: Quicunque &c* (ff. 3a–b)

This poem is a translation of Propertius 2.12 in the numbering of the Loeb edition.

### Textual Notes

| | |
|---|---|
| Title | In the MS "11" is written above an illegible deletion (possibly "9"). There is also a canceled subtitle: "or a picture of Cupid". |
| 5 | pow'r] ⟨power⟩ MS |
| 22 | man] ⟨thing⟩ MS |

## "I looked & in a moment run" (f. 3b)

There are no corrections to the text of this poem.

## "O Tell if any fate" (f. 4a)

### Textual Notes

| | |
|---|---|
| 1 | There is an illegible deletion after "Tell". |
| 2 | Can] {does} MS |
| 6 | sighs & service gain] ⟨sighs either bring relief⟩ MS |
| 8 | pain] ⟨grief⟩ MS |

## "Young Philomela's powrfull dart" (f. 4a–b)

### Textual Note

| | |
|---|---|
| 2 | gentle] ⟨rivall⟩ MS |

## "Since bearing of a Gentle mind" (ff. 4b–5a)

There are no corrections to the text of this poem.

# "When my Nancy" (ff. 5a–b)

This is an early version of the "Song" ("When thy beauty"), first published in Pope's edition.

### Textual Notes

| | |
|---|---|
| 5 | This line is canceled in the MS, but we have let it stand since it is required by the form and appears (only slightly altered) in the poem as printed in 22. |
| 8 | rise in] ⟨run on⟩ MS |
| 14 | Now] ⟨Still⟩ MS |
| 18 | This line is underlined in the MS, probably to indicate TP's intention to revise it. |

# "Hark the thundring Drums" (f. 5b)

Lines 9–16 are written in a slightly different hand, probably indicating a break in transcription; there are no corrections.

# "As Celia with her Sparrow playd" (ff. 6a-b)

### Textual Notes

| | |
|---|---|
| 11 | Pretty] ⟨little⟩ MS |
| 16–30 | This page (f. 6b) is probably not written in TP's hand. |

# Scriblerian Epigrams

These twelve epigrams are contained on a single folded sheet (folded size 156 × 101 mm); the manuscript is autograph and is headed "Epigrams." Six of the epigrams are Scriblerian in subject matter: five refer to one or more of the Scriblerians themselves, and three refer to their known enemies. Three further epigrams are translations of epitaphs on Renaissance humanists (Platina, Faber, and Erasmus). These too reflect Scriblerian interests. The presence of the remaining three epigrams on the same sheet suggests that they, too, may have had some Scriblerian connection that is not now apparent. All the topical allusions place the epigrams in 1713–14. Apart from a brief visit to Ireland about September-October 1713, TP is known to have been in London for the whole of 1713 and until October 1714. The period of maximum Scriblerian activity was between February and May 1714; for a full account of Scriblerian interests, plans, and activities, see the *Memoirs of Scriblerus,* ed. Charles Kerby-Miller (New Haven: Yale University Press, 1950).

The manuscript is evidently (with the exception of the unfinished epitaph on Faber) a fair copy, but with a few corrections. The last three epigrams are written in a smaller and more restrained hand; they may have been added later than the others, or TP may simply have been anxious to get them all on the same sheet. The epigrams were first published, with commentary, by the present editors as "Scriblerian Epigrams by Thomas Parnell," *Review of English Studies* 33 (1982): 148–57.

Because of the unusual interest of these poems, we have provided a full commentary on them; since they are so short, it has seemed best to present this in the form of a single long note on each poem, instead of dividing the material between headnote, textual notes, and explanatory notes.

## "Our Carys a Delicate Poet"

"Cary" here is not Henry Carey (d. 1743, author of "Sally in our Alley" and burlesque plays, and whose *Poems on Several Occasions* appeared in

1713) but Walter Cary (1686–1757), in 1713 known as an Oxford wit, and later (1722–57) an MP and minor office-holder. The fullest account of Walter Cary is James M. Osborn, "Addison's Tavern Companion and Pope's 'Umbra'", *Philological Quarterly* 42 (1963): 217–25. Pope told Spence that Cary was one of Addison's "chief companions before he married," and that Cary "had scarce anything either in the *Spectators* or *Guardians*—perhaps a little song or a copy or two of verses. Steele, whom he always flattered greatly, mentioned him [as a contributor, in *Spectator* No. 555] purely to do him a service. . . . It had its effect and got him all the reputation he ever had" (Spence's *Anecdotes*, ed. Osborn, 1 : 78, 212; Nos. 183, 497). Cary is one of nine Oxford poets listed in an epigram recorded by Thomas Hearne in his diary on 6 April 1713: "The following verses written in the Boghouse of Mother Gordon's at Heddington. 'Alma novem claros peperit Rhedi[ci]na Poetas, / Trap, Young, Bub, Stubb, Crab, Fog, Cary Tickel, Evans.' All bad Poets" (*Remarks and Collections*, ed. D. W. Rannie [Oxford, 1898], 4 : 151). A later and more favorable account of Cary is found in *Characters of the Times* (1728), an anonymous pamphlet that defends and praises various Whig wits and others attacked or ridiculed in the Pope-Swift *Miscellanies*. Cary gets the longest entry in this pamphlet (over three pages), but the best the author can say of him is that he is "the Author of several very agreeable Copies of Verses in *Tonson's* Miscellanies" (p. 36). It is further suggested, however, that Cary has been too busy with weighty affairs of State to cultivate poetry; if he had been able to spare the time, he would undoubtedly have excelled Pope (pp. 38–39). These references show that Cary had contrived to acquire the reputation of being a poet without actually publishing much. His association with Addison would, in 1713–14, have made him obnoxious to Pope and therefore to TP. Pope ridiculed Cary as a small poet in "The Three Gentle Shepherds" (written about 1713; TE 6 : 112) and as a fop in "To Eustace Budgell" (written 1714; TE 6 : 123).

TP's epigram was probably suggested by Martial 2.88: "Nil recitas et vis, Mamerce, poeta videri / quidquid vis esto, dummodo nil recitas." Pope wrote a version of the same epigram: "They say A——'s a Wit, for what? / For writing? no,—for writing not." Pope's version was written in 1717 or earlier (TE 6 : 186), and is so close to TP's as to suggest that he was influenced by it as well as by Martial. (The connection between Pope's epigram and Martial's was pointed out by John Fuller in *Notes and Queries* 15 [1968]: 206–7.)

## On Mr. Pope Drawing Dr. Swift's Picture

This epigram can be dated in 1713, when Pope was studying painting under Charles Jervas; and most probably between May and September of that year. On 30 April Pope wrote to his friend John Caryll that he had been "almost every day employed in following your advice in learning to paint" (*Pope Corr.* 1 : 174). On 23 August he told Gay that he had "thrown away three Dr. *Swift*'s, each of which was once my Vanity" (*Pope Corr.* 1 : 187). On 31 August he made a similar remark in a letter to Caryll, adding that "my masterpieces have been one of Dr. Swift, and one Mr. Betterton" (*Pope Corr.* 1 : 189). By October, however, Pope had turned his energies to his proposed translation of the *Iliad*. His learning to paint is also the subject of another epigram in this series, "Once Pope under Je[r]vais." There is a general account of Pope as a painter in Ault, *New Light on Pope*, pp. 68–81.

## After the French Manner

This epigram must be later than October 1713, when Pope began to circulate his proposals for printing by subscription his translation of the *Iliad;* and some time earlier than 15 April 1714, when Tonson published Gay's *Shepherd's Week*. Lack of punctuation makes the syntax hard to construe; we take line 4 to mean "Philips has paid Tonson a fee to buy himself a reprieve". Gay's *Shepherd's Week* was in part a parody of Philips's pastoral manner. The epigram suggests that Philips has bribed Tonson to delay the publication of Gay's poem, and has thus bought himself a reprieve from looking ridiculous (as he will when the poem appears). Philips, however, was unemployed and impecunious at the time; where could he have found the money to bribe Tonson? TP seems here to be alluding to the accusation that Philips kept in his own hands the money paid to him (as secretary to the Hanover Club) by club members for subscriptions to Pope's *Iliad*. Pope makes this charge against Philips in a letter to John Caryll of 8 June 1714, adding that "it is to this management of *Philips,* that the world owes Mr. *Gay's Pastorals*" (*Pope Corr.* 1 : 229).

What TP thought of here as "the French Manner" was probably the style of epigram written by Boileau, Voiture, and such lesser writers as the abbé de Chaulieu, whose "Sur la Première Attaque de Goutte" (1695) is the original of TP's "An Imitation of Some French Verses," published in Pope's edition of his poems.

## An Impromptu like Martial

If a specific date for this epigram is needed, the most plausible is June 1714, before Gay left London as secretary to the earl of Clarendon on his mission to Hanover. Gay told Swift of his appointment in a letter of 8 June, and we know that he had great difficulty getting from the treasury the money he needed (for his trip to Hanover, see W. H. Irving, *John Gay* [Durham, N.C.: Duke University Press, 1940], 102–5). TP might well have been tempted to poke fun at the bustling self-importance of the idle poet turned busy diplomat. There was some question of TP joining this embassy to the future George I in the capacity of chaplain; but he did not go (*Swift Corr.* 2:35).

In the manuscript, this epigram has been crossed out with a large cross.

## On a Certain Poets Judgement

"Midas" in this poem is probably Thomas Tickell, who in a series of essays in the *Guardian* (Nos. 22, 23, 28, 30, 32; published between 6 and 17 April 1713) had lavishly praised the pastorals of Philips and barely mentioned those of Pope. Tickell was a close associate of Addison and (like Walter Cary, with whom he is linked in the epigram quoted above in the note on "Our Cary's a Delicate Poet") a minor Oxford wit. Apollo's revenge in TP's epigram refers to the *Guardian* paper that Pope himself wrote (No. 40, 27 April 1713), in which he compared his own pastorals with those of Philips, ironically giving Philips the preference. TP's epigram was probably written not long after Pope had thus made both Tickell and Philips look foolish, and about the time that Pope began work on his translation of the *Iliad*.

The story of the judgment of Midas is from Ovid *Metamorphoses* 11.146–93.

## To Mistress ———

The poet Sappho is complimented as a tenth Muse in several epigrams in the *Greek Anthology* (Loeb ed., 3:Nos. 66, 189, 506; 5:No. 310), and the same idea would naturally suggest itself for application to a contemporary woman writer. There is no evidence as to whom TP had in mind, but in the Scriblerian context it is tempting to propose Lady Winchelsea, to whom both Pope and Swift addressed complimentary poems. Pope was on friendly terms with her in 1713–14. In a letter to Caryll of 15 December 1713, he speaks of having recently dined with her. In 1714 he wrote his "Impromptu, To Lady Winchelsea," a reply to her defense of women poets against his ridicule in the "Cave of Spleen" episode in the expanded *Rape of the Lock* (TE 6:120). Lady Winchelsea was Mrs. Finch until, in August 1712, her husband succeeded to the earldom; but her friends might continue to think of her as "Mrs. Finch." A poem described as "by the Honourable Mrs. Finch" was published in *Pope's Own Miscellany* (as *Poems on Several Occasions*, an anthology that he edited, is now usually known) in 1717.

In line 4, TP seems (at least on its first occurrence) to have written "wert" before writing "art" over it; he may have done so the second time the word occurs, but the reading there is illegible.

## On Platina

This epigram is the first of a group of three translations of Renaissance Latin epitaphs that TP probably read in Paolo Giovio's *Elogia Doctorum Virorum*. Giovio's best-known work is his *Historia sui Temporis* (Florence, 1550–52). A rather unattractive figure, Giovio accumulated considerable wealth through papal favor (he was appointed bishop of Nocera in 1528) and the venality of his pen. Part of his fortune he used to build a villa, on the site of the younger Pliny's on the shore of Lake Como, and to furnish it with a gallery of portraits of famous leaders and writers. This gallery achieved great renown, and Giovio compiled two books to give it a permanent literary form: *Elogia Doctorum Virorum* (Venice, 1546), and *Elogia Virorum Bellica Virtute Illustrium* (Florence, 1551). Both employ the same format: for each of the worthies included, a brief biographical sketch by Giovio (in Latin prose) is followed by one or more Latin poems in the subject's praise, collected from other authors. The idea behind these books is one that would particularly have appealed to Pope, who would later collect portraits of his eminent friends in his villa at Twickenham. Probably Pope and TP read Giovio together in 1713–14. We know that Pope had some acquaintance with the *Elogia Doctorum Virorum* by the time he wrote the *Dunciad*, for he alludes to Giovio's account of Camillo Querno ("A" version, 2.11; TE 5:97; the line became 2.15 in the "B" version). Giovio's sketch is translated at length in "Of the Poet Laureate," appended to the 1743 edition of the *Dunciad* (TE 5:412–17; this piece had originally appeared in the *Grub Street Journal* in 1730). There is a modern edition of the *Elogia* by Renzo Meregazzi, as volume 8 of Giovio's *Opera* (Rome: Istituto Poligrafico dello Stato, 1972), and an English translation, as *An Italian Portrait Gallery*, by Florence Alden Gragg (Boston: Chapman and Grimes, 1935). Both omit most of the poems.

Platina (Bartolomeo Sacchi, 1421–81), a prominent Italian humanist, is best known for his *Vitae Pontificum* (Venice, 1479). The other works of Platina to which TP alludes are his *De Honesta Voluptate* (Rome, c. 1475) and his dialogue "Contra Amores" (first printed as an appendix to the

Cologne, 1540, edition of the *Vitae Pontificum*). Platina is not known to have written any "lives of Heroes" (line 2); the phrase must be a misunderstanding of "ducum vitas" (here to be taken as "lives of popes").

We have not been able to trace the poet "Prosperus Spiriteus" outside Giovio's work (where other poems are credited to him). The poem on Platina is here reprinted from the *Elogia* (the text is based on the Antwerp, 1557, edition, p. 44, and checked against the Basle, 1571, edition, p. 48):

> Qui res Pontificum sacras, et gesta piorum,
>   Quique ducum vitas nobile fecit opus:
> Quique modum docuit, quo laudet honesta voluptas,
>   Et quo ne iuvenes torqueat acer amor:
> Pluraque, quae longum est, properans censere, Viator,
>   Omnia sidereae pignora mentis erant.
> Vivit adhuc Platina: et quanquam concesserit Orco:
>   Nil tamen in vatem Parca severa potest.

### Textual Notes

| | |
|---|---|
| 1 | force of] ⟨holy⟩ MS |
| 5 | who] ⟨and⟩ MS |
| 10 | TP seems first to have written "Will kill yᵉ Body", then "yᵉ Body falls but still yᵉ Writer lives", before arriving at the final wording. |

## *Jac[obus] Faber Stapul[ensis]*

The original of this unfinished epigram is by Julius Caesar Scaliger (1484–1558). It commemorates the French Protestant and translator of the Bible into French, Jacobus Faber Stapulensis (Jacques Lefèvre d'Étaples, c. 1455–c. 1536). The text is again reprinted from the *Elogia* (Antwerp, 1557, p. 249, checked against Basle, 1571, p. 263, which has "sui" for "fui" in line 1, and against two editions of Scaliger's poems, which agree verbally with Giovio's text):

> Invidiosa utriusque fui sapientia mundi
>   Mortalis, Stapulae quem genuere, Faber.
> Iacta alios, qui egeant laudis mea Gallia vestrae.
>   Nanque mea potius Gallia laudis eges.

The difficulty of the first couplet makes TP's failure to translate it understandable. Faber himself is speaking from the grave: "People envied me for my knowledge when I was alive, as they still envy my reputation; but far from my wanting the praises of France, it is France that needs a good word from me."

TP's couplet was first written thus: "To have a Nations praise woud glory be / But here a Nation has its praise from thee."

## Erasmus

Simon Vallambert was a doctor as well as a man of letters. He wrote medical treatises in addition to poems and a translation of Plato's *Crito*. His works were published between 1541 and 1565 (*Les Bibliothèques Françoises de la Croix du Maine et de du Verdier,* ed. Rigoley de Juvigny [Paris, 1772–73], 2:415–16, 5:476–77). His epigram on Erasmus is here reprinted from Giovio (Antwerp, 1557, p. 211, checked against Basle, 1571, p. 224):

> Hoc quanquam tumulo mortale cadaver Erasmi
>   Mors claudis, id ferme est nihil.
> Non huius virtus, spes, fama, scientia, possunt
>   Claudi. quid o Mors hic habes?

In the manuscript, this epigram is deleted with an oblique stroke. Before crossing it out, however, TP made several revisions. In line 3 he seems to have written first "above y$^e$ sky", then (perhaps to avoid the repetition of "above", used again in line 5) wrote "thro" (this reading is doubtful, but "thr" is clear) over "above", before deleting the word and writing "lofty" above the line (above the deleted "above/thro"; there is no room for it where it must have been intended, after "y$^e$", where we have placed it). In line 4, "y$^e$ wide" replaces canceled "all y$^e$".

Parnell's copy of Erasmus's *Moriae Encomium* (Leiden, 1648) is now in the Cashel Diocesan Library; see Robert S. Matteson, "Books from the Library of Thomas Parnell," *The Library* 6 (1984): 372–76. The Erasmus is No. 7, p. 374.

## "Once Pope under Jevais [i.e., Jervais]"

The subject matter of this epigram places it between April and September 1713 (for references, see the notes above on "On Mr. Pope drawing Dr. Swift's Picture"). The idea of Jervas becoming a bad poet is presumably a jest; his only known literary enterprise was a translation of *Don Quixote*, posthumously published in 1742.

In line 1, "Jevas" has been corrected by "Jevais"; in line 3, "Painter" is written over a word not now recoverable.

# Out of Greek

The original of this epigram is from the *Greek Anthology*, where it is attributed to Lucian: "All that belongs to mortals is mortal, and all things pass us by; or if not, we pass them by" (Loeb translation; 4: No. 31).

In line 2 of the epigram, "fleet" replaces canceled "pass".

# An Epitaph Desird on one Wheeler

Punning epitaphs are commonly found in jest-books of the seventeenth and eighteenth centuries. *Wits Recreations* (1640), for example, has such pieces on men called Stone, Pricke, Fish, Bell, Cofferer, and Death. Otto Aicher's large-scale collection of (mostly Latin) epitaphs of all kinds, *Theatrum Funebre* (Salzburg, 1675), has punning epitaphs on Erasmus and on one "Thesaurus." James Jones's English collection, *Sepulchrorum Inscriptiones* (Westminster, 1727), has epitaphs that play on the names of Webbe, Stone, Warner, and Kitching. Punning was a Scriblerian game of which Swift was especially fond; TP's epitaph may have been written as part of a poetic game played by the Scriblerians.

# Miscellaneous Poems

These poems are in no sense a group, but are here printed for the first time from loose manuscripts among the Congleton papers.

## "In Biddy's Cheeks"

The authenticity of this poem is established by a small fragment (a MS approximately $52 \times 99$ mm) containing the last six lines in TP's hand. The MS of the whole poem (on a single sheet about $194 \times 235$ mm), folded to make four pages (size of folded page about $194 \times 119$ mm) is nonautograph.

F. la contains the (nonautograph) text of the poem; at the foot of f. 1b (upside-down from the point of view of the text of the poem) is written, "Wrote Extempore by a Gentleman on seeing."; this may have nothing to do with the poem. F. 2 is blank; a piece approximately $45 \times 105$ mm has been torn out, which contained (on f. 2a) at least four lines, of which the last two began with "w".

There are no corrections made to the nonautograph text (which is not clearly divided into stanzas, although we have taken the poem to be so structured). The autograph fragment, as finally worded, is as follows:

> And Biddys' Lillys bleachd to grey
>    Appear in Catys hairs
> Yet all the world of Biddy boast
>    And none of Caty sings
> While she deserves the figures most
>    Who better shows the things.

In the third line, "Biddy" replaces canceled "Caty". In the sixth line, TP wrote first "most appears"; canceled this in favor of "better claimes"; finally changed "claimes" to "shows".

# "Oft have I Read"

The text of this poem is in TP's hand, written on part of a sheet that must once have measured about 286 × 207 mm, but of which nearly half has been lost. The sheet is folded to make four pages, and the poem is written on a page of about 161 × 104 mm. At the bottom of the MS, "sky falls we may Catch Larks" has been written in another hand; the significance of these words is obscure.

## Textual Notes

| | |
|---|---|
| 5 | fare] ⟨fair⟩ MS |
| 13 | those] ⟨the⟩ MS |
| 14 | swains & nymphs] ⟨Nymphs & swains⟩ MS |
| 16 | retrieve] ⟨retrieves⟩ MS |

## For Philip Ridgate Esq.

The manuscript of this poem is a single sheet (185 × 270 mm), folded to form four pages. Lines 1–25 are written on f. 1a in a column, lines 26–27 are written at a right angle to these but on the same page. The title (or perhaps address) is written on the verso. The text of the poem is autograph; but the manuscript is endorsed in another hand "Tho.ˢ Parnell / This letter was sent by Dʳ Parnell with a fflute and / one of his Books to Philip Ridgate LLD." The only correction to the text of the poem is in line 18, where "reason" replaces canceled "nature."

Philip Ridgate was a slightly younger contemporary of TP's. He entered Trinity College, Dublin, in 1695, at age fifteen (TP entered in 1692, at age fourteen), having attended the same school (Mr. Davis, Dublin) as TP's younger brother, John. Ridgate graduated B.A. in 1699 (two years later than TP), but both men took their M.A. degree at the same time in 1700. Ridgate was admitted to the degree of LL.D. in 1716 (all the foregoing information is from G. D. Burtchaell and T. U. Sadleir, *Alumni Dublinenses*, new ed., Dublin, 1935). The address "For Philip Ridgate Esq" is perhaps more likely to have been used before Ridgate obtained his LL.D. than after; but this is not conclusive evidence for a date before 1716.

**Explanatory Notes**

| | |
|---|---|
| 3 | Orpheus] See Ovid *Metamorphoses* 11.2. |
| 4 | Bory] rustic dance (*OED*, s.v. "boree"), not specifically Irish. |
| 25 | The two opening words are partly obscured by fraying at the foot of the page. |
| 27 | "'Sblood, she was bred from a whistle." For illustrations of contemporary Irishisms, at which TP is here poking fun, see Alan Bliss, *Spoken English in Ireland, 1600–1740* (Dublin: Cadenus Press, 1979). |

# "When Haizy Clouds"

This poem is one of two translations from Boethius preserved in autograph texts on the same manuscript, a single sheet (160 × 95 mm) now much frayed. The first poem on the sheet is the translation of book 1, metre 4, that is also found in the "Satires" Notebook (f. 40a), where it is printed in this edition. The second poem, printed here, is a translation of book 1, metre 7. There are several corrections (recorded in the textual notes), and the entire poem has been canceled with a large cross.

The image of the ocean frying in line 5 may seem strange, but it is found in Dryden's translation of the *Aeneid* 7.737: "White Foam at first on the curl'd Ocean fries".

**Textual Notes**

| | |
|---|---|
| 5 | frys] This is either written over a deleted word (not now legible), or else TP made a false start in writing it. |
| 6 | ⟨& thickning stopps the piercing eyes⟩ MS |
| 8 | Oft runs astray] ⟨Will often stand⟩ MS |
| 9 | the piercing sight] ⟨unclouded eyes⟩ MS |
| 10 | The original opening of the line (not now recoverable) has been overwritten with two words, of which the first is probably "still" and the second illegible. This second reading has itself been heavily canceled. |
| 11 | still woud you tread] ⟨Unerring move⟩ MS |

## *Caius Rubrius Urbanus*

The autograph text of this poem is preserved on a single sheet (154 × 100 mm). It is a translation of a Latin inscription from Janus

Gruterus, *Inscriptiones antiquae totius orbis Romani* (Heidelberg, 1602–3). TP is perhaps more likely to have read it in the edition by Graevius (Amsterdam, 1707).

The Latin original is as follows. For ease of reading, we have removed the quasifacsimile elements (such as the period after every word in the inscription) and set out the verse as such:

*Romae, in domo Lud. Matthaei.*

C. RUBRIUS URBANUS SIBI ET ANTONIAE DOMESTICAE CONIUGI SUAE ET CN. DOMITIO URBICO RUBRIANO FILIO SUO ET LIBERTIS LIBERTABUSQUE POS-TERISQUE EORUM ET M. ANTONIO DAPHNO FECIT

Hic pater recubat in lecto, ollam nummorum plenam complexus et manu, et brachio sinistris. ex ea aureos plures dextra ante se versat. adsidet ad pedes filius habitu militari, gladio accinctus, nummosque aliquot quasi decidentes excipit manu dextra. stat iuxta tripes, supraque eum aliae tres ollae. sequuntur versus:

> QUI DUM VITA FUIT SEMPER VIVEBAT AVARUS
>     HEREDI PARCENS INVIDUS IPSE SIBI
> HIC ACCUMBENTEM SCULPI GENIALITER ARTE
>     SE IUSSIT DOCTA POST SUA FATA MANU
> UT SALTEM RECUBANS IN MORTE QUIESCERE POSSET
>     SECURAQUE IACENS ILLE QUIETE FRUI
> FILIUS A DEXTRA RESIDET QUI CASTRA SECUTUS
>     OCCIDIT ANTE PATRIS FUNERA MOESTA SUI
> SED QUID DEFUNCTIS PRODEST GENIALIS IMAGO
>     HOC POTIUS RITU VIVERE DEBUERUNT

## Textual Notes

In the last sentence of the English prose preamble, "on" appears to be a correction written over something else; and it is followed by a canceled "of".

| | |
|---|---|
| 5 | here] {thus} MS |
| 9 | the] ⟨his⟩ MS |
| 10 | warr] ⟨range⟩ MS |
| 11 | fell] ⟨lyes⟩ MS (?) |

# Latin Verses on Set Themes

These verses are found on a single sheet (folded to make four pages; folded size 145 × 97 mm) preserved among the Congleton papers. They are perhaps undergraduate exercises; they certainly read like verses on set themes. TP's Latin has been transcribed exactly, with two small exceptions intended to make for easier reading: the tailed *q* is transcribed as "que," and the line over a vowel used to indicate a following *m* has been replaced by *m*. Readings in square brackets are conjectural, the edge of the paper having frayed with some loss of text. Corrections made to the verses are recorded. TP's Latin sometimes seems rather strained, not unnaturally given that these are probably academic exercises, and our translations give the general sense rather than a literal rendering.

## Ex Otio Negotium

These verses are an exhortation to the triumvir Mark Antony to leave the pleasures of his life with Cleopatra and to make serious preparations for the struggle with Caesar, before it is too late.

*Translation.* Business before pleasure. "Why, Antony, do you allow your strength to slip away in idleness? Why are you letting the soft embraces of the bed put shackles on your better judgment? The time to act is now, while you can fight from a position of equality; act now, before it is too late. Look how busy Caesar is. Success seems to follow him, so both cities and individuals are going over to his side. By your neglect, you have already lost half the world; now, if you want to achieve supreme power, you have the whole to conquer."

## "Gratia ab Officio quod Mora Tardat Abest"

These verses contrast the initial popularity among the women of Greece of the Trojan War, with their very different feelings when the war lasts longer than they expect. The title is adapted from Ovid *Ex Ponto* 3.4.52: "gratiaque officio quod mora tardat, abest" ("homage which is delayed receives no favour"; Loeb translation). TP uses the line in a rather different sense, to mean something more like "when a task takes too long, it becomes irksome".

*Translation.* "When the Greeks were sailing to Troy to revenge the abduction of Helen, and ship after ship was cutting through the rough seas, the women all prayed 'Oh! Let Troy be taken quickly, let it be taken quickly!', and they kept their altars constantly smoking with incense. But after nine years had failed to bring either the doom of Troy or the return of the Greeks to their old homes, the prayers of the women were altered: 'Send us back our men, gracious Jupiter, send us back our men, even if they have not accomplished their mission. There is no satisfaction in glory when it is bought at such expense of time. Are you now selling cities, at so many years each? Enough is enough; we will give anything to have our men back.'"

## *Labor Omnia Vincit*

The moral of TP's account of a chariot race recalls a fable of Babrius (Heracles and the Ox Driver; No. 20 in the Loeb edition) in its treatment of the lazy man who calls on the gods for assistance instead of helping himself. The title ("Work conquers all") is adapted from Virgil *Georgics* 1.145 (which has "vicit"). TP evidently consulted Virgil's description of the games in *Aeneid* 5, from which he borrowed "finibus omnes . . . prosiliunt" (5.139–40) and "ocior alis fulminis" (5.319). In line 11, TP's "Juvamen", though clearly in the MS, seems meaningless and should probably read "Juvantem," and our translation assumes the latter reading.

*Translation.* "Dawn breaks, and an Olympic race is about to begin. Already each contestant imagines himself the winner! They wait expectantly. The trumpet sounds! At once each speeds forward from the starting line. The sun is hidden by the clouds of dust they raise; the earth resounds with the horses' hooves. Swifter than winged lightning, the first passes the winning post; the second is not far behind. Everyone claps the winner, and they present him with the laurel crown of victory, which he raises to heaven in thanks to the gods. But the third chariot has stuck fast in the ground! The driver calls on the gods, instead of helping himself. He calls on Hercules to help him, but in vain. He goes on calling, but the god ignores the prayers of the lazy."

## "In Vitium Ducit Culpæ Fuga si Caret Arte"

The point of these verses is to chide both Stoics and Epicureans for their extremism. The title is from Horace *Ars Poetica* line 31, but applied to morality rather than writing. In line 1, "Zenonis" is written over canceled "stoicorū".

*Translation.* Unless we are careful, the attempt to avoid doing the wrong thing may itself lead to wrongdoing. "While the followers of Zeno (the Stoics) treat their bodies roughly, and deny that they are troubled by passions and desires, softer Epicurus laughs at them from his gardens: 'What numbers are misled by that mad passion! My friends, come to my party garlanded with roses, and bid Thais hurry herself; the best may well be the one who shows himself furthest from that crowd (the Stoics).' But Epicurus, is not your triumph over the Stoics rather rash? We have to accept both the pains and the pleasures of life."

## "—Natura Beatis / Omnibus esse dedit"

The theme of these verses anticipates TP's later interest in the problem of providential order. The epigraph is from Claudian *In Rufinum* 1.215–16: "Nature has given everyone the chance of being happy, if they only knew how to use it."

*Translation.* " 'Come, Lord Apollo, speak: tell me why Nature plays the stepdame as she does, why she showers one man with wealth, titles, and honors, but unfairly condemns another to ill fortune?' Such was once the complaint of a miserable wretch at the entrance to a temple. In reply, a divine voice shook the air, speaking as follows: 'You are a fool, to condemn Nature with your ungrateful grumblings! Nature is good to everyone, though in different ways. Those whom fortune raises, fortune may equally make miserable; those who do not receive gifts from fortune, are also exempt from her blows' ".

## "Mors Sola Fatetur Quantula"

In these verses, Narcissus, still looking at his own image in the river Styx, laments his lost beauty (for the story of Narcissus, see Ovid *Metamorphoses* 3.339–510). The epigraph is from Juvenal *Satires* 10.172–73: "Only death reveals the insignificance of the little bodies of men." The lack of punctuation makes these verses difficult to construe, and some of TP's Latin seems rather forced. Line 7 reads "Hos ne", but we have corrected it to "Hosne" as the meaning requires.

*Translation.* "When Narcissus, fascinated by his own image seen reflected in the clear waters of a stream, wasted away and died, the mad youth is said to have continued to gaze at himself in the river Styx. But when he realized how his appearance had changed, he is said at first to have thus bewailed his death: 'To think of the face, which (fool that I was) I died looking at! To think that death has taken away its beauty! I had thought that my good looks would be left me in the Elysian fields. "Such a face brings to mind Venus!" So the nymphs told me, and my reflection in the pool told the same story. But this river tells a different tale; this river favors everyone alike.'"

## *In Cameram ubi Anatomia Perag[it]*

TP's starting point in these verses is the myth that Prometheus made man out of clay (Pausanias 10.4; alluded to in Horace *Odes* 1.16.13). Trinity College, Dublin, did not have its own anatomy school until 1711; probably TP saw the demonstration (if the poem describes a real experience) at the College of Physicians. In line 9, "sanguinis" replaces canceled "Corporis"; and in line 10, "refert" replaces an illegible deletion, possibly "ducit".

*Translation.* "It is said that it was Prometheus who put man together, and who kindled his mind with fire from heaven. Nor was it long before sharp and powerful sorrows began to torment men in a thousand different ways! In this room we are studying the disjointed limbs of a body; just suppose it were possible to rediscover the secret of that heavenly fire! Before such divine knowledge and skill, death would retreat and life and vigor return! Blood would once again flow through the lifeless corpse, and sense return to the organs that had expired! Even as it is, this mutilated corpse teaches us, as though it could speak itself, the nature of our constitution and how its ills may be cured. Wonderful! What has mortality to fear, what will not be possible, when even death itself thus shows us the road to life."

# Fragments

The first three of these fragments are from a prose essay or meditation; the last three are apparently unfinished poems. It is possible that more complete manuscripts of the unfinished poems once existed, but they are not now among the Congleton papers, and the chance of their surviving elsewhere seems remote.

## Three Verse Passages from a Prose Meditation

These passages are found in a prose meditation written on a single leaf, folded to make four pages (folded size 164 × 105 mm). Holes for stitching are present, and the manuscript may once have formed part of a notebook; the text as we have it may therefore be incomplete.

(1) The meditation begins with a vision of God manifesting itself in a storm; the first verse passage is then introduced as follows: "Letts to yᵉ field quitt yᵉ town for all here is sweet all flourish[es] a pure air & warm wind makes every thing fruitfull half fresh half warm."

(2) The idyll continues, but then a storm arises and the second verse passage is introduced as follows: "hear how yᵉ rain falls how the thunder rolls & the birds scream see how the vessels are beaten at sea while the seamen are confounded while yᵉ waves look darkly blew in hollows & froath atop."

(3) Descriptions of morning, day, night, and a stream follow; the third verse passage is an allegorical application of the idea of the stream to the human mind. The last two words of the passage are conjectural, the MS being frayed.

## "The First who lovd me"

This poem, untitled and evidently incomplete, is found in TP's hand on a single sheet, now rather frayed (about 161 × 104 mm). There are a number of revisions, and in a few places the manuscript is blotted.

## Textual Notes

5       then] ⟨&⟩ MS

7       The grant obtaind] ⟨Now yᵉ boats took⟩ MS

8       loosd] ⟨broke⟩ MS

10     A new] These words are written over an illegible original reading, which may have been "To ne[w]".

15     But] ⟨Then⟩ MS

19     In my] ⟨I made⟩ MS

21     sits & heares] ⟨sat & heard⟩ MS (the final reading may be "hears" rather than "heares")

23     The color of the ink changes at this point, possibly indicating a break in transcription.

28     in] ⟨wᵗʰ⟩ MS

30     first softly warbling] ⟨Warbling at first⟩ MS

34     Two canceled lines follow in the MS: "A thousand Nymphs & of yᵉ Noblest blood / With snowy bosomes ore the wa". The last word would presumably have been "waves".

# Two Fragments

These two fragments are found on the same manuscript, a single sheet folded to make four pages (folded size 162 × 103mm). "When ore my temples" is on f. 1a; "When Popry's arbitrary yoak" is on f. 2b (and upside-down from the point of view of the other poem; the designation of front and back here is obviously arbitrary).

## Textual Notes *("When ore my temples")*

4       plumes] TP seems to have tried "wings" and also to have written and canceled "plumes" before settling finally on "plumes". In the process of revising he inadvertently left an extra "on" uncanceled, which we have removed from the text. sable] ⟨dusky⟩ MS (At one point, the line was to have read "the dusky"; TP must have intended to omit "down", but it was never canceled.)

5       ⟨Now with officious Zeal [?]⟩ MS

6       The line seems first to have read, "& purple pinnions to my shoulders ty", then to have been revised to read, "& in my fancy clear an azure Sky", before TP arrived at the final version.

7       TP perhaps first wrote "Gray running mist forsakes a neigh-

bring plain". Above "Gray running" he wrote and canceled "The scudding" (or perhaps "The sounding"). He then began a new line with "Then draws" but canceled this and wrote the final version of line 7 in the text.

8     There is a canceled word (perhaps "wan" or "was") between "the" and "beautys".

10     Four canceled lines follow in the MS:

> Where Poizd & aloft I sail in chearfull air
> & Joy to view my new-born earth so fair
> while silver waters to the bottom seen
> lave the soft Margin of the circled green

In the third canceled line, TP began "Where azure", then changed "azure" to "limped" before rewriting "while silver". In the fourth line, TP tried "a" and "its" before arriving at "the circled green".

11     glittring] {chearfull} MS
12     earth] ⟨world⟩ MS

### Textual Notes *("When Pop'rys arbitrary yoak")*

5     Joy] ⟨Pride⟩ MS
6     great] ⟨fair⟩ MS
8     Ore] This word (which might possibly be "One" or "Her" or "Are") is followed by a blank line.

# Appendix 1
# Doubtful and Lost Poems

All the poems printed in this edition as TP's can be regarded as being reasonably certainly his. There must remain a degree of doubt attached to the poems published in *Pancharis,* since Curll is our only authority for TP's authorship; and it is always possible that new evidence may be found that will lead to the removal of a poem from the canon. Besides the poems we have printed, there are a number of poems connected with TP in some way but which we have not printed as his. Information about these is gathered in this appendix, at the end of which we have printed an annotated text of an inventory of TP's writings preserved among the Congleton papers.

(1) Poems of which TP may have been part author. TP can be regarded as joint author of the Scriblerian invitations, sent jointly by the members of the Scriblerus Club in 1714 to invite the earl of Oxford to join them. These invitations are printed in TE 6 : 115–19, and with much fuller annotation in Charles Kerby-Miller's edition of the *Memoirs of Scriblerus,* pp. 351–59. The only part of any of these verses that can reasonably be attributed to TP himself is a couplet written in his hand as part of an invitation in which the authors signed their individual couplets. The sentiment too is TP's: "For Frolick Mirth give ore affairs of State, / To night be happy, be to morrow great" (quoted from Kerby-Miller's ed., p. 353).

In July 1714 Pope and TP went from Binfield to visit Swift, then living in quiet seclusion in the village of Letcombe Basset. According to the account that Pope later sent to Arbuthnot (in a letter of 11 July 1714), he and TP composed the following verses as they rode to visit Swift:

> How foolish Men on Expeditions goe!
> Unweeting Wantons of their wetting Woe!
> For drizling Damps descend adown the Plain
> And seem a thicker Dew, or thinner Rain;
> Yet Dew or Rain may wett us to the shif[t]
> We'll not be slow to visit Dr Swift.

For Pope's letter, see *Pope Corr.* 1:233–35; the verses are quoted from p. 235.

(2) A Poem which has been attributed to TP. The "Ode, for Musick, on the Longitude," printed anonymously in 1727 in the "Last Volume" of the Pope-Swift *Miscellanies* (pp. 172–73), is attributed to TP in a letter of 23 December 1714 from Sir Richard Cox to Edward Southwell (see C. J. Rawson, "Parnell on Whiston," *Papers of the Bibliographical Society of America* 57 [1963]: 91–92). The attribution is close in time to the probable date of the poem (1714), but the "Ode" is so unlike anything else by TP that we have not felt able, on the strength of that letter alone, to admit the poem to the canon.

(3) Poems found among the Congleton papers, but which we do not regard as TP's. There are seven of these:

(*a*) An untitled, thirty-six-line poem beginning, "As in my chair, in dolefull dumps I satt". The poem is evidently incomplete, and is probably the beginning of a longish satire. It is not in TP's hand, nor at all in his style, and nothing about the poem suggests his authorship.

(*b*) "A New Ballad to y^e tune of Fair Rosamond," a poem of eighty-eight lines beginning, "Now Ponder well you Ladies fair". It is not in TP's hand, and there is nothing to suggest his authorship.

(*c*) "For The Hon^ble M^r Justice Parnel," a twelve-line verse invitation beginning, "Wee know you are in nightgown cl[ad]". It is not in TP's hand, and the recipient (presumably TP's younger brother, John) did not become a judge until after TP's death.

(*d*) An untitled poem of twenty lines in ballad meter, beginning, "Strange Havock did the poyson make". It is not in TP's hand, and there is no evidence to connect it with him.

(*e*) An untitled poem of twelve lines beginning, "Wouldst thou O Marlborô make thy tryumphs shine", and advising the duke to be more open-handed. The Congleton manuscript was evidently part of a larger sheet, from which it has become detached at a fold, and contains only lines 1–9 of the poem. The whole poem, however, is found in British Library Lansdowne MS 852 (f. 22b). The poem refers in line 7 to "thy Brother Treasurer", which must date the poem before Godolphin's dismissal in August 1710. The subject of the poem seems improbable for TP at any date; there is further negative evidence in that Lansdowne MS 852 contains a transcript of TP's "Anacreontic" ("Gay Bacchus"), which is attributed to TP by name.

(*f*) "Advice to a Painter," a poem of 144 lines beginning, "What hand? what Skill? can form the Artfull Peice". This poem was printed in 1697, and its politics are wrong for TP at that date, not to mention the poem being far too accomplished for him, when it is compared with the poems of about that date preserved in the "Schoedinger" Notebook. The poem is reprinted in *Poems on Affairs of State* 6 : 12–25. As with poem *(e)* above, there is a transcript in BL Lansdowne MS 852 (ff. 11–12).

*(g)* An untitled Latin poem of twenty-six lines beginning, "Hic etiam, Princeps, studio spectacula cernis", together with an additional passage of six lines beginning, "Clamores inter Laetos & publica Vota", evidently an alternative opening. It seems to be a speech of welcome addressed to a dignitary visiting a college. It is not in TP's hand, and there is no evidence to connect it with him.

In a similar category to the above is the poem "The 6 1ˢᵗ verses of yᵉ 69 psalme," a poem of twenty lines found in the "Schoedinger" Notebook, but not in the part containing TP's poems and not in his hand. Schoedinger thought it might be by TP's father.

It would be natural in a family with a poet of some importance in its past for poetic manuscripts to be associated with that poet, which would easily account for the above manuscripts finding a place with genuine TP poems. But we have felt that, in the cases of poems not in TP's hand, some positive evidence is needed before they can be attributed to him. In the case of the above poems, external evidence, where it exists (as in the case of "Advice to a Painter") counts against TP's authorship. On the other hand, the criterion of a poem being "not in TP's style" is undoubtedly subjective, so that these poems should be regarded as being in limbo rather than as having been definitively rejected.

(4) Lost poems. The Congleton inventory (printed below) lists a number of works by TP that are not now extant and that must be presumed lost. Some are certainly poems (for example, "Addison's Song Burlesqued"), others could be in prose or verse. Psalm 137, of which TP is recorded as having made a version "in Heroick Verse," was often translated. One version in heroic couplets was published in the *Oxford and Cambridge Miscellany Poems* ([1708]), pp. 147–49, and later reprinted in John Nichols's *Select Collection* (1780). It is called "Paraphrase on the cxxxviiᵗʰ Psalm" and begins, "Upon the Banks which fam'd *Euphrates* laves". Another version, as "Psalm CXXXVII" and in a mixture of stanzas and couplets beginning, "In *Babylon*, near proud *Euphrates* Stream", was published in *A Miscellany of Poems by Several Hands*, ed. J. Husbands (Oxford, 1731), 9–11. But there is no evidence to connect either of these versions with TP.

## The Congleton Inventory

This untitled inventory, preserved among the Congleton papers, lists printed as well as manuscript works. It is written on a single sheet, folded to make four pages (folded size 315 × 205 mm); the sheet is now badly

damp-stained and torn, some parts having become detached. We have
supplied missing words or letters conjecturally in square brackets, and
also summary notes identifying the various works where necessary and
indicating where they are to be found.


[f. 1a:]

The Hermit, or a vindication of Providence. [Pope's ed.]
War between the Vertues & vices; A translation out of Prudentius. [lost]
An Ecclogue on Health. [Pope's ed.]
A Rapsody of Divine meditation in Prose & Verse. [Possibly the essay
    from which we have printed three verse fragments.]
Solomon's Prayer at yᵉ Dedication of his Temple. [lost]
Heads of a Treatise on Divine Poetry, designd as a preface to the Gift of
    ⟨D⟩ Poetry. [lost]
An Essay on yᵉ Original, Alteration, & Excellency of yᵉ English
    Tongue— Designd as an Introduction to an English Gram. [lost]
Satyrs & other [?] In a [v]ellu[m] [notebo]ok. [Probably to be identified
    with the "Satires" Notebook.]
Reflections, Divine, Moral, Political, Poetical &c in another Vellum Pocket
    Book. [Not identified]
Notes on Select Texts beginnng at Genesis. [lost]
An Essay on Style. A Translation from yᵉ Greek. [lost]
Proposals for improving yᵉ English Tongue.[lost]
The 137 Psalm in Heroick Verse. [lost, but see the note above on "Lost
    Poems"]
Against Indolence in Love. In imitation of Gower [lost]
Donne's 3ᵈ Satyr, imitated. [Published by Pope in 1738.]
The Travels of yᵉ Passions. [lost]
A Collection of Hebrew Proverbs [lost]

[f. 1b:]

    Steels Miscellanies
A Hymn on Contentmᵗ.
Song.—My Days have been &ᵗ
To a young Lady / Miss ⟨Lady⟩ Tollet [?; the word could be "Joliet", or
    some variant of either word.]
Anacreontick—Gay Bacchus
[These are the four poems first published in *Poetical Miscellanies*, 1714;
    the identification of the "young lady" is intriguing. Unfortunately, we
    do not know whether the compiler of the list had a manuscript of the
    poems, a copy of the printed book, or was adding the name from
    recollection.]

Song—Thyrsis a young & amorous swain [Pope's ed.]
Judgment of Paris [1758]

To a Musician [This could be either the poem on Viner or the verse
  epistle to Ridgate; unless it is to be identified with one of these (neither
  of which seems very likely), the poem is lost.]
The Vigil of Venus. [Pope's ed.]
Hesiod or the Birth of Woman [Pope's ed.]
The Church Yard A Night Piece [Probably the same as "A Night Piece on
  Death" in Pope's ed.]
The Vision of Piety [*Dublin Weekly Journal,* 1726; 1755 and 1758 eds.]
Elizium [1755, 1758; also in "Satires" Notebook]
On y^e Peace in 1713 [1758]
An Essay on y^e Styles of Poetry In a Letter. [Either the *Essay* as published
  in 1713, or an earlier version of it.]
The Life of Zoilus [*Homer's Battle,* 1717]
A Fairy [Tale] [Pope's ed.]
The Book Worm [Pope's ed.]
Rape of y^e Lock in Monkish verse [*Poems on Several Occasions,* 1717;
  Pope's ed.]
The Rapture [possibly "Rupture"] Supposed to be a Plan for a Poem on
  y^e Times w^ch was dropd out of a Gentleman's Pocket. [lost]
An Imitation of some Verses w^ch were written by y^e Abbe de Chaulieu
  [Pope's ed.]
On Happiness in this Life [1758]
On M^rs Ar. F. leaving London. [1758]
A Riddle. [*Miscellanea,* 1727; 1758]
On the B^sp of S—— who had like to be burnt lately in his Study. [1758;
  Swift's *Works,* 1765]
Addisons Song Burlesqued [lost]
Anagram on a Quaker [lost]

[f. 2a:]

1. The Gift of Poetry containing

| | |
|---|---:|
| Moses | 866 |
| Deborah | 374 |
| Hannah | 256 |
| David | 1158 |
| Solomon | 802 |
| Jonah | 230 |
| Hezekiah | 240 |
| Habakkuk | 216 |
| | 4142 |

The Affections of Divine Poetry Containing

| | |
|---|---:|
| A Hymn for Morning | 44 |
| Noon | 48 |
| Evening | 38 |
| The Soul in Sorrow | 46 |

| | |
|---|---|
| The Happy Man | 60 |
| The Way to Happiness | [3]6 |
| The Convert's Love | 48 |
| On y^e Divine Love | 40 |
| A Desire to Praise | 64 |
| On Contentment | 48 |
| | 32 |
| | 504 |

[all the above were published in 1758; "The Gift of Poetry," "Moses," "Deborah," and "Hannah" are also contained in BL Add. MS 31114]

Bacchus's Entertainment, or ⎫
the Drunken Metamorphosis ⎭    90
[*Dublin Weekly Journal,* 1726; 1758 ed.]

[f. 2b:]

Essays

On y^e Eloquence of y^e Pulpit [lost]
On y^e Art of writing History [lost]
On y^e Fabulous in Prose [lost]

Two Epistles of Martin Scriblerus giving [an account of ?] his Travels & containing y^e Air & Argument of Modern Essays. [These cannot readily be identified with any published part of the *Memoirs of Martinus Scriblerus.* Chapter 16, containing "*some Hint of his* Travels," is closely linked to *Gulliver's Travels.* Chapter 17 includes a project for piping air from one region to another, and may be what "y^e Air" refers to. The wording makes this improbable, though air is a Scriblerian theme. See Kerby-Miller's ed., pp. 164–65, 168.]

An Abstract of Heraclides Ponticus his Vindication of Homer [lost]
The Birth & fall of Beauty [This prose essay survives among the Congleton papers.]
A Fable on Contentment [Not identified]
Sermon on our Behaviour in church. [lost]

Published by M^r [Pope; a list of the contents of his edition follows, but not in the exact order of the 1722 printing:]
Hesiod, or y^e Rise of Woman
Song. When thy Beauty appears et[c]
Song. Thirsis et[c]
Song. My Days have been so wondrous frree et[c]
Anacreontick—When Spring came on
Anacreontick—Gay Bacchus

A Fairy-Tale
The Vigil of Venus
The Battel of Frogs & Mice
To Mr. Pope
Part of y$^e$ l Canto of y$^e$ Rape of y$^e$ Lock
A Translation of part of y$^e$ l Canto of y$^e$ Rape of y$^e$ Lock into Leontine
    verse after y$^e$ manner of y$^e$ ancient monks
Health. An Ecclogue. The Flies an Ecclogue
An Elegy. To an old Beauty. The Book Worm. An Allegory on Man. In
    Imitation of some French Verses. A Night Piece on Death. A Hymn of
    Contentm! The Hermit. Spectator N$^o$ 460. 501. Guard. 56. 66. Library

# Appendix 2
# "The Hermit"

While this edition was in press, we discovered two variant texts of "The Hermit" in rare separate printings of the poem:

1. The first appears in a volume titled *The Hermit; a Poem. Being an Enquiry into the Hidden Mysteries of Divine Providence*. The imprint is London: for J. Wakelin . . . and J. Wyatt . . . 1752. It is described on the title page as "The Third Edition," and in ambiguous relation to this statement the title page continues: "To which is added, (by way of Introduction) A Discourse on the same Subject, By Mr. ADDISON: With Notes and other Remarks." There is a copy at Yale (Sterling Library: Ik P243 750 Bb). Foxon (P72) records a separate edition of the poem as having been advertised (not by Wakelin & Wyatt) in 1748, claiming to be reprinted from a Dublin edition. Foxon was unable to locate either printing, and they have likewise eluded us.

The 1752 "Third Edition" is a compilation of theodicean material and contains: an "Introduction," abbreviated from *Spectator* No. 237; an anecdote deriving ultimately from Plutarch's "Life of Timoleon," but with an added moralization; "The Hermit," supplied with an epigraph from Milton ("—I may assert Eternal Providence, / And justify the Ways of GOD to Men."), and varying from Pope's text in some forty passages; a brief "Conclusion," introducing a passage from Pope's *Essay on Man*.

The variations in the text of "The Hermit" must be regarded as of unproven authenticity. It seems curious that the editor of the volume did not make any claims for his text, as one would have expected. If the 1752 variants derive from an authorial manuscript, it must have been a very late one, for the text agrees with Pope in all cases against the 1755 "Variations." Substantially the same set of variants as are found in 1752 are also found in a New Haven, 1784 printing of the poem (copy at Yale: Ik P243 750c) and in a transcript made about 1789 and entered in a commonplace book kept by Thomas Binns of Liverpool (also at Yale: Osborn Shelves c 139 pp. 16–29). It is hard to explain these variants in any other way than as deriving somehow from an authorial manuscript. Discovery of copies of the unlocated editions of 1748 might help solve the problem. Meanwhile, we print a collation of 1752 with Pope's text:

5        the] 22; his 52
17       Scene] 22; sea 52
25       Pilgrim-Staff] 22; pilgrim's staff 52
38       kind] 22; kinds 52
42       In 52 there follows a passage of four lines not found in 22,
         then a variant of 22's line 43 (which in 52 does not begin a
         new paragraph):

> But here the youth enjoin'd the eager sire,
> Who into hidden truths did much inquire:
> If he'd in silence each event behold,
> He would to him, some wond'rous things unfold.
> Agreed;— and now the closing hour of day

54       them] 22; 'em 52
71–77    In 52 these lines occur in a different order and with some
         variations:

> Now on they pass— when far upon the road
> The wealthy spoil, the wiley partner shew'd.
>     As one who spies a serpent in his way,
> Glist'ning and basking in the summer ray,
> Disorder'd stops, to shun the danger near,
> Then walks with faintness on, and looks with fear:
> So seem'd the sire, he walk'd with trembling heart,

78       52 appends a footnote: "On account of his promise at first
         setting out."
91       Doors] 22; door 52
103      eager Wine] 22; dead small beer 52
104      them both to dine] 22; 'em both to cheer 52
116      this] 22; his 52
         In 52 there follows a passage of four lines not found in 22,
         then a variant of 22's line 117 (which in 52 does not begin a
         new paragraph):

> Just sunk to earth, the miser in surprize
> Receiv'd the glitt'ring gift with startled eyes;
> But e'er he could recover from his fright
> The generous guests were gone quite out of sight.
> Now the brisk clouds in airy tumults fly,

121–22   These lines are not found in 52, nor does 52 begin a new
         paragraph at line 123.
125      52 appends a footnote: "To steal the cup from the most
         generous man, and give it to a wretch that would scarce admit
         them within his gate."

| | |
|---|---|
| 126 | and] 22; but 52 |
| 131 | Lodging] 22; Mansion 52 |
| 140 | No new paragraph in 52. |
| 149 | dappled] 22; dapple 52 |
| 163 | trod] 22; went 52 |
| 164 | Oaks] 22; oak 52 |
| 170 | Father's] 22; hermit's 52 |
| 171 | madly] 22; mildly 52 |
| 177 | thro'] 22; in 52 |
| 178 | on] 22; like 52 |
| 179 | gradual] 22; dazzling 52 |
| 190 | These] 22; Their 52 |
| 195 | these] 22; the 52 |
| 199 | Means] 52 appends a footnote: "Second means— God often appoints wicked and abandoned wretches to be his instruments of justice upon others, for some ends tending to public good, tho' unperceived by human eyes." |
| 225 | Heart] 22; soul 52 |
| 226 | his] 52 appends a footnote: "Child of his age,— a child born to him when in years, on which he doated too fondly." |
| 234 | Wrack] 22; wreck 52 |
| 235 | that] 22; the 52 |
| 236–37 | 52 has a longer version of these lines and an appended footnote: |

> This very night, (by secret plot contriv'd)
> Of life and wealth his master he'd depriv'd;
> Had he in this conspiracy prevail'd;
> What funds of charity would then have fail'd.*
>    *He gave largely to the poor.

| | |
|---|---|
| 246 | bending] 22; blending 52 |
| | begun] 22; began 22 |

2. The second appears in an eight-page pamphlet with no title page or imprint but which has been identified as printed by James Chattin in Philadelphia in 1753 (Evans, *American Bibliography*, 7084, locating a single copy in the Historical Society of Pennsylvania; there are other copies at BL [11633.a.24] and at the Houghton Library at Harvard [Aldrich, 168.15]). In this edition the text of "The Hermit" occupies pp. 1–5; no author is given. The remaining three pages contain three pieces of devotional prose: one attributed to William Penn, two anonymous. Parnell's poem is supplied with an epigraph, based on lines 206–7 of the poem itself: "Now taught by this, confess th' Almighty just, / And where thou can't unravel, learn to trust."

The most notable variants are six omissions totaling nineteen lines, and the fact that 1753 has no paragraphing. There are no additions. None of the variants is shared with either the 1752 edition or the 1755 "Variations." Like those of 1752, their authenticity is unproven. The collation that follows indicates verbal differences between the BL copy of Evans 7084 and Pope's text; for convenience, the former is cited as "53":

| | |
|---|---|
| 1 | unknown to] 22; remote from 53 |
| 5 | Remote from] 22; Unknown to 53 |
| 10 | This] 22; Hence 53 |
| | Doubt] 22; Doubts 53 |
| 13–20 | Omitted in 53. |
| 23–26 | Omitted in 53. |
| 27 | Then] 22; He 53 |
| 37 | Question Answer] 22; Questions Answers 53 |
| 47–48 | Omitted in 53. |
| 49 | noble] 22; generous 53 |
| 56 | Hospitably] 22; hospitable 53 |
| 61–62 | Omitted in 53. |
| 65 | Goblet] 22; Vessel 53 |
| 72 | Summer] 22; summers 53 |
| 129 | again involve the Sky] 22; involve the azure Sky 53 |
| 130 | Omitted in 53. |
| 165 | the bending] 22; them bending 53 |
| 177 | breathe thro' purpled] 22; breath'd thro' purple 53 |
| 178–79 | Omitted in 53. |
| 202 | not] 22; nor 53 |
| 207 | you] 22; thou 53 |
| 225 | the Child] 22; this Child 53 |
| 233 | was] 22; is 53 |
| 234 | Wrack] 22; Wreck 53 |
| 246 | bending Hermit] 22; Hermit, bending, 53 |

# Checklist of Eighteenth-Century
# Editions of Parnell

On the model of Foxon's *English Verse* (though with some variations) this is "not a descriptive bibliography, but a short-title catalogue with frills" (Foxon, p. xi). The main points to note are that titles are abbreviated as indicated by ellipses (. . .), and no attempt has been made to reproduce the capitalization of the original title; imprints are usually quoted in full, but their punctuation has been rationalized; and in the collation, page numbers inferred are printed in italic.

The bibliography lists (in the "A" section) all the first and important printings of TP's poems, and (in the "B" section) all the eighteenth-century collected editions that are known to us. It excludes reprintings of individual poems, or of small selections of poems, in miscellanies. Section "B" is intended primarily as a guide to the collected editions, illustrating what readers at any particular point during the century are likely to have found in an edition of TP's *Poems*.

At the end of each entry, the copies examined are listed. The following abbreviations are used for libraries:

| | |
|---|---|
| BL | British Library, London |
| Bodley | Bodleian Library, Oxford |
| Clark | William Andrews Clark Memorial Library, Los Angeles |
| Harvard | Houghton Library, Harvard University |
| Huntington | Henry E. Huntington Library, San Marino |
| Illinois | Library of University of Illinois at Urbana-Champaign |
| LC | Library of Congress, Washington |
| TCC | Trinity College, Cambridge |
| ULC | University Library, Cambridge |
| V & A | Victoria and Albert Museum, London |
| Yale | Beinecke Rare Book and Manuscript Library, Yale University |

These copies are listed primarily to indicate the basis of our descriptions; we have not attempted to provide a census of copies.

In both sections we have added bibliographical references to the sources of (in most cases) fuller descriptions than we give. Those frequently cited are referred to by the following short titles; references are to numbered items unless a page reference is specified:

Case  Arthur E. Case, *A Bibliography of English Poetical Miscellanies, 1521–1750*. Oxford: Oxford University Press, 1935.
Foxon  D. F. Foxon, *English Verse, 1701–1750*. 2 vols. Cambridge: Cambridge University Press, 1975.
Gaskell  Philip Gaskell, *A Bibliography of the Foulis Press*. 1964; 2d ed. Winchester: St. Paul's Bibliographies, 1986.
Griffith  R. H. Griffith, *Alexander Pope: A Bibliography*. 2 vols. Austin: University of Texas, 1922.
Rothschild  *The Rothschild Library*. 2 vols. Cambridge: Privately printed, 1954.

## A. First and Other Important Printings

A1. *An essay on the different styles of poetry. . . .*
London, printed for Benj. Tooke, at the Middle-Temple-Gate in Fleet-street, 1713.
*8vo:* A-E⁴ F²; *i–viii* 1–36
*Copies:* BL (1078.m.6(6)); ULC (Acton d.54.13(2); Williams 408(14)); TCC (Rothschild 1512; with a presentation inscription from TP to "Edw: Smyth Esq"); Illinois (Nickell 30; presentation inscription from TP "For Benj. Everard Esq"); Clark (*PR3616.E78).
*References:* Foxon P70–71; Rothschild 1512.

A2. [dh:]*The horse and the olive: or, war and peace.*
Printed for John Morphew, near Stationers-Hall.
Folio half-sheet; imprint at foot of verso.
*Copies:* Clark (*fPR3616.H81); Harvard (EB7. A100. 712h2).
*Reference:* Foxon P77.

A3. *Poetical miscellanies, consisting of original poems and translations . . . Published by Mr. Steele*
London, printed for Jacob Tonson at Shakespeare's Head over-against Catherine-street in the Strand, 1714.
*8vo:* A-X⁸; *i–xvi 1–3* 4–134 "13" 136–316 "217" 318 *319–20.*
TP's poems, "A Hymn on Contentment," "Song" ("My Days have been"), "To a Young Lady," "Anacreontick" ("Gay Bacchus"), are on pp. 56–68 (E4b–F2b). E4 is a cancel in all the copies examined. On the title page the date is misprinted "MDDCXIV"; this was corrected when the volume was reprinted. There is an engraved frontispiece.
*Copies:* BL (1077.1.26); ULC (X.19.28; Williams 680); Clark (*PR1171.S81); Huntington (147842).

*References:* Case 279; Griffith 24; Iolo A. Williams, *Points in Eighteenth-Century Verse* (London: Constable & Co., 1934), pp. 85–87.

A4. *Homer's Battle of the Frogs and Mice, with the remarks of Zoilus. To which is prefixed, the life of the said Zoilus. . . .*
London, printed for Bernard Lintot, between the Temple-Gates, 1717.
*8vo:* A–F⁸; *i–xlii 1* 2–30 *31–54.*
For the differences between ordinary and fine-paper copies, see our headnote to the poem.
*Copies:* BL (C.133.c.2(1)); ULC (Syn 7.72.12(5); Williams 580); Clark (*PR3616.B31); Huntington (215468). Presentation copies from TP to Pope, at Harvard (A1707.5*), to Benjamin Everard, at Illinois (Nickell 30), and to Swift, at V & A (Dyce 4914). The latter was probably given by Swift to Esther Johnson (Stella) and has her signature on the title-page.
*References:* Foxon P73–74; Griffith 74–74a.

A5. *The works of Mr. Alexander Pope . . .*
London, printed by W. Bowyer, for Bernard Lintot, between the Temple-Gates, 1717.
*4to:* π⁴ a–c B–3I⁸ 3K²; *i–xxx 1–2* 3–10 *11* 12–17 *18* 19–23 *24* 25–29 *30* 31–35 *36* 37–46 *47–49* 50–72 *73–75* 76–114 *115–16* 117–19 *120–21* 122–29 *130* 131–37 *138* 139–47 *148* 149–57 *158* 159–66 *167–71* 172–98 *199–201* 202–43 *244–47* 248–69 *270–73* 274–86 *287* 288–93 *294* 295–99 *300–3* 304–47 *348–51* 352–64 *365* 366–67 *368–71* 372–414 *415–17* 418–35 *436.*
TP's poem "To Mr. Pope" is on c1a–2a, signed "T. Parnell". The volume has a portrait frontispiece.
*Copy:* BL (C.59.i.20).
*Reference:* Griffith 79.

A6. *Poems on several occasions. . . .*
London, printed for Bernard Lintot, between the Temple Gates, 1717.
*8vo:* A⁴ B–N⁸ *N⁸ O–P⁸ Q²; *i–viii 1* 2–192 177–228.
TP's "Translation" is on pp. 153, 155, facing the passage from *The Rape of the Lock* on pp. 152, 154. TP's poem is unsigned.
*Copy:* V & A (Dyce 7612).
*Reference:* For a detailed discussion of the volume, see Norman Ault's introduction to his reprint, *Pope's Own Miscellany* (1935).

A7. *A miscellaneous collection of poems, songs and epigrams.*
*. . . Published by T. M. Gent . . .* [2 vols]
Dublin, printed by A. Rhames, 1721.
*12mo:* [Vol. I:] A–L¹²; *i–xxiv* 1–240.
"On the Death of Mr. Viner" is in vol. 1, pp. 55–58 (D4a–D5b).
*Copies:* BL (11632.de.6); Clark (*PR1217.M91).
*Reference:* Case 320.

A8. *The pleasures of coition; or, the nightly sports of Venus: a poem . . . With some other pieces. . . .*
London, printed for E. Curll, at the Dial and Bible over against Catherine-Street in the Strand, 1721.
*8vo:* A⁴ B–G⁴; *i–iv* 5–56.
"On the Death of Mr. Viner" is on pp. 53–56 (G3a–G4b). The volume has an engraved frontispiece. A second edition was published later in 1721.
*Copy:* Clark (*PA8477.B6P4E).

A9. *Pancharis queen of love: or, woman unveil'd. Being the "Basia" of Bonefonius. . . .*
London, printed for E. Curll, at the Dial and Bible, over against Catherine-Street in the Strand, 1721.
*8vo:* A² B–G⁴ H²; *i–iv 1* 2–52.
TP's poems, "Chloris," "On the Castle of Dublin," "Love in Disguise," "On a Lady with a Foul Breath," "On the Number Three," "Epigram," are on pp. 37–47. The volume has an engraved frontispiece.
*Copy:* BL (164.l.57).
*Reference:* Case 322.

A10. *Poems on several occasions. . . .*
London, printed for B. Lintot, at the Cross-Keys, between the Temple Gates in Fleet-street, 1722.
*8vo:* A⁴ B–P⁸; *i–viii 1* 2–26 "28" 28–45 "49" 47–67 *68–71* 72–180 *181–82* 183–221 *222–24.*
*Copies:* BL (993.k.24); ULC (Y.21.65(1); Williams 615); TCC (Rothschild 1513; a presentation copy from Pope to Edward Harley, later second earl of Oxford); Clark (*PR3616.A1 1722); Huntington (113455); Illinois (Nickell X821/P84p, and two other copies); V & A (Dyce 7222).
One of the ULC copies (Y.21.65(1)), as described above in the headnote to "The Vigil of Venus", has both the cancellans and the cancelland of D8. In some copies (Clark, Nickell, Dyce) the cancellans D8, probably as the result of an error of imposition, reverses pp. 47 and 48. This error was evidently detected, and most copies have these pages in the correct order. There are also some variants in press-figures. In the copies examined, these involve signatures D, E, K, L, and P, but a full treatment would be beyond the scope of this bibliography.
*References:* Foxon, p. 554; Griffith 130; Rothschild 1513.

A11. [dh] *The Dublin weekly journal.* No. 62. 4 June 1726.
TP's poems "Piety" and "Bacchus" were first printed in this issue, introduced by a letter from "Musophilus" (James Arbuckle).
*Copy:* ULC (Hib 3.725.3).

A12. *Miscellanea. . . .* [2 vols]
London, printed in the year, 1727.

*12mo:* [Vol. 2] $A^4$ B–$I^6$ $K^2$ $\chi^1$ $2A^2$ 2B–$2I^6$ $2K^3$; *i–viii 1* 2–22 *23–25* 26–37 *38–41* 42–66 *67–69* 70–99 *100 i–ii i* ii–iv i–ii *3* 4–101 *102.*
TP's "A Riddle" is in vol. 2, pp. 79–80 (H4a–b).
*Copy:* Huntington (92048).
*Reference:* Case 343 (I & II); Griffith 177–78.

A13. *The works of Alexander Pope.* . . . Vol. II, Part ii.
London, printed for R. Dodsley, and sold by T. Cooper, in Paternoster-row, 1738.
*8vo:* $\pi^4$ $A^8$ $M^2$ $A^8$ $B^3$ B–$D^8$ $E^4$ F–$G^8$ $H^2$ *$K^8$ $\chi^2$ $L^4$; *i–iv i* ii–iii *iv 1–3* 4–9 10 11–19 *20 1–3* 4–13 *14* 15–21 *22 i–ii* iii–iv *5* 6–31 *32–35* 36–53 *54* 55–56 *57–59* 60–71 *72* 73–77 *78–81* 82–92 *151–53* 154–63 *164–66 i–iv* 161–68.
TP's version of "The Third Satire of Dr. John Donne" is on pp. 151–63.
*Copies:* Bodley (Don.f.172); TCC (Rothschild 1627; this set is a presentation copy from Pope to Lord Orrery, and has several signatures not found in the Bodleian copy, from which the above collation was taken); Yale (Ik P810 737). The second B3 is signed "A3."
*References:* Griffith 507; Rothschild 1627. For a detailed discussion of the problems associated with the printing and publication of this volume, see Maynard Mack, "Pope's Horatian Poems: Problems of Bibliography and Text," *Modern Philology* 41 (1943): 33–44; reprinted in Mack's *Collected in Himself,* pp. 106–21.

A14. *The works in verse and prose* . . . *Enlarged with variations and poems, not before publish'd.*
Glasgow, printed and sold by R. and A. Foulis, 1755.
*8vo:* $\pi^4$ A–$2F^4$; *i–viii 1* 2–39 *40–43* 44–105 *106–8* 109–43 *144–47* 148–200 *201–2* 203–10 *211* 212–14 *215* 216–20 *221* 222–24 *225* 226–32.
*Copies:* ULC (7720.e.95(1)); Huntington (228953); BL (1607/2845).
*Reference:* Gaskell 303.

A15. *The posthumous works* . . . *Containing poems moral and divine: and on various other subjects* . . .
Dublin, printed for Benjamin Gunne, bookseller in Caple-street, 1758.
*8vo:* $A^4\chi^4$ B–$2O^4$; *i–iii* iv–v "vii" *vii–ix* x–xiii *xiv* xv *xvi 1* 2–197 "298" 199–286 *287–88.*
The edition was also issued in London, with a cancel title page, but retaining Gunne's catalogue of books.
*Copies:* BL (1608/31); ULC (Hib.7.758.11). With London title page: BL (992.h.32); ULC (Williams 613, 614).

*Reference:* Williams, *Points in Eighteenth-Century Verse,* pp. 91–92.

A16. *The works of Dr. Jonathan Swift* . . . Volume VIII, Part II.
London, printed for W. Johnston, in Ludgate-Street, 1765.

*4to:* A–2N⁴; *i–ii* iii–vii *viii 1* 2–140 *141–42* 143–279 *280*.

TP's poems "To Dr. Swift" and "On Bishop Burnet" are on pp. 143–45, 149.

*Copies:* BL (90.d.8); Huntington (100400); Yale (1986 +93 8).

*Reference:* Hermann Teerink, *A Bibliography of the Writings of Jonathan Swift*, 2d ed., rev. A. H. Scouten (Philadelphia: University of Pennsylvania Press, 1963), No. 87, p. 86.

## B. Collected Editions

In listing the contents of the various collected editions, "Pope's selection" means the poems printed in 1722; "the 'Affections' group" means the sequence of poems from "A Hymn to Morning" to "On Divine Love" as printed in 1758; "the Biblical poems" means the sequence from "The Gift of Poetry" to "Habakkuk"; the other abbreviated titles used are self-evident. In all the editions, the poem we have printed from the manuscript as "The Heroins or Cupid Punishd" is called "Elysium," and we have retained that title in the following list.

B1. *Poems on several occasions . . .*
London, printed for B. Lintot, at the Cross-Keys, between the Temple Gates in Fleet-street, 1722.
*8vo:* A⁴ B–P⁸; *i–viii 1* 2–26 "28" 28–45 "49" 47–67 *68–71* 72–180 *181–82* 183–221 *222–24*.
*Contents:* Pope's selection.
Same as A10 above, where further details are given.

B2. *Poems on several occasions . . .*
Dublin, printed by A. Rhames, for J. Hyde, R. Gunne, R. Owen, and E. Dobson, 1722.
*12mo:* π¹A-B b C–F¹² G¹⁰; *i–vi 1* 2–43 *44 i–xxiv 45–46* 47–132 *133–34* 135–59 *160*.
*Contents:* Pope's selection, with the "Zoilus" prose evidently added as an afterthought (the Preface and the "Life of Zoilus" are unpaged and occupy signature "b"; the regular pagination resumes with the "Battle" itself and the "Remarks").
*Copy:* BL (11631.aa.22).

B3. *Poems on several occasions . . .*
London, printed for Bernard Lintot, at the Cross-Keys between the Temple Gates in Fleet-street, 1726.
*8vo:* A⁴ B–R⁸; *i–viii 1* 2–67 *68–70* 71–179 *180–82* 183–221 *222–56*.
*Contents:* Pope's selection; pp. 223–56 comprise a catalogue of "Books Printed for Bernard Lintot," unnumbered but an integral part of the sequence of signatures.
*Copies:* BL (992.h.31); ULC (Williams 616); Bodley (12.θ.1079; the imprint has the misprint "Kyes" for "Keys").

B4. *Poems on several occasions.*
Dublin, 1727.
This edition is mentioned by Griffith (1 : 1, p. 100) and by Schoedinger (p. 140), but we have been unable to locate a copy.

B5. *Poems on several occasions . . . The sixth edition with additions.*
Dublin, printed by R. Reilly on Cork-Hill, for R. Gunne, and R. Owen, booksellers, 1735.
*12mo:* $\pi^1$ A–B b C–G$^{12}$ H$^{11}$; *i–vi 1* 2–43 *44 1–8* 9 *10–24 43–47* 48–70 71 *72–132 133–37* 138–58 *159–60* "160" 162–85 *186.*
*Contents:* Pope's selection, with the addition of the "Zoilus" prose (as in the Dublin, 1722, edition, and oddly retaining the same irregularity in the signatures, although with page 9 numbered), and the *Essay on the Different Styles of Poetry.*
*Copies:* BL (1507/1070); ULC (Hib.8.735.9); Clark (*PR3616.A1 1735).

B6. *Poems on several occasions . . .*
London, printed for H. Lintot, at the Cross-Keys against St. Dunstan's Church in Fleetstreet, 1737.
*8vo:* $\pi^1$ A$^4$ B–P$^8$ 2A–D$^8$; *i–ii i–viii 1* 2–67 *68–70* 71–179 *180–82* 183–221 *222–24 i–iii* iv–xii *13* 14–39 *40* 41–42 *43* 44–64.
*Contents:* Pope's selection, with the addition (at the end) of the "Zoilus" prose; $\pi$1 is the additional title page that refers to the prose.
*Copies:* ULC (Williams 617; has the prose but not the second title page); Huntington (447512; complete); Clark (*PR3616.A1 1737; without the added prose and the second title page).

B7. *Poems on several occasions . . . The seventh edition with additions.*
Dublin, printed by A. Reilly, for R. Gunne and R. Owen, booksellers, 1744.
*12mo:* A–I$^{12}$; *i–vi 1* 2–43 *44 i–xxiv 45–47* 48–70 *71* 72–86 "78" 88–132 *133–37* 138–58 *159–60* "160" 162–83 "175" 185 *186.*
*Contents:* same as Dublin, 1735 (B5); here the "Life of Zoilus" is integrated into the sequence of signatures, but is again unpaged; and the misprinted page number "160" (for 161) is curiously repeated.
*Copy:* BL (992.a.32).

B8. *Poems on several occasions . . .*
London, printed for H. Lintot, J. and R. Tonson and S. Draper, 1747.
*8vo:* A–S$^8$; *i–viii 1* 2–63 *64–66* 67–173 *174–76* 177–215 *216–19* 220–28 *229* 230–54 *255* 256–57 *258* 259–79 *280.*
*Contents:* same as London, 1737 (B6), with the "Zoilus" prose again at the end.
*Copies:* BL (1465.e.12); ULC (7720.d.448; Williams 618); Clark (*PR3616.A1 1747); Huntington (68834).

**B9.** *Poems on several occasions . . .*
Glasgow, printed by Robert Urie, and sold by the booksellers in town and country, 1748.
*12mo:* $\pi^2$ A–U$^6$ X$^4$; *i–iv* iii–v *vi* 7–59 *60–62* 63–71 *72* 73–95 *96–98* 99–213 *214–16* 217–47 *248–50*.
*Contents:* Pope's selection, with the addition of the "Zoilus" prose and (now first collected) "Piety" and "Bacchus."
*Copy:* BL (1486.df.27).

**B10.** *Poems on several occasions . . .*
Glasgow, printed by Robert Urie, 1752.
*8vo:* A$^4$ B–2F$^4$; *i–v* vi 7–11 "21" 13–53 *54–56* 57–65 *66* 67 "8" 69–89 *90–92* 93–113 *114* 115–36 "173" 138–40 *141* 142–67 "198" 169–95 *196–98* 199–230 *231–32*.
*Contents:* same as Glasgow, 1748 (B9).
*Copy:* BL (1568/9260).

**B11.** *The works, in verse and prose . . . Enlarged with variations and poems, not before publish'd.*
Glasgow, printed and sold by R. and A. Foulis, 1755.
*8vo:* $\pi^4$ A–2F$^4$; *i–viii 1* 2–39 *40–43* 44–105 *106–8* 109–43 *144–47* 148–200 *201–2* 203–10 *211* 212–14 *215* 216–20 *221* 222–24 *225* 226–32.
*Contents:* Pope's selection plus the "Zoilus" prose; "Variations"; "Bacchus"; "Elysium"; "To Dr. Swift"; "Piety"; "Ecstasy."
Same as A14 above, where further details are given.

**B12.** *Poems on several occasions . . .*
London, printed for J. and R. Tonson in the Strand, 1760.
*12mo:* B–L$^{12}$ M$^8$; *i–iv* iii–v *vi* 7–42 *43* 44–61 *62–64* 65–158 *159–60* 161–94 *195–96* 197–205 *206* 207–46 "147" 248–52 *253–54*.
*Contents:* Pope's selection; "Piety" and "Bacchus"; the "Zoilus" prose.
*Copies:* BL (11631.aaa.27); ULC (Yorke d.337; Williams 619). In both ULC copies p. 109 is numbered "10."

**B13.** *Poems on several occasions . . . The eighth edition with additions*
Dublin, printed for Henry Saunders, in Castle-street, 1767.
*12 mo:* A$^1$ B-S$^6$ T$^3$; *i–ii* i–ii *3* 4–41 *42–45* 46–51 *52* 53–69 *70–73* 74–79 *80* 81–85 *86* 87–94 *95* 96 *97* 98–116 *117* 118–59 *160–65* 166–84 *185* 186–209 *210*.
*Contents:* Pope's selection, with the "Zoilus" prose; *An Essay on the Different Styles of Poetry.*
*Copies:* ULC (Hib.8.767.5); BL (1607/2486); Bodley (Vet A5f.1163). In the ULC copy p. 32 is not numbered.

**B14.** *The works in verse and prose . . .*
Glasgow, printed by Robert & Andrew Foulis, printers to the University, 1767.

*8vo:* π⁴ A–2F⁴; *i–viii 1* 2–39 *40–43* 44–105 *106–8* 109–43 *144–47* 148–
200 *201–2* 203–10 *211* 212–14 *215* 216–20 *221* 222–32.
*Contents:* same as Glasgow, 1755 (B11), of which this is a reprint.
*Copy:* BL (12271.a.16).
*Reference:* Gaskell 468.

B15. *Poems on several occasions . . . A new edition, to which is prefixed "The
life of Dr. Parnell," written by Dr. Goldsmith.*
London, printed for T. Davies, in Russell Street, Covent-Garden,
1770.
*8vo:* π³ a–b⁸ c² B–Q⁸ R²; *i–vi* i–xxxv *xxxvi* i–iii *iv* 5–51 *52–54* 55–148
*149–50* 151–60 159–82 *183–84* 185–93 *194* 195–238 241–42 *243–44.*
*Contents:* Goldsmith's "Life"; Pope's selection; "Piety" and "Bacchus";
the "Zoilus" prose.
Apart from the importance of Goldsmith's "Life," this is the first
illustrated edition, with two engraved full-page illustrations, one each for
"Hesiod" and "The Hermit."
*Copies:* BL (239.g.24); ULC (Williams 620).

B16. *Poems on several occasions . . .*
Dublin, printed by John Murphy, printer and bookseller in Skinner-
Row, 1771.
*12mo:* π² a¹² A–I¹² K⁴; *i–iv* i–xxiv *i–iv 1* 2–43 *44* i–xxiv 45–47 48–53
*54* 55–59 *60* 61–68 *69* 70 *71* 72–132 *133–37* 138–161 "132" 193–96 *197–
98* 199–223 *224.*
*Contents:* Goldsmith's "Life"; Pope's selection, with the "Zoilus" prose;
*An Essay on the Different Styles of Poetry;* "Piety" and "Bacchus."
*Copy:* ULC (Hib.7.771.20). A1 is missing from the only copy we have
examined.

B17. *Poems upon several occasions . . .*
London, printed for T. Davies, in Russell Street, Covent-Garden,
1772.
*8vo:* A² B–M⁸ N⁶; *i–iv i* ii–xxviii i–ii 1-29 *30–32* 33–83 *84–86* 87–110
"11" 112 *113–14* 115–58.
*Contents:* Goldsmith's "Life"; Pope's selection; "Piety" and "Bacchus";
*The Horse and the Olive;* the "Zoilus" prose.
*Copy:* Bodley (Douce P423).

B18. *Poems upon several occasions . . .*
London, printed for T. Davies, in Russel-Street, Covent-Garden; J.
Dodsley, in Pall-Mall; and R. Baldwin, in Pater-noster-Row, 1773.
*8vo:* A² B–M⁸ N⁶ O⁸ P⁴; *i–iv i* ii–xxviii i–ii 1–29 *30–32* 33–83 *84–86*
87–110 "11" 112 *113–14* 115–58 *159* 160–68 *169* 170–74 17–21 *180–82.*
*Contents:* Goldsmith's "Life"; Pope's selection; "Piety" and "Bacchus";
*The Horse and the Olive;* the "Zoilus" prose; "The Third Satire of Dr. John
Donne"; "An Essay of the Learned Martinus Scriblerus concerning the
Origin of Sciences."

This is a reissue of the London, 1772, edition (B17), with the addition of an "Appendix" containing "The Third Satire of Dr. John Donne" and the "Essay" of Scriblerus, both now for the first time printed in an edition of TP.

*Copies:* BL (1480.aa.4); ULC (7700.d.641); Bodley (Vet.A5.f.2685).

B19. *Poems on several occasions . . .*
Dublin, Thomas Ewing, 1773.
*4to:* π² b–k B–U *X X–3T²; *i–ii i* ii–xxxiii *xxxiv–xxxv* xxxvi–xxxvii *xxxviii 1* 2–37 *38* 39–51 *52–57* 58–63 *64* 65–70 *71* 72–80 *81–96* 93–116 *117* 118–19 *120–21* 122–43 *144–45* 146–49 *150* 151–52 *153* 154–56 *157* 158–60 *161* 162–64 *165* 166–69 *170* 171–75 *176* 177–78 *179* 180–83 *184* 185–87 *188* 189–200 *201* 202–6 *207* 208–11 *212–15* 216–22 *223* 224–30 *231* 232–39 *240* 241–47 *248* 249–54 *255–56.*
*Contents:* Goldsmith's "Life"; Pope's selection, with the "Zoilus" prose; "Piety" and "Bacchus."
This handsome quarto edition has an engraved medallion portrait of TP at the head of "Hesiod."
*Copies:* BL (78.g.24; 1488.i.5); ULC (Hib.4.773.4; Williams 442).

B20. *The poems . . .*
Edinburgh, printed for J. Balfour and W. Creech, 1773.
*8vo:* π³ A–G⁸ H⁴ I²; *i–vi i* ii *3* 4–37 *38–40* 41–124.
*Contents:* Pope's selection (excluding the "Visions"); "Piety" and "Bacchus"; *The Horse and the Olive;* "Elysium," "To Dr. Swift," "The Third Satire of Dr. John Donne," "Ecstasy."
This edition has an additional title page, "The British Poets. Vol. 37."
*Copy:* BL (11604.a.37).

B21. *The works in verse and prose . . . Enlarged with variations and poems, not before publish'd.*
Edinburgh, printed by Alex. M'Caslan, and sold at his shop, opposite to the Chapel of Ease, Cross-Causeway, 1773.
*12mo:* π² A–N⁶; *i–ii 1–3* 4 5 6–22 *23* 24–33 *34* 35–59 *60–62* 63–130 *131–32* 133–58.
*Contents:* Pope's selection, with the "Zoilus" prose; "Piety" and "Bacchus." Despite the wording of the title page, this edition contains neither "variations" nor new poems.
*Copy:* BL (1578/63).

B22. *Poems on several occasions . . .*
Glasgow, printed by Robert & Andrew Foulis, printers to the University, 1773.
*12mo:* π² χ¹ A–L⁶ M²; *i–vi 1* 2–38 *39–40* 41–102 *103–4* 105–12 *113* 114–16 *117* 118–22 *123* 124–26 *127* 128–31 *132* 133–35 *136.*
*Contents:* Pope's selection (omitting the "Visions"); "Variations"; "Bacchus," "Elysium," "To Dr. Swift," "Piety," "Ecstasy."
*Copies:* BL (238.a.47); ULC (7720.e.164).
*Reference:* Gaskell 559.

B23. *Poems upon several occasions . . .*
London, printed for John Bell, No. 132 Strand, 1774.
*8vo:* A⁴ B–2B⁴; *i–ix* x–xviii "xxi" xx *xxi* xxii *23–25* 26–33 *34–37* 38–44
*45–47* 48–53 *54–61* 62–71 *72–77* 78–82 *83* 84–87 *88–89* 90–95 *96–99*
100–102 *103–7* 108–9 *110–13* 114–15 *116–19* 120–21 *122–25* 126–27
*128–31* 132–34 *135–37* 138–40 *141–43* 144–45 *146–49* 150–52 *153–55*
156–57 *158–61* 162–68 *169–71* 172–75 *176–79* 180–81 *182–85* 186
*187–91* "162" 193–200.
*Contents:* an unacknowledged abridgment of Goldsmith's "Life"; Pope's
selection (omitting the "Visions"); "Piety" and "Bacchus"; *The Horse and
the Olive;* "The Third Satire of Dr. John Donne."
*Copies:* BL (11630.b.38); ULC (Hib. 8.774.3, Williams 621).

B24. *Poems on several occasions . . . The ninth edition with additions.*
Dublin, printed by Henry Saunders, in Great Ship-Street, 1776.
*12mo:* A¹ B–S⁶ T³; *i–ii* i ii *3* 4–41 *42–45* 46–51 *52* 53–69 *70–73* 74–79
*80* 81–85 *86* 87–94 *95* 96 *97* 98–116 *117* 118–46 "14" 148–59 *160–65*
166–84 *185* 186–209 *210*.
*Contents:* Pope's selection, with the addition of the "Zoilus" prose; *An
Essay on the Different Styles of Poetry.*
*Copy:* BL (11631.aaa.28).

B25. *Poems on several occasions . . .*
Glasgow, printed by Andrew Foulis, 1777.
*12mo:* π⁴ A–L⁶ M²; *i–viii* 1 2–38 *39–41* 42–102 *103–4* 105–12 *113*
114–16 *117* 118–22 *123* 124–26 *127* 128–31 *132* 133–35 *136*.
*Contents:* same as Glasgow, 1773 (B22).
*Copy:* LC (PR 3616.A1 1777).
Reference: Gaskell 626A.

B26. *The poetical works . . . Containing those published by Mr. Pope, together
with his whole posthumous pieces. In two volumes. With the life of the author.* [2
vols]
Edinburg, at the Apollo Press, by the Martins, Anno 1778.
*12mo:* [Vol. 1] A–O⁶ P⁴; *i–v* vi–xxii *xxiii* xxiv *25* 26–30 *31* 32–33 *34* 35–
36 *37* 38–40 *41* 42–48 *49* 50–53 *54* 55–63 *64* 65–72 *73* 74–81 *82* 83–92
*93* 94–111 *112* 113–14 *115* 116–117 *118* 119–21 *122* 123–25 *126* 127–
31 *132* 133–34 *135* 136–44 *145* 146 *147* 148–49 *150* 151–53 *154* 155–59
*160* 161–64 *165* 166 *167* 168–71 *172–73* 174–75 *176*. [Vol. 2] A–P⁶; *i–iv*
*5* 6–20 *21* 22–26 *27* 28–32 *33* 34–61 *62* 63–75 *76* 77–84 *85* 86–126 *127*
128–55 *156* 157–63 *164* 165–71 *172* 173–79 *180*.
*Contents:* This was the first edition to break significantly with Pope's
arrangement. Not only were the "Visions" omitted (as they had been in
some earlier editions), but the order of the poems was changed, integrat-
ing the posthumous and miscellaneous poems with Pope's selection. This
edition contains, apart from Pope's selection, all the poems published in
the 1758 *Posthumous Works, The Horse and the Olive,* "The Third Satire of
Dr. John Donne," and (here first collected ) "To a Young Lady."

There are additional engraved title pages (and in vol. 1 an engraved frontispiece) headed "Bell's Edition," as this edition is usually known.
*Copies:* BL (1066.b.30); Bodley (Vet.A5.f.801).

B27. *The works of the English poets. With prefaces, biographical and critical, by Samuel Johnson.* Vol. 44.
London, printed by J. Rivington, for C. Bathurst [etc], 1779.
*8vo:* a² B–2C⁸ 2D²; *i–iv 1–2* 3–34 *35–36* 37–290 *291–92* 293–403 *404.*
*Contents:* the same as Bell's (B26), except that it excludes "To a Young Lady" and adds "To Dr. Swift." The same volume also contains the poems of Ambrose Philips.
*Copy:* BL (11601.cc.7).

B28. *Poetical works . . .* [2 vols.]
London, printed by Fry and Couchman, Moorfields, Anno 1786.
*12mo:* [Vol. 1] A–O⁶ P⁴; *i–v* vi–xxii *xxiii* xxiv *25* 26–30 *31* 32–33 *34* 35–36 *37* 38–40 *41* 42–48 *49* 50–53 *54* 55–63 *64* 65–72 *73* 74–81 *82* 83–92 *93* 94–111 *112* 113–14 *115* 116–17 *118* 119–21 *122* 123–25 *126* 127–31 *132* 133–34 *135* 136–44 *145* 146 *147* 148–49 *150* 151–53 *154* 155–59 *160* 161–64 *165* 166 *167* 168–71 *172–73* 174–75 *176.*
[Vol. 2] A–P⁶; *i–iv* 5 6–20 *21* 22–26 *27* 28–32 *33* 34–61 *62* 63–75 *76* 77–84 *85* 86–126 *127* 128–55 *156* 157–63 *164* 165–71 *172* 173–79 *180.*
*Contents:* same as Bell's 1778 edition (B26), of which this is a line for line reprint; the type, however, has been reset.
*Copies:* V & A (Dyce 7218); Bodley (12.θ.1520–21).

B29. *The poetical works. . . .*
Glasgow, printed by Andrew Foulis, printer to the University, 1786.
*Folio:* π² χ¹ b–c A–5E² χ²; *i–ii i–v* vi–x *xi* xii *1* 2–3 *4* 5–7 *8* 9–11 *12* 13–15 *16–17* 18–19 *20* 21–23 *24* 25 *26* 27 *28* 29 *30* 31–33 *34* 35–38 *39–40* 41–50 *51* 52–61 *62* 63–71 *72* 73–84 *85–87* 88–93 *94* 95–99 *100* 101–8 *109* 110–11 *112* 113–14 *115* 116–19 *120* 121–124 *125* 126–27 *128* 129–31 *132* 133–34 *135* 136–46 *147* 148–49 *150* 151 *152* 153–54 *155* 156 *157* 158–61 *162* 163 *164* 165–67 *168* 169 *170* 171–74 *175* 176–78 *179* 180–93 *194* 195–200 *201* 202–3 *204* 205–6 *207–8* 209–41 242 243–57 *258* 259–68 *269* 270–317 *318* 319–51 *352* 353–61 *362* 363–72 *373* 374–82 *383* 384–88 *389–92.*
*Contents:* same as Bell's edition (B26), the arrangement of which it follows, but with the addition of "To Dr. Swift" and the "Variations."
*Copies:* ULC (Williams 443); BL (75.i.1).
*Reference:* Gaskell 681, Rothschild 1514.

B30. *The works of the English poets.* Vol. 27.
London, printed by A. Strahan for J. Buckland [etc.], 1790.
*8vo:* A² B–X⁸; *i–iv 1–2* 3–34 *35–36* 37–315 *316–20.*
*Contents:* This was the most complete collection to date, including everything previously printed except "To a Young Lady," and collecting

for the first time "On the Death of Mr. Viner" and the poems published in *Pancharis*.

*Copy:* BL (237.d.27).

B31. *The poetical works.* . . .
Edinburgh, printed by Mundell and Son, Royal Bank Close, Anno 1794.

*8vo:* π⁴ A–D⁸ E⁶ [etc.; E7 is the title page for Garth's poems]; *i–iii* iv–viii *1* 2–75 *76* [etc.].

*Contents:* same as B30.

There is an additional engraved title page for the series, "A Complete Edition of the Poets of Great Britain," of which TP's poems form part of vol. 7 (which contains the works of eleven other poets).

B32. *Poetical works.* . . . *Cooke's edition* . . .
London, printed for C. Cooke, No. 1, Paternoster-Row; and sold by all the booksellers in Great Britain and Ireland.

*12mo:* A–X⁶; *i–v* vi–xiii *xiv 15* 16–18 *19* 20–22 *23* 24 *25* 26–30 *31* 32–35 *36* 37–48 *49* 50–54 *55* 56–61 *62–63* 64–75 *76* 77–90 *91* 92–97 *98* 99–114 *115* 116–34 *135* 136–44 *145* 146–51 *152* 153–81 *182* 183–202 *203* 204ʹ–8 *209* 210–15 *216* 217–21 *222* 223–51 252.

*Contents:* same as B30.

The additional engraved frontispiece and title page are dated 1796.

*Copy:* Bodley (Vet.A5.f.2183(1)).

B33. *The poetical works* . . . *Cooke's edition* . . .
London, printed for C. Cooke, No. 17, Paternoster-Row; and sold by all the booksellers in Great Britain and Ireland.

*18mo:* A–X⁶; *i–v* vi–xiii *xiv 15* 16–18 *19* 20–22 *23* 24 *25* 26–30 *31* 32–35 *36* 37–48 *49* 50–54 *55* 56–61 *62–63* 64–75 *76* 77–90 *91* 92–97 *98* 99–114 *115* 116–34 *135* 136–44 *145* 146–51 *152* 153–81 *182* 183–202 *203* 204–8 *209* 210–15 *216* 217–21 *222* 223–51 *252*.

*Contents:* same as B30.

The engraved plates are dated 1796–97.

*Copy:* BL (11613.h.1).

B34. *Poems* . . .
Manchester, printed at the office of G. Nicholson, No. 9, Spring-gardens, sold by T. Knott, No. 47, Lombard-street; and Champante and Whitrow, Jewry-street, London, Anno 1797.

*12mo:* A–B⁶; *1–2* 3–9 *10* 11–24.

*Contents:* "The Hermit"; "Hymn to Contentment"; "Elegy to an Old Beauty"; "Night-Piece"; "Imitation of Some French Verses"; "Song" ("My days have been"), retitled "Love and Innocence"; "Song" ("Thyrsis"); "Health"; "Anacreontick" ("When spring came on").

*Copy:* Bodley (2705.f.151).

# Index of First Lines

# General Index

Parnell's works are entered under their titles.